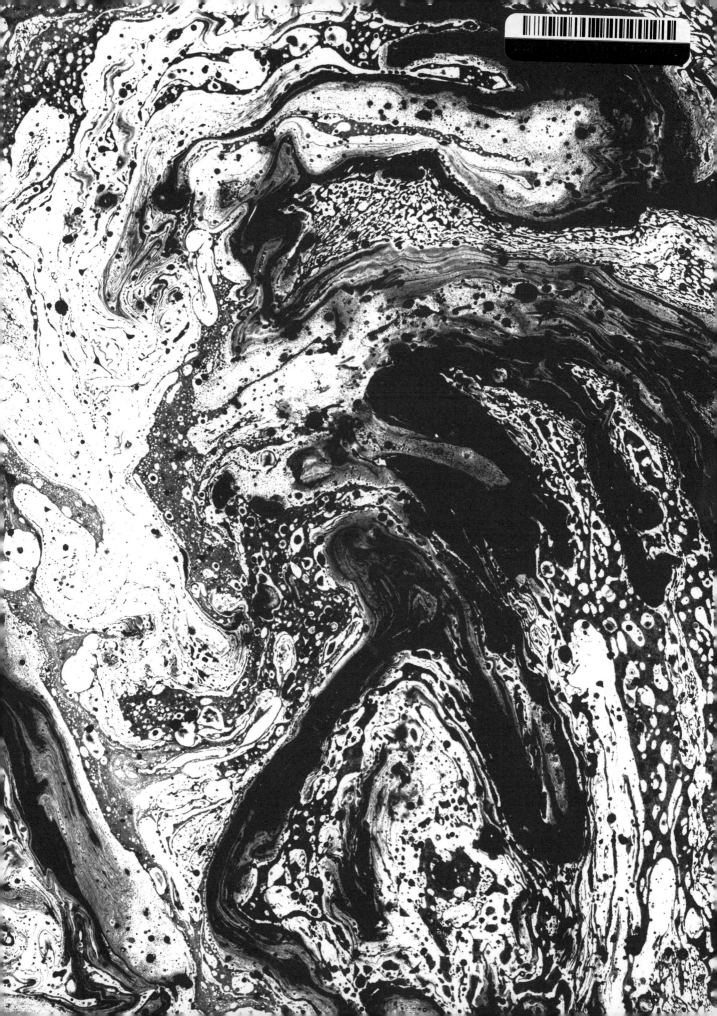

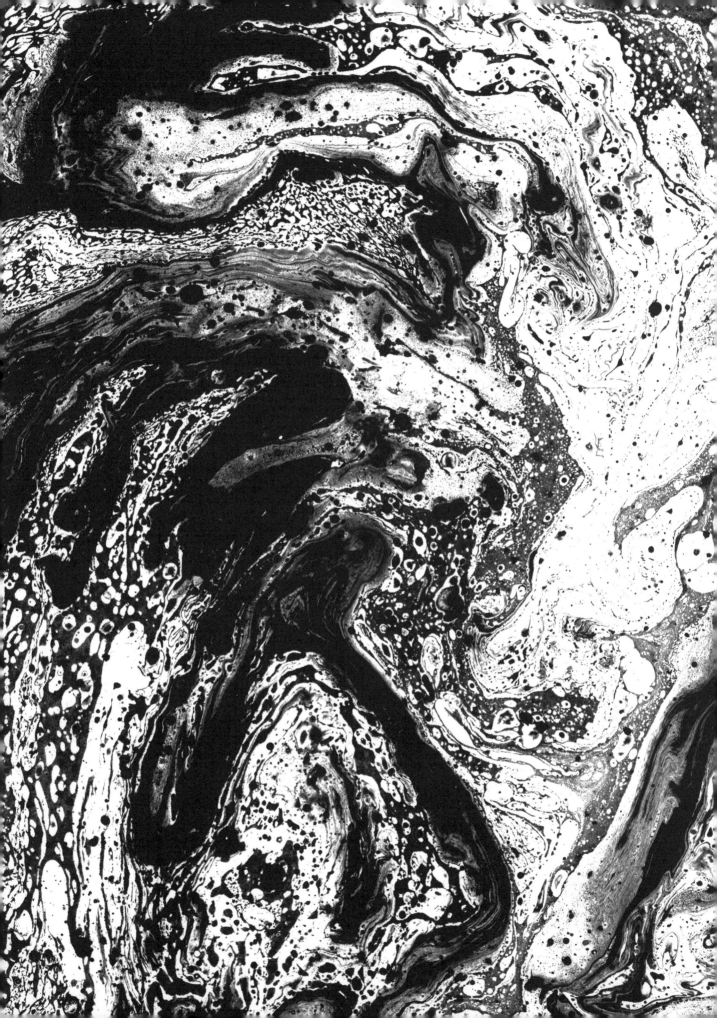

SIGNATURE
DISHES
THAT
MATTER

SIGNATURE

curated by

Susan Jung

Howie Kahn

Christine Muhlke

DISHES

Pat Nourse

Andrea Petrini

Diego Salazar

Richard Vines

THAT

narrative texts by

Christine Muhlke

illustrations by

Adriano Rampazzo

MATTER

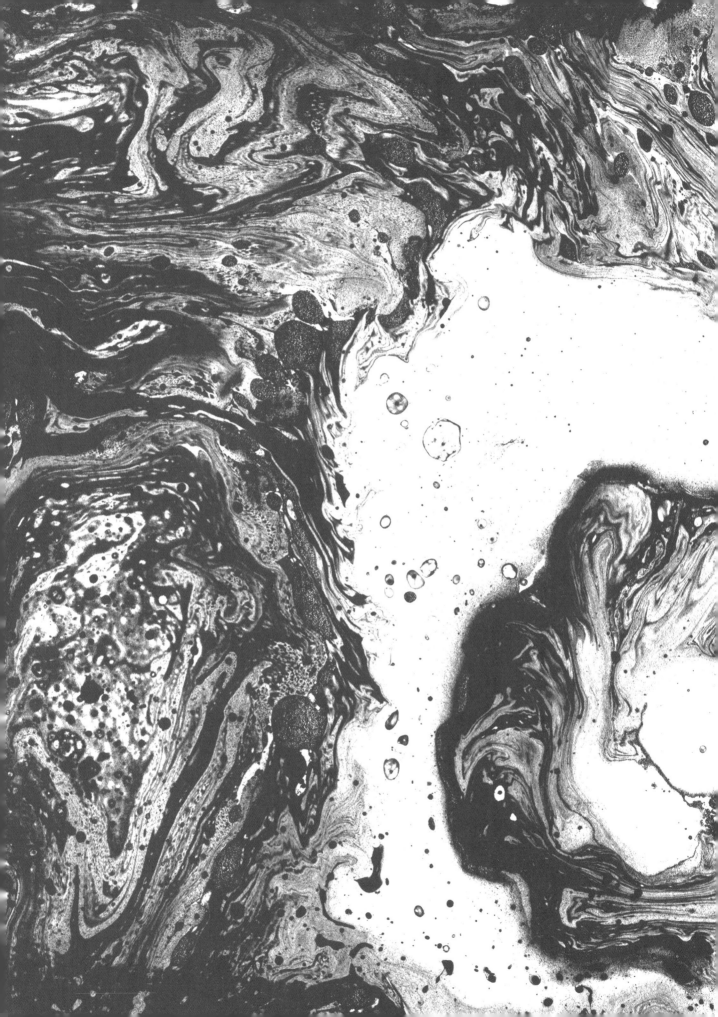

foreword

Mitchell Davis

7

curator statements

10

signature dishes

17

recipes

257

bibliography

440

index

442

Mitchell Davis

Two hours standing in line at a Los Angeles parking lot. Five hours driving mountainous Swiss roads in a tiny Fiat Punto. A last-minute overnight flight to Paris. These are just some of the lengths I have gone to to sample a signature dish.

The idea that any combination of ingredients—whether served on elegant china or in a paper bag—could be worth such effort, no matter who's cooking, may be foreign to some. But signature dishes afford more than just a taste of something new. They are the flavor of history. What is striking as you flip through the beautifully illustrated pages of this book is that a menu of signature dishes is so much more than a meal. It's an encyclopedia of cuisine; a window into our collective culinary unconscious.

There are many ways that these dishes come to hold their positions of prominence. A place may have been the first to serve something, as with Le Procope's Gelato in eighteenth-century Paris (page 18) or it can be the last, such as the Grand Marnier Soufflé at La Grenouille in New York (page 83). A chef may have invented something totally new, like with Ferran and Albert Adrià's Spherical-I Green Olives at elBulli (page 199), or perfected something very old, like Fergus Henderson's Eccles Cake at St. John (page 160). A signature dish can also emerge from a particular moment in time, for example the twenty-four-carat gold risotto at Gualtiero Marchesi (page 120) or the caviar Beggar's Purses at Quilted Giraffe (page 121) that typify the high-flying 1980s, or from a good story, such as Prince's punishingly hot fried chicken, stemming from a Nashville man's infidelity (page 64), or Massimo Bottura's childhood memory of the crunchy part of the lasagna that inspired his famous dish (page 165). Or, it can be something that is just so damn delicious that you can't get it out of your mind, like Zuni Café's roast chicken for two (page 138). The genesis of these dishes and the mythologies that swirl around them infuse them with meaning that outstrips their recipes and taste.

This delectable book is a celebration not only of the dishes that have stood the test of time, but also of the chefs and restaurants who made them famous. It stretches back over centuries and across continents, charting chronologically the dishes that punctuate the landscape of global food. As such, it is a combination of history lesson, travel guide, and cookbook curated by an international team of award-winning journalists, editors, critics, and writers. Coincidentally, I know and have worked with all of them— they are the first people I would ask to tell me what and where to eat. (Could that be why I can tick off more than a 120 of these entries from my bucket menu?)

Often a signature dish leaps from its association with a particular restaurant or chef into the culinary vernacular— in short, it becomes a trend, an icon, something you can't believe ever didn't exist. Think Eggs Benedict (page 40), Caesar Salad (page 56), Tuna Tartare (page 131), Whole Roasted Cauliflower (page 202), Avocado Toast (page 158). How many people on my recent flight to Amsterdam might have known to acknowledge their indebtedness to chef Joshua McFadden's Brooklyn farm-to-table restaurant Franny's for the Kale Salad (page 204) they were served in flight?

Obviously, not all signatures are entirely original. Sometimes a confluence of cultural attention or a new context takes something out of the ordinary and puts it into the spotlight. We know that Nobu Matsuhisa's signature Black Cod with Miso (page 136) is a common Japanese staple and that David Chang's Pork Buns (page 197) at Momofuku are based on a traditional Taiwanese snack, but that doesn't detract from their impact, and the way in which the dishes brought these cuisines into focus for many diners. Could the late French chef Joël Robuchon be given credit for inventing buttery *pommes purée* (page 119)? Not if you had tasted my mother's mashed potatoes. But no one can deny the deliciousness of these dishes that have become the chefs' signatures.

In this era of heightened sociopolitical awareness and sensitivity, one can't avoid the question of cultural appropriation, especially when talking about the more traditional dishes that rise to the level of noteworthiness. Not every gifted cook has equal access to the mechanisms of power that turn a soup into a sensation, a mole into madness. In order to pay proper due we must acknowledge the power dynamic between the creator and the created, the consumer and the consumed. Nor can we deny the negative impact such elevated status might convey. In Bangkok, Jay Fai's remarkable Crab Omelet (page 116) was a sought-after signature long before Michelin anointed her stall with one of their coveted stars. Though the attention was welcome recognition of a lifetime's hard work, the impact has been a lot to bear. Likewise, at Jiro Ono's legendary sushi restaurant in Tokyo (page 88), the demand for tables is so great that they have had to suspend reservations altogether for the foreseeable future.

The nature of what the signature signifies has changed over time. Escoffier's Peach Melba (page 38) was created and named to honor the Australian opera diva Nellie Melba, not Escoffier himself. Oysters Rockefeller, Tournedos Rossini, Carpaccio (pages 43, 26, 72), and many other signature dishes were named for someone besides the cook. Today the chefs themselves are usually honored by the dishes that become their signatures. This is a relatively recent phenomenon.

Very early in my career as a food writer I interviewed the late Paul Bocuse (pages 95, 103) about nouvelle cuisine, of which he was considered one of the fathers (at that time, it's worth mentioning, no mothers were included). Despite the culinary clichés people associate with that movement—small portions, undercooked vegetables, unnatural combinations, reduction sauces dabbed on plates—Bocuse told me the most important innovation of the era was putting the chef's name on the door. The phenomenon of the chef-owner, according to Bocuse, had the biggest impact on the cooking, allowing creativity to blossom and the chef-artiste to emerge. Behold the context for the modern signature dish.

For many reasons, the Cronut® (page 237) reflects another turning point in the trajectory of the signature dish. Tellingly, it's the only entry in this collection with a registered trademark, a legal protection that pastry chef Dominique Ansel sought in early 2013 before the first Cronut® was ever sold. The Cronut® was also one of the first signature dishes to become a global social media sensation, the acquisition of which became a gourmet's badge of honor. Barely three weeks after its debut, when people started lining up in the early morning hours outside Ansel's New York pastry shop to purchase one of his limited-edition croissant-donut hybrids, I landed in Tokyo to find copycat Cronuts® already for sale in department store food halls. In November of 2013 at the annual James Beard Foundation fundraising gala, we auctioned custom-flavored Cronuts® for $5,000 apiece.

Of course, the way that a rock band's greatest hit doesn't reflect the totality of its oeuvre, neither does a signature dish represent the breadth of a chef's cooking. Once the novelty of a fabulous new dish wanes, for some a signature can risk becoming a kind of creativity-stifling albatross, the thing that can never be taken off the menu. Initially Ansel tried to get out from under the weight of his Cronut® success to assert his versatility as a pastry chef. But eventually he turned all the attention into an international empire that gave him the creative freedom he so deserved. Because signatures are often uniquely complicated creations, they can require dedicated complements of cooks to produce. How many cornets of salmon tartare (page 159) must Thomas Keller's team have prepared? I myself have happily eaten what seems like hundreds, maybe more. Rather than an hors d'oeuvre, if you think of Keller's complex cornets as culinary calling cards, you begin to appreciate the value of all that repetitive effort.

Long before social media, signature dishes trafficked in the fear of missing out. As this book proves, you don't need to have three Michelin stars to make something people will go to great lengths to consume, such as the food truck with the fusion mash-up Korean beef Short Rib Taco (page 210), or the pizzeria with the best Margherita (page 33). To the real food explorer these peaks are as important to conquer as Bocuse's foie-gras-and-truffle-enriched Soupe Elysée (page 103).

But these days, as much as experiencing something in its original form, sharing the experience has become a modern foodie's mission. Post a picture of Chen's Mapo Tofu in Chengdu (page 28) or the Tsukemen ramen at Taishoken's in Tokyo (page 81). Take a selfie while sipping the soup out of the *xiao long bao* at Din Tai Fung in Taipei (page 100). We are consuming photos as much as we are consuming food, and sharing those photos has become part of sharing the meal. This phenomenon has only increased the import and impact of the signature dish.

I have a copy of a 1992 menu from a lunch at Restaurant Girardet in Crissier, Switzerland, where chef Frédy Girardet was once considered the best in the world. That's before the Internet broke out of computer science labs, before cell phones, before global gastronauts gallivanted around the world to eat. Printed on the back of that menu is a list of fifty mouthwatering-sounding dishes under the heading *Le brigade de Frédy Girardet a déjà exécuté les spécialités et compositions suivantes,* "Here are some of the special dishes Girardet's kitchen has created in the past." To my surprise, then and now, they were not serving these dishes on the day we were there, nor necessarily ever again (I asked). Rather they were giving us Girardet's bona fides, self-solidifying his genius, making sure we knew that the meal we were about to have would soon move from lunch into the realm of culinary dreams. Reading them today I still wonder what these dishes would have tasted like, who got to eat them. They were proto-signature dishes purposely kept out of the realm of public consumption. Boy, have things changed.

Once any food is consumed, all we have left are the stories we share. Kept to ourselves, food is primarily nutrients seasoned with memory. When we think about it, talk about it, share the experience, that's when food becomes cuisine. In this transformation, signature dishes play a particular role. They are both almighty, making gastronomic giants, and democratizing, giving us bite-size goals. When you look at the history of food through the window of signature dishes, you see the movements and madness that have shaped our food culture. In flavor and technique, each dish carries with it traces of its time—from the richness and regality packed into the laminated layers of Carême's Mille-Feuille (page 22), to the engineered entrepreneurship of the Big Mac (page 90), to the resonant techno-emotional creativity of Ferran Adria's Smoke Foam (page 173), to the naturalistic austerity of Magnus Nilsson's King Crab and Almost-Burnt Cream (page 226). Each dish reflects its maker and its moment. As such, this compendium is not just a collection of recipes or stories, or even an aspirational bucket list of meals to consume—it is a definitive canon of cuisine.

Susan Jung

_____

Susan Jung trained as a pastry chef and worked in hotels, restaurants, and bakeries in San Francisco, New York, and Hong Kong, before becoming the food and drinks editor of the *South China Morning Post* in Hong Kong. She is academy chair for Hong Kong, Macau, and Taiwan for the World's 50 Best Restaurants and Asia's 50 Best Restaurants.

curator statements

Trying to come up with a list of signature dishes for this book was extremely difficult. It was a similar experience to those times in which people ask me, "What's your favorite restaurant?" There's so much I like, so it's impossible to name just a few. For inspiration, I started by looking at my own Instagram feed, and saw that even though I am constantly visiting new restaurants in Hong Kong and in other countries, there were certain dishes at specific restaurants that I was eating (and posting about) over and over again.

For me, a signature dish is something that I immediately equate with a certain restaurant or chef. Seventh Son = Suckling Pig; The Chairman = Steamed Flowery Crab with Shaoxing Wine and Chicken Fat; Tam Kwok-fung, at whichever restaurant he's working at = Glutinous Rice-Stuffed Suckling Pig. It's impossible for me to go to those restaurants and not eat those dishes.

The problem is that when you start to think of signature dishes, it's hard to stop. Even now I can think of more that I wish I had nominated. I'm sure some of the other curators also can name dishes they wish they had included in their selections. Starting this conversation to celebrate the dishes that have made history, changed the way we eat, or simply just brought people joy, is the fantastic thing about this book.

Howie Kahn is the co-author of the *New York Times* bestseller *Sneakers*, the author of *Becoming a Private Investigator*, and the founding host of *Prince Street*, a food and culture podcast, heard in more than two hundred countries. He is a James Beard Award winner and a contributing editor for the *Wall Street Journal Magazine*. His writing has also appeared in *GQ*, *Wired*, *Travel + Leisure*, and dozens of other publications worldwide.

"Why do certain dishes matter?" is a question I consider almost daily. It's one of the bedrock questions of a career writing about food. What really makes a plate resonate? Is it staggering innovation? Is it creativity so singular that it begins to rival even the thinking behind works of art? Is a dish's importance owed to resourcefulness and research, the way chefs can draw from what they've learned and who's around them to bring kitchen and cultural discourse to new levels? Is it about influence? Not the influence of social media, but the way something edible can, with time, trigger industrial, regional, or even global change? Or, is it mainly about how a single plate of delicious food can open doors to explaining the lives of others in surprising, trenchant ways?

When the idea for this book came about, I jumped at it mostly for the chance to think even more deeply about the issues above. This volume is set in the context of restaurants. There are, of course, way more dishes in the world that matter. Ones my grandmother—and yours—cooked. Ones you made imperfectly for a loved one. Ones that keep people alive.

But for a food writer and food lover, like me, the dishes here amount to an important and grounding exercise in critical and historical thinking. So much of what we say in print about food is about taste and reaction: what we love or hate, how we feel, precious memories triggered by a bite. Much of it is also dictated by what's brand-new even if what's brand-new only matters because of what has been.

Treating "what matters" as scholarship, even as a study of our own invention, feels like an especially timely endeavor to undertake during the broader global moment in which context is simultaneously being fought for and eroded. Searching for "why," in all regards, is now especially timely. I filtered my set of dishes through the questions above, while also questioning myself. To write about what matters is to constantly check your own values. Could mine help expand a dialogue about restaurants and chefs and our growing fascination with the genre of food? I hope they can.

Compilations like this one, of course, strive to be definitive. But they're most useful if understood and embraced as imperfect. The best compilations spark debate. They leave room to consider their readers' experiences. The best resource, in the end, becomes a package: the book to start and then the intentional action of a deeper, more thorough and more empathetic conversation. Evaluating which dishes matter can help us move toward that moment.

Christine Muhlke

Christine Muhlke is the editor-at-large for *Bon Appétit* and the founder of the food consultancy Bureau X. The former food editor of the *New York Times Magazine*, she has co-authored books with Eric Ripert and Aldo Sohm of Le Bernardin, David Kinch of Manresa, and Eric Werner of Hartwood.

Pat Nourse

Australian journalist and critic Pat Nourse is the creative director of the Melbourne Food & Wine Festival. A travel writer and restaurant reviewer with some twenty years' experience, he was an editor at *Gourmet Traveller* for fourteen years, and his work has been published in the likes of *Saveur*, *Travel + Leisure*, Fool, *Afar*, *Lucky Peach*, and *Gourmet*. He has also been the chair of voting for Oceania for the World's 50 Best Restaurants since 2006.

In today's dining world, we tend to think that every dish is, if not exactly original, then at least a relatively new invention. But if, like me, you've been eating around the world and interviewing great chefs for decades, you'll know that there are certain touchstone dishes that chefs can't help but pay homage to, whether it's Michel Bras' Gargouillou from 1978 (page 13) or Christian Puglisi's Beef Tartare from 2010 (page 224), going all the way back to Escoffier and Carême.

When I thought about which dishes to nominate for this book, I thought about those that not only changed the course of cooking, plating, and serving, but also those that could be found in countless iterations around the world. The instant dissemination of images across the Internet has certainly changed the game in the last decade. In my mind, though, it makes the global impact of a dish that was served in the hills of rural France four decades ago and is still relevant today that much more significant.

It wasn't until I began researching and writing this book that I truly understood its importance. Just as each generation thinks it invented sex, we don't give credit to those who were cooking centuries ago. Nor did we Eurocentric fanboys (and girls) pay sufficient attention to the incredible innovations that were taking place around the world, especially in Asia, for centuries before that. It also taught me that, in many ways, all of the dots connect if you just step back far enough to look. That, and that sometimes the most exciting and powerful stories came from chefs I'd never heard of before.

When so much of our food media culture today is focused on chefs, looking at the last few centuries through the lens of the dishes that have stood the test of time tells us a lot about what's really durable. While I wouldn't say that there's nothing new under the sun exactly, it's interesting to discover how many ideas that we think are new turn out to have deep roots. Conversely, there are more than a few dishes we might consider to be deep-rooted products of tradition that in fact have only been with us for a few generations. This fascinating project allows us to reflect on the development of gastronomy, and on our preconceptions about food culture.

My own process of choosing dishes for our initial long list of dishes was partly a matter of letting the mind's eye roam around the map, thinking about which dishes are emblematic in each part of the world, and then also applying the same sort of thinking to eras. Which of these could be said to be truly *sui generis*? Which represented a significant step in culinary evolution? Which of them will still be with us fifty years from now?

Chefs don't choose their signatures—it's the pressure of time and the loyalty of diners that confer this quality on these dishes, like things worn to a shine by the passing of many hands. There's something beguiling about that, something that I hope speaks to a quality beyond fashion. "By their works shall you know them": in *Signature Dishes That Matter* there is a wealth of understanding to be gleaned.

Andrea Petrini is a writer, journalist, food curator, and cultural activist living mostly in France. He has put his pen to many books, including for *Cook It Raw*, books by Marc Veyrat, Luca Fantin, Rodolfo Guzman, Ana Ros, and Terry Giacomello; and collaborations with an eclectic range of publicatons. When he is not road managing the avant-garde chefs posse GELINAZ! or curating a new cookbook exhibition in Seoul or Los Angeles with art theorist Nicolas Bourriaud, he sits as the chair of the World Restaurant Awards judging panel.

A specter haunts the food scene: it's the specter of hauntology. This concept, first conceived by philosopher Jacques Derrida, is used by contemporary critics such as Mark Fisher and Simon Reynolds to describe society's reliance on the aesthetics and constructs of the past, particularly in reference to artistic endeavors—art that is defined by its preoccupation with nostalgia. But in the chef-driven world of restaurants, which has little or no connection with the other arts, nobody seems to acknowledge this phenomenon. Had I been asked the question: "Who would you like to share the findings of this book with?" I would have answered, no questions asked: British journalist and musicologist Simon Reynolds, who wrote one of the most astonishing books of the past decade, *Retromania*, about the way that we are all stuck in the cult of what is behind us. We could have had fun pulling the legs of all those chefs who are so stubbornly convinced of being progressive and therefore "moving forward" that they don't even realize how grounded they are in the nostalgia of the past.

Are sons doomed to repeat the flaws of their fathers? Did, for example, Michel Guérard and Michel Bras even imagine, forty years ago, when they created their very first Tartelette or Gargouillou (page 113), that they were to become the forerunners of a veggie-obsessed generation, stuck on repeat mode? Is a dish truly iconic because it has really changed the world as we knew it, or simply because it haunts us every time we step out into the streets? How long can a dish stand on its own terms before it gets morphed, cloned, copycatted, serialized *ad infinitum*, until it becomes something else and loses its own original sense?

The past always catches us, and yes, we should always keep in mind that The Dead Don't Die. They come back, they mutate, they transform, they allure us into never-ending daydreams. Had we been cutting bread together, Reynolds and I, we might have been trying to pin down how and why simple dishes or fragile concepts—like the inflated "sustainability"—have merely become evergreen but useless tools, a password on the road to nowhere, a brand in the hands of the brands.

An iconic dish is like art: when it comes with a message, well that's bad news. A man's gotta do what a man's gotta do: cut his daily steak, and not choke on an empty slogan. God save us from sustainability. Let's turn the page and find out—dish by dish, ingredient by ingredient, technique by technique, thought by thought—what real "sustainable thinking" could be. That's the humble purpose of this playlist of personal favorites; iconic dishes from our haunted past that dare to speak their name.

Diego Salazar is an award-winning journalist based in Lima and Mexico City. He is the author of *No hemos entendido nada*, a book on the state of the media industry in social media times. His work has been published in media outlets from Latin America, Europe, and the United States, where he is a regular contributor to the *New York Times en Español*. He is also an academy chair for the World's 50 Best Restaurants.

When deciding which dishes to include in this compilation, the first thing to be considered was, of course, how to define what a signature dish is. From my point of view, the main issue when we talk about a signature dish is how influential the dish actually is. Of course, the dish has to be well-known, it has to have traveled beyond the chef or restaurant's town or country, but mainly the dish has to have influenced other cooks: either to make their own versions of it, or to make them see a particular ingredient or preparation in a new way, a way they haven't thought of before the dish was created.

One of the things I was particularly surprised by while looking for dishes that match that idea was how many dishes wouldn't fit the description, because they weren't created in a restaurant kitchen but in a home. I had to leave many dishes out because I realized they were, at least in origin, part of the cultural and food tradition of a country or region and they couldn't be traced or ascribed to a professional cook, but rather a home cook. In that process, I also discovered the deep imbalance in the recognition male and female cooks receive. In most cases, when a dish is ascribed to a professional cook, that cook almost certainly is a man. While when a dish is ascribed to tradition or to a home cook, almost certainly that cook is a woman. Of course, this is testimony to the inequality we still see in professional kitchens around the world.

This book is important because one of the problems of the food world, particularly today when we can see what any cook or kitchen is doing or working on through social media, is that a lot of cooks in restaurants around the globe like to take credit for recipes or ideas they didn't develop by themselves, without granting recognition to those who inspired them. It is important to be able to trace back the ideas, concepts, and recipes for great dishes to their original creators, not only to pay respect to them but also to understand how interconnected creativity is in our world nowadays.

London-based Richard Vines is chief food critic at Bloomberg. He has been writing about restaurants for fifteen years and is the past UK and Ireland chair of the World's 50 Best Restaurants awards. He is a graduate of the London School of Economics. He has been a journalist for more than four decades and was formerly on the staff of *The Times* in London. He spent thirteen years in Asia, working for *China Daily*, the *Asian Wall Street Journal*, and the *South China Morning Post*, where he was foreign editor. He joined Bloomberg in 1995.

For me, a signature dish is one that is distinctive and memorable for the right reasons. It's not enough for a dish to be creative or beautiful or surprising. It needs to be capable of producing "madeleine moments." Signature dishes were thin on the ground when I first came to London to study in the mid-1970s. The few that existed were generally cooked by continental chefs in grand hotels that were too expensive for students, or even ordinary working people. The restaurants I visited were mainly curry houses or trattorias.

When I returned from overseas in the mid-1990s, a process of change was already underway, with the emergence of British chefs such as Fergus Henderson. That process has accelerated in the past twenty years, and dining has also democratized as incomes have risen and gastronomy has become more affordable.

My focus when considering the dishes for this book was largely on the UK, and the difficulty was in deciding what to leave out, rather than on which dishes to include. There are talented chefs across the nation, cooking in a variety of styles, though many of these chefs trained under French masters, whose DNA is in their food.

My personal favorite dishes reflect past and present. Pierre Koffmann's Stuffed Pig's Trotter with Morels (page 106) and Heston Blumenthal's Meat Fruit (page 229) are the products of culinary tradition and of technical innovation. What they have in common is great flavor. Cooking and presentation have both evolved, but it's taste that triumphs.

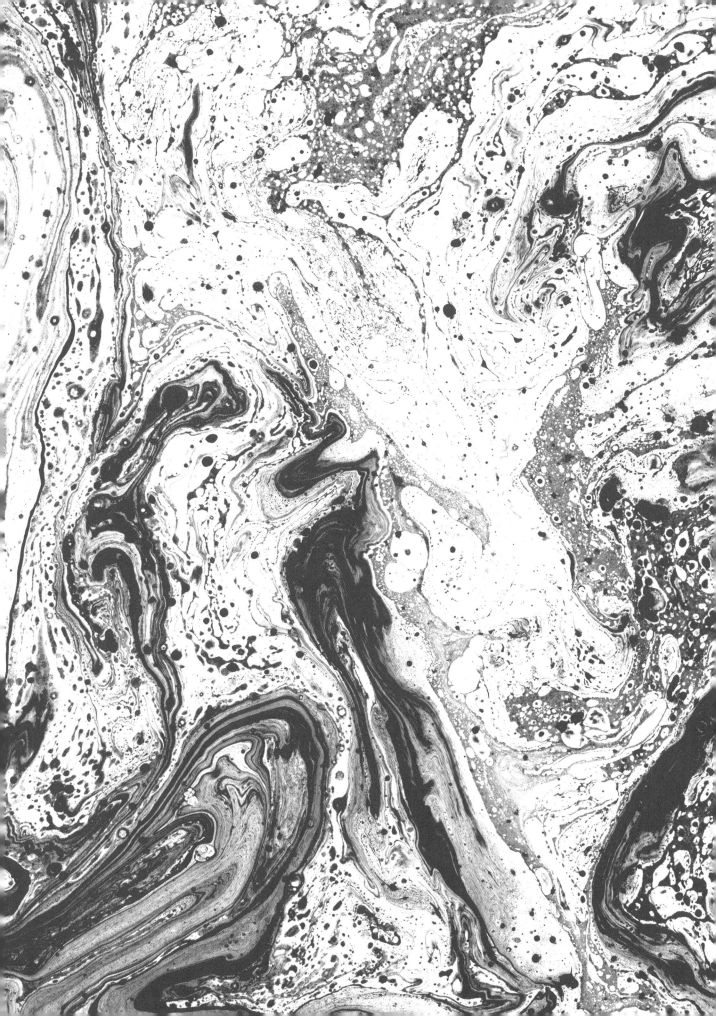

signature dishes

Procopio Cutò LE PROCOPE
France 1686

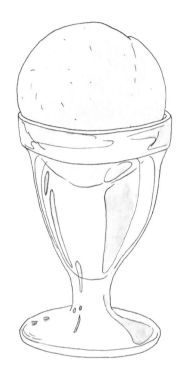

recipe → p 258

Gelato

"Ice cream is exquisite. What a pity it isn't illegal." So said a character in the Voltaire play *L'Écossaise*, set in a Paris café modeled after Le Procope, a café located across the street from the famous theater La Comédie Française. Le Procope was opened by Procopio Cutò (also called Francesco Procopio dei Coltelli), who had immigrated from Sicily, an area with a long history of enjoying *sorbetti*. These honey-sweetened fruit-flavored ices (which were brought to the Italian island by the Arabs) could be widely enjoyed in the summer months, thanks to the bounteous snow brought down from Mt. Etna. It is said that Cutò's grandfather, a fisherman, had invented a *sorbetto* machine that received a patent from the king; it became his grandson's inheritance. Until then, ices were only available to the rich because of the high cost of the ingredients required in the preparation.

Sorbets and ice creams were first brought to France for the wedding of Catherine de Medici to Henry II in 1559. But it was Cutò who finally made them more widely available to the public at his café, one of the first in Paris (up until then, coffee was mostly sold by street vendors or at fairs). In addition to coffee, Le Procope sold a variety of cold drinks, liqueurs, and ices. It is said that Cutò made his gelato by substituting sugar for honey and adding salt to the ice to speed up the freezing process, serving his creation in egg-shaped cups. His success was sealed when he received a royal patent to sell the dessert exclusively. Because of his proximity to the theater, his lavishly decorated café was a favorite of the likes of Balzac, Victor Hugo, Robespierre, and Benjamin Franklin. Cutò served his gelato in such a beautiful, unique environment that it became indelibly associated with him. The café remains open to this day.

selected by **Christine Muhlke**

Thomas Rule RULES
United Kingdom 1798

recipe → **p258**

Red Grouse

Rules, the oldest restaurant in London, was founded in 1798 by Thomas Rule. Known for their classic game cookery, a dish of particular note is their red grouse—the UK's only indigenous, wild bird—sourced from the restaurant's sporting estate, Lartington Hall. Known for its herbaceous minerality, which many attribute to its diet, the red grouse is additionally valued because it is a fast-moving and elusive target and requires great skill to catch. A brochure passed around with the menu details the culinary mission of the restaurant, which is to serve the finest, natural ingredients infused with nothing but the flavor of context. The brochure mentions that grouse tastes of heather, and snipe of bog, or "sweetly rotting wild mushrooms."

For many centuries the restaurant was known as a locale for celebration, oysters, and wild game paired with large amounts of claret and cigar smoke. During World War II, when rations were strictly enforced in restaurants, Rules was able to provide their diners with an unlimited amount of sustenance in the form of traditional—though by then considered alternative—national cuisine, as grouse, rabbits, and pheasants were not subject to rationing laws. Despite having lived out its golden years, Rules is still critical to the development of global gastronomy. Waiters still write down orders on papers stuffed into old shotgun cartridges, which are then sent down a copper pipe to the kitchen. At Rules, the diner is deeply connected with both the food he or she is eating and the land from whence it came, as well as fully insulated from the world outside by the exclusive nature of the fine-dining world.

selected by **Richard Vines**

Marie-Antoine Carême PÂTISSERIE DE LA RUE DE LA PAIX
France early 1800s

recipe → **p 259**

Vol-au-vent

Bouchée à la reine

These savory hors d'oeuvres, the original name of which translates to "Queen's Mouthfuls" or "Queen's Nibbles," were first created for Marie Leczinska, the Queen of France and wife of Louis XV. What today we call vols-au-vent, the *bouchées à la reine* were an ephemeral indulgence, emblematic of the cooking of Marie-Antoine Carême, who perfected and recorded the dish some years later. Puff pastry cases, their tops sliced off and reserved, were filled with a rich white sauce of chicken stock, cream, butter, flour, and egg yolk, and a savory mixture of poached chicken breast, black truffle simmered in white wine, and button mushrooms gently cooked in butter and finished with lemon juice. (Sweetbreads and calves' brains were also considered acceptable additions.) Once filled, the reserved pastry "hats" were placed back on and served hot, to be eaten in one bite. Later, larger versions for sharing were created.

Carême made his career as the first celebrity chef by devising elaborate, lavishly expensive dishes to delight the ruling class. It is to him that today's chefs owe not only the development of haute cuisine, with its technical sauces and regal pageantry, but also its cataloging. Although Escoffier would complete the systemization of French cuisine a century later, it was Carême who was the first to break down cooking into its building blocks—beginning with a bouillon, then the four mother sauces, and so on—writing recipes that could be combined to create fantastical banquets. Capitalizing on his reputation as chef to the rich, cooking for kings in Russia and England, and the new ability to mass-produce and distribute his cookbooks inexpensively, Carême's recipes spread throughout the world, establishing French cuisine as the world standard—a reputation that endured for another two hundred years.

selected by **Susan Jung, Pat Nourse, Andrea Petrini**

Zheng Chunfa JU CHUN YUAN
China early 1800s

recipe → **p 261**

Buddha Jumps Over the Wall

A soup with as many ingredients as origin stories, the only common thread being that the scent of its cooking is so heady, it could entice monks to break their vows of vegetarianism and jump over the monastery wall for a bowlful. Also known as Fu Shou Quan, or "wish for good fortune and long life," the creation is credited to Zheng Chunfa, a Qing Dynasty chef for a senior local official named Zhou. The official returned home one day insisting that Zheng replicate a soup made with pork, duck, chicken, seafood, and vegetables that he had just tasted at a banquet held by the financial authority of Fuzhou, the capital of the Fujian province. Zheng added more seafood and delicacies such as shark fin, abalone, ginseng, sea cucumber, dried scallops, and pigeon eggs to the banquet recipe until the ingredient list topped twenty, plus another dozen or so condiments and seasonings (today, the list of ingredients can include up to thirty items). The soup is cooked over the course of days in an earthenware crock—originally the narrow-mouthed jar used for making Shaoxing wine—to concentrate the aromas. It was so delicious that he was able to open his own restaurant in Fuzhou.

The most iconic dish of the Qing Dynasty, today the soup is renowned for more modern reasons: its price and its sustainability. The *2005 Guinness World Records* listed London's Kai restaurant as the source of the world's most expensive soup: it was selling for £108 ($140) a bowl and had to be ordered five days in advance. In 2000, the killing of sharks for their fins was banned by the United States, with similar laws reaching the UK in 2009 and the EU in 2013. (In 2013, China declared it illegal to serve the soup at government functions.)

selected by **Susan Jung, Pat Nourse**

21

recipe → **p 262**

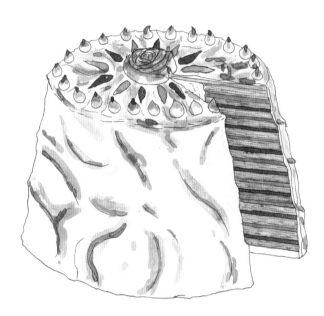

Mille-feuille

Gateau de mille feuilles à la ancienne

An invention attributed to royal chef Marie-Antoine Carême, father of *grande cuisine*, at the turn of the nineteenth century, the Mille-feuille is a classical dessert composed of alternating layers of paper-thin puff pastry and either a whipped cream, pastry cream, or jam. Usually served with a combed icing or glaze on top, the Mille-feuille can be either sweet or savory, though it is more often found in its dessert form. While it is closely associated with Carême, the Mille-feuille first appeared in *The Modern Cook*, written by Vincent La Chapelle in 1733. Carême is noted as a later appreciator of this work, however, so we know that the original pastry was not actually invented by him. He simply perfected the puff pastry technique, and recipe, that we know today. As with most classic French pastries, a similar variant exists in many countries around the world, despite the nation's assertion of culinary ownership.

Carême was considered the "king of cooking," the first celebrity chef, not because he invented a single dish, but because he invented a structure for French cuisine. He approached the culinary arts from a taxonomical perspective, aligning himself with the trend toward rational empiricism in the scientifically enlightened nineteenth century. By creating a self-contained system of practices, he was able to elevate cooking from a craft to an art. He was inspired by architectural displays of pâtisserie and created similar "structural" designations in the way in which he named his dishes, often naming them first by their main ingredient and then relating them to specific regions in France where the ingredients could be found. This in effect Frenchified unknown recipes to appeal to the local, nationalistic population.

selected by **Christine Muhlke**

recipe → **p 263**

Peking Duck

Ask any Beijinger who makes the best Peking Duck and, after an eye roll (because they get the question all the time), they'll reluctantly give you the name of a restaurant. The problem is, no one can agree. Do you like it lean or fatty? Cooked over live fire or in the traditional cylindrical oven? The best place to begin is at the beginning: at Bianyifang, which has been serving the Imperial banquet favorite since the 1800s. While the ovens might look different these days, the method remains the same: they line the walls with sorghum stalks to burnish the ducks' skin, placing the ducks in the oven as soon as the flames die out. The result is beautifully lacquered amber skin and juicy, rosy, exquisitely fatty meat. Presented tableside, the duck is traditionally served in three courses: the translucent, crackling skin is served with a dipping sauce of sugar and garlic; the carcass is thinly sliced into up to 120 pieces, which are rolled up in pancakes along with sweet plum sauce and batons of cucumber and scallion; the remaining duck and bones are served as a broth.

Perhaps even more impressive than the balance of textures of the finished dish is the care that goes into making it. Only Peking-breed ducks, which have been killed at sixty-five days, are used. Air is pumped into the duck through the neck cavity to separate the skin from the fat, which enables it to crisp so beautifully. The multitude of steps throughout the three-day process include glazing the uncooked skin with maltose syrup and marinating it with a rub of five-spice powder. While some prefer ducks cooked in the style of rival restaurant Quanjude, hung over the embers of peach or pear wood, saying that it renders more of the fat for exceptionally crispy skin, Beijingers agree that this is one dish that requires no update.

selected by **Susan Jung**

recipe → **p 263**

Lamb Cutlets Reform

Cotelettes de mouton à la Reform

The French-born chef Alexis Soyer, who began as an apprentice cook at the Palace of Versailles at the age of eleven, fled France during the July Revolution of 1830 and went to England to cook for the well-to-do. While he did make his name cooking for the rich, including at London's Reform Club and preparing a breakfast for two thousand guests at Queen Victoria's coronation, he also invented the "magic stove," the first portable tabletop cooking device, set up soup kitchens in Ireland during the famine of 1840, and fed soldiers at the Crimean War front at his own expense, where he and Florence Nightingale reorganized the provisioning of the hospitals. As a result, he became one of England's first celebrity chefs.

One of his most memorable dishes was Lamb Cutlets Reform, said to have been made for a club member with a late-night request. They were first prepared with mutton, but as the taste for young lamb grew, Soyer—who preferred the flavor of sheep raised in the South Downs to those from Wales—sliced it into cutlets, leaving a section of bone exposed, i.e., a modern chop. (A woodcut demonstrating his new technique appeared in his 1849 cookbook of two thousand recipes, *The Gastronomic Regenerator*.) The cutlets were coated in breadcrumbs and chopped ham and broiled (grilled), then set on a bed of mashed potatoes. Most remarkable was the piquant sauce, a complex mixture of stocks, consommé, secondary sauces, herbs, vinegars, and "preserved tomatas" that required many hands to boil, press through "tammies," or muslins, and blend to the perfect sweet-tart consistency. The dish remains on the menu at the Reform Club to this day. Other chefs have taken it up using simplified sauces—London chef Mark Hix uses beef stock, tarragon vinegar, and red currant jelly.

selected by **Pat Nourse**

recipe → **p 264**

Soufflé Potatoes

Pommes soufflées

When chef Jean-Louis-François Collinet invented *sauce béarnaise* at his hotel restaurant just outside of Paris after the second French revolution, it was fully intentional. His invention of *pommes soufflées*, however, was an accident. (Luckily a happy one.) He was charged with preparing a dinner for Queen Marie-Amélie and her notable friends in honor of the inaugural journey of the new passenger steam train linking Paris to Saint-Germain. He was in the midst of deep-frying thinly sliced ovals of potatoes when he was informed that her party would be delayed. Collinet pulled the potatoes from the oil and set them aside. When he later went to reheat them, this time in hotter oil, they inflated into crisp, oval pillows of air with a lightly golden shell. It turns out that frying the potatoes at a lower temperature created a waterproof skin around each slice. When allowed to cool and then submerged in hotter oil, the steam has nowhere to go, so it pops and puffs. The delicately shattering chips (crisps) were a success, and came to represent the haute-cuisine *pomme de terre* in all its painstaking perfection. (Suffice it to say that the success rate of perfectly puffed potatoes is not 100 percent.) The method was taken to America by Collinet protégé Antoine Alciatore, who opened Antoine's restaurant in New Orleans in 1840. To this day, they are served throughout the city, still accompanied by a ramekin of—what else?—béarnaise sauce. They remain a marvel of science: pommes soufflées are the most traditional recipe included in Nathan Myhrvold's cookbook *Modernist Cuisine.*

selected by **Christine Muhlke**

Casimir Moisson MAISON DORÉE
France 1859

recipe → p 264

Tournedos Rossini

The Italian composer Gioachino Rossini was as known for the forty operas he had written by the age of forty (most notably *The Barber of Seville*) as he was for his considerable appetite. The amateur cook, who spent most of his adult life in France, counted chefs such as Marie-Antoine Carême among his best friends, and they named plenty of dishes after him—most of them containing truffles. But it was a recipe invented by the Maison Dorée chef Casimir Moisson for which he is best remembered. Tournedos Rossini is a lavish entrée consisting of a thick round of buttery, pan-fried filet mignon (fillet steak in the UK; chateaubriand elsewhere) on a toasted crouton. The beef is crowned not only with a lobe of foie gras that is pan-seared in beurre noisette (brown butter) but also generous shavings of black Périgord truffle, more of which appear in the Madeira demi-glacé that surrounds the plate. Operatic indeed.

While the dish is often attributed to Carême because of their close friendship, it is widely held that Casimir Moisson, chef at the popular Maison Dorée, created the dish in Rossini's honor. It's not surprising the restaurant appealed to Rossini—it had two entrances, one for the general public and another for the rich and famous. As for the term "tournedos," one story goes that Rossini was pestering Moisson in the kitchen to such an extent that he told him to *tournez le dos*, or "turn your back." Another suggestion is that the maître d' serving the dish had to turn his back on diners so as to preserve the secret of the final preparations. Long associated with haute cuisine, Tournedos Rossini fell out of favor with nouvelle cuisine in the 1970s, as it is the antithesis of light and modern. It does live on, however: Daniel Boulud said that it was the inspiration for his DB Burger (see page 184).

selected by **Christine Muhlke**

recipe → **p264**

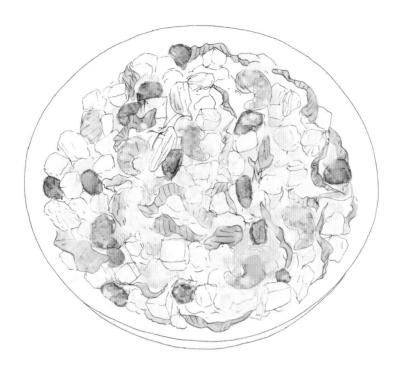

Russian Salad

Salade Olivier

What began as a lavish still life designed by a French chef to play to the Russian nobility's fondness for French culture gradually became the most Russian of dishes. What Lucien Olivier first served at the elegant Hermitage restaurant in Moscow was a gathering of the most expensive ingredients: caviar, grouse, pheasant, lobster, venison, veal tongue, crayfish, and other seasonally changing items—meats and seafood that were only available to the wealthy. In the center of the display were potatoes and hard-boiled eggs. To the chef's horror, the Russian diners mixed everything together on their plates. So, rather than object, he reconfigured the dish as a salad, dressing it with a secret Provençal sauce, which he forbade any of his cooks to see him prepare.

With the downfall of the aristocracy and the arrival of Communism, such a salad would seem to be distinctly anti-State. So in 1930, Olivier's former apprentice, Comrade Ivanov, updated it at the Moskva Hotel, exchanging grouse for the more proletariat-friendly chicken and carrots for the crayfish, with canned peas and potatoes lowering it further to meet the masses. The industrialized production of mayonnaise made it widely available, a cheap source of calories and protein for the people. And so it became the binding element of many dishes, especially this salad, which over time became an endlessly mutable amalgam containing diced chicken, potatoes, eggs, pickles, and canned peas, drenched in sweet, vegetable oil-based "Provansal" mayo. As White Russian emigrés took it with them, it became known around the world simply as Russian Salad. Today, it is centuries—and worlds—away from the French chef's original creation. A ghost of a gilded age.

selected by **Pat Nourse**

Mrs. Chen CHEN XINGSHENG
China 1862

recipe → **p 265**

Mapo Tofu

Ma po dou fu

No dish is more internationally emblematic of Sichuan cuisine than this blistering creation, with its bold flavors and comforting texture. It was first made by Mrs. Chen, a woman who ran a small restaurant with her husband, Chen Chunfu, by the Bridge of the 10,000 Blessings (Wanfu Bridge) near the north gate of Chengdu in the late 1800s. It is said that men lugging vats of canola (rapeseed) oil to sell in the city's market would often stop at her restaurant. It is speculated that one day a porter gave her some oil and asked her to make him something to eat using bean curd, so she wok-fried cubes of tofu and, heeding the region's taste for *ma-la* (a mixture of numbing and spicy flavors, one of twenty-three unique flavor combinations in the region's cooking), served it in a pool of dark-red chili oil seasoned with ground *huajiao* (Sichuan peppercorns) just before serving. Additional flavorings grew to include minced beef (now pork), fermented black beans, chili-bean paste, and local baby leeks called *suanmiao*. It was called *ma po dou fu*, which translates to "pockmarked old woman's bean curd," either in reference to the smallpox scars on Mrs. Chen's face, or because the ground meat makes tiny indentations in the tofu as it's being tossed together. The silken texture of the firm tofu and slight chewiness of the meat and beans is a soothing counterpoint to the tingling punch of the glossy brick-red oil, which leaves the mouth and lips buzzing. After Danny Bowien and Anthony Myint of San Francisco's Mission Chinese Food rose to success with their take on mapo tofu in 2012, restaurants around the United States have offered their own renditions. Unfortunately for Americans, the processing required for exporting the Sichuan peppercorns renders them considerably less infernal.

selected by **Pat Nourse**

Adolphe Dugléré CAFÉ ANGLAIS
France c.1867

recipe → **p 265**

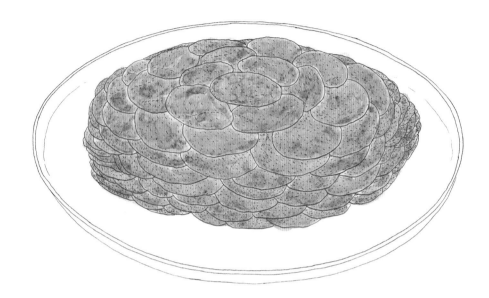

Anna Potatoes

Pommes Anna

Using just three ingredients—potatoes, clarified butter, and salt—the beautiful concentric shingled appearance and sublime crisp-tender texture of this dish relies on a steady hand in both layering the potatoes and flipping the two-piece copper "Anna" pan designed especially for the recipe.

Adolphe Dugléré was a student of Marie-Antoine Carême and, like many of the best chefs of the mid-1800s, started out as the head chef for a wealthy house—in this case that of Baron de Rothschild—before working at a restaurant. In 1866 he arrived at the Café Anglais in Paris and through his exacting standards for quality produce and the restaurant's inclusion in the International Exposition, he helped to make it known globally. It was the century's most illustrious restaurant: its appeal to politicians and powerful businessmen—and their courtesans—linked it to a certain kind of Second Empire power, epitomized by characters who dined there in the novels of Balzac, Flaubert, Proust, and Henry James. Dugléré was known for naming dishes after his famous clients, and even named a sole dish after himself. It is said that he named this potato side dish, created to resemble a delicate, upside-down cake, after Anna Deslions, one of the most fabled courtesans of the Second Empire, who frequented the restaurant near the Opéra Comique.

The pattern achieved by these crisp, scalloped potatoes can later be seen in dishes like Paul Bocuse's Red Mullet with Potato Scales (see page 95), which in turn influenced Daniel Boulud's sea bass wrapped in sheets of potato at his New York restaurant.

selected by **Pat Nourse**

İskender Efendi KEBAPCI ISKENDER

Turkey 1867

recipe → **p 265**

Iskender Kebab

İskender kebap

Turkish immigrants arriving in Germany in the 1960s made the doner ("spinning") kebab a staple of drunken, late-night snackers throughout Europe. (Mahmut Aygun of Hasir restaurant in Berlin claims to have invented it in 1971.) But one must go back to Ottoman Empire Turkey, a century before, to locate its real roots. It was there, on the main street of Bursa, that İskender Efendi, who had helped his uncle grill meat at a restaurant during childhood summers, turned away from the traditional method of roasting a whole lamb horizontally over a wood fire. He turned the spit vertically at his father's restaurant and developed a newly shaped charcoal grill, which he placed behind the meat, from which he had removed all of the bones and nerves and formed into a pyramid shape.

The resulting method helped prevent the dripping fat from causing flare-ups on the roasting embers, thereby eliminating the meat's strong cooking odor, while the constantly spinning skewer of the new mechanism allowed the meat to be evenly exposed to the heat. Thin, tender shavings of the spiced and basted lamb were layered on pillowy flatbreads, then called *alaturca*, and served with yogurt and tomato paste, with fried sheep's milk butter poured over the dish tableside to enrich the flavor even further. In its original iteration, the kebab is a knife-and-fork dish; not something to be wrapped in foil and eaten with one hand, a pint of beer in the other. Efendi's family, the İskenderoğlu, still operate the restaurant in Bursa.

selected by **Pat Nourse**

recipe → **p 266**

Baked Alaska

This dessert first appeared in France as the *omelette surprise* or *omelette à la norvégienne* in the 1830s: layers of cake and ice cream were topped with meringue and broiled (grilled) to a golden brown while the ice cream inside remained magically frozen. The omelet named for the country of Norway was possible thanks to the early-nineteenth-century research of the American-born scientist Benjamin Thompson, aka Count Rumford, who, in addition to inventing the double boiler and the kitchen range, discovered that the air bubbles that are contained in meringue make them a great insulator from heat.

By 1867, an expat French pastry chef named Charles Ranhofer had become famous for his elaborate, expensive feasts at Delmonico's, which is known as one of New York's first French fine-dining restaurants. Ranhofer was known for naming the restaurant's dishes for famous people, such as Veal Pie à la Dickens and Peach Pudding à la Cleveland, in honor of President Grover Cleveland. To mark the signing of the Alaska Purchase, a treaty with Russia that signed the northern territory over to the US, Ranhofer, who began his pastry apprenticeship at the age of twelve, debuted a dessert called "Alaska, Florida," in which he layered "a very fine vanilla-flavored Savoy biscuit paste" with apricot marmalade, banana and vanilla ice creams, and meringue before quickly browning the conical creation in the oven. The price tag—the equivalent of $40 (£30) in today's currency—caused a stir, even during the Gilded Age.

The recipe appeared in Ranhofer's 1894 book, *The Epicurean*, a collection of more than one thousand recipes that has been compared to Escoffier's masterpiece works. Escoffier in turn included the *omlette norvégienne* in his *The Complete Guide to the Art of Modern Cookery* in 1903.

selected by **Christine Muhlke**

Annette Poulard LA MÈRE POULARD
France 1888

recipe → **p 266**

Omelet

"Joan of Arc, at point of lance; Drove the English out of France; Madame Poulard did better yet: she brought them back with her omelette."

So wrote an American in 1908 in the guest book of the restaurant and auberge La Mère Poulard, just two decades after Annette Poulard had begun serving her famous omelets in the historically holy town of Mont Saint-Michel. Madame Poulard began feeding the religious pilgrims who made their way to the tiny island during low tide with the ingredients she had on hand, namely Normandy's salted *beurre de baratte* (hand-churned butter) and eggs. These were omelets in name and form only. Madame Poulard whipped her ingredients—which some say included extra egg whites . . . or perhaps crème fraîche?—for at least five minutes in a thick copper bowl before pouring them into a butter-slicked, long-handled copper skillet (frying pan), custom made for her in a nearby town. She cooked the mixture over a wood fire in a large fireplace until it transformed into a puffy, soufflé-like omelet with a golden bottom and slightly trembling center. The ethereally light and frothy result is served either *nature* (plain) or alongside hearty accompaniments such as *lardons*, lobster, or a ratatouille-like vegetable stew. Today it is listed on the menu at €35 ($40/£30), and it is a French tradition—and craft—that guests are more than willing to support. As that 1908 article citing the poem noted, Madame Poulard made her diners feel that they were witnessing an artist rather than an artisan: "Madame Poulard paid her visitors the compliment of treating them as persons to whom cooking as a fine art was a delicate tribute."

selected by **Susan Jung**

recipe → **p 267**

Pastrami Sandwich

More than the pizza slice or the bagel, the pastrami sandwich on rye bread is the most nostalgic dish for New Yorkers of a certain age. Today, Katz's is one of the longest-standing New York City delis serving it, having opened on the Lower East Side in 1888 and expanded in 1910, during a period when the neighborhood was home to many of the two million Yiddish-speaking Jews who immigrated to New York from Eastern Europe. At the time, the city had been transformed by the wave of Germans who arrived starting in 1840, bringing with them many things, including rye bread and the delicatessen, which, loosely translated, means "to eat delicious things."

The first Jewish delis celebrated an abundance of beef, since it was more available in America than it had ever been at home. Affordable kosher cuts such as brisket were brined to make corned beef, already an American classic. What the Yiddish newcomers did in the 1880s was to adapt a recipe for preserving meat from Turk-ruled Southeastern Europe that rubbed the brined beef with spices like paprika, cinnamon, ginger, red pepper flakes, cloves, garlic, ground coriander, and peppercorns before smoking it for six or so hours, then boiling and steaming. The resulting "pastrami" (from the Turkush *bisturma*) was thinly sliced against the grain and served on bread, with a balance between fat and lean slices. The pastrami recipe at Katz's, which is now run by the third generation, is, of course, a closely held secret. When chefs from around the world visit New York, they always stop here. Besides pastrami's renewed popularity in the US, a new generation of Jewish deli-style restaurants have popped up as far away as London and Paris—making this sandwich one of the most iconic in the world.

selected by **Christine Muhlke**

recipe → **p 267**

Oysters Rockefeller

More than 120 years after the introduction of this seminal New Orleans starter, its true recipe remains a secret to everyone except for the restaurant's owner and a member or two of the family, as does the reason for its invention. It is said that Jules Alciatore, working in the kitchen of the high-end French restaurant that had been founded by his parents in 1840, came up with this dish in the face of a shortage of imported snails. His attempt to make something that adapted the essence of garlicky escargot butter to broiled oysters from the nearby Gulf Coast was so buttery, he named it for John D. Rockefeller, then the richest man in America.

Back then, oysters were so common as not to be considered a delicacy. Who knows why Alciatore and his family guarded the recipe so fiercely. (A 1948 approximation by *New York Herald Tribune* food writer Clementine Paddleford in a story about the ten most closely guarded secrets of Antoine's guessed at spinach, celery, cooked lettuce, and onion, along with bread crumbs, anchovy, and Worcestershire sauce.) Almost forty years later, the Antoine's owner mentioned in his cookbook, which did not include the recipe, that spinach was decidedly not part of Oysters Rockefeller. Could it be sorrel? Watercress? Collard greens? To this day, no one can be entirely sure.

What is known is that the secrecy around this decadent dish, with its rich sauce of greens, transformed a cheap bivalve into an American success story. A 1938 card telling the diner his number of the dish, not unlike La Tour d'Argent's certificate for its fabled *canard à la presse* (see page 38), shows Alciatore's son serving his own son the millionth order of Oysters Rockefeller. The caption concludes, "The recipe is a sacred family secret." Sometimes an air of mystery is the best ingredient.

selected by **Howie Kahn, Pat Nourse**

recipe → **p 267**

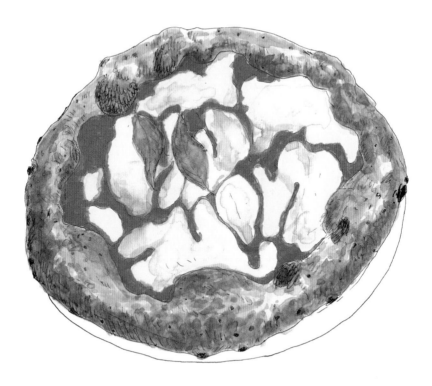

Pizza Margherita

There have been mentions of pizza in Italy dating as far back as 997 AD. The soft yet crisp-edged dough, baked in ovens built from the heat-retaining lava stones of Mount Vesuvius and topped with tomatoes, herbs, and garlic or anchovies, was typically folded into a *libretto* (little book) and eaten by hand. But it is the *pizza napoletana*, or Naples-style pizza, that is most commonly associated with the dish today. And there is no pizza more iconic than the Margherita. Its simple composition of crushed tomatoes, fresh mozzarella, and basil leaves —all widely available from the surrounding Campania region—has endured since its alleged creation by Raffaele Esposito at Pizzeria di Pietro e Basta Così for the Italian Queen Margherita of Savoy during a visit to the city in 1889. The red, white, and green ingredients are said to have represented the colors of the *Tricolore*, the country's flag.

Over the following decades, its popularity was disseminated by Italian emigrants, reaching New York City in 1905, with the opening of Gennaro Lombardi's pizzeria—which, like Pietro (though purchased by the Brandi brothers in the 1930s and given their name), is still open today.

As pizza's popularity spread throughout America, cheaper ingredients and more toppings have diluted the authenticity of the original. But over the last decade, genuine Naples-style pizza has taken root around the world, as chefs look to celebrate locally sourced ingredients. Do all of these twenty-first-century Margheritas meet the rigorous standards codified for pizzaiolos by the Associazione Verace Pizza Napoletana, which specify such factors as oven temperature and the paddle used to remove pizzas from the oven? No. But when done well, there is no more perfect pie.

selected by **Pat Nourse**

recipe → **p 268**

Spotted Dick

Little has changed at Sweetings, the fish and seafood restaurant that opened in the City of London in 1889. For more than a century, it has served almost the exact same menu. It only started accepting credit cards in 2001, and served just lunch until 2018, when it began hosting a monthly dinner club. For a restaurant with such simple, time-honored British fare, it's fitting that its most famous dessert is Spotted Dick.

The traditional British recipe with the eyebrow-raising name has been around since 1849, when the famous Victorian chef Alexis Soyer served the suet pudding speckled with dried currants at London's Reform Club, a recipe that he included in his 1854 cookbook, *A Shilling Cookery for the People*. A descendant of the meat-based medieval puddings, Spotted Dick combines beef suet with milk, baking soda, flour, lemon zest, and raisins or dried currants—hence the "spots." The dough is placed in a cloth bag and steamed or boiled, and the resulting domed "pudding" is served in a puddle of sweet custard sauce. (A word about that name: while in the nineteenth century it was slang for everything from policemen to dictionaries, it is commonly held that "dick" could be a corruption of the last syllable of the word "pudding.")

Like the old-fashioned Eccles cakes served for dessert at St. John (see page 160), the homely, unapologetic Englishness of the Spotted Dick served at Sweetings has inspired a new generation of chefs who have moved away from the French pastries that long defined desserts in Michelin-starred restaurants. In fact, St. John's founder, Fergus Henderson, proposed to his wife, Margot, at Sweetings—though it was the restaurant's Black Velvet, a silver tankard of Guinness and champagne, not this dessert, that set the mood.

selected by **Richard Vines**

recipe → **p 268**

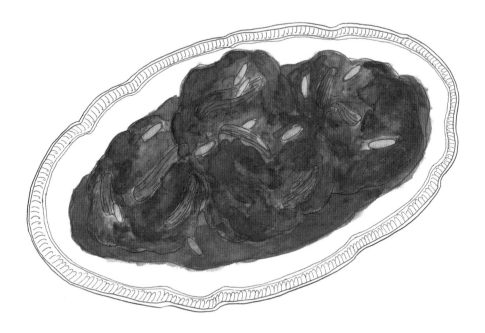

Oxtail Stew

Coda alla vaccinara

The most emblematic of Rome's *quinto quarto* dishes, this oxtail stew is poor in ingredients but rich in flavor. In the late 1800s, the workers on the lowest rung at the slaughterhouse in the Testaccio neighborhood, including the *vaccinari*, or butchers, had their pay supplemented with offal, or the "fifth quarter" of the butchered carcass—the meat of the first four regions designated to higher ranks. (The first *quarto* was sold to the nobles, the second to the clergy, the third to the bourgeoisie, and the fourth was for the soldiers.) The offal was hard to keep fresh due to the lack of refrigeration, so workers would take the organs, hooves, brains, tails, etc. to nearby restaurants —such as Checchino, which was across the square from the slaughterhouse—to have them cooked for them. Checchino stewed the lard-seared oxtails for six hours with garlic and onion in white wine, tomatoes, and water, before adding celery, pine nuts, and raisins—just as it does today, with the restaurant still being run by the same family. (Across town at Armando al Pantheon, the sauce is enriched with such special-occasion ingredients as chocolate or cocoa powder.)

This Roman style of poverty cooking, known as *cucina povera*, stood out even in a city that prides itself on its simplicity. (Another popular dish at Cecchino is rigatoni with a sauce made from tomatoes, suckling lamb intestines, and pecorino.) It soon became tightly wound into the city's cuisine, with such dishes as *trippa alla romana*. In recent years, *quinto quarto* food has seen a resurgence in Italy as a way to stay connected to their past. Their modern nose-to-tail movement is in evidence at restaurants like Trippa in Milan.

selected by **Pat Nourse**

Frédéric Delair LA TOUR D'ARGENT
France 1890

z

recipe → **p 269**

Pressed Duck

Canard à la presse

Beginning in 1890, the Parisian restaurant La Tour d'Argent made a spectacle of tableside carnage—and one hell of a dish. Server-turned-owner Frédéric Delair knew it was iconic, too: he gave each person to whom his invention was served a numbered tag to commemorate the duck that was enjoyed. That number reached well over one million before the restaurant's new chef retired the dish in 2016.

The show will be missed. The diner was presented with a roast duck in a copper pan, which was then wheeled on its white linen-covered cart to a server at a stage-like station in the center of the restaurant. The skin was removed, and the breasts, legs, and liver removed and set aside. (The liver was puréed in a blender and briefly reduced over a burner.) The remainder of the carcass was placed in a silver-plated duck press, based on the original designed in Rouen in the mid-1800s, from which flowed blood enriched with the bone marrow and intestines once the wheel was cranked. This blood was poured into a silver tray set over flames, to which the liver, Cognac, Madeira, and veal stock were added and reduced by three-quarters before being strained and spooned over a slice of the breast meat. The legs were sent back to the kitchen and crisped up, to reappear as a second course.

It was the ultimate show, refined in its brutality. (The Challans breed of ducks were known to have been strangled rather than hanged, so that they retained their blood.) One of the restaurant's original silver-plated Christofle presses sold for €40,000 ($45,430/£34,700) at auction. Pressed duck is still served at Restaurant Daniel in New York, while at The Grill nearby, the show and flow are used to create a rich poultry jus for pasta. Unfortunately, no numbered tags are given.

selected by **Christine Muhlke, Pat Nourse**

38

recipe → **p 269**

Waldorf Salad

In the dining world of the late 1800s, both hotel restaurants and their maîtres d'hôtel held enormous sway, catering to the tastes of the rich in London, Paris, and New York. At the latter's Waldorf Hotel (later Waldorf Astoria), the Swiss-born Oscar Tschirky was known as defining the art of hospitality for New Yorkers. As evidenced by *The Cook Book by "Oscar" of the Waldorf*, he is credited with introducing such dishes as Lobster Newburg and sometimes Eggs Benedict (see page 42). But it is for the Waldorf Salad that he is best remembered.

When the hotel opened in 1893, a writer declared that it "brought exclusiveness to the masses." The same could be said for the salad that Tschirky composed for an opening-night "society supper" for 1,500 guests—cold salads and fruit salads both being popular at a time when lunches went until late in the afternoon, just nudging up against the evening. Employing just apple and celery and dressed with "good mayonnaise," the Waldorf Salad immediately lent itself to new iterations, such as the sprinkling of walnuts on top—as the recipe appeared in Escoffier—or the addition of walnut oil to the mayonnaise. As *The New Yorker* food writer Sheila Hibben lamented, it had "bred the sorry mixture of sweet salads that remain very much on the gastronomical scene." It was a trend that continued unabated as the salad's popularity spread to American homes. Its notes of once-elegant simplicity were embellished, post-War style, with canned mandarin orange sections, shredded coconut, and miniature marshmallows.

selected by **Diego Salazar**

Auguste Escoffier SAVOY HOTEL

United Kingdom c.1893

recipe → **p 269**

Peach Melba

La pêche Melba

The legendary French chef, Auguste Escoffier invented this simple fruit-topped ice cream sundae for the Australian opera singer Nellie Melba, who was a frequent guest at his restaurants when she performed at London's Royal Opera House at Covent Garden. The dessert's debut for the soprano was much more dramatic than the version that subsequent customers received.

In 1892, Melba was in London to perform in Wagner's *Lohengrin* and sent Escoffier tickets to the performance. Moved by the dramatic production, during which Melba sang while riding in a swan-shaped boat, the following evening he fêted her with *pêches au cygne*, or swan peaches. The dessert featured slices of peeled, lightly sugared ripe peaches served over vanilla ice cream, the silver dish arriving on top of a swan carved from ice. Within a few years, Escoffier and his employer, César Ritz, had opened the Ritz-Carlton in London, having been run out of the

Savoy for embezzlement. Escoffier added a raspberry purée to differentiate the dish, now renamed *La pêche Melba*.

In his autobiography, Escoffier lamented the more elaborate versions that later appeared at other restaurants, writing, "Pêche Melba is a simple dish made up of tender and very ripe peaches"—he recommended the Montreuil variety, blanched for just two seconds, "vanilla ice cream, and a purée of sugared raspberry. Any variation on this recipe ruins the delicate balance of its taste." In his recipe, he also suggested the addition of slivers of fresh almonds, "but never use dried."

One wonders what Escoffier would have made of the Melba that chef Ferran Adrià served in his honor at the last dinner at his restaurant elBulli in 2011. Interestingly, the dishes Adrià created at elBulli were always numbered, from 1 to 1846—the last of which happens to be the year Escoffier was born.

selected by **Pat Nourse**

recipe → **p 270**

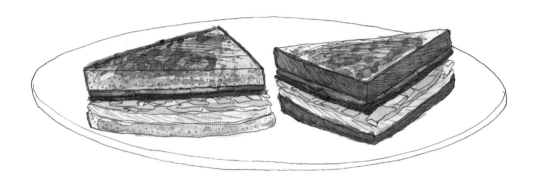

Club Sandwich

One of the most iconic of American sandwiches (apologies, hamburgers and grilled cheese), the Club Sandwich has murky origins but a clear and consistent recipe. Some speculate that it was created at Manhattan's Union Club, while others argue that it resembled, and was named for, the double-decker club cars that the Pennsylvania Railroad began running in the United States in 1895. (It was also argued by American food writer James Beard that the original had only two slices of bread.) However, the most popular theory finds its creation in a gentlemen's club and casino in Saratoga Springs in upstate New York in the late 1800s, a time when sandwiches were most commonly associated with ladies' lunches. The recipe has never wavered, minus that extra slice or two: toasted white bread layered with bacon, cold sliced chicken or turkey, lettuce, tomato, and mayonnaise. The winning combination of warm and cold, crisp and creamy has proven unbeatable.

Today, Club Sandwiches are as closely associated with room service in international five-star hotels as they are with American diners and members of country clubs. Guy Savoy serves a foie gras version at his Las Vegas outpost. The Beverly Hills Hotel offers an avocado supplement for the Club Sandwich that is said to make up a quarter of the orders at its poolside Cabana Café, where it has been served for over a century. But really, like the BLT (bacon, lettuce, and tomato) that it closely resembles, a Club Sandwich is best left unadulterated. An early recipe that appeared in *The New York Times* in 1907 does tempt: "Go to the club. Drink six toasts. Eat a slice of meat. Drink six more toasts."

selected by **Diego Salazar**

Oscar Tschirky WALDORF HOTEL
United States 1894

recipe → p 270

Eggs Benedict

This indulgent recipe gave rise to Americans' desire for a luxurious breakfast item with a little bit of French technique involved—and eventually became the basis for that very American idea of brunch, the weekend restaurant service that is now a worldwide phenomenon, created to both soothe hangovers and make a lot of money selling booze before dinner.

As one of the creation stories for this dish goes, one morning in 1894, a hungover Wall Street bon vivant named Lemuel Benedict asked the maître d' at his favorite fine-dining restaurant to bring him buttered toast, bacon, two poached eggs, and a pitcher of hollandaise (a thick French "mother" sauce made from egg yolks, butter, vinegar or lemon juice, and herbs such as tarragon)—all of which he layered upon the toast. The maître d', known as Oscar of the Waldorf, was impressed by Benedict's creation and added it to the menu, substituting an English muffin and Canadian bacon (round slices of smoked lean pork, similar to British back bacon, but without the fat). Another story set during the same era has a Mrs. LeGrand Benedict, unable to find anything she wanted on the breakfast menu at Delmonico's, asking the restaurant's famous chef, Charles Ranhofer (see Baked Alaska, page 31), to invent something for her. (Ranhofer's 1894 cookbook, *The Epicurean*, contained a recipe for Eggs à la Benedick [sic].)

Whatever the truth may be, much of Eggs Benedict's popularity lies not only in its illusion of fanciness but also its endless adaptability. In the United States, the Canadian bacon may be swapped out for that regional favorite the crab cake in Washington, D.C., while in New Orleans, it could have artichoke hearts, creamed spinach, and shrimp, aka Eggs Sardou. Also, it remains a fantastic hangover cure.

selected by **Christine Muhlke**

recipe → **p 270**

Crepes Suzette

As one of several origin stories around this dessert goes, a fourteen-year-old apprentice waiter named Henri Charpentier was preparing crepes for Prince Edward VII at a Monte Carlo hotel. He accidentally set fire to the cordials as he was making the sweet, buttery orange sauce using various liqueurs with which to coat the crepes, and in a moment of panic decided to serve the sauce anyway. Much to his surprise, the resulting caramelization married the flavors in perfect balance. The Prince enjoyed the dessert immensely, as did his dining partner, a young companion named Suzette. Other tales link the dish to Oscar Tschirky of the Waldorf Astoria in New York, who published a similar recipe for un-flamed crepes in 1896; Monsieur Joseph of Restaurant Marivaux next to the Comédie Française in Paris, who made the crepes that the popular actress Suzette served onstage in 1897, setting them aflame for dramatic flair; and Escoffier himself, who published the recipe in 1903 (although also not flambéed).

Tableside preparations, according to the food historian Paul Freedman, date back to the feasts of the Middle Ages, while modern flambéing in home cooking began in the nineteenth century, including the famous flaming Christmas pudding in Charles Dickens's 1843 novella *A Christmas Carol* and omelets set ablaze with rum and kirsch in cookbooks of the 1860s and 80s. In a restaurant, flambéing at the table is performance art. This fantastical dessert, which enjoyed a resurgence at the end of the twentieth century in Parisian restaurants such as Alain Ducasse's Benoit, arguably set the stage in the twenty-first century for elaborate tableside dishes, like the Baked Alaska at New York's Eleven Madison Park.

selected by **Christine Muhlke**

Caroline and Stéphanie Tatin HÔTEL TATIN
France c.1898

recipe → **p 271**

Tarte Tatin

As the legend goes, sometime in the late 1890s, Stéphanie Tatin, the commandress of the kitchen at the Hôtel Tatin in the Loire Valley, which she ran with her sister, Caroline, found herself confronted with a mishap: instead of putting her dough into the lidded cast-iron dish before layering sliced apples, butter, and sugar over the top, she performed these actions in reverse, putting the apples in first. Realizing her mistake, she decided to add the pastry on top and cook the tart anyway, resulting in a sweet, sticky caramel that pooled at the bottom of the pan. Rather than disappoint the customers who filled the dining room that night, Tatin not only served the tart as it was, she served it warm—a deviation from the traditional room-temperature apple tart of the era. This serendipitous sweet became an instant hit, and was affectionately referred to as "*tarte des demoiselles Tatin*" (tart of the unmarried Tatin women).

Because the original recipe for what came to be known as Tarte Tatin was never written down, the dish became wrapped up in the construction of a French nationalist mythos at the turn of the twentieth century. As sugar became more accessible to both the upper and lower classes, the Tarte Tatin began to represent a luxury that everyone could enjoy—a symbol of regional unity; an identity builder.

Though its first appearance in print was in the 1903 *Bulletin de la Société Géographique du Cher* (a regional journal), the dish was truly popularized at the Paris restaurant Maxim's, when it was added to their menu in the 1930s. With phrases like " … as French as Tarte Tatin," it's clear that this caramelized confection—the iconic French upside-down cake—still holds the same symbolic value in the national cultural conscience.

selected by **Susan Jung, Pat Nourse, Diego Salazar**

Motojiro Kida RENGATEI
Japan 1899

Tonkatsu

In Meiji-era Japan (1868–1912), the formerly closed country was quickly trying to establish itself as a modern nation. This, of course, meant experimenting with the cuisines of other countries. Motojiro Kida of the new Tokyo restaurant Rengatei, which specialized in Western dishes, tried a recipe that appeared in an 1872 cookbook for French-style *côtelettes de veau*, or veal cutlets. The strips of loin coated with stale breadcrumbs were sautéed in butter then placed in the oven, but Kida deemed them too soft and oily for the Japanese palate and opted for the traditional tempura method, dredging the cutlets in flour, egg, and soft panko breadcrumbs and deep-frying them in vegetable oil instead. Since veal was too expensive, he tried it with the pork that was then more commonly available. The resulting thin, crisp-fried cutlet was served with a knife and fork, also a rarity at the time. (It later came to be precut into chopstick-friendly slices.) It was originally called *katsuretsu*, a Japanization of the word "cutlets," and was shortened to *katsu*, which became the term for breaded and fried dishes. In the 1930s, the name for the crisp pork cutlet changed to *tonkatsu*, *ton* being the Chinese character for pig.

Over time, the restaurant's recipe evolved: to deal with a dearth of cooks, the restaurant substituted sliced raw cabbage for the original hand-cut carrots and potatoes. (Cabbage also benefitted from being available year-round.) Kida also replaced the French demi-glacé sauce with a mixture of two kinds of imported Worcestershire sauce for a sweet and tangy counterpoint to the fatty meat. Served as a set meal with rice and miso soup, Rengatei's Tonkatsu has endured for more than a century. It is also the basis for such popular variations as *katsu sando* (a cutlet sandwich) and *katsu kare* (cutlets with curry).

selected by **Susan Jung**

Chin Heijun SHIKAIRO
Japan 1899

recipe → **p 272**

Nagasaki Champon

Because Japan was a closed country for so long, the existence of fusion dishes is relatively small. But during an open moment in the late Meiji period near the turn of the twentieth century, an immigrant from China's Fujian province opened a hotel and restaurant in Nagasaki, then the only port open to the outside world. In his desire to feed something nutritious and affordable to the poor young Chinese students visiting Dejima Island near the bustling port city, owner Chin Heijun called upon a favorite soup from back home, *tonniishiimen* (also similar to Korean *jjamppong*). His soup was made by sautéing pork, cabbage, bean sprouts, mushrooms, and local seafood, such as squid, shrimp, and fish cake (*chikuwa*), in lard. To this he added a creamy, milky-white broth—not unlike that for *tonkotsu ramen*—made by simmering pork bones and several whole chickens and additional chicken bones together for three to four hours. Thick, chewy wheat noodles were cooked in the substantial stock for extra flavor. Initially called "Chinadon," or "Chinese udon," Chin changed it to "Champon." It quickly became popular in Nagasaki's Chinatown, and was soon considered a Japanese dish. Today, it is said that there are more than one hundred Chinese restaurants in the rebuilt city of Nagasaki, but there are more than a thousand restaurants offering champon. And while ramen may be the noodle soup most associated with Japanese food around the world, the Ringer Hut champon chain has outlets throughout Asia and the United States.

selected by **Pat Nourse**

Louis Durand PÂTISSERIE DURAND

France 1910

recipe → **p 272**

Paris-Brest

Created by the owner of a bakery outside of Paris to celebrate a bicycle race between the cities of Paris and Brest—the 1891 precursor of the Tour de France—this pastry was made in the shape of a wheel. Once baked, the sliced (flaked) almond –topped *pâte à choux* ring is sliced in half horizontally, filled with a pralineed hazelnut pastry cream whipped with butter (called crème mousseline). The pastry cream is piped with a fluted tip, which creates vertical stripes that mimic spokes of the wheel, and can be made in a large or individual size.

Although the Durand family has guarded the recipe for more than one hundred years, versions appear in patisserie cases and on restaurant menus across France, whether it's a limited-edition Ispahan interpretation by Pierre Hermé (see page 171) or a chocolate and walnut version served by Cedric Grolet at Le Meurice. In the United States, the French chef Ludo Lefebvre brought the classic dessert to the attention of Los Angeles dwellers at Trois Mecs in the 2000s, and at influential New York restaurant Le Coucou, Daniel Rose put pastry chef Daniel Skurnick's rendition on the menu, in which the crème mousseline is lightened with whipped cream in lieu of butter. At Theodore Rex in Houston, chef Justin Yu skews savory, flavoring his filling with Swiss cheese and layering it with burnt honey caramel. Even today, the Paris-Brest is a dessert that only an endurance cyclist could consume without care.

selected by **Susan Jung, Pat Nourse**

Alfredo di Lelio ALFREDO ALLA SCROFA
Italy 1914

recipe → **p 272**

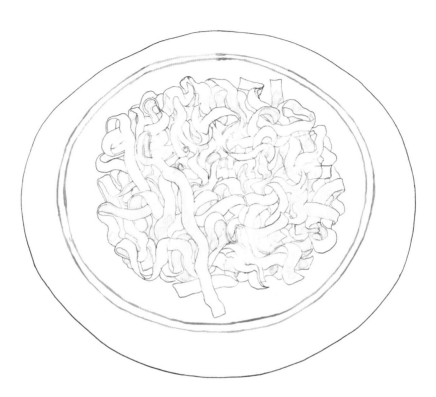

Fettuccine Alfredo

Celebrities and food writers brought this pasta from Rome to America in the late 1920s. Like many imports to the States, it was made much bigger, richer, and more complicated. Today, Americans consider Fettuccine Alfredo one of the top pasta dishes—one that an Italian would not recognize.

After giving birth to her son, Roman restaurateur Alfredo di Lelio's wife, Ines, lost her appetite. To entice her to eat, di Lelio added copious amounts of Parmesan and butter to fettuccine. It worked, so he put it on the menu at his restaurant, where he prepared it tableside on a warm platter. Then, in 1927, the American movie stars Douglas Fairbanks and Mary Pickford had the fettuccine several times while vacationing in Rome. (They loved it so much, they gave di Lelio a gold fork and spoon set engraved with their signatures and the note "To Alfredo—the king of the noodles.") Back

in Hollywood, they served it to friends. The dish's reputation was further boosted by the *Saturday Evening Post* columnist George Rector, who wrote, "Alfredo doesn't make fettuccine. He doesn't cook fettuccine. He achieves it."

Di Lelio sold the original restaurant in 1943 and retired, but in 1950 decided to open a new restaurant in a different location, called Alfredo di Roma (subtitled *il vero Alfredo,* or "the real Alfredo.") Postwar American tourists visiting Alfredo's further popularized the dish back home. In 1966, the Pennsylvania Dutch noodle company began selling Fettuccine Egg Noodles, the package for which included a recipe for "Alfredo's Sauce." This version called for cream and Swiss cheese in addition to the butter and Parmesan. By the 1970s, American Alfredo sauce had become rich and gloopy, sometimes even containing flour and cream cheese.

selected by **Christine Muhlke**

recipe → **p 273**

Josef Keller CAFÉ AHREND
Germany 1915

Black Forest Cake

Schwarzwälder kirschtorte

Today's versions of this German classic have strayed far from its roots, with some using buttercream instead of whipped cream, chocolate sprinkles in lieu of shavings of dark chocolate, and sticky glacéed cherries in place of fresh sour cherries soaked in the *kirschwasser* (cherry brandy) that is common in the Black Forest thanks to thousands of distilleries. Then again, the cake itself is said not to have originated in the fabled German region but several hundred miles away in Bad Godesburg near Bonn, where the pastry chef Josef Keller was working.

Playing upon a traditional dessert of kirsch-poached cherries with whipped cream from the southern portion of the Black Forest, Keller allegedly began with a base of chocolate pie crust (shortcrust pastry), layering it with chocolate sponge cake, sour cherries, whipped cream, plenty of kirsch, and chocolate shavings. Some think that the cake evokes the traditional women's dress from the Black Forest, a black pinafore worn over a white puff-sleeved shirt and a hat topped with red pompoms that look like giant cherries. Others say that the chocolate curls resemble the dense trees of the region. Today, the original recipe is held by Claus Schäfer, the son of Keller's apprentice, who makes the famous cake at his own café in Triberg, deep in the Black Forest.

The cake didn't trickle down to home cooks until 1951, when the popular German food scientist and inventor Dr. August Oetker included a recipe in his cookbook, *Backen macht Freude*. It spread around the world during the second half of the century. Today, the term "Black Forest" has become synonymous with the simple pairing of chocolate and cherries.

selected by **Pat Nourse**

49

Louis Diat RITZ-CARLTON HOTEL
United States 1917

recipe → **p 273**

Vichyssoise

Créme Vichyssoise glacée

Louis Diat elevated the traditional French potato-leek soup, or *potage parmentier*, to the height of elegance for restaurant and home cooks alike—a spot it maintained for decades until it crashed from favor in the 1980s. In the summer of 1917, the chef was reflecting on his favorite childhood dishes, including the potato-leek soup that his mother and grandmother used to make while he was growing up near the spa town of Vichy. He and his brother would pour milk on it to cool it down. Diat resolved to make it worthy of the Ritz, which meant straining the potato-leek purée twice before adding milk, half-and-half (single cream), *and* heavy (double) cream. Minced chives were sprinkled on top to add color to the pure-white soup, as well as to underscore the leeks. He named it *Crème Vichyssoise glacée*, or iced Vichy cream—a confusing moniker for the French, since "Vichy" typically refers to a dish of carrots with butter

and sugar. (And following the events of World War II in Vichy, the name took on a more sinister association. In 1941, a group of chefs tried to change the name to *crème gauloise*.)

The first night that it was served, the American financier Charles M. Schwab ordered a bowl, then immediately requested a second helping. It remained on the dinner menu every night that summer, and every summer thereafter, until the requests for it grew to the point that it was put on the lunch menu as well and kept on year-round. (At the time, leeks were hard to find in the US; one of Diat's vegetable suppliers contracted with a farmer to grow them for the Ritz.) Diat originated several hundred dishes during his career, including Chicken Gloria Swanson and Fillet of Sole Lincoln. To his great chagrin, it was this soup that made his legacy.

selected by **Pat Nourse**

recipe → **p 273**

French Dip Sandwich

Legend has it that the French dip sandwich was created by accident. When Philippe Mathieu, a French immigrant who opened his first sandwich shop in 1908 in Los Angeles, inadvertently dropped a French roll into a pan of savory beef drippings, a sandwich staple was born. A hurried fireman took it as-is and returned the following day with friends. Angelenos' love of soggy sandwiches quickly spread. While a long-standing debate over the recipe's true origins remains between Philippe's the Original and Cole's P.E. Buffet (which serves its jus, or gravy, on the side), these days Philippe's can feed up to 3,000 people a day. The popularity of hot dunked sandwiches reached other cities in the United States as well, such as Chicago's hot Italian beef and the beef on weck in Buffalo, New York.

The traditional French dip consists of thinly sliced roast beef on a freshly baked seven-inch French roll (softer and thicker than a baguette, with a lightly crackling exterior), often with Swiss cheese. Once assembled, jus is ladled over the sandwich. The jus derives from the pan drippings of the roasting meat: the restaurant adds water to the concentrated drippings throughout the day, then adds chicken stock to half of the meat juices and simmers it down overnight. There are four dip styles, indicating the amount of moisture the customer wants for the roll: dry, single-dipped, double-dipped, and wet (in which the entire sandwich is submerged). It's often served with a side of Philippe's house-made hot mustard.

The iconic sandwich has received a modern revival in restaurants across the country in recent years. In New York City, 4 Charles Prime Rib and Minetta Tavern elevate the sandwich form in a white tablecloth setting.

selected by **Pat Nourse**

Marie Bourgeois HÔTEL BOURGEOIS
France 1920

recipe → **p 274**

Hot Pâté

Pâté chaud de la mère Bourgeois

While la Mère Brazier and la Mère Fillioux are the most commonly remembered "mothers" of Lyonnais cuisine from the 1930s, Marie Bourgeois made many significant contributions to the region's cooking at her restaurant in a small village outside of Lyon. She, too, was one of the first women to be awarded three stars by the Michelin guide when it debuted in 1933, and had already been the first woman named to the secretive dining association the Club des Cent. She is known for many of her recipes, including her Bresse chicken with morels, her îles flottantes with pink praline and her gratin of crayfish tails. But it was her *pâté chaud*, or hot pâté, that drew the likes of Charles de Gaulle, Josephine Baker, and the Aga Khan to the tiny village where she cooked.

Pâtés had been cooked in dough-lined terrines since medieval times as a means of preserving the fatty, flavorful farce in the absence of refrigeration. Louis XIV made them especially popular. But it was the Lyonnais who came to claim mastery of the form, none more so than la Mère Bourgeois. Stunningly executed, rich, hearty, and luxuriously excessive, hers was also unique in that it was served warm and sauced with a Madeira and black truffle reduction. The lard-lined pastry case was filled with alternating layers of farce (made from sautéed foie gras scraps and Bresse chicken liver) and thin strips of chicken, pork, and veal that had been marinated for twenty-four hours in Madeira and chicken stock. At the center of the layers was a decadent log of foie gras and black truffles. No wonder it was said that Mère Bourgeois began her terrine on Monday in order to serve it on Saturday. Such pâtés continued their popularity thanks to the likes of Paul Bocuse, Georges Blanc, and Bernard Loiseau.

selected by **Howie Kahn**

52

recite → **p 274**

Eugénie Brazier LA MÈRE BRAZIER
France 1921

Chicken in Half Mourning

Volaille demi-deuil

Eugénie Brazier's rustic yet refined *cuisine lyonnaise* made her the first chef to hold six Michelin stars simultaneously, both at her Lyon restaurant, La Mère Brazier—where she was the first woman in France to hold three stars—and her countryside lodge, Le Col de la Luère. At both restaurants she served the same menu: a salad of artichoke hearts and foie gras followed by a young hen from the nearby region of Bresse, slices of black truffle slipped beneath its skin before it was poached. Served with plum pickles and an enriched reduction of its broth, the chicken was so tender that it was sliced before the guest with a table knife, the only showy note in what the food writer Elizabeth David described in *An Omelette and a Glass of Wine* as "an extraordinary restaurant" where "everything, the food, the wine, the service, could be best described as of a sumptuous simplicity, but lighthearted and somehow all of a piece."

Brazier's unchanging menu was inspired by the Burgundian farm girl's brief time working as a washerwoman for La Mère Fillioux, one of the most famous of the "mother" chefs in Lyon in the 1800s and the inventor of the *poularde* recipe. Opened in an old grocery store in 1921 when she was just twenty-six, Brazier's restaurant was instantly popular. Bocuse arrived at Le Col de la Luère fresh from the army in 1946 and learned simplicity and rigor in sourcing from her kitchens. Just as Brazier made her name with Fillioux's recipe, Bocuse built his reputation upon his tribute to La Mère Brazier by poaching his *poularde demi-deuil* not in a muslin cloth but in a pig's bladder, a masterful piece of showmanship originated by her peer, Fernand Point at La Pyramide (see page 61), and one that bypassed her secret, "to cook 15 at a time . . . at least."

selected by **Howie Kahn**

53

recipe → **p 275**

Green Goddess Dressing

With Caesar and Cobb, we remember the salad itself. But who knows what was in the original Green Goddess Salad beyond its vibrant, herby dressing? Well, in addition to a dressing blended from sour cream, mayonnaise, many anchovies, and chives with generous amounts of tarragon and parsley, as well as tarragon vinegar, the salad that Philip Roemer invented for the actor George Arliss—who was staying at San Francisco's Palace Hotel while performing in the play *The Green Goddess*—featured lump crabmeat scooped into a canned artichoke heart, then considered a luxury. The dressing is said to have descended from the *sauce au vert* that typically accompanied smoked or grilled eel during the reign of Louis XIII. Almost a century after its creation, the dressing is still served at the Palace Hotel, albeit alongside a more refined version of the salad (without the canned artichokes), the dressing now lightened with olive oil and containing considerably more herbs.

Even when it was a popular bottled salad dressing in the 1960s and 70s (it was knocked off the shelves by balsamic vinaigrette in the 80s), Green Goddess had a California association, thanks to its herbal freshness and aura of health, if only because of its color. In the late 1990s, Los Angeles chefs like Suzanne Goin at Lucques blended watercress into a homemade mayonnaise for her take. For her contribution to Dan Barber's wastED dinner in 2015, Osteria Mozza chef Nancy Silverton set fried sardine skeletons over a bowl of Green Goddess. Other chefs go full California and blend in avocado. In the South, it remains popular as an accompaniment to fried oysters and other shellfish.

selected by **Pat Nourse**

recipe → **p 275**

Caprese Salad

Insalata Caprese

This iconic Italian appetizer is said to have been invented for a dinner in honor of the Futurist poet and writer Filippo Tommaso Marinetti. The author of the revolutionary art manifesto *The Futurist Cookbook* would certainly not have been happy with traditional food, and he apparently considered pasta too heavy. And so the chef at the Grand Hotel Quisisana on the island of Capri arranged slices of the tomatoes that grew so well on the island with leaves of basil that seemed to sprout from every terraced yard. When paired with cool, creamy slices of mozzarella and finished with olive oil, the resulting combination was far greater than the sum of its summery parts. (The fact that the red, white, and green resembled the Italian flag did not go unnoticed.) A few decades later, when the Egyptian King Farouk asked for a quick meal at the hotel during closing time, he was served a sandwich made with the Caprese salad. He spread the word amongst his jet-set cadre, who helped take the "recipe" with them as they traveled around the globe. (Farouk was also served a version of the salad with squid ink standing in for the basil to mimic the Egyptian flag, which did not make the cut.) The salad is now synonymous with Italian food—and with summer dining, its fast, fresh simplicity having become almost a formula as chefs substitute other vegetables or fruit and herbs. The mozzarella, however, remains untouchable.

selected by **Christine Muhlke**

Caesar Cardini CAESAR'S PLACE

Mexico 1924

recipe → **p 275**

Caesar Salad

Necessity is the mother of invention. Or so the story goes. This simple yet alchemical salad was allegedly thrown together on July 4, 1924, when the Tijuana outpost of Italian-born chef Caesar Cardini's San Diego restaurant was overrun with holidaying Americans in search of booze during Prohibition. The French-trained Cardini took what he had left in the kitchen—romaine lettuce, raw egg, croutons, Worcestershire sauce, Parmesan, lemon juice, and olive oil—and prepared it tableside in a large wooden bowl in order to make it seem impressive. The lettuce spears coated in the umami-rich dressing—originally intended as finger food—were so popular that the restaurant became a tourist attraction. By 1948, Cardini had to patent the recipe for his dressing, which he and his daughter Rosa began bottling and selling in Los Angeles.

In 1953, a group of French chefs deemed Caesar's salad the most important American dish of the previous fifty years.

In facy, Cardini's brother, Alex, claimed that while his brother had developed the dressing, it was he who first made the salad for pilots based in nearby San Diego. (Called "Aviator's Salad," it used lime juice and garlic, with anchovies in lieu of Worcestershire.) Another cook at the restaurant claimed the dish as his own, having adapted it from his mother's recipe.

The stories behind Caesar salad can't compare to the countless variations on its greatness, the most recent being the 2007 version in which Joshua McFadden, then the chef at Franny's in Brooklyn, New York, rebelled by using chiffonaded lacinato kale (cavolo nero) in lieu of romaine (see page 204).

selected by **Pat Nourse, Diego Salazar**

Luis Federico Leloir MAR DEL PLATA GOLF CLUB
Argentina 1925

recipe → **p 276**

Salsa Golf

A popular sauce born out of boredom—and not by a chef, but a teenager. In 1925, Luis Federico Leloir and his friends were eating at the country club in Mar del Plata, Argentina. Tired of the usual plain mayonnaise *aderezo,* or dressing, that usually accompanied a cocktail of raw shrimp, Leloir asked the kitchen to send out a tray of condiments with which to experiment. The winning sauce was a combination of mayonnaise and ketchup, with a few drops of Cognac and Worcestershire sauce added (some say it was hot sauce). He dubbed it Salsa Golf.

"There's nothing special about the anecdote," said Víctor Ego Ducrot, author of *Los sabores de la patria.* "It was just a bunch of bored kids doing what bored kids do." What makes it so notable, he says, is that both the sauce and its inventor went on to play major roles in twentieth-century Argentina.

The popularity of the sauce grew slowly until big brands like Fanacoa started mass-producing it in the 1960s, joined by Hellmann's, which had started making regional varieties in South America, in the 1970s. Fast-forward to 1980, and every cocktail party was kicked off with hearts of palm with salsa golf (*palmitos con salsa golf*) and shrimp cocktail (*cóctel de camarones*). Today, it's still a popular condiment throughout Argentina, used on everything from salads and grilled meat to pizza and fast food, while a combination of mayo and ketchup is essential in countries like Colombia and Puerto Rico.

As for Leloir, in 1970, he won the Nobel Prize for chemistry. He and his colleagues stopped briefly to drink champagne out of pipettes to celebrate. "If I had patented that sauce, we'd have a lot more money for research right now," he later said.

selected by **Pat Nourse**

recipe → **p 276**

Chiffon Cake

The Brown Derby restaurant was the place to be during Hollywood's Golden Age: where deals were made, the elite mingled and martini-ed, and stars were born. One such star was the Chiffon Cake (and the Cobb Salad, page 65). Harry Baker, an insurance salesman turned caterer, started selling his cake to the restaurant, where it quickly received great fanfare. It was similar to an angel food cake, which uses up to a dozen egg whites but no fat, but somehow more glamorous: light as air, but richer, taller, and prettier. He guarded the original recipe so closely that he even went to the length of disposing of his own garbage so that no one would rifle through it in search of his secret.

Twenty years later, he sold the recipe to General Mills, which marketed it as the first new cake in one hundred years. In 1948, housewives around the country opened up their *Better Homes & Gardens* magazines to find Betty Crocker's Orange Chiffon Cake, made billowy but moist thanks to vegetable oil instead of the usual shortening or butter. For the diet-conscious starlets and starstruck of the time, what could be better? Over the decades, the cake has been dolled up with ice cream, whipped cream, and various flavors, made from boxes of Betty Crocker and from scratch. It's gone in and out of fashion, usually in sync with which fats we deem acceptable; but it will forever be an American classic that changed the way many Americans bake.

selected by **Pat Nourse**

Jean Baptiste Virlogeux SAVOY HOTEL

United Kingdom 1929

recipe → **p 277**

Omelet Arnold Bennett

Yet another classic born of a finicky regular at a high-end restaurant—in this case at London's Savoy Hotel. That's where, in 1929, the English author Arnold Bennett was staying while researching the second of his books set there, *Imperial Palace* (1930). Although the dish was developed by a French chef, it has a distinct English accent—one that has made it an enduring favorite, with chefs like Marcus Wareing and Hugh Fearnley-Whittingstall adapting it. It remains on the menu at the Savoy (currently called the Savoy Grill) to this day. The food writer Diana Henry declared the Omelet Arnold Bennett one of the ten dishes you can't leave the UK without trying, up there with roast beef and Yorkshire pudding. The version served at The Wolseley in London is particularly popular.

The fluffy open omelet is topped with smoked haddock that has been cooked in milk and cream infused with bay leaves and nutmeg. The cooking liquid is then used to make a béchamel, which is added to a hollandaise sauce and then cut with whipped cream. Once the eggs are almost set, the fish and sauce are added off the heat, along with a sprinkling of grated Parmesan. The golden-brown omelet is served in the pan in which it was cooked—usually as an incredibly rich breakfast dish, but sometimes also as an appetizer to share for lunch or dinner. Bennett died two years after his namesake dish was invented—of typhoid resulting from tap water that he drank in a Parisian restaurant against the waiter's advice.

selected by **Pat Nourse, Richard Vines**

recipe → **p 277**

Lobster Roll

There are as many origin stories as there are versions of this American classic. As legend has it, the Connecticut style —chunks of hot, fresh-picked lobster meat drenched in butter and served on a toasted split-top hot dog bun—was first served at Perry's in Milford, Connecticut, when a salesman driving on the new highway in front of former fish salesman Harry Perry's just-opened seafood shack asked for something special. Perry served him hot buttered lobster on bread and put it on the menu once he'd sourced long, buttery rolls from a local bakery. He picked the meat himself and made the rolls four at a time, toasting the bread on a small grill and serving the sandwiches dripping with butter. Soon after, he'd posted a neon sign claiming "Home of the Famous Lobster Roll."

In 1937, the first mention of a lobster roll appeared in *The New York Times*, albeit in reference to one served in Cape Ann, Massachusetts, a "quick lunch delicacy" dressed with mayonnaise and seasonings on a hot dog roll, a style also popular at Maine seafood shacks (these versions both served cold, as opposed to Perry's hot sandwich). While chef Jasper White had served an upscale version at his Boston restaurant, Jasper's, in the late 1980s, it was New York City chef Rebecca Charles, who had lived in Maine, who served the lobster roll at her restaurant, Pearl Oyster Bar, that made headlines in 1997. Her lobster roll, dressed simply with jarred mayonnaise and lemon juice and served on a store-bought bun (she had tried making both components and decided the store-bought versions were most authentic), helped spread this icon of American summers, of docks and seagulls and sunburns. Soon, it was replicated from coast to coast. Everywhere, that is, except Connecticut.

selected by **Susan Jung**

Fernand Point LA PYRAMIDE
France 1930s

recipe → **p 278**

Chicken in a Bladder

Poularde en vessie

"If the divine creator went to the effort of giving us delicious and exquisite things to eat, the least we can do is prepare them well and serve them with ceremony," Fernand Point wrote in his posthumously published cookbook, *Ma Gastronomie.* This chicken dish was no exception. The fabled Bresse chicken from eastern France arrived at the table inside an inflated pig's bladder. Once punctured, the aroma of black truffle was transported to the table. The original sous-vide technique, the bladder allowed the chicken to be delicately poached and flavored by the steam generated by chicken broth, Madeira, and brandy, further infused with foie gras and black truffle. The result was juicy, tender, and exquisitely luxurious.

The recipe can be traced to the "*mères*" of Lyon, the female chefs who learned their craft as cooks for wealthy families before opening their own restaurants. It was Mère Fillioux who first popularized the dish around the turn of the twentieth century, about thirty-five years before Point opened La Pyramide in Vienne, just south of Lyon. It was there that the twenty-four-year-old chef began to put in motion the philosophy behind what would become nouvelle cuisine, thanks to protégés like Paul Bocuse, Alain Chapel, and Jean and Pierre Troisgros. Point's dedication to local, seasonal ingredients, coupled with a desire to move French food beyond Escoffier to embrace something lighter and more modern was totally new at the time. Also new was Point's desire to be in the dining room as well as in the kitchen, thereby allowing him to serve large portions to his guests and make sure they were happy.

Today, the classic version is served by Éric Fréchon at Le Bristol in Paris, while in New York, Daniel Humm of Eleven Madison Park places a celery root (celeriac) inside the bladder.

selected by **Christine Muhlke**

Pat Olivieri PAT'S KING OF STEAKS
United States 1933

recipe → **p 278**

Philly Cheesesteak

The street-cart sandwich that came to represent a city. The Philadelphia cheesesteak was born when an Italian immigrant's young son, who was selling hot dogs and fish cakes on a corner in South Philly, tired of his offerings one day and asked his brother, Harry, to run to the butcher shop for some scraps of meat. Harry came back with thinly sliced beef, which Pat crisped up on his griddle with some onions and served it all on a hot dog bun. As the legend would have it, a cab driver who frequented their cart liked what he smelled and asked Olivieri to make him his off-menu sandwich. He spread the word to his cabbie friends, and told Olivieri that he should stop making hot dogs to focus on his new creation. A street star was born.

Cheese didn't enter the picture for another decade when, it's said, the manager at Olivieri's busy new brick-and-mortar restaurant on the same corner melted provolone on his sandwich. (While there were rival steak sandwich places by then, Pat's was the first to offer cheese, thereby inventing the cheesesteak. When the sprayable cheese product Cheez Whiz was invented in 1952, the bright orange goo quickly made its way onto cheesesteaks.) Today, the nomenclature while ordering a cheesesteak—made internationally famous when Sylvester Stallone ate one in the 1976 movie *Rocky*—can be intimidating. It's important to always lead with the cheese: "One Whiz with" is a cheesesteak with Cheez Whiz and fried onions, while "One Provolone without" is a provolone-topped sandwich without fried onions. If it's your first time in the City of Brotherly Love, it's best to order one of each.

selected by **Susan Jung, Diego Salazar**

Guo Zhaohua and Zhang Tianzheng FUQI FEIPIAN
China 1933

recipe → **p 278**

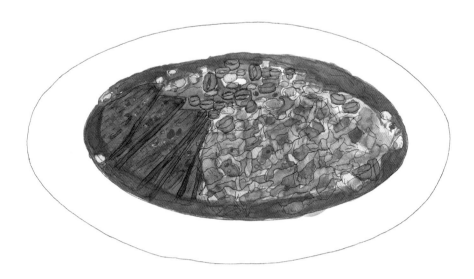

Husband and Wife Lung Slices

Fuqi feipian

This dish might not have the most appetizing name. But the Chengdu couple who introduced it at their stall in 1933 hit upon a winning combination: thin slices of cold beef and offal, such as tripe, tendon, tongue, heart, and, yes, lung, served cold in an electrifying sauce of Sichuan peppercorns, sesame paste, five-spice powder, scallions, and red chili oil that both numbs and illuminates the mouth. On top of that, it offers a tantalizing range of textures, with crisp peppercorn husks, fresh celery, cilantro (coriander), and toasted peanuts contrasting against the slick, tender, and chewy pieces of meat and lacy-edged odd bits.

Fuqi feipian derived from a Qing Dynasty street-food dish of cold, thinly sliced beef supplemented with cow organs in order to lower the price, making it a favorite of students and rickshaw drivers. Guo Zhaohua and Zhang Tianzheng's flavorful additions created a new sensation, and to this day, countless variations, including one with rabbit, have thrived. In 2017, it got a new life in America, when *GQ* food critic Brett Martin tasted the appetizer version served by Chongqing natives at Pepper Twins in Houston. They renamed it "Mr. & Mrs. Smith," a more palatable play on the original name and the Brad Pitt/Angelina Jolie movie. As Martin described his experience, "I had not realized how much I was sleepwalking until flavor hit me in the face. The dish is a numbing, burning, textural masterpiece, and the kind of thing a budding empire is built on." Now that Americans are more open to both Sichuan flavors (see page 235) and nose-to-tail options, look for more husbands and wives—and perhaps their lungs—to follow.

selected by **Pat Nourse**

Thornton Prince III PRINCE'S HOT CHICKEN SHACK
United States 1936

recipe → p 279

Hot Chicken

Hot chicken is fried chicken that is spicy to the bone. Eating it is a rite of passage for those who both live in and travel to Nashville, Tennessee. And, as those who have survived that first taste (clinging to the slices of white bread served underneath to soak up the blood-red oil and attempting to douse the fire with the sweet dill pickle slices on top) will agree: Hot Chicken is not a food, it is an addiction.

No one outside of the family that has owned Prince's since the 1930s knows what Hot Chicken really is. As the family legend goes, Thornton Prince III's girlfriend got her revenge on him after he came home late one night by making his fried chicken unbearably spicy, adding cayenne and other spices. Except he loved it and started selling it out of his home. He then opened the BBQ Chicken Shack, which eventually moved near the Grand Ole Opry. (At the time, Southern businesses were segregated. At Prince's, African-Americans sat in the front, while the whites entered through a rear door and sat in back.) Now located next to a nail salon in a run-down strip mall, Prince's is a pilgrimage site for those who seek the miraculous transformation wrought by such powerful spice. (Sweating, crying, euphoria, and gastric breakdown are common when ordering anything above "mild" on the menu, which goes up to XXXHot.) Regulars are known to wake up in the middle of the night craving the made-to-order chicken, which is why Prince's stays open until 4 a.m.

"Nashville Hot Chicken" is now its own category. Restaurants touting their own recipes have opened throughout the South, as well as in New York, Chicago, and even Melbourne.

selected by **Christine Muhlke, Pat Nourse**

Robert Cobb THE BROWN DERBY

United States 1937

recipe → **p 279**

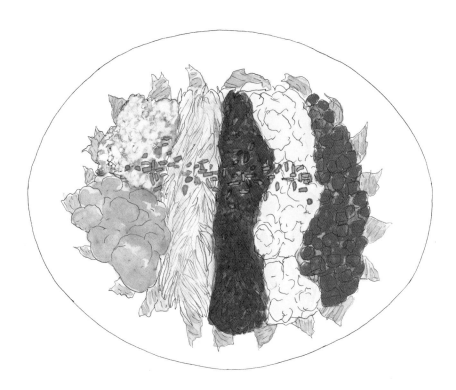

Cobb Salad

The original chopped salad, this is another restaurant invention born of scarcity that has lent itself to countless riffs. It is said that the owner of this Los Angeles celebrity canteen was rummaging around the kitchen in search of a late-night snack. He grabbed what he could from the fridge, chopping up romaine, lettuce, watercress, and chicory and topping it with chopped chicken breast, hard-boiled eggs, bacon, tomato, Roquefort, and that abundant California staple, avocado. Doused with a French dressing made with oil, vinegar, sugar, Worcestershire, and mustard powder, it's said that it was so good that the owner of Grauman's Chinese Theatre, who was there for that midnight meal, came back the next day and requested the "Cobb Salad." Movie moguls would regularly send their drivers to pick up cartons of the salad, and the lure of the restaurant's famous clientele also helped to create an aura around the dish. Over the years and throughout multiple locations (including one in Disney World), the Brown Derby has sold more than four million Cobbs.

Robert Cobb wasn't a chef, which is perhaps what has made this filling, protein-dense salad so appealing to Americans: they know that no matter where they eat one, whether in a shabby diner or a hotel room halfway around the world, it will look and taste almost exactly the same. (It's the Club Sandwich of salads, not to mention the only salad that most men will deign to order as a lunch entrée.) And of course, it gives chefs license to riff with all manner of meats and cheese.

selected by **Pat Nourse**

recipe → **p 280**

Prime Rib

Certainly Lawry's was not the first restaurant to serve prime rib, but it is the name most closely associated with this extravagant dish, also known as standing rib roast or rib of beef. When the restaurant opened in 1938, the dinner—a mere $1.25 (95 pence)—included a Jurassic-size hunk of rare, tender beef *au jus*, paired with steaming Yorkshire pudding, mashed potatoes with gravy, and creamed corn or spinach. (The restaurant opened with a full menu; within six months, every entrée had been taken off except for prime rib.) What makes Lawry's unique is the way that they carve the prime rib to order tableside, using custom carts designed by cofounder Lawrence Frank. The Art Deco–style stainless steel "silver" carts are five feet (1.5 m) long, weigh nearly nine hundred pounds (408 kg) when fully loaded—helped in part by the charcoal pans in the lower section—and are wheeled around the grand dining room throughout the evening, catching the eyes of customers eager to witness the performance. At the original location, the floors had to be reinforced so that they wouldn't collapse under the weight. At the time, a cart cost $3,200 (£2,420); today, they can sell at auction for more than $30,000 (£22,700). Carving staff must train for six months in order to be able to wear a Royal Order of Carvers medallion around their necks. While tableside prime rib service never went out of style, it has found a new audience among chefs. Today, it features at such restaurants as Mission Chinese Food (which owns a vintage Lawry's cart), The Grill, and Thomas Keller's TAK Room in New York City. Los Angeles resident Roy Choi, who grew up with Lawry's as the special-occasion ideal, put a prime rib rice bowl on his menu at the casual Chego in 2010.

selected by **Susan Jung, Christine Muhlke**

recipe → **p 280**

Gunkan Sushi

Gunkanmaki

Sushi has evolved to take many forms since its first recorded mention in a fourth-century Chinese dictionary. The word sushi derives from an antiquated word meaning "sour-tasting," and the dictionary details a process in which salted fish was placed on cooked rice and allowed to lacto-ferment for months to slow the bacterial growth in the fish (and create the sour taste). By 1824 in Edo (now Tokyo) a sushi stall owner sped up the process by adding rice vinegar and salt to the rice and allowing it to sit for a few minutes before forming it into a bite-size ball and placing a piece of raw fish on top. This *nigiri* (hand-pressed) form became the norm—what Westerners associate with sushi today, along with *makizushi* (rolled sushi).

In 1941, the Tokyo sushi chef Hisaji Imada created a new kind of *nigiri* at his restaurant, which was just a ten-minute walk from the Tsukiji fish market. Called *gunkanmaki*—warship or battleship roll—Imada constructed it by wrapping a band of toasted nori, or seaweed, around the sushi rice to create an oval, with the nori higher than the rice, creating a wall and leaving a space above the rice that could be filled. Imada's *gunkanmaki* form allowed him to use ingredients that were too soft or fine to top regular *nigiri* or *maki*, such as uni, *ikura* (salmon roe), oysters, quail eggs, and *negitoro* (chopped tuna belly and scallions), thereby expanding sushi into a new realm of textures. Imada ran Ginza Kyubey until his death in 1985. His son, Yosuke, then took over, followed by his own son, Kagehisa, maintaining the level of quality while expanding the family's empire.

selected by **Pat Nourse**

67

Ignacio Anaya VICTORY CLUB
Mexico 1943

recipe → p 280

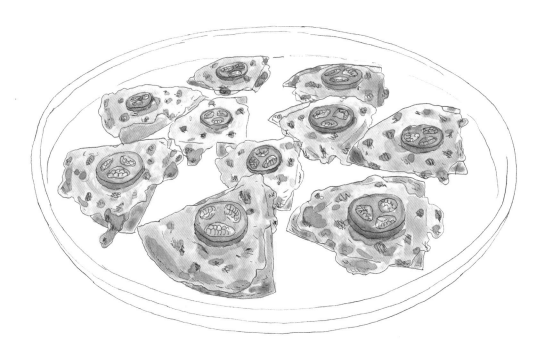

Nachos

Nacho's especiales

Like Caesar Salad (see page 56), nachos trace their roots to a Mexican border town, hungry Americans, a kitchen's depleted pantry, and a very resourceful cook. When a group of about a dozen wives of American military men stationed at the base in nearby Fort Duncan, Texas, found themselves hungry in Piedras Negras, Mexico, after a day of shopping—only to discover that most of the nearby restaurants had closed at that hour—Ignacio Anaya, the maître d' (some accounts list him as chef) at the Victory Club, went into the kitchen to make them something from what was left at that late hour. Anaya sliced and fried some tortillas to make chips, covered them with shredded cheese and sliced jalapeño peppers, and put it into the oven for a few minutes, until the cheese was melted and bubbling. He served the ladies the snack, which he named after himself —or rather, his nickname, Nacho. *Nacho's especiales* were born.

A church cookbook from nearby Eagle Pass, Texas, later included Anaya's recipe, which became a Mexican (and American) staple. Indeed, the dish points to an early example of border cuisine, in which the Americans living in Southern California, Texas, New Mexico, and Arizona appropriated Mexican classics like tacos, burritos, guacamole, enchiladas, and chili con carne into their own regional cuisines.

In 1960, the inventor and his son, Ignacio Anaya, Jr., tried to patent the recipe in San Antonio, Texas. They were told that after seventeen years, the dish now belonged to the public domain. Anaya Jr., who owned Nacho's Restaurant in Piedras Negras, also served as the judge for the Mexican city's annual nachos contest. Countless variations of nachos have been introduced over the years, but the alchemy of the original —salty, crispy, creamy, spicy—remains unbeatable.

selected by **Pat Nourse**

Helen Chock HELENA'S HAWAIIAN FOOD
United States 1946

recipe → **p 281**

Poke

Poke (pronounced poh-kay, meaning "to cut or section") had centuries of culinary history on the Hawaiian islands before it was popularized—first in 1970s Hawaii and then worldwide. Originally associated with the native Polynesians who populated the islands, the dish consisted of raw chopped reef fish seasoned with seaweed and sea salt—which also acted as a preservative—and mixed with roasted, ground candlenuts, or kukuis. The ingredients evolved as the islands' population became more mixed. Japanese immigrants arriving in the late 1800s began marinating the raw fish in soy sauce and sesame oil, and adding green onion and wasabi. Korean immigrants added kimchi. Most historians agree that the dish was not called "poke" until the 1970s, around the same time that fishermen began catching more ahi tuna. The fish was plentiful enough to be affordable to home cooks and supermarkets.

If you're in Hawaii and looking to try authentic poke, you couldn't go far wrong by visiting Helena's Hawaiian Food, a Honolulu institution that has been serving traditional recipes unchanged since it was first opened by novice cook Helen Chock in 1946. In recognition of this, Helena's was awarded the Regional Classic Award by the James Beard Foundation in 2000.

Poke gained further acknowledgment in the early 1990s when Sam Choy, a chef associated with the Hawaii Regional Cuisine movement, launched an annual poke contest for chefs from across the state. Later, Australian chef Bill Granger (see page 158) added avocado to the poke at his Honolulu location before bringing it to his influential restaurants in Australia, London, and Japan. Today, every major city in the world has fast-casual outlets selling approximations of the humble, traditional dish.

selected by **Howie Kahn**

69

recipe → **p 281**

French Onion Soup

Soupe à l'oignon

Mentions of onion soup in France can be found as far back as 1649, in a political pamphlet titled "Mazarin's Last Onion Soup." The first recipe appeared two years later in the cookbook *Le vrai cuisinier françois* [sic], a book that marked the break from the cuisine of the Middle Ages. It took four centuries of evolution—the onions, sautéed in butter, slowly shading from blonde to golden brown, the addition of toasted bread and cheese—before it became the soup we now know: a hefty crock of caramelized onions in beef broth topped with slices of baguette that are hidden beneath grated Gruyère or Emmental cheese before being broiled (grilled). Outside of its home, the rich, bubbling, life-affirming soup-as-meal is known as "French Onion Soup." But in France, it is just onion soup, a dish that has come to be associated with late-night dining, whether because of hard work or revelry.

Beginning around the turn of the twentieth century, places began staying open late around the Les Halles market in Paris, offering gratinéed onion soup as an affordable restorative for those who had just finished or were about to begin working at the nearby food stalls, and for those fashionable nightbirds who were still out on the town and needed a way to "wash their stomachs" so they could begin drinking anew. Starting in 1947, it became associated with Au Pied de Cochon, a twenty-four-hour restaurant near the market. It uses white onions from Cévennes, gently browned in butter, then simmered in beef stock with thyme and bay leaves. Soup crocks are filled three-quarters of the way, topped with buttered toasts, then layered with grated cheese and broiled (grilled). It remains the preferred restorative of Parisian night owls, even though the market itself has long since retreated to the outskirts of town.

selected by **Christine Muhlke**

recipe → **p 281**

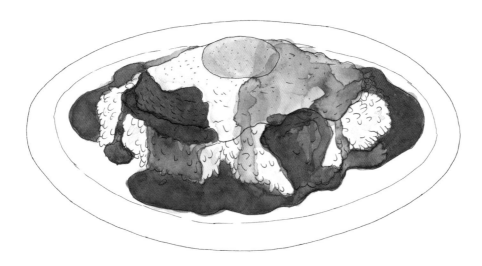

Loco Moco

The food of Hawaii can't help but be fusion: for centuries, the islands have been populated by migrating Pacific Islanders, Puerto Ricans, Caucasians from Portugal and America, Asians from Japan, Korea, Southeast Asia, and the Philippines, and more. The "local" food that began to appear in the 1920s and 30s—spread through lunch trucks, mom-and-pop shops, and the homemade lunches traded by school kids and plantation workers—mixed all of these nations onto one heaping plate, such as spaghetti with meat sauce mixed with Spam and hot dogs. Starchy and heavy, it was food that haole (non-Polynesian) American tourists never saw. So when the owners of the Lincoln Grill in the town of Hilo were asked by local teenagers to make them something that was an affordable alternative to American-style sandwiches and less time-consuming to eat for breakfast than Asian fare, they put two scoops of white rice on a plate, added a hamburger, and doused the whole with brown mushroom gravy. (The fried egg was added later.) Allegedly called Loco Moco (loh-KOO moh-KOO) after one of the teens' nicknames, Loco, it is the original Hawaiian fast food meets comfort food, what's known as "local grind," as opposed to the buffet fare served at upscale resorts and tourist restaurants on the island. It is eaten at breakfast, lunch, and dinner, with either chopsticks or a knife and fork.

Today, in an effort to serve food that reflects Hawaii's heritage, chefs are translating the traditional Loco Moco for their higher-end Pacific Rim restaurants. Hawaiian chef Sam Choy places a crab cake atop fried rice and sautéed Maui onions, while Alan Wong pairs nori-flecked rice with a pork-and-shrimp patty and a quail egg.

selected by **Pat Nourse**

Giuseppe Cipriani HARRY'S BAR

Italy 1950

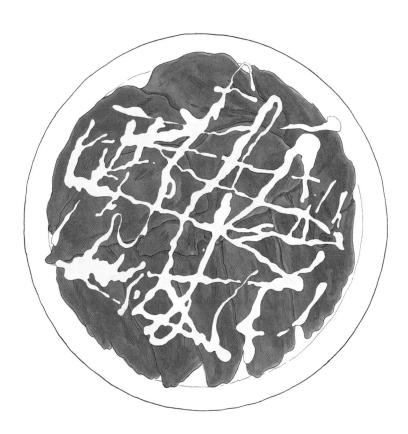

recipe → **p 282**

Carpaccio

The dietary restrictions of the rich and titled can indeed yield contributions to the culinary canon. In 1950, the successful Venetian restaurateur Giuseppe Cipriani needed to please an ill countess, whose doctor had placed her on a strict diet and ordered her not to eat any cooked meat. Raw meat it would be.

"To make her happy," Cipriani wrote in his 1978 memoir, "I thought of slicing fillet of beef as thinly as possible. But the meat by itself was rather insipid, tasteless." And so, a sauce: "I squirted a little sauce on the raw beef and named it in honor of the painter for whom Venice was then holding a show. More importantly, I found that the color of the beef presented to the countess resembled the reds to be found in his paintings."

The sauce that made the soon-infamous pattern on the nearly translucent slices of beef consists of an aioli spiced with Worcestershire, and mustard powder, and thinned with chicken or beef stock. The dish was a sensation, ordered by wealthy travelers from around the globe. And it was through them that it spread. By the time Giuseppe's son, Arrigi (Harry), opened a Cipriani in New York City in 1985, beef carpaccio could be found everywhere from New York's Le Cirque to São Paolo. In 1986, Gilbert Le Coze, a young French chef in New York, made the carpaccio at Le Bernardin with pieces of raw tuna (see page 133) with an Asian-inflected, aioli-based sauce, while at his eponymous restaurant in France, Michel Guérard made it using duck before expanding to seafood —even jewel-like rows of translucent lobster.

selected by **Pat Nourse, Diego Salazar**

recipe → **p 282**

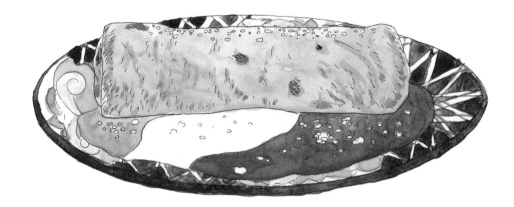

Chimichanga

Chimichangas el Charro

The chimichanga is a colossal creation, one that seems like the epitome of an Americanized Mexican dish: a deep-fried burrito. A large flour tortilla (18 inches/46 cm in diameter) is stuffed with meat, refried beans, onions, grated cheese, rice, and more, the packed parcel held together with toothpicks and dropped into a deep fryer until crisp and browned. Served garnished with salsa, sour cream, shredded lettuce, cheese, and guacamole, it is not for the faint of heart or stomach. But the "chimi" has been an essential part of the Sonoran Mexican–style food of southern Arizona, which was once a part of Mexico and borders the Mexican state of Sonora.

Its origin stories differ. Some assert that fried burritos exist in Mexico under a similar name, while Frontera Grill chef Rick Bayless claims they were invented in Baja, Mexico, where they're known as *chivechangas*. But Tucson, Arizona, claims to be the US birthplace of the fried packet. Many say that it was invented when El Charro Café owner Monica Flin accidentally dropped a burro (the local name for burrito) into a vat of boiling oil. Rather than use a Mexican swear word starting with *ch*—there were children underfoot in her kitchen—she uttered *chimichanga*, the world for "thingamajig." (Flin's great-niece, Carlotta Flores, suggests that her great-aunt first fried a burro to cover up the flavor of the goat that was a popular Mexican filling in the 1920s.) The restaurant now sells more than 10,000 chimis a week at its two locations. In an effort to be more healthful, El Charro now uses canola oil rather than lard for frying. Flores said that they tried posting the calorie count alongside each chimi on the menu (starting at 1,200 for plain beef), but, she told *Sunset* magazine in 1999, "Let's just say my customers didn't appreciate it."

selected by **Diego Salazar**

73

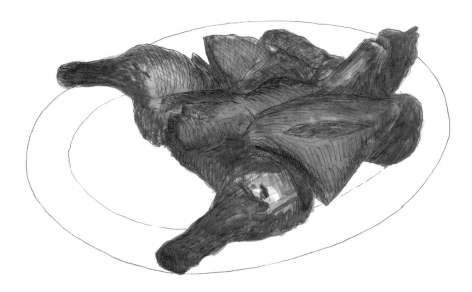

recipe → **p 283**

Piri-Piri Chicken

The spicy piri-piri sauce beloved in South Africa (also known as peri-peri) can be traced back to the fifteenth century, when Portuguese settlers discovered the searingly hot bird's eye chile native to the south of the continent and made a marinade with European ingredients such as red wine vinegar, olive oil, garlic, paprika, and bay leaves. While both Portuguese-Mozambicans and Portuguese-Angolans claim to have created the magical blend, which Mozambican chefs brought to Johannesburg, today it is most often associated with the Nando's franchise, which began serving Piri-Piri Chicken in the South African capital in 1987 and now has cult status around the globe.

While celebrities like David and Victoria Beckham and Prince Harry might favor the Nando's in the UK, they owe a debt to Radium Beer Hall in Johannesburg. Opened in 1929, the city's oldest surviving beer hall and grillhouse was first known for illegally serving blacks alongside whites in defiance of the laws. In the 1950s, it also became known for its Piri-Piri Chicken, a dish that eventually attained national icon status. Marinated overnight and grilled over charcoal, it is served with piri-piri sauce, which is essentially a puréed version of the marinade. Succulent and spicy—the peppers rate 175,000 units on the Scoville heat scale, ranking them just below the powerful Thai chiles—the chicken is best accompanied by a crisp salad, plenty of napkins, and, of course, a beer.

selected by **Pat Nourse**

recipe → **p 283**

Green Gumbo

Gumbo z'herbes

In New Orleans, Holy Thursday is indeed a holy event: locals would head to Dooky Chase's to indulge in Leah Chase's *gumbo z'herbes* before fasting until Easter Sunday. Until her passing in 2019, Chase made over fifty gallons of the stew just once a year, as she did for the six-plus decades that she cooked at her family's restaurant. Unlike the other gumbos on her menu, Chase loaded this one with between seven and eleven types of greens—always an odd number according to Creole superstition—including mustard greens, collards, turnip greens, watercress, carrot and beet tops, kale, cabbage, and spinach. They're stewed down before being puréed or chopped, then sprinkled with flour. While some claim this was descended from *sauce feuilles*, a "sauce of leaves" found in West Africa, this isn't a vegetarian dish: its goal is to provide days' worth of sustenance. And so there are no fewer than five kinds of meat,

including chicken, ham, brisket, beef stew meat, and smoked and hot sausages, simmered until tender and then seasoned with thyme and filé powder (made from ground sassafras leaves). Served over rice, each bite of the green-topped gumbo offers a new flavor and texture, be it sharp and vegetal, beefy and tender, or spicy and porky. Asked by Sara Roahen why she only served it once a year, Chase said "Leave things be special."

It's not just Leah Chase's stew that is so special in New Orleans. It is Chase herself. Starting in 1945, when she married into the family, she worked to make Dooky Chase's a white-tablecloth restaurant for African Americans, with food to rival that of the whites-only restaurants she worked for. Despite the city's "no race-mixing" policy, integrated groups sometimes met in the private dining rooms. It was here that many of Dr. Martin Luther King's protests were mapped out.

selected by **Howie Kahn**

recipe → **p 284**

Royal Hare

Lièvre à la royale

How fantastic to have the fate of a dish shaped by a writer! And, better yet, for the writer to be Colette, that voluptuary of Bordeaux who spent her later decades living in the Palais Royal, also home to the fabled restaurant Le Grand Véfour in Paris. When its chef and owner, Raymond Oliver, cooked a luncheon to celebrate her birthday, Colette requested that *lièvre à la royale* be on the menu. Here the debate began. Oliver, who hailed from Gascon, wanted to make the traditionally rich autumn (fall) dish in the Périgord style, in which the wild hare was deboned, stuffed with a farce of foie gras, truffle, and its organs, rolled into a ballottine and simmered in red wine until it was as tender as silk. Slices were served in a sauce thickened with the animal's blood, as well as foie gras and egg yolks. (The dish, it is said, was first made for King Louis XIV, who had but two teeth.) But Colette wanted it in the Poitou style advanced by

senator Aristide Couteaux in 1898, the game cooked whole in two bottles of Burgundy with up to sixty cloves of garlic and thirty shallots. "What an idea to embalm a hare in foie gras!," she growled at Oliver. And so he made both the traditional version and Collete's, stuffing the hare with a farce of pork, lard, mushrooms, egg, spices, Armagnac, garlic, shallots, and its lungs, liver, and heart, cooking the ballottine in Chambertin wine for four hours and serving it with a blood-enriched sauce.

Although the addition of so many aromatics was considered heresy, Colette wrote of Oliver's dish, with its nearly black sauce, "Who among you, readers, when savoring the authentic *lièvre à la royale*, melting, hot, in the mouth, doubts that 60 cloves of garlic cooperated in its perfection?" Hare stayed on the menu for decades. In the 1970s, Paul Bocuse perfected a twelve-hour version spiced with clove, juniper, and bay.

selected by **Susan Jung, Christine Muhlke, Pat Nourse**

recipe → **p 285**

Bananas Foster

When tasked with coming up with a dessert for a dinner in honor of New Orleans Crime Commissioner Richard Foster, Ella Brennan, the manager of her uncle's restaurant, fussed and carried on, then reached for what was closest at hand: bananas. Split and sautéed in butter, brown sugar, and cinnamon, then flambéed with rum and banana liqueur, Brennan served them à la mode (with ice cream). The dessert was inspired by childhood breakfasts of caramelized bananas and by Baked Alaska (see page 41), the flambéed meringue dessert that was popular at rival restaurant Antoine's.

The newly christened dessert was an instant hit. Luckily, bananas were readily available to the Brennans: in the mid-twentieth century, New Orleans was a major port for the fruit trade due to its convenient proximity to banana-producing cities in Central and South America. It is said that freighters packed with bananas, which had become common in the United States starting in the 1870s, clogged the Mississippi River. Ella's father, John Brennan, had ties to the banana industry both through his own produce company, which often had a surplus of the fruit, and through his wife's family, who were involved with the Standard Fruit Company. In the 1950s, labor crises began to plague the banana industry, resulting in the downfall of the New Orleans fruit trade. Bananas Foster then gained even more symbolic value as an iconic dish of New Orleans because it harkened back to a time when the city was the banana capital of America. This emblem of regional nostalgia is, to this day, Brennan's top-selling dessert, the restaurant flambéing roughly eighteen tons of bananas annually.

selected by **Susan Jung**, **Christine Muhlke**

Peng Chuang-kuei PENG'S GARDEN HUNAN RESTAURANT
China 1955

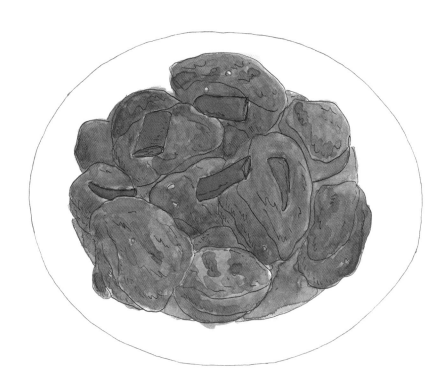

recipe → p 285

General Tso's Chicken

One of the most popular Hunanese dishes in America, General Tso's Chicken is a story of revolution and immigration, as well as of culinary appropriation. Peng Chuang-kuei was a banquet chef for Chinese Nationalist party officials in Hunan, who brought him to Taiwan with them in 1949. In 1955, he had run out of ideas while cooking for a four-day visit by the US joint chiefs of staff. So he marinated pieces of chicken in soy and egg yolk, wok-fried them until crisp, adding plenty of red chiles, then stirred them into a thickened sauce of soy, rice vinegar, chicken stock, and tomato paste (purée). He named it for the Hunanese general Zuo Zongtang (whose last name when Romanized is Tso), who had crushed rebellions in the nineteenth century. "Originally the flavors of the dish were typically Hunanese—heavy, sour, hot and salty," Peng told Fuchsia Dunlop, the author of *The Revolutionary Chinese Cookbook*.

The dish followed him to his Taipei restaurant, which happened to be visited in 1971 by Chinese restaurateurs who had opened restaurants in New York City. In search of new regional cuisines and chefs, rival restaurateurs David Keh and T. T. Wang coincidentally both dined at Peng's and noted the relatively unknown dish. At their new Hunan restaurants in the United States, they added sugar to their General Tso's chicken to make it more palatable to Americans. Both received four-star reviews from *The New York Times*. By the time Peng arrived to open a restaurant, New Yorkers already knew the dish and deemed his version too savory and sour, considering the others to be the original. Although Peng's restaurant closed, he trained many chefs who then spread his dishes across America.

In a twist, Peng's invented tradition has been adopted by Hunanese food writers and influential chefs as authentic.

selected by **Christine Muhlke**

Ichiro Mashita TOKYO KAIKAN

United States 1960s

recipe → **p 286**

California Roll

Imagine being a Japanese sushi chef in California in the 1960s. To Americans of the era, tuna was grayish-pink and came precooked in a can. Edible seaweed paper was pure science fiction. And so chefs who have laid claim to inventing the California Roll, like Ichiro Mashita and his assistant, Teuro, had to consider what the person on the other side of the counter might want: when Mashita left Japan, his sushi master told him that "Americans wouldn't be able to appreciate sushi. He advised me to put it on skewers." Barring that, he replaced fatty tuna (some accounts say that it wasn't always easy to source tuna at the time) with the similarly textured avocado that has been so abundant in Southern California since the 1800s, added crab and cucumber, and rolled it "inside out" so that the vinegared rice was on the outside of the roll as opposed to the nori. This California Roll soon gave way to other novelty rolls, such as the Philadelphia (smoked salmon and cream cheese) and Hawaiian Rolls (avocado, tuna, and pineapple).

The "misbegotten invention," as *The New York Times* restaurant critic Mimi Sheraton called it in 1981, eventually made its way to Japan. But unlike, say, the Chinese adoption of General Tso's Chicken as an "authentic" Hunanese dish decades after it was popularized in New York (see opposite), sushi masters in Japan refuse to serve the *kashu-maki*, a literal translation of "California Roll." In America, it proved to be the ideal gateway to authentic sushi and sashimi—not unlike Nobu Matsuhisa's lightly cooked New-Style Sashimi of 1987 (see page 141). Between 1988 and 1998, the number of sushi restaurants in the US tripled, and California Rolls began being sold in supermarkets.

selected by **Diego Salazar**

79

Pedro Solari CEVICHERIA PEDRO SOLARI
Peru 1960s

recipe → **p 286**

Ceviche

Cooking has never been said to be child's play. But in the case of the twelve-year-old Pedro Solari, it led to one of the most important inventions in Peruvian cuisine. When his mother was running behind in preparing a lunch for sixty guests, he offered to make the ceviche. At the time, traditional ceviche was a time-consuming affair, with pieces of fish left to marinate in bitter orange or lime juice for hours or days, adding ingredients like milk in complex proportions. (Ceviche had been popular in Peru since the Incas, the fish marinated in *chicha*, or corn beer, until the Spanish arrived and planted citrus groves.) But the guests were already arriving, so Pedro threw together fish, lime juice, fresh chiles, onions, and salt and served it in under five minutes, unintentionally modernizing ceviche.

For more than eighty years, Solari has sat at a small table in his twenty-seat, elaborately decorated open-air *cevichería* in Lima, making each bowl himself with the help of his longtime assistant, Teresa. He arrived at sole as his fish of choice when he sampled what a fishmonger had thrown away—sole being considered trash fish at the time, with sea bass as the choice of wealthy diners. Solari insists that each serving be made fresh in the moment, just before eating, and contain only those five simple ingredients. "The chef's touch is crucial," he has said. "Not anyone can combine these flavors in the right proportion." His repositioning of ceviche inspired the likes of Javier Wong and Gastón Acurio, who has said: "How to define that person who, in five minutes, gave me a culinary lesson that I had been seeking fruitlessly for years?" While Solari has many admirers, he has no disciples. Instead, he said, he has an epitaph: "Whoever hasn't eaten my food is screwed." ("*Quien no haya comido mi comida que se joda.*")

selected by **Diego Salazar**

Kazuo Yamagishi TAISHOKEN
Japan 1961

recipe → **p 286**

Tsukemen

Called The God of Ramen, Kazuo Yamagishi began his apprenticeship at a ramen shop in Tokyo's Nakano district at the age of seventeen. He later opened Higashi-Ikebukuro Taishoken and introduced what he called "special made *morisoba*," cold noodles with sauce for dipping that were inspired by having seen his colleagues eat noodles after dipping them in a cup of soup. (Until the 1950s, ramen noodles were called *shina soba*, or Chinese noodles, a reference to the wheat noodles introduced to Japan by Chinese immigrants around the 1860s. They became especially popular after World War II, when low rice yields led to an increased reliance on wheat products such as bread and noodles.) The dish morphed into *tsukemen*, or "dip ramen." The customer is served an enormous bowl of chilled, snappy, chewy wheat noodles, which are slightly thicker than regular ramen noodles, alongside a bowl of hot broth to which such toppings

as egg, *menma* (fermented bamboo shoots), scallions, and nori have been added, as well as the essential slice of pork leg cooked in soy sauce. While the texture of the noodles (made using *kansui*, an alkaline solution that gives the noodles their springiness) is important, it is the broth that Yamagishi has spent decades training hundreds of apprentices to master. The broth requires half a day to prepare and contains chicken bones, pig's feet, burlap (hessian) bags filled with dried mackerel and sardines, ginger, leeks, and more. It is then clarified using chicken skin, broken eggshells, and ground pork. With its richness, bitterness, sweetness, and umami, it is a humble yet heroic dish, one that has inspired the likes of American chefs David Chang and Ivan Orkin, as well as triggering a *tsukemen* boom in Japan in recent years, with new ramen shops dedicated to the style.

selected by **Pat Nourse**

Cecilia Chiang THE MANDARIN
United States 1961

recipe → **p 287**

Tea-Smoked Duck

If anyone is to be credited with the introduction of authentic Chinese food to the United States, it's Cecilia Chiang. Rather than serve the gloopy Cantonese chop suey and egg foo yung that were offered by the city's restaurateurs when she opened in San Francisco's Chinatown in 1961, she dared to serve the more refined recipes of her native Shanghai. The most evocative dish was her Tea-Smoked Duck, which was on no other menu at the time (and for which she had no recipe). The traditional process calls for duck to be rubbed with five-spice powder and Sichuan peppercorns and left to cure overnight, then steamed and placed in a smoker filled with a mixture of rice, black tea, brown sugar, dried orange peel, and star anise. It is caressed by the aromatic wisps of smoke until cooked to an ideal medium-rare.

Chiang was set on preserving the cultural heritage of her homeland through her food. But instead of attracting Chinese customers that valued traditional cuisine, or Americans interested in experiencing a unique facet of (what in reality is) a mosaic of Chinese food culture, The Mandarin remained nearly empty for two years. It was saved by an extremely favorable review from *San Francisco Chronicle* columnist Herb Caen, which designated it as a hidden gem sincerely selling real Chinese food—made with mysterious, exotic vegetables and employing such unfamiliar tools as the wok. Over time, Chiang came to be known as the ultimate word on Chinese cuisine in America, teaching her techniques to greats like Julia Child, James Beard, Alice Waters, Jeremiah Tower, and Marion Cunningham, and mentoring chefs such as Corey Lee at Benu.

selected by **Howie Kahn**

Charles Masson LA GRENOUILLE
United States 1962

recipe → **p 287**

Grand Marnier Soufflé

La Grenouille, founded by Charles Masson in midtown Manhattan in 1962, is one of the last strongholds of French haute cuisine in the city, an era that was ushered in by the 1939 World's Fair. It was there that Masson held his first job in America, having arrived with his mentor, the legendary Henri Soulé, for whom he had worked at the Café de Paris in France. The dish for which La Grenouille is most known is its Grand Marnier Soufflé, an ethereal dessert made even more heavenly by the addition of Grand Marnier liqueur. Masson likely featured this dish as an ode to his wife, Gisèle, who purchased the restaurant behind his back, handed him the keys, and told him to get to work. The story goes that a very pregnant Mme. Masson had requested a Grand Marnier Soufflé at the Waldorf-Astoria to satisfy a craving. When they told her they couldn't make it, the exasperated Masson furiously scribbled the recipe on a napkin and handed it to the waiter. The kitchen obliged her request. The very next morning, their son Charles was born.

Food aside, what's most memorable about Masson was his dedication to creating an aesthetic harmony in his restaurant, from the elaborate flower arrangements that changed daily, to the discontinued peach-tinted lightbulbs that he bought in bulk, ten thousand to an order, to avoid compromising the special ambiance he worked so hard to cultivate. Today, La Grenouille has been around long enough to have become influential again. Its elegance and aesthetic harmony—and its Grand Marnier Soufflés—can be traced to the new French movement that includes Le Coucou, Frenchette, Manhatta, and The Grill in New York.

selected by **Howie Kahn**

Sam Panopoulos SATELLITE RESTAURANT
Canada 1962

recipe → p 288

Hawaiian Pizza

An original—and divisive—flavor combination that came from pure experimentation, the Hawaiian Pizza was invented almost 4,500 miles from the Polynesian source: the name hailed from the brand of canned fruit that Chatham, Ontario, restaurant owner Sam Panopoulos placed on a standard tomato-and-cheese pie "just for fun," alongside bits of chopped ham. The Greek immigrant and his brother weren't exactly strangers to midcentury fusion: their casual restaurant served breakfast and burgers alongside Chinese food. But, as Panopoulos noted, the North American palate of the mid-1960s was bland at best: "Those days nobody was mixing sweets and sours and all that," he recalled. "It was plain, plain food."

At the time, pizza was considered "ethnic" food in Canada, unlike in the nearby American city of Detroit, where Panopoulos had tried it. In fact, he had to make his own pizza boxes by cutting rounds from cardboard he got at a furniture store. Because of the novelty of pizza itself, there were no preconceptions around what could or couldn't top it. Hence the canned pineapple, which was popular at the time, thanks to the tiki trend that had blossomed in Canada after World War II. Somehow, the sweet-salty combination just worked.

Or did it? There are those who consider it unholy. In 2017, the Icelandic president told schoolchildren he would ban pineapple pizza if he could—a statement he later retracted by saying that he did not have the power. "Presidents should not have unlimited power," he wrote. "I would not want to live in such a country. For pizzas, I recommend seafood." Canadian president Justin Trudeau's response? "I have a pineapple. I have a pizza. And I stand behind this delicious Southwestern Ontario tradition. #teampineapple."

selected by **Pat Nourse**

84

recipe → **p 288**

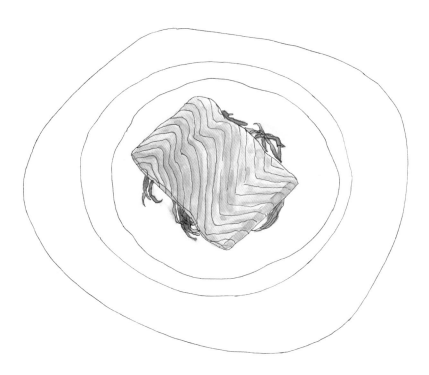

Salmon Escalope with Sorrel

Escalope de saumon à l'oseille

The dish that defined *nouvelle cuisine* might not seem so revolutionary today, but its break with Escoffier's classic cooking was radical at the time. It wasn't the pairing of fish with sorrel, a combination that had been served by Jean Delaveyne in 1956. It was how the fish was cooked and served that marked such a break. Until then, salmon was typically cut into thick steaks rather than fillets. It was poached and then served on a warmed plate, with sauce spooned over it. But the Troisgros brothers put years of thought into their new dish. First, inspired by the avant-gardist chef Alex Humbert, who sliced his salmon into fillets, they cut it into "scallops," which they then flattened and sliced in half horizontally to create large, thin fillets. While on vacation in Basque country, they had been impressed by how the fishermen grilled salmon over embers until the flesh was just rare. They experimented with Tefal's newly invented nonstick pans to enable them to cook the fish quickly and without oil, searing it for just 25 and 15 seconds per side. The fish was immediately plated on top of a sauce made from a velvety reduction of fish fumet, shallots, crème fraîche, Sancerre, and vermouth into which a few leaves of lemony sorrel had been quickly "melted," a final squeeze of lemon added before the plate was rushed to the diner. What's so radical about that? Well, no one had served a sauce beneath fish before, allowing its quality to shine—and certainly not such a light sauce. That sauce created its own conundrum: because the brothers refused to serve bread at the table and the sorrel sauce was too liquid to be eaten with a fish knife, they worked with Lyonnais silversmiths to design a flattened spoon that could both cut and gather sauce. Eventually, the sauce spoon eclipsed the fish knife in fine dining.

selected by **Christine Muhlke**

Alba Campeol and Roberto Linguanotto LE BECCHERIE

Italy 1962

recipe → **p 288**

Tiramisu

"How does a dessert that was barely known in New York three years ago suddenly become so popular?" asked Marian Burros in *The New York Times* in 1985. In New York, it was because the Istrian-raised chef Lidia Bastianich served tiramisu at her restaurant when it opened in 1981, at a time when Italian ingredients like mascarpone were just becoming available. Even then, the decadent creation was only a decade old. Tiramisu hails from the Veneto region, where the custardy zabaglione (egg yolks beaten with sugar) was often eaten with whipped cream and traditional Venetian cookies called *baicoli*. When mixed with rich mascarpone, zabaglione was also given to children and the elderly for strength.

As Le Beccherie co-owner Alba Campeol tells it, her mother-in-law fed her the mixture to shore her up after the birth of her son. One particularly tiring day, she added a bit

of espresso to it as a pick-me-up, or *tiramisù* in the Venetian dialect. It was so good that Campeol told Le Beccherie's pastry chef, Roberto "Loli" Linguanotto, about it as soon as she arrived at work. He had the idea to dip the crisp cookies in espresso and layer the zabaglione between and above them, dusting the top with chocolate. Word quickly spread; within a few years, the influential critics of the Academy of Italian Cuisine hosted their meeting there.

There are hundreds of variations on the dessert, some containing liqueur, which some chefs deem inauthentic. But authenticity seems beside the point considering how many claims there are on the original source. What is sure is that it captured the world's attention in a way that only gelato had. As the New York-based chef Pino Luongo said in 1985, "It's the first Italian dessert that competes with the French."

selected by **Diego Salazar**

Teressa Bellissimo ANCHOR BAR

United States 1964

recipe → **p 289**

Buffalo Wings

This spontaneously devised bar snack, assembled from the odds and ends available at hand late one night at a bar in Buffalo in northwestern New York State, is more than just an iconic American dish. It has become its own flavor, added to snacks from dips to chips. The stories told about the chef and bar co-owner Teressa Bellissimo differ, even within her own family: did she come up with the recipe when her son Dominic was tending bar one Friday and asked her to whip up something for his drunk friends, or did she improvise when the weekly delivery for her spaghetti sauce included chicken wings instead of the meatier backs? The fact remains that first she halved the wings into flats, the part with two bones (aka wingettes), and drumettes, which resemble miniature drumsticks. Then she deep-fried them, tossed them in vinegar-based cayenne pepper hot sauce and butter, and served them with carrot and celery sticks and blue cheese dressing grabbed from the kitchen's salad station. The wings were such a sensation, they were famous in Buffalo within weeks. Soon there were three variations offered: mild, medium, and hot. (There is, according to *The New Yorker*'s Calvin Trillin, a competing story: the Buffalo-based African American owner of John Young's Wings 'n Things said that he was the creator of wings, which he fried breaded and whole and coated with spicy "mambo sauce," telling Trillin that African Americans have been eating chicken wings since thirteenth-century Spain.) Long considered the least desirable part of the chicken by chefs, either thrown away or used for stock, wings are now said to be in short supply every year during the Super Bowl. And it put the city of Buffalo, a once-prosperous city that had fallen on hard times, back on the map.

selected by **Susan Jung, Diego Salazar**

Jiro Ono   SUKIYABASHI JIRO
Japan 1965

recipe → p 289

Sushi

Jiro Ono didn't invent sushi. He was about twelve centuries too late for that. But during the decades he has spent mastering his craft at his ten-seat Tokyo sushi counter in the basement of an office building, he came to be seen as the true modern artisan of Edo-style sushi. For Ono, sushi began not with the best fish (which he, of course, chose himself daily at the Tsukiji fish market), but the best rice. At Sukiyabashi Jiro, the cooked rice, sprinkled with rice vinegar, is served at "skin temperature" to stabilize the flavor. The fish and seafood that appear on the hinoki wood counter before diners during the twenty-two-course, $271 (£208) meal (which is so much in demand that reservations have been suspended until further notice) is served at room temperature, sliced at precisely the right moment, and brushed with just enough soy sauce or sweet tsume sauce. In fact, Ono's sushi is all about timing: each batch of rice is timed

to the diner's reservation. Every piece of nigiri sushi is served at exactly the right temperature and stage in its aging to ensure the best texture. As a result, the diner has to both keep up with the master's pace and respect his rules, including how to pick up the piece of sushi, how to dip it correctly into the soy sauce (not rice first), and why diners should not turn the nigiri upside down. The payoff? Sushi crafted to melt in the mouth.

Ono began his training in kitchens at the age of seven, and is still working into his nineties—a lifetime of experience and rigorous devotion that have allowed him to home in on the smallest details of the meal. As Anthony Bourdain told Vice of his experience at Ono's three-Michelin-starred counter, "He looks at you and examines the shape of your mouth and your left hand and right hand as he forms his nigiri." Jiro Ono didn't invent sushi. He just perfected it.

selected by **Susan Jung**

88

Pedro Arregi ELKANO
Spain 1967

recipe → **p 289**

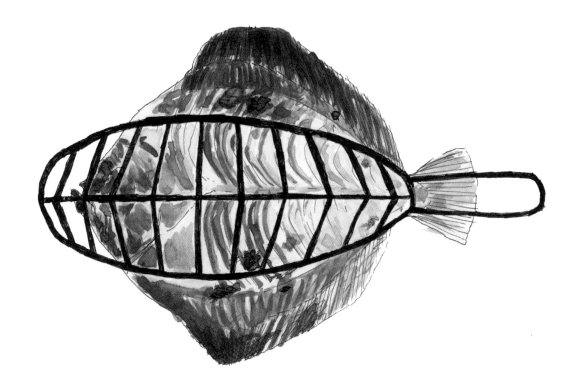

Grilled Turbot

Rodaballo a la parrilla

Decades before local, seasonal, and nose-to-tail eating were fashionable, not to mention the trend toward minimalist plating, Pedro Arregi was championing them at his seaside restaurant in the fishing town of Getaria, outside San Sebastián. Here, whole grilled turbot is served without accompaniment, sauce, or fanfare. And none are required.

Since the restaurant opened in 1964, boats have delivered freshly caught fish to the dock below the restaurant. (Elkano was inspired by the charcoal grills that fishermen set up in their boats to eat their fresh catch.) Pedro, like his son, Aitor, who now runs the restaurant, worked closely with the fishermen to learn not only where the fish are from, when they were caught, and what they ate, but also if they were in season (i.e., before or after spawning), as he insisted that the quality of the fish could not be corrected or improved through cooking.

It is said that Arregi invented the metal baskets in which the seasoned turbot are grilled, crisping their fins over charcoal that has been burning for at least two hours and liquefying the gelatin inside the head and cheeks. During cooking, the fish is basted using a secret sauce, referred to as "holy water." A mixture of olive oil, lemon juice, and salt, only three people have been responsible for making it since the restaurant opened, and it is always prepared after the kitchen has closed.

The whole fish arrives at the table, the pin bones around the perimeter browned and crisp, its flesh collagen-rich and tender. The chef debones the fish for the guests, then tells them to explore the range of flavors and textures in the flesh near the head, spine, tail, and the prized cheeks.

It is a dish of the utmost simplicity and respect.

selected by **Susan Jung**

Jim Delligatti McDONALD'S
United States 1967

recipe → **p 290**

Big Mac

Almost thirty years after McDonald's revolutionized the burger business, the owner of several McDonald's franchises located near Pittsburgh, Pennsylvania, made the American dream food even bigger. In searching for a burger that would boost profits and draw new customers after McDonald's repeatedly turned down his requests for a double-patty burger, Jim Delligatti sandwiched two beef patties between not two but three sesame seed buns, adding cheese, lettuce, pickles, onions, and a "special sauce." (Long believed to be Thousand Island dressing, in 2007 it was revealed to be a combination of mayonnaise, sweet relish, yellow mustard, cider vinegar, garlic powder, onion powder, and paprika.) The resulting burger creation, initially called "The Aristocrat" and "The Blue Ribbon Burger," appealed to Americans' growing appetite not just for hamburgers, but for bigger, more loaded, special burgers.

Delligatti later admitted that the idea was not brand new, telling the *Los Angeles Times*, "this wasn't like discovering the light bulb. The light bulb was already there. All I did was screw in the socket." McDonald's began selling the burger in 1968, and the Big Mac was cemented in the national consciousness following an advertising campaign whose jingle quickly listed the burger components. By 1980, the *Economist* had created the Big Mac Index, which compared the valuation of global currencies based on the price of a Big Mac in each country —a standard that came to be known as burgernomics.

As concerns around health and ingredient quality began to slow McDonald's domination in the 2000s, the race to create the most decadent, ethically sourced burger was sweeping restaurants, such as Daniel Boulud's DB Burger (see page 184) and the Black Label burger at New York's Minetta Tavern.

selected by **Diego Salazar**

recipe → **p 290**

Gourmet Salad

La salade gourmande

In France in the 1960s, a *salade composée*, or composed salad, was basic bistro fare, under the gastronomic radar with its ordered disorder. In 1965, the young chef Michel Guérard disrupted that disorder and put a salad where none had gone before: on a fine dining menu. His wasn't just a green salad. His was a *salade gourmande*, with green beans, the tips of white asparagus, shaved black truffle, and thin slices of foie gras—a revolutionary idea at the time. Make that a *salade folle . . .* or crazy salad. It upended everything the French thought of salad at the time, and transformed Guérard's career in the process.

Guérard, the son of a butcher, began his career as a pastry chef at the Hôtel de Crillon in Paris before working with the rebellious and influential chef Jean Delaveyne at Camélia in Bougival (outside Paris). Delaveyne, the first chef to pair salmon with sorrel, among other innovations, served a similar *salade gourmande*, which his protégé took with him when he purchased a North African bistro just outside of Paris sight unseen and turned it into Le Pot-au-Feu. Chefs Paul Bocuse, Alain Chapel, Roger Vergé, Raymond Olivier, and Pierre and Jean Troisgros all came to support him. In 1970, these men became known as the founders of nouvelle cuisine, a seminal movement whose practitioners sought to free themselves from the Escoffier-era rules of French fine dining, moving toward a lighter, more natural cooking—alas, away from the heaviness of foie gras. In fact, Guérard continued to lighten his cuisine throughout the decades, becoming focused on health, and establishing *la cuisine minceur* ("slimming cooking"). It has served him well: in 2019 he was the only living father of nouvelle cuisine, still in his kitchen at his health spa in Eugénie-les-Bains.

selected by **Christine Muhlke, Andrea Petrini**

recipe → **p 291**

Key Lime Pie

The origin of this sweet, creamy, electrifyingly tart yellow (not green!) pie has multiple sources, be it the nineteenth-century sponge fishermen of the Florida Keys, where the sour, golf-ball-size citrus had thrived since its introduction by the Spanish, or a certain "Aunt Sally," the cook of a self-made millionaire in Key West—or, as some say, the Borden company, which manufactures the sweetened condensed milk that is as essential to the no-cook filling as the egg yolks and lime juice, whose acid naturally sets it. (Until an overwater causeway was built in the 1930s, residents of the Keys had no access to fresh milk and had to make do with the canned version that Borden introduced in 1856.) Among Floridians, where the pie originated is as hotly contested as the decision to use a graham cracker crust or a pastry shell; whether to top it with meringue and bake it or finish it with whipped cream.

What is agreed upon is that it was the Miami restaurant Joe's Stone Crab that brought the Key Lime Pie to America, as tourists have flocked to the family-owned crab shack for decades. Their delicate yet heavy, massive yet somehow-not-enough slice is as essential to a meal there as the fresh-caught stone crab, making the Key Lime Pie a globally recognized and iconic regional dessert. As for the limes themselves, they hail from a Malaysian variety. The trees thrived in the coral-enriched soil of the Keys until a 1926 hurricane wiped out South Florida's citrus plantations. They were replanted with milder Persian limes, which are easier to pick and transport than the spiky Key lime trees. Even today, Key limes are mostly a backyard crop in the United States, making them even more sought-after and special.

selected by **Diego Salazar**

recipe → **p 292**

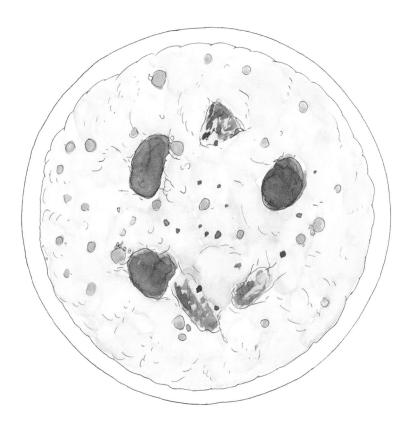

Mushroom Cappuccino

Bouillon de champignons comme un cappuccino

In an attempt to lighten the traditional French *velouté*, Alain Chapel looked to the Italians, frothing the top of his creamy mushroom soup into a foam and serving it in a coffee cup. It was a transgression that suited the boundaries that the practitioners of nouvelle cuisine—a group that included Chapel, Paul Bocuse, Michel Guérard, and Pierre and Jean Troisgros—wished to break through. Acclimatization prompted chefs to import "exotic" foreign ingredients and techniques, while transgression encouraged the use of common or accepted cooking techniques and ingredients, but in ways that were not yet deemed legitimate. Chapel, the son of a restaurateur who took over his father's kitchen outside of Lyon at a young age, had worked at La Pyramide under Fernand Point, whose quest to modernize French cuisine led him to simplify traditional dishes and to embrace seasonal, local produce of the highest quality.

The soup base itself was not revolutionary. It consisted of wild and button mushrooms, fish stock, butter, crayfish tails, cream, and chervil. It was the technique and playful presentation that sparked so many versions in the 1990s and early 2000s, from Eric Ripert at Le Bernardin to Iñaki Aizpitarte at Le Chateaubriand, from Thomas Keller at The French Laundry to Alain Ducasse—who worked in Chapel's kitchen and was greatly influenced by him. The concept of an ethereal foam—the idea being that the surface area is increased and therefore the flavor intensified—drove elBulli chef Ferran Adrià to experiment with whipping canisters and lecithin or gelatin to sustain the illusion.

selected by **Christine Muhlke**, **Andrea Petrini**

Alain Chapel ALAIN CHAPEL

France 1970

recipe → **p 292**

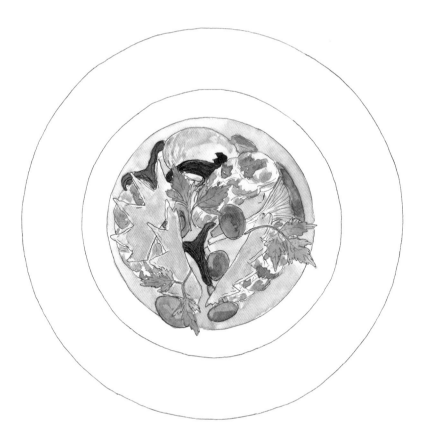

Stew of Cockscombs and Chicken Kidneys

Ragoût de crêtes et rognons de coq

Although Alain Chapel was a pioneer of nouvelle cuisine alongside Paul Bocuse, Michel Guérard, and Pierre and Jean Troisgros, and the youngest Frenchman to be awarded three stars at the age of thirty-five, he never obscured his Lyonnais roots. He grew up in the kitchen of his father's bistro in the fabled culinary city, and trained with Paul Mercier at Fernand Point's La Pyramide, where he learned both a profound respect for seasonal ingredients and to think beyond Escoffier while celebrating the region's food. And so he took the classic Lyonnais dish *poulet aux écrevisses*—a version of chicken Marengo, the Napoleonic marriage of surf and turf (in this case chicken and crayfish)—and didn't stop with the flesh of the bird. He used the unlovely, less-used bits of the region's *poulet de Bresse* as well—kidneys, cockscombs, and more—bringing them into the Michelin sphere with crayfish from the streams running through nearby Nantua, morels, veal stock, truffle juice, and chervil. The resulting ragoût was exuberant and refined, a dish that looked back to simpler times, when all of an animal was used, while predating the nose-to-tail movement by almost fifty years.

Of the many chefs who were inspired or taught by Chapel, including Pierre Gagnaire, Thierry Marx, Heston Blumenthal, Michel Troisgros, and David Kinch, this particular dish had a profound effect on one of Chapel's most celebrated disciples, Alain Ducasse, who included it in his *Grand Livre de Cuisine*. Ducasse recognized that Chapel was one of the first chefs to emphasize the importance of produce, revealing ingredients at their seasonal best. As Chapel himself said in his book *La cuisine c'est beaucoup plus que des recettes*, "The produce alone is the truth. The produce alone is the star, and not the chef."

selected by **Andrea Petrini**

Paul Bocuse L'AUBERGE DU PONT DE COLLONGES
France 1970s

Red Mullet with Potato Scales

Rouget en écailles de pomme de terre

The visual playfulness of this trompe l'oeil dish earned it homages from chefs around the world. Paul Bocuse, one of the fathers of nouvelle cuisine in the 1960s and 70s, tiled a slender fillet of red mullet with perfect circles of blanched potato dipped in clarified butter. When crisped in the pan (itself a masterful feat of fish cookery), the rounds transformed into golden scales. In keeping with his philosophy of light sauces—poured beneath, rather than over, the fish, in the style of the new French cooking (see Salmon Escalope with Sorrel, page 85)—Bocuse deftly composed a fanciful olive-leaf design by swirling dots of veal stock into an ephemeral sauce of orange juice, rosemary, vermouth, and liquid crème fraîche.

Bocuse, who was born into a family of Lyonnais chefs dating back to the seventeenth century, claimed that he came up with the idea after seeing a cold salmon decorated with cucumber slices while at a food show. "I remember that I cut the potato scales with the tube from an aspirin container," he recalled. (Today, the cooks in his kitchen, where the dish is still made, punch out the rounds with an apple corer.) When Daniel Boulud, then a young chef at Le Cirque in New York City, went to make his version in the late 1980s, he didn't have apprentices doing it all day, *comme chez* Bocuse. So he wrapped sea bass with vertical potato slices. (Boulud also said that the Swiss chef Frédy Girardet did a zucchini-scaled red mullet not long before.) Los Angeles-based French chef Michel Richard did his Bocuse-Girardet rendition with potato chips and scallops. In the twenty-first century, the dish was referenced using clams and fennel at Eleven Madison Park in New York, wild oyster with broccoli stems at Noma in Copenhagen, and Amazon river fish and native potatoes at Gustu in La Paz, Bolivia.

selected by **Christine Muhlke**

Ali Ahmed Aslam SHISH MAHAL
United Kingdom 1970s

recipe → p 294

Chicken Tikka Masala

One of Britain's most popular dishes is a prime example of melting-pot cuisine: a recipe that is said to have been spontaneously invented by a Punjabi cook to please a customer in Glasgow, Scotland, Chicken Tikka Masala even found popularity in India. (A reverse-engineered journey not unlike that of General Tso's chicken, page 78, which first found fame in New York City before working its way back to Hunan, where the chef was originally from.) As the story goes, Ali Ahmed Aslam served boneless pieces of tandoori chicken to a customer, who said that it was too dry; did the cook have any gravy? Aslam, who was eating tomato soup at the time, had the idea to make a quick sauce from yogurt, tomatoes, and mild spices that he thought would appeal to the Scots' palate.

In 2001, a Glasgow lawmaker urged the European Union to grant Chicken Tikka Masala "protected designation of origin"

status and thus recognize the dish as a regional specialty. "Chicken Tikka Masala is now a true British national dish, not only because it is the most popular, but because it is a perfect illustration of the way Britain absorbs and adapts external influences," Foreign Secretary Robin Cook said in a 2001 speech on British identity that claimed CTM, as it's also known, as proof of the country's multiculturalism. (The motion did not pass.)

The speech set off an outcry among chefs in India, some claiming that a version of the dish has existed since the Mughal period centuries prior; others pointing out a similar version in a 1965 version of Mrs Balbir Singh's *Indian Cookery*. But what is a recipe, anyway? A 1998 survey by *The Real Curry Restaurant Guide* found forty-eight recipes for the dish, the only common ingredient being chicken. And pride.

selected by **Richard Vines**

Francis Coulson SHARROW BAY COUNTRY HOUSE HOTEL
United Kingdom 1970s

recipe → **p 294**

Sticky Toffee Pudding

For a country as crazy about traditional puddings (desserts) as England is, it's funny to think that two of its most famous weren't invented until the 1970s. Perhaps that's because during the early years of that decade, a trend for nostalgic British sweets was sweeping the country, which restaurants were happy to indulge and escalate. But it turns out that the emerging winners may have had roots in midcentury North America. Banoffi Pie (see page 101), which first appeared in Sussex in 1971, was an adaptation of an American dessert called Coffee Toffee Pie. Icky Sticky Toffee Pudding, as it was called when it went on the menu at the celebrated Lake District hotel Sharrow Bay in the 1970s, has multiple claims upon it, which trace back to Canada. Both, it must be said, are incredibly sweet and endearingly indulgent.

Sharrow Bay's moist sponge cake, which started as a loaf cake but evolved to individual molds, is studded with chewy chopped dates and drenched in a rich butterscotch sauce. It is served with fresh cream. Although Sharrow Bay still claims to have invented the dish, swearing its staff to secrecy in perpetuity, owner Francis Coulson himself admitted to the food writer Simon Hopkinson that he had taken it from Mrs. Martin at the Old Rectory restaurant in Lancashire, who published it in her 1971 cookbook. (By turn, she admitted that she had learned the recipe from two Canadian Air Force pilots who stayed there, which could explain the sponge's muffin-like texture.) Like Banoffi Pie, Sticky Toffee Pudding has remained an untouchable classic, left alone by chefs to soak up the glory like so much butterscotch sauce.

selected by **Christine Muhlke**

Jacques Pic MAISON PIC
France 1971

recipe → **p 295**

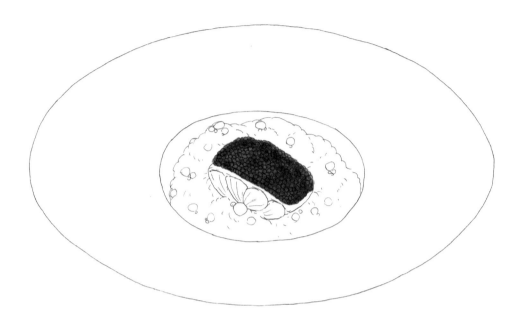

Loup au Caviar

"Jacques Pic was well respected and loved in our profession . . . he had style and creativity and his name was synonymous with excellence. Among the dishes for which he became famous [was] his . . . *filet de loup au caviar* . . . . It was delectable cuisine, but more important was the spirit in which it was given. For Jacques Pic's greatest quality was his modesty and generosity." So wrote Raymond Blanc in Pic's obituary in the *Independent* in 1992.

The modesty and generosity of Jacques Pic's cooking was on full display in his Loup au Caviar, a small fillet of Mediterranean sea bass completely hidden beneath a stripe of wild Aquitaine caviar, surrounded by a champagne cream sauce. There was no garnish or accompaniment, nor was there any need. The dish's relatively few ingredients spoke for themselves, the caviar's iodine quality catalyzing the natural sweetness and salinity of the fish. With both a Japanese purity and a certain French classicism, Pic's creation was emblematic of both the nouvelle cuisine movement of which he was quietly a part, as well as the traditional foundation of his family's 1889 restaurant near Lyon, where his father received three Michelin stars in 1934. It was also unique because it was the first time that caviar was plated on a hot dish. (Another of Pic's firsts was his introduction of an eight-course tasting menu called "Rabelais," a jump from the three-course structure.) Pic's daughter, Anne-Sophie, took over the restaurant five years after his untimely death at the stove. Her attempt to remove the iconic entrée from the menu lasted two weeks, until customers told her they'd traveled there just to taste it. Today, her version features an aerated sauce, lighter than her father's flour-thickened accompaniment. In 2007, Anne-Sophie Pic was the first woman since La Mère Brazier to receive three stars, keeping her family's tradition alive.

selected by **Susan Jung, Christine Muhlke**

Juan Mari Arzak RESTAURANTE ARZAK

Spain 1971

recipe → **p 295**

Scorpion Fish Cake

Pastel de kabrarroka

This is the dish that defined and ignited the playful genius of Spanish haute cuisine. The young Basque chef, who had been working the line under his mother since 1966 in the family's 120-year-old restaurant in San Sebastián, Spain, wanted to elevate the region's food to the international fine-dining level—a New Basque Cuisine to rival the nouvelle cuisine that had recently emerged to challenge tradition in France. Inspired by chefs like Paul Bocuse, Arzak examined the humble ingredients, rustic techniques, and unadorned presentation that made Basque cooking special, then set about translating them into his own style. He set aside five tables in the dining room to create his own mini-restaurant showcasing his inventive dishes, but, he said, no one came.

And then he took scorpion fish, a hideous fish common to the Cantabrian Sea that was most often used in soup stock,

and whipped it into a custardy base to make an elegant molded terrine. It was a light and refined marriage of Basque and French, one that soon launched Arzak's new style of cooking into the spotlight. The dish evolved into bite-size portions coated in the shreds of phyllo-like *kataifi* dough and skewered to create avant-garde bites resembling lollipops. *La nueva cocina* was born. Arzak's cooking has inspired the likes of Ferran Adrià, Juan and Jordi Roca, and Jose Andrés, all of whom celebrate local Spanish ingredients with humor and forward-thinking techniques.

More than four decades later, *pastel de kabrarroka* is said to be the most copied dish in Spanish restaurants and tapas bars alike. Cans of the pâté can also be found in supermarkets. Arzak's daughter, Elena—the family's fourth-generation chef—has maintained the restaurant's Michelin stars.

selected by **Howie Kahn, Diego Salazar**

recipe → **p 296**

Soup Dumplings

Xiao long bao

A dainty dumpling is chopsticked from bamboo steamer into a soup spoon. Black Chinkiang vinegar is sprinkled on top, and a few threads of ginger are added. A tiny nibble is taken from the crest of the wrapper's eighteen elegant pleats, from which steamy, intensely meaty yet light broth rushes into the mouth. What remains is a tender ball of minced pork and a toothsome yet featherweight skin. It is a one-bite roller coaster ride of an experience—one that diners gladly do tens of thousands of times a day around the world at Din Tai Fung's locations in Asia, Europe, Australia, and the United States.

The owners of Din Tai Fung in Taipei, Taiwan, China, didn't invent the *xiao long bao*, the soup-filled buns named for the steamer in which they are cooked. (Translated, it means "little basket bun.") Instead, their invention is said to have originated in a restaurant in Nanxiang, a district of Shanghai, in the 1870s,

when the owner added aspic to the pork mince in his dumplings. During steaming, the gelatinous aspic transformed into silky soup. Din Tai Fung was started by Yang Bingyi, an immigrant from the mainland, and his wife in 1972. In order to sustain the cooking oil store that they owned, the Yangs began selling homemade snacks. Taipei was also a haven for the former cooks of wealthy Chinese families and government officials during the Cultural Revolution, so it was easy for Yang to hire an excellent cook from one of the restaurants to which he delivered oil. Yang's wife and kitchen apprentices gradually learned the technique for *xiao long bao* and within a decade, the couple had transformed every story of the building they had bought into dining rooms. The success of Din Tai Fung's buns stems from rigorous standardization, but unlike many global chains, it still allows for magic.

selected by **Susan Jung, Howie Kahn**

recipe → **p 296**

Banoffi Pie

A pie so gloopy and indulgent, it's often been mistaken as American—a fact that upset the owner of the British restaurant where it was invented so much that he offered a £10,000 ($13,000) reward to anyone able to prove that it originated anywhere other than the county of East Sussex, in the south of England. True, the combination of caramelized sweetened condensed milk (aka toffee, aka dulce de leche), bananas, whipped cream, and instant and freshly ground coffee layered in a tart crust *was* an adaptation of the coffee toffee pie made at the famous San Francisco bakery Blum's and that the Hungry Monk's young chef Ian Dowding had picked up from a previous job—but it was a recipe that didn't work very well. Dowding set about tinkering with the recipe and, at his sister's suggestion, tried using cans of slow-cooked sweetened condensed milk as the toffee base. Nigel Mackenzie wanted to add another dimension, so Dowding experimented with different fruit. Apple? Not bad. Mandarin orange? Revolting. Mackenzie suggested banana, and they knew they'd cracked it, creating a flavor pairing that was more than the sum of its parts. Speaking of which, the name "banoffee" is a portmanteau of banana and toffee; Mackenzie later changed the spelling to "banoffi" to make it seem more exotic. The pie's invented name allowed the two to track its success as it spread from England to the United States, Australia, and beyond, becoming a flavor for everything from ice cream to cookies and candy. The word banoffi even warranted an entry in *The Oxford English Dictionary* in 2002. Dowding wrote that he doesn't mind that he never made a penny from it, or that he rarely even receives credit for the recipe. He just likes that years from now, "someone, somewhere will be making banoffi pie."

selected by **Pat Nourse**

Chui Fook Chuen FOOK LAM MOON
China 1972

recipe → **p 297**

Crab Steamed with
Egg White and Huadiao Wine

In China, from the Qing Dynasty (1644–1912) right up until the end of the Republic of China in 1949, the best chefs worked in the homes and palaces of the nobility and, later, government officials. The lavish banquet food that they prepared was prized for both its complexity and its delicacy, with expensive ingredients being foremost. (See Braised Abalone, page 127.) Chui Fook Chuen began his cooking career as the house chef for prominent families. He started his own catering company for Hong Kong's elite, cooking traditional Cantonese grand cuisine for two decades, until, in 1972, he opened the restaurant Fook Lam Moon, which means "good fortune arriving at your door." Among his signature dishes were fried chicken, dried abalone with goose web, and roasted suckling pig—a dish that followed his son, Chiu Wai-kan, to his restaurant Seventh Son (see page 241.)

For this classic Cantonese dish, delicacy and premium ingredients are in perfect harmony. Originally, the crab was steamed and served whole in the traditional style. Its modern incarnation was developed in 2010 by chef Chan Lau Leung. Here, a single stone crab claw is gently steamed with slices of ginger, its juices then mixed with chicken stock, egg white, sugar, and *huadiao*—semi-dry Shaoxing, a cooking wine derived from rice and wheat. The egg mixture is then returned to the steamer until it is gently set, resembling an ethereal take on the Japanese steamed egg custard, *chawanmushi*. The result is pure and subtle, the wine and egg bringing out the fresh sweetness of the crab. Today, this dish is on the menu at many high-end restaurants in Hong Kong. In the United States, it is one of the dishes that Corey Lee painstakingly re-creates at his restaurant In Situ. To Lee, it represents the best of Hong Kong cooking.

selected by **Howie Kahn**

recipe → **p 297**

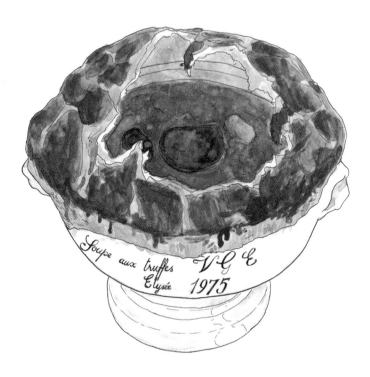

Black Truffle Soup Elysée

Soupe aux truffes Elysée

Today, the tureen in which this soup is served at the late chef's restaurant bears the legend of its origin: "PAUL BOCUSE Soupe aux truffes Elysée, VGE 1975," the day that the chef was awarded the Légion d'Honneur medal. Even five decades later, the dome of golden puff pastry emitting the aroma of truffles (first served at a banquet honoring the French president Valéry Giscard d'Estaing) is still synonymous with French fine dining. Its recipe is not necessarily evocative of the nouvelle cuisine, which Bocuse is often credited with creating in the 1960s as a lightened approach to traditional French food. Instead, the double-clarified consommé of beef and chicken stocks is enriched with cubes of foie gras, julienned black Périgord truffle, sautéed mushrooms and Noilly Prat vermouth, then encased in a cap of buttery pâte feuilletée. It could not be more traditional—or luxe.

At the banquet—where the other chefs included Michel Guérard, Roger Vergé, Jean and Pierre Troisgros, and Maurice Bernachon—Bocuse told the president the origins of the dish: it was a combination of both a beef and chicken soup with a shaving of truffles that he was served by farmers in the Ardèche region, and a truffle hidden beneath flaky pastry in the style of an English chicken pie that he enjoyed on a hunting trip in Alsace. It is also the direct lineage, it could be said, of Bocuse's apprenticeship with the legendary Fernand Point at La Pyramide and his time cooking with La Mère Brazier. While the dish became internationally famous and was emulated by chefs, it also became a popular dish for home cooks In his memoir, *32 Yolks*, Le Bernardin chef Eric Ripert writes about making it in culinary school. And at Daniel Humm's restaurant the NoMad, it is listed on the menu under its original name.

selected by **Christine Muhlke, Pat Nourse, Diego Salazar, Richard Vines**

recipe → **p 297**

Veal Prince Orloff

Mignon de veau Prince Orloff

"We have maintained the style of menu designed by Auguste Escoffier, circa 1880," read the bottom of maître chef Michel Bourdin's menus at the London hotel the Connaught. Escoffier brought lavish French food to London in 1890, when he opened the Savoy hotel with the Swiss hotel manager César Ritz. In Bourdin's opinion, it was the golden age of cooking —one that, while it may have gone out of fashion, remained the height of excellence: "It is classic, like Chanel, Monet, or Mozart. Not many people do that any more. . . . Even in France, they can't find a great French restaurant the way they expect it, so they have come to England to find it."

What they found at the Connaught were recipes like Veal Prince Orloff, which was a painstakingly technical dish to assemble. Dating from Russia in the mid-1800s, it required roasting a saddle of veal, then carefully carving it into two loins,

cutting them into 1-inch slices, then reassembling it to resemble the original roast. A mushroom purée, an onion soubise, and a slice of black truffle were then inserted between each slice, the entirety coated in rich Mornay sauce, sprinkled with Parmesan, and baked again.

After taking over the Connaught in 1975, Bourdin's cooking remained a benchmark in British gastronomy for more than twenty-five years. His kitchen was also a training ground for the likes of Pierre and Jean Troisgrois, Philippe Braun of Jamin, and the American chef Larry Forgione. Bourdin was interested in encouraging good kitchen practices, forming the Club du Neuf with the Roux brothers and Peter Kromberg to train a new generation. He once told a reporter that it takes fifteen years to make a chef, providing he gets them at the age of sixteen, "before they know everything and lack the patience to learn."

selected by **Richard Vines**

recipe → **p 298**

Chicken Manchurian

"Now when I see it on the menu at McDonald's, I feel really proud," Nelson Wang told food writer Vir Sanghvi. Wang's off-the-cuff response to club members' requests to make them something unique became one of the most copied dishes in India—from restaurants all the way down to street carts— and launched Indo-Chinese cooking. Like its chef, the dish is an unabashed amalgam of Indian and Americanized Cantonese food: crispy fried pieces of battered chicken swim in a thick, Bengali-inspired sauce of garlic, green chiles, ginger, and cilantro (coriander). But rather than add tomato sauce, Wang reached for soy, chicken stock, and sugar. Crunchy, spicy, sweet, and salty, it was irresistible to the Indian palate.

The Kolkata-born son of Chinese immigrants, Wang worked his way into restaurant kitchens in Bombay after a few years spent as a limbo dancer and fire-eater in nightclubs. When he started cooking, Chinese restaurants served bland dishes like chop suey and sweet-and-sour pork. There was no appetite for spice until one restaurant began importing chefs from Hong Kong, and suddenly Sichuan peppercorns were in everything. So when that fateful request was made, Wang decided to put together "all the things that Indians like." Asked what to call it (neither the Chinese cooks nor the Indian clientele had ever seen anything like it), Wang opted for "Chicken from Manchau," or "Chicken Manchurian," since in China, those from the former region of Manchau are considered barbarians—and this, he said, "was really a dish for barbarians." But the word has entered the culture. "I want to tell all these fancy people who tell me that the dish is from Manchuria, 'Find me Manchuria on the map!' . . . The only Manchurian thing that remains is my creation."

selected by **Pat Nourse**

Pierre Koffmann LA TANTE CLAIRE
United Kingdom 1977

recipe → **p 298**

Stuffed Pig's Trotters with Morels

Pieds de cochon aux morilles

How did a French chef change British cuisine? By serving pig's feet. Humble, traditional, and extremely tedious to make, Pierre Koffmann served the stuffed trotters of his Gascon childhood—a dish credited to the Touraine chef Charles Barrière—with just a ladle of potato purée spiked with fried cracklings. Surprisingly, the high-end clientele at his London restaurant loved it. As his protégé Marco Pierre White explains of the dish in *Marco Pierre White in Hell's Kitchen*, "it is a dish fit for a king, being both stylish and pleasing to the eye."

The nine-hour recipe requires first laboriously deboning the trotters, then poaching them in port and veal stock; making a filling of morels and sweetbreads bound with chicken mousse; baking the stuffed feet; and reducing the stock into a translucent, jewel-like glaze. The marriage of low-end and high-end ingredients was remarkable at a time when fine dining, even in London, still meant haute cuisine. Within six years of opening, Koffmann had earned three Michelin stars.

Koffmann passed on the simplicity and honesty of his food, as well as his demand for perfection, to a generation of cooks who went on to change British cuisine, including Gordon Ramsay, Michel Roux Jr., and Marcus Wareing. Marco Pierre White, in what was the first "cover" in the history of cuisine, put "Braised Pig's Trotters Pierre Koffmann" on his menus. And certainly Fergus Henderson's nose-to-tail ethos and no-fanfare plating can be linked to Koffmann. By 2009, five years after Koffmann closed his restaurant, a one-week pop-up at Selfridges stretched into eight, during which he sold more than 3,200 of the little back feet (the rear foot, he insists, being larger). "When I die, I will have a pig's trotter on my tombstone," the chef told Vice at the age of seventy.

selected by **Christine Muhlke**, **Pat Nourse**, **Richard Vines**

recipe → **p 299**

Roast Tronçon of Turbot with Hollandaise Sauce

When Christopher Richard Stein opened his Seafood Restaurant in Padstow, Cornwall, on England's southernmost coast, he was breaking new culinary ground by going so far from London, with its century-old seafood restaurants like Scott's, Sweetings, and J. Sheekey—to be so close to the source of his country's best seafood. Indeed, it is Stein whose ensuing popularity (once his TV series for the BBC became successful, he shortened his name to the more media-friendly Rick) made the region a dining destination, drawing chefs like Paul Ainsworth, Nathan Outlaw, Jamie Oliver, and April Bloomfield in ensuing decades. This dish exemplified the simplicity of Stein's approach. To best showcase the delicately flavored, firm-textured turbot from the region, he opted for the steak-like tronçon cut to highlight its meaty thickness and juiciness. He served this grand fish humbly, removing it from its typical associations with Escoffier-level French dining. It was, as Stein saw it, made "in the English style," deeming it "probably a nicer way of eating this fish than anything more elaborate." Then again, with a hollandaise sauce spooned over the top and a pool of *fines herbes* sauce—fish stock and lemon juice flavored with chervil, parsley, tarragon, and chives—it was a reminder that in the 1970s, food "in the English style" was still French at its core. What was even more interesting was that it was allowed to stand on its own on the plate without accompaniment or garnish, a style that was later emulated by chefs such as Fergus Henderson at St. John in London.

selected by **Richard Vines**

recipe → **p 299**

Pistachio Soufflé

Soufflé aux pistaches

Like his Stuffed Pig's Trotters (see page 106), the Pistachio Soufflé that Pierre Koffmann served at La Tante Claire in the 1970s was an instant favorite, one that he kept on the menu for twenty-six years (and revisited when he opened Koffmann's at the Berkeley Hotel from 2010 to 2016). Like his trotters, it showed how the Gascon chef could extract incredible flavor from even the simplest ingredients—in this case, eggs, milk, sugar, butter, flour, pistachio paste, and chocolate—thanks to his masterful French technique. This flawless, high-rising soufflé, which was inspired by his favorite ice cream flavor as a child, made a huge impression on Londoners at the time for two reasons: the bottom and sides of the ramekins were prepared not with the typical coating of butter and sugar, but with butter and grated dark chocolate, which melted into a bittersweet sauce as the individual soufflés baked. And after the waiter placed the dessert before the guest, he deftly inserted a dainty quenelle of pistachio ice cream into the center of the high-rising soufflé, adding a touch of dramatic flair as it began to glide down and melt into the golden-edged, pastel-green dessert, which somehow managed not to be overly sweet, thanks to the delicate nuttiness of the pistachio—not a common flavor at the time. After the success of Koffmann's soufflé, other restaurants began their own tableside takes, inserting ice cream, crème anglaise, whipped cream, and other sweet delights. The trend was revived in London around 2014 by restaurants like Brawn, Balthazar, and The Ledbury, with The Delaunay even serving an oatmeal soufflé at breakfast.

selected by **Richard Vines**

recipe → **p 300**

Truffled Zucchini

Courgette à la fleur et aux truffes

At the restaurant of the Negresco Hotel in Nice, chef Jacques Maximin single-handedly elevated the zucchini (courgette) blossom. Though the stuffing of delicate, eye-catchingly orange blooms is a tradition that dates back centuries before, he presented something novel. Known for playing with regional peasant dishes and revising them with nouvelle technique, he chose to leave the fragile flower attached to the female squash. He worked on the recipe for a month until he arrived at the following technique: after lightly poaching the vegetable, he stuffed the flowers with a subtle, mousselike interpretation of the traditional Provençal *farce*, made using squash peelings, *pain de mie*, eggs, crème fraîche, garlic, and basil, and rested them upon a reduction of vegetable juices mounted with truffle-infused butter and folded into whipped cream, finally topping the least expensive vegetable with the most expensive mushroom—truffle slices. Two years later, at Le Louis XV in nearby Monaco, his friend Alain Ducasse showcased the region's seasonal baby vegetables in a tiny casserole, serving them luxed up with black truffle (see page 140).

In order to ensure that the zucchini was of the correct size and texture, Maximin researched varieties with a local agricultural organization, finally finding seeds in Los Angeles that he gave to his market supplier to grow for him. Maximin's attention to regional identity through biodiversity and flavor predated the farm-to-table movement of the early 2000s and arguably presaged the now-essential relationship between chefs and farmers. He was one of the first to recognize that flavor comes from the ingredients, not just preparation—a founding tenet of enterprises like Dan Barber's Blue Hill at Stone Barns near New York and Alain Passard's farms outside of Paris.

selected by **Pat Nourse**

recipe → **p 301**

Blackened Redfish

Paul Prudhomme, the iconic face (and hat) of New Orleans cuisine, was splitting his time between a wine and cheese shop and a local television gig when he met Terry Flettrich. Though their plans to open a culinary school didn't pan out, it was Flettrich who introduced him to Ella Brennan, the owner of the restaurant Commander's Palace. She was serendipitously looking for a new executive chef and coaxed Prudhomme into being the first American to ever hold the position. He became known for playing with French-Acadian influences and flavor profiles, spawning what the Brennans called "nouvelle Creole." One day, a waiter began waxing poetic about his desire to eat a fish that had just come out of the water. On a whim, Prudhomme requested that a piece of fish, buttered and aggressively seasoned with paprika, cayenne, onion and garlic powders, and dried thyme and oregano, be put on the stove to blacken like their "Indian-style" steak. He loved it, but Mrs. Brennan wasn't moved, only agreeing to put it on the menu at their other restaurant, Mr. B's, and insisting it "grilled" instead of "blackened." When Prudhomme left to open K-Paul's, his position filled by a young Emeril Lagasse, he brought the Blackened Redfish recipe with him, using a cast-iron skillet (frying pan), preheated for almost ten minutes to achieve that striking char. He began serving the dish in 1980, and as soon as word spread, the fervor was almost uncontrollable. Tables were limited to one order each, but eventually the trend caught on nationally, and the redfish population was critically depleted. In the words of the food editor Michael Batterberry, "Getting into K-Paul's was harder than getting into East Germany." And in the words of Lagasse, the redfish was "so monumental . . . they had to put a ban on the product."

selected by **Pat Nourse**

Alice Waters CHEZ PANISSE

United States 1980

recipe → **p 302**

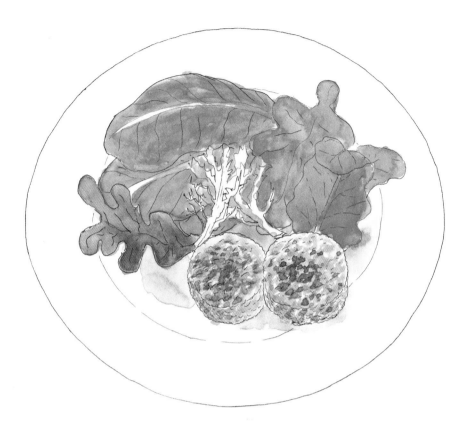

Baked Goat Cheese with Garden Lettuces

When Craig Claiborne first published a recipe for this salad in an article about Chez Panisse for *The New York Times* in 1981, it sparked a food revolution. Countless variations of warm, breaded discs of marinated fresh goat cheese followed.

At the time, artisanally made goat cheese was almost impossible to find in the United States. In 1980, California cheesemaker Laura Chenel showed up at Chez Panisse with fresh *crottins* from her year-old venture. Alice Waters placed a standing order, allowing the salad to stay on the menu—and Chenel to quit her waitressing job. (By the time she sold her company in 2006, she was selling over two million pounds of goat cheese annually.) Inspired by the salads of mesclun (mixed lettuces) that she had eaten while living in France, Waters encouraged friends and neighbors to plant lettuces around their homes, guaranteeing her a supply that thrives to this day. Dressed in a simple red wine vinaigrette, the salad is accompanied by garlic-rubbed slices of toasted baguette.

The interplay of warm cheese, crisp breadcrumbs, and cool seasonal greens wasn't the only influential thing to emanate from this humble Berkeley restaurant. As Claiborne wrote in the introduction to his article, "Where American gastronomy is concerned, there is one commodity that is rarer than locally grown black truffles or homemade foie gras. That is a chef of international repute who was born in the United States. Even rarer is such a celebrated chef who is a woman."

selected by **Christine Muhlke, Diego Salazar**

Fulvio Pierangelini GAMBERO ROSSO
Italy c.1980

recipe → **p 302**

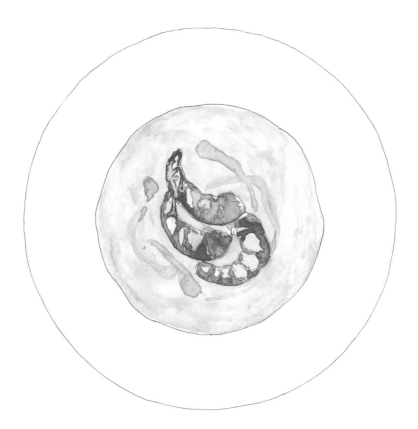

Chickpea Purée with Red Shrimp

Passatina di ceci e gamberi rossi

Of those who were able to dine at Fulvio Pierangelini's beachside restaurant in the small fishing village of San Vincenzo on the Tuscan coast before it closed in 2008, many will recall the haunting simplicity of this dish. The fluid chickpea purée was as sensual as Joël Robuchon's Potato Purée (see page 119), but relied simply on good dried chickpeas, a clove of garlic, and a sprig of rosemary. (Though the chef himself refused to adhere to a specific recipe, simply allowing himself to be moved by the sincerity of the ingredients.) Passed through a sieve then lightened with a hand blender and a little olive oil, the cream is topped with quickly steamed prawns that retain their sweetness and silken texture. Evocative of a fisherman's dish—land and sea meeting on the plate—albeit one with more spontaneity and skill. "You have to learn the techniques perfectly, then forget them," the chef has said.

Pierangelini has said that he first made the dish when he invited the famous winemakers Piero Antinori and Nicolò Incisa della Rochetta to dinner at his house. (They, however, preferred to argue about wine than discuss the plate in front of them.) In the thirty years, give or take, during which the seemingly simple puree was served, it influenced countless chefs, including David Chang of Momofuku, who used it as starting point for a pasta made with fermented chickpeas.

But Pierangelini's cuisine was never about modernity or flash. And that has been the most lasting influence. Like this dish, it was rooted in being able to evoke emotion with as few brushstrokes as possible. As he told the cooks gathered at chef René Redzepi's annual MAD Symposium in 2014, "Don't forget that simplicity is the ultimate goal."

selected by **Andrea Petrini**

Michel Bras BRAS
France 1980

recipe → **p 303**

Gargouillou

The most beautiful "salad" you will ever eat. From its microseasonality—the dozens of elements are gathered that day—to its inclusion of the plant in all of its stages (root, leaf, bud, flower, fruit, seed, "soil"), not to mention its naturalistic plating, Michel Bras's translation of the fields of the Aubrac region of France has caused countless chefs to plate his or her own moment in nature. Alain Passard at L'Arpège, David Kinch at Manresa, Andoni Aduriz at Mugaritz, Dominique Crenn at Atelier Crenn, Kyle Connaughton at SingleThread (who spent a year on the Gargouillou station at Bras' restaurant in Hokkaido, Japan). All were inspired by this poetic expression of place.

Named after a traditional Aubrac stew made with potatoes, water, and ham, Bras' Gargouillou was inspired by the chef's runs through the mountains. The dish is reimagined as a painterly salad in which each type of young vegetable is prepared differently, lightly sautéed or left raw according to its maturity and flavor, then joined by wild herbs and flowers, foraged mushrooms, and pearls of parsley oil. (The ham is there, either as a paper-thin slice sautéed in butter, or an infused emulsion that coats the vegetables.) Raw and cooked, wild and farmed, rustic and "haute," traditional and modern, local and international, the dish was a radical departure for French food in the late 1970s.

Since then, as Wylie Dufresne told the Food Snob blog, Bras' style "has been copied by every chef in the world. We've taken a page out of the Bras book—the schmear, the spoon drag, putting food on a plate like it fell off a tree." More than the plating style, it is Bras' exploration and elevation of the nature surrounding him that has influenced subsequent generations.

selected by **Susan Jung, Howie Kahn, Christine Muhlke, Pat Nourse,** Diego Salazar

Guy Savoy GUY SAVOY

France 1980

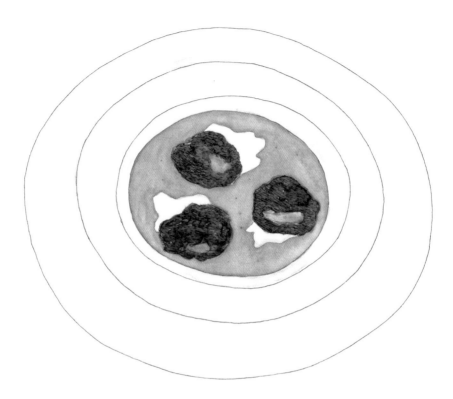

recipe → **p 306**

Artichoke Soup with Black Truffle

Soupe d'artichaut à la truffe noire

The Burgundian chef Guy Savoy, who grew up helping his mother run her restaurant before apprenticing with a local pastry chef, spent three years apprenticing with the Troisgros brothers in Roanne, at a time when nouvelle cuisine still held sway. While the young cook came away from Troisgros with a deep understanding of teamwork and precision—indeed, the influential restaurant critic Christian Millau mentioned him in an article on the restaurant at the time, writing, "In 10 years, we'll be talking about this commis with a great future"—when Savoy finally opened his own restaurant in Paris in 1980, he placed the importance on emotion: the profound feelings that a perfect bite could evoke.

Indeed, Savoy's signature dish has caused many diners to weep with joy in the decades since it first appeared on his menu. A classic creamy velouté of artichokes and leeks is enriched with shavings of Parmesan and black truffle. Savoy takes the indulgence even further, serving a buttery *brioche feuilletée* alongside, its many layers marbled with mushroom purée. Sliced in half to show off its faultless architecture in cross section, the brioche is toasted and, for good measure, slathered with truffle butter. (He gives the diners permission to dunk it into the soup, well aware of the childlike response it provokes in the hushed dining rooms of his posh, three-Michelin-starred restaurant along the Seine.) The soup is so popular that it appears on the menu year-round, truffle season be damned, as well as at his outpost in Caesars Palace in Las Vegas. It is proof positive of the red neon phrase that Savoy hung in his kitchen: "Cooking is the art of being able to instantly transform ingredients laden with history into joy."

selected by **Richard Vines**

Néstor BAR NÉSTOR
Spain 1980

Spanish Omelet

Tortilla de patatas

San Sebastián has long been the gastronomic center of Spanish Basque country, holding more Michelin stars per capita than any city in the world. Even tiny *pintxos* (or tapas) bars in the city's Old Town experiment with innovative bites. But one of the city's most celebrated dishes is also its simplest: the tortilla served at Bar Néstor. Not to be confused with the Mexican cornmeal tortilla, the Spanish version is an omelet made in a skillet (frying pan) using only olive oil, potatoes, caramelized onion, and of course, lots of eggs. The peasant dish has been a staple on the Iberian peninsula for centuries; it is a practical and economical way to stretch the basic ingredients that most home cooks in Spain have on hand into something filling and delicious. If prepared with skill and good ingredients, the top will be lightly crisped but the center will remain a bit *baveuse*, the soft egg straddling the line between cooked and runny.

The mustachioed Néstor and his wife set out a freshly made tortilla twice daily at his eponymous bar—one at 1 p.m. and another at 8 p.m.—roughly sliced into sixteen or seventeen pieces and served only to those customers who ducked beneath the half-closed metal shutters before opening time and put their names on the list. So perfect is their creation, it has become a sensation not only in San Sebastián, but across the world—a site of pilgrimage at which foodies can sample the legendary tortilla, as well as Néstor's *txuleta* steak and tomato salad.

By perfecting a foundational culinary tradition, Néstor inspired local institutions at all levels to reimagine the classics, arguably leading to reinventions such as the potato crisp tortilla at Ferran Adrià's elBulli in nearby Roses. In essence, Néstor's minimalism helped those cooking around him to fuse their desire to innovate with the desire to remain true to their roots.

selected by **Christine Muhlke**

Supinya Junsuta RAAN JAY FAI
Thailand 1980s

recipe → p 307

Crab Omelet

Khai jeaw poo

Supinya Junsuta has been cooking solo for over four decades in her native Bangkok. So Junsuta, known as Jay Fai, doesn't understand why the inspectors from the Michelin Guide have only now awarded her tiny restaurant a star—the only street-food stall to receive one. In fact, the septuagenarian, who wears protective ski goggles and a black knit cap while standing over a wok of bubbling oil set over high charcoal flames, would like to give back the award so she can cook more than just the Michelin-cited recipes requested by tourists who have stood in line for hours. At the top of everyone's list: the *khai jeaw poo*, or crab omelet. Fai has elevated the traditional recipe to cult status: despite the street-food setting in which it's served, people are willing to pay more than $30 (£23) for one of the torpedo-shaped omelets, each containing a luxurious amount of fresh chunks of sweet crab just barely bound by egg and flour. Cooking them one at a time, Fai meticulously shapes the batter as it cooks, gradually rolling it into cylinders plumper than a forearm, pouring in more egg as needed in order to perfect the shape. Despite the crackling, golden-brown exterior, the omelet is miraculously light on the tongue.

The popularity of Fai's dish speaks to the increased global appreciation of Thai street food. (She demonstrated it onstage at René Rezepi's MAD Food Symposium to huge applause.) Her Michelin star, ironically, came just as the city of Bangkok announced that it would move to ban street food vendors from much of the city, claiming that they were blocking sidewalks. Although her shophouse is safe from developers and urban planners, the cuisine that it represents is potentially in danger.

selected by **Susan Jung**

recipe → **p 307**

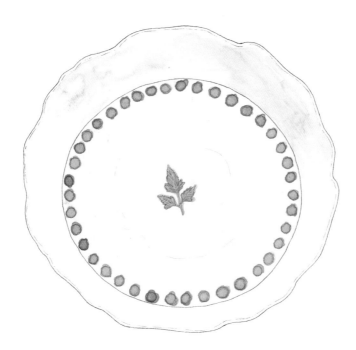

Caviar Jelly with Cauliflower Cream

Gelée de caviar à la crème de chou-fleur

Cooks who worked in the Jamin kitchen during its 1980s heyday still have dreams in which they're tasked with plating this high-wire dish during the peak of dinner service. Each dot of perfectly spaced chlorophyll-tinted mayonnaise was carefully dropped onto the cauliflower cream from a coffee spoon just before it was sent into the dining room. There was no room, or time, for error. The effect dazzled diners before they had even lifted a spoon—even those who thought it controversial for a three-star Parisian restaurant to serve cauliflower, considered food for *paysans* (peasants) at the time.

What lay beneath those dots was made with an even higher level of refinement and precision, cauliflower included. The cauliflower cream was featherlight, a velvety sauce made with reduced chicken stock, cornstarch (cornflour), egg yolk, and heavy (double) cream. Even more foundationally French was the clarified lobster jelly, the masterful base of which was a traditional veal-foot consommé whose natural gelatin made the lobster-infused stock transform into liquid on the tongue, rather than leave the blocky traces associated with commercial gelatin. Even without the salinity and subtle acidity of the 20 grams (0.7 ounce) of caviar hiding at the bottom of the bowl, the dish was a marvel of texture and complexity, of subtlety gleaned from the chef's life-changing visits to Japan and a palpable obsession with perfection. While it upheld nouvelle cuisine's dedication to seasonal ingredients, it was a departure from its restrictions. Instead, the dish fused elements of Japanese cooking with the rigor of haute cuisine techniques.

Joël Robuchon always said that a chef's role was to tell the truth of the flavor at the heart of each ingredient. In this creation, each ingredient told nothing but.

selected by **Christine Muhlke**, **Andrea Petrini**

Michel Bras BRAS

France 1981

recipe → **p 309**

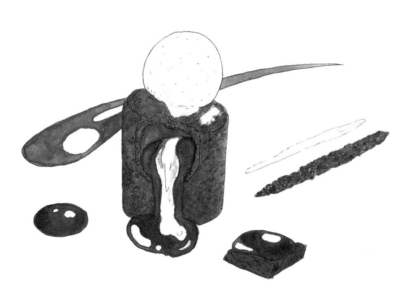

Chocolate Coulant

Coulant au chocolat

The dessert that launched a thousand imitations—to the point that American food writer Mark Bittman dubbed what came to be known as molten lava cake "the Big Mac of dessert." The original was a technical marvel: melted ganache oozes from a dark chocolate shell of crisp dough. Bras invented it to evoke an afternoon his family spent cross-country skiing: chilled to the bone, they were re-energized by sipping cups of hot chocolate around the family table. Bras said in an interview that "translating an emotion in a dessert isn't necessarily easy," but he spent the next two years realizing his masterpiece, which he finally arrived at by inserting a sphere of frozen ganache into cookie dough set into a tall cylindrical mold. The dessert was an instant success, spreading to kitchens throughout France. By 1991, Alain Ducasse told a reporter, "It reached a point where we were practically obliged to make it."

Six years after the *coulant* debuted in France, Jean-Georges Vongerichten put a similar cake on his menu at Lafayette in New York. For his cakes, the melting center was the result of his accidentally underbaking five hundred cupcakes for a private event. His mistake earned him a standing ovation from the guests. The four-ingredient Chocolate Valhrona Cake went onto the menu the next day. It wasn't until he added it to the menu at JoJo in 1991 that the cake took off, jumping to restaurants like Bouley and Le Cirque across the city—and country—within months. Called lava cake or molten chocolate cake, the hugely popular dessert found its way into chain restaurants, theme parks, and coffee shop chains.

At Bras, the coulant has evolved to include more than one hundred iterations over the decades. Today, Bras' son, Sébastien, heads up the restaurant. The coulant remains.

selected by **Christine Muhlke, Pat Nourse, Diego Salazar**

Joël Robuchon JAMIN
France 1981

recipe → **p 310**

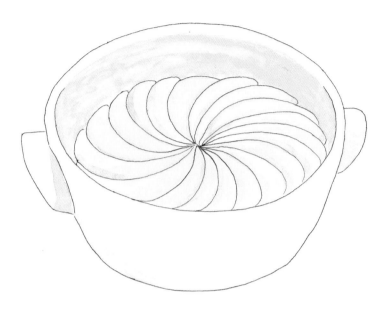

Potato Purée

Pommes purées

"I owe everything to these mashed potatoes," Joël Robuchon once said. It's odd that one of the world's most famous and creative chefs, who once held a record of thirty-two Michelin stars simultaneously, is best known for his mashed potatoes. But anyone who has tasted Joël Robuchon's potatoes would understand. Made with 500 grams of butter to each kilo of "la ratte" variety potatoes (1 part butter to 2 parts potato), they were more silken sauce than solid; pure richness on the plate.

Robuchon first served them alongside pig's head with sage at his restaurant Jamin—not unlike L'Escoffier's 1912 menu of truffled pig's foot and potato purée, which used approximately the same ratio of butter to potatoes. In 1981, France was emerging from nouvelle cuisine, and both purées and potatoes were decidedly out of fashion in high-end restaurants. Robuchon's purée became an immediate sensation.

This signature dish was nothing new; nor was the traditional French method of pushing boiled, unpeeled potatoes through a food mill, then cooking out the moisture before adding butter, then milk. But Robuchon's attention to the quality of his ingredients and the rigor and attention he focused on technique (not to mention that golden butter ratio) propelled this purée to signature-dish status.

Today, served in individual cocottes at the various L'Atelier de Joël Robuchon locations around the world, it continues to make diners marvel. And it has inspired chefs from Thomas Keller to Eric Ripert and Gordon Ramsay, both of whom cooked at Jamin in the 1980s. Indeed, Ripert once told a reporter who asked him what single dish he could eat for the rest of his life, that it would be Robuchon's "braised pig's head with mashed potatoes."

selected by **Susan Jung, Howie Kahn, Christine Muhlke, Diego Salazar, Richard Vines**

recipe → **p 311**

Rice, Gold, and Saffron

Riso, oro e zafferano

The 1970s was arguably the most critical decade in the evolution of global gastronomy since the 1800s. With the transition from haute to nouvelle cuisine, French chefs like Paul Bocuse were lauded as harbingers of a new dining culture, veering away from rich, classic recipes in favor of lighter dishes, with aesthetically stimulating presentation and carefully sourced produce. The concept was not contained to France. *Nuova cucina italiana* was the Italian iteration, and the father of the movement was Gualtiero Marchesi, who arguably caused the greatest alteration to the national palate since Pellegrino Artusi's first regional Italian cookbook in 1891. To Marchesi, 1970s Italian cookery was an embarrassing display of pastoral romanticism lacking any professional utilization of technique. He aimed to legitimize the cuisine as equal to French—a tension fired by the Michelin Guide's disregard of Italian talent.

Marchesi opened his first restaurant in Milan in 1977 and won one Michelin star within six months, his second the following year. In 1985, he received his third star as a result of this dish: golden saffron risotto gilded with a square of gold leaf. Considered his masterpiece, the dish encapsulated Marchesi's principles: not only did it engage the palate in innovative ways, it also sparked contemplation about historical context and dinner theater. This dish transformed the landscape because it was simultaneously figurative, literal, meta, ephemeral, and theatrical. It embodied the dualities of danger and attraction, toxicity and nourishment. With saffron considered the gastronomic version of gold since Medieval times, to pair the risotto with actual gold was an acknowledgment that cuisine is a tradition passed down through the generations and enriched over time.

selected by **Christine Muhlke**

Barry Wine QUILTED GIRAFFE
United States 1981

recipe → **p 311**

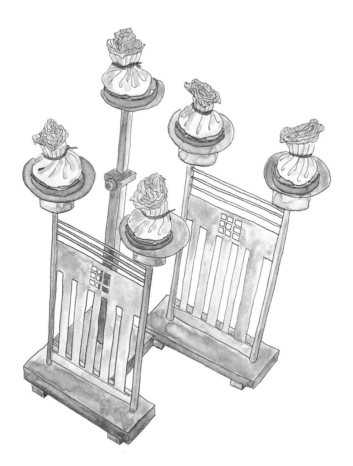

Beggar's Purses

The ultimate symbol of 1980s American excess, by way of France. Discovered by New York City chef Barry Wine at the Vieille Fontaine restaurant outside of Paris, these chive-wrapped crepe bundles filled with crème fraîche and caviar were topped with gold leaf. Requiring considerable dexterity to prepare without tearing either the thin crepe membrane or the chive sprig, they were a lavish interpretation of a Versailles-worthy amuse-bouche. At the time, high-end New York City diners were familiar with French food, having been sustained on the courtly fare at Le Pavillon and Le Dôme since the 1960s. But at the Quilted Giraffe, the freethinking, self-taught chef was serving what he called New American cuisine, which, in his vision, drew upon French and, eventually, Japanese ideas as well. It was groundbreaking at the time, and earned him four stars from *The New York Times.*

These singular bites were served on a silver pedestal and eaten with the hands. You tilted your head back to await the flavor and explosion of richness. Literally: each one was a $30 (£23) supplement on the $75 (£57) prix-fixe menu when they debuted in 1981. By 1990, they were $50 (£38) apiece. According to one server, investment bankers would order them by the dozen, "just as a way to spend money." (No wonder *American Psycho's* Patrick Bateman brought dates here.) In the kitchen, chef Tom Colicchio (who would go on to co-found Gramercy Tavern) and others made them in six-second intervals. Quilted Giraffe acolyte David Kinch served an homage filled with lightly smoked vegetables in albacore tonnato sauce at his California restaurant Manresa. And at Corey Lee's Benu in San Francisco, a filling of egg-yolk puree is complemented with black truffle, Iberico ham, and Parmesan.

selected by **Christine Muhlke**

Alain Senderens L'ARCHESTRATE

France 1981

recipe → **p 312**

Roast Lobster with Vanilla Butter Sauce

Homard à la vanille

An unorthodox pairing from one of the founding fathers of nouvelle cuisine, *The New York Times* food critic Craig Claiborne described it as "a triumph of taste over logic." How could vanilla be on the same plate as shellfish, watercress, and spinach? In the mind of Alain Senderens, who actively explored exotic and ancient flavors in the food served at his Michelin-starred restaurant named after the Greek gastronomic poet, finding new combinations for unfamiliar flavors and breaking down categories was second nature. And so the vanilla seeds were scraped into a finished beurre blanc and poured over the roasted lobster before serving. The vanilla's effect was not to bring sweetness to the plate. Rather, it enhanced the flavor of the shellfish, making it taste more intensely of itself.

When Senderens consulted on the Maurice restaurant in New York City, he brought the dish with him. It had an impact on his head chef, Christian Delouvrier, who went on to open Lespinasse, and also inspired American chefs David Bouley and Wolfgang Puck to create their own homages. In France, Michel Guérard, a cofounder of nouvelle cuisine, added vanilla to a hollandaise. And, of course, the impact of Senderens on his protégé, Alain Passard, cannot be underestimated. Passard sought to find the exotic side of French produce by challenging or revealing its true nature. He added vanilla to a tomato salad with lemon verbena and to an avocado soufflé.

Even when Senderens returned his three Michelin stars and removed the tablecloths in his eponymous Paris restaurant in 2005, the dish remained on the menu. "I don't want to feed my ego anymore," he told *The Times*. "I am too old for that. I can do beautiful cuisine without all the tra-la-la and chichi, and put the money into what's on the plate."

selected by **Christine Muhlke**

Wolfgang Puck SPAGO
United States 1982

recipe → **p 313**

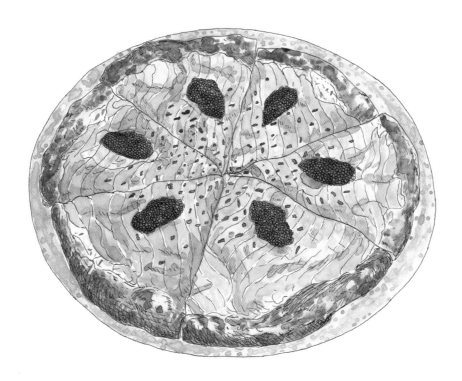

Pizza with Smoked Salmon and Caviar

Making pizza a luxury item was unheard of when the French-trained, Austrian-born chef Wolfgang Puck introduced this at his celebrity canteen on the Sunset Strip in West Hollywood. He specialized in what he deemed spa cuisine—California ingredients given the French treatment, with some Asian influences thrown in. But not all of his customers ate light. Legend has it he realized that he had run out of brioche for his smoked salmon plate when Joan Collins placed an order. Panicked, Puck substituted pizza dough instead, topping it with dill, crème fraîche, and smoked salmon—like a bagel and cream cheese for the rich and famous. To gild the lily, caramelized onions and a dollop of caviar were added to each slice. Not only was a star born (it's still the official pizza of the Oscars Governors Ball), but pizza's horizons expanded far past Italy, and Puck became America's first name-brand chef.

The smoked salmon pizza marked the moment when heavy cheese and meat were replaced by lighter, fresher, more seasonal toppings—a style that became known as California pizza. It also ushered in a generation of stunt pizzas and high-end hybrids (see also: truffle oil, foie gras, gold leaf). It helped Puck to open new restaurants, launch a catering arm, start Wolfgang Puck Worldwide, Inc., and roll out his franchise restaurants. Books, television shows, product lines, newspaper columns, and more are all part of the Puck brand.

The chef once visited his friend, the late Paul Bocuse, at his restaurant in France. He was shocked to see a pizza with smoked salmon on the menu. "I said, 'Paul, what the heck?'" the chef recalled in an interview with Michelin. "He showed me the name of the pizza, and it was 'Spago Pizza.' That was a proud moment for me."

selected by **Howie Kahn, Christine Muhlke, Diego Salazar**

123

recipe → **p 314**

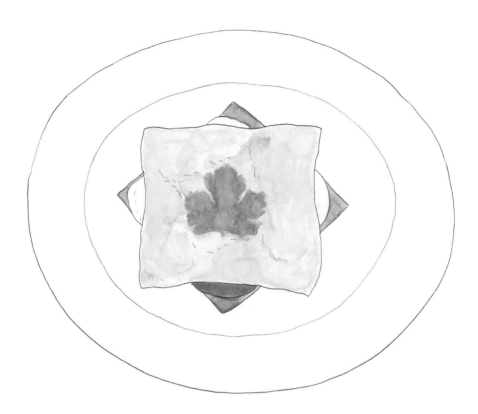

Open Raviolo

Raviolo aperto

In Italian cuisine, pasta was traditionally seen as a filling, economical course, never able to achieve the status of haute cuisine. It was simply what came between the antipasto and the main course. And filled pasta? It was a way to use up leftovers. In the early 1980s, Gualtiero Marchesi, the Milanese chef who made his name by gilding saffron risotto with gold leaf (see page 120), sought to deconstruct ravioli, both literally and metaphorically. He was inspired by a bad restaurant meal, during which the ravioli was so poorly made that it split open on the plate. It triggered a new dish and a new presentation—this in a country that saw culinary innovation as heresy. His Open Raviolo was a radical deconstruction, not only of the pasta's physical form, but also its filling. In this case, the "ravioli" was two sheets of pasta—one spinach, the other egg—between which he placed scallops sautéed in butter and white wine, the sauce then reduced with ginger juice. Ginger? Scallops? Butter? In *Italy*? The concept tilted toward nouvelle cuisine in its simplicity and lightness. Indeed, Marchesi had been influenced by the time he spent cooking at Ledoyen in Paris and Troisgros in Rouanne.

The dish embodied two of Marchesi's precepts, that beauty is essential—"form is matter"—and that "simplicity is a point of arrival, not a point of departure." It was radical at the time, and Marchesi was to be the first Italian chef to earn three Michelin stars. Protégés Davide Scabin and Carlo Cracco have paid homage to the dish. And it could be said that Marchesi's reframing of Italian cuisine in an artistic mindset (a later dish was based on a Jackson Pollock painting) gave birth to such chefs as Massimo Bottura.

selected by **Andrea Petrini**

recipe → **p 314**

Crème Brûlée

France, England, and Spain all lay claim to this iconic dessert. "Burnt cream," a sweet pudding made from the rich springtime milk of calving cows upon which a layer of sugar was burnt with a hot iron can be traced as far back as fifteenth-century England, where it later became associated with King's College, Cambridge, and called Cambridge Cream. In France, the earliest appearance of a dessert called Crème Brûlée is in the 1691 cookbook *Le Cuisinier Roïal et Bourgeois,* written by Versailles chef François Massialot. That version, made from a custard of egg yolks and milk with a burnt sugar crust, most closely resembles today's. And then there is the *crema catalana* of Spain, a cornstarch-thickened milk custard that dates to the 1400s.

It was the Spanish dessert, in fact, that Sirio Maccioni, owner of New York's Le Cirque restaurant, tasted while on vacation in Barcelona in 1982. He was immediately smitten and asked Alain Sailhac, Le Cirque's chef who happened to be visiting the Maccioni family on vacation, to re-create the dish for them. Realizing they had used up all the white sugar in the vanilla-enhanced custard, the dessert was topped with grated brown sugar before broiling, resulting in a thinner crust and more delicate dish. Le Cirque's pastry chef, Dieter Schorner (who originally scorned the dish, but afterward perfected it) later told a reporter that when French chef Paul Bocuse tasted it, he declared it the best dessert he'd had all year. It soon became popular in France, where it had never been a favorite, and iterations including ingredients such as coffee, ginger, lavender, and even foie gras took off in the United States.

Crème Brûlée requires a delicate touch so as not to curdle the custard while caramelizing the sugar. The introduction of affordable portable blowtorches helped to spread its popularity.

selected by **Christine Muhlke**

Olivier Roellinger LES MAISONS DE BRICOURT
France 1983

recipe → **p 315**

John Dory Back from India

Saint Pierre retour des Indes

On the plate, the entrée that made Olivier Roellinger's career could be said to be a fillet of John Dory with apple purée, mango, cabbage, and curry spices. What set it apart—aside from its exoticism, which was new at the time—was that it told a story of both history and place. The John Dory came from the bay that Roellinger could see from the windows of his family's Brittany home, which the chemical engineering student turned chef, driven by his passion to create new flavors, had opened as a restaurant. The cabbage came from a field facing the sea. And the curry powder was a blend that Roellinger had made following a conversation he'd had with someone who'd written his thesis on the French East India Company, who told him not only of the exotic silks and woods that made their way through the nearby town of Saint-Malo in the eighteenth century, but of the spices that entered then, too. Fascinated by the idea of the

historical gastronomical moment, he used his imagination as he blended the fourteen spices—including cardamom, ginger, coriander, star anise, vanilla, peppercorns, and cacao—into Retour des Indes, or Back from India, a heady mixture that spoke of a romantic era of globalization and maritime epics.

From that moment forward, Roellinger's cuisine was one that told a story through spices, incorporating them in a sometimes unexpected manner, as was echoed by his contemporaries Alain Senderens (see page 122), Pierre Gagnaire, Michel Troisgros, and Alain Passard (see pages 134 and 169). While rooted in France, these chefs were fearless when it came to looking to Asia and beyond for flavor inspiration. Roellinger, who returned his Michelin stars in 2008 for want of a quieter life, has also built a successful company out of sourcing and blending spices.

selected by **Andrea Petrini**

recipe → **p 317**

Braised Abalone

In 1983, chef and restaurateur Yeung Koon Yat was considering closing his six-year-old Hong Kong restaurant. The rich—i.e., those who spent money on fine cuisine—were moving away and in order to survive, a restaurant had to either lower prices or step up its culinary game considerably. The result was a wave of culinary creativity not unlike California's food revolution of the 1980s. In Yeung's case, he wanted to invent a dish that would create a craze. And so he became The Abalone King.

In China, sun-dried abalone has long been considered one of the more precious good-luck texture foods. One kilo (2.2 lb) can fetch over $7,000 (£5,350). Except Yeung didn't like the centuries-old Cantonese recipe that called for it to be cooked for days, rendering it tender but flavorless. So he developed a way to cook it in a humble clay pot, layered between bamboo sheets, with pork spareribs and an old stewing hen. The richest possible stock was added occasionally during the braising. After twelve hours, only the abalone and its reduced sauce are served. Connoisseurs know to nibble the rich, slightly sticky shellfish from the outside in, in a circular manner, working through the layers of texture until they reach its "honey heart."

Fellow cooks were shocked that he broke with tradition. But Yeung, known as Ah Yat, held firm. "It was very, very difficult in the beginning," he told the *Los Angeles Times*, "but it's important to contribute to your profession. I am a chef, and a chef must be aware of developments in society, of cultural changes—he must grow with modern times." He was bold enough to serve his modern invention to Chinese leader Deng Xiaoping. In a sentence that would make Yeung's career, the supreme leader declared it the best he had ever eaten. The Abalone King was crowned.

selected by **Susan Jung**

recipe → **p 317**

Samgyetang

In Korean and Chinese medicine, the belief is that you should fight fire with fire. And so on the special occasions to mark the three most sweltering, oppressively humid days of the year (Chobok, Jungbok, and Malbok), South Koreans eat hot chicken soup. Not only that, this *samgyetang* contains many ingredients said to create heat in the body and therefore promote health. Westerners think their chicken noodle soup is restorative? This traditional soup—in which a small chicken is stuffed with glutinous rice, fresh whole ginseng, garlic, scallion, gingko nuts, chestnuts, astralagus root, jujube dates, and pumpkin, sunflower, and sesame seeds and simmered for hours in stock—contains numerous medicinal herbs, including that four-year-old ginseng root, said to promote longevity. All that heat causes the body to sweat, thereby eliminating more toxins.

This is why there are such long lines outside of Samgyetang, the restaurant set in an old temple-style building in Seoul's historic Bukchon Hanok Village, every summer. Said to be the first Seoul restaurant specializing in *samgyetang*, it is certainly recognized as the best, with a consistently high quality that transcends its touristy reputation. Almost every diner at the 400-seat restaurant orders his or her own stone *dol-sot* casserole filled with the piping-hot whole-chicken soup in the hopes of tapping into its purported ability to restore energy and replenish lost nutrients. While the cloudy white broth itself is mild, the treasures tucked inside the cavity of the young (forty-nine-day-old) bird are full of surprising flavor, especially when dipped into a dish of salt. To increase one's heat even further, it is often paired with fiery *insam-ju* (ginseng wine).

selected by **Susan Jung**

recipe → **p 317**

Saffron Mashed Potatoes

Saffron Mashed Potatoes, or what the inventive London chef Simon Hopkinson prefers to refer to as "saff mash," were invented after an influential trip he took in 1983 to restaurant Michel in Marseille. While finishing a bowl of bouillabaisse, Hopkinson was struck by the hazy terracotta hue of the broth at the bottom of the bowl. He began to crush his leftover potatoes in the remaining liquid to soak up the last bits of deep flavor when the idea came to him: saffron mash! He could emulate the flavor profile of the bouillabaisse by substituting olive oil for the usual butter and integrating a bit of garlic and hot pepper sauce; the saffron not only imparted a layer of minerality to the flavor of the riced potatoes, but also infused them with a golden tone that drastically elevated what had come to be known as a simple dish as common and English as fish and chips or mushy peas.

Nostalgic for the smooth, rich "creamed potatoes" served onto plates with silver spoons in British hotels throughout the 1960s, Hopkinson set out to correct the tuber travesties occurring in the fine-dining establishments around him. The fashion of the time, which Hopkinson described in *The Economist*'s *1843* magazine as "cardiac-arrest-inducing, butter-cream-slop that is the darling of Michelin-obsessed chefs," he could see as nothing but "the work of a kitchen devil." His golden purée became a global sensation—the first notable reintegration of what was once a pivotal spice in the world of gastronomy—after it was popularized in his kitchen at Bibendum. Considered one of the leaders of the British "back to basics" movement, Hopkinson quickly became the superstar of the city's burgeoning food scene, with chefs Rowley Leigh and Rick Stein soon found saff-mashing in his wake.

selected by **Richard Vines**

recipe → **p 318**

Salt-Baked Squab Pigeons

Pigeonneau de Bresse en croûte de sel

When Le Manoir aux Quat'Saisons opened in the British countryside in 1984, the country hotel immediately became known for the classical French cooking of its chef, Raymond Blanc. Blanc's menus combined the showy presentation and luxe ingredients of Carême with the country cooking of his native France, with most ingredients supplied by the bounty of his *potagers* (kitchen gardens)—a rarity at the time, such traditions having gone the way of Versailles. Blanc's technical mastery of food for the elite is on brilliant display in Blanc's signature squab pigeon baked in a salt pastry crust that has been sculpted to evoke the game bird beneath—head, eyes, beak, wings, and all. When the little *pièce montée* is brought to the table, Blanc wrote in the introduction to his recipe in the 2011 cookbook *Kitchen Secrets*, "there is always a small silence." And then, *le déluge*: "The waiter elegantly severs the head from

the body in the good old-fashioned Republican way . . . la Guillotine!" (For home cooks not accustomed to fine-dining birds, he had to include the comment that while the squab may look like a pigeon loitering in London's Trafalgar Square, "it is in fact a bird with the most unctuous flesh and refined flavor.")

In his restaurant, this sense of refinement was underscored by the squab's accompaniments: a classic sauce made from a reduction of the necks and wings with Madeira and mushrooms, alongside a crisp fanned disc of pommes Maxim, fricasseed mushrooms, and pan-fried foie gras. Subsequent trends could not erode the popularity of this dish, which remains on the menu to this day. As Blanc himself said of the nature of a signature dish, it "represents the value and style of a restaurant: its texture, its classic values. It lasts through time and doesn't follow any fashion."

selected by **Richard Vines**

130

Shigefumi Tachibe BRASSERIE CHAYA
United States 1984

recipe → **p 320**

Tuna Tartare

Beverly Hills in the 1980s proved to be sushi's gateway to America—albeit in un-sushi-like form. Like Nobu Matsuhisa's groundbreaking New-Style Sashimi (see page 141), which was created in 1987, Shigefumi Tachibe's Tuna Tartare made raw fish more palatable to diners in a country that still preferred its seafood fried, smoked, or canned. Unlike Nobu's sashimi, which arose from a customer's distaste for raw fish, the genesis was a vegetarian customer who asked for an alternative to the steak tartare served at the casually elegant Japanese-French restaurant. And so Tachibe, who had worked in Japan, where he learned both Japanese and French cooking, as well as in Florence, Italy, simply used what was right in front of him to expand upon the idea of steak tartare—itself a 1920s French take on an ancient dish that is more concept than recipe (see page 224).

In addition to diced ahi tuna mixed with capers, onions, pickles, and crushed green peppercorns in a house-made Dijon-tarragon mayonnaise, Tachibe's version also added a distinctly Californian touch: thin slices of avocado. It was part of the restaurant's mission to lighten traditional French fare for the restaurant's body-conscious celebrity clientele by incorporating Japanese elements. Chaya CEO Yuta Tsunoda, whose family began the restaurant empire behind Chaya as a small teahouse in Japan almost four centuries prior, felt the city was asking for it at that time. To say that the dish was widely emulated throughout the 1980s (and still today) is an understatement along the lines of saying that people really took to the molten chocolate cake originated by Michel Bras. Today, the dish is in the Smithsonian National Museum of American History, alongside Tachibe's sushi knife.

selected by **Diego Salazar**

Anne Rosenzweig ARCADIA
United States 1985

recipe → **p 321**

Lobster Club Sandwich

The Club Sandwich (see page 39) is an American classic. Its origins are murky: was it first made in the club car of a train? Or perhaps served in a gentlemen's club? What is known is that this simple but substantial sandwich, made from two or three slices of toast layered with chicken breast, bacon, lettuce, and tomato, has become a safe if uninspired order in coffee shops, cafés, and hotels around the world. As the American food writer Michael Stern said, "Club sandwiches are sort of like having a .38 tucked in your pocket. One seldom avails oneself of it, but it's good to know they're there."

And then, in 1985, the New York City chef Anne Rosenzweig decided to offer something that would break down the formality of her Upper East Side restaurant, where she was setting down the first roots of what came to be known as New American cuisine with her seasonally led menus. "I wanted

something that was really huge, that might fall apart in your hands," she told *Newsday* in 1986. "But I wanted something classic, too, ingredients that would be elegant and luxurious." So she tucked just-steamed lobster meat between three slices of house-made brioche toast slicked with lemon-Dijon mayonnaise. The bacon was applewood-smoked, the tomatoes were vine-ripened, the seasonal greens, such as mâche or arugula (rocket), grown herself. "Hot and cold, and crunchy, and the creaminess of the dressing, there's all that going on. It's so ephemeral. It lasts such a short time. The first few bites are heaven." At $24.50 (£18.75), it was the height of decadent comfort food. Her sandwich was not only the impetus for the ensuing gourmet sandwich craze, it became the name of her second restaurant, The Lobster Club, which served elegant yet affordable comfort food.

selected by **Christine Muhlke**

132

Gilbert Le Coze   LE BERNARDIN
United States 1986

recipe → **p 322**

Tuna, Shaved Chives, and Extra-Virgin Olive Oil

While Japanese chefs at Matsuhisa and Brasserie Chaya in Los Angeles would begin to transform Americans' perceptions of raw fish starting in 1994, it took a Frenchman to do the same for New Yorkers. When the Parisian chef Gilbert Le Coze and his sister, Maguy, opened their second restaurant in New York in 1986, they didn't know they would have so much difficulty sourcing ingredients such as high-quality seafood and fresh herbs. As the grandson of a fisherman and the son of a restaurateur in coastal Brittany, Le Coze immediately set about convincing the fish market sellers to get him the quality and variety he demanded. In the meantime, sushi-grade tuna was the best fish he could get. Le Coze tried out recipes on his sister. "After tasting several experiments, I told Gilbert the tuna was so bad, it would be better raw," she wrote in the restaurant's first cookbook. And so tuna carpaccio was born.

A play on the beef carpaccio (see page 72) that was so popular at New York's new Harry Cipriani outpost at the time, Le Coze took a Japanese-Mediterranean approach, pounding each slice until it formed a transparent veil across the plate, then minimally embellishing it with olive oil, lemon juice, chives, white pepper, and salt. As *The New York Times* wrote of the Le Cozes in an early four-star review, "I would like to see their passports confiscated and their movement restricted to this fish-starved island." As Ruth Reichl wrote in a review one year after his death in 1994, "Mr. Le Coze's cooking changed American dining. His style, impeccably fresh fish cooked with respect and simplicity, was soon so widely copied that people forgot who had invented it. That did not seem to bother Mr. Le Coze. " What was most important to Le Coze was that New York chefs gained access to beautiful seafood.

selected by **Christine Muhlke**

133

Alain Passard L'ARPÈGE
France 1986

recipe → **p 322**

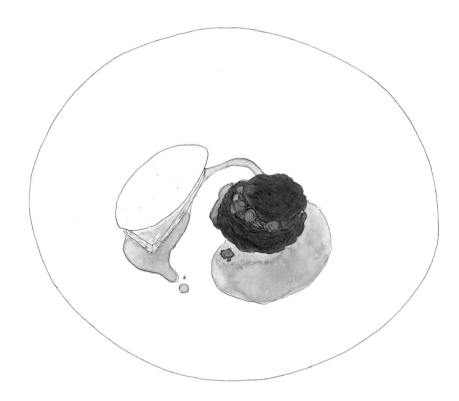

Confit Tomato with Twelve Flavors

Tomate confite aux douze saveurs

More than a decade before the Parisian chef moved to an all-vegetable menu, he was already exploring and expanding the possibilities of produce. In 1986, he put diners at attention by sending out a reminder of the true nature of a tomato. As Adam Gopnik wrote in The *New Yorker*, the visionary brilliance of the tomato stuffed with fruit, ginger, spices, as well as orange zest and a variety of chopped nuts before being basted with caramel for hours, is that it "demonstrates, with a stubborn, sublime logic, an extremely abstract botanical point: tomatoes are not vegetables; they are fruit." How could we have forgotten? Or perhaps we never really knew.

The dish can trace some of its flavors to the honey- and clove-basted canard à l'Apicius that Passard prepared while working for Alain Senderens at L'Archestrate, a restaurant that Passard later purchased from his mentor in 1986. In addition to its remarkable flavor and intellectual provocation—both of which were ahead of their time—what was also notable about the dessert was that it seemingly concluded the era of *la grande cuisine* in which dishes were finished tableside. (Before it arrived at the table, the dish required hours of hands-on attention from the fish, meat, and legume stations—who all shared the kitchen's one stove; if not constantly basted, the tomato flesh would collapse around the stuffing, ruining the dish. In the Arpège kitchen, one could always hear the chefs imploring, "*Arose les tomates! Arose les tomates!*" "Baste the tomatoes!")

Following its success, three-star restaurants began offering vegetal desserts, such as Le Grand Vefour's artichoke tart with candied carrots. By the 2000s, the dessert had oddly trickled down to US television, appearing as Tomato Saltambique on "*The West Wing*" as a favorite of the president.

selected by **Pat Nourse, Andrea Petrini**

recipe → **p 323**

Salmon Rillettes

Although every dish served today over the course of a meal at Maguy Le Coze and Eric Ripert's New York City seafood restaurant, Le Bernardin, is memorable, it is the welcoming gift to the table that has had the most unforgettable impact on diners since it debuted on Gilbert Le Coze's original menu over three decades ago. A maritime take on the hearty French classic *rillettes de porc*, that rich, flavorful spread made from shredded braised pork mixed with lard that is slathered onto bread or toasts during aperitif hour, Le Coze sought to make salmon as silken and indulgent, worthy of the restaurant's four stars, which have gone untarnished since its opening in 1986. Having begun cooking at his family's restaurant and inn in a Brittany port as a teenager, Le Coze—the grandson of a fisherman—became known for treating fish like meat, basing preparation and cooking time on each fish's individual character, a new philosophy in the culinary world that earned him stars first at his restaurant in Paris, and then in New York.

Poached in white wine with shallots and sliced into generous cubes, these rillettes get their "fat" from more refined sources: diced Scottish smoked salmon and homemade mayonnaise, the gently folded mixture brightened with lemon juice, chives, and white pepper. Translucent toasts of thinly sliced baguette accompany the bowl of rillettes to the table and are continually replenished, as even seasoned regulars can't help themselves from emptying the not-insignificantly-sized portion. After all these years, Mlle. Le Coze still makes her daily 12 o'clock snack from that morning's preparation, sneaking into the walk-in refrigerator, still-warm slice of toasted baguette in her hand. Such is the enduring allure of a signature dish.

selected by **Howie Kahn**

Nobu Matsuhisa MATSUHISA

United States c.1987

recipe → **p 323**

Black Cod with Miso

One of the most famous and successful chefs in the world—and the dish that helped him build his empire. This Black Cod with Miso helped expose Nobu Matsuhisa's diners to Japanese food at a time when Americans weren't yet accustomed to sushi. Like David Chang's Pork Buns a decade later (see page 197), the sweet mirin and sugar glaze on the meaty, delicately flavored fish skewed an Asian recipe for Western palates. And, like those buns, this dish proved easy to replicate by copycat restaurants while adding a telltale cheffy credibility.

Although this recipe—a traditional method of preserving fish in sake lees and miso—has been served in Japan for centuries, Matsuhisa made it sweeter, adding sugar, mirin (sweet rice wine), and milder white miso to the three-day marinade. The fermented mirin and miso also impart irresistible umami. The introduction of miso as a starring ingredient was novel in America—until then, it was associated with macrobiotic restaurants and health food stores.

At the time, black cod was a cheap, widely available fish, and the recipe is easy to make, even by home cooks: placed under the broiler (grill), the sugars caramelize into an amber shell while insulating the fish from overcooking. The cod's simplicity and spare presentation—placed simply on a banana leaf with miso dots and ginger—meant that as the restaurant spread across the world, a cook in Dubai could make it taste exactly as another in London or Kuala Lumpur.

As *New York* magazine restaurant critic Adam Platt wrote of the dish, "Certain dishes are like that famous obelisk in Kubrick's *2001: A Space Odyssey*. When it lands in their midst, the apes have never seen anything like it, and they are changed forever. Miso cod was one of those dishes."

selected by **Christine Muhlke, Diego Salazar**

Alain Ducasse LE LOUIS XV
Monaco 1987

recipe → **p 324**

Rum Baba

Baba au rhum

Alain Ducasse did not invent this dessert. Rather, he reinvigorated the plump, sweet, rum-and-sugar-soaked pastry for the twentieth century, lightening the batter, reducing the amount of sugar, adding lemon and orange zests to the sugar syrup and honey to the yeasted brioche dough, and, in the most memorable flourish, serving the dish tableside: the diner is given his or her choice of five different rums with which to anoint the little cake, which is then finished with sweetened whipped cream, accented with vanilla.

While the baba, as it is commonly called, is associated with bourgeois French pastry, its roots are Polish. The story goes that the exiled Polish king Stanislaus I was enamored of the traditional raisin-studded Alsatian cake, the *kouglof*, but found it too dry. He soaked it in rum and named the result after Ali Baba, his favorite character from the *One Thousand and One Nights*. Appropriated by the French, it took its place in nineteenth-century literature in the works of Diderot, Zola, and others. The lowered price of sugar during that time made such sweets more accessible to the working class, while they still maintained their air of luxury. By the mid-nineteenth century, a version without raisins served with whipped cream and fruit was named a *brillat-savarin*, or *savarin*, after Jean Anthelme Brillat-Savarin, the author of *Physiologie du Goût.*

By the time Ducasse put his baba on the menu, its reputation was one of a dated, uninspired pastry more associated with childhood dessert than *la grande cuisine*. By adding his own touches, he added a fresh sense of wonder to the nostalgia.

selected by **Richard Vines**

Judy Rodgers ZUNI CAFÉ
United States 1987

recipe → **p 324**

Zuni Roast Chicken with Bread Salad

Roast chicken is like heaven: everyone has their way of getting there, and everyone is probably mostly right. But Judy Rodgers's roast chicken is a religion all on its own—one whose every step and logic has been prodded for fallacies, of which there are none. From the first night she took the helm at San Francisco's legendary Zuni Café until her death in 2013, Rodgers—a student of Alice Waters and greats in Italy and Southern France—served roast chicken with bread salad for two. It's a deeply rustic dish, in no way trendy or flashy, but that's the point. She honed her recipe for years and outlined it in small type over five pages in the restaurant's 2002 book, *The Zuni Café Cookbook*: first, pick a small bird for its optimal meat to fat ratio. Next, roast at a very high heat: 475°F (245°C) approximates the wood-burning oven that is at the heart of

much of the restaurant's food. And most significantly, salt generously, days ahead of cooking. Every protein that entered the back door of Zuni Café was salted before being refrigerated —Rodgers was dry-brining before there was a term for it. The method has since become second nature to home cooks and chefs seeking a succulent, tender bird that's well seasoned inside and out. At Zuni, the buttery chicken with crisp skin is served carved on a warm bread salad, a scrappy sort of stuffing—made using the restaurant's leftover bread—that's vinegary and schmaltzy in every bite but certainly second fiddle to the archetypal roast chicken. If you ever see a roast chicken for two on a menu or a dry-brined roast chicken or turkey recipe, know Rodgers's salt-sprinkled fingerprints touched it.

selected by **Susan Jung, Howie Kahn, Christine Muhlke, Pat Nourse**

Foo Kui Lian TIAN TIAN HAINANESE KITCHEN
Singapore 1987

recipe → **p 326**

Hainanese Chicken and Rice

When the Hainanese began immigrating to Singapore from the southern Chinese island of Hainan, they were relegated to the servant class, working (and cooking) for British colonialists. They served them a traditional dish of boiled chicken and rice, known as Wenchang chicken, that seemed simple enough for their taste buds. What became known as Hainanese chicken and rice—eventually the national dish of Singapore—is hauntingly subtle in flavor and cleverly resourceful in its technique. After a whole chicken is gently poached in water, it is dunked in ice so its skin tightens and seals in the juices. White rice is cooked in the resulting broth with aromatics and chicken fat, and the chicken and rice are finally served with a drizzle of sauce and dipping sauces.

After the British left Singapore during World War II, the Hainanese needed new jobs and started selling, among other things, chicken and rice. In 1971, as part of Singapore's efforts to improve the quality of life in the newly established nation, street carts were concentrated into hawker centers. Among all the dishes, the unflashy Hainanese chicken and rice became the star, with people forming near-religious loyalty to their favorite carts. That served at Tian Tian, which Foo Kui Lian opened in the Maxwell Food Centre in 1987, became considered the best, with TV cameos, write-ups in nearly every guidebook, and chef fans who have helped the dish travel around the globe and even earned the stall a Michelin Bib Gourmand award. These hawker centers are in limbo as the older generation retire and their children take desk jobs. Luckily for Tian Tian, Foo Kui Lian's daughter left her accountant position to expand the restaurant's legacy. That said, Mom still arrives at the kitchen at 6 a.m. to make sure everything's running smoothly.

selected by **Howie Kahn**

Alain Ducasse LE LOUIS XV

Monaco 1987

recipe → **p 327**

Provençal Garden Vegetables Stewed in Shaved Black Truffle

Cocotte de legumes des jardins de Provence mijotée à la truffe noire ecrasée

Decades before vegetables became the star of the plate at many restaurants, Alain Ducasse gave them a starring role at his Monte Carlo flagship. At the time, the concept was revolutionary for a luxury three-star restaurant, where costly proteins such as lobster and lamb were still at the center of a dish. (Michel Bras had introduced his vegetal symphony, Gargouillou, page 113, in Laguiole, France, in 1978, but Bras's eponymous restaurant was not as internationally celebrated as Le Louis XV.) Ducasse attributes the dish's inspiration to southern French chef Mimi Brothier, whom he once described in the *Sunday Times* as "a lady who slow-cooks with her heart."

The often-miniaturized assortment of peak produce was sourced from farms in neighboring Provence, highlighting the agrarian connection to the kitchen. The vegetables were cooked very slowly in their own moisture, with a minimal amount of vegetable or chicken stock added; the colorful, seasonally changing assortment embellished with crushed black truffles, both in and out of season. Not only delicious but beautiful to behold, it introduced a generation of cooks (and diners) to the endless possibilities of cooking with vegetables.

As Ducasse's empire expanded over the decades into multiple countries, the dish developed into what came to be known as a "cookpot," declared by Ducasse a "glocal" dish, meaning that it is capable of becoming local no matter where it is in the world, as long as it relies upon that region's best ingredients. The cookpot also presaged Ducasse's evolution toward a more healthful, vegetable-based cuisine. Today such dishes are cooked by his chefs de cuisine, Dominique Lory at Le Louis XV, Jean-Philippe Blondet at The Dorchester in London, and Romain Meder at the Plaza Athénée in Paris.

selected by **Susan Jung, Howie Kahn, Christine Muhlke, Pat Nourse, Andrea Petrini, Diego Salazar, Richard Vines**

Nobu Matsuhisa MATSUHISA
United States 1987

recipe → **p 328**

New-Style Sashimi

Raw fish that isn't raw fish: less a Zen koan than the dish that weaponized sushi-bar fare for a non-Japanese audience. Sushi purists may consider this dish a travesty, but the more generous among them must admit that giving customers what they want isn't such a crime. The dish came about when a diner at Matsuhisa's original Beverly Hills restaurant said that she would not eat raw fish. The chef went back into the kitchen with the plate of snapper sashimi, wondering what to do. Put it in the oven? Run it under the salamander? It would be ruined. His eyes fell upon a pan of hot olive oil, which he drizzled on the fish. "The fish was not really cooked, just about 10 percent," he later wrote in the *New York Times*. "So it was a bit of a joke, but it was enough to make it acceptable to her, and it pleased me."

The contrast in temperature and texture made the fish feel silkier in the mouth. Matsuhisa eventually began using sesame oil in lieu of olive oil, topping each slice with ginger, garlic (unheard of in Japanese cuisine), and chives for complexity and serving it with a sauce of soy and yuzu. Matsuhisa's preference for strong flavors such as chile and garlic, influenced by his time cooking Japanese food in South America, set him apart from Japan's practitioners of subtlety and purity. Indeed, these bigger flavors and Westernized approach are what made him the world's most popular Japanese chef and restaurateur.

This fusion, born of compromise, became a triumph—one that helped open the gates to experimentation at every level. As Matsuhisa wrote, pleasing his client was a gamble that paid off, both in terms of his reputation and his creative evolution: "So many chefs seem to feel they must not compromise. But I don't think you'll get far that way, and you'll miss so many inspirations along the way."

selected by **Susan Jung, Pat Nourse**

recipe → **p 328**

Grilled Squid with Chile

Calamari ai ferri con peperoncini

This three-ingredient dish has been on the menu since the first day that self-taught cooks Ruth Rogers and Rose Gray opened their canteen for an architecture firm in a converted oil warehouse on the Thames. It was their philosophy on a plate. At the time, restaurant Italian food in London meant spaghetti Bolognese and tiramisu, a greatest hits of heavy dishes with none of the attachment to regionality and seasonality that mark the cuisine in the country itself. By grilling whole squid and serving it with a sauce of fresh red chile and olive oil alongside a wedge of lemon and a pile of spiky arugula (rocket) that they'd grown from seeds brought back from Italy, where Gray had lived and Rogers had in-laws, they changed not only Italian food in London, but restaurant cooking itself.

Rogers and Gray could cook so essentially because they brought an attention to Italian ingredients that had never been seen before. Freshness and seasonality were key, down to the olive oil, which they sourced every autumn. As the canteen became a successful restaurant, they began to import both the highest quality ingredients and humble ones that were not yet available in the UK, such as those red chiles, lacinato kale (cavolo nero), and fresh ricotta. Eventually, the scored squid bodies were cooked in a wood-burning oven, like those they had seen in the Tuscan countryside.

The chefs' style spread not just because other restaurateurs wanted to emulate their success, but also because they taught their philosophy to young cooks who went on to fame, including Jamie Oliver, April Bloomfield, Hugh Fearnley-Whittingstall, Samuel and Samantha Clark, Jess Shadbolt, and Clare de Boer.

selected by **Howie Kahn, Christine Muhlke**

recipe → **p 329**

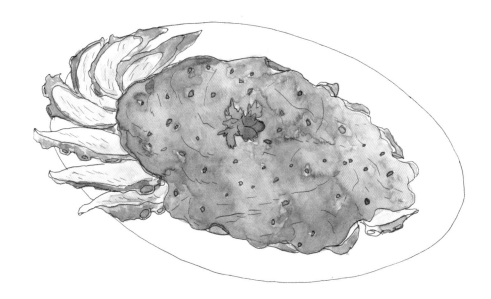

Octopus in Olive Sauce

Pulpo al olivo

Although the Japanese make up less than 1 percent of the population in Peru today, their influence on the cuisine has been significant—and vice versa. (See Nobu Matsuhisa, pages 136, 141, and 180.) Chef Rosita Yiruma, the daughter of Japanese immigrants, was one of the first chefs to blend Japanese and creole in her cooking. Her most emblematic dish paired thin, chilled slices of boiled octopus—which was commonly returned to the sea when it became tangled in Peruvian fishermen's nets—that had been mixed with vinegar and lemon juice and topped with a creamy black olive and lemon mayonnaise, mayonnaise having become central in Peruvian cooking in the mid-twentieth century. Yiruma invented it for a regular at the restaurant she ran out of her home who told her that he had tasted octopus with a "lead-colored sauce" and wondered if she had tried it. Her creation was considered the first Nikkei dish.

The term *nikkei*, the Japanese word for emigrants and their children, was used by food writer and poet Rodolfo Hinostroza in the late 1980s to describe the kind of food that chefs in Lima were serving at the time: Peruvian dishes mostly made with seafood, applying Japanese techniques and/or flavor codes. Yiruma's dish became a huge success and quickly spread to *cevicherías*, or seafood restaurants, in Lima. Decades later, you can still find it at *cevicherías* around the country. Chefs like Gastón Acurio, Micha Tsumura, and Diego Oka pay homage to her dish, as does Albert Adrià at Pakta, his Nikkei restaurant in Barcelona.

selected by **Diego Salazar**

Michael Clifford CLIFFORD'S

Republic of Ireland 1988

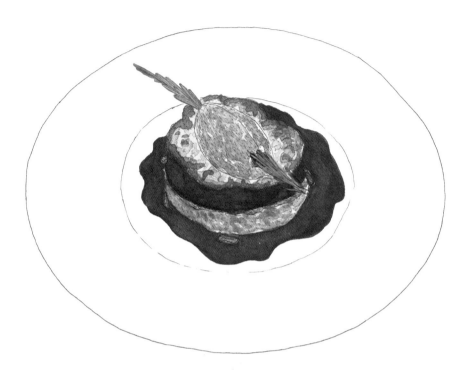

recipe → **p 329**

Gâteau of Clonakilty Black Pudding

In 1988, black pudding was merely an old-fashioned breakfast "sausage," a cheaper alternative made with pork or beef, plus blood and oatmeal or barley to thicken and bind it. (The word "pudding" allegedly comes from *boudin*, the French word for sausage.) Said to have first been made over a thousand years ago, it was seen as food for poor families, fried up with bacon as a way to make it stretch further. As chef Michael Clifford wrote himself in the introduction to this recipe in his cookbook, *Cooking with Clifford: New Irish Cooking*, "Surely after a thousand years it deserves a facelift!" He used the spiced beef version of blood pudding made in the town of Clonakilty as the basis for an elegant appetizer at his Michelin-starred County Cork restaurant. Drawing upon his experience cooking in London and Paris, where he was influenced by nouvelle cuisine, Clifford lay crisped slices of the beef-based black pudding between "cakes" of fanned-out slices of buttery potatoes spread with a mushroom-apple purée, then surrounded the gâteau with smoked bacon and a reduction of sherry vinegar and pork stock mounted with butter. As he wrote, "My gateau . . . uses simple ingredients which are easily available, but oh! The difference they make to this lovely honest food."

By elevating this lovely, honest breakfast food to a fine dining ingredient—at the dinner table, no less—Clifford and other chefs who were advancing Irish cuisine at the time, including Gerry Galvin and Eugene McSweeney, helped to restore it to its rightful place. Within years, it could be seen on everything from pizza to toasts, and the butcher shop that had been making Clonakilty pudding for a century was able to open a second production facility in order to keep up with demand.

selected by **Andrea Petrini**

recipe → **p 329**

Phillip Searle OASIS SEROS
Australia 1988

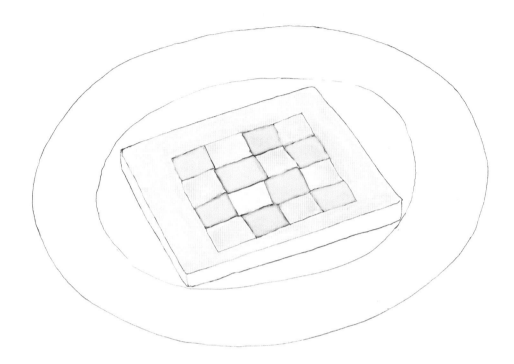

Chequerboard of Star Anise Ice Cream, Pineapple Sorbet, and Liquorice

One of Australia's most legendary desserts has rarely been imitated, but its influence is enduring. At his Sydney restaurant, the self-taught chef Phillip Searle was known for his early embrace of Asian flavors and textures in the context of fine dining. In a rare combination, the innovative and single-minded perfectionist also created the desserts. For this dish, he approached ice cream with the eye of both a technical perfectionist and the radical artist he had been to create a stunning mosaic of vanilla ice cream inset with a grid of pale squares of pineapple sorbet and star anise ice cream, each surrounded by a thin black frame of licorice gel. It was a game for the palate. There was no other sauce or garnish on the plate, and none was necessary: it had all of the power of a meditative Agnes Martin painting. As British chef Rowley Leigh wrote of

the masterpiece in the *Financial Times*, "Such was the virtuosity of this dish that I am not sure many chefs have tried to copy it."

Searle continued to serve the dessert when he moved to Blackheath in Australia's Blue Mountain region to open the wood-fired restaurant and bakery, Vulcans. The chequerboard continued to impress, as did Searle's disciplined focus. His influence can be seen in the desserts of his protégée, Christine Manfield, and helped to give rise to the extreme gelato movement that has taken hold of the country at places like Gelato Messina and N2 Extreme Gelato, where layered cakes and unusual flavors are the norm. He also influenced chefs such as Chui Lee Luk (who began her career cooking with Manfield) and Peter Gilmore of Quay, who told *Gourmet Traveller*, "Phillip is the rarest kind of chef: an original thinker."

selected by **Pat Nourse**

recipe → **p 332**

Chocolate Nemesis

"We found a recipe for a cake and called it Chocolate Nemesis," Ruth Rogers told *Waitrose Food*, speaking of the origins of both the architects' canteen that she opened with fellow self-taught cook Rose Gray and the cake that's been on the menu ever since. The molten chocolate cakes that were being made by Michel Bras in Laguiole, France (see page 118) and Jean-Georges Vongerichten at Lafayette in New York City had debuted in 1981 and 1987 respectively. This cake, too, is as miraculous as it is decadent: it contains only four ingredients, none of which are flour. There are: 10 eggs, 2¾ cups (575 g) sugar, 1½ pounds (675 g) 70% chocolate—the equivalent of about eight bars—and 1 pound (450 g) butter. The resulting cake is impossibly light in texture but incredibly rich on the tongue, a distinct departure from the fresh, light, seasonal Italian fare that Rogers and Gray made popular in the early

1990s—a style that remains to this day, when their restaurant has become one of the most celebrated in London.

The "nemesis" in its name alludes not only to how addictive and rich it is, but also to just how bedeviling it is to make as well as the restaurant's version. The recipe included in the chefs' *River Café Cookbook* has been the scourge of home cooks, who find the intuitive instructions too vague to allow for the cloudlike perfection of the original. ("Bake for 1½–2 hours or until set—test by placing the flat of your hand gently on the surface of the cake," they read. But how firm should it feel? Trickier still is the unmolding. . . .)

Perhaps the best iteration of the cake outside of London can be found at King in New York City, where River Café alumnae Jess Shadbolt and Clare de Boer serve it to Americans who believe they've struck the gluten-free jackpot.

selected by **Christine Muhlke, Richard Vines**

Dolester Miles CHEZ FONFON AND BOTTEGA CAFÉ
United States 1988

recipe → **p 332**

Coconut Pecan Cake

In 2018, after making desserts for the Alabama chef Frank Stitt's restaurants—including Highlands Bar & Grill, Chez Fonfon, Bottega, and Bottega Cafe—for more than thirty-five years, the self-taught, sixty-one-year-old Dolester Miles won the James Beard Award for Outstanding Pastry Chef in America. The only person who was surprised that evening was Miles herself. All along, patrons knew that her coconut pecan cake was iconic, elevating the homestyle Southern coconut cake to another level of excellence. There has even been a movement to declare it the official state dessert of Alabama. While coconut cake traditionally aims to be light and fluffy, Miles decided to amplify the richness of the coconut, adding ground pecans, those staple Southern nuts, to the buttery batter, which contains both coconut milk and cream of coconut; brushing each of the cake's four layers with simple syrup before smoothing on a filling of egg yolks, butter, sweetened condensed milk, and toasted shredded coconut; and finishing it with a Chantilly cream frosting dusted with yet more finely crushed toasted coconut as opposed to the traditional snowy flakes (in the restaurants the cake is served in a puddle of silky crème anglaise).

The Southern food scholar John T. Edge told *The New York Times* that, as the pastry chef in a high-end Alabama restaurant, Miles's excellence depends on bridging two factions: "She has to meet the standards of a diner's grandmother, but Dol also meets the expectation of the fine-dining customer. That straddle is hard to manage." So is her endurance in the kitchen for all these years. This dish matters for both of those reasons.

selected by **Howie Kahn**

recipe → **p 333**

Fried Black Pudding with Oysters, Apple, and Onion in Mustard Sauce

When Gerry and Marie Galvin opened their first restaurant in Kinsale, Ireland, in 1974, "There wasn't a huge interest in more than steak and potatoes in Ireland. It was truly a different era," Marie recalled. But Gerry changed that with his unique approach to food that was fresh, organic, and traditional, combining classic Irish ingredients in original, iconoclastic ways, frequently using a modern French base, as he was inspired by the creativity of his French peers, Paul Bocuse, Michel Guérard, and Roger Vergé. A decade later, when the Galvins left to open a restaurant in an old manor house in Galway, Kinsale was considered a mecca of food in the country—and Galvin the father of modern Irish cooking.

His signature dish was first served at a grand dinner celebrating the Euro-Toques society at Dublin's Trinity College in the late 1980s. A first course made with Clonakilty black pudding (an old-fashioned blood sausage that was then considered peasants' breakfast food) in Irish mustard sauce with the surprising addition of warm oyster, onion, and apples, his epiphany-inducing take on surf and turf—of the quotidian with the regal—was a success that soon made it to the Drimcong menu, and put Irish cuisine on the world map. As the food writers John and Sally McKenna, who were at the dinner, put it: "In effect, he was saying to us, great culinary art can be seen and shown in the simplest thing, so long as you have the artistry—and the courage—to create it and to present it, and to be proud of it. When I recall him on that night, he seems in retrospect to have been floating above the ground, he was so in the moment, so in the flames of creativity."

selected by **Andrea Petrini**

Alain Solivérès LA BASTIDE DES GORDES

France 1989

recipe → **p 334**

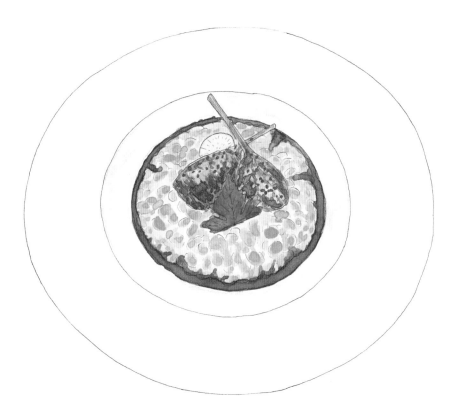

Spelt Risotto

Risotto d'épeautre

It's hard to imagine a time when "alternative grains" were thought of as *too* alternative. At least, that was the initial reception that Alain Solivérès, the twenty-six-year-old chef at La Bastide de Gordes in Provence received when he tried to put a risotto made from spelt on the menu at this fine-dining restaurant, where Alain Ducasse was consulting at the time. The young cook, who had trained with Jacques Maximin at the Hotel Negresco in Nice, with Alain Senderens at Lucas Carton in Paris, and with Ducasse at Le Louis XV in Monte Carlo, was so enamored by the nutty flavor of the heritage grain—an ancient variety of wheat that was referred to at the time as *céréale du pauvre*, or poor person's grain—that he was given by his truffle dealer that he sent it out as a complimentary course to a VIP critic. Who cared if it wasn't a "luxury" ingredient? The ensuing review described the risotto—itself a slightly edgy choice of preparation at the time—as a masterpiece, and so it went on the menu, following the young chef to Paris, first at l'Élysées du Vernet and, eventually, to Taillevent, where it became a menu "fetish item."

The rich risotto, made with white wine and chicken stock, served as a blank canvas for many iterations, including frog's legs, marrow, morels, lobster with curry, and cockscombs and kidneys, a nod to Alain Chapel's legendary Ragoût de Crêtes et Rognons de Coq from 1970 (see page 94). When Solivérès first discovered spelt on the slopes of Mt. Ventoux in the Luberon, they were only growing 660 pounds (300 kilos) per year. As other chefs like Éric Fréchon at Le Bristol and Ducasse himself began experimenting with their own spelt risottos, the poor-man's grain has become richly valued.

selected by **Andrea Petrini**

recipe → **p 334**

Pig's Trotter Carpaccio

Carpaccio de manitas de cerdo

Three years after opening a restaurant next to their parents' bar in Girona, Joan and Josep Roca sometimes had so few customers that they played foosball (table football) in the middle of the restaurant. Joan was still in a creative phase, figuring out what his food would be. He looked to what was happening in France, and spent some time in the kitchens of fellow Spaniards Santi Santamaría at Can Fabes and elBulli with Ferran Adrià—both of whom had been influenced by Juan Mari Arzak and other seminal Basque chefs. Roca returned home, ready to interpret a Catalan classic in his own voice. Playing with the typical dish of whole stewed pig's trotters served hot in tapas bars, he decided to expand upon the cold carpaccios that were popular at the time, inventing a delicate, fantastical terrine. The translucent mosaic was made from deboned trotters, carrot, onion, and bay leaves and rolled into a cylinder before being chilled and sliced 0.3 mm thick. The symmetrically arranged slivers were accompanied by variations on wild *Boletus edulis* mushrooms (*porcini* in Italian; *cèpes* in French), including an infused oil, sautéed mushrooms, and a caramel made from powdered mushrooms, as well as white beans and diced tomato. Roca has said that this is the first dish with which he was truly satisfied. It is also the one that helped to turn around the fortunes of El Celler de Can Roca. While the carpaccio has evolved over the years at the restaurant, variations of the original can still be seen on Catalonian menus at every level. Like Juan Mari Arzak's Scorpion Fish Cake (see page 99), which even made its way to grocery-store shelves, the popularity of the pig trotter carpaccio is evidence of what happens when the avant-garde enters the mainstream.

selected by **Diego Salazar**

Edna Lewis GAGE & TOLLNER
United States 1989

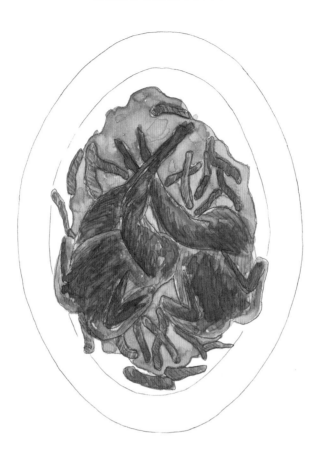

Panfried Quail with Country Ham

While the crab cakes and chicken fried in lard, butter, and country ham that Edna Lewis made after she took over Brooklyn's Gage & Tollner at the age of seventy-two may have become more famous, this dish stands as the most influential and prescient. Lewis was dedicated not only to honoring and preserving the traditional Southern foodways that she had grown up with as the granddaughter of slaves in rural Virginia, but also to cooking with seasonal, authentic Southern ingredients that are close to the land (no matter how humble they may have seemed to diners at an expensive restaurant in the midst of an unparalleled economic boom). As both peer and mentor to the likes of James Beard, Lewis was one of the first torchbearers for real Southern cuisine. "We weren't ready for her then," Chez Panisse owner Alice Waters, who was close with Lewis, told the *New York Times Magazine*. "Now we are."

For this dish, she pan-fried thyme-rubbed quail and julienned country ham in copious amounts of butter, the pan deglazed with the juice of just-crushed grapes. It was served with spoonbread, a rich, comforting pudding made with fresh corn and cornmeal. Lewis's Southern pride can be seen in the food of Sean Brock, Mashama Bailey, Frank Stitt, and others who, inspired by Lewis, have made it a point to reconnect the food of their heritage with the seasons and local ingredients of their regions. As M.F.K. Fisher wrote in her introduction to Lewis's 1976 book, *The Taste of Country Cooking*, Lewis's food was "in the best sense American, with an innate dignity, and freedom from prejudice and hatred, and it is reassuring to be told again that although we may have lost some of all this simplicity, it still exists here . . . and may be attainable again."

selected by **Christine Muhlke**

recipe → **p 336**

Shepherd's Pie

London restaurant The Ivy dates to 1917, but the most popular items on its menu date to the 1990s, when chef Mark Hix was the culinary director of the restaurant group Caprice Holdings, which also owns the restaurants J. Sheekey and Le Caprice. This classic English dish hasn't been off the menu since. A combination of cottage pie, which uses ground beef, and shepherd's pie, which uses lamb, Hix enriched the traditional recipe with rich veal stock, red wine, tomato paste, and mushrooms for umami, bringing depth to the celery/carrot/onion trio. Puréed parsnips are added to the mashed potatoes for earthy sweetness, the mixture piped into an elaborate pattern on top and baked until burnished. This is comfort food at its best, albeit with plating suitable for a high-end restaurant. For the celebrities who have long made The Ivy their canteen, reconnecting with better versions of their favorite childhood dishes in an elegant setting helped restore the image of British cooking at a time when high-end restaurants in London meant French (see: the Roux brothers at Le Gavroche, Pierre Koffmann at Tante Claire, Marco Pierre White at Harveys). And for the British public, reading about Tracey Emin tucking into a shepherd's pie while Madonna dined nearby in a conical bra certainly had an impact that rippled for a decade, as did plentiful Victoria Beckham and Kate Moss sightings. Perhaps Chrissy Teigen's Instagram posts about her shepherd's pie experience at The Ivy will revitalize it for another generation.

At the same time, shepherd's pie was beginning to be celebrated by the burgeoning gastropub movement. By the late 1990s, the restoration of pub food took on enough momentum to jump the pond to America, where April Bloomfield (see page 193) served the pie at The Spotted Pig when it opened in 2004.

selected by **Richard Vines**

Uncle Hung GOLDEN CENTURY
Australia early 1990s

recipe → **p 336**

XO Sauce Live Pippies

Modern Australian food owes much to the contributions of its immigrants, especially those from Asia. Just two weeks after Eric and Linda Wong arrived in Sydney from Hong Kong in 1989 they bought a run-down Chinese restaurant. Among the Hong Kong traditions that they brought with them was the desire to serve live seafood—but at the time, there was a limited availability to choose from. What was available were the local clams, pippies, which the head chef cooked with his own-recipe XO sauce (another Hong Kong favorite). The tank-to-wok pippies doused in the umami-rich sauce and served over fried vermicelli became the restaurant's signature dish, a late-night favorite of chefs and pop stars. (Regulars know that the tanks are restocked with fresh seafood at midnight.) The rich, pungent sauce accentuates the sweetness of the pippies, the juices mingling with the crispy noodles.

XO sauce was invented in the 1980s by Hong Kong's elite Cantonese chefs. (The name is a reference to XO, or extra-old, Cognac.) While each chef has his own recipe, it typically contains a pricey combination of dried scallops and shrimp (prawns) cooked down into a paste with garlic, scallions (spring onions), dried Chinese ham, ginger, anchovies, fresh chilies, sugar, and oil. The sauce is rich, complexly layered, and almost fruity, with the scallops lending a floss-like chewiness. The sauce has entered the cooking of such Golden Century regulars as Kylie Kwong, Neil Perry, Jock Zonfrillo, Andrew McConnell, and Tetsuya Wakuda before emigrating to London and the United States via traveling chefs such as Momofuku's David Chang, who declared Golden Century's pippies as "the best dish in the world."

selected by **Pat Nourse**

Richard Corrigan BENTLEY'S
United Kingdom 1992

recipe → **p 337**

Irish Stew

A rustic Irish stew elevated to Michelin-level refinement in one of London's poshest districts? The larger-than-life Irish chef Richard Corrigan accomplished exactly that. "The French might call it a white *daube*," he told Vice, of the traditional lamb stew recipe, "but it's the most delicious, wholesome, gorgeous thing you're ever going to eat." Originally the humblest of peasant dishes, this stew made use of what most Irish farmers had on hand: potatoes, water, and the meat of a sheep that had come to the end of its usefulness for wool and milk. In the hands of Corrigan, who made his reputation with robust, evocative food like that cooked at his first London restaurant, Lindsay House, the dish is warmth and sustenance itself.

While the ingredient list remains essentially the same, Corrigan goes deep on sourcing and variety. Instead of chunks of lamb, he prefers to use the scrag end of the shoulder or filleted middle-neck, leaving the bones in to give the initial poaching liquid body. He then removes the meat and bones and adds veal stock, onions, thyme, and two types of potatoes: a starchy (floury) variety, such as the British King Edward, which dissolves into the stew and thickens it, followed by a waxy variety like Pentland Javelin added toward the end so they retain their shape. Sometimes he sneaks in bacon brought over from a family-owned butcher shop in Ireland's Tipperary County (he has yet to find a satisfactory bacon in the UK, he has said). While there have certainly been more complex dishes on Corrigan's menus, it is personal food like this that stays on diners' minds. As a review in the *Independent* said, Corrigan's "talent and the sort of big-heartedness . . . shows on the plate. He gives you close to perfect food, and lots of it. Hell, it is better than perfect. It is exciting."

selected by **Richard Vines**

Tetsuya Wakuda TETSUYA'S
Australia 1992

recipe → **p 337**

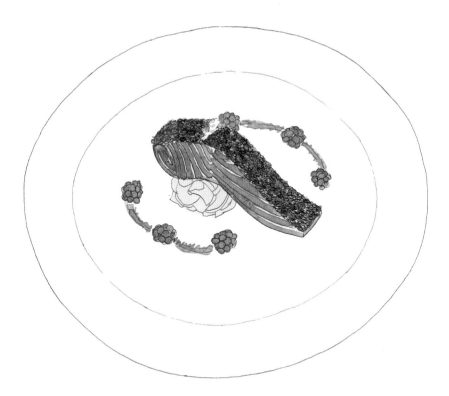

Confit of Petuna Ocean Trout with Fennel Salad

This landmark dish was a marriage of Japanese and French cooking, with ingredients that could only be at home in Australia during the early 1990s, when the country's cultures had come together to create a new cuisine. By gently cooking the orange-fleshed fish on a bed of mirepoix in herbed oil in the French style, the ocean trout retained its exquisite texture and jewel-like hue—it still appears vibrant and raw. A flavor-some kombu crust and pearls of ocean trout roe added subtle textural complexity with a nod to the chef's native Japan, while raw fennel tossed in lemon-scented oil evoked Australia's Italian immigrants. The dish caused a sensation in Australia. To this day, it remains the country's most photographed entrée.

It began with the produce. In the late 1980s, Tasmanians began farming Atlantic salmon so that chefs no longer had to import it from Scotland or Canada, giving rise to its popularity in restaurants. In 1991, Wakuda, who had moved to Australia from Japan only a decade before, went to Tasmania in search of unique ingredients. He found Petuna, a company that had just begun sustainably farming fish off the coast. Wakuda originally wanted to use their salmon, but supply was low, so they steered him toward ocean trout, a species with similar orange flesh that had been introduced to Australia in the nineteenth century.

Wakuda's elevation of the unheralded fish led to its celebration around the world. His slow-cooking method soon appeared on distant shores, such as at Jean-Georges Vongericthen's JoJo in New York. But it was really in Australia, where chefs like Neil Perry, Christine Manfield, and Phillip Searle were exploring the country's ingredients and multicultural influences to find their own language, that a new cuisine was born.

selected by **Christine Muhlke, Pat Nourse**

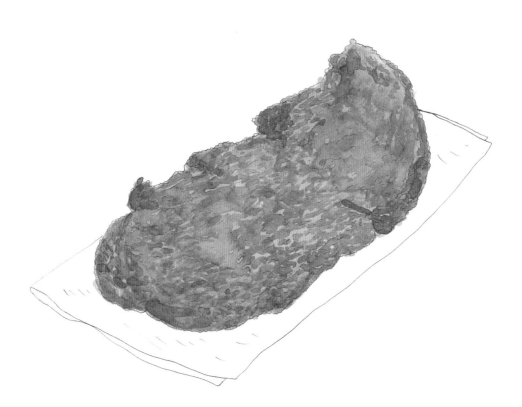

recipe → p 338

Large Fried Chicken

Taiwan always had a strong fried chicken game: those heavily spiced bites known as popcorn chicken can be found at nearly every night market, street cart, and sit-down restaurant. But somehow, a fast-food stall created what would become one of the country's greatest fried chickens and hottest exports by *not* turning chicken into crispy two-bite kernels. It opted for a different pop culture route: the chicken got supersized, and then it exploded. Sure, the Large Fried Chicken from Wang's was an exemplary fried chicken—shatteringly crisp, well seasoned, not greasy—but there must have been something more to catapult it from being sold from beneath a 7-Eleven overhang in the 1990s (under the name Wang's Large Fried Chicken) to selling 3,000 cutlets a day at the ensuing Hot-Star Chicken stall at Taipei's Shilin Night Market, to now one hundred locations worldwide. For any kind of food to be exportable, a good hook is essential (see: 100-Layer Lasagne, page 218), and this chicken's certainly got one: the cutlet is cartoonishly large—the company says it's bigger than your face. The souped-up size also has a taste benefit: Hot-Star has special cutlet-slicing techniques and machines that help to pound the chicken extra-thin so the ratio of meat to crackling coating is nearly equal. Sold in a paper sleeve for less than $3 (£2.35), it's like fried chicken in burger's clothing—universal and oh so irresistible.

selected by **Pat Nourse**

recipe → **p 339**

Smoked Salmon Consommé

A dish of technique, bold restraint, and impeccable sourcing, yielding a hot consommé of jewel-like clarity and balanced richness that played against the coolness of a saffron cream. The young chef Tim Pak Poy called upon both the classical French roots of this Sydney restaurant and his time exploring Australian ingredients with Cheong Liew at Neddy's in Adelaide. Indeed, it could be said that Liew's Four Dances of the Sea (see page 166), with its celebration of the continent's seafood sources and immigrant cuisines, had an impact on this consommé, which was made from five species of fish—four of which were indigenous to the east coast of Australia.

Snapper heads and the bodies of flathead, scorpion cod, and yellowfin leather jackets were simmered with the smoked collars and pectoral fins of Tasmanian farmed salmon—the salmon being essential for its fattiness. (Pak Poy, who took

a perfumery course in Paris, believed that the oils from the salmon encapsulated the smoky flavor and carried it throughout the dish.) A variety of aromatics, as well as lemon flesh and Chardonnay, imparted acidity and freshness, which were amplified during a clarification process (that included fish trimmings, egg white, onion, chervil, and dill). The smoky, slightly oily consommé, with its gently acidic backbone, broke through the cool saffron cream, with the saffron's musky properties emerging in the end. Served in custom-made Limoges porcelain cups that were custom designed by chef Anders Ousback and glazed only on the rim, even the physical experience of drinking the soup was calibrated and sensually remarkable, making it emblematic of a moment when modern Australian cuisine was coming of age, thanks to chefs like Neil Perry, Sean Moran, Phillip Searle, and others.

selected by **Pat Nourse**

Bill Granger BILLS
Australia 1993

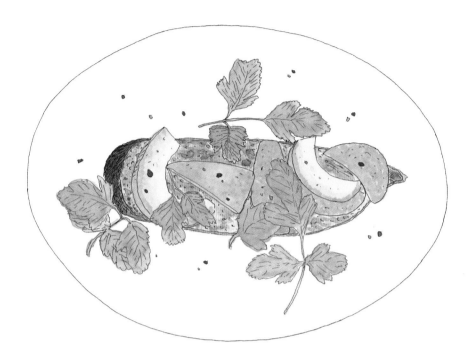

recipe → **p 340**

Avocado Toast

Bill Granger made this dish a global phenomenon when the twenty-two-year-old cook with no formal restaurant experience put it on the menu of his tiny café in 1993. Though Granger might sometimes be blamed for the plight of millennials who are deferring their student loans to support their attachment to all things avocado, things might have been very different if it hadn't been for an unfortunate landlord in need of a tenant.

Said landlord had opened a café in the Darlinghurst area of Sydney, but due to complaints from neighbors, was stuck with the limited opening hours of 7:30 a.m. to 4 p.m. Luckily art-school dropout Bill Granger was looking for a venue for his lunch-focused café. He only put breakfast on the menu because it meant he could open early and it would help to pay the rent.

His limited staff and kitchen made simple dishes that any cook could replicate a necessity. And because Sydney is essentially a beach town where people are conscious about looking good in a bathing suit, the food had to be healthy. So Granger arranged avocado quarters on toasted slices of sourdough bread and added lime juice, olive oil, chili flakes, and cilantro (coriander). The dish—and his restaurant—soon became so popular that he opened other locations in Sydney and Melbourne, as well as London, Tokyo, Seoul, and Hawaii. In the following decades, as young Australians began traveling the world on work visas, bringing their Aussie café culture with them to places like London, New York, and Los Angeles, they also brought their favorite dishes—especially Avocado Toast. Within a few short years, variations on this virtuous-seeming yet indulgent (and Instagrammable) dish made it the symbol of the wellness movement, a no-recipe recipe that encapsulates a lifestyle of sun, sea, and breakfast whenever you wish.

selected by **Christine Muhlke**

recipe → **p 340**

Cornets

One of the first dishes ever served at the French Laundry when it opened in 1994, these amuses-bouches were created not only to amuse the palate, said the chef, but to make you smile when you see them. More than twenty years later, they're still working their magic at The French Laundry, as well as at Keller's restaurant Per Se in New York. The cones bring together two elements that were well known by the mid-1990s—salmon tartare, in this case finely diced with an almost Japanese precision, and crème fraîche—in a classic tuile in a way that both brought humor and playfulness into tasting-menu American fine dining and literally helped to reshape canapés for caterers for decades to come.

Thomas Keller wasn't smiling when he came up with the idea in 1990. Nor was he in the kitchen. Rather, he was upset that he had to leave New York City, where the financial crisis had caused him to close his restaurant, Rakel. He was about to move back to the West Coast, where his new employer wanted him to come up with an impressive passed hors d'oeuvre for a food and wine benefit. After a final dinner with friends in Chinatown, they went to their usual spot for dessert: the all-American ice cream chain Baskin-Robbins. When the server placed Keller's order in the standard silver holder and said, "Enjoy your cone," the idea took root: turn a sesame seed–flecked tuile into a cone and fill it with tuna tartare (it eventually became salmon) and sweet red onion crème fraîche. "The cone is just a vehicle," Keller has said. "You can really use anything." A little French, a little Japanese, and ultimately American, these cones are proof of the power of the diner's first bite.

selected by **Christine Muhlke, Diego Salazar**

159

Fergus Henderson ST. JOHN

United Kingdom 1994

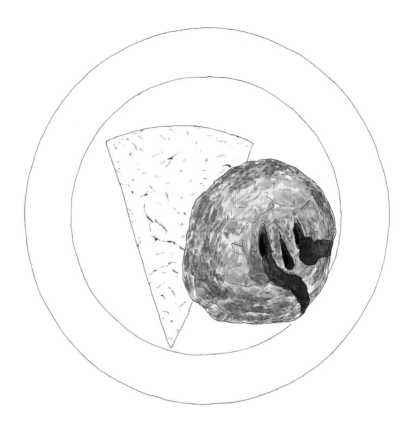

recipe → **p 342**

Eccles Cake and Lancashire Cheese

The savory courses at London's St. John have been influential for their austere gluttony, that combination of minimalist presentation and maximalist intent. Pig's head and potato pie. Roast Bone Marrow with Parsley Salad (see page 163). Deep-fried calves' brains. Dessert is certainly no exception. Though the cakes and trifles tend toward the prettier side of the St. John spectrum, the restaurant's best-known dessert is its Eccles Cake: a simple dish that epitomizes Fergus Henderson's approach to food. While the word "cake" evokes something rich, frosted, moist, and celebratory, these humble stuffed buns are of the sixteenth-century sort, which means they look like they could be savory meat pies. Instead, the little rounds of puff pastry—a departure from the traditional lard, yet another sly joke from the chef and his original baker, Dan Lepard—are

filled with a mixture of dark brown butter, sugar, currants, allspice, and nutmeg. Slashed three times to represent the Holy Trinity (they were allegedly first sold during a sixteenth-century religious festival called Wakes week), brushed with egg whites, and dipped in sugar before baking, the cakes are a fitting way to end a meal at such a quintessentially British restaurant—especially when enjoyed with a slice of mild Lancashire cheese. (Eccles Cakes hail from the town of the same name, not far from Manchester in the county of Lancashire.) While the cakes are sometimes referred to as "dead fly pie" thanks to the appearance of the filling, they are delicious enough to have made it through the centuries. The spirit of serving something so seemingly traditional, so frumpy, so comforting and personal has been both a reassurance and an inspiration to chefs.

selected by **Richard Vines**

recipe → **p 342**

Vegetable Casserole in Textures

La menestra de verduras en texturas

Of all the dishes that Ferran Adrià has created, he has said that he wants to be remembered for the 1994 invention that marked the beginning of the evolution in his restaurant toward what he calls "techno-emotional cuisine." Adrià developed this plate as a distinct homage to Michel Bras' Gargouillou from 1978 (see page 113). But rather than vary the concept or the ingredients in order to arrive at an edible snapshot of the terroir of his own corner of the Mediterranean, Adrià sought to offer a completely new experience, one that guided diners through techniques and manipulations that he had developed in his kitchen over the years. And so the guest is presented with a multicolored plate of unrecognizably retextured vegetables: a quenelle of salty almond sorbet rests on a disc of avocado, surrounded by renditions of tomato purée, cauliflower mousse, peach granita, basil jelly, corn mousse, and beet foam, a fresh almond perched between each new iteration to provide the only crunch on the plate. With the elements so radically broken apart, the flavors are identifiable only by taste, thereby marking the beginning of the restaurant's era of deconstruction and its revolutionary move toward the technical-conceptual kitchen. Adrià believed that in order for elBulli to continue to evolve, it needed to expand the concept of creativity itself—not to find new ways to vary and juxtapose existing concepts, but to invent entirely new ones. This iconic dish is the first and most impactful manifestation of that philosophy.

selected by **Diego Salazar**, **Richard Vines**

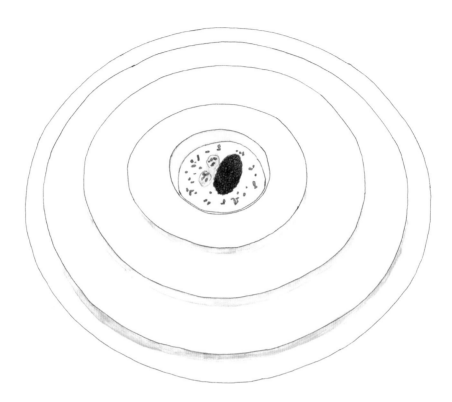

recipe → **p 345**

Oysters and Pearls

An unassuming name for a spectacular dish—one that helped shape both careers and how dishes were named for more than a decade. Thomas Keller has become best known for his precision and perfectionism, but that means that the best part of his cooking—and his influence—tends to get overlooked. While Keller's dishes are in fact meticulous and often flawless, they are elegantly playful, too. This is the man who put salmon tartare in a miniature ice cream cone, after all (see page 159), and who launched the tasting-menu-only restaurant he opened in a former steam laundry in California's rural wine country (Yountville) with a tiny course called Coffee and Doughnuts. But the most influential and famous of his fun dishes is this one, where Island Creek oysters and white sturgeon caviar come together in a pearl tapioca sabayon to riff on the life and treasures of a bivalve. Through his lens, the dish tells a story about the natural world and his relationship to it. In the years after this first went on the menu at The French Laundry, and even today, narrative has become an integral part of fine dining in almost every country. But Keller remains the narrative king.

This singular bowl, in which tapioca is elevated to the status of fine pearls, has inspired the likes of David Chang, who riffed on it to create a dish of uni, tapioca, and tofu. And in the case of Grant Achatz, who worked at The French Laundry before opening Alinea, tasting this dish at the age of twenty-three shaped his entire career. He told *Saveur*: "It was exciting. Revelatory. As you get older, those moments get rarer. It's harder to get excited." And while the age of modern fine dining that Keller ushered in may not be so exciting to the younger generation, we must all remember that it used to be fun, thanks to dishes such as this.

selected by **Susan Jung, Howie Kahn, Andrea Petrini, Diego Salazar**

Fergus Henderson ST. JOHN
United Kingdom 1994

recipe → **p 346**

Roast Bone Marrow and Parsley Salad

The pure, primal simplicity of this salad—singed bones on a plate with grilled bread, a pile of flaky salt, and a small salad of "disciplined" parsley with caper and shallot dressed with lemon juice and olive oil—made chefs everywhere rethink the layers of visual and technical complication they had built into their food. It also gave them license to return to ingredients both humble and strange. The nose-to-tail movement launched with this recipe (which, to be precise, was taken from a calf's leg).

St. John's defining dish has been on the menu since day one. Fergus Henderson, who trained as an architect, had made it for a friend who came in after service at the French House, the Soho restaurant that he had opened with his wife, Margot. With nothing on hand but marrow bones, parsley, and capers, he thought they would make "a splendid marriage." (Henderson

had been cooking marrow bones since watching a pivotal scene in the 1973 film *La Grande Bouffe.*) The participatory element of spooning the molten marrow onto the bread, sprinkling it with flakes of coarse salt, and adding a pinch of bracing herb salad was key to Henderson, whose food and personality combine both delight and a touch of conceptual art.

Over the next twenty-five years (and counting), marrow bones have become menu staples around the world, allowing chefs to serve other parts of the skeleton, thereby saving money and reducing waste in the kitchen—movements that were partially put into motion by this dish. These bones also redefined British cooking within the country and put it on the map as a global influence.

selected by **Susan Jung, Howie Kahn, Christine Muhlke, Pat Nourse, Andrea Petrini, Diego Salazar, Richard Vines**

Claudia Fleming GRAMERCY TAVERN
United States 1994

recipe → **p 347**

Chocolate Caramel Tart

Pastry chef Claudia Fleming's creations for New York's Gramercy Tavern in the late 1990s and early 2000s were groundbreaking for their seasonality, purity, and elegance, underscored by a nostalgia for classic American desserts and candies. She left a career in modern dance to study pastry in France. Upon her return to the United States, Fleming took the rigorous French technique and playful combinations she learned while apprenticing with Pierre Hermé at Fauchon in Paris and married them with the rustic seasonal approach of California's Lindsey Shere at Chez Panisse and Nancy Silverton at Spago and Campanile to develop her own graceful style that favored maximum flavor in deceptively minimal presentations.

In 1994, Fleming joined chef Tom Colicchio and restaurateur Danny Meyer to open Gramercy Tavern, a tasting menu restaurant serving seasonal American food. Of her many influential recipes, her Chocolate Caramel Tart stands out. It layered a buttery caramel filling (slightly sharpened with crème fraîche) and a dark-chocolate ganache glaze in a chocolate cookie shell. Childhood flavors with a grown-up touch that was distinctively Claudia Fleming: large flakes of fleur de sel on top to spark the palate as they melt on the tongue, cutting through the tart's intense richness. At the time, fleur de sel was still new in the US. And it certainly wasn't being used to finish desserts. But Fleming had attended a cooking demonstration by Phillipe Conticini, then at Petrossian Boutique and Café in New York City, and tasted a sample of dark chocolate topped with the salt. From that moment on, she told *The New York Times*, "using salt as a garnish seemed suddenly natural."

And from the moment Fleming's tartlets hit the table, American pastry chefs began reaching for the salt, too.

selected by **Christine Muhlke**

recipe → **p 348**

The Crunchy Part of the Lasagne

La Dame et Son Chevalier

In one of Massimo Bottura's most memorable dishes, memory is in fact the motivation. This deconstructed lasagne sprang from his childhood recollections of sneaking into the kitchen to eat the edges of the toasted top layer of his mother's just-baked lasagne before the pan left the kitchen—those crispy bits tinged with concentrated juices from the ragù. And so he set out to evoke the pleasure of that limited, fleeting texture by making a crisp "cracker" rolled out from three dehydrated pasta purées: one made from spaghetti with tomato sauce, one from spaghetti with Parmesan, and another with fresh herbs, the red, white, and green reflecting the colors of the Italian flag, naturally. After being fried, the pasta cracker is smoked and torched to give it that essential burnt flavor. The resulting "lasagne" is set into a disc of hand-cut beef ragù topped with a foamy béchamel.

The first iteration of the dish took its name from a painting of a Ferrari that was hanging in his Modena restaurant and which, like Bottura's food, evoked criticism in an early review. Perhaps, the chef thought, the writer did not understand the fundamental contradictions underlying the surrounding Emilia-Romagna region, that it is a land of slow food and fast cars. Could Bottura, like Enzo Ferrari, take lasagne to its lightest, fastest extreme? He designed the original version to evoke the air jets of a Ferrari—four sharp triangles, alternating between triangles of Parmesan-Reggiano wafers and crisp spinach pasta that had been boiled and baked. Like the driver of the race car in the painting *La Dame et Son Chevalier,* Bottura saw this dish as risking everything at high speed. Luckily for him, the risk paid off.

selected by **Richard Vines**

recipe → **p 350**

Four Dances of the Sea

The first recorded East-West dinner—a collaboration between Chinese-American chef Ken Hom and Jeremiah Tower of Chez Panisse—occurred in California in 1980, one year after the label "fusion" was applied to cuisine. But East-West cooking had already begun in the unlikely city of Adelaide, Australia, in 1975, when Kuala Lumpur-born chef Cheong Liew opened his first restaurant, Neddy's, and began applying Asian cooking techniques to Western ingredients, presenting them with a European accent. When he opened The Grange in 1995, he felt that he needed to launch with an upscale dish, one that reflected not only the country's (and the chef's) many cultures and influences, but also the seafood that was pulled in from Australia's surrounding waters. And so he developed Four Dances of the Sea, a strong multicultural statement containing four conceptual "islands" on the plate—to be eaten in order of increasing flavor—that represented Japanese, modern Australian, Mediterranean, and Malay cuisines.

First, he "soused" snook by curing it in sugar and salt before marinating it with such ingredients as rice wine and mirin, serving it with wasabi mayonnaise and avocado. Next came cuttlefish sashimi with squid-ink tagliatelle swirled in a dressing of oyster and soy sauces, sesame oil, and balsamic. Octopus was dabbed with a chile-cilantro (coriander) aioli as a nod to his time cooking in a Greek restaurant. Finally, representing Liew's Malaysian heritage, prawn sushi was flavored with tamarind juice, palm sugar, and a *rempah* spice paste—containing galangal, turmeric, candlenut, chili, and cloves—cooked in coconut cream atop a disc of glutinous rice "sushi" on smoked banana leaf. This seminal plate embodied Liew's philosophy, of loving the planet, its people, and the land.

selected by **Pat Nourse**

recipe → **p 353**

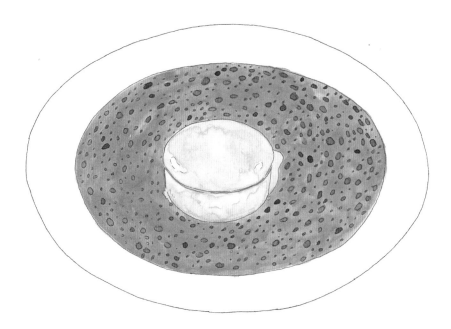

Lasagne of Crab with a Cappuccino of Shellfish and a Champagne Foam

Known as a chef's chef, Phil Howard told *Food and Wine* magazine that "flavor, not process, was always at the core" of his food. But the signature dish at his Mayfair restaurant deftly married both. It was a marvel of progressive French cuisine as interpreted through British products—luxury comfort food with serious finesse. It layered generous portions of flaky crabmeat bound with a delicate diver scallop mousse between wafer-thin sheets of parsley pasta that was steamed rather than baked. In the bowl, it was enriched by a frothy and aromatic take on a classic seafood bisque and brightened by the acidity of an effervescent champagne foam, made with the scallop trim and coriander seeds. The simple harmony of flavors was more powerful than any technical innovation.

Howard, who abandoned a degree in microbiology to dedicate himself to cooking, beginning at the Roux brothers'

catering division before moving on to London restaurants Harveys and Bibendum (with Simon Hopkinson, see page 129), was just twenty-four when he opened The Square. His startling maturity was present in this early dish, which was created in the decade that bridged the time between when Michelin-starred UK restaurants were still classically French (see La Tante Claire, The Connaught, Harveys, and Le Gavroche) and when they began to highlight seasonal ingredients and recipes from the UK and beyond.

In his cookbook, *The Square*, Howard was able to overcome his humility when it came to the creation: "In general, given that I use classical combinations of flavors and mostly traditional cooking techniques, it has all been done somewhere before," he wrote. "However, I do claim this one."

selected by **Richard Vines**

Pierre Gagnaire PIERRE GAGNAIRE

France 1996

recipe → p 356

Langoustine Five Ways

When the "*avant-gardiste*" French chef Pierre Gagnaire opened Twist in Las Vegas in 2009, he brought a signature dish with him from his Parisian flagship. Americans in the middle of a desert were treated to a master class in modern French technique centered around one luxurious ingredient from a faraway sea. Five plates and bowls in an array of sizes were placed before diners, each spotlighting a different preparation and range of flavors that borrowed from France, Asia, Spain, even a glimpse of India. In the original line-up there was a mousseline with chopped strawberries and cardamom butter (or sometimes curried grapes); a pan-fried tail with brown butter, Spanish chorizo, piquillo peppers and langoustine shell powder; tartare of raw shelled langoustine with crisp bok choy and a grapefruit syrup spiced with piment d'espelette; a cold bouillon with edamame and a jelly made with langoustine bisque; and grilled langoustine with potatoes, dried bacon bits, and *beurre meunière* (brown butter with lemon juice). Like Gagnaire's food, the course was unpredictable, iconoclastic, playful, and experimental in terms of its flavor combinations and textural contrasts. Later incarnations saw langoustines poached in sake and grilled with Iberico ham.

A dish that could be seen as show-offy and pretentious was really a meditation on a delicate and fleeting ingredient whose rich, sweet nature has many potential expressions—not unlike the *menestra de verduras en texturas* served at elBulli in 1994 (see page 161), a groundbreaking dish at the restaurant that explored the potential for different textures for vegetables, or a presentation of pigeon cooked three ways that Pierre Gagnaire's protégé, André Chiang, served at his Singapore restaurant, Restaurant André.

selected by **Diego Salazar**

Alain Passard L'ARPÈGE
France 1996

L'Arpège Egg

Chaud-froid d'oeuf avec sirop d'érable et vinaigre d'xérès

Since its debut in 1996, chefs have referenced this dish—from David Kinch's seasonal amuse-bouche at Manresa to Michael Laiskonis's predessert at Le Bernardin. Daniel Berlin, David Chang, Jean-Georges Vongerichten, Kyle Connaughton, and many others have tapped into the magic that Alain Passard made within a single shell. The French have long been known as the masters of egg cookery; Alain Passard's contribution has certainly earned its place in the twentieth-century canon.

In this version of an *oeuf à la coque*, or soft-boiled egg, hot and cold, sweet and savory, bitterness and umami blend for two ideal bites. The gently coddled yolk is sprinkled with chives, then layered with salted whipped cream, aged sherry vinegar, maple syrup, and salt. While the egg preparation requires a delicate hand, the dish itself is uncomplicated.

The mastery comes from Passard's deep understanding of flavor and balance—not to mention his connection to the joy that can be sparked by a great dish. As David Kinch wrote in his cookbook, *Manresa*, "Anyone can feed you; few can make you feel." The grace and restraint embody what Passard protégé Pascal Barbot referred to as the chef's "elegance of gesture."

Passard's lack of interest in embracing molecular gastronomy, as well as his decision to stop cooking animal tissue in 2001, caused him to fall out of favor. But young chefs began to appreciate his attachment to vegetables and their terroir to create a cuisine of place, as well as to the purest essence of cooking. The kitchen at L'Arpège gave rise to Mauro Colagreco, Magnus Nilsson, Bertrand Grébaut, Tatiana Levha, Ludo Lefebvre, Fumiko Kono, and others.

selected by **Howie Kahn, Christine Muhlke, Pat Nourse**

Davide Scabin COMBAL

Italy 1997

recipe → **p 358**

Cyber Egg

"Eggs are perfect in all aspects, starting from the shell, a fantastic natural packaging. Nature gave them everything and this became a challenge for me. I wondered how I could improve perfection." Those were the Turin chef's thoughts while bored in the pastry laboratory one day, as he told Paolo Marchi at Identità Expo in Milan. Scabin, who had started off serving the hidden experimental menu at his *prix fixe* restaurant only to regulars, was staring into a bin of flour when a container of eggs caught his attention. He decided to work on rethinking the shell only—not inventing a new dish, but rather rethinking the egg itself. He lined one of the wells in the egg container with a double layer of plastic film, spooned in caviar, an egg yolk, diced shallot, and ground black pepper. Closed and twisted, the plastic inflated around the egg, a brave new shell.

When punctured with a blade, the contents flowed into the mouth before the diner had a chance to consider what they might be. Expectations removed, the response to the egg was physical rather than analytical or anticipatory.

Scabin originally served the dish in a medical sample container, giving the diner a razor blade with which to slice it open. That quickly morphed into the original plastic wrap shape, accompanied by a scalpel for hastening the transfer from "shell" to tongue. Brash, disruptive, and provocative, the egg recalled the recipes of poet and founder of Futurism, Filippo Tomasso Marinetti. It also became the matrix of twenty-first-century food design, the forebear of dishes like Alvin Leung's Sex on the Beach, an edible condom filled with ham and honey, served at Bo Innovation in Hong Kong.

selected by **Andrea Petrini**

Pierre Hermé LADURÉE
France 1997

Ispahan Macaron

When the nine-year-old aspiring pâtissier Pierre Hermé was learning to make macarons in 1976, the only flavors were chocolate, vanilla, coffee, and raspberry. The little confections —light, chewy-crisp almond-flour meringues surrounding a dollop of creamy ganache—were pleasant if rather unremarkable. "It gave me great latitude for creativity," recalled Hermé, who went on to make his name with them. At the age of fourteen, he apprenticed with the legendary Gaston Lenôtre, before moving on to helm the pastry departments at Fauchon and Ladurée in Paris, where he introduced new macaron flavors every month. It was at Ladurée that he introduced the Ispahan, a large macaron consisting of raspberry meringues sandwiching rosewater cream with lychee and fresh raspberries. After tasting roses in Bulgarian cuisine in the mid-1980s, Hermé sought the right partner for their perfume until he found the fruity

ripeness and strong acidity of raspberry. He used this pairing in the Paradis cake. It took him another decade before he hit upon the idea of adding lychee, whose exotic floral notes balanced the whole. (As for the name, Ispahan was the capital of the ancient Persian Empire.) When Hermé left to open his eponymous bakery in Tokyo in 1998, Ladurée kept the rights to and recipe for his pastry. But Hermé quickly translated the flavors into an individual macaron, which remains the bestseller at his locations in France and Asia. By the time Hermé published his *Ispahan* cookbook in 2013, he had forty-two Ispahan recipes, from waffles to cocktails.

In addition to being a remarkable pastry, the Ispahan macaron was part of a revolutionary new luxury brand, with its seasonal collections, special launches, and targeted marketing. Pastry has never been the same.

selected by **Susan Jung, Howie Kahn, Christine Muhlke**

Massimiliano Alajmo LE CALANDRE
Italy 1997

recipe → **p 360**

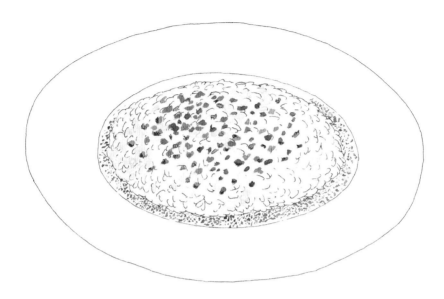

White Risotto with Coffee Powder and Pantelleria Capers

Risotto bianco con polvere di caffè e capperi di Pantelleria

"We must always study the ingredients and their search for a dialogue with taste," Massimiliano Alajmo told *Italia Squisita*. In this case, the French-trained Italian chef from a family of restaurateurs used the risotto associated with his region, the Veneto, as a blank screen for vibrant flavor, thereby freeing it from its tradition-bound association with (some would call it the dictatorship of) seafood, vegetables, or saffron.

Massimiliano Alajmo was inspired by the briny-sweet capers grown on the island of Pantelleria by Gabrio Bini and was seeking a radical pairing that would somehow harmonize with them. To him, the caper subtly evoked the flavor of Indian coffee. It wasn't until he was asked to prepare a lunch for his brother, with whom he runs the family restaurant, and a renowned coffee roaster from Verona that the idea to dust the caper-studded rice dish with powdered coffee took hold.

Like Gualtiero Marchesi's groundbreaking gold risotto of 1981 (see page 120), Alajmo's creation evolved Italian cuisine by adding a new accent to the national culinary language. By treating such disparate yet familiar flavors as capers and coffee as a spice and adding them to a dish that had for centuries been associated only with herbs or saffron, if that, he made the familiar bracingly avant-garde. (Another famous risotto from Le Calandre dusts a classic saffron risotto with bitter licorice powder to an electrifying effect.) Chefs who took up this philosophy of the playful, minimalist evolution of Italian cuisine include Niko Romito, Antonia Klugmann, and Enrico Crippa.

selected by **Andrea Petrini**

Ferran Adrià ELBULLI

Spain 1997

recipe → **p 361**

Smoke Foam

Espuma de humo

Ferran Adrià introduced his first foam in 1994, a white bean *espuma* rising from a sea urchin shell. The technical innovation—achieved by whipping liquids with nitrous oxide in a siphon originally developed as a way for pastry chefs to quickly froth cream—was an immediate provocation: what kind of chef feeds diners flavored air? And what, exactly, does it have to do with cooking? The discovery fueled even more creativity in the restaurant's laboratory, in turn helping it to earn its third Michelin star in 1997. Adrià's reaction was, of course, to be even more provocative. For his four hundredth recipe, he sought to achieve the impossible: he devised a way to get diners to eat smoke.

By placing water over the pungent smoke of green firewood and leaves, adding a touch of gelatin, and whipping it in one of the kitchen's now-ubiquitous iSi siphons, Adrià was able to make water and smoke ingestible. He topped this frothy essence of pure nothingness, served in a small glass, with croutons of grilled bread seasoned with olive oil—his twisted twist on the classic Spanish snack. "It is an iconic dish, used to arouse a reaction," Adrià told the writer Colman Andrews in *Ferran: The Inside Story of elBulli and the Man Who Reinvented Food.*

While even dedicated supporters of the restaurant agreed that the acrid flavor made it one of the restaurant's least delicious dishes to date, they also agreed that Adrià's ability to transform an ephemeral material into an edible, solid state was pivotal. It was, some said, an edible expression of Adrià's message that everything is possible.

selected by **Richard Vines**

recipe → **p 361**

Carrot and Celery Root Ravioli

Raviolis de carotte et céleri-rave, poudre de truffe

In a clear prophecy of the natural cuisine to come, the Haute-Savoie chef Marc Veyrat crafted pasta-less "raviolis" of thinly sliced envelopes made from carrots, celery root (celeriac), artichoke, and turnip—all grown or foraged nearby—with herb-enriched vegetable purées tucked inside. No meat. No sauces. And certainly no butter, eggs, oil, or cream. But this was luxury food, to be served for thousands of francs at a Michelin-starred restaurant (he received his third in 1995), and so black truffles were dehydrated, their aromatic powder sprinkled on top.

In a region known for its heavy potato gratins, sausages, polenta, and gnocchi (the area was part of a kingdom linked to northern Italy until the 1860s), Veyrat's move toward lighter fare was revolutionary, as was his dedication to

a cooking based on mountain herbs, roots, and *legumes oubliés*, or forgotten vegetables, foraged from the surrounding slopes—also a rarity at the time. But, guided by the French food critic Christian Millau, who advised him to move away from nouvelle cuisine to develop his own style based on local ingredients when he opened his first bistro in 1979, as well as the chefs he considered his "spiritual fathers," Joël Robuchon, Alain Senderens, and Michel Guérard, Veyrat continued their movement away from heavy sauces, as well as upheld their celebration of seasonal produce. It could be said that Veyrat's attention to the ingredients and traditions of his remote surroundings presaged the hyperlocal movements that began to take root in Scandinavia and America in the early 2000s.

selected by **Andrea Petrini**

Gabriela Cámara CONTRAMAR
Mexico 1998

recipe → **p 362**

Snapper a la Talla

Pescado a la talla

If you mention Contramar to anyone who's been to the Mexico City restaurant, they will immediately respond, "That fish!" True, the colorful grilled snapper that the young chef Gabriela Cámara opened her Condesa restaurant with is as dramatic as it is delicious. The dish—in fact, the restaurant itself—was inspired by the simple grilled fish that she ate with friends at a beachside restaurant while vacationing in Zihuatanejo on the Pacific coast. Her version features a butterflied, boneless red snapper that's been scored and slathered with a spicy red chile salsa and, unusually, a pepper-less salsa made with parsley and garlic, before being charred on a charcoal grill (char being an important flavor in Mexican grilling). What looks like the most delicious version of the Mexican flag arrives at the table with fresh tortillas, lime slices, an avocado-tomatillo salsa verde, and a grilled salsa roja.

Cámara opened Contramar, which means "against the sea," to bring the best-quality fish to Mexico City, which, while not lacking in access to fresh seafood, had few restaurants that focused on it. Her menu is simple but perfectly executed, such as the three-ingredient tuna tostadas that, like the grilled fish, followed her to the menu at her San Francisco restaurant, Cala. "This food is so simple that you have to be honest," she has said. "If the ingredients are not good, the food isn't good." The food at Contramar also takes pride in traditional Mexican recipes and ingredients, another trend that the incredible and enduring popularity of the restaurant helped to inspire in Mexico City. And, it must be said, with the arrival of the age of Instagram, the visual impact of this Rothko of a fish has helped lure countless new diners to the city.

selected by **Howie Kahn**

175

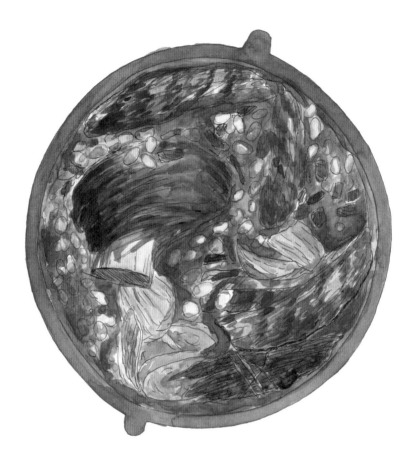

recipe → **p 363**

Cassoulet

Cassoulet, uniquely emblematic of southern French peasant dishes, is in its most basic form a white bean stew cooked low and slow with pork, tomato, onion, garlic, herbs, and stock. As legend tells, this iconic Languedoc dish was first invented in 1355 during the Hundred Years War at the Siege of Castelnaudary. With their defenses weakening, the townspeople scrounged up what they could to make a large-scale meal just fortifying enough to sustain their soldiers through battle.

Fast-forward to New Year's Eve, 1998. Mark Firth and Andrew Tarlow were hosting a party to thank the employees and workers behind their about-to-open restaurant, Diner, set in a salvaged Pullman dining car in a then-abandoned part of Brooklyn in the shadow of the Williamsburg Bridge. Chef Caroline Fidanza had to get crafty: not only had the gas not been turned on yet, but there was a snowstorm *and* a power outage. Add to that the pressure that Firth and Tarlow had hired her without tasting her food. So she chose something comforting and classic, evocative of time and technique: cassoulet. Fidanza's recipe included duck leg confit, sausage, and cured pork shoulder. She and Tarlow carried it over to the old train car in a couple of *cazuelas*. "There's a romance to this dish, and dinner that night had this feeling that it was coming from another place, not the bombed-out part of Brooklyn we were living in, but the South of France," Tarlow told the website, Taste. The cassoulet was a hit, and when the restaurant opened four days later, the homey but profound dish came to embody the spirit and identity of the restaurant itself. Fidanza's cooking style matched with Firth and Tarlow's loose yet detail-oriented hospitality to give rise to what many remember to be an organic, democratic, and engaging dining experience.

selected by **Howie Kahn**

Gabrielle Hamilton PRUNE
United States 1999

Canned Sardines with Triscuits, Dijon Mustard, and Cornichons

Everyone has that snack that sustained them through difficult times. For Prune chef Gabrielle Hamilton, such a snack earned a spot on the menu at her New York City restaurant. Sardines and Triscuits is exactly that: fat, canned sardines on a plate alongside store-bought Triscuit crackers, a dollop of Dijon mustard, some cornichons, and a sprig of parsley. For Hamilton, who once told NPR that she never serves food that was "learned in a stainless steel kitchen . . . or conceived in a dream," preferring to serve food that she knows intimately from a lifetime of being close to it or "eating it at an originating source," this dish speaks to survival: when she was a sixteen-

year-old who'd just moved to New York City and was living off of a jar of change, she bought sardines at the bodega for 35 cents (27 pence) as an affordable source of protein.

This story, the off-the-shelf ingredients, and the unobtrusive plating all speak to Hamilton's desire not to have a restaurant-y restaurant, all of which were a welcome change in late-1990s dining. Even Hamilton herself admitted that people don't go to a restaurant for someone to open a can, but her belief in her vision—coupled with her success—inspired a new generation of women to enter the kitchen.

selected by **Howie Kahn, Pat Nourse**

Gabrielle Hamilton PRUNE
United States 1999

recipe → **p 365**

Deviled Eggs

Comfort food certainly had its place in American restaurants of the 1990s. But the food that Gabrielle Hamilton put on the menu at her tiny East Village restaurant in New York City was comforting to her personally, crafted in what seemed to be private shorthand for only her friends and neighbors to understand. (She once wrote that she wanted to make food that would appeal to "the woman upstairs in my building who sells pot.") And so the snack menu at the four-seat bar included Deviled Eggs, a dusty, outmoded housewives' dish that wasn't seen outside of potluck suppers, with the exception of down-home Southern restaurants. But there they were, a confident strike against trend and technique. As it turns out, they were just what New Yorkers had been missing.

Deviled Eggs first appeared in an Andalusian cookbook from the 1300s, which recommended combining the hard-boiled yolks with cilantro (coriander), coriander seed, onion juice, chile, and the soy-like *muuri* sauce. By the time the term "deviled" was used, in the 1700s, their popularity had spread across Europe. Americans adopted the recipe in the 1800s, adding mayonnaise to an "egg farci" recipe in Fanny Farmer's *Boston Cooking-School Cookbook.* Adding paprika became popular in the 1920s, following an increase of Hungarian immigrants.

Hamilton's eggs are made the traditional way, blending the yolks with Hellmann's mayonnaise and Dijon mustard, piping them into the whites, and topping with parsley. (No paprika.) Many luxury versions have followed—topped with truffles, uni, shredded duck, all the way up to the caviar-and-gold-flecked oeuf mimosa at l'Atélier de Joël Robuchon in Montreal—but it's the unembarrassed, unembellished version on the zinc bar at Prune that brought it home for chefs.

selected by **Christine Muhlke, Pat Nourse**

178

recipe → **p 365**

Grilled Anchovies

Anchoas a la brasa

During the same decade that Ferran Adrià and Andoni Aduriz were revolutionizing Spanish cuisine, Victor Arguinzoniz was distilling Basque food to its very essence, using only embers. The self-taught cook had grown up in a nearby village with no heat or electricity; all food was cooked in the hearth, imbuing his childhood memories with the scent of smoke. So, beginning in 1989, he set about designing the kitchen in his rural pub in Axpe, outside of Bilbao, around grills, learning which wood produced the best flavors to infuse the ingredients selected from the region's hills, forests, farms, and waters.

His first breakthrough dish was anchovies from the nearby Cantabrian Sea—the same waters from which Elkano sources its legendary turbot (see page 89)—which he butterflied and sandwiched together, flesh to flesh, and grilled on an open-mesh grill pan close to the embers for just two minutes per side, occasionally spraying them with a mixture of olive oil and Basque txakoli wine. The rosy flesh is delicate and buttery, with just a hint of smoke to the skin. Even diners from other countries, who might have been otherwise wary of anchovies, experienced them as never before, in their best and purest state. Arguinzoniz's primal yet calculated technique also showed visiting chefs that you could cook even the most delicate proteins over fire, with results just as transportive as the scientific pyrotechnics being showcased at the time. Within two decades, moveable grills like those that Arguinzoniz had designed (based on ships' sails) could be found in the best kitchens, and wood salesmen built entire companies on teaching chefs which type of wood imparted the most complementary smoke. But few restaurants will ever be able to get anchovies this fresh, or cook them with such humility.

selected by **Howie Kahn, Diego Salazar**

Nobu Matsuhisa MATSUHISA
United States c.2000

recipe → p 366

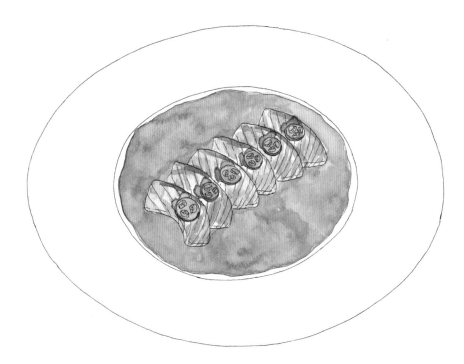

Yellowtail Sashimi with Jalapeño

Nobu Matsuhisa learned the craft of sushi while a young cook in Tokyo. When he moved to Peru to work as a chef for hire, he saw that the Japanese weren't the only ones to have mastered the possibilities of raw or very lightly cooked fish. His explorations of the country's ceviches and *tiraditos*, with their bright citrus and hot chiles, have expanded the lexicon of sushi and Japanese food in America. Whether or not "Asian fusion" is considered a compliment or an insult simply depends on who's using it: the fact is that it is combinations like this that have moved the needle furthest.

His ethereal yet flavorful appetizer of yellowtail with jalapeño was catnip to diners in Los Angeles, who were familiar with the green chiles through the city's vibrant Mexican food culture. The health-minded combination, which was also appealing to celebrity regulars like Robert De Niro, who backed Matsuhisa

in his first New York City restaurant, began as a meal for his staff. Eager to use up the scraps of hamachi (yellowtail) after cooking for a charity event, the chef went to make a *tiradito*: the traditional Peruvian dish of thin slices of raw fish topped with vegetables and cilantro, dressed with a spicy chile and citrus sauce just before serving so that the fish does not "cook" in the marinade. Realizing that he was out of chile paste, he used slices of jalapeño instead, pouring a yuzu-soy mixture around the pieces of fish. Simple and elegant yet powerful, Yellowtail Jalapeño became a staple in Japanese restaurants outside of Japan, where it is still seen as heretical. As the dish became popular at his more than thirty restaurants on six continents, Matsuhisa also used fatty toro, which he seared lightly and dabbed with grated garlic beneath the slices of green chile.

selected by **Howie Kahn, Pat Nourse, Diego Salazar**

recipe → **p 366**

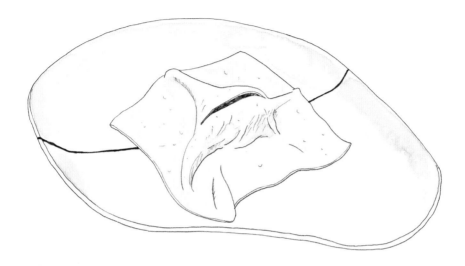

White Milk and Black Truffle

Le blanc du lait et le noir de la truffe

Chefs are artists, it's true. But in their own medium. Sometimes, however, they bring a canvas to life on a plate. Michel Troisgros, the second generation chef behind the stoves of his family's fabled restaurant, La Maison Troisgros, had developed his cooking skills beyond his hometown of Roanne, cooking with Roger Vergé, Alain Chapel, Frédy Girardet, Michel Guérard, and Alice Waters. He also developed a love of art along the way, particularly of painting. Based on his passion for the taste of milk, Troisgros worked with the fabled cheesemaker Hervé Mons to develop a curd as thin as the skin that forms on heated milk. Arriving eventually at the form of a milky veil, Troisgros used it to cover a "pesto" made from the season's black truffles. Its stark, minimalist appearance concealed an almost alchemical flavor combination. While experimenting with a plate of it,

the skin tore, revealing a gash of black. "I made a Fontana!" Troisgros exclaimed excitedly, referring to the Italian painter Lucio Fontana, whose textured canvases split to reveal hidden voids. Troisgros sent out unbroken samples to four friends at dinner one night when he realized that he needed to add a tableside element in order to make it as impactful visually as it was on the tongue. And so the "canvas" is slashed with a knife in front of the diner, thereby adding an emotional reaction that magnifies the power of the dish. Troisgros said that his love of art finds its way to the plate purely subconsciously. "I never say, hey, I'm going to make a Fontana or a Rothko, another painter I admire," he told French gastronomy website Atabula. "It happens . . . like a natural gateway between cooking and art."

selected by **Andrea Petrini**

Peter Gilmore QUAY
Australia 2001

recipe → p 367

Crisp Confit of Pork Belly, Seared Sea Scallops, Shiitake, Jellyfish, Sesame

This is one of the rare signature dishes that has evolved over the course of almost two decades, continuing to refine, explore, and advance both ingredients and techniques in a way that goes far beyond simply adapting a recipe to incorporate the produce of the moment. The Australian chef Peter Gilmore first served it in the late 1990s, when he was the head chef at DeBeers. He was experimenting with the Chinese idea of pairing proteins, Chinese food having been a fundamental part of the authentic fusion that was Australian cuisine for a century. "For me, combining a confit pig belly and sea scallops made a lot of sense texturally," he told Australia's *Good Food* magazine. "The fact that they could be plated very geometrically was a bonus." It was first served as two batons of crisp-succulent pork belly with two sea scallops balanced on top; a salad of jellyfish and shiitake mushrooms alongside. "It was my first really

special dish I think," said Gilmore, who put it on the menu at his first restaurant, Quay, when it opened in Sydney in 2001.

The dish was cited in Quay's first review, and a generation of chefs from this era—the flowering of Modern Australian cuisine—were inspired to pay greater heed to the contrast of natural textures in a dish, texture being fundamental to Gilmore's style. (It also set off the pork belly craze on the continent.) The entree has since had many incarnations, evolving to feature smoked pork jowl as the base. Other components have included silken tofu and shaved green-lipped abalone, and pressed shaved cuttlefish, jamón butter, lightly fermented shiitake, and a crumble made from puffed Japanese rice, dehydrated Jerusalem artichoke, roasted kombu, and sesame seeds, all underscored by house-made umami powder.

selected by **Pat Nourse**

recipe → **p 368**

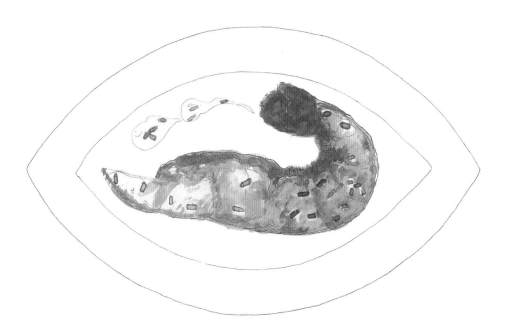

Home-Smoked Scottish Lobster
with Lime and Herb Butter

In a tribute to the flavors and ingredients of his native Scotland, Andrew Fairlie received considerable acclaim for this dish, which he served at his eponymous restaurant in the posh Gleneagles resort. Fairlie, an unusually calm and reserved chef who was temperamentally at odds with his fellow celebrity chefs from the UK, sadly passed away in 2019. He was known for applying classical French technique to seasonal Scottish produce from the seas, farms, and hillsides around him, such as lamb from his brother, who worked as a shepherd. At twenty, he was the first recipient of the scholarship sponsored by the Roux brothers, of the fabled restaurant Le Gavroche, to send young chefs from the British Isles to study in France. There,

Fairlie spent time with Michel Guérard at Les Prés d'Eugénie in Les Landes, as well as at the Hôtel de Crillon in Paris. (Cited less often is Fairlie's turn as the head chef at the Disneyland hotel outside of Paris, where he made gourmet pizzas for the California Grill.) He went on to become Scotland's only two-star Michelin chef; Michel Roux himself declared Fairlie's restaurant "a temple of gastronomy in Scotland."

At this temple, the empty shells of lobster sourced from the northern tip of Scotland were smoked for twelve hours over oak chips made from old Auchentoshan whisky casks, then returning the meat to the deeply aromatic shells and gently roasting the split halves with lime juice, herbs, and butter.

selected by **Richard Vines**

Daniel Boulud DB BISTRO MODERNE
United States 2001

recipe → **p 369**

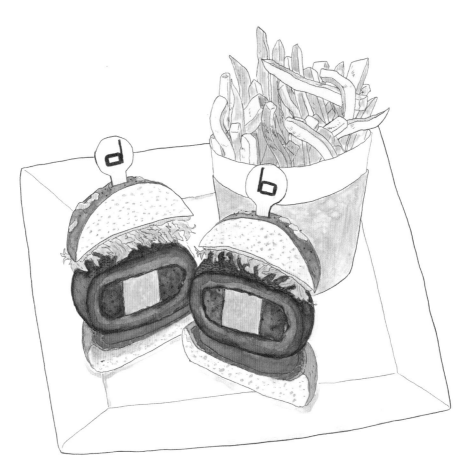

DB Burger

How does a three-star French chef do a burger in New York City? Quite decadently. When Daniel Boulud introduced his DB Burger at his newly opened Times Square bistro in 2001, the idea of fine-dining chefs skewing casual was still something new, and "gourmet" burgers made from custom beef blends were not yet on the map. Granted, the "21" Club generated an uproar in 1950, when it introduced the first haute burger, made with duck fat and fennel seeds. It cost $2.75 (£2) at a time when McDonald's was charging just 15 cents. But when Boulud's burger was put on the menu at $32 (£24.50), the entire nation paid attention. (Little did they know that it was his response to French farmers rioting against McDonald's.)

Boulud's creation took almost three days to make. The burger's center is based upon Boulud's most popular dish, braised shortribs—in this case a mixture of shredded oxtail and short ribs braised in red wine with aromatics and minced truffle. This filling is rolled around a torchon of foie gras and chilled. Later, a puck of it will be tucked inside a patty made from a mixture of ribeye, short rib, flatiron, and sirloin (rump) steak, ground in-house. The toasted house-made Parmesan-topped potato bun is spread with mustard (French) and mayonnaise, followed by fresh horseradish and a dollop of tomato confit. (In truffle season, a $110/£84 "Royale" version is available.) Finally, tomato, onion, and frisée are added before the burger is cleanly bisected with an electric knife.

Boulud's burger paved the way for the Black Label burger (2009) made from dry-aged ribeye at Minetta Tavern in New York, even Hubert Keller's $5,000 (£3,830) foie-topped Fleur Burger 5000, served with a bottle of Pétrus, in Las Vegas (2011).

selected by **Christine Muhlke**

Heston Blumenthal THE FAT DUCK

United Kingdom 2001

recipe → **p 370**

Nitro-Poached Green Tea and Lime Mousse

Heston Blumenthal has been using liquid nitrogen in the kitchen at the Fat Duck since the late 1990s. He had been interested in the science of food since he read Harold McGee's *On Food and Cooking* as a teenager, and enlisted Dr. Peter Barnham, a physicist at Bristol University, to help him find a way to use the −320°F (−196°C) product to transform liquids, including alcohol, into crystalline solids in seconds. The effect was pure drama, a tableside feat that impressed upon diners that nothing during that meal would be what it seemed.

Blumenthal's most groundbreaking dish using liquid nitrogen was actually a cocktail. Before the meal, a server wheeled an opulent cart across the dining room, parking it before the diner. On it sat a cauldron filled with liquid nitrogen. A ball of dense foam was squirted into a silver soup spoon from a whipping siphon, then plunged into the liquid nitrogen to cryo-poach it, basting it with the other spoon. It was then removed from the bath, dusted with matcha, and served to the diner on a chilled plate with a spritz of lime-grove scent from a perfume atomizer. One bite of the crackling orb released a mousse of lime juice, green tea, and vodka into the mouth. When the diner exhaled, puffs of "smoke" emerged from his or her nose. This was a vodka sour unlike any other.

Blumenthal had calibrated the recipe to cleanse the palate. The lime juice removed any alkaline residue, the astringent polyphenols in the green tea got the saliva flowing, and the alcohol in the vodka dispersed fat molecules. Above all, though, it was fun. So much so that the theatrical smoke-and-mirrors effect was later put into use by Ferran and Albert Adrià, Dominique Crenn, Daniel Humm, José Andrés, and others.

selected by **Howie Kahn, Christine Muhlke**

Martin Picard AU PIED DE COCHON
Canada 2001

recipe → **p 371**

Foie Gras Poutine

The early 2000s in North American cuisine were meat-heavy, with a tendency toward extreme nose-to-tail. At his Montreal restaurant Au Pied de Cochon, chef Martin Picard—one of the country's most respected chefs—took it to a new level, marrying his Michelin-starred French background and love of luxury ingredients with rustic Canadian fare and Québécois *casse-croûte* (diner) food to punishingly brilliant effect.

Picard has found few things on which a lobe of seared foie gras could not be placed—at one point, it appeared on twelve menu items, including lobster, pizza, and a burger. In this instance, foie gras found its way onto poutine, the downmarket Canadian dish of French fries soaked with brown gravy and topped with cheese curds of the most industrial quality. Following its introduction in rural Quebec in the late 1950s, poutine became a favorite of drunken students, along the lines of a late-night doner kebab or slice of pizza. In Quebec, canned poutine sauce is sold in supermarkets alongside gravy. Picard's gravy, however, adds pork stock and foie gras to the classic chicken velouté base. He also fries the potatoes in duck fat. The fresh curds are handmade by a local cheesemaker. And the four-ounce (115g) slab of duck liver was raised by farmers selected by Picard for their humane practices.

After the dish gave Anthony Bourdain the foie sweats on his television show *No Reservations* in 2006, the gourmand hybridization of Picard's poutine was mimicked around the world, from chicken tikka to cheesecake poutine. Obama even served Prime Minister Justin Trudeau smoked duck poutine canapés at the White House. (Granted, their size was much more "diplomatic" than Picard's.)

selected by **Susan Jung, Christine Muhlke**

Yotam Ottolenghi and Sami Tamimi OTTOLENGHI
United Kingdom 2002

recipe → **p 372**

Eggplant with Buttermilk Sauce

At Ottolenghi, their London deli and restuarant, the Israeli-born chef Yotam Ottolenghi and Palestinian-born chef Sami Tamimi cast Middle Eastern food in a new light in the West by filtering it through a lens that included Mediterranean and Asian sensibilities. They weren't serving the hummus, falafel, and baba ghanoush typically associated with the region. Rather, they were celebrating its bright, acidic, herb-y flavors and the freshness and abundance of its produce. And so they roasted eggplant—still unloved and little used at the time, beyond the occasional eggplant Parmesan and ratatouille—to melting softness and topped it with a creamy, garlicky dressing, topping it with za'atar (an herb blend) and jewel-like pomegranate seeds. Variations of the dish have graced the menus ever since, as the restaurant has expanded into mutliple locations.

Eggplant. Greek yogurt. Za'atar. Pomegranate. These were not yet common ingredients, but through the popularity of Ottolenghi's vegetarian column in the *Guardian* food section, not to mention the stratospheric success of his second book, *Plenty*, in the United States—which featured the eggplant dish on the cover—they became essential. Grocery chains in the UK began selling za'atar and sumac; US grocery stores started stocking pomegranates year-round. And a global appetite for Eastern Mediterranean food, as it came to be known, spread around the globe, from Zahav in Philadelphia to Kismet in Los Angeles, Miznon in Paris to The Palomar in London. It can also be said that the visual impact of this recipe led to a new, more naturalistic wave in food photography and styling, as well as set in motion the possibility for a beautiful dish to go viral.

selected by **Christine Muhlke**

187

recipe → **p 372**

Eternity by Calvin Klein

To say that a pastry chef's desserts taste like perfume might well be considered an insult. Unless that pastry chef is Jordi Roca, whose hypercreative desserts have explored such concepts as smoke, anarchy, and music. For Eternity, he served no less than a deconstructed fragrance on the plate, the edible elements miraculously harmonizing in the mouth to render the olfactory edible.

Roca had been reading the book *Perfume* by Patrick Süskind when the kitchen received a delivery of bergamot. He was struck by the noble scent that emanated from the thick skin of the Italian citrus. He commented to his brother, Josep, the restaurant's wine director, that bergamot was something that one was used to smelling rather than tasting. Josep commented that it smelled like the scent he was wearing, Eternity by Calvin

Klein. And so Roca worked with the perfumer to determine the other natural notes in the fragrance and to bring them to the plate. Bergamot ice cream, basil cream, cubes of both orange blossom water and maple syrup gelée, and tangerine slush and segments are each delicious on their own. Together, they are truly Eternity. (A scent strip accompanies the plate as verification.) At first Roca was hesitant to tell diners what had inspired the dessert for fear they would think he was using artificial essences. The success of his effort to link taste and smell led him to adapt over twenty-five famous perfumes, and to even launch a scent based on one of his desserts. His only fragrance failure? "We've never been able to get Chanel No. 5 to taste good," he told *Time* magazine. "Too many aldehydes."

selected by **Susan Jung**

Gastón Acurio ASTRID & GASTÓN
Peru 2003

recipe → **p 373**

Peking Guinea Pig

Cuy Pekinés

Peruvians have been eating *cuy*, or guinea pig, since millennia before the country had a name. But the Andean staple was rarely served in the coastal cities, where it was considered peasant food. And the most common preparation in twenty-first-century restaurants, called *chactado*, proved to be a bit of a hurdle for even the most adventurous visitors: deep-fried and served whole—head, legs, and all—with boiled potatoes and corn. In 2003, Acurio, who was already internationally renowned for his modern interpretations of Peruvian dishes at his Lima restaurant Astrid & Gastón, set out to find a new way to serve *cuy* that brought the poor man's protein into a fine-dining environment. He created an entrée that spoke just as strongly to the country's rich heritage of indigenous produce as it did to its long tradition of mixing Amerindian, Spanish, Chinese, African, Italian, and Japanese cuisines. A fan of the

Peruvian-Chinese fusion cuisine known as Chifa, Acurio decided that it was time to treat *cuy* with the same regard as a first-rate meat like duck. So he made Peking Guinea Pig, in the Peruvian style.

A rosy filet of guinea pig is served on a purple corn tortilla in lieu of a Chinese pancake, topped with a crisp wafer of the lacquered skin. Rocoto chiles, one of hundreds of Peruvian varieties, form the base of a sweet, hoisin-like sauce, which combined with a topping of julienned pickled turnips balances the richness of the fried skin. Not only was a classic invented, but Acurio also opened up the dialogue about guinea pig as being worthy of a fine-dining restaurant. Guinea pig has since appeared not only on high-end Peruvian menus, but is now also exported to other countries. Now that sustainable proteins are in demand, it seems that *cuy*'s time may have come.

selected by **Diego Salazar**

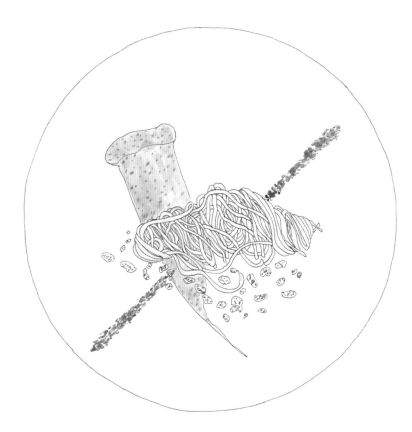

recipe → **p 374**

Shrimp Noodles

What is a noodle, exactly? How much science should there be in a restaurant kitchen? These were just two of the questions raised when the experimental New York chef Wylie Dufresne debuted his delicious Frankenpasta at wd~50. Inspired by a conversation with Heston Blumenthal at his restaurant, The Fat Duck, in the UK, Dufresne began working with a powdered "meat glue" that allowed him to transform puréed shrimp (prawns) into linguine-like strands of pasta. (No simple feat, it required piping the forcemeat into an extruder, dropping the noodles into an immersion circulator set at 165°F/74°C, then cutting each noodle by hand.)

The idea of carb-free noodles caused a buzz in the media and online forums, leading Dufresne to apply for a patent for the technique and wonder what else he could make them with. Sesame paste? Milk? It also led to questions about the alchemic process used to make them. It turns out that meat glue—aka transglutaminase (a product created by the same company that commercialized MSG), which binds proteins to create a uniformly textured meat product—had been approved by the Food and Drug Administration and the US Department of Agriculture and was already widely in use by supermarket meat and sausage companies. The glue allows chefs to stick together even unlike proteins to create a uniform-looking whole. "You could make a medieval beast if you wanted to," said Dufresne.

The wd~50 dish got other chefs thinking about what to do with the glue. Sean Brock made lobster cheese puffs at McCrady's, while a chef in Australia presented the dish almost exactly as Dufresne did, plating the noodles with smoked yogurt, tomato powder, and tiny shrimp (prawn) chips.

selected by **Howie Kahn, Andrea Petrini**

Heston Blumenthal THE FAT DUCK
United Kingdom 2003

recipe → p 375

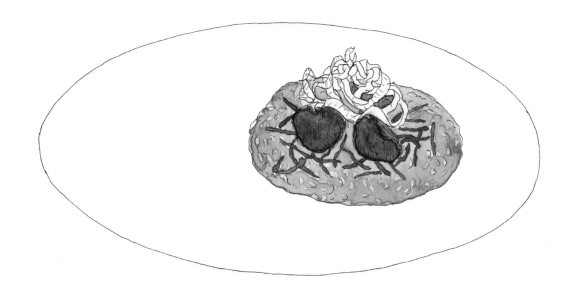

Snail Porridge

Before Heston Blumenthal launched himself into the molecular gastronomy stratosphere, he created a dish that used only the diner's mind to play tricks on them. In this case, he brought together two things that evoked images of "gray and gloopy," depressing foods: breakfast porridge and snails. But this rich, surprisingly savory, oat and barley "porridge" wasn't for breakfast. Instead, the vibrant green, risotto-like base brought together all of the delicious things with which snails are associated: a compound butter made with parsley and garlic, further enriched with ham, shallots, porcini, and almonds. The snails themselves were braised for hours in herbed chicken stock before being quickly sautéed in yet more butter. Topped with ribbons of *pata negra* ham and translucent

arcs of fennel in a walnut-oil vinaigrette, there was nothing gray nor gloopy about any component on the plate.

Blumenthal scientifically crafted each recipe at The Fat Duck to provoke a response or challenge a perception—what he has called "multi-sensory cooking." In the case of this dish, "It's just the name." The dish pulled upon the self-taught chef's classic French background. "If I'd called it risotto with garlic butter and snails, it wouldn't have had the same impact," he told the *Telegraph*, stressing the importance of menu wording.

The starter was an immediate sensation, becoming one of The Fat Duck's most popular dishes. By the time he removed it from the menu before reopening in 2015, Blumenthal jokingly called it "the bane of my life."

selected by **Susan Jung, Andrea Petrini, Richard Vines**

Iñaki Aizpitarte LA FAMILLE
France 2004

recipe → **p 377**

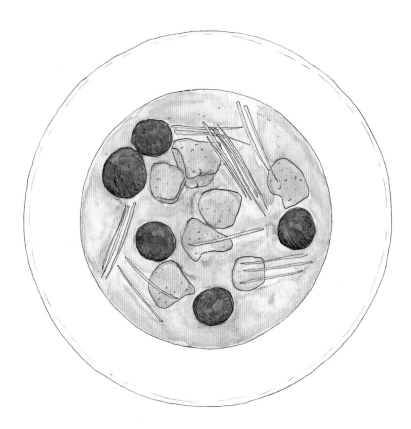

Foie Gras and Miso Soup

An East-meets-West combination that introduced the young European culinary scene to miso as a starring ingredient. Self-taught chef Iñaki Aizpitarte put the soup on the menu at his first restaurant, La Famille, where he served challenging, cerebral inventions in a relaxed environment—an instant success that led to the opening of Le Chateaubriand in 2006. It was from the latter restaurant that the fusion dish became a symbol of the new bistronomy, of which Aizpitarte eventually became seen as the leading practitioner. "He is the creator of the 'neo-bistro'—the contemporary restaurant of Paris," Alain Ducasse, an early supporter, told *WSJ.* magazine.

Aizpitarte's drive to experiment and to destroy (if not simply disregard) the codification of classic French cooking can be summed up in this dish, in which the only recognizably French ingredient is foie gras. But the cubes are raw, cooked only by the simmering duck broth poured over them. At the time in Paris, ingredients like house-pickled radish, miso, lemongrass, ginger, and shiso were only tasted in Asian restaurants or at a handful of fusion-leaning restaurants. But at La Famille, everything went: one might be served cubes of oyster terrine in sea water with a nori cappuccino and cilantro mousse, or a dessert of chocolate pudding spiked with piment d'espelette. In the case of this soup, it combines the subtlety of Japanese food with a cri de coeur against French fine dining. This soup caused many young chefs in Paris and elsewhere to wonder what they could do to loosen up the codes—and have fun in the process.

selected by **Howie Kahn**, **Andrea Petrini**

192

recipe → **p 378**

Devils on Horseback

In the summer of 2004, April Bloomfield, a British chef well trained in the simple yet exacting ways of The River Café in London, took the helm at a cramped, chaotic bar/restaurant in New York's Greenwich Village—in fact, New York's first gastropub. The Spotted Pig was revolutionarily casual and democratic: it didn't accept reservations, and it wasn't seeking Michelin stars (though Bloomfield would get them). The food was hearty, porky, nibbly, seasonal, and very British, so it makes sense that one of her star dishes is a snack from Victorian England. Devils on Horseback, which consists of a prune or other dried fruit wrapped in bacon, was a savory served after dinner in the early twentieth century. (Its saintly kin is Angels on Horseback—oysters wrapped in bacon—but that wouldn't fit the vibe of The Spotted Pig.) In Bloomfield's kitchen, Devils on Horseback were made with prunes plumped in humble PG

Tips tea from the UK and highbrow Armagnac, stuffed with a slice of pickled pear, wrapped in bacon, and then basted with chile-spiked pickling liquid before being broiled (grilled). In one bite, it's salty, sweet, smoky, and very good with booze, not to mention a perfect representative of the chef-led bacon explosion of the early 2000s. This thoughtful take on an old-school British snack would bring acclaim to Bloomfield's elevated pub food and encourage other chefs to eschew French technique in favor of cooking downmarket comfort food their way (see Danny Bowien and Anthony Myint's Chongqing Chicken Wings, page 235, or Martin Picard's Foie Gras Poutine, page 186). Moreover, the word "gastropub" was added to the Merriam-Webster dictionary eight years after Bloomfield's British invasion—*that's* how many gastropubs opened in the United States after The Spotted Pig.

selected by **Howie Kahn**

recipe → **p 379**

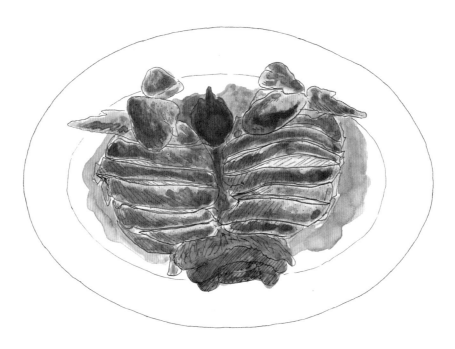

Smoked Chicken

Sometimes, looking back is the best way to advance cuisine. In the case of the Smoked Chicken served at Kin's Kitchen, diving into nostalgic Cantonese home-cooking recipes and so-called peasant food helped to reconnect Hong Kongers with flavors and ingredients that had almost been lost. The well-known food and art critic Lau Kin-Wai partnered with his son, Lau Chun, and the executive chef Kwong Bing-Kwan, who had been cooking traditional food for Chinese government officials (the highest position for a chef in that country) for more than four decades. The trio opened a restaurant where Kwong updated and upgraded traditional recipes, using the best locally sourced ingredients—difficult in Hong Kong, where more than 90 percent of food is imported.

Allowing Kwong to stay true to his principles has paid off: the restaurant won a Michelin star in 2011 and has since expanded.

"I'm pig-headed," Kwong has said, explaining his unexpected success. "Over the years, my co-workers often complained about me not updating my time-consuming and labor-intensive methods. I also insist on using the freshest ingredients available, and you won't find MSG, chicken powder, or meat tenderizer in my kitchen. But if I don't stick to my practices, my customers will be disappointed."

The dish uses "full term" birds that are more than one hundred days old and have been raised without antibiotics, intensifying their flavor. The chicken is braised in soy sauce, then slowly smoked over fresh and dried rose petals mixed with brown sugar and fresh sugar cane. Cut into multiple pieces and served simply, without sauce or garnish, the tender meat has smoky, faintly floral notes as well as a deep caramel flavor from the soy and sugars.

selected by **Susan Jung**

Jean-Charles Rochoux JEAN-CHARLES ROCHOUX

France 2004

recipe → **p 380**

Chocolate Truffles

Jean-Charles Rochoux opened his eponymous chocolate shop in Paris's 6th arrondissement in 2004, after getting his start in the pastry department with chef Guy Savoy and working with famed chocolatier Michel Chaudun. He makes all of his creations in a laboratory beneath the shop, his specialties being chocolate-dipped fruit, available Saturdays only—as the line will attest—and lifelike chocolate sculptures of a whimsical nature, from looming toads to an elephant trumpeting to his neighbors. He even does custom figurines (popular at his Tokyo and Dubai locations). Despite this, Rochoux is known for his humility, as well as his attention to quality and elegance.

But it is his truffles that have garnered the passion not only of Parisians, who have their share of talented chocolatiers from which to choose, but of a global audience. It's not simply because they are unlike the common round variety. Working like a sculptor, Rochoux uses a *guitar*, a hefty tool similar to a cheese wire that allows the bittersweet chocolate ganache to be sliced into exact cubes. Using an *enrobeur*, his perfectly molded treats of dark chocolate, fresh cream, and Normandy butter are gently and evenly dusted with cocoa powder to enhance the richness of the rich yet ephemeral ganache below. Fresh for only a handful of days due to their dairy content, these truffles require as much care and strategy in planning out their celebratory consumption as does their highly technical fabrication. Asked what the true secret of his truffles is, Rochoux simply demurs, "*C'est l'amour.*"

selected by **Susan Jung**

195

Margaret Xu Yuan YIN YANG KITCHEN
China 2004

recipe → p 380

Yellow Earth Chicken

With the popularity of one dish, the self-taught chef Margaret Xu Yuan has helped to change how Hong Kong restaurants source their ingredients. When the advertising design director began serving food in her home in the New Territories district of Yuen Long, she either grew the produce at her own farm or bought it at the local market—a radical idea in a country where "farm to table" and "organic" were still relatively new concepts. The popularity of her food led her to open on Hong Kong Island, where she stuck to her ethos. At the time, she was the only chef in Hong Kong with her own farm.

Xu's food tells the culinary history of Hong Kong. It is mainly based on time-honored Hakka techniques that she learned from female home cooks and Shaolin monks, along with influences of Cantonese, Chiu Chow, and British Colonial settlers. But it all has a personal stamp. In the case of her

Yellow Earth Chicken, that stamp is visible: after learning live-fire cooking techniques in a Hakka village, she devised the oven herself by inverting one terracotta planter (in Chinese, the word for terracotta translates as "yellow earth") over the other, so they are lip to lip, cutting off the bottom of the upper planter to form the lid. Set over a wood fire, the high temperature and closed environment (not to mention that the chickens hang from a custom rack so that the fat renders and the juices circulate) make for moist chicken with thin, crackling skin. The head-on bird is rubbed with rock salt, its cavity filled with minced wild ginger, curry leaves, mandarin wine, and extra-virgin olive oil. Xu cuts the bird with scissors at the table, serving it with a condiment made from wild ginger and olive oil. Although Xu's menu changes seasonally (even daily), the Yellow Earth Chicken has remained since day one.

selected by **Susan Jung**

David Chang MOMOFUKU NOODLE BAR
United States 2004

recipe → **p 381**

Pork Buns

In 2004, the French-trained, Virginia-raised chef David Chang revolutionized Japanese ramen for New Yorkers at his East Village noodle counter. But the dish that cemented his reputation wasn't noodles, but a simple bun that the chef added to the menu after he'd become disillusioned by a slow start to the business, and decided to cook whatever he felt like. Steamed Pork Buns were the perfect mash-up for the time. They were his homage to the *char siu bao* he ate in Beijing and the milder Japanese version, *nikuman*, that he bought from convenience stores while living in Tokyo—as well as the Peking duck, served on steamed buns rather than the traditional scallion (spring onion) pancakes, that he ate regularly at Oriental Garden in New York's Chinatown.

While the pillowy *bao* (essentially steamed white bread made with milk powder) and sweet hoisin sauce were sourced in Chinatown, the roasted cured pork belly and quick-pickled cucumber were perfected in Chang's mad lab. (A few dabs of sriracha are optional.) The result was brilliantly engineered to hit all of the tongue's pleasure centers. These buns, served in a loud, late-night spot where more attention was given to the playlist than to the décor, were the perfect distillation of the moment that Chang had brought about: pork worship (especially belly; ethically sourced), raucously casual dining with a fine-dining backbone, and the naissance of modern ethnic cuisine by the first-generation children of immigrants who fearlessly mixed their childhood favorites with the array of ethnic cuisines they grew up eating in the United States. These buns not only started Chang's empire, initially at the noodle bar and later at Ssäm Bar, but a new way of personalizing cuisine that has spread around the world.

selected by **Howie Kahn, Christine Muhlke, Pat Nourse, Andrea Petrini, Diego Salazar**

Richard Ekkebus AMBER

China 2005

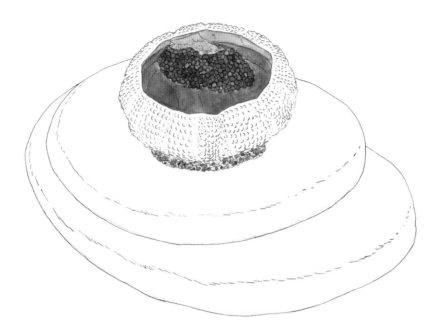

recipe → **p 383**

Aka Sea Urchin in a Lobster Jelly with Cauliflower, Caviar, and Crispy Seaweed Waffles

Sometimes a dish becomes so popular that its creator can't take it off the menu. The dilemma becomes the choice between evolving in the kitchen and pleasing returning guests. When Amber chef Richard Ekkebus retired this sea urchin course at his Hong Kong restaurant in 2016, after serving it for eleven years, fans launched an #occupyamber campaign on Facebook and Twitter to get it to stay. While it didn't work, the iconic pairing did return in 2018 as part of the newly renovated restaurant's classics menu. Not only that, chef Corey Lee came to Hong Kong to learn the formula so that he could immortalize the dish at his San Francisco restaurant, In Situ, which highlights seminal recipes from chefs around the world.

What was causing such emotional attachment? A luxurious, masterfully subtle combination of sea urchin tongues from Hokkaido with lobster jelly, cauliflower purée, and cauliflower mousse, crowned with a gold-leaf-tipped quenelle of Schrenkii-Dauricus caviar. The texture comes not from the pop of the roe, but from spinach, tapioca, and seaweed crackers served alongside. It is an unforgettable dish of refined power, relying not only on that combination of seafood, caviar, and cauliflower that chefs such as Joël Robuchon (see pages 117 and 119) and Thomas Keller understand, but also on an essential principle of flavor that Ekkebus—a Dutch-born, French-trained chef who worked with the likes of Alain Passard, Pierre Gagnaire, and Guy Savoy—came to under-stand after more than a decade of cooking in Hong Kong and listening to guests' feedback. And so dashis replaced traditional French stocks in his kitchen, and the lobster consommé in his jelly is girded with seaweed. This melding of French and Japanese continues to redefine fine dining in the twenty-first century.

selected by **Susan Jung**

Ferran Adrià and Albert Adrià ELBULLI

Spain 2005

recipe → **p 385**

Spherical-I Green Olives

The dish that brought molecular gastronomy to the world, Ferran and Albert Adrià's spherical olives were one of the most accessible—and influential—examples of art imitating life. For the fourth course at elBulli, diners popped what looked like an olive into their mouths. The smooth green oval burst on the tongue, filling the mouth with an intensely flavored juice tasting of the ideal olive. Even after this became the restaurant's most iconic dish, it never failed to surprise and delight.

Albert Adrià came upon the reverse-spherification technique when he visited the laboratory in a food factory and saw a bottle of sauce in which little spheres were floating. The technique was created by Unilever in the 1950s as a drug delivery system. When he asked the chemist how it was done, he was handed a bag of alginate. Back at the elBulli lab, Adrià added water to the sodium alginate in one bowl, and calcium chloride and water in another. When a spoonful of the liquid calcium was dropped into the alginate, a thin, gel-like skin formed around it. When punctured, liquid escaped. "I began to tremble and sweat," recalled Adrià on the Netflix series *Chef's Table*. "And I asked myself, 'Where is the limit?' That moment, I realized that I don't see a ceiling. And from then on, our techniques really took off." The olives were the result of two years of development.

Spherification traveled around the world, with balls both sweet and savory appearing at restaurants like José Andrés's Minibar and Grant Achatz's Alinea. Trompe l'oeil "caviars," "yolks," "ravioli," and other bursting bites were enabled by the Adriàs' own brand of powders. To this day, the olives remain on the menu at Tickets, Albert's tapas bar in Barcelona, proving that although the trend has moved away from molecular gastronomy, genuine deliciousness will always be in favor.

selected by **Susan Jung, Christine Muhlke, Pat Nourse, Diego Salazar, Richard Vines**

Enrico Crippa PIAZZA DUOMO
Italy 2005

recipe → **p 386**

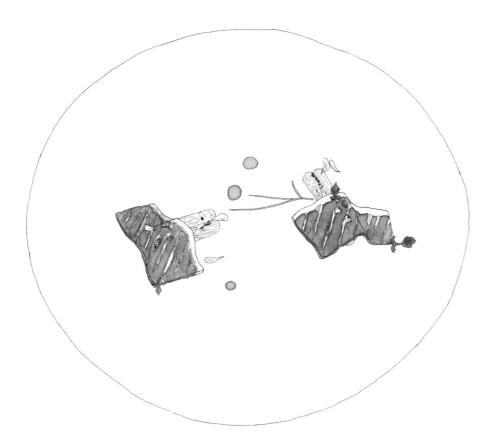

Tuna Nigiri and Maccheroncini

Nigiri di tonno e maccheroncini

One of the first dishes served by Enrico Crippa at his restaurant in Alba, this is the distillation of his Italian heritage, his time spent cooking in Japan, and his appreciation of seasonal herbs and flowers from his garden. Made to resemble a piece of sushi, or *nigiri*, Crippa boiled rice-flour *maccheroncini* pasta, rolled them into a cylinder and glazed them with a mixture of rice vinegar and gelatin before slicing them into bite-size portions. Each piece was topped with raw tuna and decorated with black sesame seeds, yellow calendula flowers, dried red shiso flowers, and fresh red and green shiso leaves. To finish, there was a drizzle of herb oil and extra-virgin olive oil and a few flakes of Maldon salt. As food writer Andrea Petrini described it, it was so simple, it was almost a political statement. And in a country like Italy, transforming pasta into something so completely "other" was indeed a strong opening salvo.

This wasn't fusion for fusion's sake. Crippa had trained with the Italian master Gualtiero Marchesi, who broke the mold in Italian fine dining in the 1970s when he gilded saffron risotto (see page 120) and deconstructed ravioli (see page 124). After cooking with Ferran Adrià at elBulli and Michel Bras in Laguiole, where Crippa learned to pay careful attention to the ingredients coming from the surrounding nature, he spent three years cooking with Marchesi again—this time in Kobe, Japan. There, he learned not only about perfection in presentation, but also in produce. It also reminded him of the importance of simplicity, to which he found comparisons in Mediterranean food and his own minimalist cuisine. It was in Kobe and Osaka that he fell for the sushi that inspired this dish: the fact that he was able to manifest such an experience in the hills of Piedmont is a testament to his creativity.

selected by **Andrea Petrini**

Andoni Luis Aduriz MUGARITZ
Spain 2005

recipe → **p 386**

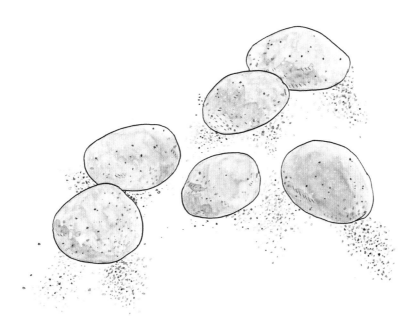

Edible Stones

At Mugaritz, even the welcome is presented as a challenge: the first dish at this farmhouse in rural Basque country is a bowl of rocks, which you are instructed to dip into garlic confit and eat. With your hands. Except those beautiful, smooth gray stones, which look like they could be from a nearby riverbed, are potatoes coated in crackling kaolin clay. Tender and steamy within, the playful trompe l'oeil masterpiece of the humble and familiar instills the trust required to cross over into the world of Aduriz, where the senses are stimulated in ways that are alternately subtle and jarring, sensual and intensely cerebral.

An early disciple of Ferran Adrià, Aduriz has been celebrated as a chef's chef since he opened Mugaritz in 1998. During a trip to Peru, he saw Andean potatoes that were preserved using a pre-Hispanic method called *tunta*, not unlike freeze-drying. Around the same time, he knew someone who was obsessed with kaolin, the clay that can be used for everything from making paper to explosives. His kitchen's experiments with a pharmaceutical grade of the clay as a coating coincided with their exploration of the milk sugar lactose to create different textures—neither of which application had been used in a kitchen before.

Though minimal in appearance, these "stones" push boundaries and pull the strings of diners' expectations. They have since become the signature dish of Mugaritz, one whose spirit and presentation have changed the way that diners (and chefs around the world) see.

selected by **Diego Salazar, Richard Vines**

Eyal Shani NORTH ABRAXAS
Israel 2006

recipe → **p 387**

Whole Roasted Cauliflower

By 2006, vegetable cooking had been elevated by the likes of Alain Passard, Dan Barber, and Charlie Trotter. For most of the world, however, humble ingredients like cauliflower had little sex appeal. But then the Tel Aviv chef Eyal Shani went over to his business partner Shahar Segal's house for the Passover seder. When he asked what was for dinner, he was told to look in the oven. There, in lieu of meat or fish, he saw a whole cauliflower roasting "in its full golden glory." It was a recipe from Segal's mother. Shani told the newspaper *Haaretz*, "I said to myself, 'Good God, another week and I would have invented this dish myself. Now it's his for keepsies.'"

The cauliflower first appeared at his flagship restaurant North Abraxas before it was introduced to his more casual sandwich outlet, Miznon, which has branches in New York, Paris, and Vienna. Whole cauliflower is cooked in salted water and allowed to dry. The cooks then dip their hands into olive oil and let the excess drip off before rubbing it into the vegetable, which is then roasted until deeply browned and sweet. The dramatic presentation also creates a sense of generosity, transforming a vegetable into something that can be shared like a piece of roasted meat. (Alon Shaya, who was the first to adopt the whole cauliflower at his eponymous New Orleans restaurant, underscored this idea by serving it with a steak knife sticking out of it.)

In addition to becoming popular at restaurants in the United States (both vegetarian and non), whole cauliflower has trickled down to the celebrity chef level, thereby putting a vegetable not only at the center of a plate, but at the center of the table.

selected by **Richard Vines**

Raphael Duntoye LA PETITE MAISON
United Kingdom 2007

Whole Roasted Black Leg Chicken

Poulet "La Petite Maison"

"It is the most thrilling dish to arrive on a London menu in years," *Guardian* restaurant critic Jay Rayner wrote of Raphael Duntoye's decadent roast chicken at the London franchise of the Niçoise restaurant started in the 1990s by Nicole Rubi. So good, in fact, that he advised readers on the best approach to dining at the restaurant: "If you choose to go, and I think you should, here's what you do: before drinks, menus or even the word 'hello' has been offered, tell your waiter that you want the whole black leg chicken and that it should go in the oven now." That's because the whole heritage bird, stuffed with many cloves of garlic and a plump lobe of foie gras, requires over an hour to roast before it arrives at the table, black legs dangling over the edge of the casserole, paired with a sizable fried crouton with which to soak up the flavorful juices and smear

with rosy foie. According to Rayner, it is the only restaurant chicken that can stand up to the pinnacle bird—that served at L'Ami Louis in Paris—and guests agree: it appears on the menu at every location that La Petite Maison has opened since the Mayfair original, from Miami to Hong Kong and beyond.

The Nigerian-born Duntoye left a career in engineering to study cooking. His best school, however, was with Pierre Koffmann at London's La Tante Claire. There, he learned about the importance of flavors and textures: "You don't put things on a plate for the sake of it," Duntoye told the *South China Morning Post*. That philosophy has followed him to La Petite Maison, where he lets the flavors of the French-Mediterranean ingredients shine through, feet and foie included.

selected by **Richard Vines**

recipe → p 388

Kale Salad

It's hard to believe that in Nigella Lawson's 1999 book, *How to Eat*, she lamented that people no longer ate kale like they used to. Brits were, however, eating the Italian variety known as cavolo nero, lacinato, or Tuscan kale, at London's River Café, where it was used in the ribollita soup for authenticity's sake. With the popularity of *The River Café Cookbook* overseas, the bumpy, dark-green variety (lacinato)—as opposed to the frilly kind that in the United States was then only seen garnishing salad bars and fruit plates—began to be grown in the US for the new crop of Italian restaurants that drew upon the restaurant's seasonal, rustic food.

And so it was in the kitchen of the Brooklyn restaurant Franny's that chef de cuisine Joshua McFadden, frustrated with the quality of the limp, flavorless, greenhouse-grown mesclun greens that were available during the long winter, reached for a bunch of lacinato with which to make—gasp—a salad. The sturdy, chiffonaded greens were matched with a vibrant, muscular vinaigrette made from olive oil, lemon juice, crushed garlic, and wisps of shaved Pecorino Romano cheese. The dressed kale was left to sit for five minutes to allow the leaves to soften slightly, then finished with breadcrumbs and yet more Pecorino. Once the recipe appeared in Melissa Clark's column in *The New York Times*, an unlikely star was born, rescuing kale from the compost heap of unloved vegetables and making it the salad star of the late 2000s. Soon there were kale Cobbs and kale Caesars, kale salad with goat cheese and kale salad with burrata. Kale salad also became the poster dish of the health and wellness movement, symbolic of an organic, farm-to-table lifestyle that was the opposite of molecular cuisine and nose-to-tail excess.

selected by **Christine Muhlke**

Jeremy Fox UBUNTU
United States 2007

recipe → **p 389**

Cauliflower in a Cast-Iron Pot

"I like to impress with everyday vegetables," said Jeremy Fox, who had worked at the farm-focused Manresa before helming this vegetarian restaurant attached to a yoga studio in Napa, California. And impress he did: his food helped to revolutionize vegetable cuisine (a term he preferred to "vegetarian") in America by lifting it to a fine-dining level of complexity and flavor in a relaxed setting. Never before had such a chef been celebrated by the likes of Oprah and the "Today Show". Fox's signature dish? The one that he made when he was trying out for the job: a trio of cauliflower preparations in a cozy individual cast-iron pot, the likes of which were just starting to appear in American restaurants. This was met with a decadent, deeply flavored meditation on an unloved vegetable—the kind Fox associated with vegetable medleys languishing on banquet steam tables.

While the ingredients themselves were few—butter, the vadouvan curry mixture that was just beginning to migrate from French kitchens to the United States, cauliflower, butter, cream, and lemon—the textures were many. Florets roasted in vadouvan-infused brown butter until caramelized and finished with lemon juice and zest rested between layers of creamy cauliflower purée, then briefly baked and doused with more copper-hued vadouvan butter before being garnished with raw cauliflower slivers or grated "couscous." Served with orange supremes, flowering cilantro (coriander) from Ubuntu's garden, and vadouvan-buttered toasts made from day-old bread, it looked more like a luxurious serving of *oeufs en cocotte* than hippie food. "It was making something that was really humble and common into something decadent, while still being vegetarian," said Fox. "It was a good crossover dish."

selected by **Christine Muhlke**

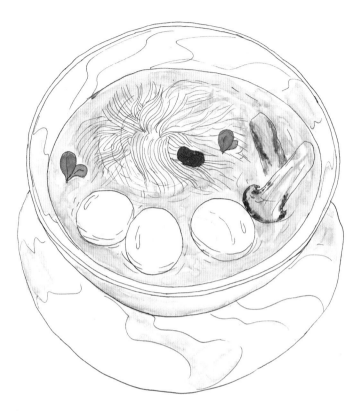

recipe → **p 390**

Chrysanthemum Tofu Soup with Fish Balls and Matsutake Mushrooms

This ethereal dish was invented in the rule of Qing Emperor Qianlong (1711–1799) but refined by Joseph Tse at his three-Michelin-starred restaurant, The 8, in a Macau hotel and casino complex (the number eight is a symbol of good fortune). This traditional imperial banquet dish, based on the famous Huiayang-style Wensi Tofu (Huiayang being celebrated as one of the four most important culinary traditions in China), is not expensive because of its ingredients (consommé made from two types of chicken, fish balls, tofu, matsutake mushrooms). Rather, it's the labor-intensive preparation: Tse, who has more than fifty years of kitchen experience, says that only two chefs in the Greater China region are dexterous enough to be able to slice a cube of soft tofu so thinly with a cleaver that, once steamed, it fans out into the form of a many-petaled blossoming chrysanthemum—a feat that requires up to fifteen minutes and 108 delicate cuts to create the gorgeous, vermicelli-fine strands. (There is a metal tofu press available for home cooks, but what fun is that?) Of course the light, airy fish balls, made of grouper, are delicious, but this stunning broth is a strong reminder of why some consider tofu to be China's fifth invention, alongside printing, paper making, compasses, and gunpowder.

selected by **Susan Jung**

Enrico Crippa PIAZZA DUOMO
Italy 2007

recipe → **p 391**

Salad 21 . . . 31 . . . 41 . . . 51

Drawing from his time cooking with Michel Bras, Ferran Adrià, and Gualtiero Marchesi, Enrico Crippa (see also page 200) has said that it's often easier to be innovative than traditional, because the only benchmark for something new is whether or not it tastes good. When Crippa created this signature salad it was totally new. And totally delicious. The name hails from the number of natural ingredients arranged in the bowl, which varies with the season—though Crippa says that the number often stretches above one hundred. Every morning at 7:30 a.m., Crippa harvests at the two farms that grow for him in fields and greenhouses, where they have even managed to transplant succulents foraged from the seaside and grown in sand and water. The greens, herbs, and flowers are taken to the restaurant, then cleaned to order so as not to compromise their freshness.

A deep, high-sided bowl, at the bottom of which sits a shallow pool of dashi scented with candied ginger to flavor the final leaves and refresh the palate, is lined with tall leaves such as endive and chicory, as well as crisp tuiles. Within that frame, a salad mixture seasoned with sesame seeds, nori, julienned strips of candied ginger, Barolo vinegar, and olive oil is layered with herbs such as shiso, mint, and basil, then finished with an undressed layer of leaves, sorrels, microgreens, and bright flowers. Tiny vegetables and hazelnuts might appear, depending on the season and size. Crippa insists that the salad be eaten with tweezers, going from top to bottom in order to enjoy the concentration of flavors. Salty, floral, earthy, bitter, briny, sweet, it is the full expression of a seasonal moment with no manipulation or intervention beyond the lightest of dressings.

selected by **Andrea Petrini**

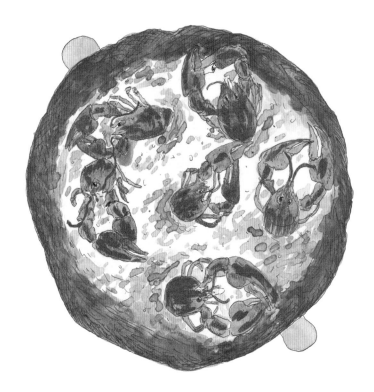

recipe → p 392

Rabbit and Crayfish Stargazy Pie

During his seventeen-year tenure as the chef director of Caprice Holdings, Mark Hix made sure that London's chicest restaurants served food that highlighted both British heritage and regional produce—while, of course, delighting and comforting their celebrity clienteles. At Soho's The Ivy, for example, Hix brought back the Shepherd's Pie in the 1990s (see page 152). Over a decade later, at the seafood restaurant Scott's, he opted to elevate a much less comforting pie. In fact, the Stargazy Pie made diners downright uncomfortable. (That is, until they tasted it.) Hix's offering of a rich rabbit and crayfish version of the traditional whole-sardine pie, in this case thickened with a creamy cider sauce and encased in suet pastry, had not long before helped him win BBC television's competition, *Great British Menu*. With the heads and claws of whole crayfish rising heavenward out of the puff pastry crust,

the pie looked like a grotesque kaleidoscope. Hix chose crayfish as a way of using an out-of-favor ingredient that, despite being delicious, is often seen as vermin due to its sheer abundance.

The dish's roots were born of famine: the original Stargazy Pie was allegedly created in the 1600s when a fisherman in the Cornish village of Mousehole braved stormy seas to bring back fish for his starving neighbors, who baked the entire haul into a communal pie. (It is so named because the fish appear to be looking at the sky.) Traditionally made with sardines layered with bacon and hard-boiled egg in a creamy mustard sauce, it is still eaten every December 23 in Mousehole to mark that day.

Hix's Stargazy Pie not only put a spotlight on regional British cuisine that brightened in subsequent years, it also piqued the public's interest in historic dishes, a trend that was followed by the likes of Heston Blumenthal's Meat Fruit (see page 229).

selected by **Richard Vines**

Andoni Luis Aduriz MUGARITZ

Spain 2007

recipe → **p 393**

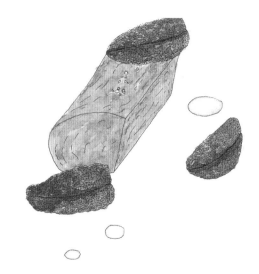

Duck Foie Gras Charcoal Grilled with Sea Urchin Caviar and a Spicy Touch

In the *Mugaritz* cookbook, Andoni Luis Aduriz describes the traditional preparation of foie gras as thin slices of liver "toasted with absolutely no compassion" over a hot fire, resulting in "an unpleasant purée of emulsified fat sandwiched between two charred crusts" that is served with "aggressive garnishes" of fruit. It was time for a radical rethink.

In 2002, his team in the Basque countryside outside of San Sebastián began their study. They worked with professors at the University of Granada to understand how a liver works, and what makes for the best quality foie gras for cooking. (The key: hand-fed ducks, which are raised by small producers, store their fat in small cores, which stabilizes the foie during cooking.) Next, they conducted experiments in the kitchen to determine a cooking method that allowed them to serve perfectly cooked, uncharacteristically thick slices (1½–2

inches/4–5cm) with a texture that was melting rather than oozing. The resulting experience was the ultimate magnification of the pleasures of foie gras.

The Mugaritz technique begins with gentle poaching in a bain-marie, after which the lobe is flash-frozen, grilled over charcoal, then slowly roasted at a low temperature on a tilted baking sheet so that the liver does not come into contact with any fat. Finally, it is allowed to reach its finished temperature of 133–136°F (56–58°C) outside of the oven.

When served with similarly silken lobes of brined sea urchin—here dubbed "caviar" for its salinity—the result is a symbiotic interplay of softness. A crash test on what (and who) is melting. This uniformity of texture was revolutionary in European fine dining.

selected by **Howie Kahn, Andrea Petrini**

Roy Choi KOGI BBQ
United States 2008

recipe → **p 394**

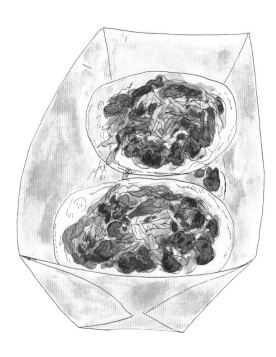

Short Rib Taco

When Roy Choi parked his new food truck outside of a Los Angeles club at midnight in November of 2008, he didn't know that he would transform food culture. "The first couple weeks we were out there, people were laughing at us because they just couldn't conceptualize what it was," he said. What the trained chef was experimenting with was "LA on a plate": tacos that married both the Korean barbecue and Mexican street food that Choi had grown up eating. By serving marinated Korean short ribs, chopped and crisped up carnitas-style, on corn tortillas topped with cabbage-chili salsa, shredded lettuce, cilantro (coriander) relish, and a sauce made with *gochujang* paste, rice vinegar, and sesame oil, Choi proved that fusion could be authentic and heartfelt. He also proved that chef-driven food could be served from a truck, democratizing the restaurant by putting it on wheels and taking his affordable, high-quality food to new neighborhoods daily. ("Our vinaigrette has 14 ingredients, our marinade has 20 ingredients, our meats are all natural meats," Choi told a reporter. "And we sell it for $2.") It was the beginning of the food-truck trend, which has since spread throughout the world, giving chefs a way to build a reputation without the crushing overhead costs of a bricks-and-mortar restaurant. Choi was also one of the first to use social media to build a cult food following: a "new-media consultant" helped get the word out about the Kogi truck's hour-by-hour location on a new platform called Twitter. And finally, Choi showed that Los Angeles had more internationally influential culinary firepower than anybody at the time—perhaps with the exception of the late Los Angeles food writer Jonathan Gold—ever imagined.

selected by **Howie Kahn**

Christina Tosi MOMOFUKU KO
United States 2008

recipe → **p 394**

Cereal Milk Panna Cotta
with Caramelized Cornflakes

This dish is a New Yorker's proverbial madeleine—the taste of childhood that, in the case of its creator, launched an entire business. Cornflakes steeped in cream and barely set with gelatin: a no-pastry-chef-required dish that was put together on the fly. Its flashback personality and flawless execution encapsulated the type-A stoner ethos that was driving Momofuku Ko, a tasting-menu counter on New York's Lower East Side. Its chef, David Chang, had already launched his career with his tweaks to ramen and Pork Buns (see page 197); now he was aiming for Michelin. So why didn't he have a pastry chef?

When he realized that he needed to offer diners something sweet, he asked Christina Tosi, who had been helping him set up food-safety procedures at Momofuku Noodle Bar, to return to her roots. Tosi had been the pastry chef at Wylie Dufresne's wd~50 and had begun at David Bouley's eponymous restaurant. Ambitious and with a genuine love of junk food, Tosi needed to create an easily replicable recipe with a lot of personality. While looking for inspiration at a nearby deli, she stopped in the cereal aisle and thought about the best part of a bowl of cereal: the milk that's left at the end. Her toasted corn flakes were rounded out with brown sugar and salt.

Chang knew that Tosi had struck a nerve, and encouraged her to use cereal milk in every possible combination. Soon, she opened Momofuku Milk Bar, a bakery where junk food and nostalgia entered an unholy (and brilliant) union. Since opening, the bakery has expanded to multiple locations. The unapologetic pleasures contained in this dish gave license to American pastry chefs to reconnect with their lunchboxes.

selected by **Howie Kahn, Christine Muhlke**

David Kinch MANRESA
United States 2008

recipe → **p 395**

Into the Vegetable Garden

While this representation of a moment in a California garden was inspired by Michel Bras's Gargouillou (see page 113), Kinch's interpretation influenced a new generation of American chefs, from Jeremy Fox (a Manresa alum) at Ubuntu to Jeremiah Stone and Fabián von Hauske at Contra and Kyle Connaughton at SingleThread. Drawing upon what he called Bras's garden's worth of vegetables at all stages of growth, which he tasted in Laguiole in 1992, Kinch first began evolving this dish in 2006, when the restaurant began partnering with a nearby farm to grow all of its vegetables. As he wrote in the *Manresa* cookbook, "We realized that we could put together a *gargouillou* that was not just about our seasons or our region, but about one farm containing hundreds of cultivars of plants and vegetables. Why couldn't a single dish represent a small plot of land, evoking the great effort that supplies and inspires the Manresa kitchen?"

Over time, Kinch came to see the dish—with its components of roots, shoots, flowers, fruits, leaves, seeds, and so on—as more of a concept than a plate of food: a mirror held up to a moment in nature. Although the ingredients change daily, each plate contains a raw element, a cooked element, a root purée or herb oil, a flower or seed, as well as an edible dirt made from dried potato, chicory root granules, almond flour, sugar, and butter, and a frothed vegetable "dew." It takes the cook assigned to the dish all day to clean and prepare the produce, then place it into the 120 containers from which he or she will arrange each plate *à la minute*.

The beauty and popularity of Into the Vegetable Garden also had an impact on chefs, inspiring them to work with farms to grow exclusively for their restaurants, thereby controlling the integrity of their food from seed to plate.

selected by **Christine Muhlke**

René Redzepi NOMA
Denmark 2008

recipe → **p 397**

Langoustines and Sea Flavors

In a fine-dining landscape that was still leaning toward the molecular and the overwrought, René Redzepi's decision to serve a dish with just two elements, place them on a big slab of beach rock, and instruct diners to eat it with their hands was practically Luddite—lo-fi acoustic in an era of power ballads. The effect? It jolted an entire generation of chefs into returning to simplicity . . . while dishwashers around the world sorted out the best way to get those rocks clean.

The course was intended as an edible snapshot of the Danish coast. A fat, sautéed langoustine tail from the Faroe Islands (a remote Danish territory whose cold, deep waters produce some of the finest seafood) lay on the foraged beach stone near some edible "rocks" that were a mayonnaise-like emulsion of oysters and parsley with grapeseed oil and lemon juice,

speckled with butter-crisped rye bread crumbs and dusted with a powder of dried dulse seaweed. Eight ingredients and no equipment more complicated than a Thermomix. (A blender would do for the home cook, which meant this was one of the only conceivably makeable recipes in the *Noma* cookbook, perhaps another reason why its influence spread to faraway kitchens.) And yet it told a complex and delicious story. Better yet, it was fun for diners to eat.

Rocks and slate are certainly nothing new on the table, but those literal reminders of terroir have appeared at restaurants like Faviken in Sweden and at Eleven Madison Park in New York, where Daniel Humm was said to have been inspired by the pure simplicity of the dish.

selected by **Pat Nourse, Andrea Petrini**

213

recipe → **p 397**

Strawberry Watermelon Cake

What began as a gift for a friend's wedding became the world's most Instagrammed cake. Such was the rise of former Quay pastry chef Christopher Thé's creation, two layers of meringue-like almond dacquoise filled with rose-scented whipped cream and slices of cool, succulent watermelon, prettily decorated with strawberries, rose petals, grapes, pistachios, and fragrant rosewater syrup. "When I first made it, I asked myself what would romance taste like and developed these aromas that get your emotions going," Thé told the *Sydney Morning Herald*. Customers at the side-street bakery and café in Sydney's Newtown neighborhood certainly agreed. But it was with the rise of Instagram in 2012 that the cake became Australia's first viral pastry sensation, with lines almost 1,000 feet (300 m) long forming outside the bakery by early 2013. Today, busloads of

Chinese tourists who have followed the cake on WeChat make the Rosebery branch of Black Star Pastry their first and last stop, arriving equipped with coolers and ice packs to bring home slices to friends. (Thé has noted that the flavors are especially appealing to the Asian palate.) The bakeries sell over sixteen thousand slices of the cake a week, requiring the bakery to order more than 2 tons of watermelon, 23 gallons (100 liters) of rosewater, and 237 gallons (900 liters) of cream. Since taking control of the business in 2018, Chinese-born entrepreneur Louis Li has put plans into place to expand Black Star Pastry to Asia and America, citing that the cake is a phenomenon, not just a fad: "This is a Sydney pastry that's so iconic it could equal the lamington as the best-known Australian pastry."

selected by **Pat Nourse**

Ben Shewry ATTICA
Australia 2008

recipe → p 398

A Simple Dish of Potato Cooked in the Earth In Which It Was Grown

This potato earned its starring spot at the center of the plate. Ben Shewry's dish is a distillation of place and the cook's personal history, combining a variety of hyperlocal Australian ingredients to underscore what is quite possibly the perfect tuber, earth-enhanced and custardy—even more remarkable for the fact that it arrived at its essence and perfection not by adding butter or truffles, but by being cooked in dirt.

"There isn't a plate of soil-cooked potatoes on the menu because soil is in vogue," Noma chef René Redzepi told *Bon Appétit*. "No, everything he does is integral, as opposed to just cerebral concepts with no roots in yourself, which is the way most of us cook." Instead, Shewry's potato is born of the memory of a childhood *hangi*—a New Zealand barbecue in which food is buried in the earth and cooked over hot stones —and a music festival on his uncle's farm.

The peeled Virginia Rose potatoes—chosen from thirty-nine varieties that Shewry tasted—are cooked between layers of jute in a pan filled with the dirt from which they were harvested two weeks earlier, then served in a burnt coconut with cheese curds cold-smoked with local mallee wood, a floss made from fried chicken that's been marinated in fish sauce, deep-fried foraged saltbush that is native to the Australian coast, ground coconut ash, and coffee-bean dust.

The Melbourne chef is part of a global movement of men and women who strive to create food that reflects the countryside around them. This dish has inspired Shewry's peers, including David Chang, Magnus Nilsson, and others. At Core by Clare Smyth, the Northern Irish chef was moved to create a main dish around a potato, in this case served with herring and trout roe and seaweed beurre blanc, an evocation of the coast.

selected by **Pat Nourse, Andrea Petrini**

215

Kwok Keung Tung THE CHAIRMAN
China 2009

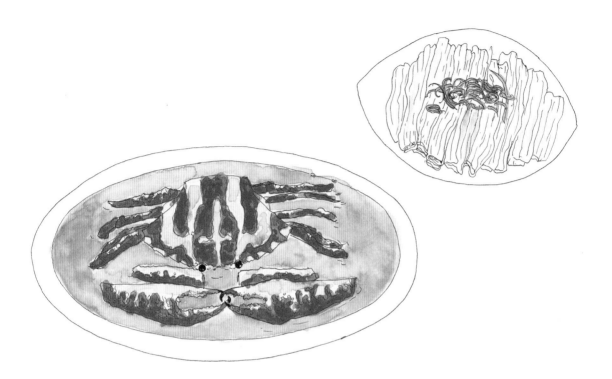

recipe → p 399

Steamed Flowery Crab with Shaoxing Rice Wine and Chicken Fat

Owner Danny Yip changes the menu frequently at his impossible-to-get-into Hong Kong restaurant, which highlights seasonal, locally grown produce from the New Territories in favor of the luxury ingredients and lavish presentations that are so popular in the city. But chef Kwok Keung Tung's old-fashioned Cantonese crab dish has remained on the menu since day one. In fact, you'll find it on practically every table in the two-story restaurant. Following the Cantonese culinary principle of always preserving the food's natural flavor, this simple recipe of indigenous flowery crab steamed with aged Shaoxing wine and chicken stock and fat, its shell framing handmade layered rice noodles, is pure alchemy. While the crabmeat is a delicacy—the crabs are bought live off the boat at dawn every morning—the magic occurs when its drippings and roe combine with the oxidized wine and chicken fat, thereby softening the wine and deepening the flavor, as well as the addition of clam juice to bring all of the flavors into focus. (The restaurant refuses to use MSG in its food, also an anomaly in Hong Kong.) The result is a most memorable sauce that pools beneath the chewy yet delicate noodles. The dish has since been put on the menus of countless restaurants around Hong Kong, but Yip has said that Kwok Keung Tung holds the secret of its excellence: "People have tried it at other restaurants. It might look exactly the same but taste different. Ours has more umami."

selected by **Susan Jung**

recipe → **p 400**

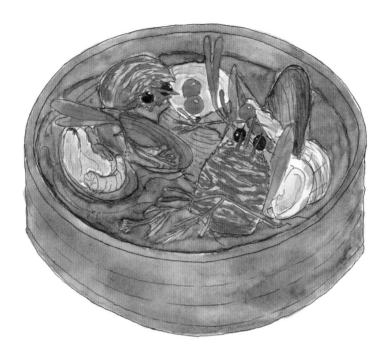

Shellfish Rockpool

Tom Kitchin's four-year-old son was the inspiration for this dish, which evokes a Scottish "rockpool" at the edge of the sea at low tide. An ever-changing combination of an incredible array of local shellfish and sea vegetables, such as sea plantain, samphire and sea aster, are arrayed in a bowl. A traditional chilled shellfish and tomato consommé—modernized with the fragrance of cardamom, fennel, ginger, and star anise—is poured over the elements tableside, the tide coming in for the diner, who is also given a scroll map indicating where each element hails from. It's all part of Kitchin's philosophy of "nature to plate," in which he applies the French technique he learned while working with Pierre Koffmann at La Tante Claire, Alain Ducasse at Le Louis XV, and Guy Savoy in Paris and applies it to the best Scottish and English ingredients.

"I wanted to produce something that would be a surprise to eat—like a rockpool itself, with lots of hidden ingredients, so that each bite becomes a discovery," Kitchin told the *Independent*.

Like Michel Bras's Gargouillou (see page 113), David Kinch's Tidal Pool, René Redzepi's Vegetable Field, and Andoni Aduriz's Vegetables: Roasted and Raw, Kitchin created an edible snapshot of a specific place and time. Mimicking its natural environment underscores the philosophy (and sensation) for the diner, thereby strengthening their understanding of the connection between nature and food. Rockpool is eating local at its finest, thereby modernizing and celebrating Scottish cuisine. No wonder he became Scotland's youngest chef-proprietor at the age of twenty-nine.

selected by **Richard Vines**

Mark Ladner DEL POSTO
United States 2009

recipe → **p 401**

100-Layer Lasagne

Del Posto's 100-Layer Lasagne, invented by chef Mark Ladner in 2009, is a feat of edible architecture. There are fifty layers of paper-thin dough interspersed with alternating layers of Bolognese, *besciamella*, and marinara sauces. The Bolognese sauce alone requires eight hours of cooking, while making the paper-thin pasta takes no fewer than four or five. It cooks for just under forty minutes every day at 1:30 p.m. and then must rest for three hours. The lasagne—which, despite its fragile composition, is incredibly rich and substantial—was originally carved tableside as though it were a majestic roast. (It is so tall that the thin slice must be served on its side.) But it proved too tricky for service, so they began caramelizing individual slices in the kitchen to seal the layers.

Ladner created this recipe at a time when the cultures of identity in fine-dining restaurants were beginning to assimilate. In an effort to set themselves apart, establishments like Bouchon in Healdsburg, California, and Restaurant Daniel in New York began elevating old-school comfort food, in so doing redefining the dishes through their respective culinary lenses. Though the lasagne was an incredibly well thought out, strategic addition to the menu—one that helped to change the perception of Italian cuisine in America from something humble and nonna-esque to decidedly high-end—the same can't quite be said for the concept behind the number of layers. When asked by the *New York Magazine* why he chose one hundred layers, Ladner explained, "Well, I started with twenty and just kept going. One hundred seemed like a nice even number." Ladner, who left the restaurant in 2016, revealed that he was lucky to have someone with an architectural degree working in the kitchen with him, allowing him to go higher.

selected by **Diego Salazar**

recipe → **p 404**

Beef Heart

Corazón

Virgilio Martínez was a pro skateboarder as a teenager. While skating around Lima, he fueled his days with street food, such as the barbecued beef hearts marinated with chiles known as *anticuchos*. Riffing on his favorite snack from that period, Martínez and his wife, executive chef Pía León, begin most meals at Central with beef hearts, in this case powdered over a dollop of potato purée in a small hand-glazed ramekin. To them, there's no better introduction to an already formidable national cuisine than his own dressed-up take on two of Peru's seminal ingredients: the potato—to which he feels a responsibility bordering on ambassadorial duty—and beef heart, which, to the couple, is symbolic of Peruvian food.

Rather than serve *anticuchos*, Martínez dries the beef heart, preserving it with a paste made from Maras salt and indigenous chiles such as *ají panca*, as well as herbs and grasses that evoke the high-altitude Andean hills upon which the country's cattle graze. Although the heart can be hung from a hook in a refrigerator to dry over the course of nineteen hours, Martínez recommends suspending it in a windowed room in a particularly windy spot. In his cookbook, he explains further: "This process works best if done in the mountains, at this specific altitude, in a dark room with a window facilitating the entrance of the wind. We've learned this from doing this process for over three years." The dried heart is then used as a seasoning in multiple dishes, including with a "ceviche" of Andean tubers. In the hands of Martínez, it is the heart and salt of Peruvian cuisine.

selected by **Howie Kahn**

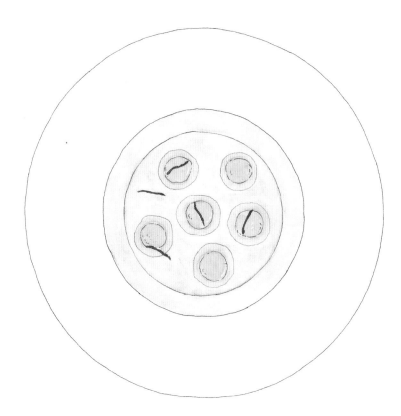

recipe → **p 405**

Onion Reduction with Parmesan Buttons and Toasted Saffron

Assoluto di cipolle, parmigiano e zafferano tostato

While it might look like a traditional bowl of *pasta in brodo*, this is not a broth. Rather, this pasta floats in an intensely flavored essence of onions, Parmesan, and toasted saffron that is as clear as a running stream. It is liquid poetry and a tribute to terroir. The saffron, which hails from the plain of Navelli in the province of l'Aquila in central Italy, is said to be one of the world's best. In order to fix its color and flavor, it is lightly toasted before being added to the onion extraction. When the onion and saffron are tasted together, the saffron component is strong. But when the Parmesan and cream-filled pasta buttons are added to the bite, the purity and harmony of the three ingredients is a revelation. In Niko Romito's philosophy of a new Italian cuisine, flavor is improved by the elimination of ingredients. Simplicity,

focus, Italian ingredients, and a sense of warmth and comfort that one gets from home-style cooking that is so often absent from fine dining—all of these ideals are central not only to this *assoluto di cipolle*, but to Romito's three-Michelin-star cuisine.

A self-taught cook who unexpectedly took over his parents' restaurant in a tiny village in Abruzzo while working as a stockbroker in Rome, Romito has been inspired by the Spanish and Nordic chefs of the last two decades to move away from the French techniques that have dominated high-end Italian restaurants and toward something more elemental and essential. It is Romito's triumph with inventions such as this dish that have inspired a new generation of chefs to create an avant-garde style that still focuses on terroir.

selected by **Andrea Petrini**

recipe → **p 406**

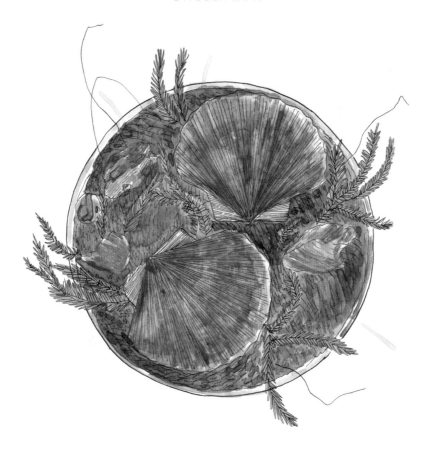

Scallop Cooked Over Burning Juniper Branches

The recipe for this dish is an exercise in the complexity of simplicity: the chef calls for "dry hay with a high herb content" for the base of the smoldering juniper branches that support the "perfectly fresh, very large and absolutely sand-free live scallops in their shells" that are quickly grilled before being returned to said shells, the only ingredients and techniques required beyond "good bread and cultured butter." Few cooks in the world have access to the quality of scallops—or hay . . . or butter—that fit Nilsson's specifications. Which is why it was easier to make the lengthy journey to a remote ski area in Sweden and get a table at the twelve-seat restaurant than it is to make the dish as it was intended at home.

Inspired by a spontaneous late-night beach barbecue in Biarritz, France, when Nilsson was twenty years old, at which he and a young woman pried oysters from a rock with a rental-car key and a bottle opener, then grilled them on the embers of driftwood and an old telegraph pole, it is as much about the process as it is about the product. At Fäviken, his restaurant on a 20,000-acre hunting estate, the scallops arrived live from waters several hours away. The juniper branches were gathered from outside the kitchen door. And the fire, it seems, came from within.

selected by **Howie Kahn**

Corey Lee BENU

United States 2010

recipe → **p 406**

Thousand-Year-Old Quail Egg, Potage, Ginger

Guests at Corey Lee's San Francisco fine-dining restaurant don't need to have a sophisticated palate in order to enjoy their experience, but they do need an adventurous one. Lee challenges them right out of the gate, with a first course based on *pidan*, a traditional Chinese recipe in which duck eggs are preserved in a highly alkaline solution until the whites become a translucent brown and the yolks an almost iridescent green. With its ammonia-like aroma and wiggly, pudding-like consistency, the classic *pidan* is polarizing to say the least. But Lee, a Korean-born chef who mastered modern French-American cooking at the fabled Lespinasse before spending almost a decade with Thomas Keller in California and New York, has added his own accent and considerable technique. He uses smaller quail eggs and reduces the alkalinity, serving

the deeply savory bite paired with a pickled ginger foam and a silken savory potage made with pork belly, potato, Savoy cabbage, and a hint of chili. Served in a simple, handmade Korean bowl, it speaks of the restaurant's lo-fi opulence and relentless attention to detail—and flavor—with which Lee has become so closely associated. The result is, like all of Lee's food, elegant, nuanced, and deeply impactful. Lee had considered serving this potentially divisive dish later in the menu, after his kitchen has had a few chances to coax the diner, but, he writes in his cookbook, *Benu*, "I think it's better to get the formalities out of the way." Not everyone can get past putting a little black egg with a green yolk in their mouths, but, Lee says, "When I see someone's egg untouched, I know that person is in the wrong restaurant."

selected by **Howie Kahn**

222

recipe → **p 407**

Radishes in a Pot

René Redzepi's playful starter winked at the concepts of both terroir and root-to-leaf dining, making the vegetables' connection with the earth edible. Sprightly radish leaves planted in a terra cotta flowerpot were set before the diner, who was instructed to pluck the radish from the "soil" and eat it, leaves and all. (Zero waste!) The crunchy soil was made from a dehydrated crumb made from hazelnuts, malt flour, butter, and lager; the creamy dip beneath the surface a mixture of herbs, shallots, capers, mayonnaise, and sheep's milk yogurt. The ingredients and technique were not complex, but the idea behind it was: connect diners to the food that is grown in rich, dark Nordic soil. In many ways, it is the very idea behind the concept of New Nordic Cuisine put forth by Redzepi and eleven other chefs as a challenge to French technique in 2004:

to translate nature into culture. To make the landscape edible.

Thanks to the Internet, the dish quickly went global, with chefs around the world encouraging diners to harvest their (locally sourced) crudités from a flowerpot, soil and all. It also helped to spur the movement to eating the stems, leaves, and roots that might be otherwise thrown away. Some reviewers of the dish noted that they had never tasted radish leaves. Edible flowerbeds—and their dirt—have been on the table since Michel Bras plated his first Gargouillou in 1980 (see page 113). Other proponents of crunchy soil have included Heston Blumenthal at The Fat Duck, David Kinch at Manresa, Dominique Crenn at Atelier Crenn, Jeremy Fox at Ubuntu, and Yoshihiro Narisawa of Narisawa.

selected by **Christine Muhlke, Diego Salazar**

Christian Puglisi MANFREDS
Denmark 2010

recipe → **p 407**

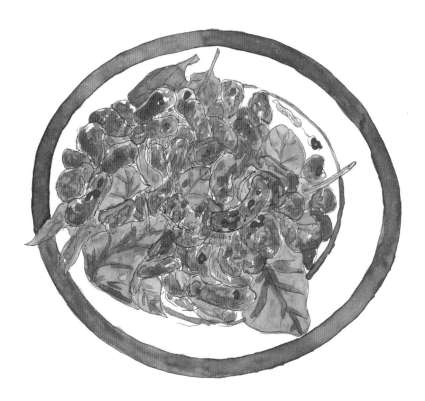

Tartare of Beef with Watercress and Rye Bread

Steak tartare has been around since 1926, when it debuted in France as "filet américain." Unlike most French food of the era, it had no codified recipe; rather, it was an adaptable concept (see Tuna Tartare, page 131) in which the bright-red patty of molded raw meat might include capers, red onion, and Worcestershire sauce, and be topped with raw egg yolk, served with baguette toasts to counterbalance its velvety texture. When Relæ chef Christian Puglisi opened Manfreds, his Copenhagen natural-wine bar, in 2010, he had only one meat dish on his menu of casual, vegetable-driven small plates. It was a way to highlight the country's excellent beef—in this case organically raised and grass-fed. In the end, that dish ended up defining what the restaurant should be.

Puglisi's interpretation of tartare stemmed from the restaurant's exploration of charcuterie. He was impressed by the supple texture of meat that had been briefly placed in the freezer and run through a meat grinder. Lightly bound by an egg "cream" made from soft-boiled eggs blended with day-old sourdough bread, canola (rapeseed) oil, and lemon juice, and finished with crisp breadcrumbs made from traditional Danish rye bread, the effect was brutal and rustic, Nordic and modern. In short, an instant sensation. Homages have appeared around the world at such restaurants as Estela in New York City (chef Ignacio Mattos's influential version, inspired by a trip to Copenhagen, is made with hand-chopped bison, fish sauce, and chile flakes) and Iñaki Aizpitarte's Le Chateaubriand in Paris.

selected by **Christine Muhlke**

Joshua Skenes SAISON
United States 2010

recipe → **p 408**

Sea Urchin Toast

This natural-born killer dish is one of the most ridiculously luxurious, explicitly obscene, infinitely Instagrammable dishes to come out of Joshua Skenes's San Francisco kitchen. Saison built its reputation on meticulously sourced ingredients (dairy from their own cow, fish from their own boat) kissed with fire and smoke and served to Silicon Valley's richest—the kind of powerful people who wear fleece vests and jeans to enjoy a $400 (£315) tasting menu, thereby expecting perfection with a casual edge. And so this orange crest of glistening uni tongues hand-harvested off the Mendocino coast atop a half-soaked tranche of toast has to have a big impact. It does. The smoke-grilled rectangle of sourdough from San Francisco's renowned Tartine Bakery is basted with an umami-loaded jus made from leftover bread, soy, brown butter, and egg yolk. Sweet, salty,

custardy, and caramelized, it's a decadent bread pudding, a *pain perdu* (or "lost") in its own excellence. The flavors are coaxed rather than dictated. Combined with the velvet and brine of the sea urchin, the experience is the epitome of casual refinement, a uniquely California style of cooking that lets the primary ingredients lead the dish.

The instantly recognizable course also came to signify a certain moment in aspirational food culture, in which posting images of iconic dishes from specific high-end restaurants around the world served as a form of culinary credibility. Such bite-size bling tells your friends that not only can you get a table, you can afford the bill. Luckily, as such genuinely delicious courses as this prove, Skenes's Saison is worth it.

selected by **Andrea Petrini**

recipe → **p 408**

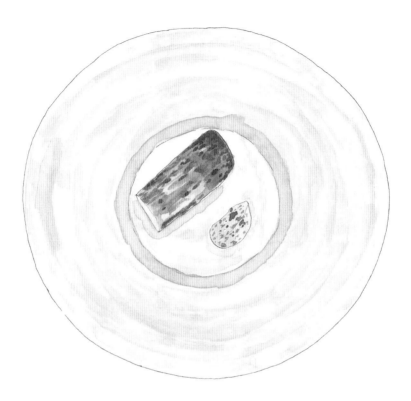

King Crab and Almost-Burnt Cream

"Do it once, perfectly" is something that Magnus Nilsson said frequently to the cooks during service at Fäviken. That's because some of the courses served at his twelve-seat restaurant had so few components, meaning there was zero room for error. Take this starter, which has two elements and four ingredients. King crab is brushed with butter and quickly seared in a hot, dry pan, then carefully rolled over with a spoon rather than flipped with a spatula, until it is exactly the right shade of gold and coral. Once out of the pan, it is misted with *ättika* vinegar—an extremely acidic white Swedish vinegar made from oxidized alcohol that is typically used for pickling (or, at higher concentrations, for removing calcium buildup from bathroom tile)—to cut through the very sweet seafood flavor of the crab. Next, fresh cream from nearby cows is poured into another hot, dry pan and left to boil undisturbed until the exact moment when it has achieved the perfect relationship between the milk proteins at the bottom being almost burned and the top layer reduced until it is creamy and caramelized. (The amount of cream having been precisely calculated in relation to the size and temperature of the pan.)

And then, one small spoonful of the condensed cream is placed alongside one baton of crabmeat on each plate. Simple, perhaps, but the sweet, pure flavors are magnified through caramelization, achieving incredible new heights. Many reviews of Fäviken also cited this as the most memorable dish, serving as a signal to chefs around the world that something so simple, if done perfectly, only needs to be done once.

selected by **Howie Kahn**

226

Jessica Koslow SQIRL
United States 2011

recipe → **p 409**

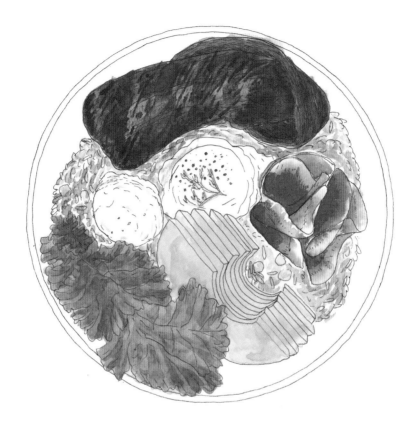

Sorrel Pesto Rice Bowl

Jessica Koslow's ricotta-jam toast may be the most photographed item on the menu at this Los Angeles restaurant and café, which serves breakfast and lunch until 4 p.m. daily. But it doesn't really get into what she knows about cooking: the rigorous selection of seasonal California ingredients, the time-consuming fermentations, the combining of global flavors in a way that feels personal instead of contrived. Those are Koslow's special powers, all of which combine in this dish, which takes the tired idea of California health food and imbues it with new vitality. (Not to mention expanding the idea of what can be eaten for breakfast.) There are many who try to imitate the worlds of flavor in this very bowl, but only Koslow has managed to hoist this New Californian ideal upon her back.

Her take on the grain bowl—a staple of 1970s macrobiotic cuisine that had been re-embraced by the healthy-leaning, breakfast-all-day movement set into motion by the likes of Bill Granger at Bills in Sydney—pushes past the clichés of kale, turmeric, and tahini. Here, she uses California-grown Kukuho Rose short-grain brown rice, tossed with dill, house-made preserved lemon peel, and a springy kale-sorrel pesto (when in season). Folds of mandolined watermelon radish, sharp feta, and a poached egg are splashed with lacto-fermented jalapeño hot sauce. In keeping with Koslow's Silver Lake diners' whims, the dish can be made vegan, or bacon *and* breakfast sausage (both house-made) can be added.

As Koslow wrote in her cookbook, *Everything I Want to Eat*: "This dish succeeding is like when the horse that no one bet on ends up winning the Kentucky Derby. At first nobody even knew it was in the race." In her hands, breakfast is disrupted, and health food is suddenly something to which to aspire.

selected by **Howie Kahn, Christine Muhlke**

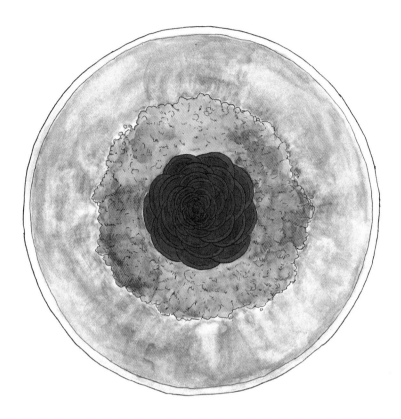

recipe → p 410

Beet Rose, Yogurt, and Rose Petal Ice

Daniel Patterson, known as a chef who is unafraid to defy convention and challenge the heroes of the food world, grew tired of seeing photographs of his dishes copied by chefs around the world—a fairly recent phenomenon facilitated by the use of social media. He was also tired of people saying that they could get food using three-star ideas cheaper at other restaurants, not giving enough credit to the creativity of the chefs inventing the original dishes. So he decided to invent something to serve at his San Francisco restaurant that was too time-consuming to replicate in service—something "deliberately, obtusely difficult," to be exact. His beet rose was an exquisite bloom composed of thirty "petals" of overlapping rounds of roasted beets cooked in beet syrup and compressed in a Cryovac, each carefully maneuvered into place. Set over

a dollop of puréed trimmings mixed with more of the reduced beet juice, another of aerated yogurt with lime juice and dusted with rose-honey granita, it was the most natural-looking plate of tweezer food to date—one almost impossible to do perfectly. "That's what our cooking is: to do stuff that looks super, super simple but is ridiculously hard," Patterson told Eater. "If we do it right, it looks like any monkey could do it, but if we do it wrong, it's a complete disaster."

And so the international copycats skipped this dish. That is, except for one chef: René Redzepi served an homage during Noma's residency in Australia. His raw, vegetal "Patterson rose" played not only with the appearance of the Coi dish, but also with the history of carpaccio (see page 72).

selected by **Andrea Petrini**

recipe → **p 412**

Meat Fruit

History repeated itself at Heston Blumenthal's London restaurant, where he modernized a recipe from the 1300s to spectacular effect. A shiny, dimpled mandarin orange sits on a wooden board, alongside a slice of grilled sourdough bread brushed with herb oil. Where's the meat in this Meat Fruit? A knife glides easily through the "orange," revealing it to be creamy chicken liver and foie gras mousse enrobed in mandarin jelly. This savory and sweet trompe l'oeil masterpiece—which required three days to make—surprised and delighted diners who had turned away from molecular cuisine in favor of casual, ethnic-influenced dining. To look so far back into England's past to create something so decadently technical was a reminder that the tattooed-chef culture hadn't won (yet). Soon, diners were having their photos taken with the dish. In New York, Eleven Madison Park's Daniel Humm created a dish of red cabbage and foie gras meant to look like the quartered vegetable. And in Paris, Le Meurice pastry chef Cédric Grolet built his name on his masterful trompe l'oeil fruit.

Blumenthal had become fascinated with medieval recipes for meat fruit about a decade before Dinner opened. He and chef Ashley Palmer-Watts set about trying to modernize the recipe for old English "pome dorres" (apples of gold) for Blumenthal's TV show *Heston's Feasts*, trying several variations that also made it into his cookbook, *Historic Heston*, in 2013. The labor-intensive recipe requires three days to prepare, with three cooks on the cold larder station working on it for five hours each day.

As Blumenthal wrote, he wanted to "create a meat fruit that the medieval chef could only dream of." If medieval chefs had had access to sous-vide machines, Thermomixes, and freezers, who knows what they could have done.

selected by **Diego Salazar**, **Richard Vines**

Esben Holmboe Bang MAAEMO

Norway 2011

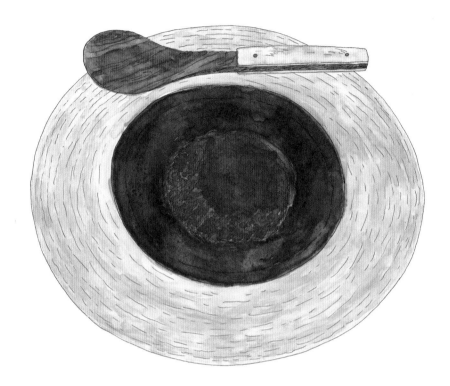

recipe → **p 414**

Rømmegrøt with Cured Reindeer Heart and Plum Vinegar

Drawing upon the New Nordic manifesto, when Danish chef Esben Holmboe Bang moved to Oslo he studied the rugged, challenging nature of his new home's climate to develop a style that put the countrys humble flavors of his adopted country into focus. "Norway used to be a very poor country, and as such our traditional dishes are very spartan," he explained in an interview with online magazine, The Bod Edit. "It's not about making delicious food in Norway, it's about surviving, so things are not necessarily made up to be delicious, but we find a way!" By exploring the centuries-old regional recipes that have evolved to work with the environment's extremes through the lens of locally sourced organic and wild ingredients, Bang gave the food of Norway bold new complexity. Within a year of opening, he had earned his first Michelin star.

One of his first breakout dishes was inspired by a traditional savory porridge that he'd tasted at a roadside café. *Rømmegrøt* is typically made with very sour cream and topped with salty cured meats. "That was really an eye-opener for me," he said. "I had never tasted anything like it! I went right back to the restaurant and made my own version of this dish." In his interpretation, he lightened the porridge and tucked it beneath a cap of powdered smoked reindeer heart—a play on the cured and smoked meats that are common in Norway, preserved for the harsh winter—and enhanced it with house-made butter and plum vinegar, part of Maaemo's extensive fermentation program. By serving dishes that use time-honored techniques and preparations, Bang has moved Nordic food onto the modern global stage.

selected by **Andrea Petrini**

recipe → **p 415**

Smoked Eel Sandwich

If the sandwich has been said to be Britain's greatest contribution to gastronomy, then the Smoked Eel Sandwich that Jeremy Lee serves as a starter at Quo Vadis is its apogee. The simple snack that the Scottish chef first created on a whim while cooking at the London Design Museum's Blueprint Café is now a signature at the nearly century-old Soho restaurant, a favorite of regulars and critics that is arguably more iconic than the dining room's stained glass windows.

When opening Quo Vadis, Lee originally wanted to serve a truffle sandwich, but the cost was prohibitive. So he considered the smoked eel (the ray-finned fish a rarity far more costly than the classic "fancy" smoked salmon), which he then sourced from Mr. Beale's Eels in Lincolnshire, resolving to lay the silken, profoundly smoky fillets on thin slices of buttered and fried Poilane sourdough slathered with Dijon mustard and nose-clearing horseradish. A dainty pile of red onion pickled in white wine vinegar and sugar accompanies the sandwich to refresh the palate from the rich indulgence of those three bites. "It arrived on the menu a very unsung dish," Lee recalled, but it received "generous, tumultuous applause. Folks got very overexcited about it, and it's been on the menu ever since."

To elevate a sandwich—that quintessentially British dish, named for an eighteenth-century earl—to something luxurious and sought-after was a key moment in advancing modern British food. "It used to be much bigger and seriously, over-the-top rich—it was absolutely outrageous," Lee has recalled of his invention. "We did all sorts of things to make up for the fact that it was a sandwich, but it was a journey to realize that it was a dish in its own right. So then it was actually a case of what we could take away."

selected by **Richard Vines**

recipe → **p 416**

Grilled Salad Smoked Over Embers, Isle of Mull Cheese, Truffle Custard, and Cobnuts

At Simon Rogan's two Michelin-starred restaurant in England's Cumbrian Lake District, he updates modern British cooking by utilizing ingredients that are either grown on his own farm or taken from the surrounding hills and shores and deepening their radically fresh flavors through carefully calibrated sauces and techniques. Inspired by the French chef Marc Veyrat, who uses the Alpine herbs and flowers around him in avant-garde fashions, this "salad" takes the hearty greens of the moment—such as a variety of kales, baby cabbage, cauliflower, celeriac, and broccoli—and slowly cooks them on a pizza stone placed over charcoal embers in a Big Green Egg smoker, adding cherrywood chips to enhance the flavor of the smoke. The low-temperature cooking coaxes new personality from the produce. The grilled vegetables are then plated upon a spoonful of loosely set truffle custard and finished with a frothed sauce made from local Isle of Mull cheese. A chile/parsley/garlic oil is dotted around the bowl, and the salad is finished with young mustard greens, black mustard flowers, sunflower seeds, and julienned truffle, as well as a tuile made from foraged cobnuts. It is a dish of humility and decadence, of local ingredients with an accent from European forests (though in fact the truffles are found in Wiltshire, England), and, above all, of confident flavors evoked through gentle textures. It could be said to be a British Gargouillou, that legendary edible landscape invented by Michel Bras (see page 113). Like that dish, Rogan's creation challenged the idea of what a salad could be.

selected by **Richard Vines**

Tam Kwok Fung JADE DRAGON
China 2012

Glutinous Rice-Stuffed Suckling Pig

Like other chefs of his generation who were starting out in China thirty years ago, Tam Kwok Fung had no formal training. Rather, he got his first restaurant job—as a cleaner—because a high school friend's father was the manager of a good restaurant. He worked his way up the ranks, gradually perfecting the classics and learning the modern Cantonese repertoire, such as this exceptional suckling pig, which is impressive even in lesser restaurants. As allegedly created by Yung "Joe" Chan at the Kimberley Hotel in Hong Kong, the recipe requires a whole suckling pig to be painstakingly deboned, filled with seasoned glutinous (sticky) rice, then tightly rolled and roasted to form a cylinder that is golden and crisp on the outside, tender and subtly seasoned within, with a slight chewiness from the rice. At the Jade Dragon

restaurant in Macau's City of Dreams casino, Tam achieved a spectacular meat-to-rice ratio by first drying and preparing the pig in the traditional way before slicing the pig in half lengthwise, deboning it and removing the meat used in the dish. The filling—a mixture of glutinous rice, mushrooms and Iberico ham—is then delicately placed inside the pig before it is rolled up and finally tied with kitchen string or wire, to keep the filling and flavorful juices from escaping. Finally, it is oven-cooked before being doused with hot oil to ensure a perfectly crispy skin. The resulting dish is served with a few pickled vegetables to cut the considerable richness of the meat. Chef Tam took this technique with him to the Wing Lei Palace in 2018.

selected by **Susan Jung**

233

Daniel Humm ELEVEN MADISON PARK
United States 2012

recipe → **p 418**

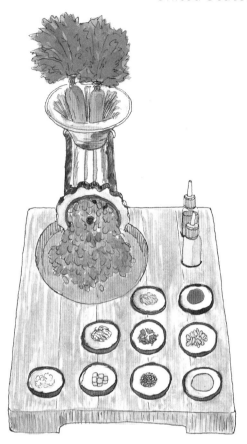

Carrot Tartare

The partners behind Eleven Madison Park, restaurateur Will Guidara and chef Daniel Humm, have attained near-celebrity status through their innovative cuisine, performative service, intentional restaurant design, and strategic collaborations. In his dishes, Humm often pays homage to the classics, but manipulates the sense memories they call to mind to create culinary metaphors. An iconic example of the drama and flare they bring to the otherwise mundane is their Carrot Tartare, which is served alongside smoked bluefish, mustard oil, and pickled quail egg yolks. As a meat grinder is clamped to the side of the diner's table, a grand speech commences, explaining that this is EMP's homage to New York's classic steakhouses: Delmonico's, Gallaghers, Keens, Sparks. As the finale of this performed lore is approached, expectations are defied when a bunch of cooked carrots is instead lowered into the meat grinder and transformed into a bright orange emulsion. Because New York State's Hudson Valley is known for carrots with a complex flavor profile, Humm decided to use them —greens and all—as his steak substitute. Each dish on the menu is paired with a story or gesture from a server or cook that helps to clarify the history, how it came to be on the menu, why the ingredients were chosen; the front- and back-of-house staff are closely integrated to create a sense of transparency between the two functions of the restaurant. What Humm does with precision and expertise is offer up a slice of the authentic, reimagined through his own lens.

selected by **Howie Kahn, Christine Muhlke, Diego Salazar**

recipe → **p 420**

Chongqing Chicken Wings

Somewhere around 2012, food got feisty and loose. Thanks to experimental, low-stakes venues like pop-ups and food carts, chefs could cook whatever they wanted. For some, that meant serving the kind of food they made for themselves: quick, post-shift meals that went down well with a High Life beer. Even media behemoth Vice had *Chef's Night Out*, a show dedicated to chronicling chefs' after-service greasy, spicy, carby escapades. Restaurants got louder, less predictable, and hotter. Why couldn't you make a really delicious, forward-thinking dish that was inspired by both the American bar snack Buffalo chicken wings and a revered, centuries-old cuisine? You can, at least when you think like Danny Bowien, a Korean-born, Oklahoma-raised culinary school dropout who, with his partner Anthony Myint, opened an "Americanized Oriental" restaurant inside a run-of-the-mill Chinese takeout joint in San Francisco's Mission district. At Mission Chinese Food, they created a phenomenon, with lines of eager diners waiting for mind-boggling, face-tingling, sorta-Sichuan food.

Exhibit A: the Chongqing Chicken Wings, which Anthony Bourdain called the best chicken wings in recorded history. They're fried, frozen, and then fried again (just like the original Buffalo chicken wings at Anchor Bar in Buffalo, New York, page 87). Then, after a toss in a powder that includes mouth-numbing Sichuan peppercorns, they get topped with a pile of whole, dried chiles. Like many of Bowien's later signature dishes, they were simultaneously nostalgic and challenging. Painfully spicy, yes, but also hard to forget. Asian-inflected wings have since become a respectable appetizer on menus from Paris to Copenhagen, though it'll be hard to find any as freaky as Bowien's.

selected by **Christine Muhlke**

Massimo Bottura OSTERIA FRANCESCANA
Italy 2012

recipe → **p 421**

Oops! I Dropped the Lemon Tart

A marvel of radical modern plating—by way of a kitchen accident. One would expect no less from Massimo Bottura, who has dragged tradition-bound Italian food into the twenty-first century by linking it with art, emotion, memory, and experience (even when that experience is potentially catastrophic). This lemon tart was meant to portray "the palate of the people": lemongrass gelato and traditional zabaglione with mint sauce, salty capers from Pantelleria, candied Sorrento lemon, Calabrian bergamot, and ginger upended Italian traditions and blurred the line between sweet and savory. It was plated like any tart until the day that the pastry chef quit unexpectedly and young chef Takahiko Kondo had to step in. As he was sending out the last two lemon tarts of the evening, one fell on the kitchen counter, splattering like a Jackson Pollock painting. Kondo's face went white, but Bottura saw the fractured plate as much more beautiful than the original: "It's a metaphor for the South of Italy!"

As Bottura writes in his cookbook, *Never Trust a Skinny Italian Chef*, "In that instant the dessert revealed itself for the first time, and the lemon tart has never been the same. It is broken again and again. The ritual reminds us that breaking is a beginning not an end. Break, transform, and recreate." The postmodern plating proved too controversial for the locals in Modena—just one of the reasons why the restaurant nearly closed for lack of business in its early days. But as Bottura's fame eventually grew, this dessert inspired swooshes, smears, and sweet-savory dots around the world. More important, it freed chefs to be playful and artistic. As Bottura told a reporter, the dish is a reminder to "keep space open for poetry in your everyday life, with which you can jump and imagine everything."

selected by **Christine Muhlke, Diego Salazar, Richard Vines**

236

recipe → **p 422**

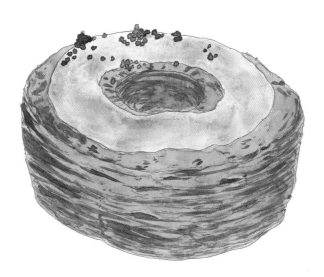

Cronut®

Before the Sconut, Rownut, Crookie, Crumbnut, and Dunkin' Donuts's New York Pie Doughnut, there was the Cronut®, a cream-filled donut-croissant hybrid that debuted at New York City's Dominique Ansel Bakery in May 2013 and was trademarked nine days later. (A staffer had suggested that Ansel make a donut for Mother's Day, but Ansel didn't have a recipe.) To make the pastry, croissant-like dough is manipulated so it stays buttery and flaky inside when plunged into hot oil to crisp up the outside. It's a baking marvel that required innovation and skill to devise, two things Dominique Ansel has plenty of: before opening his bakery, he led the pastry team at Restaurant Daniel, Daniel Boulud's New York City restaurant to its first four-star *New York Times* rating, three Michelin stars, and a James Beard award.

Food critics called his trademarked pastry a masterpiece, and it was named one of *Time* magazine's twenty-five best inventions of 2013 (along with waterless fracking and the artificial pancreas). Just like every new sneaker and cell phone, people happily stood in line for this scarce, hyped status item. During its heyday, just as the gourmet cupcake trend was fading, the Cronut®-crazed would line up hours before the bakery's 8 a.m. opening to claim only two of the few hundred made each day, pay up to $100 (£76) for a Cronut® on the black market, or settle for one of the many imitations found around the world. While today its presence on social feeds has dwindled, the Cronut® lives on as one of the few pastries with the power to propel patrons into line and online—and with popularity matched by its deliciousness and culinary craftiness.

selected by **Susan Jung, Diego Salazar**

Alex Atala D.O.M.

Brazil 2013

recipe → **p 426**

Ants and Pineapple

Imagine a two-ingredient dish capable of generating a huge ripple in the global chef community. Alex Atala's Ants and Pineapple did just that. Atala had decided to use only Brazilian ingredients at his São Paulo restaurant, in a country where fine dining was classic European cooking. He wanted to challenge his wealthy diners to think about the vast larder in their own backyard: the Amazon rainforest. By combining the primitive with the progressive and imbuing each ingredient with an origin story, Atala has helped Brazilians to not only take pride in their cuisine, but also to radically rethink what is valuable, edible, sustainable—and delicious. By presenting diners with a domed glass containing a single ant on a cube of pineapple, the whole natural world opens up to the plate and palate.

Being simple, Atala has said, is a difficult and complex task. He told an audiece at a public lecture in 2013, "One dish with three ingredients is a huge challenge for a chef. Sometimes I take out one ingredient, and then the dish has a clear message."

It helps that the ants are delicious. Atala tasted a dried saúva ant (the only species used for culinary purposes) while visiting the now-famous Baré Indian cook and purveyor Doña Brazi in the remote São Gabriel da Cachoeira region and was struck by its flavor. He asked Brazi if she had used ginger, lemongrass, and cardamom in the dish, but she told him it was the aromatic flavor of the ants. (Later, Atala brought her those spices to sample; she told him they tasted like ants.) Ants have since appeared in many dishes at D.O.M. The dish has inspired the likes of Enrique Olvera at Pujol and Ben Shewry at Attica to explore the flavor of ants in their home countries, where they are served dried and ground as a seasoning or even live as a truly fresh provocation.

selected by **Howie Kahn, Andrea Petrini**

recipe → **p 426**

Crapaudine Beetroot Cooked Slowly in Beef Fat with Smoked Cod's Roe and Linseeds

In the last decade, even the least-loved vegetables have achieved star status in restaurants. From Eyal Shani's cauliflower (see page 202) to Daniel Humm's celeriac in a pig's bladder to Yotam Ottolenghi's makeover of the once-maligned eggplant (aubergine, see page 187), our grandparents' vegetables are now at the center of the plate. In the garden pantheon, the beet now belongs to Tommy Banks. At his family's restaurant in Yorkshire, where the self-taught cook earned a Michelin star when he took over at the age of twenty-four, Banks transforms the crapaudine beet (beetroot), a torpedo-shaped heirloom varietal, into an elegantly arrayed entrée with the soul of a rustic English roast. By confiting "fillets" of the beets in beef fat for five hours before smoking them, they take on the shriveled appearance and caramelized texture of a steak. A glaze of reduced syrup made from juiced beet trimmings adds an almost barbecue-like sweetness. Carefully arranged puffs of horseradish goat curd, slivers of pickled red and gold beets, smoked cod roe emulsion, and flaxseed crackers make the meaty wedge look almost like a modern dessert.

Treating vegetables like meat, finding creative ways to avoid food waste, and working to revive heirloom varieties are now de rigueur among chefs, and it is a trend worth supporting. It is dishes such as this that make a profound impact upon diners to help them rethink what constitutes a fine-dining entrée. And Banks's beet dish is making an impact on the land around him, too: with his parents, who are farmers, he now grows more than twenty tons of beets per year just to fulfill orders for this entrée. Such is the power of a signature dish.

selected by **Richard Vines**

Enrique Olvera PUJOL
Mexico 2013

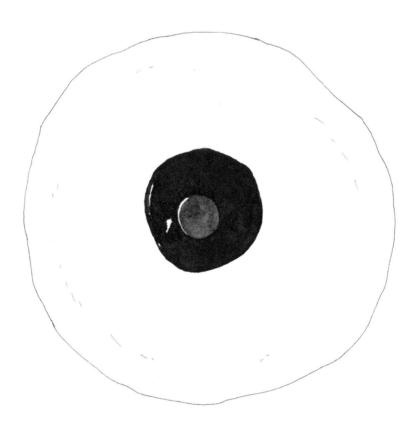

recipe → **p 428**

Mother Mole

Mole madre

What began as a celebratory gift for a former sous-chef turned into a meditation on how a country's culinary traditions can be of the utmost modernity, transmitting an ever-changing statement about time and place. Enrique has been cooking his mole—the same mole—since March 2013, when he made *mole negro* (black mole) in honor of the first anniversary of Quintonil, a restaurant opened by a former Pujol cook in Mexico City. To make the mole, a combination of spices, nuts, herbs, fresh and dried fruits, and seeds that vary from region to region, are toasted on a *comal* (griddle) and ground in a mortar and pestle. Traditionally, a portion from the enormous batch is served at the feast, with the leftovers reheated over the course of a week. For the Quintonil dinner, Olvera stretched the reheating period to fifteen days. After the event, he wondered what would happen if he continued to reheat the mole twice a day indefinitely,

feeding it with new paste when the supply dipped below 10 liters (10½ quarts), as one would a sourdough starter. This he named *mole madre.* (Olvera also likens the process to the solera system that is used to make sherry, in which old wines are combined with younger ones.) The ingredients change with the seasons: the mole might include hazelnuts, macadamias, or almonds, or a mixture of all three. The chiles, tomatoes, and fruits change, too.

"Mole is probably the best metaphor and certainly the cornerstone of Mexican gastronomy," Olvera told *T Magazine.* The magical complexity of his mole is everchanging, subtle one day, fruity or nutty the next. Because he considers this mole to be its own self-contained universe, Olvera serves it alone on a plate, surrounding a small circle of *mole rojo* (fresh red mole), and accompanied only by a basket of tortillas.

selected by **Howie Kahn, Christine Muhlke**

Chui Wai-Kwan SEVENTH SON
China 2013

recipe → **p 429**

Roast Suckling Pig

The famous Cantonese-style suckling pig served at this high-end Hong Kong restaurant was made famous by Chui Wai-Kwan's father in the 1970s at his Michelin-starred restaurant, Fook Lam Moon, often dubbed the "tycoon's canteen." Chui, one of seven brothers, worked in the kitchens of his father's restaurant, which became a successful chain, for more than fifty years. After a falling-out in 2009, he left the business. Some food lovers remain faithful to the original, while others have followed Wai-Kwan to his smaller, more modern restaurant, opened in 2013, where the suckling pig rivals that of his father's. While the recipe for a seasoned young pig roasted at high heat in a charcoal-burning oven is traditional, the result at Seventh Son is exemplary, with thin, cracking skin yielding to flavorful fat and custardy pork. Regulars at this high-end restaurant know to order the suckling pig in advance and ask for it to be plated in two servings: first the crisp skin, which is accompanied by thin pieces of steamed bread, allowing the diner to make a decadent crackling sandwich (especially delicious when a sprinkling of sugar is added). The next course is the bone-in pieces of exceptionally tender meat. It is celebratory banquet fare at its best. Wai-Kwan can often be seen greeting guests from behind the desk near the entrance of his breakaway restaurant, which has also grown into a chain of seven. And, like his father, Wai-Kwan has since earned his own Michelin star.

selected by **Susan Jung**

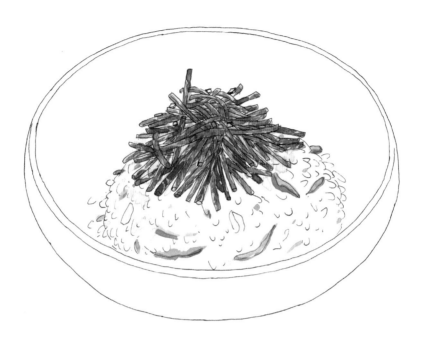

recipe → p 429

Mixed Rice with Vegetables and Korean Beef Tartare

Yukhoe bibimbap

La Yeon was the first restaurant to receive three stars in Michelin's inaugural guide to Seoul. It was a vote of confidence for chef Kim Sung-Il, who, going against the trend of fine-dining restaurants serving molecular or European cuisine, is dedicated to showcasing traditional Hansik cooking, with its reliance on top-quality Korean rice, vegetables, seafood, and beef (which, many say, is better than Japanese because it's just as tender but not nearly as fatty). Sung's food also stands out for its subtlety and delicacy, perhaps recalling the flavors of Korean food as it may have been before Portuguese settlers introduced chiles to the country in the sixteenth century. Sung's take on the traditional final rice course of the *kaiseki*-like Hansik-style meal is not a hearty, spicy bibimbap. Rather, this interpretation is a light, fresh mixture of rice and finely chopped vegetables with ruby red matchsticks of julienned frozen raw beef, or *yukhoe*, on top. When mixed into the rice, they soften and release the sweet flavor of the marinade. This rice and "beef tartare" is both the antithesis and the essence of bibimbap. Stronger flavors find their way into the course through the banchan, or accompanying small dishes. These include pickled vegetables and garlic, a bright and gently spiced pear kimchi, and a soybean soup made with a powerful shrimp (prawn) stock.

selected by **Susan Jung**

Mashama Bailey THE GREY
United States 2014

recipe → **p 430**

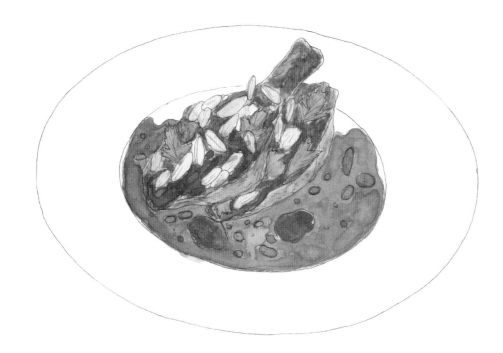

Chicken Country Captain

The origin of Country Captain, a chicken curry, is most often associated with Savannah, Georgia, a major spice trade port of the eighteenth century. Truly representative of regional Southern cuisine, the dish draws upon a hodgepodge of cultures and culinary traditions—and chef Mashama Bailey's version at The Grey has caused a sensation. Bailey's homage to Country Captain is a half-chicken, roasted and partially deboned, served on a piece of toasted sourdough soaked with pan juices and slathered in a sauce inspired by Country Captain flavors: a relish of turmeric, currants, and green bell pepper. Even though The Grey's food is defined by its Lowcountry (coastal South Carolina) and African flavor profiles, Bailey finds inspiration in the traditions and ingredients around her, paying homage to the city in subtle and inventive ways. Opened in 2014 in a formerly segregated Greyhound bus terminal, The Grey addresses the problematic history of the American South without being burdened by it: from the self-classification of its food as "soulful" as opposed to soul food, to the photos on the walls of the First African Baptist Church, and even through its business practice—a co-ownership between a white restaurateur, Johno Morisano, and a black executive chef. Bailey has had a version of Country Captain Chicken on the menu since opening week. This modern take on a Savannah classic shows the depth—both in flavor and history—of regional Southern cuisine, and is a fine example of the city's burgeoning culinary renaissance.

selected by **Howie Kahn**

243

recipe → **p 430**

Cacio e Pepe in a Bladder

Cacio e pepe in vescica

A classic Italian dish meets French haute cuisine. Elemental meets theatrical. The two traditions don't clash. In fact, the result is brilliant: a mash-up of the Roman pasta cacio e pepe and the traditional *en vessie* technique, in which a meat is gently steamed in a pig's bladder (see Chicken in a Bladder, page 61). A server arrives at the table with an otherworldly inflated orb on a plate. He shakes it dramatically, then punctures it to reveal steaming, al dente rigatoni, evenly coated in butter, black pepper, and cheese—enough for two, because this show should be shared. First, there is the exceptional flavor, the familiar cheese and pepper elements haunted by the aromas concentrated in the bladder. The *cacio e pepe* takes on a flavor similar to *pasta alla gricia*, which is traditionally made with guanciale and cheese, to become something new. Also new is the cooking technique, in which pasta is steamed within the bladder, rather than boiled. Somehow Riccardo Camanini manages to serve it perfectly cooked, even though he is unable to test it without ruining the surprise. More than just great pasta, Camanini has given it personality—a relative first in Italy.

When still a teenager, Camanini cooked with the legendary Gualtiero Marchesi before moving to England to learn from Raymond Blanc at Le Manoir aux Quatr'Saisons. He had read about the ancient Roman technique of using animal organs to cook in a book written by the Pope's chef in the 1500s. Why not try it with pasta? After a long experimentation, the combination of cheese and liquid in cacio e pepe provided the necessary elements. Not that the bladders don't occasionally explode. "It's like when you buy shoes from an artisan," Camanini has said, "you find these imperfections because they're handmade. Cuisines need to be like this."

selected by **Andrea Petrini**

recipe → **p 431**

Superiority Burger

When the talented Brooks Headley left his job as the award-winning pastry chef at New York's much-lauded Italian restaurant Del Posto to follow his dream, those who knew him well were not surprised when the dream turned out to be opening a vegetarian burger stand (!) with extremely limited seating. In fact, his tiny East Village shop is the perfect expression of Headley's background as a punk drummer (many in the US hardcore scene of the 1980s were vegetarian or vegan). The star here is the namesake Superiority Burger, a compact puck on a squishy potato roll that takes its inspiration from California's In-N-Out burger, but cranks up the umami to 11. "This is not fake meat, nor is it trying to be," Headley notes in the *Superiority Burger Cookbook: The Vegetarian Burger Is Now Delicious*. What it is is the answer to what a burger lover is supposed to love once beef—that increasingly unsustainable protein—is removed from the equation.

The burgers are a perfected mixture of roasted carrots, red quinoa, chickpeas, sautéed onions, toasted fennel seeds, potato starch, parsley, crushed walnuts, hot sauce, lemon juice, and more. The crisp, moist grain and legume croquettes are topped with roasted tomatoes (more umami!), chickpea mayo, pickles, and melted Muenster cheese. They are portable, lovable, and infinitely more satisfying than the Frankenburgers being cranked out by labs, filled with pea protein and fake blood. They are, Headley notes, "absolutely recognizable as food." Thanks to Headley, the vegetarian burger is now 100 percent delicious.

selected by **Christine Muhlke**

Riccardo Camanini LIDO 84

Italy 2014

recipe → **p 432**

Spaghettoni in Butter and Fresh Yeast

For decades, it has been surprisingly rare to find spaghetti at the higher end of modern restaurants in Italy. But in 2014, Lido 84 chef Riccardo Camanini put it back on the map when he sent out a dish of radical simplicity that became the symbol of the new Italian cuisine. In Camanini's hands, the three ingredients of pasta, butter, and brewer's yeast resulted in a completely balanced dish in which, like any great work of art, nothing could be added, and nothing taken away. Chef Alain Ducasse described it to then-president François Hollande as the best pasta he had ever tasted, then put it on the menu at his restaurant in the Plaza Athénée.

Camanini made his name with pasta, which he has been pushing in bold new directions. His Cacio e Pepe in a Bladder (see page 244), another example of a subtly reformulated classic that broke barriers, has ranked high on many critics' lists of favorite dishes. Of course, Camanini's spaghetti isn't just plain noodles with butter and a twist on Parmesan (many vegans use nutritional yeast to re-create the umami effect of cheese). This is carefully sourced spaghettoni (thick spaghetti)—made by a 120-year-old company that extrudes pasta through dies made of gold (in order to achieve a superior texture)—and purposely cooked just past al dente. The pasta water clinging to the noodles is emulsified with a mixture of three kinds of butter from Beppino Occelli in Piedmont. On the plate, the strands are sprinkled with brewer's yeast that has been dehydrated for five hours until it achieves the aroma of caramelized hazelnuts and the crisp, airy texture of meringue. On the tongue, this trinity evokes the perfect brioche (or, you could say, bread and butter), with an undercurrent of acidity. It is gone in just three bites, but the memory of this masterpiece lingers long after.

selected by **Andrea Petrini**

recipe → **p 432**

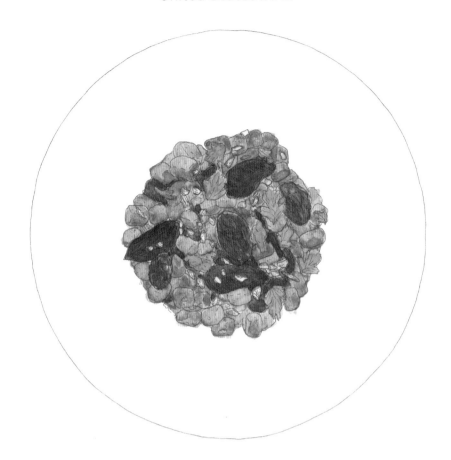

Curried Baby Goat with Sweet Potato Gnocchi

Brined, braised, and shredded, chef Nina Compton's goat curry, flavored with cashews and coconut, arrives at the table alongside delicate sweet potato gnocchi. Rather than simply serve the goat curry with rice, the New Orleans chef wanted to showcase her culinary journey and the techniques she acquired along the way. While the goat is an ode to her upbringing on the West Indies island of Saint Lucia and coming-of-age in Jamaica, the gnocchi were informed by her time cooking for chef Scott Conant at Scarpetta in Miami Beach. Compton wasn't even sure that it would sell when she added it to Compère Lapin's menu, but since opening in New Orleans' warehouse district, the restaurant has continued to buy a goat every week to fulfill the three hundred orders of curry they regularly field. Compère offers up a complex and exotic fusion of Caribbean, French, and Italian cuisines, hidden behind the humble and unassuming face of regionally identifiable dishes and iconic New Orleans plates. One doesn't feel intimidated by the food here like one might at New York's Restaurant Daniel, where Compton trained under Daniel Boulud. Instead, she's focused on making food that's universally enjoyable. She infuses an aspect of approachability into her innovative, ingredient-driven cuisine, bridging the gap for individuals who may not be so familiar with the novel flavor profiles she's serving up. Compton's ability to draw inspiration from her childhood and update it with a contemporary American sensibility are bravely declared by this signature dish.

selected by **Christine Muhlke**

recipe → **p 433**

Vegetable Pulp Burger

When the Michelin-starred farm-to-table chef Dan Barber tackled the problem of food waste, he didn't stay in the fine-dining sphere. Instead, he reached a broad spectrum of diners during a casual four-week pop-up called wastED, with a menu that included plays on dishes like chicken wings and bagels and lox. It was the juice pulp burger that struck the public's imagination, not just for its thoughtfulness and creativity, but for its legitimate deliciousness.

Concerned about how much was left behind during the production of the juice that he saw New Yorkers consuming every day (the juice company he contacted was throwing away a ton of pulp per day), Barber and his culinary director, Adam Kaye, used a base of beet, apple, and celery pulp, beefed up, so to speak, with tofu, eggs, and grains and umami-fied with mushrooms, Parmesan, miso, Worcestershire, and soy sauce.

The buns were made from day-old bread from the Balthazar bakery in Manhattan, reconstituted with milk and water, the cheese rejects from a Vermont cheesemaker. The ketchup was rendered from beets from a farmer's field trials, while the "pickle butts" were the ends sliced off by a pickle processor. The result was not an abstemious veggie burger, but something so satisfying that it enjoyed a limited, sold-out run at the popular New York City burger stand Shake Shack.

Barber not only reached new customers, he also spread the gospel by inviting guest chefs to cook for a night, bringing with them a dish that addressed the waste in their own kitchens. As a result, chefs like Grant Achatz, Daniel Humm, Dominique Crenn, Enrique Olvera, and others were challenged to create with the scraps around them. They returned to their own stoves with a new vision of how good garbage can taste.

selected by **Howie Kahn, Christine Muhlke**

recipe → **p 435**

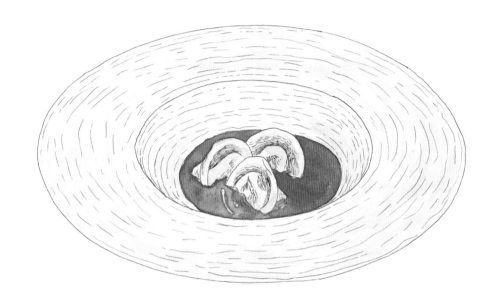

Wild Boar Cappelletti with Plum Broth

Cappelletti al cinghiale, brodo di susine

In the grapevine-covered hills of Friuli, near the Slovenian border, self-taught chef Antonia Klugmann is masterminding highly personal plates from the ingredients around her. "I love to create things that have never existed before," she said in a interview for the gastronomy symposium ChefAlps. "However, my new creations always imply personal experiences as well as continued traditions. I want people to notice this diversity when they taste my dishes." Such diversity is evident in this starter, a classic hat-shaped pasta, filled with a traditional farce of wild boar from the surrounding hills cooked with garlic, onion, celery, carrot, and rosemary and then swirled with cream. The surrounding broth, however, is the revolutionary element: what looks like tomato sauce is in fact the brightly flavored juice of ripe plums from her gardens. It is this whiplash between traditional and modern, sweet and gamey, sternness and lightness that has caused Klugmann's food to be admiringly referred to as "Dr. Jekyll and Mrs. Hyde." Deliciousness at its highest, most balanced ying and yang level.

While Klugmann, who dropped out of her law studies in Trieste to cook, admires the food of such modernists as Ferran Adrià, Massimiliano Alajmo, Pier Giorgio Parini, and Niko Romito, her food is rooted in the gardens and fields outside her kitchen window: "Customers don't come here for me but for the land and the community," she has said. "Either the land works or I become a spaceship floating in nothingness." Using the best products and applying her intellect and heart to what's around her rather than following trends or copying styles has set her apart. With Klugmann, the local is radical.

selected by **Andrea Petrini**

Hisato Hamada WAGYUMAFIA
Japan 2016

recipe → **p 436**

Kobe Beef Cutlet Sandwich

Gyukatsu sando

The *katsu sando*, a popular Japanese sandwich made from a crisp, panko-breaded fried pork cutlet on crustless, pillowy milk bread, has long been a casual food typically sold cold in convenience stores. But in 2016, the self-taught Tokyo chef Hisato Hamada gave it a serious upgrade, with a price tag to match. At his members-only Wagyumafia restaurants, which sprang from a pop-up series celebrating the luxuriously fatty beef of the country's wagyu cattle, his Kobe Beef Cutlet Sandwich swaps a thick slice from the chateaubriand cut of wagyu for the common pork, breading and frying it and topping it with a secret blend of sweet soy and vinegar before placing it between lightly grilled slices of bread. The crusts are then cut off to create a perfectly symmetrical two-bite rectangle, the rare, ruby-red flesh of the buttery beef revealed and ready for its Instagram close-up. It's hard to say whether it was social media or the countless articles about the sandwich's price tag that took it over the top: at 20,000 yen ($180/£135) for two of those little rectangles, this is not your everyday sando.

Hamada has positioned himself as a champion of preserving the tradition of wagyu beef, a time- and labor-intensive way of raising cattle. And these sandwiches seem to be accomplishing his aim of education (and profit): "A lot of Japanese people think the sandwich is crazy," Hamada told Vice. "But everybody just shuts up once they bite it. It's so obvious even my kids can understand … What I'm doing is ingredient-driven, so I want to make very simple food that people don't have to think about or study." Except, of course, they have. Cities worldwide, including Sydney, San Francisco, Los Angeles, and Paris have taken up the *sando*, adding their own cheffy spins.

selected by **Susan Jung**

recipe → **p 436**

Whole Hog Barbecue

Whole Hog Barbecue is an art that traces its history from Native American communities to Southern plantations to roadside restaurants in the 1920s, and Rodney Scott is one of the foremost practitioners of this particular style. He smoked his first pig at Scott's Bar-B-Que, his family's store in Hemingway, South Carolina, at eleven years old, and has been perfecting the twelve-hour process ever since. Today, he seasons the pork with salt, pepper, and some secret spices, then mops the skin with a sauce of vinegar, peppers, and citrus as it cooks. When the hog is done, he chops it into rough pieces and serves it either on a plate beside his famous collards or on a roll.

Scott's rise to prominence underlines the racial and class tensions that have always been at the center of barbecue. Scott and his family had been cooking in their small town in poor, rural South Carolina for nearly thirty years before receiving any kind of recognition or media attention. But in 2009, journalist John T. Edge wrote about the little shop, and suddenly, anointed by a white Southern food expert, Scott's Bar-B-Que became a pilgrimage-worthy destination for barbecue connoisseurs. Journalists and chefs poured in; the late Anthony Bourdain included Scott's Bar-B-Que in a South Carolina episode of *Parts Unknown*.

Scott's cooking is deeply regional; the wood he uses to smoke his hogs comes from Pee Dee, the South Carolina region where he's lived since early childhood, as do his hogs. Even though he's expanded his operations to include a somewhat fancier restaurant in Charleston and another in Birmingham, Alabama, he still sources his pigs from the same farmers, who respect his cooking so much they'll make the two-hour drive to Charleston to deliver the meat.

selected by **Howie Kahn, Christine Muhlke**

Calum Franklin HOLBORN DINING ROOM
United Kingdom 2016

recipe → p 437

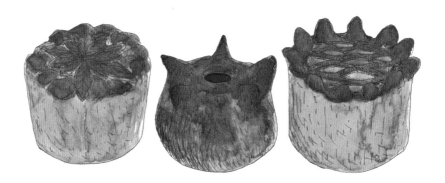

Meat Pie

When chef Calum Franklin came across a bunch of tarnished vintage molds in the basement of London's century-old Rosewood hotel, he knew that they were for savory pies. He just didn't know how to make one worthy of the equipment. He and his thirty cooks began more than six months of study into the history of the traditional English dish, updating a variety of old-school pastries with the best ingredients from the UK, whether pork or beef and vegetables from Cornwall or freshly milled flour from Northumberland. While diners may have initially expected to see the hearty, filling, plain-topped pies they knew from childhood or the country's disappearing pie and mash shops, they were stunned to find them elaborately decorated and exquisitely refined. The pies became so popular that the Holborn Dining Room opened The Pie Room (with a street-side service window called the Pie Hole) in 2017.

Because this is a twenty-first-century dish, Instagram has been key to its success. Almost 100,000 followers track Chef Calum's latest object of research and obsession, be it the weekly beef Wellington or a curried mutton pie served with mango salsa. The pork pie required meticulous recalibration once the kitchen decided that the traditional ratio of meat to pastry was too heavy, resulting in imbalanced cooking. Their rendition contains a rich yet not too heavy farce, the elaborate pastry a perfectly even gold. Not only is Franklin happy to be teaching new generations of cooks the techniques needed to make the pies that are part of the country's home-cooking history, he is also proud to be burnishing the image of British food itself. Above all, he's happy to have revived an almost-vanished art in British gastronomy.

selected by **Susan Jung**

Claude Bosi CLAUDE BOSI AT BIBENDUM
United Kingdom 2017

recipe → **p 437**

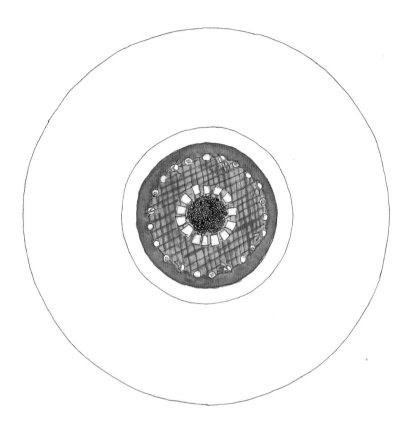

Duck Jelly

One of the most elegant forms of surf and turf in London since its debut in 2017, Bibendum chef Claude Bosi's starter of smoked sturgeon, duck consommé, and osetra caviar actually traces its roots to both Hong Kong and Paris. Bosi is a Lyon-born chef who trained with Alain Passard at L'Arpège and Alain Ducasse at the Plaza Athenée before making his name in London at his own restaurant, Hibiscus. He joined Sir Terence Conran's Bibendum (named for the Michelin Man character, whose old headquarters the restaurant is situated within) and quickly earned it a Michelin star. After tasting an appetizer of eel and duck in Hong Kong, Bosi spent two years developing this dish. He drew from the legendary Caviar Jelly with Cauliflower Cream that Joël Robuchon served at Jamin in

1981 (see page 117), placing a layer of flavorful puréed onion soubise at the bottom of the bowl and fixing it in place with a rich duck jelly set using the gelatin from duck bones and cow's feet. Diced cubes of cold-smoked sturgeon—rich and fatty, with an earthy smokiness—surrounds a generous dollop of its own eggs. Emulating Robuchon's famous, painstakingly perfectionist circle of dots near the rim of the bowl, Bosi renders his in brightly flavored fennel purée to cut the richness of the sturgeon, each dot punctuated with a miniscule slice of chive. It is a technically thrilling work of art that reminds diners of the skill required of true haute cuisine, while the unusual pairing of ingredients is a note of modern playfulness that speaks to Bosi's provocative personality.

selected by **Richard Vines**

253

Tomos Parry BRAT
United Kingdom 2018

recipe → **p 439**

Whole Turbot

A signature dish born of a signature dish, London chef Tomos Parry was so inspired by the grilled turbot served at Elkano in Spain's Basque Country (see page 89) that he made it the centerpiece of the menu at Brat, an elegantly considered restaurant with quality ingredients at the core of its cooking. Custom grills were installed on the second floor of a former pole-dancing club, and Parry spent eighteen months collaborating with a metalworker in Somerset to design the fish-shaped grill baskets. ("We probably could have got some from Spain, but where's the fun in that?" he told the *Guardian*.) He sources his turbot—"brat" being old Northumberland slang for the unattractive flatfish—not from the Bay of Biscay but from Cornwall and Devon. Parry and his cooks slowly grill the fish over low-temperature lumpwood charcoal embers for about thirty-five minutes, turning it frequently and misting it from a spray bottle with a vinaigrette until the skin has a golden, lightly blistered char. It is then allowed to "relax" in the mouth of the restaurant's wood oven to coax out the gelatinous juices, which are whisked together with the vinaigrette to make a pil-pil emulsion that bastes the fish once more before serving.

The fish that is presented is a marvel: the fins crisp enough to eat; the flesh meaty and seductively sticky from the slowly rendered gelatin. Brat's servers guide diners through the best bits—ones that they might typically overlook—including the prized nuggets of the cheeks, the rich meat to be pried from the collar, and the sweet, snowy-white fillets. As Guardian critic Jay Rayner put it in one of Brat's many glowing reviews, "This is the pinnacle of a meal with many high points."

selected by **Richard Vines**

The illustrations in *Signature Dishes That Matter* were commissioned by Phaidon to bring to life the dishes selected by the curators. Choosing to use illustration meant that a book could be created that would otherwise be impossible. The dishes included in this book range from the eighteenth to the twenty-first century, so photographs for many of the dishes do not exist. With illustration, there was the exciting opportunity to represent every dish, even if there wasn't an exact original visual representation to reference. These illustrations are not meant to be perfect recreations: they are artistic impressions, each one hand sketched and hand inked.

There was extensive research to achieve the best possible illustration for each dish. That included a wide range of historical sources— from illustrations and manuals to modern reinterpretations by culinary historians, chefs, and food writers. This allowed for the possibility to showcase, in color, dishes that had until now not been seen or depicted in a realistic way. The illustrated dishes help to create a visual narrative to accompany each page. These illustrations are inventive, colorful, and beautiful.

Under consideration were the original plating styles, the vessels in which the dishes were cooked, and any special plates that were presented to the restaurant diner. There was a need to adapt the style throughout, due to the diverse nature of the dishes— some were boldly minimal, others a riot of detail and color.

Therefore, the illustrations in *Signature Dishes That Matter* have a very important role, to guide for a complete understanding of the dish. They needed to convey both the personalities and attributes of food from all over the world.

The illustrator is Adriano Rampazzo, a former chef whose career bridges illustration and food. He is based in São Paulo.

recipes

Gelato

Procopio Cutò
Le Procope
France 1686

page 18

Red Grouse

Thomas Rule
Rules
United Kingdom 1798

page 19

The recipes included here are reproduced in their original form, using both UK and US English, in order to preserve the intention, spelling, and syntax of the author.

The recipes do not include measurement or temperature conversions, unless where originally given.

For any recipes that have been kept secret or are otherwise unavailable, a brief description of the dish appears instead.

Procopio Cuto's original recipe from his café doesn't exist, but we know that he sweetened his fruit-flavored ices with honey instead of sugar, and that he added salt to the ice for faster freezing. Gelato has more milk (and less cream) than ice cream, and is typically made without egg yolks.

You will find this wild game bird on the British Isles. They can be hunted Monday through Saturday (good luck, they are very fast). Cook this dark meat without any seasoning—so it is only flavored by the heather it eats and its natural environment. To stay true to the original process, stuff any notes about the grouse order into a shotgun cartridge, then send to your kitchen on the lower level through a copper pipe. While the original recipe does not exist, you could braise or roast it, after of course first taking out the shot.

Vol-au-vent

Marie-Antoine Carême
Pâtisserie de la rue de la Paix
France early 1800s

page 20

Having already spoken of the vol-au-vent under the head of Puff Paste (see below), I shall only observe here that after finishing it as there directed, put it in a moderate oven and take it out when it has acquired a fine reddish colour. Then empty it, but at the same time examine the inside, and if any parts of it appear too thin, fasten them on some of the pieces you have taken from the inside, and then egg the whole of the inside lightly, in order to make all of the loose parts of the vol-au-vent stick well together. Afterwards put it for a few minutes in the mouth of the oven. All these precautions are necessary to prevent the sauce from running out when the crust of the vol-au-vent is not thick enough to hold it.

To make puff paste
Twelve ounces of fine sifted flour, twelve ounces of butter, two drams of fine salt, and the yolks of two eggs.

Manner of working – Having placed the twelve ounces of flour on the board, make a small hole in the middle; in which put the two drams of fine salt, the yolks of two eggs, with nearly a glass of water; and with the ends of the fingers of your right hand gradually mix the flour with the ingredients, adding a little water when necessary, till the paste is of proper consistence, rather firm than otherwise. Then prove it by leaning your hand on the board, and working it for some minutes, when the paste will become soft to the touch, and glossy in appearance.

Care must be taken in mixing the flour with the liquid ingredients that they do not escape; and that the paste be very lightly gathered together, to prevent it forming into lumps, which render it stiff and very difficult to be worked, thereby in some degree causing failure, which is easily to be ascertained by the paste, when drawn out, immediately receding, which arises from its having been clumsily and irregularly inter-mixed. To remedy this, let it be carefully rolled out, and place here and there upon it five or six small pieces of butter, each of the size of a nutmeg; when, after well-working it as before, it will acquire the degree of softness necessary.

It is important to observe that this paste should be neither too stiff nor too soft, but of a proper medium; yet it will be better when it is a little too soft than when too stiff. The same process must be attained to in winter as in summer; though many persons pretend that this kind of paste should be made stiffer in summer than in winter, on account of the difference of the two seasons. As far as regards the hardness of butter, this mode of reasoning has certainly some truth in it; for really, inasmuch as the winter is favourable to our work, so does the summer render our operations troublesome and difficult, and prevents them sometimes from having the desired effect, particularly in the making of puff paste, which during this season cannot be easily made to look well without having been exposed to, or struck by, the coolness of the ice, which gives to the butter the same degree of hardness it has in the month of January. The reason why summer paste should not be softer than that made in winter is this; if, when the paste is soft, it be buttered, and afterwards placed on ice, as is practised in summer, the butter, which is a greasy substance, will become quickly congealed by the coldness of the ice; while the paste, which is only a moist body, will scarcely be affected by it; and, consequently, the butter being frozen and the paste soft, it will follow that, in working it, the butter not being held by a paste sufficiently firm to unite with it, will break in small pieces, and after having received the two first turns, will appear in small lumps like large peas. Then rolling it, and again placing it on the ice, the cold acts with greater force on the small particles of butter, which quickly become like so many icicles, and the paste, in consequence, will be completely spoiled; for, in baking, these particles of butter melt, and separating themselves from the →

259

Vol-au-vent

paste, render it incapable of uniting with them.

What has been here stated is not a frivolous explanation, for practice proves it in the clearest manner. The same thing happens in winter, when the butter has not been sufficiently worked, and the paste is rather soft; for though the season be favourable to the making of paste, yet care must be taken to work the butter to such a degree of softness as is necessary for making paste, which then does not require to be so very firm.

Our business during the summer season (from May to September) requires the greatest exactness and closet application. When the paste has been made as above, take three-quarters of a pound of butter, in pieces, which for twenty minutes has been in a pail of spring-water, thoroughly imbued with a few pounds of ice, well washed and pounded, and squeeze and work it well in a napkin, in order to separate the water from it, and at the same time to render it soft, and, above all, of an equal substance: then as quickly as possible, roll the paste, on a marble slab, into a square, and placing the butter in the middle, cover it with an equal thickness of paste, by raising the paste over it. After rolling it out to about three feet in length, fold it into three equal parts;

now roll it to a greater length, and put it quickly on a plate lightly sprinkled with flour, then cover it with ten pounds of pounded ice, and afterwards put a sheet of paper on the paste, and upon that a plate with one pound of ice. This plate serves to keep the surface of the paste cool, and also to prevent its becoming soft by the action of the air. After three or four minutes remove the plate, and then turn the paste upside down, instantly covering it as before. This operation should be performed three times, in the same manner, and with the same precautions. Lastly, roll it out once or twice, according to what you intend making of it, and use it as expeditiously as possible, lest the extreme heat of the season should render it too soft to handle, or prevent its having the desired effect in baking.

Thus, in less than half an hour, it is possible to make very fine puff paste; having previously every thing ready – the ice pounded, the butter frozen, and the oven quite hot; for otherwise it can not be done. This is important, as it is sometimes hours before the oven can be made hot; and therefore the paste should not be begun to be made till the oven is half heated.

Another method of making puff paste
I prepared my paste as before, rather softer, however, then usual, and worked

it for about a minute, when it became sleek and supple, as if it had been made some time. (In winter, I added to it butter that had been well worked, and then rolled it twice every four minutes, so that in twelve minutes my paste had been rolled six times.) I then let it rest for a minute, and afterwards worked my butter, keeping it all the time in the pail with ice and spring-water, where, as in the former case, I had put it before I began; then, having worked it for about two minutes, I squeezed it well in a napkin, folded it in the paste, and gave it quickly two turns, taking care to roll it lightly, in order to prevent the butter from penetrating through it. I placed it afterwards in ice between two plates, as described before, and after turning it twice in five minutes, rolled it twice more and replaced it immediately in the ice, where I left it only three minutes, and then gave it two more turns, and placed it again in the ice, where I left it two minutes longer. In the meantime, I put a very thin piece of fine paste, lightly wetted, on a small baking-plate, and after removing the puff paste from the ice, I placed in the centre a lid of eight inches in diameter, running the point of my knife along its edge, and cutting out a round piece to make a vol-au-vent, the top of which I egged lightly, and then marked, with the point of my knife, a circle of one-sixth of an inch

Buddha Jumps
Over the Wall

Zheng Chunfa
Ju Chun Yuan
China early 1800s

page 21

deep, and at the distance of three-quarters of an inch from the edge; this I did to mark the cover of the vol-au-vent, which I placed immediately in a clear oven. I have sometimes made this kind of paste with very great success, in less than fourteen minutes.

It is necessary to lightly flour both sides of the paste when you roll it, in order to prevent its turning grey in baking. And also, when the paste has been rolled for the last time, to put it into the oven in the course of four, six, or eight minutes at farthest; for, if it be left twenty or twenty-five minutes before it is baked, it will, instead of being clear and light, become dull and heavy.

What has here been stated, will show the possibility of making fine puff paste in an hour, in three-quarters of an hour, in half and hour, and even in a quarter of an hour, in summer as well as in winter. To make up sixteen pounds of flour into this kind of paste, put one pound of butter to twelve ounces of flour, and give it seven or eight turns in rolling it.

1 kg abalone
1 liter bone broth (stock)
2.5 liters Shaoxing yellow wine
1 chicken
1 duck
1 kg pig's feet (trotters)
500 g sheep's elbow
500 g pork tripe
500 g duck gizzards
250 g soaked sea cucumber
150 g tendon meat
12 boiled pigeon eggs, shelled
500 g winter bamboo shoots
500 g lard
10 g shredded scallion
   (spring onion)
5 g ginger
75 ml soy sauce
75 g crystal sugar
10 g cassia bark

Steam the abalone until soft and tender on a high heat. Add 250 ml of the bone broth and 15 ml of the Shaoxing yellow wine. Steam for another 30 minutes.

Remove the bones of the chicken, duck, pig's feet (trotters), and sheep's elbow. Cut the meats and pork tripe into bite-sized pieces and add, along with the duck gizzard, to the pot. Skim. Remove and flash boil in 250 ml of the broth, adding 85 ml of the Shaoxing yellow wine.

Put the soaked sea cucumber and tendon meat into 150 ml of water and steam on a high heat for 30 minutes.

Shell the boiled pigeon eggs. Flash boil the winter bamboo shoots.

Place the lard in a pan and when melted add the pigeon eggs and winter bamboo shoots. Deep-fry for about 2 minutes.

Leave 50 g of lard in the pan. Add the shredded scallion (spring onion) and ginger, then the chicken, duck, sheep's elbow, pig's feet, duck gizzard and pork tripe, and stir-fry with 75 ml soy sauce, 75 g crystal sugar, the Shaoxing yellow wine, the remaining 500 g of broth, and the cassia bark. Cover the pan and stew for 20 minutes. When ready, scoop out all the ingredients, leaving the broth.

Put 500 ml of fresh water into a Shaoxing yellow wine jar and heat. Drain off the boiling water. Place a bamboo grate at the bottom of the jar, add the cooked chicken, duck, sheep's elbow, pig's feet, duck gizzard, pork tripe and winter bamboo shoots. Add sliced tendon meat and flaked abalone, wrapped in gauze, and add the broth.

Cover the wine jar with a lotus leaf and invert a small bowl on top. Simmer the jar on a charcoal fire for 2 hours. Add the sea cucumber and simmer for 1 hour more. Serve.

Mille-feuille

Marie-Antoine Carême
Pâtisserie de la rue
de la Paix
France 1815

page 22

After giving two pounds and a quarter of puff paste (see page 259) twelve turns, cut out sixteen round pieces, four of which must be eight inches in diameter, four seven and a half, four seven, and four six and a half. Cut out the centres of all of them with a paste-cutter of two inches in diameter; and then cut out another round piece of six inches and a half in diameter, keeping it whole. Egg all these pieces, and after pricking them here and there, put them in a moderate oven, taking them out as soon as the paste is perfectly dry. When cold, place one of the large pieces on another of confectioner's paste, of nine inches in diameter; and then cover the top of the puff paste with half a potful of apricot-marmalade. Put upon this another large piece of puff paste, and cover it with half a potful of red currant jelly. Dispose of all the other pieces of puff paste successively in the same manner, putting the larger ones at the bottom and the smallest at the top, and masking them as you proceed with different kinds of preserves, taking care at the same time not to cover the edges, nor the openings in the centre. When the whole of your sixteen pieces of puff paste have been arranged in this manner, mask the outside of your cake, as expeditiously and regularly as possible, with the whites of six eggs, beaten up and mixed with eight ounces

of very fine pounded sugar, strewing over it some coarser sugar, which has been only bruised and not sifted. Afterwards make a small clear flame at the mouth of the oven, and hold your cake before it, but at the distance of a foot, turning it gently all the time. If the cake be put in the oven, the heat will cause it to fall, and thereby disfigure it very much. Ornament the top of the remaining piece of puff paste, that without an opening in the centre, with méringues; put also a ring of small méringues, of the size of an almond, round the edge; and with some white of egg, fix a handsome rosette in the middle. After lightly covering the whole with very fine sugar, put this piece of paste in the oven, taking it out as soon as it has acquired the same colour as the outside of the cake. When cold, decorate it tastefully with apple or currant jelly, &c. &c. The moment you are going to serve it up, fill the inside of the cake with whipt cream, flavoured with vanilla, and then place the ornamented piece of paste on the top of it. To fill this cake, six pots of preserves, of a pound each, are at least necessary: the shape at one time used to be an octagon, having a small niche in each side for a fountain; while its surface was covered with almond paste of various colours.

Ditto, à la Moderne

After preparing and baking seventeen round pieces of paste, the same as before, cover the top of one of the large ones with a half a potful of apricot marmalade; and then lay another large piece over. Mask the edges of these two pieces with white of egg, prepared as before stated; then roll them over pistachios, chopped very fine; and afterwards put them for ten minutes in a slack oven. Then mask another large piece with currant jelly, cover it as before, and after egging the edges, roll them over some coarse sugar, and put them immediately in the oven. Join the remaining pieces in the same manner, two and two, and after egging the edges as before, roll them alternately on pistachios and coarse sugar. When all your eight cakes are quite cold, place one of them on a round piece of confectioner's paste, the edge of which has been rolled in sugar. Proceed in this manner, beginning with the largest cakes, placing alternately one with a green and another with a white edge, and finally covering the top of each with a preserve. When all your cakes have been disposed of in this manner, place the last piece of puff paste, decorated as directed in the preceding recipe, on the top of the whole. In placing the cakes one on another, take them up in the centre. The inside of this cake is not filled with cream.

Peking Duck

Bianyifang
China 1827

page 23

Lamb Cutlets Reform

Alexis Soyer
Reform Club
United Kingdom 1830s

page 24

This original recipe from Bianyifang is a secret. But we can advise the following: find a specially bred Peking duck that has lived for exactly 65 days. Cook the duck in a closed oven over three days and be sure to glaze the uncooked skin with maltose syrup and marinate with a five-spice powder rub. Once the skin is lacquered, serve in three courses: first the skin with sugar–garlic dipping sauce; then the meat, cut into up to 120 pieces and rolled in pancakes with sweet plum sauce, cucumber sticks, and scallion (spring onion); and finally a broth made from the bones.

Chop a quarter of a pound of lean cooked ham very fine, and mix it with the same quantity of breadcrumbs, then have ten very nice cotelettes, lay them flat on your table, season lightly with pepper and salt, egg over with a paste-brush, and throw them into the ham and breadcrumbs, then beat them lightly with a knife, put ten spoonfuls of oil in a sauté-pan, place it over the fire, and when quite hot lay in the cotelettes, fry nearly ten minutes (over a moderate fire) of a light brown colour; to ascertain when done, press your knife upon the thick part, if quite done it will feel rather firm; possibly they may not all be done at one time, so take out those that are ready first and lay them on a cloth till the others are done; as they require to be cooked with the gravy in them, dress upon a thin border of mashed potatoes in a crown, with the bones pointing outwards, sauce over with a pint of the Sauce à la Reform (opposite), and serve. If for a large dinner you may possibly be obliged to cook the cotelettes half an hour before, in which case they must be very underdone, and laid in a clean sauté-pan, with two or three spoonfuls of thin glaze; keep them in the hot closet, moistening them occasionally with the glaze (with a paste-brush) until ready to serve; the same remark applies to every description of cotelettes.

Sauce à la Reform
Cut up two middling sized onions into thin slices and put them into a stewpan with two sprigs of parsley, two of thyme, two bay leaves, two ounces of lean uncooked ham, half a clove of garlic, half a blade of mace and an ounce of fresh butter, stir them ten minutes over a sharp fire, then add two tablespoonfuls of tarragon vinegar and one of chilli vinegar, boil it one minute, then add a pint of brown sauce or sauce Espagnole, three tablespoonfuls of preserved tomatoes and eight of consommé, place it over the fire until boiling; then put it at the corner, let it simmer ten minutes, skim it well then place it again over the fire, keeping it stirred and reduce until it adheres to the back of the spoon; then add a good tablespoonful of red currant jelly and a half dozen of chopped mushrooms, season a little more if required with pepper and salt, stir it until the jelly is melted, then pass it through a tammie into another stewpan. When ready to serve make it hot and add the white of a hard boiled egg cut into strips, half an inch long and thick in proportion, four white blanched mushrooms, one gherkin, two green Indian pickles and half an ounce of cooked ham or tongue, all cut in strips. Do not let it boil afterwards. This sauce must be poured over whatever it is served with.

Soufflé Potatoes

Jean-Louis-François Collinet
Le Pavillon Henri IV
France 1837

page 25

Soufflés potatoes are like extra-large cut chips (fries). The potatoes are peeled, washed and cut into 3-mm-thick slices.

Cook twice over:

The first time at 150°C, paying close attention that the chips don't change in colour.

Place on a kitchen towel.

The second time at 170–180°C.

The sides separate to form the astonishing soufflé potato.

Tournedos Rossini

Casimir Moisson
Maison Dorée
France 1859

page 26

This original recipe has not been found, but we know that is should be served as an entrée. Pan fry a round of buttery filet mignon and serve each piece on a toasted crouton, topped with pan-seared foie gras and black truffle shavings. Eat while listening to opera, of course.

Russian Salad

Lucien Olivier
The Hermitage
Russia 1860s

page 27

This original recipe went to the grave with Lucien Olivier. He did not even allow his cooks to see how he prepared it, using a special room away from the main kitchen to make it. You can make this at home. First, announce to anyone who is around that you are doing something very secretive and are not to be disturbed. Cube some cooled boiled potatoes, boiled eggs, vegetables, and meats and douse in homemade mayonnaise. Then come out of your room and present it heaping on a plate.

Mapo Tofu

Mrs. Chen
Chen Xingsheng
China 1862

page 28

To make this dish, fry tofu cubes in a wok with bean curd and Szechuan peppercorns, then serve in chili oil. You can add minced beef or pork, too.

Anna Potatoes

Adolphe Dugléré
Café Anglais
France c.1867

page 29

This original recipe does not exist, but with thinly sliced potato rounds, clarified butter, and salt, you can make this at home. Overlap and layer the potatoes with layers of butter, then cover and bake.

Iskender Kebab

Iskender Efendi
Kebapci Iskender
Turkey 1867

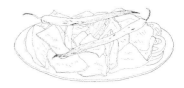

page 30

The original recipe for this kebab has remained a secret, but try this approach. Set up a vertical spit and charcoal grill behind where you'll place the boned lamb. Let the lamb cook while the skewer constantly rotates. Shave the slices and serve on Turkish flatbread—with yogurt, tomato paste (purée), and butter. Eat at the table with a knife and fork.

Baked Alaska

Charles Ranhofer
Delmonico's
United States 1867

page 31

Prepare a very fine vanilla-flavored Savoy biscuit paste. Pour into a vessel one pound of powdered (icing) sugar flavored with vanilla and a pinch of salt, add 14 egg whites, one at a time, and beat the whole forcibly to have it get quite frothy. Whip 14 egg whites to a stiff froth, and put a fourth part into the yolks, also 6 ounces potato fecula and 6 ounces flour, the two latter to be sifted together. As soon as the whole is thoroughly combined add the remainder of the beaten whites.

Butter some plain molds 2¾ inches in diameter by 1½ inches in depth; dip them into fecula or flour, and fill two-thirds full with the paste. Cook, turn them out and make an incision all around the bottom. Hollow out the cakes and mask the empty space with apricot marmalade.

Have some shaped ice cream molds, fill them half with uncooked banana ice cream, and half with uncooked vanilla ice cream; freeze, unmold and lay them in the hollow of the prepared biscuits; keep in a freezing box or cave.

Prepare also a meringue with 12 egg whites and 1 pound of sugar. A few moments before serving place each biscuit with its ice on a small lace paper, and cover one after the other with the meringue pushed through a pocket furnished with a channeled socket, beginning at the bottom and diminishing the thickness until the top is reached. Color this meringue for 2 minutes in a hot oven, and when a light golden brown remove and serve at once.

Omelet

Annette Poulard
La Mère Poulard
France 1888

page 32

In Elizabeth David's *French Provincial Cooking* (1960) she references a letter Annette Poulard sent to M. Robert Viel, a "celebrated Paris restaurateur and collector of a famous library of cookery books."

"Monsieur Viel,

Voici la recette de l'omelette: je casse de bons œufs dans une terrine, je les bats bien, je mets un bon morceau de beurre dans la poêle, j'y jette les oeufs, et je remue constamment. Je suis heureuse, monsieur, si cette recette vous fair plaisir

– Annette Poulard"

Translation: *Here is the recipe for the omelette: I break fresh eggs into a bowl, I beat them well, I put a good piece of butter into the pan, I drop in the eggs, and I stir constantly. I am pleased, sir, if this recipe makes you happy.*

Pastrami Sandwich

Katz's
United States 1888

page 33

The exact recipe for the spice blend (and the wood chip blend for smoking) of this sandwich is a secret. But we know from just looking at the sandwich, and having eaten it, that you need rye bread and beef. Cure the brisket with salt. Rub it with loads of spices (including pepper, coriander, garlic, and onion). Smoke it at a low temperature for two to three days. Then boil the meat—and perhaps you can find a Katz's employee to tell you when it is ready. To stay true to the methods at Katz's, once boiled, put the meat in a vat and put that vat in any shopping cart that you have around. Then take the meat out of the cart to steam it for up to 30 minutes. Slice the meat, put a massive stack in between two pieces of rye bread, and cut in half. Serve on a plate, with the cut sides facing out.

Oysters Rockefeller

Jules Alciatore
Antoine's
United States 1889

page 34

You will never find the original recipe, as the only person who knows the sacred secret is the owner of Antoine's (and maybe one or two employees). If you are finding a shortage of snails, and thereby considering cooking oysters for dinner, you will need to find good quality oysters, ideally from the Gulf Coast off the state of Louisiana. You could try an assortment of greens for the creamy sauce that tops the baked oysters, but do not include spinach.

Pizza Margherita

Raffaele Esposito
Pizzeria di Pietro e Basta Così
Italy 1889

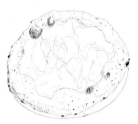

page 35

The original authentic recipe for this was never revealed, but now that pizza is such a popular dish, it can generally be figured out. You'll need crushed tomatoes, fresh mozzarella, and basil leaves. For more details about any rigorous standards you can explore guidelines at the AVPN—True Neapolitan Pizza Association. And please, no other toppings.

Spotted Dick
Sweetings
United Kingdom 1889

page 36

Oxtail Stew
Checchino dal 1887
Italy c.1890

page 37

For the spotted dick
600 g (1 lb 5 oz) plain
   (all-purpose) flour
20 g (4 teaspoons) baking powder
300 g (11 oz) shredded suet
150 g (5 oz) caster (superfine)
   sugar
350 g (12 oz) currants
2 lemons, zest only
600 ml (1 pint) milk

For the custard
400 ml (14 fl oz) milk
400 ml (14 fl oz) double (heavy)
   cream
12 free-range egg yolks
150 g (5 oz) caster (superfine)
   sugar

For the spotted dick
Sift the flour and baking powder into
a large bowl; add the suet, caster
(superfine) sugar, currants and lemon
zest. Mix to combine.

Add the milk and mix to a soft dough.

Pipe the mix into small basins and place
a small circle of greaseproof (wax) paper
on top before closing with a lid.

Place in a steamer and steam for
approximately an hour.

For the custard
Place the milk and cream into a
saucepan and bring to a simmer.

Place the egg yolks and sugar into
a bowl and whisk together until light
and frothy.

Pour on the hot milk and stir well.
Pour the mix back into the pan and
cook over a low heat until just
thickened, stirring constantly with
a wooden spoon.

Serve with the puddings.

2.5 kg of oxtail, fat removed
3 tablespoons extra virgin olive oil
1 small onion, minced
2 cloves of garlic
salt and pepper, to taste
1 glass of dry white wine
   (if possible from the Castelli
   Romani)
2 kg of peeled tomatoes
1 stalk celery, chopped
1 handful of pine nuts
1 small handful of sultanas
   (golden raisins)
grated dark chocolate

Take a large oxtail, wash it well and cut
it into small pieces (along the joints). In
a heavy-bottomed pan put a mixture of
lard and oil over a high heat and add the
tail. When browned, add the onion, two
cloves of garlic, salt and pepper.

After a few minutes, wet with a little
wine and cover with the lid. Cook for 15
minutes, then add the peeled tomatoes.
Cook for another hour, then add a little
hot water, cover well with the lid and
cook slowly for another 5–6 hours, until
the meat detaches from the bone.

Remove the threads from the celery
before boiling it, then add the boiled
celery, pine nuts, sultanas (golden
raisins) and some grated bitter
chocolate to the oxtail sauce. Boil it for
10 minutes and pour this sauce on the
tail when served, naturally warm.

Pressed Duck

Frédéric Delair
La Tour d'Argent
France 1890

page 38

---

2 ducklings from Madame Burgaud
120 g well-seasoned duck gravy

For the Tour d'Argent sauce
2 mixed duck livers
45 ml vintage Madeira
60 ml Cognac
juice of 1 lemon
2 duck carcasses

Roast the ducks in a hot oven (260°C).

Place the chopped livers in a pan and add the Madeira, Cognac and lemon. Reduce.

Remove the duck legs. Set aside and keep warm. Remove the skin from the ducks and slice the fillets lengthwise.

Crush the carcasses with pruning shears or with a knife and put them into a *presse à canard* (duck press) to extract the juices and blood. Add the duck consommé during this process and cook for 25 minutes. Keep stirring the sauce while it reduces to maintain a smooth consistency.

Pass the gravy through a sieve and adjust the seasoning.

Serve with a garnish.

Waldorf Salad

Oscar Tschirky
Waldorf Hotel
United States 1893

page 39

Peel two raw apples and cut them into small pieces, say about ½ inch square, also cut some celery the same way, and mix it with the apple. Be very careful not to let any seeds of the apples be mixed with it. The salad must be dressed with a good mayonnaise.

Peach Melba

Auguste Escoffier
Savoy Hotel
United Kingdom c.1893

page 40

Poach peaches in vanilla-flavoured syrup. Dish them into a timbale upon a layer of vanilla ice cream, and coat them with a raspberry purée.

Club Sandwich

Saratoga Club House
United States 1894

page 41

Have ready four triangular pieces of toasted bread spread with a mayonnaise dressing; cover two of these with lettuce, lay thin slices of cold chicken (white meat) upon the lettuce, over this arrange slices of broiled (grilled) breakfast bacon, then lettuce and cover with the other triangles of toast spread with mayonnaise. Trim neatly, arrange on a plate, and garnish with heart leaves of lettuce dipped in mayonnaise.

Eggs Benedict

Oscar Tschirky
Waldorf Hotel
United States 1894

page 42

Cut some muffins in halves crosswise, toast them without allowing to brown, then place a round of cooked ham ⅛ inch thick and of the same diameter as the muffins on each half. Heat in a moderate oven and put a poached egg on each toast. Cover the whole with Hollandaise sauce.

Crepes Suzette

Henri Charpentier
Café de Paris
Monaco 1895

page 43

4 eggs
3 tablespoons flour
3 tablespoons milk
a pinch of salt
1 tablespoon water

For the sauce

Small piece of orange peel
Small piece of lemon speel
2 tablespoons vanilla sugar
5 ponies of blended maraschino, curacao and kirchwasser
¼ lb sweet butter

Stir the ingredients smoothly to the consistency of thick olive oil. Heat a frying pan (skillet) with 2 tablespoons of butter. When it bubbles, pour in enough batter to cover the bottom of the pan. Move the pan to spread it thinly. After one minute, turn the pancake upside down, then continue turning until it is nicely browned. Fold in half, and again to form a triangle.

Tarte Tatin

Caroline and Stéphanie Tatin
Hôtel Tatin
France c.1898

Tonkatsu

Motojiro Kida
Rengatei
Japan 1899

page 44

page 45

Combine the sugar and peel, cover and leave for two days. To make the sauce, melt the butter in a pan. When it begins to bubble pour in three ponies of the blended cordials. This will catch fire. When the fire goes out add the sugar and peel. Plunge the pancakes into the boiling sauce. Turn them, and add two more ponies of blended cordials. Let the fire die down then serve.

200 g butter
150 g sugar
3 kg Reine des Reinettes
   (King of the Pippins) apples
200 g shortcrust pastry
   (basic pie dough)

Line a springform tin (pan) with the butter and sugar. Add the apples cut into large quarters.

Cover the apples with the shortcrust pastry. Bake at 220°C for 15 to 20 minutes.

Take the tart out of the oven and cook on high heat until it reduces down. Turn the tin regularly.

Allow it to cool for 1 hour.

Put back on high heat and continue to turn the tin until you see caramel at the bottom of the tin.

When the caramel is a red amber colour, take the tarte out of its tin.

Serve the tarte tatin lukewarm, without any accompaniments.

Dredge pork loin strip cutlets in flour, egg, and panko, then deep-fry in vegetable oil. Serve with rice and miso soup and carrots and potatoes (or sliced raw cabbage).

271

Nagasaki Champon
Chin Heijun
Shikairo
Japan 1899

Paris-Brest
Louis Durand
Pâttiserie Durand
France 1910

Fettuccine Alfredo
Alfredo di Lelio
Alfredo alla Scrofa
Italy 1914

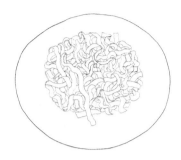

page 46

page 47

page 48

chicken and tonkotsu soup
pork slices
cabbage
scallion (spring onion)
beansprouts
small oysters
shrimp (prawns)
squid
cloud ear mushrooms
kamaboko
noodles

The soup is cooked with 2–3 whole chickens, pork bones and chicken bones for 3–4 hours. The detailed recipe of this soup and the proper heat level is a secret.

Heat an iron pan until it smokes, add the meat and let it draw out the oil, then stir-fry with the rest of the ingredients on high heat to add flavour.

Add the soup and let it boil, then add the noodles. Cook on high heat until ready.

This secret has been closely guarded by family for over 100 years, so it will not appear here. Figure out how to get pastry in the shape of a wheel, then bake the ring. Top it with sliced almonds, then slice in half horizontally. Fill with a praline-hazelnut cream whipped with butter, and top with powdered sugar. Then go ride a bicycle to commemorate its origins.

While this original recipe is officially a secret, you simply need fettuccine and lots of Parmesan cheese and butter. Please do not adapt by adding flour and/or cream cheese. Serve hot.

Black Forest Cake

Josef Keller
Café Ahrend
Germany 1915

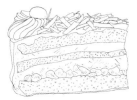

page 49

The recipe is a closely guarded secret, but if you begin with chocolate pie crust layered with chocolate sponge cake, sour cherries, whipped cream, kirsch, and chocolate shavings, you are on your way.

Vichyssoise

Louis Diat
Ritz-Carlton Hotel
United States 1917

page 50

Follow the recipe for the Soup Bonne Femme potato and leek soup (below) and strain the soup. Add 2 cups each of hot milk and light cream and bring the soup back to a boil, stirring it occasionally to prevent scorching. Strain the soup through a fine sieve, cool it, stirring occasionally to keep it smooth, and strain again. Stir in 1 cup heavy cream and chill the soup thoroughly. To serve, sprinkle each portion with finely chopped chives.

For the Soup Bonne Femme

Remove the green tops and roots from 4 leeks, clean them well, and cut them into ⅓-inch dice. There should be about 1½ cups. (If leeks are not available, use 2 onions.) Peel and dice a medium onion. There should be ½ cup. Melt 1 tablespoon butter in a large soup kettle, add the leeks and onion, and cook them slowly, covered, for a few minutes, or until they are soft but not brown, stirring occasionally with a wooden spoon. Cut 4 or 5 peeled potatoes into ½-inch dice. There should be 3 cups. Add the potatoes, 4 cups hot water and 2 teaspoons salt to the kettle, and simmer the soup, covered for 30–40 minutes, or until the potatoes are soft. Add 2 cups hot milk and 1 tablespoon butter. Taste the soup and correct the seasoning with salt.

French Dip Sandwich

Philippe Mathieu
Philippe's
United States 1918

page 51

4½ oz roast beef
French roll
2 oz Au Jus
1 oz slice cheese (optional)

Philippe's uses prime bottom round in preparing the classic sandwich. The meat, which is roasted on a mirepoix, is topped with rock salt and garlic while being roasted. The pan drippings are taken from the roasting pans and combined with a twenty-four-hour house broth (stock) consisting of vegetables, beef bones, and spices to create the "Au Jus."

Philippe's prepares the sandwich a few ways. Double dip is the house favorite, in which the top and bottom portions of the French roll are dipped in the Au Jus. Customers can also request a single dip (top portion of roll dipped) or a "wet" sandwich.

Other popular sides that accompany the sandwich are homemade potato salad, macaroni salad, and coleslaw. Pickled eggs are a must try as well.

Served with Philippe's hot mustard made in house.

Hot Pâté

Marie Bourgeois
Hôtel Bourgeois
France 1920

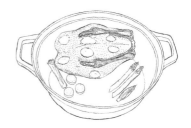

page 52

750 g pork
1 poultry bird
a bit of foie gras
some truffles
980 g flour
740 g butter
5 eggs
salt
lard
pepper

For the marinade
carrots
shallots
parsley
peppercorns
butter
glass of Madeira
1 litre stock

To make a marinade, brown carrots, shallots, parsley and peppercorns in butter, together with the Madeira and stock, until softened and cooked.

Cut up the meat and poultry. Marinate them overnight.

Make a pâté stuffing out of the foie gras, poultry liver and truffles.

Prepare the pastry with the flour, fresh butter, half a glass of water, the eggs and a pinch of salt.

Knead the butter with the flour, make a well in the middle and break in the eggs, then mix all the ingredients together.

Line the bottom and sides of a mould with a light layer of lard. Line the mould with the pastry.

Debone the bird, remove the hard parts and skin, cut the pork finely and mix the meat. Lightly season. Fill the mould with the meat and arrange the stuffing in the middle. Cover and leave to cook in the oven on a low heat for 1½ hours.

Serve hot to get the same subtle aromas that won Mère Bourgeois – the first woman to achieve this title – four Michelin stars in 1933.

Chicken in Half Mourning

Eugénie Brazier
La Mère Brazier
France 1921

page 53

1 fine truffle
1 fine bresse chicken (or any
    high-quality chicken) of less than
    a year, weighing about 1 kg
carrots
leeks
mustard
gherkins
Girotte plums in vinegar
sea salt

Slice the truffle across into circles about 4 mm thick. Slip the slices under the skin of the breast and thighs of the chicken. Fold up the chicken in a tight muslin cloth (cheesecloth). Tie it up with string under the wings and thighs to keep it in place.

In a large casserole – a *faitout* – put some carrots and the leeks. Fill it halfway with water. Bring to the boil. As the water bubbles plunge the chicken in and make sure it is just covered by the water. Leave to cook gently for 45 minutes.

It is a good idea to leave the chicken in its broth for 30 minutes before serving. Serve the chicken simply with its vegetables out on the table with mustard, gherkins, Girotte plums in vinegar and sea salt.

Green Goddess Dressing

Philip Roemer
Palace Hotel
United States 1923

page 54

1 cup mayonnaise
½ cup sour cream
¼ cup snipped fresh chives or
   minced scallions (spring onions)
¼ cup minced fresh parsley
1 tablespoon fresh lemon juice
1 tablespoon white wine vinegar
3 anchovy fillets, rinsed, patted dry,
   and minced
salt and freshly ground pepper
   to taste

Stir all the ingredients together in a small bowl until well blended. Taste and adjust the seasonings. Use immediately or cover and refrigerate.

Caprese Salad

Grand Hotel Quisisana
Italy c.1924

page 55

beefsteak tomato
fior di latte mozzarella
fresh basil
Maldon salt
oregano

The distinctive Quisisana input comes from the fior di latte mozzarella. Other recipes indicate the bufala variety, but this style of mozzarella actually came into the picture rather recently (from the 1980s), while the traditional mozzarella has always been fior di latte.

Caesar Salad

Caesar Cardini
Caesar's Place
Mexico 1924

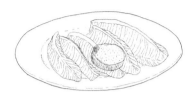

page 56

The original recipe for this classic salad has been reinterpreted many times over the years, but the basic elements always stay the same.

Crush together a few garlic cloves and anchovy fillets. Add olive oil, fresh lemon or lime juice, Worcestershire sauce, Parmesan and egg, and then toss with whole leaves of romaine lettuce.

Serve with croutons made from rounds of stale French bread, brushed with olive oil and toasted.

Salsa Golf

Luis Federico Leloir
Mar del Plata Golf Club
Argentina 1925

page 57

Chiffon Cake

Harry Baker
The Brown Derby
United States 1927

page 58

The original recipe is nowhere to be found, but the story goes that it was born out of boredom. If you mix mayonnaise and ketchup, with a bit of Cognac and Worcestershire sauce, you may get it just right. Or perhaps, when you're bored like Luis Federico Leloir was when he made this, you'll come up with another sauce. The creator of this condiment also went on to win a Nobel Prize. So maybe you will also do that.

2¼ cups sifted cake flour (spoon lightly into cup, don't pack)
1½ cups sugar
1 tablespoon baking powder
1 teaspoon salt
½ cup cooking (vegetable) oil
5 unbeaten egg yolks (medium)
¾ cup cold water
2 teaspoons vanilla
grated rind of 1 lemon (about 2 teaspoons), if desired
1 cup egg whites (7 or 8)
½ teaspoon cream of tartar

Preheat the oven (see pan size and corresponding temperature below). Sift an ample amount of cake flour onto a square of paper. Measure and sift together into a mixing bowl the cake flour, sugar, baking powder and salt.

Make a well and add in the following order the oil, egg yolks, cold water, vanilla and grated lemon rind. Beat with a spoon until smooth.

Measure into large mixing bowl the egg whites and cream of tartar. Whip until whites form very stiff peaks. They should be much stiffer than for angel food or meringue. Do not underbeat.

Pour the egg yolk mixture gradually over the whipped egg whites – gently folding with a rubber scraper just until blended! Do not stir! Pour into the ungreased pan immediately.

Bake in a 10-inch tube pan (ring mould) 4 inches deep in the preheated oven at 325°F for 55 minutes, then at 350°F for 10–15 minutes, or in a 9 × 13 × 2-inch oblong pan at 350°F for 45–50 minutes.

The cake is baked if the top springs back when lightly touched.

Immediately turn the pan upside down, placing the tube part of the pan over the neck of a funnel or bottle, or resting the edges of a square, oblong or loaf pan on two other pans. Let hang, free of the table, until cold. Loosen from the sides of the pan with spatula. Turn the pan over and hit the edge sharply on the table to loosen.

Omelet Arnold Bennet

Jean Baptiste Virlogeux
Savoy Hotel
United Kingdom 1929

page 59

100 g smoked haddock
milk, for poaching
5 g butter
150 ml whole eggs
20 ml double (heavy) cream
2 g salt
chopped chives, to serve

Glaze
40 ml Hollandaise
10 ml double (heavy) cream
1 egg yolk
20 g Parmesan cheese, grated
10 g Swiss cheese, grated
100 g mornay sauce

Mornay sauce
200 g haddock trimmings (scraps)
1 litre milk
100 g butter
100 g flour
50 g Swiss cheese, grated
50 g Parmesan cheese, grated

To make the mornay sauce, infuse the haddock trimmings (scraps) in the milk and strain. Melt the butter, add the flour and make a roux.

Add the milk and make a béchamel. Finish with the Swiss and Parmesan cheeses and strain.

For the glaze, mix all ingredients together and set aside.

For the omelet, gently poach the haddock in milk and flake.

Add the butter to a non-stick frying pan (skillet), add the whole egg liquid, cream and salt, and make a soft omelet. Place it in a copper pan, add the flaked smoked haddock, cover the omelet with the glaze and gratinate it under the salamander until golden brown. Serve garnished with chopped chives.

Lobster Roll

Harry Perry
Perry's
United States c.1929

page 60

The original recipe for the lobster roll was never documented, but we want to share a modern take on this classic dish for inspiration, so you can make it at home. Mix bite-sized lobster meat pieces with butter, lemon juice, ground black pepper, and salt. Then serve in a hot dog-style bun, buttered and grilled, and open on top.

Chicken in a Bladder

Fernand Point

La Pyramide

France 1930s

page 61

Philly Cheesesteak

Pat Olivieri

Pat's King of Steaks

United States 1933

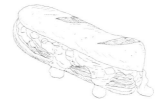

page 62

Husband and Wife Lung Slices

Guo Zhaohua and
Zhang Tianzheng

Fuqi Feipian

China 1933

page 63

Singe and clean a nice young hen from Bresse weighing about 3½ pounds (1.6 kg). Soak it in some ice water for 4 hours so the flesh will remain very white. In a separate bowl clean and soak a pork bladder adding some coarse (kosher) salt and vinegar to the water.

Pound the chicken liver in a mortar with 4 ounces (120 g) of fresh truffles, ½ pound (225 g) of foie gras, 1 egg to bind the forcemeat, salt, pepper, and a dash of brandy. Stuff the chicken with this mixture and truss it.

Place the trussed chicken into the rinsed and dried pig's bladder with the closure in the back. Add two good pinches of coarse (kosher salt, a pinch of pepper, 1 cup (250 ml) of Maderia wine and 1 cup (250 ml) of brandy. Close the opening very securely and prick the bladder a number of times to prevent it from bursting while it cooks.

Roast the chicken in a simmering consommé for an hour and a half, along with some turned potatoes, some carrots, turnips and the white part of leeks or some rice pilaf. Open the bladder at the table on serving, slitting at the back of the chicken. A subtle aroma will waft out – which prepares one perfectly to taste and enjoy the results of this marvellous hermetic cooking.

1 jar processed cheese sauce
6 tablespoons soybean oil
1 large Spanish onion, cut into
  large dice
24 oz rib eye steak, thinly sliced
4 crusty Italian rolls
sweet green and red peppers
  sautéed in oil (optional)
mushrooms sautéed in oil
  (optional)

Melt the cheese sauce in a double boiler (water bath) or in the microwave and keep warm until ready to use.

Heat an iron skillet (frying pan) or a nonstick pan over medium heat.

Add 3 tablespoons of oil to the pan and sauté the onion to the desired doneness. Remove the onion.

Add the remaining oil and sauté the slices of meat quickly on both sides. Return the onion to pan, with the peppers and mushrooms if using, and heat all the ingredients through.

Spread the cheese sauce on the rolls. You MUST spread the sauce on the roll to ensure you get a bite of cheese with every bite of meat. Divide the meat mixture between the rolls. If you like extra cheese, drizzle it on top of the steak once added to the roll.

The original recipe has never appeared anywhere. To make it at home, combine thin slices of beef with offal (such as lungs, tripe, tendon, heart). The dish should be served cold in a very spicy sauce with Szechuan peppercorns, sesame paste, five-spice powder, scallions (spring onions), and lots of red chili oil.

Hot Chicken

Thornton Prince III
Prince's Hot Chicken Shack
United States c.1936

page 64

This secret recipe has never been revealed. If you too want to get back at someone with some very spicy chicken, add cayenne pepper and incredibly hot chili to your fried chicken. Just be sure to put it on top of two slices of bread to soak up the fiery oil—all topped with a couple of sweet dill pickle slices. And if you can't quite figure it out and it's still the middle of night, you can always stop by to get some at Prince's in Nashville, since it's open until 4:00 a.m.

Cobb Salad

Robert Cobb
The Brown Derby
United States 1937

page 65

½ head of iceberg lettuce
½ bunch watercress
1 small bunch chicory
½ head romaine
2 medium tomatoes, peeled
2 breasts of roasting chicken
6 strips (rashers) crisp bacon
1 avocado
3 hard-boiled eggs, shelled and chopped
2 tablespoons chopped chives
½ cup crumbled Roquefort cheese
1 cup Brown Derby Old-Fashioned French Dressing (see below)

Cut finely the lettuce, watercress, chicory and romaine and arrange in a salad bowl. Cut the tomatoes in half, remove the seeds, dice finely and arrange over the top of the chopped greens (salad leaves). Dice the breasts of chicken and arrange over the top. Chop the bacon finely and sprinkle over the salad. Cut the avocado in small pieces and arrange around the edge of the salad. Decorate the salad by sprinkling over with the chopped eggs, chopped chives, and crumbled cheese. Just before serving mix the salad thoroughly with the French dressing.

Brown Derby Old-Fashioned French Dressing
makes about 1½ quarts

1 cup water
1 cup red wine vinegar
1 teaspoon sugar
juice of ½ lemon
2½ teaspoons salt
1 teaspoon ground black pepper
1 tablespoon Worcestershire sauce
1 teaspoon English mustard
1 clove garlic, chopped
1 cup olive oil
3 cups vegetable oil

Blend together all the ingredients except the oils. Then add the olive and vegetable oils and mix well again. Chill. Shake before serving. This dressing keeps well in the refrigerator. Can be made and stored in 2-quart Mason jar.

Prime Rib

Lawry's
United States 1938

page 66

1 bag (5 lb) rock salt
1 (4-rib) standing rib roast
   (rib of beef)
Lawry's Seasoned Salt

Preheat the oven to 350°F. In a heavy roasting pan, spread the rock salt evenly over bottom; place a wire roasting rack on top of the salt.

Sprinkle the fatty cap of the meat with Lawry's Seasoned Salt. Place the meat on the rack, fatty side up. Make sure the rock salt does not touch the beef.

Insert an oven-safe meat thermometer into the thickest part of the meat, making sure it does not touch the bone. Roast the prime rib in the oven until the thermometer registers 130°F for rare, 140°F for medium. Or roast for approximately 20–25 minutes per pound. Remove from the oven and let stand for 20 minutes before carving.

Using a sharp knife, slice the meat across the grain for serving. Discard the rock salt. Serve with vegetable sides of your preference. We recommend creamy mashed potatoes!

Gunkan Sushi

Hisaji Imada
Ginza Kyubey
Japan 1941

page 67

The recipe has not been written down and shared publicly. To attempt to make this sushi, add rice vinegar and salt to your rice. Then let the rice sit before shaping it into a small oval, wrapping nori seaweed around the sides, and topping with raw fish of your choice.

Nachos

Ignacio Anaya
Victory Club
Mexico 1943

page 68

1 tablespoon canola (rapeseed) oil
3 corn tortillas
1 cup shredded (grated) longhorn
   cheese, about 3 oz by weight
12 pickled jalapeño slices

Preheat the oven to 350°F.

Brush the oil on both sides of each tortilla, cut each into quarters, and bake them in a 350°F oven for 15–20 minutes. They will turn a darker brown, but do not let them burn.

Distribute the shredded cheese among the tortilla triangles. Place a slice of jalapeño on each.

Bake the triangles in a 350°F oven for about 5 minutes, until the cheese is bubbly. Alternately, you can place them under the broiler (grill) for a minute or so. Keep a close watch so that they do not burn.

Poke

Helen Chock
Helena's Hawaiian Food
United States 1946

page 69

Helena's recipe is simply for fish, limu and onion. The precise quantities are a secret—simply adjust to taste.

French Onion Soup

Au Pied de Cochon
France 1947

page 70

---

600 g onions
150 g unsalted butter
2 liters beef stock
a sprig of thyme
6 bay leaves
half a baguette
300 g Gruyère cheese, grated
salt and pepper

Finely chop the onions and sweat them in butter for 30 minutes.

Add the beef stock and herbs, season and boil for 5 minutes.

Ladle the soup into a bowl, add chunks of grilled baguette and then sprinkle the Gruyère on top.

Put it under the grill and then serve.

Loco Moco

Richard and Nancy Inouye
Lincoln Grill
United States 1949

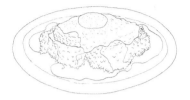

page 71

The recipe does not exist, but it can be easily approximated. On a plate, place two scoops of white rice, a hamburger, and lots of mushroom gravy. For a more modern version, add a fried egg if you'd like. You can eat this any time of day—with a knife and fork or chopsticks.

Carpaccio

Giuseppe Cipriani
Harry's Bar
Italy 1950

page 72

Chimichanga

Monica Flin
El Charro Café
United States 1950s

page 73

---

3 lb boned shell of beef/strip steak
  (2.35 kg), to yield 1½ lb after
  trimming (675 g)

For the Carpaccio Sauce
makes about 1 cup (250 ml)
¾ cup (170 ml) homemade
  mayonnaise
1–2 teaspoons Worcestershire
  sauce, to taste
1 teaspoon fresh lemon juice
2–3 tablespoons milk
salt
freshly ground white pepper

To make the sauce, put the mayonnaise
into a bowl and whisk in the Worcestershire sauce and lemon juice. Whisk in
enough milk to make a thin sauce that
just coats the back of a wooden spoon.

Taste the sauce and adjust the seasoning
with some salt and pepper as well as
more Worcestershire sauce and/or
lemon juice to taste.

For the carpaccio, trim every bit of far,
sinew, or gristle from the boned shell,
leaving a small cylinder of tender meat.
Chill the meat well. Using a razor-sharp
knife, slice the meat paper-thin.
Arrange the slices of meat on six salad
plates to cover the surface completely.
Drizzle the sauce decoratively over the
meat ribbons. Serve immediately.

---

6 flour tortillas (12 to 14 inches)
meat or poultry filling
about 1½ quarts vegetable oil
2 firm-ripe avocados (about ½
  pound each)
2 tablespoons lime juice
1 (16 oz) can red chili or enchilada
  sauce
3 cups shredded lettuce (iceberg
  and/or romaine) and/or red
  cabbage
2 cups (about ½ pound) shredded
  Jack and/or cheddar cheese
sour cream
tomato or fruit salsa

Lay one tortilla flat. Fold one-third
up over the center. Spoon one-sixth of
the filling across the doubled portion,
leaving a 2-inch border at each end.
Roll the tortilla once, fold in the ends,
then roll snugly to enclose the filling.
Secure the seam with toothpicks
(cocktail sticks). Repeat to fill the
remaining tortillas.

In a 5- to 6-quart pan (at least 10
inches wide) or a 14-inch wok over
a high heat, bring about 1 inch of
oil to 360°F. Adjust heat to maintain
the temperature.

Using a wide metal spatula, lower one
chimichanga at a time into the hot oil,
filling the pan without crowding.

Fry until golden on all sides, turning
occasionally, 6–8 minutes total per
chimi. Transfer to a paper towel-lined
10 × 15-inch pan. Keep warm in a 225°F
oven. Repeat to fry the emaining
chimichangas.

Meanwhile, peel, pit (stone), and thinly
slice the avocados. Moisten the slices
with the lime juice. In a 1- to 1½-quart
pan over medium heat, warm the chili
sauce; pour into a small bowl.

Line a platter or plates with the
lettuce. Remove the toothpicks from
the chimis and place, seam down, on
the lettuce. Sprinkle the chimis evenly
with 1 cup of the cheese and garnish
with the avocado. Serve with the
remaining cheese and the chili sauce,
sour cream, and salsa, to taste.

Piri-Piri Chicken
Radium Beer Hall
South Africa 1950s

page 74

This secret recipe can be tried at home: just marinate chicken overnight and then grill (barbecue) over charcoal. The marinade should be a purée of very hot chiles, red wine vinegar, olive oil, garlic, paprika, and bay leaves. Enjoy with a salad and beer.

Green Gumbo
Leah Chase
Dooky Chase's
United States 1950s

page 75

For the greens
6 cups coarsely chopped collard (spring) greens
5 cups coarsely chopped mustard greens
4 cups coarsely chopped turnip greens
3 cups coarsely chopped watercress
3 cups coarsely chopped spinach
3 cups coarsely chopped lettuce
2 cups coarsely chopped cabbage
2 cups coarsely chopped beet (beetroot) tops
1 cup coarsely chopped carrot tops
2 cups coarsely chopped onions
⅓ cup chopped garlic

For the meat
½ lb smoked sausage, such as andouille, chopped into 1-inch chunks
½ lb smoked ham, chopped into 1-inch chucks
½ lb beef brisket, chopped into 1-inch chunks
½ lb beef stew meat, chopped into 1-inch chunks
½ cup vegetable oil
½ lb hot spicy sausage, such as chaurice or chorizo, chopped into bite-size pieces
3 tablespoons all-purpose (plain) flour
1 teaspoon dried thyme, or 1 tablespoon fresh thyme leaves

1 teaspoon salt
½ teaspoon cayenne pepper
rice, for serving
filé powder (optional)

To make the greens, combine all the greens in a 12-quart stockpot. Add the onions, garlic, and enough water to cover the greens by 1 inch. Place the stockpot over medium-high heat and bring it to a rolling boil, then adjust the heat and maintain a lively but gentle boil and cook for 30 minutes. The greens will cook down and become tender. Use tongs or a long-handled spoon to stir the greens now and then as they simmer.

When the greens are very tender, remove the pot from the heat. Let it stand until the pot cools down enough to handle, 30 minutes or so. Meanwhile, place a large strainer (sieve) or a colander over another large cooking pot or bowl. Strain the greens cooking liquid into the other pot, and set the cooked greens aside on a platter or in a large bowl to cool to room temperature.

To make the meats, put the smoked sausage, ham, beef brisket and beef stew meat in the stockpot and add about 1 quart of the cooking liquid from the greens, reserving the remaining liquid. Place the pot over medium-high heat and bring it to →

Green Gumbo

Royal Hare

Raymond Oliver
Le Grand Véfour
France 1950s

page 76

a lively boil. Lower the heat to maintain an active, visible simmer. Cook, stirring now and then, until all the meats are fragrant and tender, 30–45 minutes.

Meanwhile, heat the vegetable oil in a large heavy skillet (frying pan) over medium-high heat until hot. Scatter in the spicy sausage and cook, tossing often, until it is nicely browned and cooked through, 10–12 minutes. Transfer the cooked sausage to a bowl, leaving 3 tablespoons of the fat in the skillet for making the roux. (Add vegetable oil if you don't have enough.)

When the cooked greens are cool enough to handle, purée them in a food processor or a blender until smooth. Work in batches, taking your time and adding some of the reserved greens cooking liquid to the food processor to help grind up the greens as needed. (You could also gently squeeze the greens to release some of their cooking liquid and finely chop them by hand.)

Heat the grease in the skillet over medium-high heat until hot but not smoking. When a pinch of flour blooms on the surface when added to the grease, scatter in the flour and stir quickly and thoroughly, combining the grease and the flour evenly into a thick, smooth roux. Continue cooking,

stirring often, as the roux turn from white to lightly browned, about 5 minutes.

Add the roux to the pot of chopped meats and stir to mix everything well. Add the puréed greens to the pot, along with 1 quart of the greens cooking liquid. Stir to mix everything together. Place the pot over medium-high heat and bring it to a gentle boil. Adjust the heat to maintain a lively simmer and cook, stirring often, until the gumbo is pleasantly thick, fragrant, and well combined, about 20 minutes.

Add the reserved sausage to the gumbo along with the thyme, salt, and cayenne. Stir to mix everything together. Cook at a gentle simmer for 40 minutes more. Remove from the heat and serve the gumbo hot or warm, with rice, passing the filé powder at the table to add as desired.

This original recipe has not been documented, but to start you will need a hare. Stuff it with pork, lard, mushrooms, eggs, spices, Armagnac, a lot of garlic, and shallots, with the lungs, liver, and heart. Cook in wine for four hours.

Bananas Foster

Ella Brennan
Brennan's
United States 1951

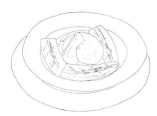

page 77

General Tso's Chicken

Peng Chuang-kuei
Peng's Garden Hunan Restaurant
China 1955

page 78

---

1 oz butter
½ cup light brown sugar
¼ teaspoon cinnamon
1½ oz banana liqueur
½ banana per person
1½ oz aged rum

Combine the butter, sugar, and cinnamon in a flambé pan.

As the butter melts over medium heat, add the banana liqueur and stir to combine.

Cook the bananas until they begin to soften (1–2 minutes).

Tilt back the pan to slightly heat the far edge. Once hot, carefully add the rum and tilt the pan toward the flame to ignite the rum.

Stir the sauce to ensure that all of the alcohol cooks out.

Serve the cooked bananas over ice cream and top with the sauce in the pan.

---

4 boned chicken thighs with skin
   (about 350 g/12 oz total)
groundnut (peanut) oil for
   deep-frying
6–10 dried red chillies
2 teaspoons finely chopped
   fresh ginger
2 teaspoons finely chopped garlic
2 teaspoons sesame oil

For the marinade
2 teaspoons light soy sauce
½ teaspoons dark soy sauce
1 egg yolk
2 tablespoons potato flour
2 teaspoons groundnut (peanut) oil

For the sauce
1 tablespoon double concentrate
   tomato purée (paste) mixed with
   1 tablespoon water
½ teaspoon potato flour
½ teaspoon dark soy sauce
1½ teaspoons light soy sauce
1 tablespoon clear rice vinegar
3 tablespoons everyday stock or
   water

Unfold the chicken thighs and lay them, skin side down, on a chopping (cutting) board. (If some parts are very thick, lay your knife flat and slice them in half.) Use a sharp knife to make a few shallow criss-cross cuts into the meat – this will help the flavours to penetrate.

Then cut each thigh into bite-sized slices, 5 mm/¼ inch or so in thickness. Place the chicken slices in a bowl.

To make the marinade, add the soy sauces and egg yolk to the chicken and mix well, then stir in the potato flour and lastly the oil; set aside while you prepare the other ingredients.

Combine the sauce ingredients in a small bowl; set aside. Use a pair of scissors to snip the dried chillies into 2-cm/¼-inch pieces, discarding the seeds as far as possible.

Heat enough oil for deep-frying to 180–200°C/350–400°F. Add the chicken and deep-fry until it is crisp and golden. (Fry in batches if needed.) Remove the chicken with a slotted spoon and set aside. Pour the oil into a heatproof container, and clean the wok if necessary.

Return the wok to a high flame with 2–3 tablespoons of the oil. Add the dried chillies and stir-fry briefly until they are fragrant and just changing colour (do not burn them). Toss in the ginger and garlic and stir-fry for a few seconds longer, until fragrant. Then add the chicken and the sauce and stir vigorously to coat the pieces in sauce. Remove from the heat, stir in the sesame oil and then serve.

California Roll
Ichriro Mashita
Tokyo Kaikan
United States 1960s

page 79

The recipe does not exist, but it is popular enough that it can easily be re-created. You will just need vinegared rice, avocado, crab, and cucumber, rolled so the rice is on the outside. Place six pieces on a plate, serve with wasabi and soy sauce, and enjoy. If you eat it in California, all the better.

Ceviche
Pedro Solari
Cevicheria Pedro Solari
Peru 1960s

page 80

sole
onion
lemon juice
Limo chiles
salt

Dice the fish. Slice the onion and soak in water for 10 seconds. Add a few drops of lemon juice to keep it from becoming bitter.

Remove the chile membranes and finely chop the chiles.

Place the fish in a glass bowl. Drain the onion and add to the fish. Follow with the chile, the lemon, and season with salt. Accompany the ceviche with cassava (yucca), corn, and chile cream, which is Tío Pedro's touch.

Tsukemen
Kazuo Yamagishi
Taishoken
Japan 1961

page 81

This original recipe was never made public. For a version to create at home, you will need a very big bowl of chilled wheat noodles with a bowl of hot broth—topped with egg, fermented bamboo shoots, scallions (spring onions), and pork leg cooked in soy sauce. That broth itself could take a half a day to prepare and traditionally included animal bones and feet, mackerel, ginger, leeks, and so much more. The noodles are dipped in the broth to eat.

Tea-Smoked Duck

Cecilia Chiang
The Mandarin
United States 1961

page 82

1 duck, about 5 lb, washed clean
2 gallons cold water
6 pieces five-star anise
1 tablespoon Szechuan
    peppercorns
6 fresh scallions (spring onions)
6 slices ginger root
1 teaspoon saltpeter
1 tablespoon salt
4 tablespoons wet jasmine
    tea leaves
vegetable oil, for deep-frying

Combine in a pot the water, anise, peppercorns, scallions (spring onions), ginger root, saltpeter and salt. Bring to the boil, and boil for about 15 minutes; then cool until lukewarm.

Submerge the duck in the lukewarm mixture for about 36 hours. Turn every 12 hours to ensure that the bird is thoroughly marinated.

Place the duck in a smoke oven over briquettes covered with the wet jasmine tea leaves for 30 minutes; then remove and steam in a bamboo steamer for about 1½ hours. Hang up to cool and allow the excess grease to drain off. (At this stage, the duck can be kept in a refrigerator for at least a week.)

Deep-fry until the skin turns dark brown. Using a sharp knife or cleaver, disjoint the thighs, legs and wings; then cut the rest into 1-inch squares.

Grand Marnier Soufflé

Charles Masson
La Grenouille
United States 1962

page 83

For the pastry cream
½ vanilla bean (pod), split
1 pint (480 ml) whole (full-fat) milk
113 g granulated sugar
6 medium egg yolks (reserve and
    refrigerate whites overnight)
34 g custard powder or cornstarch
    (cornflour)
33 g all-purpose (plain) flour
13 g sweet (unsalted) butter

For the soufflé
Unsalted butter and sugar to
    coat ramekin
140 g pastry cream (one No. 8
    ice-cream scoop)
30 g Grand Marnier
50 g egg whites
10 g granulated sugar
confectioners' (icing) sugar

Prepare the pastry cream a day ahead (it makes 6 servings, and will keep refrigerated for 3 days). Combine the vanilla and milk in a medium pan and bring to a boil. Turn the heat to low.

Cream the sugar and egg yolks in large bowl. Add the powder and flour, and mix until smooth. Pour about a ladle of the hot milk into the flour mixture, and stir to dilute everything, then pour back into the milk and whisk. Bring back to a boil while whisking quickly.

When the mixture reaches a boil, turn off the heat and add the butter. Beat the mixture with a wire whisk or an electric mixer until the pastry cream has cooled to room temperature. Store in refrigerator with plastic wrap (clingfilm) applied directly to the surface.

To make the soufflé: Preheat the oven to 400°F. Brush a soufflé ramekin (approximately 5 inches wide and 2 inches deep) with butter and fill halfway with sugar. Spin to coat well, then discard the remaining sugar.

Heat the pastry cream in a double boiler or bain-marie over high heat, adding the Grand Marnier when the cream is warm. Whisk the egg whites and sugar together by hand or with a mixer until soft peaks form. Fold the whites into the pastry-cream mixture, one half at a time.

Spoon into a ramekin, and tap it on the counter to settle. Bake for about 8 minutes.

Remove with large spatula or oven mitts (gloves), and dust with confectioners' (icing) sugar.

Hawaiian Pizza

Sam Panopoulos
Satellite Restaurant
Canada 1962

page 84

To make this original pizza-without
-a-recipe a success, you will need
a typical tomato and cheese pizza,
pineapple (canned, to be true to the
first of its kind), and some chopped
ham. Slice. Eat.

Salmon Escalope with Sorrel

Pierre Troisgros
La Maison Troisgros
France 1962

page 85

½ fillet fresh salmon (600 g)
a bouquet of fresh sorrel
4 shallots
30 cl Sancerre
12 cl Noilly Prat
30 cl fish stock
30 cl double (heavy) cream
½ lemon
salt and white pepper

Choose a meaty, thick fillet of salmon
and remove the small ridges in the
flesh. Cut into six 100 g pieces. Place
them, side by side, between two sheets
of baking (parchment) paper and gently
tap them with a mallet to even them
out to a 5 mm thickness.

Remove the stalk from the sorrel, wash,
then shred any larger leaves. Peel and
finely chop the shallots.

Combine the white wine, vermouth
and shallots in a skillet (frying pan).
Reduce until the liquid becomes syrupy.
Add the fish stock and reduce further,
then add the cream and bring to a boil.
Add the sorrel leaves, then take off the
heat. Season with salt and pepper.

Heat a large nonstick frying pan. Salt
the salmon pieces on both sides. Cook
for 15 seconds on both sides.

Ladle the sorrel sauce onto a plate and
place the salmon on top.

Tiramisu

Alba Campeol and Roberto Linguanotto
Le Beccherie
Italy 1962

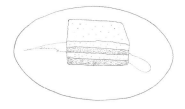

page 86

2 teaspoons sugar
1½ cups (350 ml) hot espresso
    coffee
4 egg yolks
½ cup (100 g) sugar
1 lb (450 g) mascarpone cheese at
    room temperature
30 savoiardi (ladyfinger cookies/
    sponge fingers)
2 tablespoons bitter cocoa powder

Dissolve 2 teaspoons of sugar in the
coffee while it is still hot. Let the coffee
cool to room temperature.

Beat the egg yolks and ½ cup (100 g)
of sugar in a bowl until they become
light and fluffy. Combine with the
mascarpone cheese.

Dip half of the ladyfingers (sponge
fingers) in the coffee and place them in
a serving dish in a single layer.

Spread half of the mascarpone cream
on the ladyfingers.

Dip the remaining ladyfingers in the
coffee and place them in the dish in
a second layer.

Spread the remaining mascarpone
cream on the ladyfingers.

Sprinkle with the cocoa powder and
refrigerate for 3–4 hours.

Buffalo Wings
Teressa Bellissimo
Anchor Bar
United States 1964

page 87

½ lb fresh chicken wings (12–16
   whole wings)
½ cup Frank & Teressa's Original
   Sauce

If preferred, split the wings at the joint.
Pat dry. Deep-fry at 350°F for 10–12
minutes, or bake at 425°F for 45
minutes, until completely cooked and
crispy; drain.

Put into a bowl, add the sauce and toss
until the wings are completely covered.
Serve with blue cheese dip and celery.

Sushi
Jiro Ono
Sukiyabashi Jiro
Japan 1965

page 88

This most famous of sushi masters will
not reveal his recipe, but know that his
rice is sprinkled with rice vinegar, with
the raw fish placed on top. Please
remember that the fish must be sliced
at a very precise moment when it can
be served at room temperature, then
brushed with just a hint of soy sauce.
Be sure Jiro Ono's twelve rules for
eating sushi are abided by. Also make
sure there is no music playing.
Perfection is beautiful. And delicious.

Grilled Turbot
Pedro Arregi
Elkano
Spain 1967

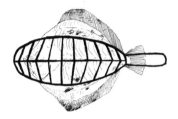

page 89

2 turbot
salt
Agua de Lourdes (a concoction of
   oil, vinegar and salt based on a
   secret recipe from Aitor Arregi's
   grandmother)

Start by preheating the grill (barbecue)
and getting the coals burning. After
gutting the fresh fish, sprinkle some
salt on either side of it. Place it in a
fish basket that has not been cleaned
in advance; this prevents the skin from
sticking and breaking. The fish should
remain as intact as possible as it is
barbecued.

Place the fish basket on the hot coals
and sprinkle it with Agua de Lourdes
several times as it is cooking. It should
be done after about 12 minutes – you
can tell that it is ready when tiny
bubbles start forming on the dark skin.

Once you have taken the turbot off the
grill, open it up carefully and remove
the bones. Sprinkle a little more Agua
de Lourdes and serve.

Big Mac

Jim Delligatti
McDonald's
United States 1967

page 90

Gourmet Salad

Michel Guérard
Le Pot-au-Feu
France 1968

page 91

The Big Mac itself is not really a secret—two hamburgers between three pieces of hamburger buns with sesame seeds. Add cheese, lettuce, pickles, and onions. It is the "special sauce" that will never be exactly revealed by McDonald's. It is now understood to be with mayonnaise, sweet relish, yellow mustard, cider vinegar, garlic powder, onion powder, and paprika. But how much of each? Experiment and perhaps you'll find out.

170 g (6 oz) young, tender, French beans, topped and tailed (trimmed)
12 fresh asparagus spears, well cleaned and trimmed or 12 tinned asparagus spears
4 beautiful leaves of salad greens, such as red chicory, red endive, radicchio trevisano etc.
1 level teaspoon chopped shallot
60 g (2 oz) fresh or preserved foie gras
1 fresh or preserved truffle, weighing 20 g (¾ oz), sliced

For the vinaigrette gourmande
salt and pepper
1 teaspoon lemon juice
2 teaspoons groundnut (peanut) oil
2 teaspoons olive oil
1 teaspoon sherry vinegar
1 teaspoon chervil
1 teaspoon tarragon

Throw the French beans into a saucepan of boiling well-salted water and cook them uncovered and at a galloping boil for 4–8 minutes, according to their size. They should be *al dente*. Take them quickly out of the water with a slotted spoon and plunge for 10 seconds in a basin of iced water. Then drain in a colander.

If you are using fresh asparagus, cook in the same water after the beans have been taken out.

Once you have washed and pared the asparagus, stand them, all tips level and pointing upwards, in a deep tin which is pierced all over with holes to make it into a sort of colander. All that is necessary is to lower the tin into boiling water in three stages, each one taking 3 minutes, or more according to the size of asparagus, with first the ends, then the middles and finally the tips of the asparagus being cooked. This means the ends, which are toughest, will have 9 minutes, the middles 6 minutes and the tips 3 minutes.

To prepare the vinaigrette gourmande, make the dressing like an ordinary vinaigrette, using a small wire whisk. Add the ingredients in the following order: salt, pepper and lemon juice, both kinds of oil, then the sherry vinegar, chervil and tarragon.

In separate bowls, dress the French beans, asparagus and sliced truffle with the vinaigrette gourmande.

Key Lime Pie

Joe's Stone Crab
United States 1968

page 92

Wash and dry the chosen salad leaves and arrange them on two plates or in a salad bowl. Pile the French beans on top in the form of a dome, scatter with chopped shallot and stud here and there with asparagus spears.

Dip a little knife in hot water and cut the foie gras in paper-thin slices. Arrange them prettily on the dome of French beans and decorate with slices of truffle.

For the graham cracker crust
⅓ of a 1-lb box graham crackers (or 150 g digestive or ginger biscuits)
5 tablespoons melted unsalted butter
⅓ cup sugar

For the filling
3 egg yolks
2 teaspoons lime zest
1 (14-oz) can sweetened condensed milk
⅔ cup freshly squeezed Key lime juice, or store bought

For the topping
1 cup heavy (double) or whipping cream chilled
2 tablespoons confectioners' (icing) sugar

Preheat the oven to 350°F. Butter a 9-inch pie plate (tart tin).

Break up the graham crackers or biscuits; place in a food processor and process to crumbs. If you don't have a food processor, place the crackers in a large plastic bag; seal and then crush the crackers with a rolling pin. Add the melted butter and sugar and pulse or stir until combined. Press the mixture into the bottom and side of a pie pan, forming a neat border around the edge. Bake the crust until set and golden,

8 minutes. Set aside on a wire rack; leave the oven on.

Meanwhile, in an electric mixer with the wire whisk attachment, beat the egg yolks and lime zest at high speed until very fluffy, about 5 minutes. Gradually add the condensed milk and continue to beat until thick, 3–4 minutes longer. Lower the mixer speed and slowly add the lime juice, mixing just until combined, no longer.

Pour the mixture into the crust. Bake for 10 minutes, or until the filling has just set. Cool on a wire rack, then refrigerate. Freeze for 15–20 minutes before serving.

Whip the cream and the confectioners' (icing) sugar until nearly stiff. Cut the pie into wedges and serve very cold, topping each wedge with a large dollop of whipped cream.

Mushroom Cappuccino

Alain Chapel
Alain Chapel
France c.1970

page 93

6 tablespoons butter
450 g button mushrooms, halved
225 g mixed mushrooms, such as
    oyster, shiitake and blue foot,
    thinly sliced, trimmings reserved
30 g dried shiitake mushrooms
375 ml double (heavy) cream
salt, to taste
cayenne pepper, to taste
12 crayfish tails, cooked and shelled
4 sprigs fresh chervil or tarragon
    leaves

Heat 3 tablespoons of the butter in a
deep frying pan (skillet) over medium
heat. Add the button mushrooms and
mushroom trimmings and cook, stirring
often, until they release their liquid,
about 10 minutes. Add 20 g of the dried
shiitakes and 950 ml of water; boil.
Reduce the heat to medium-low and
simmer until the liquid has reduced to
700 ml, about 10 minutes. Set a
fine-mesh strainer over a saucepan.
Strain the broth, pressing the mushrooms with the back of a spoon to
extract the liquid; discard the solids.
Add the cream to the mushroom broth
and bring to a boil. Reduce the heat to
medium-low and simmer until the
flavours meld, about 10 minutes. Season
the broth with salt and a pinch of
cayenne and set aside.

In a spice grinder, grind the remaining
dried shiitake mushrooms to a fine
powder. Transfer the mushroom
powder to a small frying pan over
medium-high heat and toast, swirling
the pan constantly, until fragrant, about
5 minutes. Transfer the mushroom
powder to a small bowl; set aside.

Heat the remaining butter in the skillet
(frying pan) over a medium heat. Add
the mixed mushrooms, season with salt
and cook, stirring gently, until tender,
4–5 minutes. Add the crayfish, season
with salt and cook until hot. Remove
the pan from heat and set aside.

To serve, foam the reserved broth on
high speed in a blender or with the
steamer attachment on an espresso
machine. Mound the crayfish mixture in
four teacups or small bowls, and ladle in
the broth. Spoon the foam on top, dust
with the mushroom powder, and
garnish with chervil.

Stew of Cockscombs
and Chicken Kidneys

Alain Chapel
Alain Chapel
France 1970

page 94

3 European crayfish (60 g total
    per portion)
10 g butter, plus extra for the pan
2 cockscombs and 3 chicken
    kidneys, blanched and poached
    in clear stock
few teaspoons of beurre monté
    (emulsified butter sauce)
dash of glace de volaille
    (chicken glaze)
2 spoons chicken broth
60 g small morels, washed
    thoroughly under running water
salt and pepper
chervil, to taste
2 mini puff pastries cooked just
    before serving

Poach crayfish, then shell the legs and
tails. Keep them warm in a frying pan
(skillet) with 10 g of butter.

Caramelize the cockscombs and
kidneys in a casserole dish with a bit of
melted butter, the chicken glaze and
clear stock. Take off the heat and stir in
half a spoon of broth in intervals.

Sweat the morels in a covered pan
with a couple of pinches of salt. Move
the morels to the crayfish, reserving
the juices.

Red Mullet
with Potato Scales
Paul Bocuse
L'Auberge du Pont de Collonges
France 1970s

page 95

Incorporate the juices from the morels to the cockscombs and kidneys and season with pepper. Add the morels and crayfish, binding everything with the beurre monté.

Sprinkle on some chervil, adjust the seasoning and fill the hot pastries.

2 red mullet fillets of approx. 350 g
2 large Bintjes potatoes
1 egg yolk
fine salt
2 tablespoons clarified butter
   (ghee)
1 tablespoon potato starch
olive oil
1 tablespoon veal stock (optional)
1 sprig of chervil

For the sauce
2 oranges
3 sprigs of fresh rosemary
10 cl Noilly Prat
300 g crème fraîche
salt
freshly ground pepper

Remove the fish bones using a peeler or tweezers. Cut out two rectangles of greaseproof (wax) paper slightly larger than the fish fillets. Place the fish on top, skin facing up.

Peel, wash and cut the potatoes very finely. Cut potato scales with an apple corer. Put the scales into a pan. Cover with cold water, bring to a boil, leave to simmer for 1 minute, then strain.

Dilute the egg yolk with 1 teaspoon of water and a pinch of salt. Coat the fish, skin side, with a brush.
Add the scales to a bowl with 2

teaspoons clarified butter and mix. Add 1 teaspoon of potato starch and mix carefully.

Arrange the scales on the fillets, starting at the top and letting them overlap. Leave in the fridge for 15 minutes.

To prepare the sauce, squeeze the oranges and pour the juice into a casserole dish with the rosemary and reduce at medium heat. Add the Noilly and reduce to half. Incorporate the crème fraîche and a few pinches of salt and pepper. Leave to reduce on a high heat until the sauce binds (to around half, or 10 minutes).

Meanwhile, heat 2 teaspoons of olive oil in a frying pan (skillet). Take hold of each rectangle of paper. Put it in the oil and remove the paper.

Season the fleshy side of the fillets. Leave to cook for around 6 minutes on a high heat until the scales are golden. Flip the fillets and leave to cook for a few seconds.

Strain the sauce. Ladle the sauce into dishes. Add the fillets and a bit of chervil. Serve hot.

Chicken Tikka Masala

Ali Ahmed Aslam
Shish Mahal
United Kingdom 1970s

page 96

Sticky Toffee Pudding

Francis Coulson
Sharrow Bay Country House Hotel
United Kingdom 1970s

page 97

The original recipe for this dish is unknown, but if you make a sauce of yogurt, tomatoes, and some mild spices, then marinate and cook cubes of chicken before dousing in the sauce, you'll get the idea.

50 g (2 oz) unsalted butter, softened, plus extra to butter the dish
175 g (6 oz) dates, chopped
1 teaspoon bicarbonate of soda (baking soda)
175 g (6 oz) caster (superfine) sugar
2 eggs
175 g (6 oz) self-raising flour (all-purpose flour plus 1½ teaspoons baking powder)
1 teaspoon vanilla extract
vanilla ice cream, to serve

For the sauce
300 ml (½ pint) double (heavy) cream
50 g (2 oz) demerara sugar
1 dessertspoon black treacle (molasses)

Preheat the oven to 180°C/160°C fan/350°F/Gas 4. Butter a baking tin about 20 cm x 13 cm (8 × 5 inches).

Boil the dates in 300 ml (½ pint) water until soft (some dates are softer than others, so will need more cooking), then remove the pan from the heat and drain any liquid. Add the bicarbonate of soda (baking soda).

Cream the butter and sugar together until light and fluffy, then add the eggs and beat well. Mix in the flour, date mixture and vanilla extract and pour into the prepared tin. Bake for 30–40 minutes, until just firm to the touch. To make the sauce, boil the cream, sugar and treacle (molasses) together. Pour over the top of the sponge until it is covered (there will be some left over), then place under a hot grill (broiler) until it begins to bubble. Remove, cut into squares, and serve with the remaining sauce and a scoop of vanilla ice cream.

Loup au Caviar

Jacques Pic
Maison Pic
France 1971

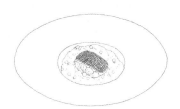

page 98

4 x 100 g skinless sea bass fillets
80 g Aquitaine caviar (20 g per
    person)
fine salt

Champagne sauce
¼ head of fennel
½ finely chopped shallot
1 button mushroom
15 g soft butter
25 cl champagne
15 cl fish stock
50 cl single (light) cream
10 cl full fat (whole) milk
fine salt

Season the fillets and steam for 2
minutes in the oven at 100°C. Remove
from the oven and let sit for 2 minutes
to finish cooking the fish. It's important
to get the temperature to 40°C all the
way through after steaming, so it will
reach 50°C after it has rested.

Champagne sauce
Sweat the sliced fennel, finely chopped
shallot, and the peeled and sliced
button mushroom in butter. Add the
champagne and reduce to half. Pour in
the fish stock and bring to the boil.

Leave the mixture to again reduce
to half.

Add the cream and milk, then heat,
making sure that the mixture doesn't
reduce. Leave to sit for 15 minutes.
Strain and add salt. Add more
champagne, to taste, if necessary.

Presentation and final touches
Spread the caviar on greaseproof
(wax) paper.

Put the sea bass on a deep plate and
cover in the champagne sauce.

Place the caviar strip on the fillet, then
pull off the greaseproof paper. Finish by
adding more sauce.

Scorpion Fish Cake

Juan Mari Arzak
Restaurante Arzak
Spain 1971

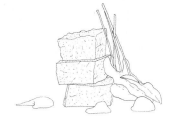

page 99

½ kg raw red scorpion fish,
    head removed
1 leek
1 carrot
salt
8 eggs
¼ litre cream
¼ litre tomato sauce (passata)
white pepper
1 dab of butter
breadcrumbs
water

Cook the red scorpion fish with the leek
and carrot, and season with salt. When
it is sufficiently cooked, remove the
bones and skin, and shred.

Beat the eggs and immediately add the
cream, tomato sauce (passata), shredded
fish, and season with white pepper.
Grease a rectangular 1½-litre mould with
the butter, sprinkle with breadcrumbs,
and add the fish mixture. Cook in
a bain-marie in the oven at 225°C for
1 hour. Cool, then unmold and cut into
small, thin rectangular pieces.

Soup Dumplings
Din Tai Fung
China 1972

page 100

Banoffi Pie
Nigel Mackenzie and Ian Dowding
The Hungry Monk
United Kingdom 1972

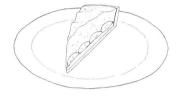

page 101

The original recipe for these soup-filled dumplings (although more strictly categorized as buns, by the Chinese) is a closely held secret, but they are typically made with ground pork and a rich broth. If you're feeling ambitious, aim for eighteen pleats on each dumpling, like those made on the originals. Once pleated, you should steam them and then eat. Use a chopstick to place the dumpling on your spoon, and add vinegar and ginger on top before taking a very small bite—or devouring in one! Just be careful, they will be hot.

butter, for greasing
12 oz uncooked shortcrust pastry
  (basic pie dough)
1½ cans condensed milk (13½ oz
  each)
¾ pint double (heavy) cream
½ teaspoon powdered instant
  coffee
1 dessertspoon caster (superfine)
  sugar
1½ lb firm bananas
a little freshly ground coffee

Preheat the oven to Gas Mark 5. Lightly grease a 10-inch x 1½-inch flat tin. Line this with the pastry thinly rolled out. Prick the base all over with a fork and bake blind until crisp. Allow to cool.

Immerse the cans, unopened, into a deep pan of boiling water. Cover and boil for 5 hours, making sure the pan does not boil dry (see Caution, below). Remove the cans from the water and allow to cool completely before opening. Inside you will find the soft toffee filling.

Whip the cream with the instant coffee and sugar until thick and smooth. Now spread the toffee over the base of the flan. Peel and halve the bananas lengthways and lay them on the toffee. Finely spoon or pipe on the cream and lightly sprinkle over the freshly ground coffee.

Caution
It is absolutely vital to top up the pan f boiling water frequently during the cooking of the cans: 5 hours is a long time, and if they are allowed to boil dry, the cans will explode, causing a grave risk to life, limb and kitchen ceilings.

Crab Steamed with Egg White and Huadiao Wine

Chui Fook Chuen
Fook Lam Moon
China 1972

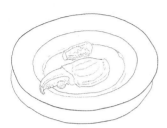

page 102

a meaty fresh crab claw
egg white
chicken broth (stock)
flour
aged Chinese yellow wine
 (Huadiao wine)

Clean the crab claw carefully and rinse well. Remove the shell after cleaning. Marinate the crab claw with just a pinch of salt and flour and some Huadiao wine for 1–2 minutes before steaming.

Prepare an egg white base – 1 part egg white: 2 parts broth.

Place the crab claw on top of the mixed egg white and broth, cover the dish and steam until the crab claw and egg white are cooked.

Prepare a sauce with chicken broth, flour and aged Huadiao wine. Drizzle the sauce over the crab claw and egg white before serving.

Black Truffle Soup Elysée

Paul Bocuse
L'Auberge du Pont de Collonges
France 1975

page 103

2 tablespoons matignon (equal
 parts carrots, onions, celery,
 mushrooms, all cut into tiny dice
 and stewed in unsalted butter)
1¾ oz fresh raw truffles
¾ oz fresh foie gras
1 cup strong chicken consommé
2 oz flaky pastry
1 egg yolk, beaten

Into an individual ovenproof soup bowl (called granitée lyonnaise) put 2 tablespoons matignon, 1¾ ounces truffles cut into irregular slices, ¾ ounce foie gras also cut into irregular slices, and 1 cup strong consommé.

Brush the edges of a thin layer of flaky pastry with egg yolk, and cover the soup bowl with it, tightly sealing the edges.

Set the soup bowl in a 425°F oven. It will cook very fast. The flaky pastry should expand in the heat and take on a golden color; that is a sign that it is cooked.

Use a soup spoon to break the flaky pastry, which should fall into the soup.

Veal Prince Orloff

Michel Bourdin
The Connaught
United Kingdom 1975

page 104

The recipe for this dish by Michel Bourdin has not been written down. To make this, you will need a veal loin, cut into one-inch slices. In between each slice, place mushroom purée, onion Soubise, and black truffles. Then reassemble back into the shape of a roast! Top the entire dish with cheese and Mornay sauce. Bake.

Chicken Manchurian

Nelson Wang
The Cricket Club of India
India 1975

page 105

Stuffed Pig's Trotters with Morels

Pierre Koffmann
La Tante Claire
United Kingdom 1977

page 106

This classic dish has long been a secret. It involves a sauce of green chilis, ginger, chopped garlic, cilantro (coriander), soy sauce, sugar, cornstarch (cornflour), and chicken stock, all coating crispy chicken pieces.

4 pig's trotters (feet)
100 g carrots, diced
100 g onions, diced
150 ml dry white wine
1 tablespoon port
150 ml veal stock (broth)
225 g veal sweetbreads, blanched and chopped
75 g butter, plus a knob (pat) for the sauce
20 dried morels, soaked until soft, and drained
1 small onion, finely chopped
1 chicken breast, skinned and diced
1 egg white
200 ml double (heavy) cream
salt and freshly ground pepper
knob (pat) of butter, to serve

Preheat the oven to 160°C/Gas 3. Place the trotters (feet) in a casserole with the diced carrots and onions, the wine, port and veal stock. Cover and braise in the oven for 3 hours.

Meanwhile, fry the sweetbreads in the butter for 5 minutes, add the morels and chopped onion and cook for another 5 minutes. Leave to cool.

Purée the chicken breast with the egg white and cream, and season with salt and pepper. Mix with the sweetbread mixture to make the stuffing.

Take the trotters out of the casserole and strain the cooking stock, keeping the stock but discarding the vegetables. Open the trotters out flat and lay each one on a piece of foil. Leave to cool.

Fill the cooled trotters with the chicken stuffing and roll tightly in foil. Chill in the fridge for at least 2 hours.

Preheat the oven to 220°C/Gas 7 or prepare a steamer, and when the water is simmering, steam the foil-wrapped trotters until heated through. Alternatively, put the trotters in a casserole, cover and heat in the oven for 15 minutes. Put the trotters on a serving dish and remove the foil. Pour the reserved stock into the casserole and reduce by half. Whisk in a knob (pat) of butter, pour the sauce over the trotters and serve very hot.

Roast Tronçon of Turbot with Hollandaise Sauce

Rick Stein
The Seafood Restaurant
United Kingdom late 1970s

page 107

25 g unsalted butter
4 × 225–275 g tronçons of turbot
salt and freshly ground black
    pepper
85 ml fish stock (broth)
¼ teaspoon nam pla (Thai fish
    sauce)
juice of ½ lemon
1 teaspoon chopped fresh fines
    herbes: parsley, tarragon, chives,
    chervil

For the hollandaise sauce
2 tablespoons water
2 egg yolks
225 g clarified unsalted butter,
    warmed
1½ tablespoons lemon juice
a good pinch cayenne pepper
¾ teaspoon salt

Preheat the oven to 190°C. Melt a small piece of the butter in a large, ovenproof frying pan (skillet) and when it is foaming, add the tronçons of turbot and cook quickly on either side until lightly browned. Season both sides well with salt and pepper and roast in the oven for about 15 minutes.

Meanwhile, for the hollandaise, put the water and egg yolks into a stainless steel or glass bowl set over a pan of simmering water, making sure that the base of the bowl is not touching the water. Whisk until voluminous and creamy. Remove the bowl from the pan and gradually whisk in the clarified butter until thick and moussey. Whisk in the lemon juice, cayenne pepper and salt.

To make a fines herbes sauce, combine the fish stock, nam pla and lemon juice in a small pan and bring to the boil. Reduce by three quarters and whisk in the remaining butter and the fines herbes.

Lift the turbot onto 4 warmed plates. Just cover the top of each tronçon with the fines herbes sauce and spoon some of the hollandaise sauce alongside. Serve with some boiled new potatoes.

Pistachio Soufflé

Pierre Koffmann
La Tante Claire
United Kingdom 1977

page 108

100 ml (3½ fl oz/scant ½ cup) milk
50 g (1¾ oz/3 tablespoons)
    pistachio paste
1 egg, plus 1 egg yolk
50 g (1¾ oz/3 tablespoons) caster
    (superfine) sugar
40 g (1½ oz/2½ tablespoons) plain
    (all purpose) flour
butter, for greasing
50 g (1¾ oz/ 3 squares) good-
    quality dark (bittersweet)
    chocolate, grated
6 egg whites
icing (confectioners') sugar,
    for dusting

For the pistachio ice cream
500 ml (18 fl oz) milk
500 ml (18 fl oz) double (heavy)
    cream
45 g (1½ oz/ 3 tablespoons) liquid
    glucose (light corn syrup)
75 g (2½ oz/ 5 tablespoons)
    pistachio paste
12 egg yolks
200 g (7 oz/1 scant cup) caster
    (superfine) sugar

Start by making the ice cream. Place the milk, cream, glucose (light corn syrup) and pistachio paste in a saucepan and bring to the boil. Meanwhile, whisk the egg yolks and sugar in a heatproof bowl. Add a little of the hot milk mixture to the eggs and whisk very →

Pistachio Soufflé

Truffled Zucchini

Jacques Maximin
Chantecler
France 1978

page 109

quickly to incorporate. Pour into the pan with the rest of the milk and cook over a low heat, stirring continuously, until a thermometer reaches 82°C (180°F). Remove from the heat and pass through a fine sieve into a water bowl set inside an ice bath – a large bowl filled with ice and cold water – and leave to cool. Once cool, churn in an ice-cream machine.

Heat the oven 230°C (450°F/Gas 8).

For the soufflés, place the milk and pistachio paste in a small pan and bring to the boil. Beat the egg, egg yolk and half the caster (superfine) sugar in a bowl until pale, then add the flour and mix until combined. Pour over the milk mixture, whisking to combine, the pour the mixture back into the pan and cook over a low–medium heat for 4 minutes, whisking continuously until the mixture is thick enough to lightly coat the back of a spoon. Pour the mixture into a bowl, cover with foil and keep in a warm place.

Thoroughly grease six individual soufflé dishes with the butter, then dust the insides with the grated chocolate. Whisk the egg whites until stiff, then add the remaining caster (superfine) sugar and whisk again until firm.

Whisk the pistachio mixture for a few seconds, to loosen, then add a quarter of the egg white and whisk vigorously. Add half the remaining egg white, stirring quickly with a spatula to remove any lumps. Add the rest of the egg white in the same way. Gently pour the soufflé mixture into the prepared dishes and bake for 10 minutes, until risen. Lightly dust the soufflés with icing (confectioners') sugar. Serve with a quenelle of pistachio ice cream gently placed on top at the last moment.

16 courgettes (zucchini), very fresh and with their flowers attached
50 g (1¾ oz) fine breadcrumbs
250 ml (scant half pint) whipping cream
10 tablespoons olive oil
a bunch of basil, chervil, and tarragon, leaves picked
2 eggs
40 g (1½ oz) preserved truffle, finely sliced, and 1 teaspoon juice from the jar or can
7 tablespoons double (heavy) cream, whipped
150 g (5¼ oz) cold diced butter
salt and freshly ground pepper

Trim the courgettes (zucchini) so that the flowers are attached to 4 inches of courgette. Peel them with a potato peeler and plunge into boiling salted water for 5–10 seconds to blanch and soften the flowers. Refresh in iced water, drain and set aside.

Soak the breadcrumbs in the whipping cream.

Soften the courgette peelings in olive oil, and put into the bowl of a mixer or food processor. Add ten leaves from the basil, the eggs and the breadcrumbs and cream. Season with salt and pepper mix to a smooth purée. Chill for a few minutes.

Blackened Redfish

Paul Prudhomme
K-Paul's Louisiana Kitchen
United States 1979

page 110

Preheat the oven and have ready an oiled baking sheet sprinkled with salt and pepper. Pack the purée into a forcing bag with a nozzle (tip).

One person, using the index fingers and thumbs of both hands, spreads out the flower very, very carefully, and inflates it by blowing gently into it. At that moment the second person uses the forcing bag to pipe the purée into the flower so that it is three quarters full. The first then twists the flower so that the ends of the petals form a natural knot, sealing in the stuffing. Repeat this process with each courgette and lay them on the prepared baking sheet. Sprinkle with a little olive oil and bake for 40 minutes.

Bring 7 tablespoons of water to the boil with a pinch of salt and a little pepper and whisk in the cold diced butter. Remove from the heat, add the slices of truffle and the truffle juice and leave to infuse in a warm place.

Sponge the excess oil from the cooked courgettes and arrange on warm plates. Remove the slices of truffle from the sauce and divide them between the four plates. Bring the sauce to the boil, simmer for a minute or so and fold in the whipped cream. Check the seasoning and pour over the courgettes. Sprinkle with the fresh herbs and serve.

¾ pound (3 sticks) unsalted butter, melted in a skillet (frying pan)
6 (8- to 10-oz) fish fillets (preferably redfish, pompano or tilefish), cut about ½ inch thick

For the seasoning mix
1 tablespoon sweet paprika
2½ teaspoons salt
1 teaspoon onion powder
1 teaspoon garlic powder
1 teaspoon ground red pepper (preferably cayenne)
¾ teaspoon white pepper
¾ teaspoon black pepper
½ teaspoon dried thyme leaves
½ teaspoon dried oregano leaves

Heat a large cast-iron skillet (frying pan) over very high heat until it is beyond the smoking stage and you see white ash in the skillet bottom (the skillet cannot be too hot for this dish), at least 10 minutes.

Meanwhile, pour 2 tablespoons melted butter in each of 6 small ramekins; set aside and keep warm. Reserve the remaining butter in its skillet. Heat the serving plates in a 250°F oven.

Thoroughly combine the seasoning mix ingredients in a small bowl. Dip each fillet in the reserved melted butter so that both sides are well coated; then sprinkle the seasoning mix generously

and evenly on both sides of the fillets, patting it in by hand.

Place in the hot skillet and pour 1 teaspoon melted butter on top of each fillet (be careful, as the butter may flame up). Cook, uncovered, over the same high heat until the underside looks charred, about 2 minutes (the time will vary according to the fillet's thickness and the heat of the skillet). Turn the fish over again and pour 1 teaspoon butter on top; cook until fish is done, about 2 minutes more. Repeat with the remaining fillets.

Serve each fillet while piping hot. Place one fillet and a ramekin of butter on each heated serving plate.

Baked Goat Cheese
with Garden Lettuces
Alice Waters
Chez Panisse
United States 1980

page 111

½ lb fresh goat cheese (one 2 x
    5-inch log)
1 cup extra virgin olive oil
3–4 sprigs fresh thyme, chopped
1 small sprig rosemary, chopped
½ sour baguette, preferably a day
    old
1 tablespoon red wine vinegar
1 teaspoon sherry vinegar
salt and pepper
¼ cup extra virgin olive oil
½ lb mesclun lettuces, washed and
    dried

Carefully slice the goat cheese into
8 disks about ½ inch thick. Pour the
olive oil over the disks and sprinkle
with the chopped herbs. Cover and
store in a cool place for several hours
or up to a week.

Preheat the oven to 300°F. Cut the
baguette in half and leave it in the oven
for 20 minutes or so, until dry and
lightly colored. Grate into fine crumbs
on a box grater or in a food processor.

Preheat the oven to 400°F. (You can
also use a toaster oven.) Remove the
cheese disks from the marinade and roll
them in the breadcrumbs, coating them
thoroughly. Place the cheese disks on a
small baking sheet and bake for about
6 minutes, until they are warm and the
breadcrumbs are brown.

Measure the vinegars into a small bowl
and add a big pinch of salt. Whisk in the
oil and a little freshly ground pepper.
Taste for seasoning and adjust. Toss the
lettuces lightly with the vinaigrette and
arrange on salad plates. With a spatula,
carefully place 2 disks of the baked
cheese on each plate and serve.

Chickpea Purée
with Red Shrimp
Fulvio Pierangelini
Gambero Rosso
Italy c.1980

page 112

100 g (3½ oz) chickpeas (garbanzo
    beans), soaked overnight and
    drained
1 garlic clove
1 fresh rosemary sprig
800 g (1¾ lb) raw prawns (shrimp),
    peeled and deveined
extra virgin olive oil, for drizzling
salt and pepper

Put the chickpeas (garbanzo beans),
garlic and rosemary into a saucepan,
add water to cover and bring to the boil,
then lower the heat and simmer gently
for about 2½ hours, until the chickpeas
are tender. Drain well, discard the
garlic and rosemary and pass the
chickpeas through a sieve into a bowl.

Steam the prawns (shrimp) for a few
minutes until they change colour.
Spoon a pool of chickpea purée on to
each of four warm dishes and top with
the prawns. Drizzle with olive oil and
season with salt and pepper to taste.

Gargouillou

Michel Bras

Bras

France 1980

page 113

Perennial vegetables

asparagus, fiddleheads, hops, bryony

Remove the base of the stalk, breaking it or simply scraping. Some of these vegetables are cooked in salted boiling water, others blanched. Refresh in cold water.

artichoke, cardoon

Remove all the leaves of the artichoke, retaining only the bottom. Remove the strings of the cardoons and cut into sections. Cook in a broth flavoured with coriander seeds, orange zest, shallots, and a few drops of aromatic oil.

Leafy vegetables with flowers

wild beet (beetroot), blond and red orache, spinach, Malabar spinach, Good King Henry spinach, lamb's quarter, comfrey, parsley

Remove the stems from most of these; when necessary remove the hard central stalk. Cook most of these leaves directly in butter or in oil. You can also cook them in boiling salted water.

cabbage, chinese cabbage, bok choy (pak choi), French oxheart cabbage, Brussels sprouts, mustard greens

Proceed in the same manner as above.

Swiss chard, borage, pascal celery

Separate the greens from the stalks. Remove the strings from the stalks with a knife. Cook everything in boiling salted water. You can finish the cooking in some leftover roast juice.

buccos (a type of cabbage), broccoli rabe, cabbage shoot

Tie in little bunches. Cook in a large quantity of salted boiling water.

broccoli, cauliflower

Separate the florets from the stalks. Select the tender stalks, peel them, and cut into fine slices. Cook the tops and the stalks separately in salted boiling water. Refresh.

watercress, clover, geslu (a type of salad), ice plant, chickweed, salads (leafy greens) of all colours and tastes

Remove the stems. These greens are usually eaten raw but some of them can be cooked.

Bulbs

garlic, bear's garlic, rocambole garlic, shallots, small onions

Peel and blanch. Cook in salted boiling water or, better yet, in a broth flavoured with coriander seeds, orange zest, wild thyme, and bay leaf with a few drops of aromatic oil. Or roast them in their skins.

Chives, scallions (spring onions), leeks, white onion

Sort and wash. Separate the white pats from the green. For better results, cook the two parts separately in water.

fennel

Remove the stalks, fronds, and the membrane. You can use the bulb raw, cook it in water or slowly in a little fat.

onions from Cevannes, onions from Lezignan

Peel. Oven-roasting the onions wrapped in an aluminium foil is a very good way to cook these sweet onions.

Root vegetables

carrots, turnips, turnip-root chervil, water parsnips, wild parsnips, parsley root, pink radishes, celeriac (celery root), Jerusalem artichoke

Peel with a knife, leaving a short length of the tops on the smaller vegatables. Cut lengthwise with a knife or a →

303

Gargouillou

mandolin, about ⅛ inch (3 mm) thick. Cook in boiling salted water. Then the parsley root and turnip-root chervil can be prepared in a purée.

beets (beetroot), crapaudine

Even though these vegatables are usually eaten cooked, you can also eat them raw, either grated or sliced in a julienne.

black radishes, long or round; daikon (mooli)

Rub with a brush and cut into slices, ⅛ inch (3mm) thick with a mandoline. You can cook them in butter.

celeriac (celery root), salsify, black salsify

Peel and cook in salted boiling water to which you have added a few drops of oil to prevent oxidization.

crosne, conopode

Clean by rubbing against one another with rock salt. Pan fry the crosne and eat the conopode raw.

burdock, bellflowers, rampion

Scrape and use raw or cooked.

Vegetables with pods
green beans, Saint fiacre green beans, snow peas (mangetout), snap peas

Snap off the stems, remove the strings, and cook in a large quantity of salted boiling water.

fava (broad) beans

Shell and cooked in salted boiling water. Refresh. Peel the individual beans.

shell beans, flageolets, lentils, chickpeas (garbanzo beans), okra, soy beans

These vegetables are better if cooked slowly and for a long time with aromatic vegetables and herbs.

Fruits
chayote, pattypan squash, summer squash, zucchini (courgette)

Slice in very thin slices, ⅛ inch (3mm), and cook in salted boiling water or pan fry in a little oil.

cucumber

Clean and place in a drainer with salt for a few hours to release some of the water. Rinse and prepare with butter or aromatic oil.

red or yellow tomatoes

Blanch in boiling water and remove the skins. Remove the seeds and use raw or cooked.

green tomatoes

Peel with a knife, remove the seeds, and cook in a marmalade.

red, yellow, or green bell peppers

Oil the skin lightly and roast in a very hot oven. Remove the charred skin and preserve in oil.

pumpkin, hard squash

Peel the thick skin and prepare a purée.

Flavoured pearls and touches

Ceps

8 oz (200 g) ceps
½ cup (10 cl) oil
¼ cup (50 g) water
2 garlic cloves
10 coriander seeds
5 peppercorns
4 sprigs of wild thyme
bay leaf
parsley
salt
juice of 1 lemon

This method can be used to prepare any kind of small, firm mushrooms. Using a knife, scrape the stems of the mushrooms. Wipe the stems and the caps with a wet cloth. Plunge in boiling water for 30 seconds. Drain and refresh. Combine the oil, water, garlic, coriander, peppercorns, thyme, bay leaf, and parsley in a frying pan. Season with salt and simmer for 5 minutes more. Season with lemon juice and adjust the seasoning.

Parsley oil

1 oz (30 g) parsley
¼ cup (5 cl) grape seed oil
salt

To make things easier, make a bigger quantity and keep some of the oil for later use. The oil can also be prepared with chives, scallions (spring onions), lovage, and other herbs. Wash the parsley, removing the longest stems. Mix the leaves with grape seed oil and a pinch of salt. Macerate for 3–4 hours. Drain in a colander. This oil can be kept for a few days in a cool place.

Country herbs

burnet, yarrow, and other plants, flowers, and roots that can be picked in nature

Sprouts

A large quantity of seeds can be used for sprouting: cereal, cruciferous, leguminous, mucilaginous, oleaginous, umbelliferae — for example alfalfa, wheat, fenugreek, green soy beans, lentils, chickpeas (garbanzo beans)

Sprouting has two phases: soaking and the actual sprouting. You can buy a seed tray, but you will also get good results using jars. The soaking time varies according to the type of seeds. For wheat and fenugreek, you need 10–12 hours; for green soy bean, lentil and chickpeas, 12–24 hours. Place the seeds in jars and cover them with a good quantity of water. Place a square of netting over the jar opening and secure it with a rubber band. After soaking, pour the water out and rinse seeds. Tilt the jar 45 degrees, so that the opening is below the base. Cover the jar with a dark cloth. Rinse twice a day. The sprouts will be ready to eat in a few days. To get good germination, it is important to meet four conditions: The seeds must always be wet, warm, aerated, and in the dark. They can keep in a cool place if they are rinsed regularly. Certain varieties of seeds can germinate in the light. →

Gargouillou

Artichoke Soup with Black Truffle

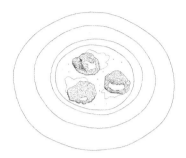

Guy Savoy
Guy Savoy
France 1980

page 114

Crystal leaves
herbs from the garden
vegetable leaves
oil
coarse grey sea salt

Wash the leaves in a large quantity of water, being careful not to crush them. It is preferable to blanch the vegetable leaves. Pat dry. Brush a drop of aromatic oil on each one and sprinkle with salt. Place on a tray lined with parchment (baking) paper. Slide into the oven. The leaves must be shiny, and as brittle as glass, with no change of color.

To finish
country (cured) ham
vegetable broth (stock)
butter
cooked vegetables
raw vegetables
garden herbs
country herbs
sprouts
flavoured pearls and touches

Fry slices of country ham in a deep frying pan.

Skim off the fat and deglaze with vegetable broth. Add a pat (knob) of butter; it will blend into the ham juice. Toss the vegetables on the plate, arranging them to give an impression of motion. Decorate with chopped garden herbs, country herbs, and sprouts. Play with flavoured pearls and touches.

We were informed that Guy Savoy wishes to keep this recipe secret, until he chooses to reveal it in a book at the end of his career—the dish includes artichokes, leek, Parmesan cheese, black truffle, and mushroom purée. Served with fresh brioche.

Spanish Omelet

Néstor
Bar Néstor
Spain 1980

page 115

2 kg potatoes, thinly sliced
1½ litres sunflower oil
1½ onions, diced (approximately
   1 cm cubes)
1 Italian green pepper, diced
14 extra-large eggs (73 g each)
extra-virgin olive oil
salt

In a frying pan (skillet), add the
sunflower oil and, over high heat, fry
the potato slices together with the
onions and green pepper. The potatoes
should not be moved. Every 10 minutes,
turn the potatoes one or two times until
some of the slices are golden brown.

Mix the potatoes with the eggs and add
a fistful of salt. The salt can be added to
taste, but it needs to be flavorful.

Grease the pan with drizzle of
extra-virgin olive oil and place over
high heat until the pan is very hot. Add
the potato and egg mixture to the pan
and reduce the heat to medium. Allow
the mixture to brown without moving it
for approximately 1 minute. With the
help of a lid or plate, flip the tortilla and
cook the other side for approximately
1 or 2 minutes, or until the tortilla is
browned on both sides yet also slightly
runny inside.

Cut and serve with bread.

Crab Omelet

Supinya Junsuta
Raan Jay Fai
Thailand 1980s

page 116

To make this secret Thai recipe, we
suggest that first you wear ski goggles
and a black cap as the chef does, and to
make this alone without any help, as she
does too. You will need lots of oil, plus
crab meat in just a bit of egg and flour.
Make one omelet at a time.

Caviar Jelly with Cauliflower Cream

Joël Robuchoni
Jamin
France 1981

page 117

500 g lobster shells
7 cl olive oil
30 g onions
30 g fennel
20 g celery sticks
30 g carrots
50 g shallots
1 small bouquet garni
1 tablespoon tomato purée (paste)
80 g caviar
1 tablespoon mayonnaise with
   added chlorophyll
a few sprigs of chervil
salt
coarsely ground pepper

For the veal foot jelly
2 veal feet, chopped in half with
   the bones loosened
40 g coarse salt

For the cauliflower cream
60 cl chicken broth
800 g cauliflower
a pinch of curry powder
30 g cornflour (cornstarch)
1 egg yolk
10 cl single (light) cream
5 cl double (heavy) cream
salt
ground pepper →

Caviar Jelly with Cauliflower Cream

For the stock (broth)
1 large egg white
1 tablespoon roughly chopped leek
1 tablespoon roughly chopped carrot
1 tablespoon roughly chopped celery
2 crushed ice cubes
1 segment of star anise

To make the veal foot jelly, boil the bones and feet in cold water with 10 g of coarse salt, then let it simmer for 2 minutes. Cool and put in a saucepan with 4 litres of water. If you need to freshen up the meat, leave it under a running tap in the pan for a few minutes. Add the remaining coarse salt. Leave to simmer for 3 hours, then strain. Remove the bones from half a foot and cut the meat into small cubes. Measure out 1.25 litres of broth.

To make the cauliflower cream, bring chicken broth to a boil with the blanched cauliflower. Add the curry powder and cook for 20 minutes. To prevent the cauliflower becoming sour, cover it with salted boiling water for 2–3 minutes, then cool under cold running water and drain it.

Strain the cauliflower, then reduce the broth to 50 cl. Mix the cornflour (cornstarch) in 4 tablespoons of cold water. Pour a small ladle of broth into the cornflour while stirring with a whisk. Pour back into the broth and let it boil for 3 minutes. Whether you're adding the cornflour into the boiling broth (or stirring the egg yolk and cream mixture), make sure to whisk gently and continuously to avoid the mixture clumping together (or the egg yolk curdling).

Mix the egg yolk with the single (light) cream. Slowly pour a ladle of broth over the mixture, stir, pour everything back into the pan while whisking. Remove from heat as soon as it starts to boil. Stir the mixture, pass through a conical strainer and season. Leave to cool completely. Adjust the consistency with double (heavy) cream if necessary.

Crush the lobster shells. Brown them in 5 cl of olive oil.

Dice the onions, fennel, celery, carrots and shallots. Add the vegetables with a bouquet garni and 2 cl olive oil to a saucepan and sweat for 5 minutes over a medium heat without letting them brown. Add the vegetables to the lobster shells with salt and pepper. Mix well and while stirring, add the tomato purée (paste), 1.25 litres of the veal jelly stock and cubed veal feet. Bring slowly to a boil, letting the mixture foam. Leave to simmer and foam for 20 minutes.

Strain the jelly mixture, then cook again until only 50 cl of liquid remains. Leave to cool, then remove the fat on the surface. While the jelly reduces, make sure to continue to skim the surface to remove any skin from the fat that forms.

For the stock, put the egg white into a terrine mould with 1 tablespoon of water and whisk to break it up. Add the chopped vegetables and ice cubes.

Bring the jelly to a boil. Pour a ladle of boiling jelly into the egg white mixture while stirring. Then pour this mixture back into the jelly, stirring slowly.

Let the jelly cook at a gentle simmer until it is clear. Make a colander out of a wrung-out muslin (cheesecloth) and place over a large bowl.

Chocolate Coulant

Michel Bras
Bras
France 1981

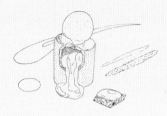

page 118

Add the star anise. Let it simmer for 30 minutes. Strain the jelly through the prepared cloth. Let it cool, then leave in the fridge to cool completely.

Warm the jelly lightly to soften. Line four bowls with 20 g of caviar in each. Pour 10 cl of the syrupy jelly. Leave to cool, then pour 5 cl of cauliflower cream over the jelly. Decorate the top with dots of the green (chlorophyll) mayonnaise. Add a leaf of chervil to finish.

Mocha centers
5 oz (120 g) couverture chocolate
¼ cup (6 cl) water
1 cup (200 g) heavy (double) cream
3½ tablespoons (50 g) butter
1 tablespoon (15 g) coffee extract

The molds
⅓ cup (80 g) butter
12 strips of parchment (baking) paper, 10 x 2¾ inches (25 x 7 cm) each
6 metal ring molds, 2 x 1½ inches (50 x 40 mm)
2 oz (50 g) cocoa powder

Biscuits
4 oz (110 g) couverture chocolate
3½ tablespoons (50 g) butter, at room temperature
⅓ cup (40 g) almond powder
⅓ cup (40 g) cream of rice (ground rice)
2 eggs, separated
½ cup (90 g) sugar

Iced double cream
¼ cup (50 g) sugar
1 tablespoon (13 g) milk powder
¼ cup (50 g) heavy (double) cream
¾ cup (175 g) milk

Caramel
½ cup (100 g) granulated sugar
1 tablespoon (20 g) glucose (light corn syrup)
¼ cup (50 g) water
2 teaspoons (13 g) coffee extract

Coffee and milk powder
¼ cup (35 g) confectioners' (icing) sugar
2 teaspoons (10 g) instant coffee
3 tablespoons (45 g) milk powder

Mocha centers

Chop up the chocolate and melt it in a double boiler (or bowl over a pan of simmering water) with the water, cream, butter and coffee extract. Let cool for 15 minutes, then pour into 6 molds, 1¾ x 1¼ inches (45 × 30 mm) each. Freeze overnight.

The molds

To prepare the molds, clarify the butter and brush it on the strips of parchment (baking) paper and on the inside of the metal rings. Insert the strips of buttered parchment paper, one on top of the other, inside each metal ring. Then sprinkle the inside of each mold with cocoa powder. →

Chocolate Coulant

Biscuits
A few hours before serving, prepare the biscuits. Chop up the chocolate and melt it in a double boiler. Remove the chocolate from the heat and let it cool for a few minutes. Stir in the butter, almond powder, cream of rice (ground rice) and egg yolks. Beat the egg whites with the sugar. Fold them into the chocolate. Place this mixture in a pastry bag. Arrange the baking molds on a baking sheet covered with parchment paper. Pipe a little biscuit mixture into the bottom of each mold and place a frozen mocha center in the middle.

Use the tip of a knife to position the center properly. Then finish filling the molds with the biscuit mix and set them aside in the freezer.

Iced double cream
Mix the sugar with the milk powder, then add the cream and milk and bring to a boil. Briefly put into the blender, then strain and churn in the ice cream machine.

Caramel
Caramelize the sugar with the glucose to any degree you wish. Deglaze with the water and coffee extract, making sure all the caramel is loosened from the bottom of the pan. Bring to a boil to obtain an even consistency. Set aside.

Coffee and milk powder
Mix together the sugar, coffee and milk powder.

To finish
Bake the biscuits for 20 minutes at 350°F (180°C). Test them for doneness by sticking a thin metal skewer into their center; they are baked when the skewer comes out warm to the touch. Remove the molds with extreme care and then carefully remove the paper strips. Place a biscuit in the center of each plate with a half scoop of the iced double cream. Spot the plates with the caramel and then use a knife to trace the coffee and milk powder along the edge of the plate. Serve immediately.

Potato Purée

Joël Robuchon
Jamin
France 1981

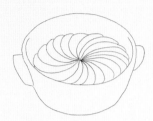

page 119

1 kg potatoes, preferably rattes or
   BF 15, scrubbed but unpeeled
coarse (kosher) salt
250 g butter, diced and kept well
   chilled until use
250 ml whole (full-fat) milk
salt and pepper

Put the potatoes into a saucepan with 2 litres of cold water and 1 tablespoon of coarse salt. Bring to a simmer, cover, and cook until a knife slips in the potatoes easily, about 25 minutes.

Drain the potatoes and peel them. Put them through a potato ricer into a large saucepan. Turn the heat to medium and dry the potato flesh out a bit by turning it vigorously with a spatula for about 5 minutes.

Meanwhile, rinse a small saucepan and pour out the excess water but do not wipe it dry. Add the milk and bring to a boil.

Turn the heat under the potatoes to low and incorporate the well-chilled butter bit by bit, stirring it in energetically for a smooth, creamy finish. Pour in the very hot milk in a thin stream, still over a low heat, still stirring briskly. Keep stirring until all the milk is absorbed. Turn off the heat and taste for salt and pepper.

For an even lighter, finer purée, put it through a very fine sieve before serving.

Rice, Gold, and Saffron

Gualtiero Marchesi
Ristorante Gualtiero Marchesi
Italy 1981

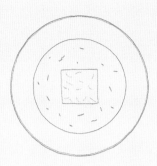

page 120

---

60 g butter
300 g Italian Carnaroli rice
100 ml dry white wine
1 litre meat stock
1 g saffron threads
    (1 dessertspoon)
1 dessertspoon onion, chopped fine
30 g grated Italian grana cheese
4 pieces gold leaf 23kt
salt

Melt 10 g of the butter in a saucepan and when warm, add the rice and stir. Moisten with 50 ml of wine and allow to evaporate. Add the stock a ladleful at a time, so that the liquid barely covers the rice. Continue until cooked, then stir in the saffron.

In another pan, place 10 g of the butter and brown the onion, add the rest of the wine, reduce the liquid to half, add the remaining butter in flakes and whip to a smooth emulsion. Pass the white butter obtained through a strainer (sieve) and use it to moisten the cooked rice together with the grana cheese.

Add salt to taste and spread on the plates, with the gold leaf at the centre of each.

Beggar's Purses

Barry Wine
The Quilted Giraffe
United States 1981

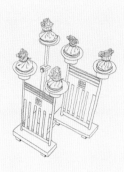

page 121

For the crepes
1½ cups milk
4 eggs
1⅛ cups pastry or unbleached
    all-purpose (plain) flour
½ teaspoon salt
½ cup (1 stick) clarified butter,
    melted

For the filling
48 chives, about 10 inches long
1¼ lb beluga caviar, chilled
1 cup crème fraîche
4 tablespoons (½ stick) unsalted
    butter, melted

Combine the milk, eggs, pastry flour, and salt in a mixing bowl. Whisk well, and then pour through a fine-mesh sieve into another bowl. Just before you cook the crepes, add 1 tablespoon of the clarified butter to the batter and stir in well.

Heat the crepe pan over medium-high heat until very hot. Lower the heat to medium. Brush the pan with a little of the melted butter, and when it sizzles, pour in 2 tablespoons of batter. Swirl the pan to form a crepe about 4½ inches in diameter. Cook just until the first side is set (do not brown), about 45 seconds to 1 minute, then turn the crepe and cook on the other side for 5 seconds. The crepes should be as thin as possible, with no holes. Remove the

crepe from the pan and repeat the process, brushing the pan with butter as needed. Stack the cooked crepes as they are done, and when you have used up the batter (you should have 48 crepes), wrap them tightly in plastic wrap (clingfilm) to keep them from drying out.

Bring a saucepan of water to a boil. Using tongs, dip a bunch of 12 chives in the boiling water and blanch for 10 seconds (this softens the chives). Repeat with the remaining chives, and place them on paper towels to dry.

Lay several crepes out on a piece of cooking parchment (no more than 12 at one time, so they wont dry out). Place 1 teaspoon of caviar in the center of each crepe, and top it with ⅓ teaspoon of the crème fraîche. Pull the edges of the crepe up around the filling, making small pleats to create a ruffle at the top. Holding the ruffled top with one hand, carefully tie a single chive around the neck, and make a double knot to hold it securely. Snip off any excess length of chive, and repeat with the remaining crepes and filling.

Brush the purses with the melted butter and serve them at room temperature, while the caviar is still cold.

Roast Lobster with Vanilla Butter Sauce

Alain Senderens
L'Archestrate
France 1981

page 122

2 lobsters, weighing about 1 kg
(2¼ lb) each
2 tablespoons olive oil

For the sauce
2 teaspoons butter
5 shallots, finely chopped
250 ml (9 fl oz) dry white wine
3 tablespoons white wine vinegar
150 g (5 oz) butter, at room
temperature, cut into cubes
salt, freshly ground pepper
1 vanilla pod (bean), split in half
lengthwise

For the garnish
1 tablespoon butter
700 g (1½ lb) fresh young spinach,
stems removed
2 large bunches watercress, leaves
only
salt, freshly ground pepper

The lobster

Place the oven dish on the middle shelf
and preheat the oven to 475°F/240°C/
Gas Mark 9.

With the blunt edge of a cleaver or a
hammer, crack the lobster claws. Place
the lobsters in the hot oven dish, pour a
tablespoon of olive oil over each one
and roast for 15 minutes or until red.
When the lobsters are cool enough to
handle, remove the meat from the claws
and detach the tails from the heads with
a twisting motion. With a pair of
scissors, cut the shell on the underside
of each tail in half lengthwise and
remove the meat. With the tip of a
knife, scrape out any blackish matter
near the top of the tails, then cut the
tail meat into slices about 5 mm
(¼ inch) thick. Place the slices of
lobster and the claws on a plate, cover
with aluminium foil and keep warm.

The sauce

Make a *beurre blanc*, heating the
2 teaspoons butter in a saucepan and
cooking the shallots. Then add the wine
and vinegar and cook until almost
reduced. Add the butter a piece at a
time, whisking until thick and creamy.
When all the butter has been added,
taste for seasoning, then with the tip
of a knife scrape some of the pulp from
inside the vanilla pod (bean) into it. Stir
the sauce, then strain it into a clean
saucepan, rubbing on the shallots with
a wooden spoon to make sure all the
sauce and vanilla goes through. Reserve.

The garnish

Melt the butter in a large pan and add
the spinach and watercress. Stir until
the vegetables have wilted down, then
simmer, uncovered, for 5 minutes,
stirring occasionally; season.

To serve the lobsters

Reheat the sauce to warm over a low
heat, whisking constantly.

Place bed of spinach and watercress on
each plate, arrange the pieces of lobster
on top, spoon the sauce over the
lobster, and serve immediately.

Pizza with Smoked Salmon and Caviar

Wolfgang Puck
Spago
United States 1982

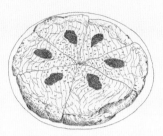

page 123

1 quantity of Pizza Dough (see below)
¼ cup extra virgin olive oil
1 medium red onion, cut into julienne strips
¼ bunch fresh dill, minced, plush 4 small sprigs for garnish
1 cup sour cream or crème fraîche
freshly ground pepper
16 oz smoked salmon, sliced paper-thin
4 heaping tablespoons domestic golden caviar
4 heaping teaspoons black caviar

Before you are ready to bake the pizzas, preheat the oven with a pizza stone inside for 30 minutes to 500°F.

After the dough has been rolled or stretched into four 8-inch circles, place the pizzas on a lightly floured wooden peel. Brush the center of each pizza to within 1 inch of the edge with olive oil and sprinkle it with some of the red onion. Slide the pizza onto the stone and bake 8–12 minutes or until crust is golden brown.

Mix the dill with the sour cream or crème fraîche and freshly ground pepper to taste. Transfer the pizzas to heated dinner plates and spread them with the sour cream mixture. Divide the salmon and arrange decoratively over the cream.

Place a spoonful of golden caviar in the center of each pizza, then spoon a little of the black caviar into the center of the golden caviar. Cut each pizza into fourths and serve immediately.

Pizza Dough
makes four 8-inch pizzas
1 package active dry or fresh yeast
1 teaspoon honey
1 cup warm water (10–115°F)
3 cups all-purpose (plain) flour
1 teaspoon kosher (coarse) salt
1 tablespoon extra virgin olive oil, plus additional for brushing
Toppings of your choice

In a small bowl, dissolve the yeast and honey in ¼ cup warm water.

In a mixer fitted with a dough hook, combine the flour and salt. Add the oil, yeast mixture, and the remaining ¾ cup of water and mix on low speed until the dough comes cleanly away from the sides of the bowl and clusters around the dough hook, about 5 minutes. (The pizza dough can also be made in a food processor. Dissolve the yeast as above. Combine the flour and salt in the bowl of a food processor fitted with the metal blade. Pulse once or twice, add the remaining ingredients, and process until the dough begins to form a ball that rides around the side of the bowl on top of the blade).

Turn the dough out onto a clean work surface and knead by hand 2–3 minutes longer. The dough should feel smooth and firm. Cover the dough with a clean, damp towel and let it rise in a warm spot for about 30 minutes. (When ready, the dough should stretch easily as it is lightly pulled.)

Divide the dough into 4 balls, about 6 ounces each. Work each ball by pulling down the sides and tucking under the bottom of the ball. Repeat four or five times to form a smooth, even, firm ball. Then on a smooth, unfloured surface, roll the ball under the palm of your hand until the top of the dough is smooth and firm, about 1 minute. Cover the dough with a damp towel and let rest 15–20 minutes. At this point, the balls can be wrapped in plastic wrap (clingfilm) and refrigerated for up to 2 days.

To prepare each pizza, dip the ball of dough into flour, shake off the excess flour, place the dough on a clean, lightly floured surface, and start to stretch the dough. Press down on the center, spreading the dough into an 8-inch circle, with its outer rim a little thicker than the inner circle. If you find this difficult to do, use a small rolling pin to roll out the dough.

Open Raviolo

Gualtiero Marchesi
Ristorante Gualtiero Marchesi
Italy 1982

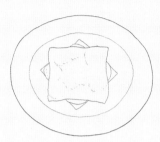

page 124

For the dough
100 g fresh dough for ravioli
4 leaves parsley
100 g fresh spinach-flavoured
  dough for ravioli

For the filling
4 kg scallops
220 g butter
8 cl white wine
8 dessertspoons of juice from one
  or more pieces of ginger grated
salt

Roll out the white ravioli dough in a thin strip. Lightly press the parsley leaves with the flat of a knife to break their central rib and space them out on the strip of dough. Fold the dough in two and then in four, so each piece contains a parsley leaf. Feed a piece through the pasta maker, then give it a quarter turn and feed through to keep it square. Form four 10 cm-square pieces, taking care that the parsley leaf remains in the centre.

Work the green dough as thin as the white dough and cut it into similar 10 cm-square pieces.

Simmer both kinds of pasta in salted water until al dente and drain.

Shell the scallops, clean, retain only the white flesh and the coral, and wash under cold running water. Fry lightly in 20 g butter for 30 seconds, add the wine and drain after a few seconds. Combine the juice of the ginger with the pan drippings and simmer for 1 minute, then combine the obtained sauce with the remaining butter (200 g), ensuring it is cold.

Put on each plate a spoonful of sauce, then a square of green pasta topped with the scallops. Give a half turn to the plate and add the white pasta so that each corner of the white pasta emerges from under the green. Pour a little sauce all around and serve.

Crème Brûlée

Alain Sailhac
Le Cirque
United States 1982

page 125

4 cups heavy (double) cream
1 vanilla bean (pod), split, seeds
  scraped out and reserved
pinch of salt
8 large egg yolks
¾ cup plus 2 tablespoons
  granulated sugar
½ cup packed light brown sugar

Heat the oven to 300°F. Place eight 6-ounce ramekins in a roasting pan. Combine the cream, vanilla bean (pod) and seeds, and salt in a saucepan set over low heat and warm for 5 minutes.

Gently whisk the egg yolks and granulated sugar in a large bowl. Gradually pour in the hot cream and stir gently to combine. Strain the custard into a pitcher (jug); discard the vanilla bean and use a spoon to skim off any bubbles on the surface of the custard.

Pour the custard into the ramekins, filling them almost to the rim. Place the roasting pan in the oven and carefully pour warm water into the pan until it reaches halfway up the sides of the ramekins. Loosely cover the pan with aluminium foil. Bake until set, 1–1¼ hours. Remove the ramekins from the water bath and allow to cool.

John Dory Back from India

Olivier Roellinger
Les Maisons de Bricourt
France 1983

page 126

Cover the ramekins individually and refrigerate for at least 3 hours, or for up to 2 days.

When ready to serve, heat the broiler (grill). Uncover the ramekins and place them on a baking sheet. Top each with 1 tablespoon brown sugar and, using a metal spatula or your finger, spread the sugar evenly over the custards. Broil (grill) the custards about 4 inches from the heating element until the sugar browns and caramelizes, 30 seconds– 1 minute. Alternatively, use a blowtorch, if you have one, to caramelize the sugar on top of the custard.

1.6 kg (or 2 smaller 800 g) John Dory (ask the fishmonger to keep the head and trimmings when filleting the fish)
1 sweetheart cabbage
1 apple
2 mangoes
1 bunch of land cress, or preferably garden cress
½ pear
a little lemon juice
1 fresh turmeric root
a couple of handfuls of kelp for steaming
butter, to taste

Spice mix
1 teaspoon mace
½ star anise
1 teaspoon coriander seeds
½ teaspoon grilled caraway seeds
½ teaspoon Sichuan pepper
½ teaspoon bitter orange peel
1 clove
2 tablespoons ground turmeric
½ teaspoon black pepper
1 cm cinnamon stick or ½ vanilla bean (pod)
a dash of cayenne pepper
1 teaspoon lily petals

Fish stock
reserved John Dory head and trimmings
1 carrot
1 onion
2 leeks, white only
1 small celery stalk
1 clove garlic
butter, for sweating the vegetables
200 ml sweet white wine
1 litre water
thyme
parsley
bay leaves
orange zest
1 slice fresh ginger

Spice broth
1 onion
50 g ginger root
2 stalks lemongrass
2 cloves roasted garlic
3 sprigs mint
3 sprigs fresh coriander (cilantro)
5 cl coconut milk

The caramel
50 g sugar
1 tablespoon crushed green cardamom
5 cl rice vinegar
200 ml chicken broth →

John Dory Back
from India

Preparing the spice mix

At least 7-8 hours in advance, dry-fry the spices in a large pan, leaving out the vanilla (if using), cayenne pepper and lily petals. When the kitchen is filled with a nice aroma, add the remaining spices and mix to a fine powder using a powerful coffee grinder.

Preparing the fish stock

Rinse the fish bones and head. Chop the carrot, onion, leek whites, celery and garlic to make a mirepoix. Sweat in the butter, then add the sweet white wine. Boil for 1 minute. Add the bones and cover to the top with 1 litre of water. Add the herbs, orange zest and ginger. Gently bring to a simmer and cook for about 30 minutes without skimming to clarify. Once done, sieve the mixture and refrigerate. The stock can be kept for up to 4–5 days. You can also make it into ice cubes.

Preparing a 'spice broth' and the caramel

Roughly chop a peeled onion and some ginger. Fry the mixture until translucent. Add 1 tablespoon of the spice mixture and stir with a wooden spoon. Next, add 300 ml of fish stock, minced lemongrass and roasted garlic cloves, then leave to simmer for 30 minutes.

In the meantime, start making the caramel. Add the sugar to a pan and when it reaches a golden colour, add the cardamom. Dilute with the rice vinegar. Finish by pouring in the chicken broth. Let it simmer for 20 minutes.

Mix the caramel and spice broth and add the mint and fresh coriander (cilantro), followed by the coconut milk. Remove from heat and leave to cool for at least 6 hours.

Execution

Discard the larger leaves of the cabbage, rip off the others, removing the larger stems, and then cut the leaves into 5 mm strips.

Peel the apple and mangoes and cut into 1 cm cubes, removing the pips and stones (seeds and pits). Cover the fruit and cook into a compote. Take off the lid towards the end to make sure it doesn't become too runny.

Wash the watercress and remove the larger stems. Peel and finely dice the turmeric and ginger (wear gloves to avoid turmeric stains). Blanch them separately.

Peel and finely dice the pear evenly to make a 'matignon'. Mix in a bit of lemon juice to stop the pears turning black.

Final stages

Divide the fish into four equal portions of two or three pieces each. Cover with clingfilm (plastic wrap) and set aside on a plate.

Cook the crunchy cabbage in boiling water with the lid off. Cool in cold water, then warm in a pan with a knob of salted butter.

Warm up the mango compote. Heat up the broth, whipping in some fresh butter to give it some body. Adjust the seasoning.

Add the kelp to a pan of water. Place the fillets in the upper part of a steam cooker layered against the sides so the fish is well imbued with the iodine aroma. Steam for about 3 minutes.

To serve

Arrange the cress across one half of the plate and the crushed cabbage on the other half with a quenelle of compote on top. Place the fillets asymmetrically. Add a dash of pear matignon to each fillet. Finish by adding a bit of coriander (cilantro) on top of the compote.

Braised Abalone
Yeung Koon Yat
The Forum
China 1983

page 127

This recipe has not been written down.
To try this at home, you will need a
high-quality dried abalone to rehydrate
and cook in a clay pot for 12 hours until
tender. Layer bamboo sheets, pork
spare ribs, and a hen. Serve the abalone
with its reduced sauce.

Samgyetang
Tosokchon Samgyetang
South Korea 1983

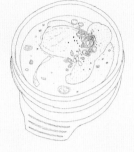

page 128

The specific recipe for this chicken
soup meant to be eaten in the summer
is a secret. A small chicken is stuffed
with rice, whole ginseng, garlic, scallion
(spring onions), gingko nuts, chestnuts,
pumpkin, sesame seeds and much
more—then simmered for several
hours. Serve in a stone bowl.

Saffron Mashed Potatoes
Simon Hopkinson
Bibendum
United Kingdom 1983

page 129

1 kg (2 lb) floury potatoes, cut into
   chunks
a generous teaspoon of saffron
   threads
1 large garlic clove, finely chopped
200 ml (7fl oz) creamy milk
200 ml (7 fl oz) virgin olive oil
Tabasco sauce, to taste
salt

Boil the potatoes in fish stock or water
with some salt. Heat together the
saffron, garlic and milk, cover and
infuse while the potatoes are boiling.

Add the olive oil to the milk infusion
and gently reheat. Drain and mash the
potatoes – I think the best texture
achieved is through a mouli-légumes.

Put the potatoes into the bowl of an
electric mixer, switch on and add
the saffron mixture in a steady stream.
Add Tabasco to taste and adjust
the seasoning.

Allow the purée to sit in a warm place
for about 30 minutes so that the saffron
flavour is fully developed.

Salt-Baked Squab Pigeons

Raymond Blanc
Le Manoir aux Quat'Saisons
United Kingdom 1984

page 130

For preparing the squabs

2 Anjou squabs (450 g in total),
   wings, neck, heart and liver
   removed and reserved for the
   sauce, cleaned and oven ready
1 tablespoon rapeseed (canola) oil

Make two small holes high on the sides of each squab and slip the legs inside. This will prevent the legs from opening when the squab is cooked in the pan and will help it to cook more thoroughly. As the legs are tucked in, they will not pierce the pastry crust. Do not season the squabs (the pastry crust will do this).

Heat the oil in a medium frying pan or skillet over a medium heat. Sear the squabs for 7 minutes on each thigh and 1 minute on each breast to crisp and colour the skin and to partially cook the legs, but not to cook the breasts. Leave to cool.

For the sauce

2 tablespoons duck fat.
reserved squab necks, wings,
   hearts and livers (see above),
   roughly chopped
4 shallots, peeled and finely
   chopped.
100 g flat cup mushrooms, cleaned
   and finely sliced
3 tablespoons dry Madeira

3 tablespoons ruby port
200 ml brown chicken stock
1 tablespoon whipping cream
a pinch of sea salt
freshly ground white pepper

Heat the duck fat in a medium saucepan over a medium heat and sear the squab necks and wings for 3–4 minutes to colour lightly. Add the shallots and mushrooms and cook for a further 2 minutes.

Add the Madeira and let bubble until reduced right down, then add the port and cook for 2 minutes. Pour in the chicken stock, stir in the cream and return to a simmer. Let simmer for 10 minutes, skimming occasionally. Chop the squab hearts and livers into 5-mm pieces and add them for the last minute.

Strain the sauce through a fine conical sieve into a jug (pitcher), pressing hard with a wooden spatula to extract as much flavour as possible. Season with salt and pepper to taste and set aside.

For the salt crust

600 g strong white flour
350 g good quality fine sea salt
6 organic/free-range medium
   egg whites (180 g)
175 ml cold water (approximately)

Combine the flour and salt in an electric mixer fitted with a dough hook. Mix at slow speed for 1–2 minutes, then add the egg whites and increase to medium speed. Finally, with the motor running, slowly add the cold water until the dough just holds together. Gather the dough, shape into a ball and flatten to a 2-cm thickness. Wrap in clingfilm (plastic wrap) and set aside until ready to assemble.

For wrapping the squabs

egg wash (2 organic/free-range
   egg yolks, beaten with 1
   tablespoon water)
plain (all-purpose) flour, to dust
4 cloves
1 tablespoon rock salt, to sprinkle

Divide the salt crust pastry in half and flatten each portion to a disc, about 3 cm thick. Roll one half of the dough between two sheets of greaseproof (wax) paper to a thickness of 5 mm.

Using a small knife and plate as a guide, cut out a circle 28 cm in diameter and set aside. Gather the trimmings (about 320 g) and roll out to a 5-mm thickness on a lightly floured surface.

For the wings, cut out an oval shape, about 10 cm long. Cut the oval in half lengthways to make 2 wings. Place one on top of the other, and using a small knife, cut into wing shapes. Separate the wings, brush with egg wash and score lines.

For the head, gather 50 g from the remaining dough trimmings and roll into a tight, perfect ball. Using your index finger, press and roll one-third of the way down the ball to create a neck and head. Use your fingers to flatten the base of the neck so it can be easily stuck to the main body. Pinch the middle of the head to create the beak.

In the centre of each large circle of dough, lay a squab, breast down, with the neck end facing away from you. Lightly brush the edge of the dough with egg wash. Fold the two sides over the squab so they overlap, press and seal.

Turn the squab away from you so it is sitting upright, tucking the dough underneath to create a firm base. There must be no holes, or the cooking time will be altered significantly. Using your hands, flatten the overlapping dough to form the bird's tail.

Repeat with the second squab and the other half of the dough.

Place the wrapped squabs on a baking tray lined with greaseproof (wax) paper. Lightly brush the insides of the wing with egg wash and press them against the sides of the squabs. Brush the bases of the heads with egg wash and press firmly in position, slightly higher on the base then they would naturally be so that they stay in place. Use your fingers to smooth where they join around the bases.

Generously brush egg wash all over the wrapped squabs, except the bases. Push 2 cloves into the sides of each head, for the eyes. Lift each squab and sprinkle rock salt over the breasts. Refrigerate until ready to cook (up to a maximum of 6 hours).

For the pommes maxim
3 Mayan Gold, Belle de Fontenay, Maris Piper or Agria potatoes, peeled
1 tablespoon duck fat
a small pinch of sea salt

Shape each potato into a cylinder, 3 cm in diameter. Using a mandoline, cut the potatoes into 2-mm thick slices. Do not wash them, as you want to retain the starch to hold them together during cooking.

Divide the duck fat between two tartlet rings placed in a small frying pan (skillet) or blini pans, 10 cm in diameter.

Place one potato slice in the middle of the mould and overlap the remaining slices around it.

Over a medium heat, pan-fry the pommes maxims for 11 minutes on each side, until crisp and golden, turning once. Keep warm.

For the pointed cabbage (optional)
¼ pointed cabbage, very finely sliced
10 g unsalted butter
60 g water
a pinch of sea salt
a pinch of freshly ground black pepper

Put all the ingredients into a medium saucepan, cover and set aside, ready to cook quickly just before serving.

To bake the wrapped squabs
Preheat the oven to 240°C/Gas 9. For this dish, the cooking time is calculated for squabs taken directly from the fridge. Place the squabs on a baking tray and bake for 22 minutes for medium or 20 minutes for medium-rare. Remove from the oven and leave to rest for 12 minutes. Observe the cooking time precisely. The heat builds up slowly at first, but as it cannot escape it intensifies during the final 5 minutes. Even as little as 2 or 3 →

Salt-Baked Squab Pigeons

Tuna Tartare

Shigefumi Tachibe
Brasserie Chaya
United States 1984

page 131

minutes less or more cooking time would under- or overcook the squabs. During the resting time, the temperature will keep rising as it has its own momentum. Our cooking time is for two dressed squabs of 225 g. After removing the squabs, turn the oven down to 170°C/Gas 3.

For the foie gras
125 g foie gras (2 slices), removed from the fridge
a dash of Xérès sherry vinegar
sea salt and freshly ground black pepper

In a medium frying pan (skillet) over a medium heat, pan-fry the foie gras for 30 seconds on each side. Season with a tiny pinch each of salt and pepper. Deglaze the pan with a dash of sherry vinegar and turn the foie gras in the liquid. Transfer to a small ovenproof frying pan (skillet) and reserve.

To serve
20 g unsalted butter, melted
100 g wild mushroom fricassée

Sit the glorious squabs on a carving board and brush with melted butter for a final glaze. Put the pan of foie gras into the oven at 170°C/Gas 3 for 2 minutes to finish.

Cook the cabbage at full boil for 3 minutes until tender; spoon into a warmed small cassolette.

Pan-fry the mushroom fricassée for 2 minutes; spoon into a small cassoulette. Bring the sauce back to the boil and pour into a sauceboat.

Reheat the pommes maxim under a grill (broiler).

Unfortunately the work doesn't stop here, as the squabs must be freed from their salt crust. To impress your guests, present the dish and carve the squabs in front of them. First slice off the head, then, with a spoon and following the inside of the wings, slice open the crust. Free the squab by lifting it with a fork. Transfer the salt crusts to a plate – they are inedible. Slice off the legs at the joint, then slice off the breasts by sliding the blade against the carcass. Of course, if you are not too confident (though you should be if you have got this far), you can do this in the privacy of your kitchen. Keep the carcasses as they will make an excellent sauce.

Divide the cabbage between plates, in a mound. Reshape the squab breasts over it. Position the pommes maxim and top with foie gras. Scatter some wild mushroom fricassée around the plates and drizzle over the sauce.

1 lb tuna (Ahi if possible)
5 fl oz olive oil
1 tablespoon Dijon mustard
2 egg yolks
1 pinch minced tarragon
1 pinch minced chives
1 tablespoon finely chopped onion
1 tablespoon finely chopped sweet pickles
1 teaspoon finely chopped capers
1 tablespoon crushed green peppercorns
juice of ¼ lemon
salt and black pepper
12 slices Melba toast or toasted sliced baguette
½ avocado, sliced

Cut the tuna into ¼-inch dice.

Slowly whisk the olive oil and Dijon mustard into the egg yolks to make a creamy mayonnaise.

Mix the tarragon and chives with the chopped vegetables, mayonnaise and other seasonings, then add the lemon juice. Sprinkle salt and black pepper on top.

Mix the tuna with the vegetable/seasoning mixture and spread on Melba toasts or toasted sliced baguette. Top with thin slices of avocado.

Lobster Club Sandwich

Anne Rosenzweig
Arcadia
United States 1985

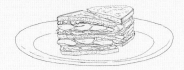

page 132

2 cups crisp cold greens (salad leaves), such as romaine, frisée, red leaf lettuce
2 fresh ripe tomatoes, sliced (cold)
16 slices (rashers) apple-smoked or double-smoked bacon, fried crisp
1 lb cooked, cold lobster tail meat, sliced on the bias ½ inch thick

For the brioche
1¼ pounds (5 sticks) unsalted butter
1 cup sugar
1 tablespoon salt
6 cups all-purpose flour
2 cups milk
1 oz cake yeast, or 1½ packages active dry yeast
10 large eggs, beaten

For the lemon mayonnaise
2 egg yolks
1½ teaspoons Dijon mustard, at room temperature
¼ cup freshly squeezed lemon juice, at room temperature
1½ cups soy oil
1 tablespoon plus 1 teaspoon grated lemon zest
salt and freshly ground black pepper, to taste

Make the brioche: Cream together the butter, sugar, and salt in a large bowl. Add the flour and beat until the mixture resembles small peas.

In a small saucepan, heat the milk to lukewarm. Remove from the heat and stir in the yeast. Set aside until foamy, 5–10 minutes. (If the yeast doesn't foam, start over.)

Add the yeast mixture to the flour mixture and stir well. Add the beaten eggs. If you have a mixer with a dough hook, process at low speed for 10 minutes. If you are mixing by hand, beat until the dough has a sheen and pulls away from the sides of the bowl into a rough ball. Add more flour if the dough is too sticky. Remove to a clean bowl, cover, and set aside in a warm place to rise until doubled in bulk, 3 hours.

Punch down the dough. Cover and refrigerate until doubled in bulk, overnight.

Preheat the oven to 350°F.

Remove the dough from the bowl and allow to soften for about 15 minutes. With a sharp knife, cut the dough into 4 pieces. Roll out each piece into a cigar shape on a lightly floured board. Wind each brioche into a tight coil and press the seam closed with your fingertips. Bake on baking tiles or a baking sheet until the bottoms sound hollow when tapped, 50 minutes. Cool on a wire rack.

Make the lemon mayonnaise: In a small bowl, whisk together the egg yolks, mustard, and lemon juice until thick. Add the oil drop by drop, whisking constantly, until the mayonnaise begins to emulsify. At this point the remaining oil can be added in a thin stream, until the mayonnaise is thick. Fold in the lemon zest and season with salt and pepper. Cover and refrigerate for at least 1 hour, or until you are ready to proceed with the rest of the recipe.

Assemble the sandwiches: Slice each brioche lengthwise into 4 even slices. Toast lightly. Spread mayonnaise on each toasted slice. Layer each bottom slice with the lettuce, then the tomato, bacon, and lobster. Top with a slice of toast and repeat the layering two more times to make four triple-decker sandwiches.

Tuna, Shaved Chives, and Extra-Virgin Olive Oil

Gilbert Le Coze
Le Bernardin
United States 1986

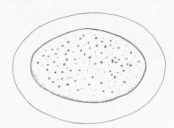

page 133

Confit Tomato with Twelve Flavors

Alain Passard
L'Arpège
France 1986

page 134

The tuna

approximately 3 oz per order
  yellowfin tuna, pounded flat
  between two layers of plastic
  wrap (clingfilm), sinew and
  blood removed
fine sea salt and freshly ground
  white pepper, to taste
2 teaspoons extra virgin olive oil

The garnish

1 teaspoon shallot, minced
1 teaspoon chives, sliced
½ lemon

Season the tuna with salt and pepper. Generously brush the tuna with olive oil. Sprinkle a few shallots over the tuna, then generously sprinkle with chives. Wipe the plate well (to the edge of the tuna), and squeeze lemon juice over the tuna at the last minute.

8–10 small cherry tomatoes
200 g apples
200 g pears
75 g pineapple
2 g fresh ginger
brown sugar, for caramelizing
10 g walnuts
10 g almonds
10 g pistachios
4 g untreated orange zest
4 g untreated lemon zest
2 vanilla pods (beans)
1 g fresh mint
1 g ground cinnamon
1 g ground anise
4 cloves

Cut off the top of the tomatoes and take out the insides, making sure to remove all the seeds.

Chop the apples, pears, pineapple and ginger into small sticks. Coarsely chop the walnuts, almonds, pistachios, orange zest and lemon zest.

Pour a thin layer of brown sugar in a frying pan (skillet). Add the apple, pear and pineapple sticks. Keep on a high heat and caramelize for a few minutes.

Add the orange zest, lemon zest, ginger, walnut, pistachio and almond pieces. Caramelize for 1 minute.

Add the vanilla, chopped mint and cinnamon, anise and cloves. Leave to caramelise for another minute. Take everything off the heat.

Stuff the inside of the tomatoes with the mixture of fruits, dried fruits and spices.

Cover the bottom and ovenproof frying pan (skillet) with a thin layer of brown sugar. Caramelize the tomatoes for 1 minute over a low heat.

Remove the skillet (frying pan) from the heat and finish cooking for 5 minutes in a preheated oven at 200°C, making sure to throw some water on the tomatoes regularly.

Serve the tomatoes with a scoop of vanilla ice cream.

Salmon Rillettes

Gilbert Le Coze
Le Bernardin
United States 1986

page 135

---

1 bottle dry white wine
2 tablespoons chopped shallots
2 lb fresh salmon fillet, fat
    trimmed, cut into 1-inch cubes
6 oz smoked salmon, fat trimmed,
    cut into small dice
2 tablespoons thinly sliced fresh
    chives
¼ cup fresh lemon juice
1 cup mayonnaise
toasted sourdough or baguette
    slices, for serving
fine sea salt and freshly ground
    white pepper to taste

Place the wine and shallots and 1
teaspoon of salt in a large saucepan and
bring to a boil. Add the fresh salmon
and poach for 40 seconds. Drain in a
sieve and run cold water over just to
stop the cooking. Drain well in a sieve
and refrigerate until cold. Discard the
poaching liquid.

Place the smoked salmon in a large
bowl and stir in the chives. Add the
poached salmon and use the side of
a wooden spoon to shred the salmon
as you mix. Stir in the lemon juice,
mayonnaise and pepper. Add salt to
taste. Refrigerate until ready to serve.
(The recipe can be made up to 6 hours
ahead). Serve with toasted sourdough
or baguette slices.

Black Cod with Miso

Nobu Matsuhisa
Matsuhisa
United States c.1987

page 136

To make this recipe, cover black cod
fillets in miso and let marinate for a
couple of days. Then grill or broil the
pieces until browned, and bake for
10-15 minutes. At Nobu they are topped
with pickled ginger shoots when served.

Rum Baba

Alain Ducasse
Le Louis XV
Monaco 1987

page 137

For the babas
14 oz (400 g) flour
1 teaspoon (4 g) salt
5 oz (140 g) butter
4¼ (17 g) teaspoons yeast
4¼ (17 g) teaspoons honey
1 lb 1½ oz (500 g) eggs

For the syrup
1 quart (1 liter) water
1 lb 1½ oz (500 g) sugar
1 orange, zested
1 lemon, zested
1 scraped vanilla bean (pod)
    and seeds

For the garnish
1¾ oz (50 g) apricot glaze
old rum, to taste

For the vanilla whipped cream
seeds from ½ vanilla bean (pod)
1 quart (1 liter) heavy (double)
    cream
7 oz (200 g) granulated sugar

Making the babas
Combine all the ingredients except the eggs, then knead the resulting dough while adding the eggs one at a time. The dough needs to come away from the walls of the mixing bowl and become elastic and smooth. Let sit for 5 minutes on an oiled marble surface. Use your hand or a pastry (piping) bag to half-fill buttered 2 × 2-inch (5 × 5-cm) cylinder (ring) molds with the dough. Let the dough rise to the top of the molds in a warm proofer (86–95°F/30–35°C). The dough should rise a little over the edge.

Bake at 400–425°F (200–220°C) for about 25 minutes, turning the baking sheet halfway through baking. The baking time will depend on the size, desired color and humidity content. Once finished baking, remove and let cool on a rack.

Preparing the syrup and vanilla cream
Mix together all the syrup ingredients. Bring to a boil, let steep (infuse). Plunge the babas into the hot, but not boiling syrup. Use a skimmer to turn. Make sure the babas are thoroughly soaked in the syrup. Drain on a rack.

Split the ½ vanilla bean (pod) in half lengthwise, scrape it out, collect the seeds, and mix into the cream. Beat together with sugar until the cream is semi-firm.

Finish and presentation
Place the babas on a plate and cover with apricot glaze. Cut in half when serving and drizzle with rum. Serve with vanilla cream.

Zuni Roast Chicken with Bread Salad

Judy Rodgers
Zuni Café
United States 1987

page 138

For the chicken
1 small chicken, 2¾ to 3½ lb
2 tender sprigs fresh thyme,
    majoram, rosemary, or sage,
    about ½ inch long
salt
about ¼ teaspoon freshly cracked
    black pepper

For the salad
Generous 8 oz slightly stale
    open-crumbed, chewy, peasant-
    style bread (not sourdough)
6–8 tablespoons mild-tasting olive
    oil
1½ tablespoons champagne
    vinegar or white wine vinegar
salt and freshly cracked black
    pepper
1 tablespoon currants
1 teaspoon red wine vinegar, or as
    needed
1 tablespoon warm water
2 tablespoons pine nuts
2 garlic cloves, silvered
¼ cup silvered scallions (spring
    onions/about 4), including a little
    of the green part
2 tablespons lightly salted chicken
    stock or lightly salted water
a few handfuls of arugula (rocket),
    frisée, or red mustard greens
    (leaves), carefully washed and
    dried

324

Seasoning the chicken (1–3 days before serving; for 3¼- to 3½-pound chickens, at least 2 days): Remove and discard the lump of fat inside the chicken. Rinse the chicken and pat very dry inside and out. Be thorough – a wet chicken will spend too much time steaming before it begins to turn golden brown.

Approaching from the edge of the cavity, slide a finger under the skin of each of the breasts, making two little pockets. Now use the tip of your finger to gently loosen a pocket of skin on the outside of the thickest section of each thigh. Using your finger, shove a herb sprig into each of the four pockets.

Season the chicken liberally all over with the salt and pepper (we use ¾ teaspoon sea salt per pound of chicken). Season the thick sections a little more heavily than the skinny ankles and wings. Sprinkle a little of the salt just inside the cavity, on the backbone, but don't otherwise worry about seasoning the inside. Twist and tuck the wing tips behind the shoulders. Cover loosely and refrigerate.

Starting the bread salad (up to several hours in advance): Preheat the broiler (grill).

Cut the bread into a couple of large chunks. Carve off all of the bottom crust and most of the top and side crust (reserve the top and side crusts to use as croutons in salads or soups). Brush the bread all over with olive oil. Broil (grill) very briefly to crisp and lightly color the surface. Turn the bread chunks over and crisp the other side. Trim off any badly charred tips, then tear the chunks into a combination of irregular 2- to 3-inch wads, bite-sized bits, and fat crumb. You should get about 4 cups.

Combine about ¼ cup of the olive oil with the champagne or white wine vinegar and salt and pepper to taste. Toss about ¼ cup of this tart vinaigrette with the torn bread in a wide salad bowl; the bread will be unevenly dressed. Taste one of the more saturated pieces. If it is bland, add a little salt and pepper and toss again.

Place the currants in a small bowl and moisten with the red wine vinegar and warm water. Set aside.

Roasting the chicken and assembling the salad: Preheat the oven to 475°F. (Depending on the size, efficiency, and accuracy of your oven, and the size of your bird, you may need to adjust the heat to as high as 500°F or as low as 450°F during the course of roasting the chicken to get it to brown properly. If that proves to be the case, begin at the temperature the next time you roast a chicken. If you have a convection/fan-assisted function on your oven, use it for the first 30 minutes; it will enhance browning and may reduce overall cooking time by 5–10 minutes.)

Choose a shallow flameproof roasting pan or dish barely larger than the chicken, or use a 10-inch skillet (frying pan) with an all-metal handle. Preheat the pan over medium heat. Wipe the chicken dry and set it breast side up in the pan. It should sizzle.

Place in the center of the oven and listen and watch for it to start sizzling and browning within 20 minutes. If it doesn't, raise the temperature progressively until it does. The skin should blister, but if the chicken begins to char or the fat is smoking, reduce the temperature by 25 degrees. After about 30 minutes, turn the bird over (drying the bird and preheating the pan should keep the skin from sticking). Roast for another 10–20 minutes, depending on the size, then flip back over to recrisp the breast skin, another 5–10 minutes. Total oven time will be 45 minutes.

While the chicken is roasting, place the pine nuts in a small baking dish and set in the hot oven for minute or two, just to warm through. Add them to the bowl of bread. →

Zuni Roast Chicken with Bread Salad

Hainanese Chicken and Rice

Foo Kui Lian
Tian Tian Hainanese Kitchen
Singapore 1987

page 139

Place a spoonful of the olive oil in a small skillet (frying pan), add the garlic and scallions (spring onions), and cook over medium-low heat, stirring constantly, until softened. Don't let them color. Scrape into the bread and fold to combine. Drain the plumped currants and fold in. Dribble the chicken stock or lightly salted water over the salad and fold again. Taste a few pieces of bread – a fairly saturated one and a dryish one. If it is bland, add salt, pepper, and/or a few drops of vinegar, then toss well. Since the basic character of bread salad depends on the bread you use, these adjustments can be essential.

Pile the bread salad in a 1-quart baking dish and tent with foil; set the salad bowl aside. Place the salad in the oven after you flip the chicken the final time.

Finishing and serving the chicken and bread salad: Remove the chicken from the oven and turn off the heat. Leave the bread salad to continue warming for another 5 minutes or so.

Lift the chicken from the roasting pan and set on a plate. Carefully pour the clear fat from the roasting pan, leaving the lean drippings behind. Add about a tablespoon of water to the hot pan and swirl it.

Slash the stretched skin between the thighs and breasts of the chicken, then tilt the bird and plate over the roasting pan to drain the juice the drippings. Set your chicken in a warm spot (which may be your stove top), and leave to rest while you finish the bread salad. The meat will become more tender and uniformly succulent as it cools.

Set a platter in the oven to warm for a minute or two.

Tilt the roasting pan and skim the last of the fat. Place over a medium-low heat, add any juice that has collected under the chicken, and bring to a simmer. Stir and scrape to soften any hard golden drippings. Taste – the juices will be extremely flavourful.

Tip the bread salad into the salad bowl. (it will be steamy-hot, a mixture of soft, moist wads, crispy-on-the-outside-but-moist-in-the-middle-wads, and a few downright crispy ones.) Drizzle and toss with a spoonful of the pan juices. Add the greens (salad leaves), a drizzle of vinaigrette, and fold well. Taste again.

Cut the chicken into pieces, spread the bread salad on the warm platter, and nestle the chicken in the salad.

While the recipe has not been documented, it can be made by poaching a chicken then cooking white rice in the broth. Serve with a sauce made from scallions (spring onions) and ginger, and cucumber slices.

Provençal Garden Vegetables Stewed in Shaved Black Truffle

Alain Ducasse
Le Louis XV
Monaco 1987

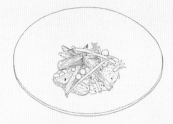

page 140

---

4 courgettes (zucchini) with
    flowers
8 baby leeks
4 purple artichokes
8 carrots with tops
4 turnips with tops
8 round red radishes
500 g baby broad (fava) beans
500 g garden peas
100 g green beans
2 bulbs fennel
8 green asparagus
1 lemon
30 g black truffle
coarse (kosher) salt
4 tablespoons plus 2 teaspoons
    olive oil
35 g butter
½ litre of fond blanc (chicken stock)
2 tablespoons mature wine vinegar
Fleur de sel (salt)

Wash the vegetables. Open the flower of the courgettes (zucchini) and remove the pistil (the small white part of the flower). Cut the green part of the leeks and take out the first layer.

Squeeze some lemon and add the lemon halves to a bowl of water. Break off the first petals of the artichokes, leaving ½ cm at the base. Use a knife to round it off. Shorten the stalk of the artichoke to 2 cm, then peel it. Cut the hearts in two and take out the choke

(the core of the artichoke) if there is one. Put them into the lemon water.

Cut the roots off the carrots, turnips and radishes. Keep 1 cm of the tops. Peel the turnips, grate the carrots and add all three vegetables to a bowl of room temperature water.

Shell the broad beans and garden peas. Cut the ends off the green beans, keeping the pointy part.

Cut the base off the fennel and remove the outer layer. Halve, then quarter the core. Peel the asparagus.

Place the truffle on baking (parchment) paper. Cut it into large chunks and then crush with a fork, pressing down on the pieces of truffle.

Boil water and add some coarse (kosher) salt. Add the green beans, asparagus and courgettes for 20 seconds, then the garden peas and baby broad beans for 10 seconds.

Drain and plunge the vegetables into cold water with ice cubes to stop them cooking and retain their green colour.

Heat up 2 tablespoons of the olive oil and 20 g of butter in frying pan (skillet). Throw in the carrots, turnips, leeks,

artichokes and fennel. Season and mix. Leave to sweat for 3–4 minutes on a low heat, until they become translucent.

Heat up 2 teaspoons of oil and 5 g of butter in a sauté pan. Sweat the radishes with the lid on, with 2 tablespoons of *fond blanc*, until they are soft. Then drain them.

Soften the vegetables with the rest of the fond blanc. Cover and leave to cook for 5–6 minutes. Ensure that they stay crunchy.

Add the green vegetables and truffle. Bring to a boil and then leave to cook for 2–3 minutes. Add the radishes and 1 tablespoon of olive oil. Strain the vegetables and save the cooking water.

Heat up the vegetable cooking water in a sauté pan with 1 tablespoon of oil. mature wine vinegar to bind the sauce. Pour the sauce over the vegetables in a soup dish and sprinkle with *fleur de sel*.

New-Style Sashimi

Nobu Matsuhisa
Matsuhisa
United States 1987

page 141

Chef Nobu uses thin slices of red snapper for this dish, topped with ginger, garlic, sesame seeds, and yuzu soy sauce. Just before serving, heat some olive–sesame oil and pour over the fish. Your mostly raw fish will now be lightly cooked.

Grilled Squid with Chile

Ruth Rogers and Rose Gray
The River Café
United Kingdom 1987

page 142

6 medium squid, no bigger than
  your hand

For the sauce
12 large fresh red chillies, seeded
  and very finely chopped
extra virgin olive oil
sea salt and freshly ground black
  pepper

To serve
225 g (8 oz) rocket (arugula) leaves
8 tablespoons oil and lemon
  dressing
3 lemons

Clean the squid by cutting the body open to make a flat piece. Scrape out the guts, keeping the tentacles in their bunches but removing the eyes and mouth.

Using a serrated knife, score the inner side of the flattened squid body with parallel lines 1 cm (½ inch) apart, and then equally apart the other way to make cross-hatching.

To make the sauce, put the chopped chilli in a bowl and cover with about 2.5 cm (1 inch) of the oil. Season with salt and pepper.

Place the squid (including the tentacles) scored side down on a very hot grill (broiler), season with salt and pepper and grill for 1–2 minutes. Turn the squid pieces over; they will immediately curl up, by which time they will be cooked.

Toss the rocket (arugula) in the oil and lemon dressing. Arrange a squid body and tentacles on each plate with some of the rocket. Place a little of the chilli on the squid and serve with lemon quarters.

Octopus in Olive Sauce

Rosita Yiruma
Salón Rosita
Peru 1987

page 143

1 egg
¼ tablespoon salt
2 tablespoons of lime juice
½ cup oil
10 large, pitted black olives
½ lb octopus, boiled for 40
    minutes, frozen and cut into
    very thin slices
chopped parsley, to serve

Put the egg, salt, and lime juice into a blender and liquefy. Then, put in a thin stream of oil. When the mayonnaise is ready, empty into a bowl, leaving a little at the bottom of the blender.

Put the pitted olives in the blender, which already contains some of the mayonnaise, and mix well until a smooth sauce is formed. To this add the previous mixture and mix with a spoon until it is a uniform consistency.

On a small platter, arrange the octopus slices in a single layer. Cover them with the olive sauce. Garnish with chopped parsley.

Gâteau of Clonakilty Black Pudding

Michael Clifford
Clifford's
Republic of Ireland 1988

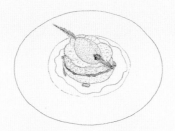

page 144

3 large potatoes, peeled
1 cooking apple, sliced
butter, for cooking
200 g mushrooms
1 clove of garlic
1 tablespoon sherry vinegar
50 ml pork stock (broth)
16 slices of Clonakilty black
    pudding (blood sausage)
25 g smoked bacon, diced
salt and black pepper

Cook the sliced apple in a knob of butter without colouring. Sauté the mushrooms with the garlic. Put both into a liquidizer and purée.

Parboil the potatoes and slice very thinly. Arrange into eight fans. Brush with melted butter and season well. Grill (broil) until golden.

For the sauce, reduce the vinegar by half, add the pork stock, season and finish with butter.

Fry the pudding and bacon until crispy. Reheat the apple and mushrooms, add a knob of butter and season well.

Place one potato fan on a plate, then a layer of purée, then the pudding and top with another potato fan. Place a small quenelle of purée on top. Place the bacon around the outside of the plate and pour the sauce around.

Chequerboard of Star Anise Ice Cream, Pineapple Sorbet, and Liquorice

Phillip Searle
Oasis Seros
Australia 1988

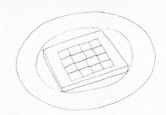

page 145

Plain ice cream
In a saucepan, add 1 litre of milk and 1 litre of cream with 400 g of caster (superfine) sugar and bring to just boiling.

In the bowl of a planetary mixer, beat 24 egg yolks with another 400 g of caster (superfine) sugar until white and creamy. Gradually pour the milk, sugar and cream mixture onto the beaten egg yolks. Whisk until combined.

Remove the bowl with the cream preparation, place onto a bain-marie and stir continuously with a wooden spoon until it thickens. Immediately pour in an additional 1 litre of cream to halt the cooking. Strain the preparation while still hot through a fine sieve and allow to cool. It is now ready to churn.

Star anise ice cream
Use exactly the same ingredients and method as above except in the saucepan with the litre of milk, cream and sugar, add 15 roughly pounded star aniseeds and be careful NOT to bring to the boil. Proceed as in the recipe above, but when you strain the preparation press on the aniseed debris to extract flavour. Allow to cool. This is now ready to churn.

Pineapple sorbet
Take a very ripe large pineapple. Cut away the skins and 'eyes' and remove →

Chequerboard of Star Anise Ice Cream, Pineapple Sorbet, and Liquorice

the core. Cut into small pieces. Be careful to preserve the juices. For each 200 g of pineapple pulp and juice, add 40 g of caster (superfine) sugar and 40 g warmed liquid glucose (light corn syrup). Mash the preparation with your hands, then place in a food processor (preferably blender) and purée. Pour the sorbet into a fine sieve (preferably conical) and press heavily so there is only a minimum amount of pulp left in the sieve. This is ready to be churned.

Liquorice confection

Take 200 g of good quality soft liquorice stick and chop it up finely. Put 200 g of caster (superfine) sugar into a saucepan and just cover with water. Cook the sugar and water to the soft ball stage, then add the chopped liquorice to the saucepan. Stir constantly on low heat until a homogenous black. While hot, press through a fine sieve and refrigerate. It is ready to use.

Begin layering the chequerboard

To mould the ice cream, you will preferably need a stainless steel oblong mould with square sides, measuring approximately 5 inches across the base, 8 inches long and 6 inches high. Place the mould in the freezer.

Take about 600 ml of pineapple sorbet and churn it. Remove from the churn

and place it into a stainless steel bowl and soften to 'just pouring consistency'. Pour a layer in the bottom of the frozen mould, 1¼ inches deep (you might have some left over). Bang the mould on the bench so that the layer becomes even and horizontal. Place the mould in the freezer. Every time you put a layer in you will need to follow the 'banging' procedure. Freeze until hard.

Remove the mould from the freezer and with a pastry brush 'paint' a layer of the liquorice confection over the surface of the frozen layer of pineapple sorbet. Place it back in the freezer.

Take about 600 ml of star anise ice cream and churn it. Place it into a stainless bowl and slightly soften and pour the ice cream on top of the painted sorbet layer (bang the mould) – you might have some star anise ice cream left over. Freeze that layer.

When it's frozen paint it with liquorice confection. Place the mould back in t he freezer.

Repeat the process with the pineapple sorbet to make the third layer, following all the same procedures. Do exactly the same for the fourth layer, which is star anise ice cream. In the mould we have a 1 inch layer of pineapple sorbet, a fine layer of liquorice, 1 inch layer of star

anise ice cream, a fine layer of liquorice, 1 inch layer of pineapple sorbet, a fine layer of liquorice and a 1 inch layer of star anise ice cream.

Cutting the layers

Put the moulded ice cream and two chopping boards into the freezer over night. Prepare to cut the block. Precision, judgement, dexterity and speed are the tools to your success. You need a sink full of very hot water in which you can unmould the block onto one of the paper lined boards; two frozen boards that are covered with baking (parchment) paper on the upper side; a very long bladed knife; a very tall jug (pitcher) full of boiling water; the container of liquorice confection with the paint brush in it.

Dip the mould into a sink full of hot water, very briefly, and unmould onto one of the frozen boards. Return it to the freezer to stabilize for about 30 minutes.

Remove the moulded block of ice cream from the freezer along with frozen board number two. Look at the block. You need to divide the block into four length-wise slices. That means you are going to make three lengthwise cuts. Mark the top as a guide. Each slice will be 1¼ inches wide.
Dip the knife into the boiling water in the jug for 5 seconds, wipe the blade

and quickly cut the first slice, keeping the knife blade perfectly vertical. Lay the first slice on frozen board number two. Paint the surface with the liquorice confection. Dip the knife in the boiling water in the jug again, wipe the blade, cut the second slice (keeping knife blade vertical). Lay the second slice on top of the liquorice covered first slice, but turn it over so that you can see the beginnings of alternative ice cream/ sorbet squares. Paint the second slice with liquorice, dip the knife into the boiling water again, wipe the blade to make the final cut of the moulded block (this is the most difficult). Place on the third slice, turning again. Paint with liquorice and finish with the fourth slice. When you are observing the block from the end you need to make sure the squares alternate. Dip the knife in the hot water again and square up the sides and tops. Freeze overnight.

Finishing the chequerboard

Finish the ice cream by placing a plain ice cream border around the ice cream. Ok, you need a new mould – 6½ inches across the base, 8 inches long and 7 inches high. Place the mould in the freezer. Churn 600 ml of plain ice cream and make a layer in the bottom of the mould, preferably ¾ inch deep. Bang the mould on the bench and freeze over night.

Remove the moulded block (which is on the board) from the freezer and paint three of the sides with liquorice confection. Refreeze for 4 minutes, remove from the freezer and turn it over, still on the frozen board, and remove the baking paper stuck to the bottom. Paint that surface too. Once again with a hot bladed knife, cut the ends to even them up and place this chequerboard (still on the frozen block) back in the freezer.

Churn the remainder of the plain ice cream and place in a stainless steel bowl to soften slightly. Remove the new mould (with a single layer) from the freezer. Remove the painted chequerboard block. With a clean pastry brush, brush a small quantity of the softened plain ice cream onto the layer in the new mould.

Centre the painted chequerboard block into the new mould onto the just painted surface and carefully pour the plain ice cream down the sides, being careful to expel any air bubbles. Continue filling the mould leaving ½ inch from the top of the mould. Freeze overnight with the chopping board onto which you are going to unmould the final project.

To unmould the ice cream, dip the mould into a sink full of hot water for 3–4 seconds and invert it onto the frozen chopping board lined with baking paper, then place immediately back into the freezer. It is now ready to serve.

To serve

Dip the long bladed knife into boiling water, wipe the blade and cut a slice a bit less than ½ inch thick, once again keeping the blade of the knife as vertical as possible. Serve each slice on a frozen plate that has been in the freezer.

Chocolate Nemesis

Ruth Rogers and Rose Gray
The River Café
United Kingdom 1988

page 146

Coconut Pecan Cake

Dolester Miles
Chez Fonfon and Bottega Cafe
United States 1988

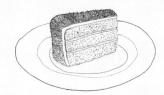

page 147

---

10 whole eggs
575 g (1 lb 5 oz) caster (superfine)
  sugar
675 g (1½ lb) bittersweet chocolate,
  broken into small pieces
450 g (1 lb) unsalted butter,
  softened

Preheat the oven to 160°C/325°F/Gas 3.
Line a 20 × 5-cm (8 × 2-inch) round
cake tin (pan) with greaseproof (wax)
paper, then grease and flour it.

Beat the eggs in a mixer with a third of
the sugar until the volume quadruples
– this will take at least 10 minutes.

Heat the remaining sugar in a small pan
with 250 ml (8 fl oz) water until the it
has completely dissolved to a syrup.

Place the chocolate and butter in the
hot syrup and stir to combine. Remove
from the heat and allow to cool slightly.

Add the warm syrup to the eggs and
continue to beat, gently, until completely combined – about 20 seconds, no
more. Pour into the cake tin and place
in a bain-marie of hot water. It is
essential, if the cake is to cook evenly,
that the water comes up to the rim of
the tin. Bake in the oven for 30 minutes
or until set. Test by placing the flat of
your hand gently on the surface.

Cool in the tin before turning out.

For the cake
1 cup firmly packed sweetened
  shredded coconut
¾ cup pecan halves, toasted
2 cups sugar
2¼ cups all–purpose flour
1 tablespoon baking powder
¾ teaspoon salt
12 tablespoons (1½ sticks) unsalted
  butter, softened
¼ cup cream of coconut (such as
  Coco Lopez)
4 large eggs
1 teaspoon coconut extract
1 cup plus 2 tablespoons
  unsweetened coconut milk
2 cups sweetened (shredded)
  coconut, for toasting

For the filling
2 large yolks, lightly beaten
¾ cup sweetened condensed milk
4 tablespoons unsalted butter
1 tablespoon cream of coconut
1 cup sweetened shredded coconut

For the simple syrup
1 cup sugar
1 cup water

For the icing
1 cup heavy (double) cream
¼ cup confectioners' (icing) sugar
1 teaspoon coconut extract

To make the cake, preheat the oven to
350°F. Grease two 9-inch round cake pans
and line the bottom of each with a circle
of parchment (baking) paper. Grease the
parchment paper, then dust with flour,
tapping out any excess. Set the pans aside.

Finely grind the coconut in a food
processor, then transfer it into a bowl.
Add the pecans to the processor, along
with 2 tablespoons of the sugar, and
finely grind them. Set aside. Sift
together the flour, baking powder, and
salt into a large bowl. Stir in the ground
coconut and pecans, set aside.

In the bowl of an electric mixer fitted
with the paddle attachment (or use a
large bowl and handheld mixer), beat
the butter, cream of coconut, and the
remaining 1¾ cups plus 2 tablespoons
sugar on high speed until light and
fluffy, about 4 minutes. Beat in the eggs
one at a time, beating well after each
addition, then beat in the coconut
extract. Add the flour mixture in three
batches, alternating with the coconut
milk, starting and ending with the
flour mixture.

Divide the batter between the prepared
pans and smooth the top of each with
a spatula. Bake until the cakes are golden
and a tester (skewer) comes out clean,
30–35 minutes. Let the cakes cool in the
pans on a rack for 30 minutes. Run a
knife around the edge of each cake,

page 148

invert onto a wire rack, and remove the parchment. Let cool completely.

To toast the coconut, spread it out on a baking sheet and toast in the oven at 350°F, shaking it every 5 minutes or so, until aromatic and golden brown, 10–15 minutes. Let cool completely.

While the cakes are cooling, prepare the filling. Place the egg yolks in a small heatproof bowl. Combine the condensed milk, butter, and cream of coconut in a small saucepan and cook over medium-low heat for 3–4 minutes, stirring constantly, until hot. Whisk one-third of the hot milk mixture into the egg yolks. Transfer the egg mixture to the saucepan of milk and whisk constantly over medium-low heat until the consistency of pudding, about 4 minutes. Do not allow the custard to become too thick, or it will be difficult to spread on the cake.

Transfer the custard to a bowl and stir in the shredded coconut. Let cool completely. (The filling can be refrigerated in an airtight container for up to 3 days; let it stand at room temperature until it is soft enough to spread before assembling the cake.)
To make the simple syrup, combine the sugar and water in a small heavy saucepan and bring to a simmer over medium heat, swirling to dissolve the sugar. Dip a pastry brush in hot water

and wipe down the sides of the pan to dissolve any sugar crystals that cling to the sides. Simmer for 2 minutes, the remove from the heat and let cool. (Simple syrup keeps for weeks in a tightly sealed jar in the refrigerator.)

To assemble the cake, cut each cake horizontally in half. Build the layer cake in a cake pan: Place one layer in the bottom of a 9–inch cake pan. Moisten the top with some of the simple syrup. Spread ½ cup of the coconut filling in a thin, even layer with an offset spatula. Repeat to make two more layers of cake and filling, then place the last layer on top. Refrigerate the cake for about 1 hour.

To unmold, run a spatula around the edges of the chilled cake, invert a cake plate over the top, and flip the cake over onto the plate.

To make the icing, whip the cream with the confectioners' (icing) sugar and coconut extract until stiff peaks form. Spread the whipped cream on the top and sides of the cake and sprinkle with the toasted coconut. Refrigerate until ready to serve.

1 large cooking apple, peeled, cored and chopped
1 medium onion, thinly sliced
3 fl oz white wine
2 oz butter
freshly ground black pepper
8 oz black pudding (blood sausage), 2 slices per portion
4 big oysters

For the mustard sauce
10 fl oz cream
3 fl oz dry white wine
1 tablespoon wholegrain mustard
1 tablespoon lemon juice
freshly ground pepper

To make the mustard sauce, put the cream, wine and mustard into a small pan and bring to the boil. Boil, uncovered, until reduced to a pouring consistency. Add the lemon juice and season with freshly ground black pepper. (Salt is not necessary as both the pudding and oysters are well salted.)

Stew the apple and onion with the wine and half the butter until soft. Season to taste with black pepper.

Fry the pudding in the remaining butter until cooked and crisp on both sides.

Pat the oysters dry and fry them with the pudding for a minute. Serve with the mustard sauce.

Spelt Risotto

Alain Solivérès
La Bastide des Gordes
France 1989

page 149

Pig's Trotter Carpaccio

Joan Roca
El Celler de Can Roca
Spain 1989

page 150

The recipe has never been revealed, but to make it you will need spelt, white wine, and chicken stock. Top with truffles, frog's legs, or a ragout of cockscombs and kidneys.

For the pig's feet
5 kg pig's feet
2 carrots
2 onions, peeled
½ bay leaf
5 black peppercorns

Clean the pig's feet well. Place them in a pot with water and bring to a boil. Remove from the heat, change the water, and add the carrots, onions, bay leaf, and peppercorns. Bring to a boil, then reduce the heat to low. Cook for 4 hours until they are completely tender. Remove the pig's feet, drain well, debone them while they're still hot, and, using plastic wrap (clingfilm), roll into cylinders. Let cool and then freeze.

For the porcini oil
100 g dried porcini powder
300 g sunflower oil
10 g Montbrió vinegar

In an empty vacuum-seal bag, place the dried porcini powder and sunflower oil, and seal at 100 per cent. Vacuum cook with a Roner (sous-vide water bath) at 70°C for 2 hours. Cool, then add the Montbrió vinegar. Reserve.

For the sautéed porcini
200 g small porcini
20 g extra virgin olive oil
salt

Clean the porcini well. Cut into fourths and reserve. In a pan over medium heat, heat the extra virgin olive oil and sauté the cut porcini. Season with salt, remove from the heat, and reserve.

For the porcini caramel
200 g fondant
100 g glucose (light corn syrup)
100 g isomalt
50 g porcini powder
1 porcini-shaped mold

In a saucepan, place the fondant, glucose (light corn syrup), and isomalt and bring to 150°C, stirring occasionally. Remove from heat, and when it reaches 140°C, add the porcini powder. Mix vigorously until a smooth mixture is achieved, then spread on a Silpat as thinly as possible.

Once the porcini caramel has hardened, place in a Thermomix and grind until achieving a fine powder. Using a sieve, dust the powder over the porcini mold and bake at 160°C for 1 minute or until

Panfried Quail with Country Ham

Edna Lewis
Gage & Tollner
United States 1989

page 151

it melts. Remove from the mold and store in an air-tight container together with silica gel.

For the diced tomatoes
4 ripe plum tomatoes
salt

In a saucepan with boiling water, blanch the tomatoes for 20 seconds and quickly cool in an ice bath. Peel the tomatoes, remove the seeds, and cut into 3-mm cubes. Season with salt and reserve.

For the tomato sauté
500 g ripe plum tomatoes
1 clove garlic
10 g extra virgin olive oil
salt

Blanch and peel the tomatoes. Remove the seeds and reserve them for plating. Cut the pulp into small cubes. Peel and chop the clove of garlic. In a saucepan with the olive oil, sauté the garlic, add the tomatoes, and cook slowly. When they are well glazed, season with salt, remove from heat, and reserve.

For plating
cooked Santa Pau beans
chopped chives
flake salt

Cut the frozen pig's feet cylinders using a deli meat slicer in 3-mm slices and place them on a flat ovenproof plate. Drizzle the porcini oil on the plate. Add the sautéed porcini, diced tomatoes, Santa Pau beans, and a few dots of the tomato sauté. Heat the entire plate in the oven and finish with the chopped chives, flake salt, and porcini caramel.

1 cup white grapes
2 teaspoons salt
½ teaspoon freshly ground black pepper
1 teaspoon dried thyme leaves
8 quail, split and flattened
½ cup (1 stick) unsalted butter
½ lb Virginia (cured) ham, cut into 2 x ¼-inch matchsticks

Crush the cup of grapes with a pestle, then put through a sieve or vegetable mill to extract the juice, or use a potato ricer. You should have about ¼–½ cup.

Combine the salt, pepper, and thyme, crushing the thyme with your fingertips. Sprinkle both sides of the birds with the seasonings.

Melt the butter in a large skillet (frying pan) over medium heat until it foams and just begins to brown. Add the quail, skin side down. Sprinkle with the ham and cook, covered, until the juices run clear, about 4 minutes longer. Take the pan from the heat and let the quail rest, covered, for about 10 minutes.

Arrange the quail on a platter and sprinkle the ham over them.

Pour the fat from the pan. Add the grape juice and bring to a boil. Cook for 1 minute, scraping the browned bits from the bottom to deglaze the pan. Pour over the quail and serve.

Shepherd's Pie

Mark Hix
The Ivy
United Kingdom c.1990

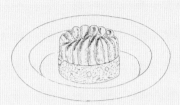

page 152

900 g each good quality minced
lamb and beef, mixed and not
too fatty
vegetable oil, for frying
500 g onions, peeled and finely
chopped
2 cloves garlic, peeled and crushed
10 g thyme, chopped finely
25 g flour
2 tablespoons tomato purée
(paste)
150 ml red wine
50 ml Worcestershire sauce
1 litre dark meat stock
8 half servings of firm mash
potatoes, with no cream added
salt and freshly ground black
pepper

Season the minced meat. Heat some
vegetable oil in a frying pan (skillet)
until it is very hot and cook the meat
in small quantities for a few minutes,
then drain it in a colander to remove
all the fat. In a thick-bottomed pan
heat some more vegetable oil and
gently fry the onion, garlic and thyme
until they are very soft. Add the meat,
dust it with the flour and add the
tomato purée (paste). Cook for a
few minutes, stirring constantly.

Preheat the oven to 200°C/gas mark 6.
Slowly add the red wine, Worcestershire
sauce and dark meat stock, bring it to
the boil and simmer for 30–40 minutes.
Strain off about 200 ml of the sauce to
serve with the pie. Continue to simmer
the meat until the liquid has almost
evaporated. Take it off the heat, check
the seasoning and allow it to cool.
To make the pie, put the meat into a
large serving dish or individual dishes
and top with the potatoes. Bake for
35–40 minutes.

XO Sauce Live Pippies

Uncle Hung
Golden Century
Australia early 1990s

page 153

1 litre water
1 kg pippies (pipi clams)
2 tablespoons peanut (groundnut)
oil or vegetable oil
2 tablespoons homemade XO
sauce (from dried seafood such
as scallops, red shallots and
chilli), or also available from
Asian grocery stores
100 ml chicken stock
1 teaspoon sugar
½ teaspoon salt
1 teaspoon soy sauce
1 teaspoon corn starch (cornflour)
mixed with 2 tablespoons water
1 bunch spring onions (scallions)
including green stems, sliced, to
serve

Heat a wok, add 1 litre of water and the
pippy cover and bring to the boil.
Removing the pippy as they open.
Drain and reserve.

Heat the oil in a wok over high heat,
add the homemade XO sauce and stir
well then add the chicken stock, sugar,
salt and soy sauce and simmer for 1
minute. Add the pippy and sauté for 1–2
minutes until the shells fully opened,
add in the corn starch (cornflour)
mixture, toss to combine and serve
garnished with spring onions (scallions).

Irish Stew

Richard Corrigan
Bentley's
United Kingdom 1992

page 154

2–3 medium necks of lamb, filleted
    and boned (reserve the bones for
    the stock)

For the stock
lamb bones
1 carrot
½ onion
1 celery stick
1 handful parsley stalks
10 black peppercorns
1 sprig rosemary
1 bay leaf
1 sprig thyme

For the stew
550 g floury potatoes, such as King
    Edward, peeled and chopped
500 g carrots, peeled and chopped
500 g swede (rutabaga), peeled
    and chopped
550 g waxy potatoes, such as
    Maris Piper or Pentland Javelin,
    peeled and chopped
½ teaspoon fresh thyme leaves
salt and black pepper
fresh chives, thyme or parsley,
    chopped, to garnish

For the stock, put everything into a
deep saucepan. Pour in enough water to
cover, then bring to a boil and simmer
on a medium heat for at least 2 hours.
Sieve the stock to remove the bones
and vegetables, then return to the pan,
boil and reduce until you have 1 litre
of liquid.

Cut the lamb into large chunks and
put into a large saucepan. Add the
stock and bring to a boil, skimming
any impurities that rise to the top, then
reduce the heat and simmer gently for
10 minutes.

Keep the two types of potatoes
separate. Add the floury potatoes first,
along with the carrots and swede
(rutabaga), to the lamb pot and
continue simmering for 10 minutes.

Add the waxy potatoes and the thyme,
season and simmer for a further 15
minutes, until the lamb is soft.

Take off the heat and leave to rest for 10
minutes before serving, garnished with
your choice of fresh herbs.

Confit of Petuna Ocean Trout with Fennel Salad

Tetsuya Wakuda
Tetsuya's
Australia 1992

page 155

350 g (11 oz) ocean trout, filleted
100 ml (3½ fl oz) grapeseed oil
80 ml (2½ fl oz) olive oil
1½ teaspoons ground coriander
1½ teaspoons white pepper
10 whole leaves basil
3 stalks thyme
¼ teaspoon finely chopped garlic
2 stalks celery, finely chopped
2 small carrots, finely chopped
3 tablespoons chopped chives
4 tablespoons konbu, finely
    chopped
½ teaspoon sea salt
2 tablespoons ocean trout caviar

Parsley oil
leaves from ¼ bunch flat-leaf
    parsley
100 ml (3½ fl oz) olive oil or
    grapeseed oil
1½ teaspoons salted capers, rinsed
    and drained

Fennel salad
¼ bulb fennel, shaved
1 teaspoon lemon juice
salt and pepper
½ teaspoon lemon-scented oil →

337

Confit of Petuna Ocean Trout with Fennel Salad

Large Fried Chicken
Wang's Large Fried Chicken
China 1992

page 156

Skin the ocean trout and cut crosswise into 70–80-g (2½-oz) pieces – they should weigh no more than 100 g (3½ oz). In a little tray, immerse the ocean trout into grapeseed oil and olive oil with the coriander, pepper, basil, thyme and garlic. Cover and allow to marinate for a few hours in the fridge. If you do not want to use too much oil, paint the surface of the fish with oil and press on the herbs.

To cook the fish, preheat the oven to the absolutely lowest setting possible.

Take the fish out of the oil and allow to come to room temperature. Chop the celery and carrots and place on the base of a baking tray. Put the ocean trout on top and place in the oven. Cook with the door open so that the fish cooks gently. Paint the surface every few minutes with the marinade.

Depending on the size and thickness of the fish, cooking takes 7–8 minutes (no more than 10 minutes). When you touch the end part, your fingers should just go through the flesh. The flesh should not have changed colour at all, but remain a brilliant orangey red, and feel lukewarm to the touch.

Remove the fish from the oven and allow to cool down immediately. Lift out of the tray and allow to come to room temperature.

To make the parsley oil, purée the parsley with the olive oil in a blender Add the capers and blend.
To make the fennel salad, finely slice the fennel on a mandoline. Toss with the lemon juice, salt and pepper to taste, and some lemon-scented oil or lemon zest.

Sprinkle the top of the fish with finely chopped chives, konbu and a little sea salt.

To serve, place some fennel salad on the base of the plate. Put the ocean trout on top and drizzle a little parsley oil all around. Dot the ocean trout caviar at regular intervals, and serve.

Wang's has yet to reveal this recipe and is keeping it secret. To attempt this, pound a very big piece of chicken super thin (or "bigger than your face" according to Wang's). The chicken should be well-seasoned and fried until super crisp.

Smoked Salmon Consommé

Tim Pak Poy
Claude's
Australia 1993

page 157

1 large snapper, head only
  (Chryophrys auratus)
2 sand flatheads (Platycephalus
  arenarius)
2 yellowfin leatherjackets
  (Meuschenia trachylepis)
2 red scorpion cods (Scorpaena
  cardinalis)
1 kg smoked salmon collars
  (pectoral fin attached)

Vegetables
3 medium carrots
3 stalks celery
2 medium leeks
1 head fennel

Aromas
½ head fresh garlic
1 lemon, flesh only
½ teaspoon dill seed
1 teaspoon fennel seed
1 teaspoon black peppercorn,
  crushed
large sprig of fresh thyme,
  tarragon and dill
parsley stalk
2 fresh bay leaves
½ bottle of good chardonnay

To clarify
1 onion
400 g fish trimmings (scraps) of
  quality white fleshed fish
1 bunch chervil
dill sprigs
200 ml egg whites

To finish
saffron (sargol)
whipping cream 35% milk fat
Pernod

Split the snapper head in half down its spine. Cut the flatheads and leather jackets into three on the bias leaving the scorpion cods whole. Rinse the collars. In a large stock pot, place the fish, smoked salmon collars, finely cut vegetables, halved head of garlic and just enough water to cover. Bring to the boil, removing scum. Simmer for 50 minutes, switch off the heat, then add the rest of the aromas. Cool for 20 minutes. Strain carefully, then cool again in a bath of cold water.

To clarify
Slice the onion in half and blacken the flesh in a cast iron pan over high heat (do not remove the skins). Pulse the fish in a food processor and place in a straight sided pot with the chopped chervil and dill. Add the egg whites and knead by hand. Pour on the cold salmon stock, add the onion and bring to the boil on a medium flame, stirring occasionally to prevent it from catching. As the stock comes to boiling point the egg whites will come to the surface forming a 'raft'. Turn down immediately and let simmer for approximately 40 minutes without stirring, until the stock is sparkling and gin clear. Strain very carefully through double muslin (cheesecloth), taking care not to break up the raft. Refrigerate overnight allowing any remaining sediment to settle.

Warm the consommé. Whip some cream and chill (season with Pernod as desired). Use a jug (pitcher) to pour the hot consommé into the vessels. Judge the temperature carefully to avoid scalding consommé through cold cream. Top with a few strands of saffron.

Avocado Toast

Bill Granger
Bills
Australia 1993

page 158

Cornets

Thomas Keller
The French Laundry
United States 1994

page 159

2 tablespoons lime juice
2 tablespoons olive oil
sea salt
freshly ground pepper
1 avocado, peeled and quartered
bread, toasted
coriander (cilantro)

Put the lime juice, olive oil, salt and pepper into a bowl and whisk until combined.

Serve quarters of avocado on the toast, drizzled with the dressing and topped with coriander (cilantro), sea salt and lots of freshly ground pepper.

For the cornets
¼ cup plus 3 tablespoons all-
   purpose (plain) flour
1 tablespoon plus 1 teaspoon sugar
1 teaspoon kosher (coarse) salt
8 tablespoons (4 oz) unsalted
   butter, softened but still cool to
   the touch
2 large egg whites, cold
2 tablespoons black sesame seeds

For the salmon tartare
4 oz salmon fillet (belly preferred),
   skin and any pin bones removed
   and very finely minced
¾ teaspoon extra virgin olive oil
¾ teaspoon lemon oil
1½ teaspoons finely minced chives
1½ teaspoons finely minced
   shallots
½ teaspoon kosher (coarse) salt, or
   to taste
small pinch of freshly ground white
   pepper, or to taste

For the sweet red onion crème fraîche
1 tablespoon finely minced red
   onions
½ cup crème fraîche
¼ teaspoon kosher (coarse) salt, or
   to taste
freshly ground white pepper
24 chive tips (about 1 inch long)

For the cornets
Make a 4-inch hollow circular stencil for making perfectly shaped rounds. Cut the rim from the top of a plastic container. Trace two concentric circles on the lid, the inner 4 inches in diameter, the outer about 4½ inches. Sketch a thumb tab that will make it easy to lift the stencil off the silicon-coated Silpat. Trim around the tab and outer circle. Remove the inner circle so that you have a hollow ring. The batter gets spread to the stencil's edges, then it's lifted off.

In a medium bowl, mix together the flour, sugar, and salt. In a separate bowl, whisk the softened butter until it is completely smooth and mayonnaise–like in texture. Using a stiff spatula or spoon, beat the egg whites into the dry ingredients until completely incorpora-ted and smooth. Whisk in the softened butter by thirds, scraping the sides of the bowl as necessary and whisking until the batter is creamy and without any lumps. Transfer the batter to a smaller container, as it will be easier to work with.

Preheat the oven to 400°F.

Place a Silpat on the counter (it is easier to work on the Silpat before it is put on the sheet pan). Place the stencil in one corner of the sheet and, holding the stencil flat against the Silpat, scoop some of the batter onto the back of an offset spatula and spread it in an even layer over the stencil. Then run the spatula over the entire stencil to remove any excess batter. (After baking the first batch of cornets, you will be able to judge the correct thickness: you may need a little more of less batter to adjust the thickness of the cornets.) There should not be any holes in the batter. Lift the stencil and repeat the process to make as many rounds as you have molds or to fill the Silpat, leaving about 1½ inches between the cornets. Sprinkle each cornet with a pinch of black sesame seeds.

Place the Silpat on a heavy baking sheet and bake for 4–6 minutes, or until the batter is set and you see it rippling from the heat. The cornets may have browned in some areas, but they will not be evenly browned at this point.

Open the oven door and place the baking sheet on the door. This will help keep the cornets warm as you roll them and prevent them from becoming too stiff to roll. Flip a cornet over on the sheet pan, sesame seed side down, and place a 4½–inch cornet mold (size No. 35) at the bottom of the round. If you are right handed, you will want the

pointed end on your left and the open end on your right. The tip of the mold should touch the lower left edge (at about 7 o'clock on a clock face) of the cornet. Fold the bottom of the cornet up and around the mold and carefully roll upward and toward the left to wrap the cornet tightly around the mold: it should remain on the baking sheet as you roll. Leave the cornet wrapped around the mold and continue to roll the cornets around molds: as you proceed, arrange the rolled cornets, seam side down, on the sheet pan so they lean against each other, to prevent them from rolling.

When all the cornets are rolled, return them to the oven, close the door, and bake for additional 3–4 minutes to set the seams and color them a golden brown. If the color is uneven, stand the cornets on end for a minute or so more, until the color is even. Remove the cornets from the oven and allow to cool just slightly, 30 seconds or so.

Gently remove the cornets from the molds and cool for several minutes on paper towels. Remove the Silpat from the baking sheet, wipe the excess butter from it, and allot it to cool down before spreading the next batch. Store the cornets for up to 2 days (for maximum flavour) in an airtight container.

To make the salmon tartare
With a sharp knife, finely mince the salmon fillet (do not use a food processor, as it would damage the texture of the fish) and place it in a small bowl. Stir in the remaining ingredients and taste for seasoning. Cover the bowl and refrigerate for at least 30 minutes, or up to 12 hours.

For the sweet red onion crème fraîche
Place the red onions in a small sieve and rinse the under the cold water for several seconds. Dry them on paper towels. In a small metal bowl, whisk the crème fraîche for about 30 seconds– 1 minute, or until it holds soft peaks when you lift the whisk. Fold in the chopped onions and season to taste with the salt and white pepper. Transfer the onion cream to a container, cover, and refrigerate until ready to serve or for up to 6 hours.

To complete
Fill just the top ½ inch of each cornet with onion cream, leaving the bottom of the cone empty. (This is easily done using a pastry/piping bag fitted with a ¼–inch plain tip/nozzle or with the tip of a small knife.) Spoon about 1½ teaspoons of the tartare over the onion cream and mold it into a dome resembling a scoop of ice cream. Lay a chive tip against one side to garnish.

Eccles Cake and Lancashire Cheese

Fergus Henderson
St. John
United Kingdon 1994

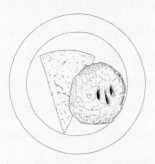

page 160

Vegetable Casserole in Textures

Ferran Adrià
elBulli
Spain 1994

page 161

To make this you will need rounds of puff pastry topped with a brown sugar-dried currant-allspice-nutmeg-butter mixture. Place more puff pastry circles on top, pinch to flatten, and "slash" exactly three times (no more, no less!). Glaze and bake for about 15 minutes. And yes, serve with this sharp and crumbly cheese.

For the almond milk
500 g whole almonds
600 g water

Using a hand blender, semiblend the almonds and water and store in the refrigerator for 12 hours until they are well hydrated.

In a blender, blend the almond mixture until you have a fine thick paste.

In batches, pour small quantities of the paste into a cheesecloth (muslin cloth) and pressit with your hands to obtain the almond milk.

For the almond sorbet
500 g almond milk
salt

Put the almond milk, seasoned with salt, into an ice cream/sorbet maker and follow machine's instructions. Keep in the freezer at -10°C.

Note: In 1999 we started adding one 2-g gelatin sheet per litre of almond milk to stabilize the sorbet.

For the beet (beetroot) purée
250 g cooked beets (beetroot)
250 g water

Blend the beets (beetroot) with the water in a blender and strain.

For the beet (beetroot) foam
500 g beet (beetroot) purée
2 (2-g) gelatin sheets, previously rehydrated in cold water
salt

Heat one-quarter of the beet (beetroot) purée and dissolve the gelatin. Remove from the heat and add the remaining beet purée. Season with salt. Strain and, using a funnel, place in a ½-litre iSi siphon. Charge the siphon with N2o and let it rest for 2 hours in the refrigerator.

For the tomato purée
6 ripe tomatoes (125 g each)
olive oil, acidity 0.4°
freshly ground white pepper
salt
sugar

Make an X-shape incision at the bottom of each tomato. With a paring knife, extract the stem (stalk) at the top of each tomato. Submerge the tomatoes in boiling water for 15 seconds. Remove with the help of a spider strainer (skimmer) and place in an ice bath. Peel the tomatoes, cut into quarters and remove the seeds. Cut into 0.5-cm cubes.

Heat a nonstick pan and sauté the tomatoes with a drizzle of olive oil. Season with white pepper, salt, and sugar. Blend the sautéed tomatoes in a blender jar until puréed. Strain through a colander, pressing it through, and let drain in a fine-mess sieve until plating this dish.

For the peach granita
200 g peach juice

Pour the juice into a container making sure it is no more than 1 cm thick.

Seal the container with an airtight lid and place in the freezer at -8° to -10°C for around 3 hours.

For the basil water
100 g fresh basil
100 g water

Separate the leaves from the stems. Blanch the leaves for 10 seconds, then place in an ice bath and drain. In a blender, blend the leaves with the water. Strain and then strain the remaining water through a cheesecloth (muslin cloth).

For the basil gelatin
100 g basil water
½ (2-g) gelatin sheet, previously rehydrated in cold water
salt

Heat one-quarter of the basil water and dissolve the gelatin. Remove from the heat and mix with the rest of the basil water. Season with salt. Let set in the refrigerator for 3 hours minimum in a container that allows for it to rise to 1 cm.

For the corn purée
2 cans (250 g each) of corn kernels

Drain the cans of corn and blend three times in a blender to make the smoothest purée possible. Strain.

For the corn mousse
100 g corn purée
¾ (2-g) gelatin sheet, previously rehydrated in cold water
salt
45 g whipping cream
Heat one-quarter of the corn purée and dissolve the gelatin, remove from the heat, and add the remaining purée. Season with salt. Let the purée cool without it setting.

Semi-whip the cream and slowly add it to the corn purée, mixing from the bottom to the top until completely incorporated. Spread the mixture to 2 cm thickness in a container. Let rest in the refrigerator for 2 hours.

For the cauliflower purée
1 (500-g) cauliflower
water

Clean the cauliflower and discard the stem (stalk). Place the cauliflower in a pot filled with cold water over high heat. When it begins to boil, drain and once again cover with cold water. Place the pot over high heat and boil until it is soft.

Once it is cooked, drain and blend in a blending jar until obtaining a superfine purée. Season with salt and pass through a sieve. →

Vegetable Casserole
in Textures

For the cauliflower mousse
200 g cauliflower purée
1 (2-g) gelatin sheet, previously
   rehydrated in cold water
salt
80 g whipping cream

Heat one-quarter of the cauliflower
purée and dissolve the gelatin. Remove
from the heat, add the remaining purée
and season with salt. Cool the purée
without letting it set.

Semi whip the cream and add it slowly
to the purée, mixing it from the bottom
to the top until it is completely
incorporated. Spread the mixture to
2 cm thickness in a container. Let rest
in the refrigerator for 2 hours.

For the avocado semicircles
1 (200 g) avocado

Half the avocado, remove the pit (stone)
and peel.

Cut into 8 semicircles, 1 cm thick each.

For plating
20 blanched almonds
salt

On the center of a round plate, place
two semicircles of avocado until
forming a circle. Season with salt.

Around the avocado, and somewhat
overlapping them, place the remaining
elaborations in the following order,
from right to left, beginning at the
bottom of the plate:

a level tablespoon of tomato
   purée.
a level tablespoon of cauliflower
   mousse.
leaving space for the granita, a
   piece of basil gelatin.
a level tablespoon of corn mousse,
   then leave another space for the
   foam.
place five blanched almonds
   between the different
   elaborations.
place a quenelle of almond sorbet
   on top of the avocado circle.

With a spatula, chop the peach granita
until achieving a scaly texture.

Finish with
A tablespoon of peach granita between
the cauliflower mousse and the basil
gelatin.

A rose of beet (beetroot) foam between
the tomato purée and the corn mousse.

Oysters and Pearls

Thomas Keller
The French Laundry
United States 1994

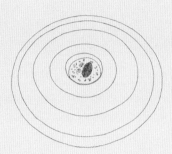

page 162

Tapioca

⅓ cup small pearl tapioca
1¾ cups milk
16 meaty oysters, such as
    Malpeque, scrubbed with a brush
1¼ cups heavy (double) cream
freshly ground black pepper
¼ cup crème fraîche
kosher (coarse) salt

Sabayon

4 large egg yolks
¼ cup reserved oyster juice
    (from above)

Sauce

3 tablespoons dry vermouth
remaining reserved oyster juice
    (from above)
1½ tablespoons minced shallots
1½ tablespoons white wine vinegar
8 tablespoons (4 oz) unsalted
    butter, cut into 8 pieces
1 tablespoon minced chives
1–2 oz osetra caviar

For the tapioca

Soak the tapioca in 1 cup of the milk for 1 hour. (Setting it in a warm place will speed up the rehydration of the pearls.)

To shuck the oysters, hold an oyster in a towel, to protect your hand, with the rounded side down. Lean the wider end of the oyster against the table for support. Push an oyster knife under the hinge at the narrow end of the shell. Don't jam the knife in, or you risk damaging the oyster. You will hear a "pop"; twist the knife to loosen the shell. Keeping the knife directly under the top shell, run the blade along the right side to cut through the muscle. This will release the top shell, which can then be removed. Slide the knife under the meat to detach the second muscle holding the oyster in place. Reserve the oyster and all its juices in a small bowl. Repeat with the remaining oysters.

Trim away the muscle and the outer ruffled edge of each oyster and place the trimmings in a saucepan. Reserve the whole trimmed oysters and strain the oyster juice into a separate bowl. You should have about ½ cup of juice.

In a bowl, whip ½ cup of the cream just until it holds its shape; reserve in the refrigerator.

Drain the softened tapioca in a sieve and discard the milk. Rinse the tapioca under cold running water, then place it in a small heavy pot.

Pour the remaining ¾ cup milk and ¾ cup cream over the oyster trimmings. Bring to a simmer, then strain the infused liquid onto the tapioca. Discard the trimmings.

Cook the tapioca over medium heat, stirring constantly with a wooden spoon, until it has thickened and the spoon leaves a trail when it is pulled through, 7–8 minutes. Continue to cook for another 5–7 minutes, until the tapioca has no resistance in the center and is translucent. The mixture will be sticky and if you lift some on the spoon and let it fall, some should still cling to the spoon. Remove the pot from the heat and set aside in a warm place. →

Oysters and Pearls

Roast Bone Marrow and Parsley Salad
Fergus Henderson
St. John
United Kingdom 1994

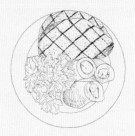

page 163

For the sabayon
Place the egg yolks and ¼ cup of the reserved oyster juice in a metal bowl set over a pan of hot water. Whisk vigorously over medium heat for 2–3 minutes to incorporate as much air as possible. The finished sabayon will have thickened and lightened, the foam will have subsided, and the sabayon will hold a ribbon when it falls from the whisk. If the mixture begins to break, remove it from the heat and whisk quickly off the heat for a moment to recombine, then return to the heat.

Stir the hot sabayon into the tapioca, along with a generous amount of black pepper. Mix in the crème fraîche and the whipped cream. The tapioca will be a creamy pale yellow with the tapioca pearls suspended in the mixture. Season lightly with salt, remembering that the oysters and the caviar garnish will both be salty. Immediately spoon ¼ cup tapioca into each of eight 4-by-5-inch gratin dishes (with a 3- to 4-oz capacity). Tap the gratin dishes on the counter so that the tapioca forms an even layer. Cover and refrigerate until ready to use, or for up to a day.

To complete
Preheat the oven to 350°F.

For the sauce, combine the vermouth, the remaining reserved oyster juice, the shallots, and vinegar in a small saucepan. Bring to a simmer and simmer until most of the liquid has evaporated but the shallots are glazed, not dry. Whisk in the butter piece by piece, adding a new piece only when the previous one is almost incorporated.

Meanwhile, place the dishes of tapioca on a baking sheet and heat in the oven for 4–5 minutes, or until they just begin to puff up.

Add the oysters and the chives to the sauce to warm through.

Spoon 2 oysters and some of the sauce over each gratin and garnish the top with a quenelle, or small oval scoop, of caviar. Serve immediately.

Roast some marrowbones. Put them on a plate. Make some toast, a parsley salad, and pile up some salt. Eat.

Chocolate Caramel Tarts

Claudia Fleming
Gramercy Tavern
United States 1994

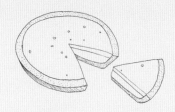

page 164

For the chocolate tart dough

8 tablespoons (1 stick) unsalted
  butter, room temperature
½ cup plus 1 tablespoon
  confectioners' (icing) sugar
1 large egg yolk
¾ teaspoon pure vanilla extract
1¼ cups all-purpose (plain) flour,
  plus more for rolling
¼ cup unsweetened Dutch-process
  cocoa powder

For the caramel filling

½ cup water
2 cups granulated sugar
¼ cup light corn (golden) syrup
8 tablespoons (1 stick) unsalted
  butter
½ cup heavy (double) cream
2 tablespoons créme fraîche
1 pinch of coarse salt

For the chocolate ganache glaze

½ cup heavy (double) cream
3½ oz extra-bittersweet (dark)
  chocolate, finely chopped

Make the tart dough: In the bowl of
an electric mixer fitted with the paddle
attachment, cream the butter and
confectioners' (icing) sugar until
combined, about 1 minute. Add the egg
yolk and vanilla, and beat until smooth.

Sift in the flour and cocoa powder, and
beat on low speed until just combined.
Scrape the dough onto a sheet of
plastic wrap (clingfilm), and form it into
a disk; wrap well. Chill until firm, at
least 1 hour and up to 3 days.

Preheat the oven to 325°F. Between two
sheets of lightly floured parchment
(baking) paper, roll the tart dough into
an 18 × 12-inch rectangle, ³/₁₆ inch
thick. Using a 2¾-inch round cutter,
cut out 24 rounds of dough, and press
them into 2¼-inch tart pans, trimming
away any excess dough. Chill the tart
shells (cases) in the refrigerator for
20 minutes.

Line each tart shell with a piece of
parchment (baking) paper and fill with
raw rice or dried lentils. Bake for 15
minutes. Remove the parchment paper
and its contents, and bake until the
pastry looks dry and set, 5–10 minutes.
Transfer the pans to a wire rack to cool.
(The tart shells can be made up to 8
hours ahead.)

Make the filling: Put ½ cup of water
into a large saucepan. Add the sugar
and corn (golden) syrup, and cook
mixture over medium-high heat,
swirling the pan occasionally, until it

becomes a dark-amber caramel, about
10 minutes. Carefully whisk in butter,
cream, créme fraîche, and a pinch of
salt (the mixture will bubble up),
whisking until smooth. (The caramel
can be made up to 5 days ahead and
refrigerated in a covered container.)
Carefully transfer the caramel to a glass
measuring cup (jug). Divide the caramel
among the tart shells while still warm
(or reheat the caramel over low heat
until it is pourable), and let stand until
the caramel is set, at least 45 minutes.

Make the ganache glaze: Put the
chocolate into a heatproof bowl.
In a small saucepan, bring the cream
to a boil. Pour the hot cream over the
chocolate and let stand for 2 minutes,
then stir with a rubber spatula until
smooth. Pour some of the glaze over
each of the tarts while still warm. Let
the glaze set at room temperature for
at least 2 hours before serving.

The Crunchy Part of the Lasagne

Massimo Bottura
Osteria Francescana
Italy 1995

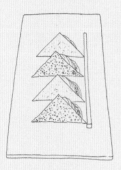

page 165

Ragù

1 yellow onion, diced
1 carrot, diced
2 celery stalks, diced
3 g extra-virgin olive oil
2 dried bay laves
1 sprig rosemary
100 g bone marrow
50 g pancetta steccata, chopped
100 g sausagemeat
200 g veal tail
100 g veal tongue
100 g beef cheek
100 g cherry tomato confit
80 g white wine
1.5 g capon stock
5 g sea salt
1 g black pepper

Pasta dough

100 g spinach
100 g Swiss chard
500 g '00' flour
8 egg yolks
1 egg
salt

Béchamel foam

30 g butter
30 g flour
500 g milk, at room temperature
120 g Parmigiano Reggiano, grated
sea salt

Tomato terrine

4 ripe tomatoes
1 g sugar
1 g sea salt
0.5 g freshly ground black pepper
3 g extra virgin olive oil
2 g agar agar

Parmigiano crackers

15 g soft butter
90 g 30-month Parmigiano
    Reggiano, grated
5 g cornflour (cornstarch)

Ragù

Make a classic soffritto by cooking the onion, carrot and celery very gently in a pan with the olive oil. Transfer to a stainless steel bowl and stir in the bay and rosemary. Blanch the bone marrow in salted boiling water and drain it on paper towels to absorb any excess liquid. Sweat the pancetta in a large, heavy-based saucepan. Add the sausagemeat and cook until browned. Remove any excess fat, then add the remaining meats, keeping them in large pieces, and cherry tomato confit. Brown them, add the wine and cook until the liquid has evaporated. Remove from the heat and add the soffritto. Put the mixture in a sous-vide bag along with a little of the stock, and seal. Cook for 24 hours at 63°C (145°F).

Open the bag and separate the liquid and solids. Place the liquid in a pan and reduce it by half over low heat. Chop the meat with a sharp knife. Put it in a large saucepan and add the liquid.

Pasta

Cook the spinach and chard in boiling water, then chill it immediately in iced water. Drain it well, dry it and pound it thoroughly.

Sift the flour on to a board and make a well in the centre. Add the egg yolks, egg and the spinach mixture gradually to the well, mixing until the dough comes together in a ball. Knead for 15 minutes, until smooth and elastic. Cover it with a clean dish cloth and leave to rest for 30 minutes.

Roll out the dough to a thickness of 1 mm (^{1}/$_{16}$ inch). Cut it into 5-cm (2-inch) triangles. Cook the pasta in salted boiling water (10 g salt per litre), drain it and dry it well. Stack the pasta, cover it carefully and let stand in the fridge for 30 minutes. Preheat the oven to 220°C (430°F). Bake for 15 minutes, until the pasta is perfectly gratinated. Let stand in a warm place for 5 minutes before serving.

Béchamel foam

Melt the butter in a pan and add the flour and salt. Cook, stirring, until it forms a smooth paste, then add the milk. Stir very well and when it starts to thicken, add the Parmigiano and keep stirring. Cook for 5 more minutes. While still warm, process it in a thermal mixer at maximum speed, then strain it, put it into a siphon and chill it. Once cold, charge with 2 charges and shake it well.

Tomato terrine

Blend the tomatoes thoroughly and strain them, adding the sugar, salt, pepper and oil. Put the liquid into a small pan with the agar agar and bring to a boil, stirring, until it has melted completely. Pour the mixture into a 10 × 15-cm (4 × 6-inch) rectangular tray and let cool. Once cold, cut it into 1 × 15-cm (½ × 6-inch) strips.

Parmigiano crackers

Knead the butter, Parmigiano and cornflour (cornstarch) together briefly. Roll it out to a thickness of 2 mm (⅛ inch) and cut it into 5-cm (2-inch) triangles, like the pasta. Bake at 200°C (400°F) for 2 minutes, or less if necessary, until lightly browned.

To serve

Place a straight line of tomato terrine along the plate. Place four spoonfuls of the ragù alongside it, topped with spoonfuls of the béchamel foam. Rest 2 Parmigiano crackers and 2 crispy pasta pieces alternately in front of them.

Four Dances of the Sea

Cheong Liew
The Grange
Australia 1995

page 166

Soused Snook

2 medium size fillets of snook or 300 g (very fresh or sashimi quality)
1 tablespoon sea salt
1 tablespoon sugar
50 ml mirin
100 ml rice vinegar
6 slices avocado
6 tablespoons wasabi mayonnaise (see below)
pickled wakame seaweed, pickled cherry with stems on, chervil leaf, to garnish

For the pickled cherries

2 kg cherries
1 litre rice vinegar
200 ml cassis
700 g sugar
1 cinnamon quill

For the wasabi mayonnaise

1 egg yolk
50 g sugar
50 ml rice vinegar
100 ml warm peanut (groundnut) oil
1 teaspoon green wasabi powder
2 teaspoons daikon juice

To make the pickled cherries, mix together the rice vinegar, cassis, sugar and cinnamon. Wash the cherries and immerse in the vinegar mix. Cover and set aside for at least 4 weeks.

Clean and trim the snook fillets, removing any bones and if possible remove the outer skin membrane from the skins. Lay the fillet skin side down and sprinkle a salt and sugar mixture evenly on both fillets for 2 hours.

Marinate the cured snook fillets with the mirin, rice vinegar and rice wine for a further 1 hour or longer. Slice the fillets at an angle diagonally and serve 3 slices per person.

To make the wasabi mayonnaise, whisk the egg yolk with the sugar and rice vinegar. Pour in warm peanut oil (50°C) slowly and whisk until it thickens. Mix the wasabi powder with the daikon juice work to a paste and add to mayonnaise.

Composition

Place two sliced avocado quarters on 6 o'clock of the plate, with ½ teaspoon of wasabi mayonnaise. Place three slices of pickled snook in front of the avocado slices, then garnish the sides of the fish with seaweed on the left and a pickled cherry on the right.

Octopus with Aioli

2 kg octopus tentacles
30 ml aioli (see below)
200 ml olive oil
40 g black olives, crushed
4 cloves garlic, crushed
¼ bay leaf
½ red chilli
½ lemon
6 parsley stalks
confit tomatoes
watercress

For the aioli

6 cloves garlic
1 large red chilli
4 coriander (cilantro) roots
1 egg yolk
100 ml olive oil
5 g sea salt
juice of ½ lemon

Peel the skin off the octopus but leave the suckers intact and dry in a dish towel.

Bring 200 ml of olive oil to a boil and add the crushed olives and fry until it's smoked.

Gently gather the small ends of tentacles and gently lower the tentacles into the pot and seal the octopus very quickly and immediately bring the temperature down as low as possible.

Add in the garlic, bay leaf, chilli, lemon and parsley stalks, cover the pot and simmer for 35-40 minutes. It should be as soft as lobster.

To make the aioli: in a mortar and pestle, pound the garlic, chilli and coriander roots into a fine smooth paste. (How good the paste is depends on the patience of pounding!)

In a mixing bowl, put in egg yolk and garlic mixture and whisk it with a fork and slowly add olive oil, whisk to a mayonnaise consistency, then add salt and lemon juice to taste.

Confit eggplant (aubergine)
Peel one large eggplant (aubergine) and cut into twice the size of matchstick. Lightly salt the eggplant and leave to stand for 20 minutes until it sweats. Dry the eggplant with a dish towel.

Heat ½ cup olive oil, with 1 crushed garlic clove until just fragrant. Add the eggplant and turn down the heat to low, cook slowly stirring the eggplant for 2 minutes; add a little more oil if it's too dry. Then remove the pan from flame and leave it to stand for 20 minutes. Finish with a squeeze of lemon and season with pepper.

Composition
Spoon a teaspoon of confit eggplant (aubergine) on 12 o'clock of the plate. Spoon a little aioli on top of the eggplant. Slice the octopus into sucker intervals and arrange on the plate, placing slices of octopus on three sides of the eggplant to from a mound. Garnish with 2 slices of confit tomatoes, and a leaf of watercress.

Raw Calamari with Black Noodles
120 g sashimi quality calamari
180 g squid ink tagliarini pasta
150 ml or 6 tablespoons Asian
    dressing (see below)
salmon roe

For the squid ink noodles
380 g plain (all-purpose) flour
2 whole eggs
80 ml fresh squid Ink
20 ml light olive oil
8 g salt

For the Asian dressing
1 teaspoon sesame oil
½ teaspoon chili oil (optional)
1 tablespoon oyster sauce
1 tablespoon balsamic vinegar
2 tablespoons sunflower seed oil
3 tablespoons extra virgin olive oil
2 tablespoons soya sauce
1 tablespoon mirin (Japanese
    sweet rice wine)
freshly ground pepper

Clean the calamari thoroughly, wipe off any ink that has smeared on the calamari with a damp cloth and chill for 30 minutes.

Cut the calamari lengthwise very thin until it's almost like a thin ribbon; repeat until the whole calamari is completely cut. Roll the ribbons into turban discs using two ribbons per disc, place on a plate, cover and chill.

Make the noodles. Make a well in the center of the flour and break in the eggs. Add the squid ink, olive oil and salt.

Using a fork beat the wet ingredients until combined. Still using the fork, incorporate the egg mixture with flour until the eggs is incorporate with the flour. Then using the heel of your hand, knead the dough and roll out into a 50-cm log wrap with cling wrap and let it rest for 40 minutes

Next, fold the log of dough in half and stretch it out into a log again. Repeat the process 5–6 times until the dough is tight and bounces back when you press it with your thumb

Roll out the dough with a pasta machine, to make sheets 1.5mm thick. Cut the pasta sheets with the tagliarini cutter on the pasta machine. Cook in rapidly boiling water with some salt. →

Four Dances of the Sea

Composition

Toss the warm squid ink pasta with the Asian dressing and let it marinade for a couple of minutes. Using a small fork, twirl into small portions and place on 9 o'clock of the plate. Place a calamari turban on top of the noodles and spoon a teaspoon of salmon roe on top of the turban.

Spiced Prawn Sushi

6 large Spencer Gulf king prawns (shrimp), shelled and deveined
pinch of salt
sugar
finely grated lime zest
60 ml peanut (groundnut) oil
40 ml coconut cream
50 ml tamarind juice
40 g light palm sugar

For the rempah mixture

20 g fresh galangal, finely grated
10 g fresh turmeric, finely grated
6 whole candlenuts, finely grated
1 whole red chilli, pound to a paste
6–10 shallots, finely chopped
3 cloves, finely chopped
15 g fresh ginger, finely grated
15 g blachan, lightly roasted in aluminium foil

Cut prawns (shrimp) into halves lengthwise, sprinkle with salt and sugar and finely grated lime zest.
Put all the rempah ingredients into a blender and blend to a smooth paste.

In a wok, heat up peanut oil, add the rempah mixture and coconut cream and stir-fry the mixture on lower then medium heat, very slowly stirring constantly until half the oil starts to separate from the solid.

Add the tamarind juice and palm sugar, cook until thickened, strain the sauce through a strainer (sieve) into another saucepan and bring sauce to a boil. Add the prawns and cook for a couple of minutes until just cooked.

For the banana leaf, gutinous coconut rice

200 g glutinous (sticky) rice, presoaked for 1 hour
20 ml peanut (groundnut) oil
10 g sea salt
80 ml coconut cream
1 large piece of fresh banana leaf
shredded cucumber
coriander (cilantro) leaves

Steam the glutinous (sticky) rice with the 20 ml of oil and salt for 15–20 minutes. Mix in the coconut cream with the cooked rice until it's nicely moist.

Toast the banana leaf with a hot iron or a frying pan. Trim off the hard stems and hard edges. Put the cooked rice on the banana leaf and roll it into a sushi log approximately 3–4 cm in diameter. Then wrap the whole rice sushi in foil and chargrill the sushi about 3–4 minutes on each side, cooking for about 15 minutes. When unwrapped, the edges of the rice sushi should be slightly brown, toasted with an astonishing fragrance of toasted banana leaf.
Cut the sushi into 4-cm logs and remove the banana leaf. Do not keep the rice in the fridge; keep at room temperature.

Composition

Cut the fresh banana leaf into 4-cm squares. Place a piece of the leaf on 3 o'clock of the plate.

Place coconut rice on the banana leaf square and place a prawn sushi on top.

Garnish with shredded cucumber and coriander (cilantro) leaves.

Lasagne of Crab with a Cappuccino of Shellfish and a Champagne Foam

Phil Howard
The Square
United Kingdom 1996

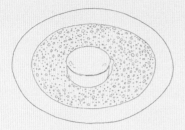

page 167

Parsley pasta dough
500 g curly parsley leaves
500 g ice cubes
650 g '00' pasta flour
30 g salt
140 g whole eggs
85 g egg yolks
25 ml olive oil

Scallop mousse
6 large scallops in the shell
    (yielding 200 g scallop meat –
    reserve the scallop 'skirts' for
    the champagne foam)
a pinch of cayenne pepper
1 large egg
200 ml double cream
a squeeze of lemon juice

Crab
1 large live cock crab, about 1.5 kg
1 quantity of scallop mousse (see
    below)
10 basil leaves, finely sliced

Shellfish cappuccino
50 ml grapeseed oil
the shell from the crab, above
100 g unsalted butter
2 shallots, sliced
½ carrot, sliced
½ celery stick, sliced
½ leek, sliced
1 teaspoon each coriander seeds,
    fennel seeds and star anise
½ head of garlic
1 tablespoon tomato purée (paste)
100 ml Madeira
2 slices of lemon
½ bunch of basil
500 ml skimmed milk

Champagne foam
'skirts' from the scallops for the
    mousse, above
200 ml white wine
200 ml champagne
3 shallots, finely sliced
1 teaspoon coriander seeds
1 star anise
1 teaspoon white peppercorns
zest and juice of 1 lemon
500 ml double (heavy) cream
a pinch of cayenne pepper

Parsley pasta dough
In a liquidizer, thoroughly blend the parsley leaves with 2 litres of water, in batches, then pass through a coarse sieve to give a "green water." Pour this into a large saucepan and place on a medium heat. Bring slowly towards simmering point. As it approaches simmering point, the green component (chlorophyll) will coagulate. Immediately remove the pan from the heat and tip the contents into a large bowl containing 500 g ice cubes. Pass through a fine sieve lined with muslin (cheesecloth), discarding the liquid and keeping the green chlorophyll. Bring up the corners of the muslin and twist into a ball to squeeze out the excess moisture. This should yield a deep green paste. You will need 100 g of the chlorophyll for the pasta dough.

Place the "00" flour, salt and a twist of pepper in a food processor. Lightly whisk the 100 g chlorophyll with the eggs, yolks and olive oil and then gradually add to the flour while the machine in running. You are looking for a crumb-like mix, which will probably not require quite all of the egg. If the mix clumps into a ball, it is too wet; if this happens, add a little more flour to obtain the right consistency.

Turn out on to a work surface, press together firmly and then knead briefly to form a smooth, firm dough. Wrap in clingfilm (plastic wrap) or vacuum pack and chill overnight. →

Lasagne of Crab with a Cappuccino of Shellfish and a Champagne Foam

Scallop mousse

Ensure the scallops are dry. If you have just removed them from the shell and washed them, leave them between 2 kitchen cloths in the fridge for an hour before puréeing. Place the scallops in the chilled food processor bowl, add a generous pinch of salt and the cayenne and blend for 30 seconds. Scrape down the sides and blend for 30 seconds longer. Scrape down the sides once more, blend for 30 seconds, then add the egg and blend for a final 30 seconds. Scrape all the purée out of the bowl and, using a spatula of a plastic scraper, pass it through a fine drum sieve. Transfer the sieved purée, including that from the underside of the mesh, into a bowl. Press a sheet of clingfilm (plastic wrap) over the surface and set aside in the fridge for 1 hour. Remove the purée with a wooden spoon. Scrape down the sides of the bowl with a rubber spatula and beat again. Add another splash of cream and beat it in, scraping down the sides once more. This is particularly important in the early stages of making the mousse, as it prevents dense lumps of protein persisting. Beating vigorously and scraping the bowl down intermittently, continue to add the cream, a little at a time to start with and then in a steady stream, until about 80 per cent has been used. This is a physical process and must be done vigorously to ensure the cream and blended scallops combine completely and homogenously.

Bring a small pan of water to the boil. Dip a teaspoon into the simmering water, then use it to scoop out a small quantity of mousse. Drop it into the water, turn off the heat and leave it to poach for 2–3 minutes. Lift it out, cut it in half and taste a piece. Focus on its texture and seasoning. If the mousse feels firm and still has a rubbery quality, you will need to add the remaining cream. This is more than likely at this stage. If it lacks seasoning, adjust is accordingly. Beat in virtually all the remaining cream and repeat the test. The mousse should now feel more supple and, whilst it should not be rubbery, it should still have a lightly springy texture. As long as it still has a definite structure and is not falling apart, beat in the remaining cream. Perform a final test and taste the mousse for seasoning, adding the squeeze of lemon juice. Transfer the mousse to a small bowl, cover and chill.

Crab

Put a large pan of generously salted water on to a boil. Kill the crab by piercing the head between the eyes with a very sharp, heavy knife, then plunge it into the boiling water and cook for 10 minutes. Remove from the water and leave to cool. Crack the claws, the legs and the body open and extract the white meat, reserving the shells for the cappuccino. Pick through the meat carefully to ensure there are no fragments of the shell in it. You will need 250 g white meat. Chill it for ½ hour, then carefully mix it into the scallop mousse. Add the basil and place the mixture in a piping (pastry) bag fitted with a large, plain nozzle (tip). Store in the fridge.

Shellfish cappuccino

Heat a large, shallow, heavy-based casserole. Add the oil, followed by the crab shells, and sauté for 2–3 minutes over a high heat. Add half the butter, followed by the vegetables, aromatics and garlic, and continue cooking for 5 minutes. Season with a generous pinch of salt, stir in the tomato purée (paste) and then place in an oven preheated to 200°C/Gas mark 6 for 5 minutes. Place back on the hob (stove), add the Madeira and simmer until it has almost completely evaporated. Add enough water just to cover, bring to the boil and simmer for 20 minutes. Remove from the heat, add the lemon and basil and leave to rest, covered, for ½ hour. Pass through a fine sieve, return to the heat and simmer until reduced to 200 ml. This should be an intensely flavoured shellfish reduction.

Champagne foam

Heat a medium, heavy-based pan and add the reserved scallop skirts. They will release a lot of juice. Allow this to evaporate completely, then add then white wine, half the champagne, the shallots, spices, lemon zest and a pinch of salt. Boil until syrupy and almost completely evaporated. Cover with the cream, bring to the boil and simmer gently for 15 minutes, without letting it reduce too much. Pass through a fine sieve, pressing on the shallots with a wooden spoon to squeeze out all the liquid, then return to the heat in a fresh pan. Simmer until it has reduced by about a third and is thick enough to coat the back of a spoon. Add the remaining champagne and the cayenne pepper, then remove from the heat and adjust the seasoning if necessary.

To assemble the lasagne

Roll out the pasta dough. Cut into three strips 30 cm long (you won't need all the pasta dough for this recipe but the remainder can be stored, well wrapped, in the freezer). Blanch the strips in a large pan of boiling salted water for 1 minute, then drain and refresh under cold running water. Lay the pasta sheets out on a kitchen towel and cut out 32 discs, using a plain 4-cm round cutter.

Cut out 8 pieces of baking (parchment) paper, 5 cm square, and on top of each set a buttered stainless steel ring mould, 4 cm diameter and 4 cm deep. Place a disc of pasta in the base of each. Pipe each ring mould one third full with crab mix, place another disc of pasta on top, then repeat this twice more, finishing with a pasta disc. You could store these in the fridge for up to a day, if necessary.

To serve

Place the champagne foam in a 500 ml foam gun, charge with 2 cartridges and set in a pan of hand-hot (lukewarm) water.

Bring the shellfish bisque to the boil. Add the remaining 50 g butter and the milk and heat to near-simmering point (about 80°C). Carefully aerate with a hand blender to check the consistency – it should form a creamy froth, which should hold for several minutes. It will not aerate if it is too cold, and will collapse if the mix has boiled – in which case, adjust the heat and re-blend.

Put the lasagne, still on their paper squares, in a steamer, cover and steam for 10 minutes. Remove from the steamer and place the lasagne, still in their rings, in eight preheated bowls. Gently lift off the rings. Blend the cappuccino once more and spoon a generous quantity over each lasagne assembly. Finish with a squirt of the champagne foam – just enough to glaze the top of the pasta.

Langoustine Five Ways

Pierre Gagnaire
Pierre Gagnaire
France 1996

page 168

Langoustine Poached in Sake, Burnt Avocado

2 medium live langoustines
50 ml good quality sake
30 g butter
½ avocado
lemon juice

For the broth

1 litre water
100 g carrots
100 g leeks
100 g celery
100 g onion
lemon skin
parsley stems (stalks)
black peppercorns

Blanch 2 medium-sized live langoustines in a vegetable broth for about 20 seconds. Cool down in ice water. Take off the shells and clean.

Bring the sake to a boil, take off the heat and poach the langoustine tails. When cooked, take out the langoustines and reduce the liquid. Stir in some cold butter and glaze the langoustine tails.

Burn an avocado half with a blowtorch until black. Cut into slices and brush with lemon juice.

Langoustine Terre de Sienne, Heart of Palm

1 large live langoustine
5 g orange skin powder
5 g curry madras powder
10 g ras le hanout
7 g paprika powder
25 g breadcrumbs
1 fresh heart of palm
lemon juice

Blanch a large live langoustine in a vegetable broth (see above) for about 20 seconds. Cool down in ice water. Take off the shells and clean.

Blend together the orange skin powder, curry madras powder, ras el hanout powder, paprika powder and breadcrumbs. Pass through a sieve. Cut the fresh palm heart into thin, long strips.

Pan-fry the langoustine in butter, and when nicely coloured take out and reserve. Let the butter cool down a little in the pan, add the spice mix and put back on the heat to foam it one time. Deglaze with a splash of lemon juice. Roll the heart of palm strips in the butter and add salt.

Broth, Daikon

500 g langoustine shells (head and claws)
50 g onion
50 g leek
10 g garlic
50 g celery
thyme
bay leaf
100 g tomatoes
15 g tomato paste (purée)
60 ml white wine
gelatine
daikon (mooli) radish

Cut langoustine heads and claws into small pieces. Roast in the oven on a large tray with a splash of olive oil until golden.

Cook the onion, leek, garlic and celery, all thinly cut, in olive oil with thyme and a bay leaf in a heavy pot. When cooked, add the chopped tomatoes and cook until all the liquid is evaporated. Add a little bit of tomato paste (purée) and cook quickly. Add the coloured langoustine shells and deglaze with white wine. Fill up with cold water to just cover the langoustine shells. Cook this broth for about 4 hours on a very gentle simmer.

When cooked, pass through a sieve and reduce the liquid to a nice dark tasty broth. Add gelatine (1 leaf for every 200 ml of broth) and cool down on ice. When set, break with a fork to obtain rough pieces. Dress in a bowl and grate daikon (mooli) on top.

Tartare Thickened with Grapefruit Gel and Lime, Fresh Corn

2 raw langoustines
olive oil
Espelette pepper
lime zest
1 corn cob (ear of corn)
salt

For the gel

grapefruits for 200 ml grapefruit
   juice
30 ml water
30 g sugar
2 g agar agar

To make the gel, press the grapefruits. Mix together the water, sugar and grapefruit juice. Bring to a boil and add the agar agar. Bring to a boil again and transfer the liquid in a bowl and cool down on ice. When the liquid is set, transfer to a blender and blend until smooth.

Cut the raw langoustine in large pieces and season with olive oil, salt and Espelette pepper. Coat in the grapefruit gel and grated lime zest.

Blanch the corn on the cob in plenty of water. When cooked, take off the kernels. Season and dress on the langoustine tartare.

Cottage Cheese Seasoned with Carcass Powder, Carrot/ Enoki Mushrooms and Parsley

40 g good quality cottage cheese
1 leafy carrot
1 packet enoki mushrooms
10 g parsley leaves
lemon juice
salt

For the carcass powder

200 g langoustine shells
   (heads and claws)
50 ml water
50 g sugar

To make the powder, cut the langoustine heads and claws in small pieces and dry on a kitchen towel. Bring the water and sugar to a boil to obtain a syrup. Add the langoustine heads to the syrup and stir over medium heat until dry. Spread out the glazed heads on a tray with a sheet of baking (parchment) paper and let dry. This can take up to several days.

Once the heads are complete dry, blend them in a blender and pass through a sieve.

Season the cottage cheese with olive oil, salt and the carcass powder. Cut the carrot into strips on a mandoline. Cut the stems of the enoki mushrooms and wash. Season with parsley, salt and lemon juice.

L'Arpège Egg

Alain Passard
L'Arpège
France 1996

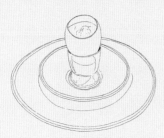

page 169

Cyber Eggs

Davide Scabin
Combal
Italy 1997

page 170

¼ cup heavy (double) cream
¾ teaspoon sugar
½ teaspoon sherry vinegar
4 eggs
4 teaspoons maple syrup
salt
1 tablespoon minced chives
freshly ground pepper

Position racks in the upper and lower thirds of the oven and heat the oven to 400°F.

Whip the cream to stiff peaks. Incorporate the sugar and sherry vinegar right at the end. Transfer the whipped cream to a pastry (piping) bag fitted with a smallish (about ½-inch-diameter) tip (fluted, if you want to get fancy). This will hold in the refrigerator for a few hours.

Cut the tops off the eggs. You'll want to take off around a sixth of the narrower end of the shell. If you have the skills and a sharp–enough blade, more power to you, do it with a paring knife. Otherwise buy a good-quality egg topper online and use that. Gently dump the contents of the eggs out into a small bowl and even more gently use your fingers to remove all the white and gooey stuff left inside the eggshell. Separate the yolks from the whites and return the yolks to their shells (save the whites for another use, such as making meringue).

Place the eggshells in ovenproof eggcups. Add 1 teaspoon of maple syrup and a pinch of salt to each eggshell. Arrange the eggcups in a shallow baking pan. Fill with about 1 inch of very hot water and place on the upper rack of the oven. Bake for 5–7 minutes. The goal is to warm the yolks, to give them some body and make them a little bit more unctuous, not to cook or poach them completely.

Remove the eggs from the pan and fill each with whipped cream. The finished egg should have a peak of piped cream rising out of the top of the eggshell like the snowcap on a mountain. Scatter that snowcap with a pinch or two of minced chives and a twist of freshly ground black pepper. Serve at once.

60 g Ossetra caviar
4 shallots, finely chopped
4 egg yolks
ground pepper, to taste
vodka, to taste

Place a square-shaped, double layer of clingfilm (plastic wrap) on a work surface, allowing in some air.

Place 15 g caviar, one finely chopped shallot, one egg yolk, ground pepper and a small dash of vodka on top of each square of clingfilm. Lift the four corners of clingfilm together, closing up into a bundle, leaving the excess air to come out, then wrap each of the Cyber Eggs again, creating two different layers of film.

To seal the Cyber Eggs, use nylon yarn with a thickness of 3 mm. Cut the excess nylon. Serve with frozen dry vodka and a scalpel, for effect. With the scalpel make an incision through the film and immediately squeeze the contents into your mouth and enjoy it.

Ispahan Macaron

Pierre Hermé
Ladurée
France 1997

page 171

For the raspberry jelly
4 g gelatine leaves
420 g raspberries
35 g caster (superfine) sugar

For the coloured sugar
100 g granulated sugar
a few drops carmine red food
    colouring or edible ruby glitter

For the macaron shells
300 g icing (confectioners') sugar
300 g ground almonds (almond meal)
110 g 'liquefied' egg whites (see
    next page), plus second portion
    110 g 'liquefied' egg whites
about 4 g strawberry food
    colouring
75 g mineral water
300 g caster (superfine) sugar
edible ruby glitter

For the lychee and rose ganache
400 g lychees (preserved in syrup)
410 g Valrhona Ivoire couverture or
    white chocolate
60 g liquid crème fraîche of
    whipping cream (35% fat)
3 g rose essence (from the
    delicatessen or health food shop)

Start by preparing the raspberry jelly.
Soak the gelatine leaves for 15 minutes
in cold water to soften.

Using a hand-held blender, blend the
raspberries and sugar to a purée. Strain
the purée to remove the pips (seeds).
Heat a quarter of the purée to 45°C.
Drain and dry the gelatine and add to
the hot purée. Stir and add the rest of
the raspberry purée.

Pour it into a gratin dish lined with
clingfilm (plastic wrap) to a depth of
4 mm. Allow to cool for 1 hour a room
temperature, then put the dish in the
freezer for 2 hours. Turn the jelly and
cut it into 1.5-cm squares. Return the
jelly squares to the freezer.

For the coloured sugar, preheat the oven
to 60°C. Put on disposable gloves. Mix
the sugar with a few drops of food
colouring and rub it between the palms
of your hands. Spread out the coloured
sugar on a baking tray. Put the tray in the
oven and dry the sugar for 30 minutes.

For the shells, sift together the icing
(confectioners') sugar and ground
almonds (almond meal). Stir the food
colouring into the first portion of
liquefied egg whites and pour them over
the mixture of icing sugar and ground
almonds but do not stir.

Bring the water and caster (superfine)
sugar to boil at 118°C. When the syrup
reaches 115°C, simultaneously start
whisking the second portion of liquefied

egg whites to soft peaks. When the sugar
reaches 118°C, pour it over the egg
whites. Whisk and allow the meringue to
cool down to 50°C, then fold it into the
almond-icing sugar mixture. Spoon the
batter into a piping (pastry) bag fitted
with a plain nozzle (tip).

Pipe rounds of batter about 3.5 cm in
diameter, spacing them 2 cm apart on
baking trays lined with baking
(parchment) paper. Rap the baking trays
on the work surface covered with a
kitchen cloth. Sprinkle every other row
with pinches of coloured sugar or ruby
glitter. Leave the shells to stand for at
least 30 minutes until they form a skin.

Preheat the fan oven to 180°C, then put
the trays in the oven. Bake for 12
minutes quickly opening and shutting
the oven door twice during cooking
time. Out of the oven, slide the shells
on to the work surface.

For the lychee and rose ganache, drain
the lychees. Blend and then strain to
obtain a fine purée. You will need 240 g.

Chop up the chocolate and melt it into a
bowl over a pan of barely simmering water.

Bring the cream and lychee purée to
the boil. Pour it over the melted
chocolate a third at a time. Add the rose
essence and stir. →

Ispahan Macaron

White Risotto with Coffee Powder and Pantelleria Capers

Massimiliano Alajmo
Le Calandre
Italy 1997

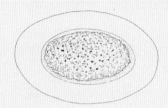

page 172

Pour the ganache into a gratin dish and press clingfilm over the surface of the ganache. Set aside in the fridge for the ganache to thicken.

Spoon the ganache into a piping (pastry) bag fitted with a plain nozzle (tip). Pipe a mound of ganache on to half the shells. Lightly press a square of frozen jelly into the centre and finish with a dot of ganache. Top with the remaining shells.

Store the macarons for 24 hours in the fridge and bring back out at the point of serving.

Liquefied egg whites
To the macaron batter, I use exclusively what I describe as 'liquefied' egg whites. Why 'liquefied'? Because the egg whites will liquefy if you sit them in the fridge for several days, preferably a week. During that time, the egg whites lose their elasticity, the albumen breaks down and they will be much easier to whisk to soft peaks without the risk of turning 'grainy'. And you don't have to worry about bacteria because they will be cooked in the oven at a high temperature.

Weigh out the egg whites indicated in each recipe described as 'liquefied' egg whites. Separate the whites from the

yolks. Weigh out the necessary quantity of egg whites into two bowls.

Cover the bowls with Clingfilm. Using the point of a sharp knife, pierce the film with holes.it s best to prepare the egg whites several days in advance, preferably a week, so that they lose their elasticity. Set the bowls aside in the fridge.

320 g Carnaroli rice
10 g extra virgin olive oil
50 g dry white wine
pinch of salt
8 espresso beans
1.2 litres hot chicken broth
60 g butter
100 g grated Parmigiano Reggiano
4 g ground espresso beans
50 g Pantelleria capers, soaked, drained and chopped
1 ristretto espresso, reduced by half

Toast the rice in a pot with extra virgin olive oil, then add the wine and evaporate.

Add the salt and coffee beans and proceed to add the simmering chicken broth, a ladleful at a time. When the rice is al dente, adjust the salt, eliminate coffee beans and energetically stir in butter and Parmigiano, then emulsify with a little broth.

Dust the serving plate with the ground espresso, ladle risotto onto the plate, spread it out, then sprinkle with the chopped capers. Draw a line of reduced espresso on the edge of the plate.

Smoke Foam

Ferran Adrià
elBulli
Spain 1997

page 173

Carrot and Celery Root Ravioli

Marc Veyrat
l'Auberge de l'Éridan
France 1998

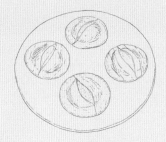

page 174

500 g smoked water
2 (2-g) gelatin sheets, previously
  rehydrated in cold water
salt
1 (100-g) slice bread
extra virgin olive oil

For the smoked water
2,000 g green firewood
500 g green leaves
500 g water

To make the smoked water, in a metal container, build a fire with the firewood and when it is lit, add the green leaves.

In a small, stainless steel saucepan, add the water and place it in the fire. Seal with an airtight lid. The smoke released when the fire is put out will smoke the water. If the water has not picked up the smoke flavor, repeat the method.

To make the smoke foam, heat one-quarter of the smoked water and dissolve the gelatin. Remove from the heat, mix in the remaining smoked water and season with salt. Drain and fill a ½ liter iSi siphon using a funnel. Charge the siphon with N2o and let it rest for a minimum of 3 hours in the refrigerator.

To make the diced bread, remove the bread's crust. Cut 20 cubes measuring 0.5 cm each. Place the diced bread on a baking sheet and toast all sides in the oven.

Fill ten shot glasses with the smoke foam. Add two cubes of bread on top of each foam. Drizzle with extra virgin olive oil.

There isn't a recipe for this dish, but you can make these round raviolis at home—just be sure not to make or use pasta. They are made with vegetables such as carrots, celery root (celeriac), artichokes, and turnips. There should absolutely not be any meat, sauce, butter, eggs, oil, or cream. Use only seasonal vegetables.

Snapper a la Talla

Gabriela Cámara
Contramar
Mexico 1998

page 175

For the red chile sauce

4 dried cascabel chiles or 1 pasilla
  chile, seeds removed
1 ancho chile, seeds removed
1 dried guajillo chile, seeds removed
1 pasilla chile, seeds removed
2 dried chiles de árbol
4 plum tomatoes, cored
¼ medium white onion
5 garlic cloves, peeled
2 whole cloves
½ cup vegetable oil
2 tablespoons fresh orange juice
1 tablespoon fresh lime juice
1 teaspoon ground achiote
  (annatto) seeds
¼ teaspoon ground cumin
¼ teaspoon Mexican or Italian
  oregano
kosher (coarse) salt and pepper

For the parsley sauce

4 garlic cloves
2 cups (packed) parsley leaves with
  tender stems
½ cup vegetable oil
pinch of ground cumin
kosher (coarse) salt

For the fish and assembly

vegetable oil (for grill)
4 (8-oz) skin-on, boneless red
  snapper fillets
kosher (coarse) salt, freshly ground
  pepper
warm tortillas, griilled salsa
roja and avocado-tomatillo
salsa verde, and lime wedges
(for serving)

To make the red chile sauce

Place the cascabel, ancho, guajillo, and
pasilla chiles in a medium saucepan and
add water to cover; bring to a simmer.
Cover, remove from heat, and let sit
30 minutes to soften. Drain.

Purée the softened chiles, chiles de
árbol, tomatoes, onion, garlic, cloves,
oil, orange juice, lime juice, achiote
seeds, cumin, and oregano in a blender
until smooth; season with salt and
pepper. The sauce can be made 1 day
ahead. Cover and chill.

To make the parsley sauce

Purée the garlic, parsley, oil, and cumin
in a clean blender until smooth; season
with salt. The sauce can be made 1 day
ahead. Cover and chill.

For the fish and assembly

Prepare a grill (barbecue) for medium
heat; brush the grates with oil.
Pat dry the skin side of each fillet with
paper towels (this will help keep the fish
from sticking). Using a sharp knife,
score flesh side of each fillet on a
diagonal about ¼ inch deep and 1 inch
apart; season with salt and pepper.
Spread 2 fillets with ½ cup red chile
sauce each, making sure to coat the
entire surface and pushing into score
marks. Repeat the process with
remaining 2 fillets using parsley sauce
this time.

Grill the fish, skin side down, until the
skin is charred and the fish is almost
cooked through, 7–10 minutes.

Carefully turn with a wide spatula; cook
until the flesh side has char marks and
easily releases from the grate, about
2 minutes. Place the fish, flesh side up,
on a platter. Serve with tortillas, grilled
salsa roja, avocado-tomatillo salsa
verde, and lime wedges.

Cassoulet

Caroline Fidanza
Diner
United States 1998

page 176

For the duck confit

1 whole duck
1 bunch of thyme
12 cloves garlic, smashed
2 tablespoons cracked whole black
    peppercorn
8 fresh bay leaves
salt

For the beans

2 lb dried tarbais or cannellini
    beans, soaked overnight
1 bunch of sage, tied with kitchen
    twine (string)
12 cloves garlic, smashed
salt

For the pork

1–2 lb boneless pork shoulder,
    seasoned with salt and pepper
    overnight
1 lb bacon, cut into lardons
1 large Spanish onion, cut into
    small dice
3 carrots, cut into small dice
4 ribs (sticks) celery, cut into small
    dice
2 tablespoons tomato paste
    (purée)
white wine
4 garlic sausages
bouquet garni of thyme, parsley
    and bay leaf
salt

For the breadcrumbs

1 baguette
a little olive oil
6 cloves garlic
½ bunch of parsley, picked, washed
    and dried

To confit the duck

Remove the breasts and legs from the
duck, season with salt and place in a
container with half of the thyme, garlic,
peppercorns and bay and refrigerate
overnight to cure.

Remove the skin and fat from the duck
carcass. Render the fat by placing it in a
heavy-duty pot with enough water to
cover the bottom of the pot and
simmering until the fat is rendered to a
liquid. Once the fat is rendered, strain
off skin and discard.

At the same time, put the duck carcass
into the oven to brown and render out
any remaining fat. Once brown, add the
fat to the pot of rendered fat above and
place the carcass in a pot, cover with
cold water and simmer to make a stock.

Reserve everything overnight.

The next day, place the duck legs and
breasts in a pot or roasting pan just big
enough to hold the parts tightly. Add
the rest of the aromatics to the duck –

the thyme, garlic, peppercorn and bay.
Remove any fat that formed on the
surface of the stock overnight and use
it along with the rendered duck fat to
cover the duck. (Don't worry if there's
not enough duck fat to cover the meat
– the skin and fat on the duck will
render out as it cooks – but if it's really
light, add some olive oil.)

Cover the duck with a lid or foil and
place in a low oven, at 300°F, to confit.
Once the duck is tender enough that
there is no resistance when pierced
with a knife, remove from the oven and
let cool in the fat.

To cook the beans

Place the soaked beans in a pot and
cover with cold water. Bring the beans
to a boil, then reduce to a simmer and
skim off any foam that rises to the
surface. Once clear, add the sage and
garlic to the pot and cook until tender.
Season with salt and turn off heat.

To braise the pork

Pat the pork shoulder dry and cut into
cubes. Place 3 tablespoons of duck fat in
a large heavy-bottomed earthenware,
enamel or cast-iron pot and brown the
pork on all sides. Remove from the pot
and set aside. →

Cassoulet

page 177

Drain off most of the remaining fat and add the bacon lardons to the pot. Brown the bacon, then add the onion, carrots and celery and some salt and allow the vegetables to deglaze the pan. Cook the vegetables until they are golden and soft, then stir in the tomato paste (purée). Add a little white wine to loosen things up, to move the paste around and coat the vegetables evenly. Add the pork back to the pot and enough stock to cover the pork two-thirds of the way. Cover the pot and braise the pork until tender.

Finishing the duck, assembling the cassoulet

Brown the duck breasts and legs in a pan. When cool, cut the duck breasts into thirds and pull the duck leg meat from the bone in large pieces. At this time also brown the sausages in a pan. Cool and cut into 1 inch pieces.

When the pork is ready, dump the pork and vegetables out of the pot and reserve. Lift half the beans out of their cooking liquid with a wire strainer (sieve) and into the pot that the pork was just in. Put the pork and vegetables on top of the beans, then the rest of the beans on top of the pork. Arrange the duck on top of the beans. Add duck stock to cover, nestle in the bouquet garni and put the pot (with a lid) into a 325°F oven for an hour to heat through.

To prepare the breadcrumbs

Meanwhile, tear the baguette into chunks, toss with olive oil and toast in a 350°F oven until crispy and golden. Allow to cool. Place the garlic in a food processor and process to break down a bit. Add the toasted bread to the food processor and process with the garlic to incorporate but not pulverize. Add the parsley and process to a not too fine crumb. (I like them on the large side.)

Finishing the cassoulet

Once heated, take the pot out of the oven. If things look dry, add a little more stock. Slice the sausages and arrange on top of the beans. Put the pot back into the oven uncovered until the cassoulet starts to bubble and the top of the beans and sausages are brown and crusty.

Once achieved, remove the pot from the oven and push down the top layer of beans and sausage into the cassoulet just a little – not fully submerging them but allowing a little of the beans and stock to pop up. If things look dry, add a little stock to the pot, then sprinkle the breadcrumbs generously on top of the cassoulet. Drizzle some duck fat or olive oil on top of the breadcrumbs and put the pot back in the oven and cook until the breadcrumbs get brown and toasty, about 30 minutes.

1 can sardines in oil (only Ruby brand, boneless and skinless in oil—from Morocco)
1 dollop Dijon mustard
small handful cornichons
small handful Triscuit crackers
1 parsley branch

Buckle the can after you open it to make it easier to lift the sardines out of the oil without breaking them.

Stack the sardines on the plate the same way they looked in the can— more or less. Don't crisscross or zigzag or otherwise make "restaurant y."

Commit to the full stem of parsley, not just the leaf. Chewing the stems freshens the breath.

Deviled Eggs
Gabrielle Hamilton
Prune
United States 1999

page 178

Grilled Anchovies
Victor Arguinzoniz
Etxebarri
Spain c.1999

page 179

8 eggs, still cold from the
   refrigerator
3 tablespoons Dijon mustard
1 cup Hellmann's mayonnaise
flat-leaf Italian parsley

Bring a large pot of water to a boil. Pierce the eggs at the tip with a pushpin to prevent exploding. Arrange the eggs in the basket of a spider and gently lower them into the boiling water. This way they won't crack from free-falling to the bottom of the pot. Let boil 10 minutes, including the minutes it takes for water to return to boil after adding the cold eggs.

Moving quickly, retrieve 1 egg and crack it all the way open, in half, to see what you have inside. (If the center has any rareness larger than a dime/5 pence, continue cooking half a minute.)

If thoroughly cooked, drain the eggs, rough them around in the dry pot to crackle their shells all over, then quickly turn them out into a frigid ice bath to stop the cooking. It helps with the cooling and the peeling to let the ice water permeate the cracked shells.

Peel the eggs. Cut them in half neatly and retrieve the cooked yolk from each. Place the hollow, cooked whites into a container with plenty of cold fresh water and let them soak to remove any cooked yolk from their cavities.

Blend the yolks in food processor with the mustard and mayonnaise. Make sure the bite of the Dijon can make itself felt through the muffle of the rich egg yolk and the neutralizing mayonnaise.

Scrape all the egg mixture from the processor bowl into a disposable pastry (piping) bag fitted with a closed star tip (nozzle), but do not snip the closed tip of the bag until you are ready to pipe. Fit the pastry bag into a clean empty quart (litre) container like you might put a new garbage liner into the bin—folding the excess over the lip of the container—to make this easier on you.

If you don't already know, you can stick your middle finger up into the punt of the processor bowl while scraping out the contents with the spatula, to hold the messy, sharp blade in place.

Remove the cooked egg whites from the cold water and lay, cavity side down, on a few stacked sheets of paper towels. Don't serve the deviled eggs wet, please.

When well drained, turn over the eggs to reveal the cavities and pipe the mixture in, more like a chrysanthemum than a soft-serve ice cream cone, please. Place on a plate and finish with finely sliced parsley.

8 fresh anchovies
20 ml olive oil
Guérande salt
1 small piece chili
20 ml Txakoli
arugula (rocket) leaves

Using a pair of scissors, clean the anchovies: Cut the tail, head, and guts. Open the anchovies in two halves, remove the bones with tweezers and extract the spine. Place under running water, clean, and dry with a dish towel.

Join two open anchovy fillets, meat sides facing in, so that they form one single anchovy with only the skin visible. Join both fillets by the tail. Repeat until you have four double anchovies.

Spray the anchovies with olive oil so that they don't become dry. Place in a barbecue grill basket and set at around 15 cm from the embers. Grill over low heat, 1–2 minutes per side, depending on the anchovies' thickness. Remove from the heat.

Plate, season with a pinch of salt, and add a few drops of a sauce made with the chili and Txakoli.

Accompany with arugula (rocket) drizzled with olive oil.

Yellowtail Sashimi with Jalapeño

Nobu Matsuhisa
Nobu
United States c.2000

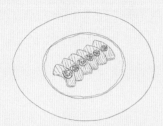

page 180

This recipe includes sliced yellowtail dipped in garlic, then topped with jalapeño and yuzu–soy sauce. Next time you're out of chili paste, perhaps you'll come up with something this original and exciting.

White Milk and Black Truffle

Michel Troisgros
La Maison Troisgros
France 2000s

page 181

The milk curd
Pour 1 litre of milk into a large bowl and heat to 32°C in a bain-marie. Take off the heat, add 20 g of rennet and stir. Pour the milk onto a plate – it should be 1 cm thick. Let it rest for 15 minutes so that it coagulates and then keep refrigerated.

Leave for one day, then using another plate, place the curd on absorbent paper. Keep cool.

The truffle pesto
Crush 60 g of puréed truffles in a mortar and season with salt, a few drops of lemon juice, virgin olive oil and a spoon of fresh cream. Keep the mixture warm.

The finishing touches
Cut the milk curd into six 12 × 12 cm squares.

Add a spoonful of truffle pesto to a hot plate. Cover with a square of milk curd and pour a few drops of olive oil over the middle.

When serving, make a slash in the milk curd with a sharp blade for a peek of the truffle. Eat with a spoon.

Crisp Confit of Pork Belly, Seared Sea Scallops, Shiitake, Jellyfish, Sesame

Peter Gilmore
Quay
Australia 2001

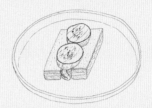

page 182

300 ml grapeseed oil, plus 50 ml for pan frying
1 small piece cassia bark
2 star anise
1.5 kg pork belly deboned, skin on
100 g fresh shiitake mushrooms
100 g fresh enoki mushrooms
sea salt
100 g dry salted jellyfish strips
150 g fine somen wheat noodles
10 ml premium Japanese soy
10 ml pure sesame oil
10 ml black rice vinegar
10 ml mirin
20 ml cold pressed grapeseed oil
1 punnet baby coriander (cilantro)
30 g blanched julienne Asian spring onions (scallions)
20 g toasted sesame seeds
16 large sea scallops

Warm 300 ml of the grapeseed oil to 70°C. Break up the cassia bark and star anise into the oil and allow to infuse for 30 minutes. Strain the oil, discarding the cassia bark and star anise, and allow the oil to cool. Place the pork belly and infused oil into a large cryovac bag and seal. Steam the pork belly at 90°C overnight for 8 hours. Remove from the steamer and carefully remove the pork belly from the bag, discarding the juices.

Place the pork belly between two silicon paper-lined heavy baking trays, then place in the fridge. Weight the trays with a stack of plates or other heavy object, but make sure the pressure is even. Allow to set for a minimum of 8 hours. Next, cut the pork belly into 16 oblong strips 2.5 cm wide and 8.5 cm long. Refrigerate until required.

To prepare the salad, slice the shiitake into 2-mm-thin slices across the mushroom, and with the enoki mushroom just remove the caps and reserve the stems (stalks) for another use. In a frying pan with 50 ml grapeseed oil, sauté the shiitake mushrooms until lightly coloured. Add the enoki mushroom caps and cook for a further few seconds, then drain the mushrooms on absorbent paper towels. Lightly season the mushrooms with sea salt, put aside and allow to cool.

Soak the salted jellyfish strips in 3 to 4 changes of cold water to remove the salt and rehydrate the jellyfish. Blanch the somen noodles in boiling water for 1–2 minutes, drain and put aside. Combine the soy, sesame oil, rice vinegar, mirin and cold pressed grapeseed oil in a bowl and whisk well.

Have all the ingredients for the salad including the spring onions (scallions), coriander (cilantro) and sesame seeds standing by to combine and dress at the last moment before serving.

You will need two large ovenproof non-stick pans to finish the pork belly. Preheat the oven to 200°C and place the non-stick pans on a medium heat, adding a smear of grapeseed oil. Place the pieces of pork belly skin side down in the pan. Increase the heat for 30 seconds, then place the pans with the pork belly into the oven and cook for 5 minutes. Remove the pans from the oven and turn the pork belly over. The skin should be very crisp and the belly hot – if the skin is not crisp, cook for a further few minutes back on the skin side. Keep warm and season the pork belly lightly with sea salt.

In two separate non-stick pans add a smear of grapeseed oil, heat the pans until very hot and sear the sea scallops for about 30 seconds until well coloured. Turn the scallops over for a few seconds and immediately remove from the pans. Combine all the salad ingredients and dress the salad. Place 2 oblong strips of pork belly in the centre of each plate leaving a small gap

in the middle to carefully place in the salad. Top with 2 seared scallops per dish and serve immediately.

Home-Smoked Lobster with Lime and Herb Butter

Andrew Fairlie
Restaurant Andrew Fairlie
United Kingdom 2001

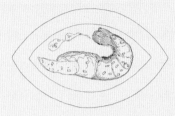

page 183

1 (1-kg) live lobster
2 generous handfuls of whisky
   barrel chips
salt and pepper, to taste

For the butter sauce
1 tablespoon double (heavy) cream
juice of 1 lime
juice of ½ lemon
250 g unsalted butter, diced
20 g each of chopped chervil,
   flat-leaf parsley, tarragon
   and chives

Bring a large pot of water to a rolling boil, seasoned heavily with sea salt. Plunge the live lobster into the water, cover with a lid and bring back to a gentle boil. Boil the lobster for 7 minutes, remove from the water and plunge into iced water.

Holding the lobster out flat on a cutting (chopping) board, split the lobster lengthways straight down the middle, being careful not to separate the tail from the body. Remove the tail meat from both halves and reserve; clean out any meat from the head and discard.

Crack the claws and knuckles and remove all the meat being careful not to break the claw meat; reserve.

Heat the smoking pan of the smoker, add a handful of the dry woodchips until they glow. Slightly dampen the remaining chips and sprinkle over the glowing embers. When the smoking chamber fills with smoke place the two empty lobster shells, cut side up, into the smoker. Smoke gently for 2 hours, remove the shells and refrigerate.

In a small saucepan, warm the cream, add the lime and lemon juices and warm to just below boiling. Whisk in the cold butter piece by piece – do not add the next piece of butter until the previous piece is melted. Season with salt and a little pepper, check for acidity and add more lime if necessary. Keep warm.

Spoon a little of the lime butter into the empty lobster shells. Neatly slice the lobster tail meat and place back into the shell. Place the knuckle meat into the head space. Neatly slice the claw and place on top of the knuckles. Drizzle a spoonful of the warm lime butter sauce over the meat. Refrigerate until needed.

Add the chopped herbs to the remaining butter sauce for service. To reheat the lobster, place in a cast iron casserole dish with a little water. Cover tightly with aluminium foil, then place

directly onto an electric stove until the foil has expanded. Leave to steam in the foil until hot through.

To serve, reheat the butter sauce with the chopped herbs. Coat the hot lobster with the warm herb butter sauce.

DB Burger

Daniel Boulud
db Bistro Moderne
United States 2001

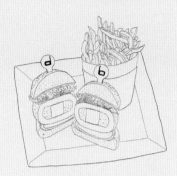

page 184

For the braised short ribs
2 cups red wine
½ cup ruby port wine
1 tablespoon olive oil
2 bone-in 2-inch thick short ribs
salt
cracked black pepper
flour, for dusting
½ medium onion, cut into
    small dice
1 carrot, cut into small dice
½ rib celery, cut into small dice
2 large shallots, peeled and split
½ small leek, white and light green
    parts only, diced and rinsed
½ head garlic, halved
2 sprigs thyme
¾ tablespoon tomato paste
    (purée)
¾ quart beef stock

Vegetable mirepoix garnish
2 tablespoons carrots, finely
    chopped and sweated
2 tablespoons onion, finely chopped
    and sweated
2 tablespoons celery, finely
    chopped and sweated

For the short rib roll and burgers
Vegetable mirepoix (see above)
2 tablespoons fresh black truffle
¾ lb grade A foie gras
3 lb ground burger meat
    (beef mince)

To serve
Parmesan buns
Dijon hot mustard
freshly grated horseradish
frisée (or arugula/rocket),
    seasoned with lemon vinaigrette
tomato confit
red onions, sliced
fresh plum tomato slices
salt and freshly ground pepper
black Périgord truffle (optional)
pommes frites
mayonnaise

For the braised short ribs
Pour both of the wines into a large
saucepan set over medium heat. When
the liquid is hot, carefully set it aflame,
let the flames die out, then increase the
heat so that the wine boils; allow it to
boil until it cooks down by half. Remove
from the heat.

Center a rack in the oven and preheat
the oven to 350°F.

Warm the oil in a Dutch oven or large
casserole over medium-high heat.
Season the ribs all over with salt and
crushed pepper. Dust half the ribs with
about 1 tablespoon flour and then, when
the oil is hot, slip the ribs into the pot
and sear 4–5 minutes on a side, until
the ribs are well browned. Transfer the
browned ribs to a plate, dust the

remaining ribs with flour, and sear in
the same manner. Remove all but
1 tablespoon of fat from the pot, lower
the heat under the pot to medium, and
toss in the vegetables and herbs. Brown
the vegetables lightly, for 5–7 minutes,
then stir in the tomato paste (purée)
and cook for 1 minute to blend.

Add the reduced wine, browned ribs,
and stock to the pot. Bring to the boil,
cover the pot closely, and slide it into
the oven to braise for 2½ hours, or until
the ribs are tender enough to be easily
pierced with a fork. Every 30 minutes
or so, lift the lid and skim and discard
whatever fat may have bubbled up to
the surface. (Not only can you make this
a day in advance, it's best to make the
recipe up to this point, cool and chill
the ribs and stock in the pan, and, on
the next day, scrape off the fat. Rewarm
before continuing.)

Carefully (the tender meat falls apart
easily) transfer the meat to a heated
serving platter with a raised rim and keep
warm. Boil the pan liquids until they
thicken and reduce to approximately
1 quart. Season with salt and pepper and
pass through a fine-mesh sieve; discard
the solids. (The ribs and sauce can be
made a few days ahead and kept →

DB Burger

Nitro-Poached Green Tea and Lime Mousse

Heston Blumenthal
The Fat Duck
United Kingdom 2001

page 185

covered in the refrigerator. Reheat gently, basting frequently, on top of the stove or in a 350°F oven.)

To shape the short rib roll
Using your fingertips, gently shred the warm and tender red-wine braised short ribs into a bowl. Add a brunoise of cooked root vegetable mirepoix, along with some chopped preserved black truffle and some reduced braising liquid from the short ribs.

Spread the warm rib mixture onto a baking sheet into a thick flat rectangle. Cut the foie gras lobe into thick slices, sear on both sides in a hot skillet (frying pan), then cool and cut into long strips. Place the foie gras in a horizontal line down the center of the short ribs and while still warm, wrap the ribs around to form a log, encasing the foie gras. Using plastic wrap (clingfilm), roll the log tightly to approximately 2¼ inches in diameter and chill until firm.

For the burger patties
Shape 6 ounces of the ground burger meat (beef mince) into a large flat circle, about ½ inch wider than the short rib log. Slice a 2-ounce piece of the short rib log and place in the middle of the ground meat disc. Wrap the meat around the disc to encase it completely. Mold the burger in your

hands into an even-shaped patty. Repeat to make 8 patties in total.

To cook and serve
Season the patties with salt and pepper and sear on all sides until well browned, and then transfer to a hot oven to reach desired doneness.

Split and toast the Parmesan buns, then drizzle both sides with mustard, freshly grated horseradish, and seasoned frisée. Top one side with tomato confit and sliced red onion, and the other side with fresh plum tomato slices and the cooked burger. For a DB Burger Royale, cover the burger with shaved black Périgord truffle. Place the other half of the bun on top and secure with skewers. Serve with pommes frites.

For the pectin base
1 kg cold water
175 g unrefined caster (superfine) sugar
16 g high methoxyl confectioner's pectin

Bring the water to the boil in a large pan. Meanwhile, combine the sugar and pectin in a jug (pitcher), then whisk the mixture into the boiled water. Continue whisking over a high heat for 1 minute. Chill the mixture over ice or in a blast chiller and set aside. (The base will keep for several weeks if refrigerated.)

For the green tea and lime mousse
95 g pasteurized lime juice*
1 g matcha tea powder
1 g malic acid
25 g vodka
55 g egg whites
325 g reserved pectin base

*To pasteurize fresh lime juice, combine it with 10 per cent of its weight in caster (superfine) sugar and seal in a sous-vide bag at full pressure. Place in a water bath set at 70°C/160°F for 10 minutes, then cool rapidly in an ice bath.

Combine the matcha and malic acid in a bowl, then whisk in the vodka to form a paste. Add the egg white, lime juice and pectin base, and mix thoroughly using a hand-held blender.

Foie Gras Poutine

Martin Picard
Au Pied de Cochon
Canada 2001

page 186

Pass this mixture through a chinois, then pour into a whipping cream canister. Charge the canister with enough gas to make the foam come out stiff and glossy, like shaving cream. Refrigerate the filled canister for at least 1 hour so that the mousse will firm up and hold its shape when dispensed.

To serve
matcha tea powder, for dusting
2 litres liquid nitrogen
reserved canister of mousse
lime grove fragrance

Place the matcha powder in a small muslin (cheesecloth) bag and tie closed.

Pour the liquid nitrogen into a Dewar flask. Squirt a small amount of the chilled mousse on to a spoon to form an egg-shaped ball of foam. Tap the spoon against the flask to knock the foam into the nitrogen to 'poach'.

Use a clean spoon to baste the liquid nitrogen over the top of the foam for 10 seconds, then roll the ball over and baste the other side for 10 seconds. The foam should be crisp on the outside, but soft and semi-liquid in the centre.

Remove the frozen foam, sprinkle matcha powder over the top, and serve immediately with a mist of lime grove fragrance.

4 slices fresh foie gras, 100 g
  (½ oz) each, 2.5 cm (1 inch) thick
4 white-fleshed potatoes (cut into
  French fries)
oil, for frying (two thirds tallow and
  one third peanut/groundnut oil)
400 g (14 oz) cheese curds

For the foie gras sauce
600 ml (2½ cups) hot PDC poutine
  sauce (available at the
  restaurant, or use store-bought
  poutine sauce)
6 egg yolks
200 g (7 oz) fresh foie gras
50 ml (¼ cup) 35% fat cream

For the foie gras sauce, set aside 100 ml (½ cup) of poutine sauce for the final presentation of the poutine. In a saucepan, bring the PDC poutine sauce to a boil.

Mix the egg yolks, foie gras and cream in a food processor at high speed. Slowly add the 500 ml (2 cups) of hot poutine sauce to the mixture.

Pour into a saucepan and heat gently, stirring constantly, until the sauce reaches 80°C (175°F). Remove the sauce from the heat. Stir for 30 seconds more. Keep warm.

For the foie gras, preheat the oven to 230C (450°F).

In a very hot pan, sear the foie gras slices until they are golden brown. Transfer the slices to a baking sheet and finish cooking in the oven for 4–5 minutes.

Cook the fries (chips) in the oil until crisp and place them on top of a mound of cheese curds in the middle of the plate. Place a slice of seared foie gras on the fries and smother in the foie gras sauce. Decorate with a few dabs of regular poutine sauce and serve immediately.

Eggplant with Buttermilk Sauce

Yotam Ottolenghi and Sami Tamimi
Ottolenghi
United Kingdom 2002

page 187

Eternity by Calvin Klein

Jordi Roca
El Celler de Can Roca
Spain 2002

page 188

For this dish you need eggplants sliced in half, then brushed with olive oil and roasted. The buttermilk–yogurt sauce brings it to a beautiful finish. Don't forget to add pomegranate seeds and a sprinkling of herbs to finish.

Composition
vanilla cream
orange blossom water jelly
basil sauce
maple syrup jelly
tangerine slush
bergamot ice cream

Vanilla cream
yields 650 g

500 g cream
1 vanilla pod (bean)
100 g egg yolks
50 g sugar
42 g cornflour (cornstarch)

Boil the cream with the vanilla pod (bean), then add the egg yolks, sugar and cornflour. Cook the mixture while stirring until it's set and smooth. Cool and reserve.

Orange blossom water jelly
yields 195 g

1 g agar-agar
200 g orange blossom water

Mix the agar-agar with one third of the water and bring to a boil; add the remaining water and spread on a tray with a thickness of 1.5 cm. When solid, cut jelly into 1.5cm cubes.

Basil sauce
yields 190 g

100 g water
50 g sugar
50 g fresh basil
3 g agar-agar

Boil 50 g water with 50 g sugar. Reserve.

Separately, bring the remaining 50 g water to a boil with and blanch the basil leaves for 20 seconds: cool quickly by submerging into iced water. When the blanching water has cooled down, place it with the syrup and leaves in the blender, liquidize and strain. Mix some of the mixture with the agar-agar, boil, add the rest of the mixture, leave to set and, lastly, run through the hand blender to break the structure and make a sauce. Reserve.

Maple syrup jelly
yields 190 g

150 g maple syrup
50 g water
1½ gelatine sheets

Dissolve the maple syrup with water and heat to 40°C/104°F. Add the gelatine sheets, previously hydrated, and when they dissolve, pour the whole

page 189

mixture in a tray with a thickness of 1.5 cm. Leave to solidify in the fridge and, when set, cut the gel into 1.5-cm cubes.

Tangerine slush
yields 650 g

500 g tangerine juice
100 g dextrose
100 g inverted sugar syrup
3 grated tangerine zests
4 gelatine sheets

Boil some of the juice to dissolve the dextrose and inverted sugar. Then, add the tangerine zest and cover for 5 minutes to infuse. Add the gelatine sheets, previously hydrated, strain and pour in the rest of the juice. Reserve in the freezer at -20°C/-4°F.

Bergamot ice cream
yields 950 g

600 g milk
300 g cream
90 g inverted sugar syrup
90 g dextrose
60 g sugar
36 g milk powder 1% fat content
6 g ice cream stabilizer
4 grated bergamot zests
120 g bergamot juices

Heat the milk, cream and inverted sugar syrup to 40°C/104°F.

Separately, mix the dextrose, sugar, milk powder and ice cream stabilizer, and add to the previous mixture. Cook until it reaches 85°C/185°F. Strain the mixture, add the grated bergamot and blast chill. Leave to ripen in the fridge for 12 hours.

Next, strain the mixture again and run through the ice cream maker. When it reaches -1°C/30°F, pour in the bergamot juice while the ice cream churns. Reserve at -20°C/-4°F.

Garnishing and plating
8 tangerine segments, peeled
    including the pith

On the plate, place three dots of vanilla cream, five dots of basil sauce, three orange blossom jelly cubes, three maple syrup jelly cubes and one tangerine segment. Serve the tangerine slush on top and garnish it with a bergamot ice cream quenelle.

Find a guinea pig and serve the filet on a purple corn tortilla, with chili sauce and pickled turnips.

Shrimp Noodles

Wylie Dufresne
wd~50
United States 2003

page 190

---

shrimp (prawn) noodles
shrimp (prawn) oil
water
15 g butter
smoked yogurt
prawn crackers
nori powder

In a small sauté pan, reheat the noodles over a medium heat with a dash of shrimp oil, water, and the butter, stirring and tossing as needed.

For each serving, paint the yogurt onto a plate and top with a generous spoonful each of warm noodles and prawn crackers. Dust the plate with nori powder.

For the shrimp (prawn) oil
200 g grapeseed oil
60 g diced onion
60 g diced carrot
60 g diced celery
10 g tomato paste (purée)
2 sprigs tarragon
60 g white wine or dry sake
400 g shrimp shells, chopped

In a large saucepan, heat about 1 tablespoon of the oil over a medium heat. Add the onion, carrot and celery and sweat until soft. Add the tomato paste (purée), tarragon, and wine and

cook, stirring, until the morepoix is tender and the alcohol is cooked down, about 10 minutes. Add the shrimp shells and the remaining oil.

For the shrimp (prawn) noodles
250 g peeled, deveined shrimp (prawns)
0.5 g activia RM
3 g kosher (coarse) salt
0.15 g cayenne pepper
shrimp (prawn) oil
cooking spray

In a food processor, purée the shrimp (prawns), activa, salt and cayenne. Pass through a coarse tamis. Transfer the mixture into a pastry (piping) bag.

Set up a water bath to 136°F, but turn the motor off.

Pipe the mixture into a noodle maker, or extruder, and extrude all of the shrimp (prawn) purée into the water bath. Cook for 2 minutes.

Using scissors, cut the noodles to the length of spaghetti and plunge them in an ice bath. Let cool.

Drain the noodles and separate them. Dress with shrimp (prawn)oil and store on parchment (baking) paper lightly coated with cooking spray.

Bring the mixture to about 200°F and cover the pot. Remove from the heat and leave at room temperature for 3 hours, then refrigerate overnight.

The next day, reheat and strain the mixture through a cheesecloth (muslin) in a paper cone filter to harvest the shrimp oil.

For the smoked yogurt
225 g plain Greek yogurt
3 g sweet paprika
kosher (coarse) salt

Spread the yogurt over a half hotel pan (restaurant service pan) and place in a smoker above another half hotel pan filled with ice. Smoke the yogurt for 3 minutes.

In a medium bowl, combine the yogurt, paprika and salt. Allow the flavours to infuse for 1 hour. Reserve.

For the prawn crackers
neutral oil, for deep-frying
4 pieces uncooked prawn crackers
tomato powder
kosher (coarse) salt

In a deep pot, heat 3 inches of oil to 375°F.

Snail Porridge

Heston Blumenthal
The Fat Duck
United Kingdom 2003

page 191

Crush a few prawn crackers with a mortar and pestle into irregular, smallish shapes. Deep-fry the cracker crumbs until they puff, about 1 minute. Pat down on paper towels, dust with tomato powder to coat, and sprinkle lightly with salt.

For the nori powder
2 sheets sushi nori

Dry the nori sheets in a dehydrator set to 155°F for 3 hours or overnight in an oven with only the pilot light lit. Blend to a fine powder.

For the duck ham
1 bay leaf
15 g black peppercorns
15 g coriander seeds
50 g sel gris
5 g sprigs of thyme
5 Gressingham duck breasts, fat scored

Snip the bay leaf into 8 pieces. Grind the peppercorns and coriander, and combine with the *sel gris*, thyme and bay leaf. Spread a layer of this mixture over the bottom of a roasting tray and place the duck breasts on top. Cover completely with the remaining salt mixture, then refrigerate for 24 hours.

Brush the salt cure from the breasts, wrap them in muslin (cheesecloth) and tie securely with string. Hang in a cellar or other cool place for at least 20 days. Remove the duck from the muslin and refrigerate until needed.

For the parsley butter
550 g unsalted butter
85 g garlic, minced
10 g lemon juice
50 g Dijon mustard
40 g ground almonds (almond meal)
15 g table salt
240 g curly leaf parsley
clarified butter

40 g ceps (porcini), cut into 1-cm dice
60 g shallots, cut into brunoise (2-mm squares)
80 g reserved duck ham, cut into brunoise

Melt 50 g of the unsalted butter in a pan, add the garlic and sauté until pale gold and fragrant.

Add the lemon juice to the pan, then transfer the mixture to a PacoJet beaker along with the mustard, ground almonds (almond meal), salt and the remaining 500 g unsalted butter.

Chop the parsley, sprinkle on top of the butter mixture and run the beaker through the Pacojet machine. Remove the beaker and freeze the mixture until completely solid. Run the frozen mixture through the Pacojet, then freeze solid again. Repeat this process until all trace of the parsley has disappeared. After the final Pacotizing, at which point the mixture will have an ice cream consistency, set aside the butter at room temperature until needed.

Heat some clarified butter in a pan, add the ceps (porcini) and sauté until caramelized. Strain and set aside. →

375

Snail Porridge

Wipe the pan clean, then heat some more clarified butter in it. Add the shallots and cook over a very low heat for 30–40 minutes, until very soft and translucent.

Fold the caramelized ceps, the cooked shallot and the duck brunoise into the reserved parsley butter. Refrigerate or freeze until needed.

For the chicken bouillon

3 kg chicken (2 good-sized chickens)
250g carrots, peeled and finely sliced
250 g onions, finely sliced
100 g celery, finely sliced
75 g leek, white and pale green parts only, finely sliced
10 g garlic, crushed
3 cloves
10 g black peppercorns
50 g sprigs of thyme
20 g parsley leaves and stems
3 g bay leaf

Place the chickens in a large pan and cover with cold water. Bring to the boil, then carefully remove the chickens and discard the water. Rinse the chickens under cold running water to remove any scum.

Put the chickens in a pressure cooker and add just enough cold water to cover them. Bring to a simmer, skimming off any scum on the surface. Add the vegetables, garlic cloves and freshly crushed peppercorns to the pan. Put the lid on, bring to full pressure and cook for 30 minutes.

Remove the pan from the heat, allow to depressurize, then remove the lid. Add the thyme, parsley and bay leaf and leave to infuse for 30 minutes.

Strain the bouillon through a fine sieve lined with several layers of damp muslin (cheesecloth). Refrigerate or freeze until needed.

For the braised snails

100 g Helix pomatia snails (shelled weight)
2 cloves
120 g onion, cut in half
40 g carrot, cut in half
90 g leeks, cut in half
2 slicks of celery
30 g garlic bulb, cut in hald
2 bay leaves
50 g sprigs of rosemary
50 g sprigs of thyme
120 g water
250 g dry white wine
50 g parsley leaves and stems

Rinse the snails in several changes of water to remove any grit. Preheat the oven to 120°C/284°F/Gas ¼–½.

Press a clove into each half of the onion, then place in an ovenproof casserole with all the other ingredients, apart from the snails and parsley, and bring to a simmer on the hob (stove).

Add the snails, cover with a cartouche and place in the oven for 3–4 hours. Remove the casserole from the oven, add the parsley and set aside to cool.

Drain the snails from the liquid and trim away their intestines and white sac. Refrigerate until needed.

For the walnut vinaigrette

75 g walnut vinegar
145 g grapeseed oil
5 g Dijon mustard

Combine all the ingredients, mix thoroughly and set aside until needed.

Foie Gras and Miso Soup

Iñaki Aizpitarte
La Famille
France 2004

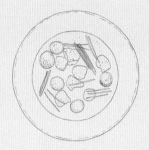

page 192

For the snail porridge
10 g fennel, shaved paper-thin
reserved walnut vinaigrette
table salt
black pepper
fleur de sel
30 g unsalted butter
12 reserved braised snails
30 g reserved chicken bouillon
10 g porridge (steel-cut)
  oats, sieved to remove the
  powdery bits
30 g reserved parsley butter, at
  room temperature
20 g Jabugo ham, cut into
  chiffonade

Dress the fennel with the vinaigrette, season with table salt, freshly ground pepper and *fleur de sel* and set aside.

Heat 20 g of the butter until foaming, then sauté the snails and season with table salt and freshly ground pepper. Add the remaining butter to the snails, then remove from the heat and keep warm.

Heat the chicken bouillon in a small saucepan. When hot, stir in the oats. Once they have absorbed the liquid, add the parsley butter and season to taste with table salt and freshly ground pepper. Adjust the consistency of the porridge with chicken bouillon if necessary until it resembles wet rice pudding. (It is important not to overcook the oats or else they will become starchy and lose their texture.)

Divide the porridge between 2 warm plates and cover with the ham. Place the warm snails on top, add the dressed fennel and serve.

white miso paste (good quality)
10 black peppercorns
75 cl chicken broth
20 very small cream Parisian
  mushrooms
160 g foie gras, cut in medium-
  sized cubes
2 baby leeks, white parts only, cut
  into julienne
fine salt

Infuse 3 spoons of the miso and the black peppercorns in the chicken broth for 10 minutes. Strain the liquid.

Cook the mushrooms for 1 minute in the broth.

Divide the broth among 4 bowls with the mushrooms. Sprinkle fine salt on the cubes of foie gras and place them in the bowls. Finish the soup by adding the julienned raw leeks to the bowls.

Devils on Horseback

April Bloomfield
The Spotted Pig
United States 2004

page 193

For the pears

450 ml dry white wine, such as
  Sauvignon Blanc
225 ml white wine vinegar
200 g caster (superfine) sugar
1 tablespoon sliced skin-on fresh
  ginger
10 black peppercorns
4 whole allspice berries
about 4 dried pequin chillies or
  pinches of red pepper flakes
1 large cinnamon stick
3 large perfectly ripe Bartlett
  (Williams) pears

For the prunes

1 English breakfast tea bag,
  preferably PG Tips
3 tablespoons Armagnac or
  Cognac
10 large pitted prunes
10 thin slices (rashers) bacon
Maldon or another flaky sea salt
2 or 3 dried pequin chillies or
  pinches of red pepper (dried
  chilli) flakes

For the pears

Combine the first eight ingredients in a pan just big enough for the pears to be submerged in the liquid in a snug fit. One at a time, peel the pears and halve them lengthwise. Use a small spoon to scoop out the tough core from each pear half, then trim off the hard bit at the base of each one. As you finish prepping each one, add it to the liquid so it doesn't brown.

Bring the liquid to the boil over medium-high heat, then turn down the heat so it simmers gently (don't rush it, or the pears will disintegrate). Cook just until the pears are tender but not very soft or mushy, 15–20 minutes, depending on the firmness of the pears.

Turn off the heat and let the pears cool in the liquid. They'll continue to cook a bit as they cool. Once cool, they'll still have a touch of snap to them, a soft crunch. They'll keep happily in their liquid in an airtight container in the fridge for up to 2 weeks.

For the prunes

Bring 225 ml water to boil in a small pan. Add the tea bag and let steep for 5 minutes, off the heat. Discard the tea bag and let the tea cool completely.

Combine the tea, Armagnac, and prunes in a small bowl. The prunes should be completely submerged in the liquid; if they're not, use a different container. Cover the bowl with clingfilm (plastic wrap) and pop it into the fridge. Let the prunes soak just until they're plump and soft, overnight or longer if necessary.

When the prunes are ready, remove them from the liquid. Reserve 2 tablespoons of the liquid.

Cut half of one of the spiced pears into 10 oblique pieces that will fit inside the prunes but are not so small that the prune envelops it completely. You want a couple of centimetres (about an inch) or so of the pear to peek out at the end of the prune. Stuff each prune with a pear piece. You might have to pop your finger into the prune first.

Lay a slice (rasher) of bacon on a cutting (chopping) board, put a prune at one end, and roll up so the prune is wrapped in the bacon. If you feel there's too much bacon, cut a little off – you want a nice balance between bacon and prune. Repeat with the remaining prunes and bacon. Covered with clingfilm, they keep overnight.

Position a rack in the middle of the oven and preheat the grill (broiler). If you don't have a grill, heat the oven as high as it will go.

Arrange the prunes seam side down in a shallow baking pan, leaving some room

Smoked Chicken
Lau Kin-Wai and Kwong Bing-Kwan
Kin's Kitchen
China 2004

page 194

---

between them. Add 3 tablespoons of pear liquid to the pan, along with the reserved prune liquor, then add a generous pinch of salt and crumble in the chillies. Baste, then cook the prunes under the grill or in the oven, basting them with the liquid every few minutes or so, until the bacon is golden and slightly crispy, about 15 minutes. Transfer the prunes to a plate or tray and drizzle with some of the liquid. If your bacon is on the sweet side, sprinkle on salt to taste. Let cool slightly before you dig in.

1 whole chicken, about 900 g

For the brine
1200 ml rock sugar
1200 ml water
600 ml light soy sauce
500 g sugarcane
4 bay leaves, 3 star anise, 1 tsaoko fruit and 1 cinnamon stick in a small cloth bag

For smoking
40 g dried rose buds
150 ml yellow slab sugar, chopped into small pieces
300 g sugarcane, cut into 8 cm long pieces, vertically cut into four pieces

Mix all the brine ingredients and bring to the boil and reduce the heat when all the sugar has melted. Place the chicken in the brine and simmer for 20 minutes. (The chicken must be fully submerged in the brine.)

When the chicken is done, place two layers of aluminium foil in a wok, then place the dried rose buds, yellow slab sugar and sugarcane in the wok. Put over a high heat and place a rack on top.

When the slab sugar starts to smoke, place the chicken on the rack, cover and smoke for 5 minutes.

When the smoking is done, let the chicken rest at room temperature for 5 minutes, then cut the chicken and serve.

Chocolate Truffles

Jean-Charles Rochoux
Jean-Charles Rochoux
France 2004

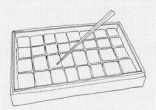

page 195

This recipe is not yet available publicly. In the meanwhile, take dark (bitter-sweet) chocolate, fresh cream, and butter (ideally from Normandy) to make the ganache. Evenly dust with cocoa powder and use a wire to slice into squares.

Yellow Earth Chicken

Margaret Xu Yuan
Yin Yang Kitchen
China c.2004

page 196

1 fresh chicken
1 tablespoon of the chicken
  marinade
1 tablespoon lychee wine (optional)
1½ tablespoons rock salt

Chicken marinade/dip
(makes one 250 ml jar)
150 ml extra virgin olive oil
100 g wild ginger (or sand ginger),
  chopped (or 1½ teaspoons dried
  Chinese wild ginger powder for
  chicken)
1 strand fresh curry leaf
1 tablespoon sea salt

Prepare the chicken marinade by mixing all the ingredients together and allow the flavours to mix. (At least overnight; can store up to a month.)

Season the inside of the chicken with 1 tablespoon of the marinade and the lychee wine. Rub the skin with the rock salt.

Hang the chicken over an enclosed charcoal oven for 1 hour, or alternatively, roast it in a preheated convection (fan-assisted) oven at 160°C, standing up, for 45 minutes.

To serve, peel off the thin skin and cut the skin into pieces with scissors. Carve off wings and legs. Shred the breast meat by hand to retain the juice in the meat.

Pork Buns

David Chang
Momofuku Noodle Bar
United States 2004

page 197

---

1 steamed bun (see below)
about 1 tablespoon hoisin sauce
3 or 4 slices quick–pickled
    cucumbers (see next page)
3 thick slices pork belly (see next
    page)
1 scant tablespoon thinly sliced
    scallion (spring onion), green
    and white
sriracha, for serving

Heat the bun in a steamer on the stove. It should be hot to the touch, which will take almost no time with just–made buns and 2–3 minutes with frozen buns.

Grab the bun from the steamer and flop it open on a plate. Slather the inside with the hoisin sauce, using a pastry brush or the back of a spoon. Arrange the pickles on one side of the fold in the bun and the slices of pork belly on the other. Scatter the belly and pickles with sliced scallion (spring onion), fold closed, and voilà: pork bun. Slather with sriracha.

Steamed buns
makes 50 buns
1 tablespoon plus 1 teaspoon active
    dry (fast-action) yeast
1½ cups water, at room
    temperature
4¼ cups (strong) bread flour
6 tablespoons sugar
3 tablespoons non-fat dry milk
    powder
1 tablespoon kosher (coarse) salt
rounded ½ teaspoon baking
    powder
½ teaspoon baking (bicarbonate
    of) soda
⅓ cup rendered pork fat or
    vegetable (fat) shortening, at
    room temperature, plus more for
    shaping the buns, as needed

Combine the yeast and water in the bowl of a stand mixer outfitted with the dough hook. Add the flour, sugar, milk powder, salt, baking powder, baking (bicarbonate of) soda, and fat and mix on the lowest speed possible, just above a stir, for 8–10 minutes. The dough should gather together into a neat, not–too–tacky ball on the hook. When it does, lightly oil a medium mixing bowl, put the dough into it, and cover the bowl with a dry kitchen towel. Put it into a turned–off oven with a pilot light or other warmish place and let rise until the dough doubles in bulk, about 1 hour 15 minutes.

Punch the dough down and turn it out onto a clean work surface. Using a bench scraper or a knife, divide the dough in half, then divide each half into 5 equal pieces, making 50 pieces in total. They should be about the size of a ping–pong ball and weigh about 25 g, or a smidge under an ounce. Roll each piece into a ball. Cover the armada of little dough balls with a draping of plastic wrap (clingfilm) and allow them to rest and rise for 30 minutes.

Meanwhile, cut out fifty 4–inch squares of parchment (baking) paper. Coat a chopstick with whatever fat you're working with.

Flatten one ball with the palm of your hand, then use a rolling pin to roll it out into a 4–inch–long oval. Lay the greased chopstick across the middle of the oval and fold the oval over onto itself to form the bun shape. Withdraw the chopstick, leaving the bun folded, and put the bun onto a square of parchment paper. Stick it back under the plastic wrap (or a dry kitchen towel) and form the rest of the buns. Let the buns rest for 30–45 minutes: they will rise a little. →

Pork Buns

Set up a steamer on the stove. Working in batches so you don't crowd the steamer, steam the buns on the parchment squares for 10 minutes. Remove the parchment. You can use the buns immediately (reheat them for a minute or so in the steamer if necessary) or allow to cool completely, then seal in plastic freezer bags and freeze for up to a few months. Reheat frozen buns in a steamer on the stove for 2–3 minutes, until puffy, soft, and warmed all the way through.

Pork belly (for ramen, pork buns & just about anything else)
makes enough pork for 6–8 bowls of ramen or about 12 pork buns
1.35 kg slab skinless pork belly
35 g coarse sea salt
50 g sugar

Nestle the belly into a roasting pan or other ovenproof vessel that holds it snugly. Mix together the salt and sugar in a small bowl and rub the mix all over the meat; discard any excess salt-and-sugar mixture. Cover the container with plastic wrap (clingfilm) and put it into the refrigerator for at least 6 hours, but no longer than 24.

Preheat the oven to 230°C/Gas 8.

Discard any liquid that accumulated in the container. Put the belly into the oven, fat side up, and cook for 1 hour, basting it with the rendered fat at the halfway point, until it's an appetizing golden brown.

Turn the oven temperature down to 130°C/Gas ½ and cook for another 1 hour–1¼ hours, until the belly is tender – it shouldn't be falling apart, but it should have a down pillow–like yield to a firm finger poke. Remove the pan from the oven and transfer the belly to a plate. Decant the fat and the meat juices from the pan and reserve for another use. Allow the belly to cool slightly.

When it's no longer hot, wrap the belly in plastic wrap or aluminium foil and put it in the refrigerator until it's thoroughly chilled and firm. (You can skip this step if you're pressed for time, but the only way to get neat, nice-looking slices is to chill the belly thoroughly before slicing it.)

Cut the pork belly into 1 cm-thick slices that are about 5 cm long. Warm them for serving in a pan over a medium heat, just for a minute of two, until they are jiggly soft and heated through. Serve at once.

Quick pickled cucumbers
2 meaty Kirby or other pickling cucumbers, cut into thin wedges through the root end
1 tablespoon sugar, or more, to taste
1 teaspoon coarse sea salt, or more, to taste

Combine the vegetables with the sugar and salt in a small mixing bowl and toss to coat with the sugar and salt. Let them sit for 5–10 minutes.

Taste: if the pickles are too sweet or too salty, put them into a colander, rinse off the seasoning and dry in a dish towel. Taste again and add more sugar or salt as needed. Serve after 5–10 minutes, or refrigerate for up to 4 hours.

Aka Sea Urchin in a Lobster Jelly with Cauliflower, Caviar, and Crispy Seaweed Waffles

Richard Ekkebus
Amber
China 2005

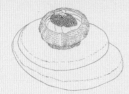

page 198

Sea urchins
50 Aka sea urchins from Hokkaido

Cut open the urchins neatly with scissors, taken out the tongues delicately with a teaspoon, rinse/dry the shells well and place in the refrigerator.

Cauliflower purée
500 g cauliflower, cleaned and cut
   into small pieces
100 g butter
1 litre milk
fine sea salt

Sweat the cauliflower in the butter without colouring but until glazed. Add the milk and a pinch of salt. Boil the cauliflower in the milk, until well cooked and soft. Mix the cauliflower in a blender until a smooth consistency, then pass through a sieve.

Cauliflower mousse
400 g cauliflower purée
2 gelatine sheets, soaked in ice
   water
800 g cream

Take 100 g of cauliflower purée and heat in a small heavy bottom saucepan. Dissolve the gelatine, mix well with the remaining cauliflower purée and cool down carefully over ice until it starts to set. In the meantime, whip the cream with a pinch of salt but only until 'half' whipped, then incorporate the half whipped cream in the cauliflower purée and mix delicately. Check the seasoning and adjust with salt if needed. Place the cauliflower mousse in a piping (pastry) bag, place the bag in the refrigerator until needed.

Lobster consommé
1 tablespoon olive oil
500 g Boston lobster, separate the
   claws, split in two and cut in 8
   regular pieces
1 vine riped Italian tomato,
   chopped coarsely
½ stem celery, peeled and diced
1 white onion, preferably Cévenne,
   peeled and chopped
20 cl Cognac VSOP
¼ litre dry white wine
1 litre chicken stock (broth), of
   good flavour
6 gelatine sheets, soaked in ice
   water
salt

In a heavy bottom saucepan, heat the olive oil, add the lobster and colour until golden brown, add the vegetables and sweat until all juices are evaporated. Deglaze with the brandy and flambé the pan until the alcohol has been burned off, add the white wine and reduce until a syrupy consistency. Add the chicken stock and add water until level with the lobster and bring to the boil, but just before the boiling point skim off all impurities (repeat this during the cooking process to obtain a clear bouillon). Keep just under the boiling point and simmer for 20 minutes. Take off the heat and leave to cool for 30 minutes. Pass the lobster bouillon carefully through a sieve covered with a pre-rinsed mousseline cloth or kitchen towel. Reduce the broth until it has a nice concentration of flavours. Reheat 1 litre of the stock and dissolve the 6 sheets gelatine in it. Check the seasoning and adjust with salt if needed. Cool down delicately over ice until the gelatine starts to set. →

Aka Sea Urchin in a Lobster Jelly with Cauliflower, Caviar, and Crispy Seaweed Waffles

Tapioca wakame waffle
400 g tapioca flour
3 litres water
40 g wakame powder, plus extra
　for dusting
5 litres grapeseed oil for frying
salt

Whisk the flour and water, put on the stove, bring to the boil, whisking continually until the mix goes clear.

Cover with clingfilm (plastic wrap) and put into the Chinese steamer powder.

Remove, season with salt and whisk in the wakame seaweed powder. Divide between six trays and spread evenly. Put into a dry oven on 65°C and leave overnight. Remove and keep in sealed bags.

Fry the waffles in grapeseed oil, at 180–190°C, and season lightly with a salt and wakame mix (ratio 1:1).

Nori seaweed waffle
10 nori sheets, toasted and ground
15 rice paper sheets
250 ml egg white
5 litres grapeseed oil for frying
salt

Blend the nori sheets in the Thermomix until it is a fine powder.

Brush the rice paper sheets with egg white. Using a small sieve sprinkle the nori powder on the rice sheets. Let it dry overnight on Silpat covered trays.

Deep-fry the waffles in smoking hot oil. Season with salt.

Plating the sea urchins
Select the 60 best and most perfect looking Aka sea urchin tongues. Place 2½ of these tongues in the centre of the cooled shells. Cover with the cauliflower mousse in a dome shape, and place on each cauliflower dome 5 Aka sea urchin tongues neatly arranged. Then place the shells in the refrigerator for 1 hour to set. After setting, cover each with 2 tablespoons of almost set jelly and place in the refrigerator for 1 hour to set.

Garnish per urchin
15 g coarse grey guerande sea salt
8 g fresh wakame seaweed
8 g fresh seaweed salad
8 g sea grapes
15 g farmed Petrossian Daurenki
　Tsar Imperial caviar
½ gold leaf

To serve
Take a large bowl, place the sea salt at the bottom, garnish with seaweeds and sea grapes. Placed the sea urchin shell on top, garnish with a dome of 15 g caviar and add the gold leaf on the top. Serve the two types of crispy waffles on the side between stone pebbles.

Spherical-I Green Olives

Ferran and Albert Adrià
elBulli
Spain 2005

page 199

For the sodium alginate solution

1.5 kg water
7.5 g sodium alginate

Mix the water and sodium alginate with a stick (immersion) blender until the mixture is lump-free.

Leave it to stand in the refrigerator for 48 hours, until the air bubbles disappear and the sodium alginate is completely rehydrated.

For the green olive juice

500 g green verdial olives

Pit the olives. Blend the olives in a liquidizer. Strain the purée through a Superbag, pressing the mixture through. Refrigerate the juice.

For the spherical-l green olive base

1.35 g calcium chloride
200 g green olive juice (previously prepared)
0.75 g Xantana

Add the calcium chloride to the juice and leave for 1 minute to hydrate well. Mix with a whisk and sprinkle the Xantana over the surface. Mix with a stick blender at medium speed. Refrigerate for 24 hours.

For the aromatized olive oil

4 cloves of garlic
500 g extra virgin olive oil
zest of 4 lemons
zest of 4 oranges
4 sprigs of fresh thyme
4 springs of fresh rosemary
12 black peppercorns

Lightly crush the garlic cloves and fry them in 100 g of olive oil without allowing them to brown. Add the remaining oil and wait for it to heat up before adding the rest of the ingredients. Store the oil in an airtight container in a cool, dry place.

For the spherical-l green olives

spherical-l green olives base (previously prepared)
sodium alginate solution (previously prepared)
aromatized olive oil (previously prepared).

Fill a 5 ml measuring spoon with the spherical-l green olive mixture. Drop the contents of the spoon into the sodium alginate solution to form spherical olives.

Make 2 olives per person. Do not allow the olives to touch one another, as they may stick. Leave the olives in the sodium alginate solution for 2 minutes.

Remove the olives from the sodium alginate solution using a slotted spoon and dip them into cold water to rinse them. Carefully strain the olives and place them in the aromatized oil without letting them touch one another. Refrigerate for 12 hours.

Finishing and presentation

2 glass jars for the olives

Put 1 piece of lemon zest, 1 piece of orange zest, 1 sprig of thyme, 1 sprig of rosemary and 4 black peppercorns into each jar. Divide the 20 spherical olives between the two jars. Cover with the aromatized oil.

Serve each jar on a slate accompanied by one slotted spoon per jar and as many medicine spoons (for serving) as there are guests.

Tuna Nigiri and Maccheroncini

Enrico Crippa
Piazza Duomo
Italy 2005

page 200

Edible Stones

Andoni Luis Aduriz
Mugaritz
Spain 2005

page 201

For the maccheroncini
32 rice pasta "maccheroncini"
salt and water, for cooking
1.7 g carrageenan kappa
100 g rice vinegar

For the tuna
8 high-quality 7 x 4-cm tuna slices
    (3 mm thick)

To finish
black sesame seeds
yellow calendula flower
tangerine zest
dried red shiso flowers
red and green fresh shiso
herb oil
extra virgin olive oil
Maldon salt

Cook the rice maccheroncini in the salted water for 10 minutes. Once cooked, put them on a tray and, while still warm, stack four pieces, two on top of the other, in order to create a small cylinder. Keep them covered with clingfilm (plastic wrap).

Boil together the gelatine kappa and rice vinegar and use it to glaze the moulded maccheroncini nigiri.

Put the nigiri onto a plate and cover half of it with tuna slices and decorate. Finish with the oils and Maldon salt.

The garlic confit
500 ml extra virgin olive oil
1 garlic bulb

Pour the oil into a small, deep saucepan and place on the cooker (stove) top over very low and steady heat, making sure it does not reach a very high temperature. Heating the oil can also be done over the edge of the cooker top. When the oil is warm, place the separated, unpeeled garlic cloves in the oil and poach them gently for approximately 2 hours. They should be tender, easy to peel and thoroughly impregnated with oil. When ready, drain the oil, peel the garlic cloves, crush them, then pass them through a chinois and set aside.

The coating
60 ml kaolin
40 g lactose
1 g black vegetable dye
0.5 g table salt
80 ml water

Place the kaolin, lactose, black dye and salt in a bowl and mix together, gradually adding the water. The mixture may seem too dry at first, but if left for an hour or so, it will liquefy and develop a yogurt-like texture suitable for coating the boiled potatoes, thick but not runny.

The potatoes
16 small Cherie potatoes (32–35 g
    each)
3 litres water
24 g salt

Gently clean the potatoes with a soft brush. Do not peel. Bring the salted water to a boil in a large saucepan, then add the potatoes. Boil for 15–20 minutes, depending on the size of the potatoes, without overcooking them. Drain them and place on a baking sheet.

The potatoes coated in clay
The potatoes (see above)
The coating (see above)

Pierce the flattest side of each potato with the tip of a skewer. Remove the skewer and insert its blunt end in the same hole until it reaches roughly the centre of the potato. Stir the kaolin mixture until thoroughly combined and of the correct consistency. Dip the potatoes into the mixture, completely covering them. Insert the ends of the skewers into the holes of a perforated baking sheet so that they are held in a vertical position.

Place the sheet in the oven at a low temperature – 50°C (120°F) for approximately 30 minutes or until the

Whole Roasted Cauliflower

Eyal Shani
North Abraxas
Israel 2006

page 202

This will contrast with the smoothness of the potato inside, which will be tender and creamy thanks to the protection of this 'shell'.

The alioli
40 g garlic confit (see above)
1 egg yolk
60 ml extra-virgin olive oil
salt

Put the garlic confit in a tall beaker, add the egg yolk and combine with a hand-held blender until the mixture forms an emulsion. Meanwhile, slowly drizzle the oil in, being careful that the emulsion does not lose stability. Once ready, add salt to taste and set aside in a covered bowl.

Presentation and finishing
Heat a few polished river stones the size of the potatoes coated in the grey clay in the oven at 70°C (160°F) for 5–7 minutes. The stones will add the finishing touch to the presentation and keep the potatoes hot for longer. Serve the potatoes in between the stones. Serve a heaped portion of alioli in smaller, individual dishes. The potatoes should be eaten with the fingers and the first bite should be taken without sauce. This will accentuate the difference in the texture between the coating and its content. After that, the potatoes should be dipped into the alioli.

1 (1½– 2-lb) head cauliflower with leaves
2 gallons water
7 tablespoons sel gris
3 tablespoons best-quality extra virgin olive oil

Preheat oven to 550°F with the oven rack in the center of oven. Trim the stem (stalk) of the cauliflower, keeping the leaves intact, so it will sit level on a rimmed baking sheet. Bring 2 gallons water to a boil in a large stockpot over high. Stir in 6½ tablespoons *sel gris* until dissolved.

Add the cauliflower to water; place a heatproof ceramic plate on top of cauliflower to keep it submerged. Boil until tender and a fork inserted in cauliflower meets no resistance, 12–13 minutes. Using a spider strainer (skimmer), gently lift cauliflower from water, and let drain in the spider, allowing water to drip back into pot. Place the cauliflower, stem side down, on a rimmed baking sheet. Let stand until cauliflower has cooled slightly and is dry to the touch, about 15 minutes.

Rub 1 tablespoon olive oil between your hands, then rub them over the cauliflower to apply a thin, even layer. (Alternatively, use a brush to spread the oil evenly over the cauliflower.) Sprinkle the remaining 1½ teaspoons *sel gris* over the cauliflower (the salt might clump in some places). Bake in the preheated oven until dark brown, about 25 minutes. Remove from the oven and carefully rub with the remaining 2 tablespoons olive oil. Serve hot.

Whole Roast Black Leg Chicken

Raphael Duntoye
La Petite Maison
United Kingdom 2007

page 203

1 poulet noir (black leg chicken), about 1.8 kg, wings removed.
300 g fresh foie gras
1 piece of bread
extra virgin olive oil
1 spring of thyme
1 garlic clove
250 ml chicken stock (broth, preferably homemade)
freshly ground salt and pepper

Clean the chicken and stuff it with the whole, raw foie gras and bread. Tie it with string. Brush the chicken with olive oil and salt. Sear it in a hot pan until golden.

Put it into an ovenproof dish and cook in a hot oven, at 220°C, for 20 minutes. Brush the chicken every 5 minutes with the juices. Remove from oven let it rest for 25 minutes.

Cut off the legs from the carcass and remove the stuffing from chicken, separating the foie gras and bread. Place the foie gras in a different pan.

In a preheated pan with olive oil, add the chicken legs, garlic clove, thyme and bread. Season with pepper and cook for 10 minutes. Remove from the heat and transfer to an ovenproof dish, reserving the juices in the pan. Sear the reserved foie gras. (Do not add any oil for this stage.)

Reheat the reserved pan with the juices, add the chicken stock and a splash of olive oil, and let simmer until thickens. This will be the sauce.

Transfer the chicken to the ovenproof dish with the legs and the bread, cook in the oven for a further 5 minutes.

Remove the chicken from oven and cut the breasts in half and do the same for the legs. Assemble the dish with the foie gras and bread in the middle of the dish along with the cut pieces of chicken. Pour all of the sauce on top and serve.

Kale Salad

Joshua McFadden
Franny's
United States 2007

page 204

1 bunch lacinato kale (cavolo nero), thick ribs cut out
½ garlic clove, finely chopped
¼ cup finely grated Pecorino Romano, plus more to finish
extra virgin olive oil
juice of 1 lemon
¼ teaspoon dried chile flakes
kosher (coarse) salt and freshly ground black pepper
¼ cup dried breadcrumbs

Stack several kale leaves on top of one another and roll them up into a tight cylinder. With a sharp knife, slice crosswise into very thin ribbons. Put the kale into a salad spinner, rinse in cool water, and spin until completely dry. Pile the kale into a bowl.

Put the chopped garlic on a cutting (chopping) board and mince it even more until you have a paste. Transfer the garlic to a small bowl, add ¼ cup pecorino, a healthy glug of olive oil, the lemon juice, chile flakes, ¼ teaspoon salt, and plenty of twists of black pepper, and whisk to combine.

Pour the dressing over the kale and toss well to thoroughly combine. Taste and adjust with more lemon, salt, chile flakes, or black pepper. Let the salad sit for about 5 minutes so that the kale softens. Top with the breadcrumbs, more cheese, and drizzle with more oil.

Cauliflower in a Cast-Iron Pot

Jeremy Fox
Ubuntu
United States 2007

page 205

½ cup (120 ml) melted vadouvan butter (see below), plus more for basting
3 lb (1.4 kg) cauliflower florets, 2 inches (5 cm) thick (2 to 3 heads, trimmed)
1 teaspoon kosher (coarse) salt, plus more as needed
ciabatta or baguette, for toasting
2 lemons
¼ cup (60 ml) whole (full-fat) milk
¼ cup (60 ml) heavy (double) cream
1 orange, segmented, and each segment cut into 3 pieces
flowering cilantro (coriander), to garnish

For the vadouvan butter
(makes 2 cups/13 oz)
1 lb (454 g) unsalted butter
10 oz (285 g) shallots, thinly sliced
4 garlic cloves, germ removed, thinly sliced
2 teaspoons madras curry powder
2 teaspoons ground turmeric
1 teaspoon fennel seeds
1 teaspoon cumin seeds
1 teaspoon kosher (coarse) salt
1 teaspoon black cardamom seeds
1 teaspoon brown mustard seeds
1 teaspoon black peppercorns
¼ teaspoon chili flakes
¼ teaspoon ground mace
⅛ teaspoon whole cloves

1 (2-inch/5-cm) thumb of fresh ginger, peeled and thinly sliced
peel of 1 orange, pith removed

Make the vadouvan butter in advance. Place all of the butter in the bottom of a pot at least twice the size of the contents you're putting into it. Sprinkle the shallots, garlic, curry powder, turmeric, fennel seeds, cumin seeds, salt, cardamom seeds, mustard seeds, peppercorns, chili flakes, mace, cloves, ginger, and orange peel on top of the butter (this way the butter will melt before the spices start toasting). Set the pot over medium heat and cook the butter slowly for about 3 hours. You don't want any of these ingredients to heat or brown too quickly, as you want slow-developing, layered, nutty flavor. Do not burn your butter—or you'll be very sad—and be sure to keep an eye on it. Stir it occasionally so the shallots, garlic, and milk solids will not stick, allowing it to simmer without ever reaching a rolling boil.

You will know that the butter is done when the shallots and garlic look almost candied—not crunchy, but translucent, glossy, golden, and jammy. The butter should be colored with turmeric and curry but with the nutty flavor of browned butter.

Remove from the heat and allow it to cool for a few minutes. Blend well with a hand-held blender until smooth and fully incorporated before moving it into airtight containers to store. Allow the butter to fully cool before you put the lids on, as trapped heat will turn the butter rancid. Refrigerate for up to 4 weeks or freeze for up to 6 months.

When ready to make the cauliflower, preheat the oven to 400°F (200°C/ Gas 6).

Stir the vadouvan butter as you would a vinaigrette (so that when you scoop it up, you are getting both the liquid and any spices that might have settled to the bottom), then toss 2 lb (900 g) of the cauliflower florets with 3 tablespoons of the vadouvan butter and the 1 teaspoon salt.

Place the tossed cauliflower in a single layer on a baking sheet and roast in the oven until the florets are slightly charred and tender, 12–15 minutes. Remove from the oven and reduce the oven temperature to 300°F (150°C/Gas 2).

Thinly slice the bread. Stir the melted vadouvan butter and brush the bread with some of it. Sprinkle with some salt and arrange the slices on a baking →

Cauliflower in a Cast-Iron Pot

Chrysanthemum Tofu Soup with Fish Balls and Matsutake Mushrooms

Joseph Tse
The 8
China 2007

page 206

sheet. Bake until crisp, 8–10 minutes. Set aside until serving time. Return the oven temperature to 400°F (200°C/ Gas 6).

Chop the cooled cauliflower into bite-size pieces and transfer to a bowl. Finely grate the lemon zest and set it aside for later. Squeeze the juice of the lemons and season the roasted cauliflower with the lemon juice and salt to taste.

Coarsely chop the remaining raw cauliflower and place it in a pot. Add the reserved lemon zest, milk, cream, and a pinch of salt. Bring to a bare simmer over medium-low heat, cover, and reduce the heat to low. Cook until the cauliflower is soft when pierced with a knife, about 30 minutes. Transfer to a blender with the cooking liquid and purée until smooth.

Spread a thin layer of the cauliflower purée in the bottom of each of four 1-cup (240-ml) cast-iron pots. Divide the roasted cauliflower pieces evenly among them and cover with the remaining cauliflower purée. Bake until just bubbling, 5–8 minutes.

Remove from the oven and spoon a tablespoon of hot, stirred vadouvan butter over the surface of each pot.

Garnish with orange segments and flowering cilantro (coriander) and serve with toasted bread.

Fresh tofu is finely sliced into 108 strands with absolute precision and then placed in a bowl of water until it miraculously blossoms into a beautiful chrysanthemum. Once the chrysanthemum tofu "blooms", it is tenderly placed in a double-boiled chicken soup that has been boiling for a few hours and is packed full of ingredients such as Jinhua ham, chicken and lean pork meat. Although remarkably rich in flavor, the soup is crystal clear, offering a blank canvas for the chrysanthemum tofu to take center stage.

Fresh fish balls, which also share a soft texture similar to that of tofu, are added to the soup. Next, the finest and freshest of matsutake mushrooms from Japan are gently placed in the soup for added aroma and a burst of flavor. For the finale, a bright red goji berry and a sprig of green parsley are sprinkled on top for a dash of color.

Salad 21... 31... 41... 51...

Enrico Crippa
Piazza Duomo
Italy 2007

page 207

---

160 g of mixed salad (greens), composed of:
leaves of Gentilina
leaves of Parella
valerian
watercress
poppy
dandelion
primrose leaves
spinach
Trevisano radicchio
Field salad (trusot)
Red beetroot (beet) leaves
Beetroot (beet) leaves
tarragon
burnet
sorrel
santoreggia savory
majoram
red mizuma
green mizuma
Chinese mustard
chervil
Mordigallina
celery
lovage
green shiso
red shiso
dill
raw fennel
nasturtium

For the amaranth chips
200 g amaranth seeds
13 g instant dashi
1.2 litres water
oil for frying

For herb flavoured oil
500 g herbs (parsley, tarragon)
1 litre olive oil (Occhipinti)

For the dressing
herb flavoured oil
Barolo vinegar
white and black sesame seeds
nori algae, finely chopped
katsuobushi
candied ginger and its juice

For the flowers
marigolds:
  red
  white
  purple
  orange
  yellow
violet flowers
primrose flowers
borage flowers
bluebottle
chive flowers
garlic flowers

For the amaranth chips
Cook the amaranth seeds as a risotto with water and instant dashi for about 40 minutes without salt.

Once cooked, spread it out between two sheets of baking (parchment) paper and let it dry.

When it is well dried, break it into irregular pieces and fry in hot oil.

For the herb flavoured oil
Boil the aromathic herbs in the oil for less than a minute, then drain, wring them out and spin.

Filter the oil through a colander lined with paper.

For the salad and the garnishment
Clean and wash well all the herbs and salads (greens). Season with all the ingredients for the dressing and put on a serving plate. Garnish with flowers.

Rabbit and Crayfish Stargazy Pie

Mark Hix
Scott's
United Kingdom 2007

page 208

2 tablespoons flour, plus extra for dusting

1 tablespoon vegetable oil, plus extra for frying

back and front legs of 4 wild rabbits, meat removed and cut into rough 2 cm chunks

1 small onion, peeled and finely chopped

a couple good knobs (pats) of butter

100 ml (hard) cider

1 litre hot chicken stock (broth)

40 live crayfish, cooked for 2 minutes in salted boiling water and refreshed

3-4 tablespoons double (heavy) cream

1 tablespoon chopped parsley

salt and black pepper

For the pastry

225 g self raising flour, plus extra for dusting (or 225 g all-purpose flour plus 1¾ teaspoons baking powder)

1 teaspoon salt

85 g shredded beef suet

60 g butter, chilled and coarsely grated

1 medium egg, beaten to glaze

Heat a heavy-based frying pan (skillet) with the vegetable oil. Season and flour the pieces of rabbit and fry on a high heat for a couple minutes until lightly coloured all over.

Meanwhile, gently cook the onion in the butter in a medium saucepan for 2–3 minutes, then stir in the flour and gradually add the cider and hot chicken stock, stirring constantly to prevent lumps forming. Add the rabbit and simmer for about an hour or until the rabbit is tender.

Meanwhile, peel the crayfish, reserving 4 whole ones for garnish, and set the meat to one side.

Break up the shells and fry in a little oil in a heavy-based pan. Add about 250 ml water and about 200 ml of the sauce from the rabbit and simmer gently for 30 minutes. Blend about a third of the sauce, shells and all, in a liquidizer until smooth and add back to the pan. Stir well, then strain all of the sauce through a fine meshed sieve into the rabbit mixture. The rabbit sauce should be a thick coating consistency – if not, drain the rabbit pieces off and simmer the sauce until thickened. Add the mix back with the rabbit, add the cream and parsley, season again if necessary and leave to cool. Stir in the crayfish meat and transfer to a pie dish and place a pie bird (funnel) in the centre.

Meanwhile make the pastry: mix the flour and salt with the suet and grated butter. Mix in 150–175ml water with the egg to form a smooth dough and knead it for a minute.

Roll the pastry on a floured table to about 1 cm thick and cut out to about 2 cm larger all the way round than the pie dish. Brush the edges of the pastry with a little of the beaten egg and lay the pastry on top, pressing the egg-washed sides against the rim of the dish. Cut 4 holes around the pastry and insert the tails of the 4 reserved crayfish so they are facing the centre, and brush with beaten egg. You can put a trim around the edge of the dish with a strip of leftover pastry. Leave to rest in a cool place for 30 minutes.

Preheat the oven to 200°C/gas mark 6. Bake for 45 minutes, or until the pastry is golden. Serve with greens or mashed root vegetables such as celeriac (celery root) or parsnip and/or small boiled parsley potatoes.

Duck Foie Gras Charcoal Grilled with Sea Urchin Caviar and a Spicy Touch

Andoni Luis Aduriz
Mugaritz
Spain 2007

page 209

For the foie gras
2 x 600-g foie gras duck livers
2 litres full fat (whole) milk
2 litres still mineral water
20 g salt

For the sea urchin roe
1.5 kg sea urchins
1 litre water
30 g salt

For the spicy touch
200 ml extra-virgin olive oil
25 g dried chillies

For presentation and finishing
1 litre sunflower oil
1 generous bunch of vine leaves
Añana salt crystals

The foie gras
Cut the large lobes of foie into 2 or 3 sections, depending on their size. If they are small, trim only 1 cm from the ends to facilitate blood draining. Put the milk, mineral water and salt into a bain-marie at a controlled temperature of 30°C (85°F). Once it reaches this temperature, add the foie pieces and keep them immersed in the mixture for 2–3 hours, depending on how much blood has drained out. This can be checked easily by pressing gently on the venous side of the piece. Once the operation is complete, remove the pieces from the dairy brine. Dry the foie gras and deep-freeze it quickly.

The sea urchin roe
Gradually cut open the sea urchins with scissors, starting from the mouth, until you make a circle that allows you to remove the roe. Prepare a brine with the water and salt. Collect the roe with a teaspoon and immerse them in the brine to wash them, then place them on greaseproof (wax) paper and refrigerate.

The spicy touch
Put the oil and dried chillies in a container and macerate at room temperature for 48 hours.

Presentation and finishing
Pour the sunflower oil into a saucepan and place over medium heat until it reaches 180–190°C (350–375°F). Brown each of the foie gras lobes until it is a lovely golden colour. Place the browned pieces on a tilted baking sheet with the cut side sloping downwards so that the fat released by the foie gras during roasting does not affect the cooking.

Now, roast the pieces at 130°C (265°F) until the core of the foie gras reaches a temperature of 56–58°C (133–136°F). Remove them from the oven and leave them to stand for 4–5 minutes in a hot cupboard at 45°C (115°F). The interior will eventually reach 60°C (140°F), a suitable temperature for the foie gras to acquire the desired texture.

Lightly perfume the baked pieces of foie gras over grilled vine shoot embers. Then cut the pieces of foie gras on a hot cutting (chopping) board with a single back and forth movement of the knife blade, which should be very long and very sharp.

Place the foie gras escalope (scallop) on the plate. Scatter a few Añana salt flakes over the dish and carefully but randomly place the sea urchin roe around the dish. Finally, add three drops of the spicy oil.

Short Rib Taco

Roy Choi
Kogi BBQ
United States 2008

page 210

Cereal Milk Panna Cotta with Caramelized Cornflakes

Christina Tosi
Momofuku Ko
United States 2008

page 211

A very popular dish, the secret recipe for this complete taco dish is not to be revealed. We do know that there are 14 ingredients in the vinaigrette and 20 in the marinade. The short ribs are marinated, chopped up and crisped, and served on corn tortillas. Plus, there is cabbage–chili salsa, shredded lettuce, cilantro (coriander) relish, and a sauce on top. Now you just need a truck to serve it out of (two tacos per person) and you are ready to go.

For the panna cotta
6 cups Kellogg's Corn Flakes
3 cups whole (full-fat) milk
2 cups heavy (double) cream
¾ teaspoon kosher (coarse) salt
¼ cup packed light brown sugar
1 tablespoon powdered gelatin
  (about 1½ packages)

For the topping
¾ cup Kellogg's Corn Flakes
3 tablespoons non-fat instant milk
  powder
1 tablespoon granulated sugar
½ teaspoon kosher salt
3½ tablespoons unsalted butter,
  melted

For the panna cotta
Heat the oven to 300°F. Spread the cereal on a baking sheet (tray) and bake until toasty, about 12 minutes. While still warm, transfer to large bowl or container and add the milk and cream. Stir to combine and let steep (infuse) 45 minutes. (Dessert will get too starchy if it steeps longer.)

Strain into a microwave-safe bowl or a saucepan, pressing to extract the liquid. (Discard the soggy cereal or eat it.) Add the salt and brown sugar, and heat just until the milk is hot enough to dissolve the sugar, watching carefully. Stir gently to dissolve the sugar. Ladle ¼ cup milk

mixture into a small bowl and mix in the gelatin. Set aside 5 minutes, then whisk the soaked gelatin back into remaining milk mixture.

Divide the mixture among 8 ramekins or silicone molds. Refrigerate until set, about 2 hours. If using ramekins, cover and reserve until ready to serve. If using molds, freeze 1 hour and pop out onto wax (greaseproof) paper (not parchment), then refrigerate until ready to serve.

For the topping
Meanwhile, make topping, if you like: heat the oven to 275°F. Put the cereal into a large bowl and crush lightly with your hands. In a small bowl, stir together the milk powder, sugar and salt. Sprinkle the mixture over the crushed flakes and add the melted butter. Toss to coat the cereal evenly. Spread on a baking sheet lined with parchment (baking) paper (or a nonstick baking mat) and bake 20 minutes, or until deep golden brown. Remove from the pan and set aside to cool. Serve immediately or store in an airtight container up to 1 week.

When ready, serve cold panna cottas in ramekins or turn out onto plates. Sprinkle generously with the corn flake topping.

Into the Vegetable Garden

David Kinch
Manresa
United States 2008

page 212

The Root Set

Carrot purée

12 oz peeled carrot, grated
kosher (coarse) salt
4 tablespoons plus 2 teaspoons
　water
3½ tablespoons extra virgin olive oil

Place the carrot, ½ teaspoon salt, and 4 teaspoons of the water in a vacuum seal bag and seal at full pressure. Cook in a large pot of boiling water for 1 hour. Remove from the bag and blend at full speed with the olive oil, the remaining 3 tablespoons plus 1 teaspoon water, and salt to taste for at least 3 minutes, until smooth. Strain, season to taste with salt, and cool.

Beet purée

15 oz beets (beetroot), well rinsed
1 cup plus 1 tablespoon water
4 teaspoons kosher (coarse) salt

Place the beets (beetroot) in a pressure cooker with ½ cup plus 2 tablespoons of the water and 1 tablespoon of the salt and cook for 28 minutes on the high-pressure setting. Once finished, peel the beets and blend with the remaining 7 tablespoons water and 1 teaspoon salt at full speed for at least 3 minutes, until smooth. Strain, adjust the seasoning to taste, and cool.

The Cooked Set

These are the vegetables that we trim to bite-size pieces of interesting shapes, then wilt or warm through in a bit of olive oil at the last moment. We want this set to be warm on the plate for temperature contrast, with the hearty greens (leaves) wilted and the previously braised, blanched, or cooked vegetables warmed through. Among the possibilities are the following:

beans of all sorts, such as Purple
　Royale romano, green flat
　(runner), baby French, cut into
　bite-size diamonds or bias cut
squashes of all sorts, such as
　crookneck Sunny Superset,
　pattypan Flying Saucer, Peter
　Pan, Starship, butternut,
　Trompetta di Albenga, Zephyr,
　Black Forest kabocha, thinly
　sliced or cut into wedges or large
　dice, quickly sautéed in oil with
　fresh basil
zucchini (courgette), such as Lunga
　Fiorentina, Raven, Romanesco,
　thinly sliced, heated raw
kales, such as Red Russian,
　Toscano, wilted raw
leeks, small and tender, blanched in
　salted water until tender
potatoes, such as Purple Peruvian,
　Ozette, Ratta, Russian Banana,
　simmered and sliced

carrots, such as Nelson, Cosmic,
　Purple Haze, Thumbelina, White
　Satin, blanched
rainbow chard, both leaves and
　stems, steamed
broccoli, cauliflower, romanesco,
　separated into florets and
　blanched in salted water until
　tender

Vegetables not to be eaten raw can be blanched in salted boiling water and refreshed in cold water.

The Raw Set

These are the more delicate shoots and leaves that we dress like a salad with a mature, buttery olive oil or herb oil and a pinch of sea salt. They might include the following:

young and tender chard leaves
　(the heart)
all carrots, thinly sliced lengthwise
younger squashes and zucchini
　(courgettes), thinly sliced
　lengthwise
apple, thinly sliced
arugula (rocket)
sylvetta arugula (wild arugula/
　rocket)
beet (beetroot) tops
chile, jalapeño, seeded and thinly
　sliced
curly cress →

Into the Vegetable Garden

wood sorrel (oxalis)
cucumber, both lemon and green,
  unpeeled but seeded and sliced
spinach, Arrowhead and Bordeaux
 young shoots
beet shoots
pea shoots
mustard, mizuna, Purple Frizzle
nasturtium leaves
radishes, thinly sliced

Remember that vegetables that are usually eaten raw can also be thinly shaved or cut into thin julienne strips to make them enjoyable as raw textural and flavor contrasts. The raw shoots and leaves can have the stems trimmed and the larger leaves torn into attractive bite-size pieces.

The Flowers and Seed Set
This is the last set to dress the garden in all its glorious colors, just like on a plant. Some examples are:

chamomile flowers
anise hyssop flowers
basil flowers, such as Thai, lemon,
  Genovese, purple opal
flowering coriander and its shoots
bronze fennel flowers
marjoram flowers, golden
parsley flowers, Italian flat-leaf
various sorrel and dock flowers
calendula flowers

chive flowers
cress flowers
mustard flowers
garlic chive flowers
nasturtium flowers
painted lady bean flowers
radish flowers
squash blossoms
violas or edible pansies

To serve
butter or extra virgin olive oil
kosher (coarse) salt
extra virgin olive oil
nasturtium vinegar, white wine
  vinegar, or champagne vinegar

To build the garden, we have small containers of the various sets ready to go. We use homemade nasturtium vinegar, made from the flowers and stems and marinated in a white balsamic vinegar with ½ clove garlic, using a large amount of the petals to achieve a beautiful color, but a white wine or champagne vinegar will work just fine.

Take a warmed plate and begin by dabbing the various purées of The Root Set on the plate—not too much, but enough for them to make their contribution. Heat up a small pan and wilt and warm through the entire contents of your Cooked Set with a

small pat (knob) of butter or bit of oil. Season with salt, then drain on a plate. Arrange the various braised items on top and around the purées. These will serve as wonderful fulcrums to hold up the more delicate leaves so the garden can be built up rather than lie flat.

Put The Raw Set in a bowl and season with a pinch of salt and a thin, small stream of olive oil. Toss the contents to coat the leaves evenly. Then, working quickly, place the leaves on top of The Cooked Set, trying to make it appear as a natural tangle in the garden.

Next, place your choices for The Flowers and Seed Set on top and around the garden. Save the most delicate element for the top, so it won't weigh down the garden. Mist the entire salad with the nasturtium or wine vinegar and serve immediately.

Langoustines and Sea Flavors

René Redzepi
Noma
Denmark 2008

page 213

This well-known dish includes a super-fresh langoustine; an oyster emulsion made from oyster juice, parsely, oil and lemon; a dried dulse powder; and a rye bread crumble. To serve, you'll need a nice local stone, onto which you should place a few dots of the emulsion, a few rye bread crumbs and a sautééd langoustine. Finish with the dried dulse seaweed.

Strawberry Watermelon Cake

Christopher Thé
Black Star Pastry
Australia 2008

page 214

250 g seedless watermelon, thinly sliced
60 ml (¼ cup) rosewater
4 tablespoons caster (superfine) sugar
40 g almond meal (ground almonds)
500 g strawberries (about 2 punnets), halved
10 seedless red grapes, halved
1 tablespoon slivered pistachios
1 tablespoon dried rose petals

Almond dacquoise
150 g almonds, coarsely chopped
150 g pure icing (confectioners') sugar, sifted
5 egg whites
135 g caster (superfine) sugar

Rose-scented cream
300 ml thickened cream
30 g caster (superfine) sugar
2 tablespoons rosewater

For almond dacquoise, preheat the oven to 200°C. Process the almonds in a food processor until finely ground, then combine in a bowl with the icing (confectioners') sugar. Whisk the egg whites in an electric mixer until soft peaks form (3–4 minutes), then gradually add caster (superfine) sugar and whisk until stiff peaks form (1–2 minutes). Gently fold through almond mixture, spread on a 30 × 40-cm oven

tray lined with baking (parchment) paper and bake until golden (10–15 minutes). Set aside to cool on tray, then cut in half lengthways.

Arrange the watermelon slices in a single layer on a wire rack. Sprinkle with 20 ml rosewater, then scatter with 2 tablespoons sugar. Stand to macerate (30 minutes), then pat dry with absorbent paper towels.

For the rose-scented cream, whisk the cream and sugar until soft peaks form, then gradually add the rosewater and whisk until stiff peaks begin to form.

Spread one-third of the rose cream evenly over one half of the dacquoise, scatter with half the almond meal (ground almonds), then top with the watermelon, trimming to fill any gaps. Scatter over the remaining almond meal, and spread over half the cream. Top with the remaining dacquoise, spread over the remaining cream and refrigerate until firm (1–2 hours).

Add the strawberries, remaining rosewater and remaining sugar to a bowl, toss to combine and set aside to macerate (15 minutes). Carefully arrange on top of the cake. Trim the edges of the cake, scatter over the grapes, pistachios and petals, and serve.

A Simple Dish of Potato Cooked in the Earth In Which It Was Grown

Ben Shewry
Attica
Australia 2008

page 215

Coconut husk ash

1 young coconut, outer green husk
  removed

Crack the top of the coconut with three sharp blows from a meat cleaver to create a triangular incision in its top. Drain the coconut water (reserve for another use), then split the coconut in half with a cleaver. Remove the flesh (and reserve for another use too). Leave the coconut husk in a warm place to dry for 4 days.

Outdoors preheat a barbeque (grill) to high. Place the coconut husk in a roasting tray and place on the grill (rack), then set the husk alight with a blowtorch. Be careful as it will burn intensely. Let the flames die down by themselves, then turn off the barbeque and leave the husk to cool. Grind the ash/husk into a fine powder in a spice mill, pestle and mortar or coffee grinder. Store refrigerated in an airtight container until needed.

Potatoes

4 Virginia Rose potatoes, peeled
20 ml grapeseed oil
Murray River salt flakes, to taste
3 kg of soil that the potatoes were
  grown in
2 dish towels, soaked in water
2 small pieces of muslin
  (cheesecloth) soaked in water

Preheat an oven to 180°C. In a bowl, combine the potatoes with the oil and season with salt. In a deep roasting tray, about 35 × 25 cm, place the half of the soil in an even layer to cover the base of the tray. Place a damp dish towel over the soil then a piece of muslin (cheesecloth) on top. Place the potatoes on the muslin, then cover with the other piece of muslin and the other wet dish towel, making sure they are sealed from the soil. Place the remaining soil on top and tightly cover with foil. Bake for 3 hours, then reduce the temperature to 100°C and bake for a further 4 hours (or up to 5). The texture of the potatoes should be soft and creamy.

Smoked curd

200 g goat's milk curd cheese
200 g fromage blanc
fine woodchips, for smoking
table salt, to taste

Place the curd and the fromage blanc in separate stainless steel bowls. Light a cold smoker using the woodchips. Place the bowls inside and smoke both at 2 degrees for 20 minutes or until lightly smoked. Combine the smoked curd and fromage in a bowl. Season with a small amount of salt to taste and whisk until smooth. It may be necessary to thin out the curd mix with a little milk if they are too stiff. Set aside in the refrigerator.

Deep-fried saltbush leaves

non-GM canola (rapeseed) oil, for
  deep frying
50 g grey saltbush leaves

Fill a small deep saucepan no more than one third full of oil and heat to 160°C. Deep-fry the saltbush leaves for 35 seconds or until crisp. Remove with a slotted spoon and drain on paper towels. Once at room temperature, store in an airtight container.

To finish

10 g coconut husk ash
5 g freshly ground ethically
  produced coffee
20 g chicken floss
8 sprigs puha (wild watercress),
  washed and picked

Place a small spoonful of curd in the centre of each plate. Sprinkle the curd with the ash, coffee and chicken floss. Place a few puha leaves in the middle of the curd. Place the potato on top of the puha and garnish with the deep-fried saltbush leaves.

Steamed Flowery Crab with Shaoxing Rice Wine and Chicken Fat

Kwok Keung Tung
The Chairman
China 2009

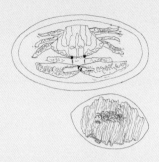

page 216

---

1 live flowery crab or mud crab
   (800 g–1 kg), cooked
1 small piece of ginger, sliced
1 stalk scallion (spring onion), cut
   to 2-inch lengths
4 pieces of chicken fat
200 g flat rice noodles

For the sauce
400 g fresh clams
400 ml 10 –15 years aged
   Shaoxing (huadiao) wine
1½ egg yolks

Clean and separate the crab into pieces, rinse well, carefully removing the yellow gills. Twist off its legs and claws. Crack the legs and claws with the back of a cleaver. Drain well and set aside.

Rinse the clams, then steam for 10 minutes on a tray. Extract the clam juice.

Mix the clam juice with the Shaoxing wine.

Arrange the crab pieces on a plate in its original shape. Pour the clam juice and wine mix on top. Sprinkle the ginger, scallion (spring onion) and chicken fat on top.

Start boiling water in a big wok. Once the water comes to a boil, place the plate of crab into the wok and steam for 6 minutes.

Take the plate out, get rid of the ginger, chicken fat and scallion (spring onion).

Pour the wine and clam sauce into a separate bowl. Whisk in the egg yolks.

Pour the sauce mix back onto the crab and steam for another 30 seconds. The crab juice will mix with the sauce and form a pool of golden liquid.

Steam the flat rice noodles in a separate plate for 5 minutes.

To serve, add the noodles to the crab plate and let them soak in the sauce.

Shellfish Rockpool

Tom Kitchin
The Kitchin
Scotland 2009

page 217

olive oil
8 mussels
2 razor clams
8 surf clams
1 shallot 1 tablespoon chopped
   parsley
50 ml white wine
50 g squid
8 squat lobster tails and heads
40 g brown shrimp
50 g fresh cooked crab
4 oysters
4 octopus tentacles, cooked
20 g keta salmon eggs
20 g Dulse seaweed
60 g samphire (sea beans)
1 scallop

For the shellfish consommé
6 carrots, thinly sliced
½ onion, diced
1 fennel, diced
½ leek, diced
1 stick celery, diced
½ bulb of garlic
1 kg langoustine bodies
1 kg lobster heads
500 g crab shells
Peel and juice of 1 orange
5 cardamom pods
20 g fennel seeds
100 g ginger
3 star anise
100 ml brandy
2 tablespoons tomato purée (paste)
1 tablespoon vegetable oil

First make the consommé. Preheat oven to 180°C. Roast the langoustine, lobster and crab shells in a roasting pan for 15 minutes

In the meantime, heat a large heavy bottom pan and add the vegetable oil. Sweat the carrots slowly until the oil becomes orange in colour and add the orange juice, cardamom pods, fennel seeds, ginger and star anise.

Add the onion, fennel, leek, celery and garlic along with the shells, then add the tomato purée and brandy before reducing until dry.

Once dry, cover with water and bring to the boil. Reduce and leave to simmer for 1 hour, skimming when required. Remove from the heat and leave to cool.

Pass the consommé through a wet muslin to remove any pieces of shell.

Heat a heavy bottom pan and add some olive oil. Add the shellfish – the mussels, razor clams, and surf clams. Add the shallot and parsley and white wine and place a lid on the pan. The razor clams should be the first to open, so as they do, take them out of the pan.

Then drop in the squid, the squat lobster tails and brown shrimp and cook in the pan. Once the mussels and surf clams have opened, take them out of the pan, and away from heat remove from the shells.

Prepare the razor clams by removing the tender flesh from the intestine.

Blanch the seaweed and samphire (sea beans) and set aside.

Start to build the dish by dividing the shellfish between the four bowls. Then add the cooked crab to the bowls evenly. Add a quarter slice of raw scallop, oysters, octopus and the salmon caviar. Garnish with all your blanched seaweed and samphire (sea beans).

To serve, pour the consommé into a jug (pitcher). Pour the consommé over each dish at the table.

100-Layer Lasagne
Mark Ladner
Del Posto
United States 2009

page 218

Fresh egg pasta dough

1½ cups (200 g) "00" flour, plus
 more for dusting
¾ cup (100 g) durum flour, plus
 more for dusting
15 large egg yolks (270 g)

Del Posto tomato sauce

4 28-oz (794-g) cans whole peeled
 San Marzano tomatoes with
 their juices
3 tablespoons (45 ml)
 extra virgin olive oil
10 garlic cloves (40 g), gently
 smashed and peeled
1 tablespoon plus 1 teaspoon
 (total 20 g) sugar
2½ teaspoons (10 g) kosher
 (coarse) salt
4 basil leaves

For the ragù Bolognese

2 oz (56 g) pancetta cut into
 ½-inch (1.25-cm) cubes
1 garlic clove (4 g), finely chopped
1½ tablespoons (22 ml) extra virgin
 olive oil
1½ medium carrots (100 g), roughly
 chopped
1½ celery ribs (100 g), roughly
 chopped
1 small yellow onion (200 g), finely
 chopped
⅔ lb (283 g) ground (minced) veal
½ lb (226 g) ground (minced) pork

1 tablespoon (12 g) kosher
 (coarse) salt
¼ cup (60 ml) dry white wine
1½ tablespoons (32 g) double
 concentrated tomato paste
 (purée)
¼ cup (60 ml) whole (full-fat) milk

For the bechamel

6 tablespoons (85 g) unsalted
 butter
1 cup plus 2 tablespoons (total 85
 g) unbleached all-purpose (plain)
 flour
3 cups (710 ml) whole (full-fat)
 milk
1 teaspoon (4 g) kosher (coarse)
 salt

To build and serve

kosher (coarse) salt
1½ quantities Fresh Egg Pasta
 Dough (see recipe)
1 quantity Del Posto Tomato Sauce
 (see recipe)
2⅓ cups (150 g) freshly grated
 Parmigiano-Reggiano cheese
 (at least 24-month aged)
3 tablespoons (45 ml) extra virgin
 olive oil
1½ teaspoons (7 g) unsalted butter

For the fresh egg pasta dough

In a large bowl, use your hands to mix together the "00" and durum flours, then form a well in the center. Add the egg yolks to the well. Using a fork, gently break up the yolks and slowly incorporate the flour mixture from the inside rim of the well. Continue until the liquid is absorbed (about half of the flour will be incorporated). With both hands, begin kneading the dough until it forms a mostly cohesive mass. Transfer the dough to a clean work surface and continue kneading and occasionally pulling apart the dough to expose moisture, then pressing it back together, until the dough is smooth and firm, 7–10 minute. (You want a firm dough. If you are having trouble kneading, wrap the dough tightly in plastic wrap (clingfilm) and let it rest 10–15 minutes, then knead again. An additional yolk can be added if the dough is too dry.)

Wrap the dough tightly in plastic wrap (clingfilm) and let rest at room temperature for at least 15 minutes or up to 1 hour before using.

To roll out the dough

Unwrap and cut the pasta dough into 4 pieces. Flatten one piece so that it will fit through the rollers of a pasta machine (rewrap the remaining pieces). Set the rollers of the pasta machine to →

100-Layer Lasagne

the widest setting, then feed the pasta through the rollers three to four times, folding and turning the pasta until it is smooth and the width of the machine. Roll the pasta through the machine, decreasing the setting one notch at a time (do not fold or turn the pasta) to the thickness desired per recipe. Cut the sheet in half crosswise, then lightly dust with "oo" flour.

Layer the sheets between dry, clean, "oo" flour–dusted kitchen towels to keep them from drying out. Repeat with the remaining dough pieces. After cutting the pasta into the desired shape, place on a durum-dusted rimmed baking sheet between sheets of durum-dusted parchment (baking) paper. (If you are not using the pasta within 1 hour, wrap the baking sheet tightly in plastic wrap (clingfilm) and refrigerate for up to 1 day or freeze for up to 1 week. Do not thaw frozen pasta before cooking.)

For the Del Posto tomato sauce
In batches use a food processor, blender, or food mill to purée the toma-toes with their juices until smooth.

In a 6- to 8-quart (5.6- to 7.5-liter) Dutch oven or wide heavy saucepan, heat the oil and garlic over a medium heat, stirring occasionally, until the garlic is very lightly golden and fragrant, about 2 minutes. Add the puréed tomatoes, sugar, and salt. Bring to a gentle simmer and cook until reduced by about two-thirds (to 2 quarts or 1.8 liters), about 1½ hours. Stir in the basil, then adjust the seasoning to taste. Remove from the heat and let cool completely. (This sauce can be kept, covered and refrigerated, for up to 3 days, or frozen for up to 1 month.)

For the ragù Bolognese
In the bowl of a food processor, combine the pancetta and chopped garlic. Pulse the mixture until it is combined and resembles a paste, then transfer to a bowl. Use a rubber spatula to scrape any remaining bits of paste from the food processor into the bowl with the paste.

Place the carrots and celery in the food processor bowl and pulse until finely chopped.

In a large skillet or frying pan, heat 1 tablespoon (15 ml) of the oil over medium-low heat. Add the onion and sauté for 5 minutes. Add the carrot and celery mixture, reduce the heat to low and cook, stirring occasionally, until the mixture (the soffritto) is tender and sweet, about 40 minutes (do not brown). Remove from the heat. (The soffritto can be made 1 day ahead and rest overnight in the refrigerator.)

In a 5- to 6-quart (4.7-to 5.6-liter) Dutch oven or heavy pot with a lid, combine the pancetta mixture and the remaining ½ tablespoon (7 ml) oil. Cook over medium heat, breaking the paste into small bits with a rubber spatula, until the fat is rendered and the bits become crispy on the edges, 5–7 minutes. Add the soffritto and cook, stirring to work the two mixtures together, for 2 minutes. Add the veal, pork, and salt. Continue cooking, stirring frequently, until the meat is broken into bits and appears cooked through, 10–15 minutes.

Make a well in the centre of the meat mixture, then add the wine to the well. When the wine comes to a simmer, stir to combine with the meat, then stir in the tomato paste (purée). Reduce the heat to low and gently cook for 1 hour, adding a touch of water if necessary to keep the sauce from drying out. The ragù is done when the meat is tender. Stir in the milk and cook for 10 minutes more. Remove from the heat and let cool to room temperature. (The sauce can be kept, covered and refrigerated for up to 3 days, or frozen up to 1 month.)

For the béchamel

In a large saucepan, melt the butter over medium-low heat. Add the flour and cook. Stirring frequently with a wooden spoon, until the mixture turns a very lightly sandy colour, 5–7 minutes (do not brown). Add about 1 cup (236 ml) of the milk, whisking constantly, until the mixture is very smooth. Repeat, fully incorporating the liquid between additions, until all of the milk has been added. Bring to a gentle simmer and cook, stirring frequently and into the edges of the pan, until the sauce is the consistency of a thick cream, about 7 minutes more. Stir in the salt, then transfer the sauce, while hot, to a pastry (piping) bag fitted with a ¼-inch (6 mm) tip (nozzle) or to a large resealable freezer bag. Set aside to cool to room temperature.

To build the lasagne

Roll out the pasta dough (see recipe below) until you can just see your hand through the pasta sheets, a scant 1 mm thick. Cut the pasta sheets into thirty 6 × 6-inch (15 × 15-cm) squares.

Bring a large wide pot of well-salted water to a boil. Set a bowl of very cold water near the range. Working in batches of four or five sheets, cook the pasta in the boiling water about 1 minute per batch, timing immediately after the pasta is slipped into the water. Using a large sieve or slotted spoon, retrieve the cooked sheets, then immediately plunge them into the bowl of cold water; let the excess water drip back into the bowl, then hang them over the side of a large empty bowl (overlapping is OK).

If the ragù is cold, gently heat it, stirring occasionally, just to loosen and slightly warm through. The tomato sauce and béchamel can be at room temperature or slightly chilled. If the béchamel is in a freezer bag, cut ¾ inch (6.3 mm) off a corner so that you can use it as a piping bag.

Place a generous 2½ cups (510 g) of the tomato sauce in a bowl. Cover and chill the remaining tomato sauce (you will use it for serving).

In the centre of a 9 × 13-inch (23 × 33-cm) rimmed baking sheet or baking dish, spread about 1 tablespoon (15 g) of the tomato sauce. Place 1 pasta sheet over the sauce. Spread about 1 tablespoon (15 grams) of the sauce on the pasta sheet, then sprinkle with 1 tablespoon (6.5 g) of the Parmigiano. In a zigzag pattern, pipe the equivalent of about 1 tablespoon (13 g) of the béchamel over the top, then sprinkle with about 2 tablespoons (30 g) of the ragù (with the addition of each ingredient, you are "sprinkling" rather than creating a solid layer of each ingredient).

Place a second pasta sheet over the filling. Using your fingers, gently press the top of the sheet from the inside out toward the edges to eliminate any air bubbles, without going so far as to push out the filling. Repeat the layering process with the remaining sauces, cheese, and pasta sheets, following the same order of ingredients for each layer.

Cover the lasagne with plastic wrap (clingfilm) and refrigerate at least 6 hours or overnight (this will help set the layers, making them easy to slice before baking).

Line a baking sheet with parchment (baking) paper. Using 1 large or 2 small spatulas, transfer the chilled lasagne from the pan to a large cutting (chopping) board. Using a large knife (ideally one with a long thin blade, such as a carving knife), trim about ⅛ inch (3.4 mm) from all four outside edges of the lasagne, then cut the lasagne in half. Gently lift and set one half to the side.

With the knife, mark the top of the remaining lasagne half lengthwise so →

100-Layer Lasagne

Beef Heart
Virgilio Martínez
Central
Peru c.2010

page 219

that when cut, you will have three long equal pieces. Cut through the layers (again pressing the knife down rather than sawing), allowing your free hand to catch and gently guide the first slice to fall onto the cutting board with the cut side facing up. Cut the piece in half crosswise. Using a spatula, transfer the cut pieces to the prepared baking sheet (if you need to gently press together the layers, its fine to do so). Repeat to form 12 total portions, placing the slices as cut in a single layer on the baking sheet. If you are not serving the lasagne within 1 hour, cover the pan tightly with plastic wrap (clingsfilm) and keep chilled until ready to serve.

To serve the lasagne
Preheat the oven to 350°F (177°C). Line a second baking sheet with parchment paper. In a large non-stick or cast-iron skillet, heat 1 tablespoon (15 ml) of the oil and ½ teaspoon (2.4 g) of the butter over medium-high heat until hot but not smoking. Add two to three lasagne slices (enough to fit in but not crowd the pan) on their sides, or cut side down, reduce the heat to medium and cook (without moving the slices) until the bottom sides are deep golden, 3–4 minutes. Using a spatula, transfer the slices to the prepared baking sheet, seared side up. Repeat with the remaining oil, butter, and slices.

Bake the seared slices until just warmed through, 4–5 minutes. Meanwhile, in a medium saucepan, gently heat the reserved tomato sauce. Spoon the warm tomato sauce onto serving plates. Top with the lasagne, seared side up. Serve immediately.

2 kg Maras salt
300 g aji panca
50 ml chicha de jora
10 g chincho
10 g huamanripa
10 g grasses from the altitude, chopped
1 beef heart

In a bowl, mix together the salt, aji panca, chica de jora, chincho, huamanripa, and grasses to make a thick paste.

Remove half of the fat from the heart and discard. Rub the heart with the paste and refrigerate for 5 hours. Using a clean cloth, wipe the cure off the heart.

Ideally, hang the heart in a cool, dark spot at 10°C (50°F) for about 19 hours in a well-ventilated room—such as a windowed room that's in a particularly windy spot. This process works best if done in the mountains, at this specific altitude, in a dark room with a window facilitating the entrance of the wind. We've learned this from doing this process for over 3 years. You can also fashion a hook in your refrigerator and hang the heart there.

We serve the heart grated like jerky; it has a firmer and drier consistency than prosciutto.

Onion Reduction with Parmesan Buttons and Toasted Saffron

Niko Romito
Reale
Italy 2010

page 220

Scallop Cooked Over Burning Juniper Branches

Magnus Nilsson
Fäviken Magasinet
Sweden 2010

page 221

Onion reduction
2 kg gold onions

Parmesan filling
300 g Parmigiano Reggiano
30 g fresh liquid cream

Home-made pasta
125 g semolina flour
125 g '00' flour
1 egg
3 yolks
salt

To finish
16 saffron pistils, toasted

To make the onion reduction, without peeling the onions, lay them in a tray and cook them in a steam oven for 1 hour at 100°C. Then remove the external leaves and blend the pulp to extract the vegetable juice, then filter with a linen cloth to obtain an almost transparent broth of "onion absolute". Adjust the seasoning with salt and keep warm.

For the filling, put the grated Parmesan into a bowl. Heat the cream and as soon as it starts to boil remove from the heat. Pour slowly into the grated Parmesan and blend with a wooden spoon. Prepare the pasta by combining the flours and the egg, yolks and a pinch of salt. Knead well and form a ball; cover with a cloth and leave to rest for 1 hour in the fridge. With a rolling pin roll two very thin doughs. On the first one, with a piping (pastry) bag distribute some "nuts" of Parmesan filling and cover with the second dough. Seal with a dough cutter to shape the buttons. Boil them in salted water for 15–20 minutes.

To finish, on each plate, add 4 saffron pistils, then place 8–10 buttons of pasta on top as soon as they are drained and carefully pour over a cup of the warm onion reduction.

some dry hay with a high herb content, or a piece of moss that covers the plate, to serve
fresh juniper branches, for the fire
6 perfectly fresh, very large and absolutely sand-free live scallops in their shells
good bread and butter, to serve

Light some birch charcoal with a hot-air blower or an electric coil – never use lamp oil or chemicals. Spray the hay or moss lightly with water.

Put the juniper branches on top of the charcoal and when they start burning, cook the scallops directly over the fire. They are finished when you hear them making a crackling noise at the edges.

Open each scallop up and pour all the contents into a preheated ceramic bowl. Separate out the scallop meat and put it back in the bottom shell. Strain off the beards and intestines quickly and pour the cloudy broth back into the shell with the scallop in it.

Put the top half shell back on, place the whole scallop on the dampened hay or moss with some fresh juniper and hot coal for a few moments, then serve right away with good bread and mature butter. No more than 90 seconds must pass between taking the scallop off the fire and serving it.

Thousand-Year-Old Quail Egg, Potage, Ginger

Corey Lee
Benu
United States 2010

page 222

---

brine of 5% salt, 4% lye, and 1%
   pu-erh tea leaves
quail eggs

For the pickled ginger
2 parts water
1 part champagne vinegar
1 part sugar
peeled fresh young ginger

For the potage
5 g butter
15 g bacon
100 g Savoy cabbage, sliced
30 g onion, chopped
1 g salt
small pinch cayenne pepper
80 g chicken stock (broth)
10 g cream

For the ginger cream
200 g cream
2 g salt
3 g sugar
10 g fresh ginger juice

Make enough brine to generously cover the eggs. Allow to soak for 12 days. Rinse thoroughly under running, room-temperature water until the water runs clear. Dry the eggs, place them in an airtight plastic bag, and store inside an opaque container. Age for 4 weeks at 68–77°F/20–25°C.

To make the pickled ginger, put the water, vinegar, and sugar into a saucepan and bring to a boil. Meanwhile, slice the ginger thinly and place in a bowl. Pour the boiling liquid over the ginger. Allow to cool to room temperature, then vacuum pack. Store in a refrigerator for at least 3 days.

To make the potage, melt the butter in a pan and sweat the bacon, cabbage, and onion. Season with salt and cayenne pepper. Cover with the chicken stock and cream. Bring to a boil, cover with a lid, and simmer until tender, about 45 minutes. Remove the bacon and discard. Purée the mixture left in the pan and pass through a chinois.

To make the ginger cream, combine the cream, salt, and sugar in a chilled mixing bowl. Whisk slowly and evenly until you've reached medium heat. Add the ginger juice and fold in evenly When you're ready to serve, cook the eggs in boiling water for 1 minute. Shock in iced water, then peel. Cut the eggs in half and season with salt and the juice from the pickled ginger. Chop a little bit of the pickled ginger and place a small amount in the center of each bowl. Place a dollop of the whipped ginger cream on top of the ginger and place the quails eggs on top. Serve the potage piping hot.

Radishes in a Pot
René Redzepi
Noma
Denmark 2010

page 223

Tartare of Beef with Watercress and Rye Bread
Christian Puglisi
Manfreds
Denmark 2010

page 224

The recipe for this dish includes raw radishes, a herb cream made of parsley, chives, tarragon, chervil, shallots, sheep milk yogurt, capers and mayonnaise, and a malt soil made of flour, malt flour, hazelnut flour, sugar, and lager. If you want to make this at home, you will need two days, as the malt soil must be made in batches and combined, to achieve the correct texture. To serve, find a flowerpot and pipe the cream into it, insert the radishes and cover with the malt soil.

For the tartare
500 g beef topside
fine sea salt

Ask your butcher to clean the meat. Alternatively, you can do it yourself by trimming off any sinew or silver skin.

Portion the beef into long strips – make sure that the thickness fits your meat grinder. Salt the strips of beef with 1.5 per cent fine sea salt by weight (e.g., 15 g salt for 1,000 g meat). Let the meat cure in the fridge for 1 hour.

Lay out the strips of beef on a flat tray or plate with space in between. Place them in the freezer for approximately 40 minutes, or until the meat is frozen on the outside, but is not completely frozen solid.

When the meat is almost frozen, it's ready to be minced (ground) in the grinder. While grinding the meat, try to preserve nice, long strips.

For the egg crème
4 large poached eggs
80 g day-old sourdough bread
    without the crust
80 g water
90 g Dijon mustard
7 g fine sea salt
15 g lemon juice
450 g rapeseed (canola) oil

Poach the eggs, whole and in the shell, in a water bath in a sous vide machine set at 65°C for 35 minutes, and let cool in cold water. Alternatively, make soft-boiled eggs, by boiling for 6 minutes before peeling.

Combine the day-old sourdough bread, water, poached eggs, and mustard in an airtight container and let the bread soak up the liquid. Keep cool in the fridge for at least a couple of hours.

Put the bread mixture into a blender together with the salt and lemon juice and blend on high speed until smooth. Turn down the speed and gradually add the oil to emulsify. You should end up with a smooth and creamy mayonnaise-like consistency. This egg cream can be made ahead of time. It holds well for a couple days in the fridge. →

Tartare of Beef with Watercress and Rye Bread

Sea Urchin Toast
Joshua Skenes
Saison
United States 2010

page 225

For the toasted rye breadcrumbs
100 g rye bread
15 g clarified butter

To serve
good quality olive oil
lemon juice
fine sea salt
plenty of fresh, green watercress
freshly ground pepper

Remove the crusts from the rye bread and cut the rest into small cubes. Let air dry for at least a half a day. With a blender, process the semi-dried cubes into fine crumbs.

Line a piece of baking (parchment) paper on a baking tray and spread the crumbs evenly on it. Drizzle the melted, clarified butter over the crumbs and toast the rye bread in the oven at 160°C for 15–20 minutes, toss them around midway through baking until they are golden brown.

To serve
Put a dollop of egg crème on each plate and sprinkle with some toasted rye breadcrumbs. Season meat the with nice olive oil, lemon juice, and salt. Mix with plenty of watercress and arrange on top of the egg crème. Finish off with freshly ground black pepper and rye breadcrumbs.

To begin, find yourself a good country levain, or other similar long fermented bread. Cut into slices to be served family style.

In a separate pot combine any bread trim, a dried seaweed, preferably kelp, and cover with water. Season this "bread sauce" with Saison Sauce (you can substitute good quality white soy sauce). Bring to simmer, and simmer until a viscous sauce. Blend with a few spoonfuls of brown butter and reserve at room temperature.

Grill the slices of levain until a deep golden color, but be careful not to burn, as we want the bread to be able to hold up to bread sauce.

Soak the grilled levain in the bread sauce and leave to soak but with the grilled top left exposed.

When ready to serve, warm the bread in the oven and top with the best quality urchin available, preferably live, and a few drops of lemon. Serve immediately.

King Crab and Almost-Burnt Cream

Magnus Nilsson
Fäviken
Sweden 2010

page 226

Sorrel Pesto Rice Bowl

Jessica Koslow
Sqirl
United States 2011

page 227

---

4 legs of king crab, raw (each leg
    a minimum of 1.5 kg)
100 ml cream
50 g butter, softened
Ättika vinegar in a spray bottle

Shell and clean the crab legs. This is incredibly difficult to get right and takes a lot of practice. You need to keep the red outer membrane of the meat entirely intact. If there is even the smallest hole, when cooked, the white meat will push out through that and the whole piece will be ruined.

For this dish you will only be using the thickest part of the leg (the segment which should have been closest to the body of the crab) the other parts will be too thin and should be used for something else. At Fäviken we generally cooked them, picked the meat and made crab sandwiches at our café in Åre, Krus. But you could make many other things too, and the picked crabmeat will freeze very well if you want to keep it for later.

Place the four segments of crab onto kitchen towel and allow them to reach room temperature.

Heat a frying pan until quite hot and pour the cream into it, it will bubble violently at first. After perhaps one

minute the cream will have reduced down and started to set at the bottom of the pan, check regularly with a spatula or spoon so that it doesn't burn – it should only almost burn! At the right moment, scrape all the contents of the pan into a frozen ceramic bowl to halt the cooking process and whisk until smooth and cool, at which point it should be the texture of mayonnaise.

While you are working on the cream, preheat another pan until very hot. Place the segments of crab in it and cook on one side until golden, turn them and keep cooking on the other side until they are medium rare to the touch. Transfer the segments to a preheated cutting (chopping) board, spray with some of the vinegar and brush with some of the soft butter. Immediately cut the end bits off and serve the crab with a small spoon of the cream. The end bits can go into the same pile of cooked crabmeat as did the rest of the legs earlier.

---

3 cups (600 g) medium-grain
    brown rice, preferably Kokuho
    Rose
fine sea salt
½ cup plus 2 teaspoons (130 ml)
    extra virgin olive oil
1 cup (25 g) lightly packed kale
    leaves (stems removed)
2 cups (50 g) lightly packed
    chopped sorrel leaves
3 tablespoons fresh lemon juice
2 tablespoons chopped fresh dill,
    plus more for serving
1 preserved Meyer lemon, flesh
    removed, peel finely chopped
2–4 small watermelon radishes,
    very thinly sliced
¼ cup (60 ml) Fermented Jalapeño
    Hot Sauce (see following page)
¾ cup (85 g) crumbled sheep's-milk
    feta
6 poached eggs
fleur de sel
freshly ground black pepper

Boil the rice in plenty of salted water until it's tender, 30–45 minutes. Drain and let cool.

Meanwhile, make the sorrel pesto: In a blender or food processor, combine ½ cup (120 ml) of the oil, kale, sorrel, and 1 tablespoon of the lemon juice. Blend until smooth, scraping down the sides as needed. Season with salt to taste. →

Sorrel Pesto Rice Bowl

In a large bowl, toss the rice with the dill, preserved lemon peel, 1 tablespoon of the lemon juice, and the pesto. Taste and add a bit more salt, if needed.

In a small bowl, toss the radishes with the remaining 1 tablespoon lemon juice, the remaining 2 teaspoons oil, and a pinch of salt. Set aside to marinate for a few minutes, until the radishes are pliable and tender.

To serve, divide the rice among six bowls. Spoon a line of hot sauce across the rice. Arrange a little clump of feta on one side and a rosette of radish slices on the other side. Set a poached egg in the middle of each bowl and season it with fleur de sel and black pepper. Garnish with a tiny sprig or two of dill.

For the Fermented Jalapeño Hot Sauce
makes about 2 ½ cups (600 ml)

20 jalapeño peppers (1 lb/455 g total)
fine sea salt or Diamond Crystal kosher (coarse) salt, as needed
1 cup (240 ml) distilled white vinegar

Cut the tops off the jalapeños, then slice each pepper in half lengthwise. Remove and discard the seeds. Chop the peppers into big pieces, put them into the bowl of a food processor fitted with a metal blade, and blend until mostly puréed but still a little bit chunky. Weigh the blended jalapeños, then use this equation to figure out exactly how much salt to add:

Grams of blended jalapeños x 0.075 = grams of kosher (coarse) salt

Stir the salt into the blended japaeños, then scrape the mash into a clean jar. (You'll need a jar that is slightly bigger than 1 pint/480 ml).

Now choose a slightly smaller jar that will fit within the jar holding the jalapeño mash, weighing the mash down so it is fully submerged. Alternatively, if you don't have a smaller jar, make a brine using the same ratio of salt to water. So, for 480 ml/2 cups water, you'll need to add 55 g/¼ cup of salt. Pour the brine into a plastic bag, get as much air out of the bag as possible, and then seal it well. Put the brine-filled bag directly on top of the mash in the jar, making sure the bag is covering the mash completely so that no air can get to the mixture. Label and date the jar, then let it sit in a dark, cool spot for 4 weeks to ferment.

Don't be afraid if you see white mold or some Kahm yeast growing on top of the mixture. Just skim it off and make sure the bag is still sealing the fermenting mixture from the air.

After 4 weeks, transfer the fermented pepper mixture to a nonreactive pot and stir in the vinegar. Bring to a boil. Remove from the heat, then carefully purée in a blender on high speed until uniform and saucy.

Store the fermented jalapeño hot sauce in an airtight container in the fridge. It will keep for at least 6 months.

Beet Rose, Yogurt, and Rose Petal Ice

Daniel Patterson
Coi
United States 2011

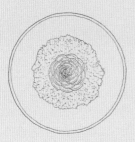

page 228

For the rose petal ice
10 g dried rose petals
400 g water
15 g honey
lemon juice
20 g sugar
salt

For the beet roses
beets (beetroot)
water
olive oil
salt and black pepper
beet (beetroot) juice
rice wine vinegar
sugar, if necessary

For the yogurt
150 g yogurt
lime juice
salt

First make the rose petal ice. Infuse the petals in hot, but not boiling water, like making a tea.

Strain through a chinois. Season with the honey, lemon juice, sugar and salt. Pour into a frozen pan and transfer to the freezer. Break with a fork every 30 minutes until it becomes completely frozen and crunchy, adjusting the seasoning with salt and lemon along the way.

To make the beet roses, roast medium to large beets (beetroot), skin on, with water, olive oil, salt and pepper. While the beets are roasting, reduce the beet (beetroot) juice by about half. Cool and season gently with salt and rice wine vinegar.

When the beets are tender, cool, peel and cut into two sizes of cylinders. Cut a sliver off one side of each to slightly flatten them. Slice approximately ⅛-inch (3-mm) thick to make the petals—you will need about 30 petals per beet rose, and about twice as many large as small. Make extra because some will break in the process of seasoning them. For the centers, peel some strips with a vegetable peeler and cut into ½-inch (1-cm) lengths.

Toss the different size beets with the reduced beet juice and season with more salt, rice wine vinegar and sugar if necessary. Keep the different shapes separate. Compress in the Cryovac on high in open containers. Remove and adjust the seasoning—the goal is to have vibrant, well-seasoned beets, neither salty, sweet nor acidic.

Purée the scraps (trimmings) with a little reduced beet juice until smooth, and season with salt and rice wine vinegar.

To assemble the roses, start by rolling a strip of beet and placing it on a working surface. That is the center. Tweezers come in handy here. Dip the bottom of a small petal of beet into the purée, and press against the centerpiece. Repeat, overlapping the first petal with the second by half, moving always in a clockwise direction. Occasionally press the petals together from the bottom to keep them tight. Gradually make the petals larger, until the rose is about 1¼-inch (3-cm) wide. Gently spread the petals outward so it looks like a rose. Refrigerate for at least 2 hours.

For the yogurt, season it to taste with lime juice and salt. Put into a siphon and charge twice.

To serve, place a dab of beet purée in the center of a frozen bowl and dispense a dollop of aerated yogurt on top of that. Spoon some of the rose petal ice around the yogurt. Place the beet rose in the center of the yogurt. Serve immediately.

Meat Fruit

Heston Blumenthal
Dinner by Heston Blumenthal
United Kingdom 2011

page 229

Parfait spheres

100 g peeled and finely sliced
    shallots
5 g peeled and finely diced garlic
15 g thyme, tied together with
    string
150 g dry Madeira
150 g ruby port
75 g white port
50 g brandy
250 g foie gras, veins removed
150 g chicken livers, veins removed
18 g salt
2 g curing salt
240 g whole eggs
300 g unsalted butter, cubed and
    at room temperature

Begin by placing the shallots, garlic and thyme in a container, along with the Madeira, ruby port, white port and brandy. Cover and allow to marinate in the fridge overnight.

Remove the marinated mixture from the fridge and place in a saucepan. Gently and slowly heat the mixture until nearly all the liquid has evaporated, stirring regularly to prevent the shallots and garlic from catching. Remove the pan from the heat, discard the thyme and allow the mixture to cool.

Preheat the oven to 100°C/212°F.

In the meantime, fill a deep roasting tray two–thirds full with water to make a bain-marie. Ensure that it is large and deep enough to hold a terrine dish measuring 26 cm wide, 10 cm long and 9 cm high. Place the tray in the oven. Place the terrine dish in the oven to warm through while the parfait is prepared.

Preheat a water bath to 50°C/122°F.

To prepare the parfait, cut the foie gras into pieces roughly the same size as the chicken livers. In a bowl, combine the foie gras and chicken livers and sprinkle with the salt and curing salt.

Mix well to combine and place in a sous–vide bag. Put the alcohol reduction, along with the eggs, in a second sous-vide bag, and the butter in a third bag. Seal all three bags under full pressure and place them in the preheated water bath for 20 minutes.

Carefully remove the bags from the water bath, and place the livers and the egg–alcohol reduction in a deep dish. Using a hand-held blender, blitz the mixture well, then slowly incorporate the melted butter. Blend until smooth. It is important to remember that all three elements should be at the same

temperature when combined to avoid splitting the mixture.

Transfer the mixture to a Thermomix, set the temperature 50°C/122°F and blend on full power for 3 minutes. Pass the mixture through a fine–mesh sieve lined with a double layer of muslin (cheesecloth).

Carefully remove the terrine from the oven, pour in the smooth parfait mixture and place the terrine in the bain-marie. Check that the water level is the same height as the top of the parfait. Cover the bain-marie with aluminium foil.

After 35 minutes, check the temperature of the centre of the parfait using a probe thermometer. The parfait will be perfectly cooked when the centre reaches 64°C/147°F. This can take up to an hour.

Remove the terrine from the oven and allow to cool to room temperature. Cover with clingfilm (plastic wrap) and place in the fridge for 24 hours.

Remove the terrine from the fridge and take off the clingfilm. To remove the oxidized layer on top of the parfait, scrape the discoloured part off the surface. Spoon the parfait into a disposable piping (pastry) bag. Holding the piping bag vertically, spin it gently to ensure all air bubbles are removed.

Place 2 silicone dome-mould trays, each containing 8 hemispheres 5 cm in diameter, on a tray. Piping in a slow, tight, circular fashion, fill the hemispheres with the parfait, ensuring they are slightly overfilled. Using a palette knife (spatula), scrape the surface of the moulds flat, then cover with clingfilm. Gently press the clingfilm on to the surface of the parfait and place the moulds in the freezer until frozen solid.

Taking one tray at a time from the freezer, remove the clingfilm and lightly torch the flat side of the parfait, being careful to only melt the surface. Join the two halves together by folding one half of the silicone mould on to the other half and press gently, ensuring the hemispheres are line up properly.

Remove the folded half of the mould to reveal a joined-up parfait sphere, and push a cocktail skewer (toothpick) down into it. Place the moulds back in the freezer for 2 hours (the spheres are easier to handle once frozen solid).

Remove them from the mould completely, and smooth any obvious lines with a paring knife. Wrap the perfectly smooth spheres individually in clingfilm and store in the freezer. They should be placed in the freezer for at least 2 hours before dipping in the mandarin jelly.

Mandarin jelly
80 g glucose (light corn syrup)
2 kg mandarin purée
180 g bronze leaf gelatine
1.6 g mandarin essential oil
7 g paprika extract

Place the glucose and 1 kg mandarin purée in a saucepan and gently heat to 50°C/122°F, stirring to dissolve the glucose completely. Bloom the gelatine by placing it in a container and covering it with cold water.

Allow to stand for 5 minutes. Place the softened gelatine in a fine-mesh sieve and squeeze out all excess water, then add it to the warm mandarin purée. Stir well until fully dissolved.

Take 250 g of the warm purée mixture and add the mandarin essential oil and paprika extract. Stir gently to combine and add it back to the mandarin mixture. Add the remaining mandarin

purée and stir again to fully combine before passing the mixture through a fine-mesh sieve.

Allow the mandarin jelly to stand in the fridge for a minimum of 24 hours before using.

Herb oil
180 g extra virgin olive oil
15 g rosemary
15 g thyme
10 g peeled and halved garlic

Place the olive oil, herbs and garlic in a sous-vide bag. Seal under full pressure and refrigerate. Keep in the fridge for 48 hours before using.

To serve
mandarin jelly
frozen parfait spheres
mandarin stalks with leaves
sourdough bread
reserved herb oil

To make the fruits, preheat a water bath to 30°C/86°F.

Place the mandarin jelly in a saucepan over a low-to-medium heat and gently melt, ensuring the temperature does not rise above 40°C/104°F. Place the melted jelly in a tall container and place →

Meat Fruit

Rømmegrøt with Cured Reindeer Heart and Plum Vinegar

Esben Holmboe Bang
Maaemo
Norway 2011

page 230

---

the container in the preheated water bath. Allow the jelly to cool to 27°C/81°F.

In the meantime, line a tray with paper towels covered with a layer of pierced clingfilm (plastic wrap). This will make an ideal base for the parfait balls when they defrost. A block of polystyrene (Styrofoam) is useful for standing up the parfait spheres once dipped.

Once the jelly has reached the optimal dipping temperature, remove the parfait balls from the freezer. Remove the clingfilm and carefully plunge each ball into the jelly twice, before allowing excess jelly to run off.

Stand them vertically in the polystyrene and place immediately in the fridge for 1 minute. Repeat the process a second time. Depending on the colour and thickness of the jelly on the parfait ball, the process may need to be repeated a third time.

Soon after the final dip, the jelly will have set sufficiently to permit handling. Gently remove the cocktail skewers (toothpicks) and place the balls on the lined tray, with the hole hidden underneath. Cover the tray with a lid

and allow to defrost in the fridge for approximately 6 hours.

To serve, gently push the top of the spheres with your thumb to create the shape of a mandarin. Place a stalk in the top centre of the indent to complete the "fruit".

Serve each meat fruit with a slice of sourdough bread that has been brushed with herb oil and toasted under the grill (broiler).

5 dl setterrømme (or 35% fat sour cream)
45 g wheat flour
70 g freshly milled wheat flour
5 dl whole (full-fat) milk
salt
plum vinegar

To serve
butter, about 15 g per portion, melted
cured reindeer heart

Put the setterrøme into a pot and heat it slowly. Sift in the flour little by little while stirring constantly. After a while, the fat will begin to separate. Ladle this out as you cook. Continue like this for 8–10 minutes.

When you have a fine, even consistency, and much of the fat has separated, begin to thin it little by little with milk, as when you are making a white sauce. When all of the milk is incorporated into the rømmegrøt, season with salt and plum vinegar.

Brown the butter. This is best done by warming the butter over medium heat. When it begins to simmer and foam, it is important to pay close attention. The butter is supposed to go through a browning process, so that the milk sugars and proteins get a rich,

Smoked Eel Sandwich

Jeremy Lee
Quo Vadis
United Kingdom 2012

page 231

caramelised flavour, but it is important that the butter does not burn. Use your sense of smell to get the right result. When you are satisfied, remove from the heat. Pour in a couple of drops of plum vinegar to give it a slightly acidic taste, and in order to stop the browning.

To serve, fill a bowl or plate with the desired amount of rømmegrøt. Grate the cured reindeer heart over the porridge with a fine grater, preferably a sharp Microplane. Pour a tablespoon of butter in the middle of each portion.

1 slice sourdough bread
butter
1 heaped teaspoon of Dijon
 mustard
30–40 g fillet of smoked eel (taken
 from an intact fish is best)
1 heaped teaspoon horseradish
 cream, of a fiery temperament

For the pickled red onion
1 good pinch sugar
2 tablespoons good white wine
 vinegar
¼ small red onion, peeled and
 thinly sliced

To pickle the red onion, combine the sugar and vinegar together in a pan and gently heat until the sugar dissolves. Remove from heat and steep the sliced onion in the pickle and let stand for an hour or so.

For the sandwich, warm a griddle (ridged grill) pan over gentle heat. Once hot, lay the slice of sourdough on the pan and brown nicely.

Generously spread butter on the toasted side of the bread, followed by the Dijon mustard, then cut the piece of toast in half.

Cut the eel into three even pieces and place on top of one of the toasted sides of the bread. Add the horseradish cream on top and place the other half of bread (toasted side down).

Return the sandwich to the griddle pan and grill on one side until brown. Carefully flip the sandwich and grill for a further few minutes.

Drain the pickled red onion and serve alongside the sandwich.

Grilled Salad Smoked Over Embers, Isle of Mull Cheese, Truffle Custard, and Cobnuts

Simon Rogan
L'Enclume
United Kingdom 2012

page 232

For the Isle of Mull cheese sauce
500 g grated Isle of Mull cheese
450 g water
2 g xanthan gum
salt and pepper

For the truffle custard
200 ml whole (full fat) milk
200 ml double (heavy) cream
30 g Black English truffle, finely
   chopped
3 egg yolks
1 whole egg
salt and pepper

For the cobnut crisp
5 g fresh yeast
70 g warm water
50 g T55 (plain/all-purpose) flour
260 g rye flour
5 g table salt
300 g sourdough starter
25 g cobnut oil
150 g peeled and chopped cobnuts

For the chilli herb oil
50 g chopped garlic
1 small chopped chilli and half the
   seeds
200 g grapeseed oil
2 g glice (emuslifier)
40 g picked flat parsley
3 g table salt

For the salad
2 baby spring cabbages
50 g cavolo nero (Tuscan kale)
50 g curly kale
25 g red Russian kale
1 large head of cauliflower
1 large head broccoli
1 celeriac (celery root)

For the garnish
black English truffle julienne
mustard frills
black mustard flowers

For the Isle of Mull cheese sauce
Melt the cheese into the water at 80°C
and leave to stand for 30 minutes. Then
pass through a fine sieve, add the
xanthan gum to slightly thicken the
sauce and season with salt and pepper.
When needed, heat and froth using a
hand-held blender.

For the truffle custard
Bring the milk and cream to the
simmer and add the truffle. Take off the
heat and infuse for 15 minutes. Add the
yolks and whole egg to a bowl, whisk
in the truffle cream and allow to cool.
Pass through a fine sieve, check the
seasoning and place in a ceramic dish,
then cover with clingfilm (plastic wrap)
and steam until just set. Keep in the
fridge until cold and needed.

For the cobnut crisp
Mix the fresh yeast with the water and
combine with the flours, salt and
sourdough starter in a mixer. Mix until
a firm dough is achieved, remove, wrap
in clingfilm (plastic wrap) and leave to
rest in the fridge for 2 hours. Roll
pieces of the dough through a pasta
machine to the lowest setting possible,
trying to keep them intact and in long
sheets. Then place them onto a lined
baking sheet, rub with a little bit of
the cobnut oil and sprinkle with the
chopped cobnuts. Next, place a piece
of silicone paper on top and cover and
press with another tray. Cook in an
oven at 180°C for 8 minutes, remove
the sheet and cook for another 4
minutes. Allow to cool, and break up
into medium-sized pieces.

Glutinous Rice-Stuffed Suckling Pig
Tam Kwok Fung
Jade Dragon
China 2012

page 233

For the chilli herb oil
Heat the garlic, chilli and grapeseed oil from cold and cook until golden. Then strain through a fine sieve and add more grapeseed oil to bring it back to 200 g. Add the glice emulsifier to the oil at 65°C. Blanch the parsley in boiling water, refresh in iced water and squeeze dry. Liquidize the oil with the parsley and 3 g of salt until you have a bright green oil, then strain through a fine sieve into a bowl over iced water and whisk until slightly thickened.

For the grilled salad
Peel and slice the celeriac (celery root) thinly, place in a vacuum pack bag and seal on full pressure. Cook in a water bath at 85°C for 1 hour, cool and slice into small ribbons. Arrange the vegetables into nice small leaves and florets. Cook the various vegetables to differing textures on a stone over the embers of a Green Egg barbecue (grill) at 200°C, constantly turning the vegetables and introducing cherry wood chips to the embers to create smoke for some of them. Season with salt and pepper.

Assembling the dish
Place a spoon of truffle custard onto the plate and arrange the grilled vegetables around. Place over pieces of the cobnut crisp, the mustard frills, flowers and a drizzle of the chilli herb oil. Finish with sprinkling over the fresh English truffle, mustard frills and flowers and spooning around some of the cheese froth.

Firstly, the suckling pig is dried and prepared in the traditional way as for BBQ suckling pig. After that, the pig is cut in half and deboned to get the skin for the dish.

The filling is cooked in advance by wok-frying glutinous (sticky) rice, morel mushrooms, mushroom jus, Iberico ham, spring onions (scallion) and soy sauce.

Then the stuffing is delicately placed inside.

The skin acts as a rolling paper, with the process being finished with kitchen string or wire to hold it all tightly in place so that the juices and the filling don't fall out.

The rolled suckling pig is placed in 180°C oven until it is golden brown with a fluffy crispy skin. Finally, it is finished with 200–220°C hot oil in a wok to ensure the crispiness of the skin when it's cut and served. The cooking time required is 30 minutes (not including the preparation time of the rice).

Carrot Tartare

Daniel Humm
Eleven Madison Park
United States 2012

page 234

Carrot bundles

8 orange market carrots, tops
    attached, no more than 3.8 cm
    (1½ inches) in diameter
75 g olive oil
15 g salt
3 sprigs thyme

Preheat a combi oven to 90°C/195°F,
full steam, and prepare an ice bath.
Cut the tops from the carrots, leaving
7.6 cm (3 inches) of the stem attached
to the carrots. Reserve the tops.

Combine the carrots, olive oil, salt,
and thyme in a sous vide bag and
seal airtight. Cook the carrots in the
combi oven until tender, about
25 minutes. Shock the sous vide
carrots in the ice bath.

When cold, remove the carrots from
the bag and drain thoroughly. Using
raffia, tie the carrots into bundles of
two, affixing the reserved carrot tops
to the top of each bundle.

Carrot vinaigrette

50 g canola (rapeseed) oil
400 g peeled and sliced carrots
40 g seeded and sliced jalapeño
70 g sliced onion
14 g salt
600 g carrot juice, from about
    8 carrots
10 cilantro (coriander) leaves
50 g olive oil
50 g orange juice
70 g lime juice
5 g sriracha sauce

Heat the canola (rapeseed) oil in a
saucepan over medium heat. Add the
carrots, jalapeño, and onion to the pan
and season with the salt. Cook, stirring
frequently, until the vegetables start to
soften, about 10 minutes.

Add the carrot juice to the pan and
bring to a simmer. Continue to simmer
the vegetables until the carrot juice has
almost completely reduced and the
vegetables are completely tender, about
15 minutes.

Prepare an ice bath.

Transfer the vegetables to a blender
with the cilantro (coriander) leaves
and blend on high speed until
completely smooth. Slowly stream
in the olive oil, being careful to
maintain the emulsion. Season the
vinaigrette with the orange juice,
lime juice, and sriracha. Pass through
a chinois and chill over the ice bath.

Apple mustard

400 g peeled and diced Granny
    Smith apples
20 g olive oil
25 g apple cider vinegar
10 g parsley leaves
1 g xanthan gum
50 g Dijon mustard
50 g drained pickled mustard
    seeds, made with yellow
    mustard seeds
3 g salt

Preheat a combi oven to 85°C/185°F,
full steam, and prepare an ice bath.

Combine the apples, olive oil, and apple
cider vinegar in a sous vide bag and seal
airtight. Cook the apples in the combi
oven until tender, about 40 minutes.
Shock the sous vide apples in the ice bath.

When cold, remove the apples from the bag and transfer to a blender with the parsley. Blend the apples until completely smooth. Continue to blend the purée on medium speed while slowly adding in the xanthan gum. Continue blending the purée until the gum is fully hydrated and the purée is thickened, about 1 minute. Pass the purée through a chinois.

Mix the purée with the Dijon and mustard seeds. Season with the salt.

7-grain toast

8 slices seven-grain bread, 3 mm (1/8 inch) thick
olive oil
salt

Preheat a convection oven to 163°C/325°F. Lightly brush each slice of bread with the olive oil and season with salt. Cut each slice of bread diagonally from corner to corner, forming triangles. Spread the slices of bread in a single layer on a baking sheet lined with parchment (baking) paper. Lay another sheet of parchment paper over the bread. Place a wire rack upside down on top of the top sheet of parchment paper. Toast the bread in the oven until crispy and golden brown, about 15 minutes. Let cool to room temperature.

Pickled apples

100 g peeled and diced Granny Smith apple, 6 mm (1/4 inch)
150 g white balsamic pickling liquid

Using a chamber vacuum sealer, compress the apple in the pickling liquid in an open container.

To finish

16 g sunflower seeds
8 pickled quail egg yolks
56 g apple mustard
smoked bluefish, for grating
horseradish, for grating
40 g drained pickled apples
sliced chives
24 g drained pickled mustard seeds, made with yellow mustard seeds
8 g sea salt
mustard oil

Preheat the oven to 175°C/350°F. Spread the sunflower seeds on a baking sheet lined with parchment (baking) paper and toast in the oven until fragrant, about 7 minutes. Let cool to room temperature.

Grind the bundled carrots through the fine die of a meat grinder at the table. Divide the ground carrots among 8 plates.

Garnish each plate with 1 drained pickled quail egg yolk, the apple mustard, toasted sunflower seeds, grated smoked bluefish, grated horseradish, pickled apples, sliced chives, pickled mustard seeds, and sea salt. Mix the ground carrots with the garnishes on each of 8 plates with the carrot vinaigrette and mustard oil to taste. Serve with the 7-grain toast on the side.

Chongqing Chicken Wings

Danny Bowien and Anthony Myint
Mission Chinese Food
United States 2012

page 235

3 lb chicken wings (either mid-
joints or whole wings)
¼ cup kosher (coarse) salt, plus
more as needed
½ cup vegetable or peanut
(groundnut) oil, plus 8–10 cups
for deep-frying
½ lb honeycomb tripe
½ cup cornstarch (cornflour), for
dredging
4 cups dried Tianjin chiles or other
medium-hot red chiles, like chiles
Japones
about ¾ cup Chongqing Wing
Spice Mix

For the Chongqing Wing Spice Mix
(makes about 1 cup)
2 tablespoons whole Sichuan
peppercorns
2 tablespoons cumin seeds
2 teaspoons fennel seeds
2 star anise
2 black cardamom pods
1½ teaspoons whole cloves
2 tablespoons plus 2 teaspoons
sugar
1 tablespoon kosher (coarse) salt
2 tablespoons plus 2 teaspoons
mushroom powder
2 tablespoons cayenne pepper

For the chicken wings, preheat the oven
to 350°F.

In a large bowl, toss the wings with the salt and ½ cup oil. Spread the wings out on a wire rack set over a baking sheet. Bake the wings for 15 minutes, or just until the skins appears cooked but not browned. Let the parbaked wings cool to room temperature, then lay them in a single layer on a baking sheet and freeze, uncovered, overnight.

The next day, clean the tripe thoroughly under cold running water, scrubbing vigorously to remove any grit. Put into a pot, cover with cold salty water by 2 inches, and bring to a boil over high heat. Boil for 10 minutes, partially covered, then reduce the heat to a simmer and cook for 2–3 hours, until the tripe is very tender. Drain in a colander, rinse, and cool completely.

Meanwhile, retrieve the wings, from the freezer and allow them to thaw at room temperature for 1–2 hours.

Make the spice mix: toast the Sichaun peppercorns, cumin seeds, fennel seeds, star anise, cardamom, and cloves in a dry skillet (frying pan) over medium heat, stirring continuously until fragrant. In a small bowl, combine the toasted spices with the sugar, salt, mushroom powder, and cayenne.

In a spice or coffee grinder, grind the spice mix to a powder, working in batches if necessary. The spice mix will keep in an airtight container for about a week before losing much of its potency.

Slice the tripe into strips about ½ inch wide and 2 inches long. Set aside.

In a deep pot or a wok (or use a deep fryer), heat about 4 inches of oil to 350°F. Meanwhile, pat the tripe strips dry with paper towels, then dredge them in the cornstarch (cornflour) shaking off any excess. Working in batches if necessary deep-fry the wings and tripe for 4–6 minutes, or until golden and crispy. They should cook in about the same amount of time.

Meanwhile, toast the Tianjin chillies in a hot, dry wok or skillet (frying pan) for about a minute over high heat, stirring continuously so the chiles cook evenly.

Drain the fried wings and tripe, shaking off as much oil as you can (or let them briefly drain on paper towels). Then transfer to a large bowl and dust them generously with the spice mix, tossing to coat. Add the toasted chiles and toss well. The chiles will perfume the dish, but they aren't meant to be eaten.

To serve, transfer everything—chiles and all—to a serving platter and present to your awestruck and possibly terrified guests.

Oops! I Dropped
the Lemon Tart

Massimo Bottura
Osteria Francescana
Italy 2012

page 236

Lemongrass gelato

200 g whole milk
50 g double (heavy) cream
3 stems lemongrass
30 g sugar
40 g sugar syrup
grated zest of 1 lemon
10 drops Villa Manodori Essenziale
    lemon oil

Process the ingredients in a thermal mixer and bring them to 85°C (185°F) at full speed. When it reaches this temperature, remove and strain the liquid. Let cool in a bowl over ice. Freeze in a Pacojet container and process just before serving.

Tart crust (case)

40 g cold butter
20 g icing (confectioners') sugar
1 egg yolk
50 g flour
2 g ground spices (a mixture of star
    anise, cinnamon, juniper, pepper
    and cardamom)

In a bowl, knead together the cold butter and sugar by hand. Add the egg yolk, flour and spices and knead thoroughly until smooth. Let rest for 2 hours in the fridge. Roll out the dough on a silicone baking mat until it is 2 mm (⅛ inch) thick. Use it to line moulds with a diameter of 8 cm (3¼ inches) at the base and 6 cm (2½ inches) at the

top to obtain the shape. Bake at 160°C (320°F) for 8 minutes.

Mint sauce

50 g fresh peppermint leaves
20 g mineral water
6 g xylitol
0.5 g mint essential oil

Bring a pan of water to a boil and blanch the mint in it for 10 seconds, then cool in iced water. Blend the mint thoroughly with the other ingredients, making sure the temperature does not go above 35°C (95°F). Pass it through a fine sieve.

Zabaglione

85 g egg yolks
50 g sugar
80 g lemon juice
80 g Amalfi limoncello

Prepare a pan of boiling water and a heatproof bowl the right size to sit over it without touching the water. Whisk the egg yolks and sugar in the bowl with a hand whisk, off the heat. When the sugar has dissolved well, set the bowl over the pan of boiling water and continue beating vigorously. As soon as the eggs are warm, and before they start to thicken, add the lemon juice and limoncello gradually, pouring them very slowly, while continuing to whisk energetically. When it is well whisked

and frothy, with a creamy texture, it is ready to be served.

Lemon powder

1 lemon

Wash the lemon, cut it into thin slices and remove the pips (seeds). Put the slices in a dehydrator at 30°C (86°F) for 5 days. Process in a thermal mixer and pass the powder through a fine sieve.

To serve

4 g candied lemon (rind and pulp)
2 g candied bergamot
1 g candied ginger
1 g lemon powder
1 g capers

Arrange the ingredients on the plate. Splash the plate with the zabaglione and add a quenelle of lemongrass gelato in the centre. Place the tart crust on top of the gelato, then gently crush it before serving.

Cronut®

Dominique Ansel
Dominique Ansel Bakery
United States 2013

page 237

ganache of your choice (see
    following pages)
flavored sugar of your choice (see
    following pages)
glaze of your choice

At-Home Cronut® pastry dough
3¾ cups (525 g) bread flour, plus
    more as needed for dusting
1 tablespoon plus 2 teaspoons (6 g)
    kosher (coarse) salt
¼ cup plus 1 tablespoon (64 g)
    granulated sugar
1½ tablespoons (11 g) instant yeast
1 cup plus 2 tablespoons (250 g)
    cold water
1 large (30 g) egg white
8 tablespoons (112 g) unsalted
    butter (84% butterfat), softened
1 tablespoon (15 g) heavy (double)
    cream
nonstick cooking spray, as needed

Butter block
18 tablespoons (251 g) unsalted
    butter (84% butterfat), softened
grapeseed oil
glaze of your choice
decorating sugar of your choice

Make the ganache
Prepare one of the ganache recipes and
refrigerate until needed.

Make At-Home Cronut® pastry dough
Combine the bread flour, salt, sugar,
yeast, water, egg white, butter, and
cream in a stand mixer fitted with a
dough hook. Mix until just combined,
about 3 minutes. When finished, the
dough will be rough and have very little
gluten development.

Lightly grease a medium bowl with
nonstick cooking spray. Transfer
the dough to the bowl. Cover with
plastic wrap (clingfilm) pressed directly
on the surface of the dough to prevent
a skin from forming. Proof the dough
in a warm spot until doubled in size,
2–3 hours.

Remove the plastic wrap (clingfilm)
and punch down (knock back) the
dough by folding the edges into the
center, releasing as much of the gas as
possible. On a piece of parchment
(baking) paper, shape into a 10-inch
(25 cm) square. Transfer to a sheet pan,
still on the parchment paper, and cover
with plastic wrap (clingfilm). Refrigerate
overnight.

Make the butter block
Draw a 7-inch (18 cm) square on a piece
of parchment paper with a pencil.
Flip the parchment over so that the
butter won't come in contact with the
pencil marks. Place the butter in the
center of the square and spread it

evenly with an offset spatula to fill
the square. Refrigerate overnight.

Laminate
Remove the butter from the
refrigerator. It should still be soft
enough to bend slightly without
cracking. If it is still too firm, lightly
beat it with a rolling pin on a lightly
floured work surface until it becomes
pliable. Make sure to press the butter
back to its original 7-inch (18 cm)
square after working it.

Remove the dough from the refrigerator, making sure it is very cold
throughout. Place the dough on a
floured work surface. Using the rolling
pin, roll out the dough to a 10-inch
(25.5 cm) square about 1 inch (2.5
cm) thick. Arrange the butter block in
the center of the dough so it looks
like a diamond in the center of the
square (rotated 45 degrees, with the
corners of the butter block facing the
center of the dough sides). Pull the
corners of the dough up and over to the
center of the butter block. Pinch
the seams (joins) of dough together to
seal the butter inside. You should have a
square slightly larger than the
butter block.

Very lightly dust the work surface with
flour to ensure the dough doesn't
stick. With a rolling pin, using steady

even pressure, roll out the dough from the center. When finished, you should have a 20-inch (50 cm) square about ¼ inch (6 mm) thick.

Fold the dough in half horizontally, lining up the edges so you are left with a rectangle. Then fold the dough vertically. You should have a 10-inch (25.5 cm) square of dough with four layers. Wrap tightly in plastic wrap (clingfilm) and refrigerate for 1 hour.

Repeat the previous two steps. Cover tightly with plastic wrap (clingfilm) and refrigerate overnight.

Cut the dough
On a lightly floured surface, roll out the dough to a 15-inch (40 cm) square about ½ inch (1.3 cm) thick. Transfer the dough to a half sheet pan, cover with plastic wrap (clingfilm), and refrigerate for 1 hour to relax.

Using a 3½-inch (9 cm) ring cutter, cut 12 rounds. Cut out the center of each round with a 1-inch (2.5 cm) ring cutter to create a doughnut shape.

Line a sheet pan with parchment paper and lightly dust the parchment with flour. Place the At-Home Cronut® pastries on the pan, spacing them about 3 inches (8 cm) apart. Lightly spray a piece of plastic wrap with nonstick spray and lay it on top

of the pastries. Proof in a warm spot until tripled in size, about 2 hours.

Fry the dough
Heat the grapeseed oil in a large pot until it reaches 350°F (175°C). Use a deep-frying thermometer to verify that the oil is at the right temperature. Line a platter with several layers of paper towels for draining the pastries.

Gently place three or four of them at a time into the hot oil. Fry for about 90 seconds on each side, flipping once, until golden brown. Remove from the oil with a slotted spoon and drain on the paper towels.

Check that the oil is at the right temperature. If not, let it heat up again before frying the next batch. Continue until all of them are fried. Let cool completely before filling.

Make the glaze
Prepare the glaze that corresponds to your choice of ganache.

Make the flavored sugar
Prepare the decorating sugar that corresponds to your choice of ganache.

Assemble
Transfer the ganache to a stand mixer fitted with a whisk. Whip on high

speed until the ganache holds a stiff peak. (If using the champagne-chocolate ganache, simply whisk it until smooth. It will be quite thick already.)

Cut the tip of a piping (pastry) bag to snugly fit a Bismarck tip (nozzle). Using a rubber spatula, place two large scoops of ganache in a piping bag so that it is one-third full. Push the ganache down toward the tip of the bag.

Place the decorating sugar that corresponds to your choice of ganache and glaze in a bowl.

Arrange each At-Home Cronut® pastry so that the flatter side is facing up. Pipe the ganache through the top of the pastry in four different spots, evenly spaced. As you pipe the ganache, you should feel the pastry getting heavier in your hand.

Place the pastry on its side. Roll in the corresponding sugar, coating the outside edges.

If the glaze has cooled, microwave it for a few seconds to warm until soft. Cut the tip of a piping bag to snugly fit a no. 803 plain tip. Using a rubber spatula, transfer the glaze to the bag and push it toward the tip of the bag. →

Cronut®

Pipe a ring of glaze around the top of each At-Home Cronut® pastry, making sure to cover all the holes created from the filling. Keep in mind that the glaze will continue to spread slightly as it cools. Let the glaze set for about 15 minutes before serving.

Consume within 8 hours of frying. (Leftover ganache can be stored in a closed airtight container in the refrigerator for 2 days. Leftover flavored sugar can keep in a closed airtight container for weeks and can be used to macerate fruits or sweeten drinks.)

Vanilla rose ganache
1 gelatin sheet (160 bloom), or 1 teaspoon (2.3 g) powdered gelatin plus 1 tablespoon (15 g) water
1¾ cups (406 g) heavy (double) cream
1 vanilla bean (pod/preferably Tahitian), split lengthwise, seeds scraped
½ cup (90 g) finely chopped white chocolate
4 tablespoons (50 g) rose water

Soak the gelatin sheet in a bowl of ice water until soft, about 20 minutes. If using powdered gelatin, sprinkle the gelatin over the water in a small bowl, stir, and let sit 20 minutes to bloom.

Combine the heavy (double) cream and vanilla bean (pod) seeds in a small pot and bring to a boil over medium heat. Remove from the heat.

If using a gelatin sheet, squeeze out any excess water. Whisk the bloomed gelatin into the cream until the gelatin is dissolved.

Place the white chocolate in a small heatproof bowl. Pour the hot cream over the chocolate and let stand for 30 seconds.

Whisk the white chocolate and hot cream until smooth. Add the rosewater and whisk until fully blended. Cover with plastic wrap (clingfilm) pressed directly onto the surface of the ganache to prevent a skin from forming.

Refrigerate overnight to set.

Whipped lemon ganache
2 gelatin sheets (160 bloom), or 2 teaspoons (5 g) powdered gelatin plus 2 tablespoons (30 g) water
¾ cup plus 2 tablespoons (188 g) heavy (double) cream
grated zest of 1 lemon
¼ cup (51 g) granulated sugar
¾ cup (117 g) finely chopped white chocolate

½ cup plus 1 tablespoon (141 g) lemon juice

Soak the gelatin sheets in a bowl of ice water until soft, about 20 minutes. If using powdered gelatin, sprinkle the gelatin over the water in a small bowl, stir, and let sit 20 minutes to bloom.

Combine the cream, lemon zest, and sugar in a small pot and bring to a boil over medium heat. Remove from the heat.

If using gelatin sheets, squeeze out any excess water. Whisk the bloomed gelatin into the cream until the gelatin is dissolved.

Place the white chocolate in a small heatproof bowl. Pour the hot cream over the chocolate and let stand for 30 seconds.

Whisk the white chocolate and hot cream until smooth. Let the ganache cool to room temperature.

Whisk in the lemon juice. Cover with plastic wrap (clingfilm) pressed directly onto the surface of the ganache to prevent a skin from forming. Refrigerate overnight to set.

Champagne-chocolate ganache

2 tablespoons (26 g) water
¼ cup plus 2 tablespoons (102 g)
   champagne
1½ tablespoons (9 g) unsweetened
   cocoa powder
½ cup (115 g) heavy (double) cream
3 large (60 g) egg yolks
3 tablespoons (38 g) granulated
   sugar
1 cup plus 1 tablespoon (165 g)
   finely chopped dark chocolate
   (66% cocoa content)

Combine the water, 2 tablespoons (26 g) of the champagne, and the cocoa powder in a small bowl. Mix to a smooth paste.

Combine the cream and the remaining 1/4 cup (76 g) champagne in a small pot and bring to a boil over medium heat. Remove from the heat.

Whisk the egg yolks and granulated sugar together in a small bowl. Stream one-third of the hot cream mixture into the egg yolks, whisking constantly until fully blended, to temper them. Whisk the tempered yolks into the remaining hot cream. Return the pot to medium heat.

Keep whisking! Continue to cook the custard over medium heat until it

reaches 185°F (85°C). The custard will turn pale yellow and thicken so that it coats the back of a spoon. Remove from the heat and whisk in the cocoa powder paste until fully incorporated.

Place the chocolate in a medium heatproof bowl. Strain the custard through a small sieve over the chocolate. Let stand for 30 seconds.

Whisk the chocolate and custard until smooth. When finished, the ganache will have the consistency of yogurt. Reserve ¼ cup (50 grams) for the glaze. Cover with plastic wrap (clingfilm) pressed directly onto the surface of the ganache to prevent a skin from forming. Refrigerate overnight to set.

Vanilla sugar

1 cup (200 g) granulated sugar
1 vanilla bean (pod/preferably
   Tahitian), split lengthwise,
   seeds scraped

Maple sugar

1 cup (200 g) granulated maple
   sugar
grated zest of 1 lemon

Orange sugar

1 cup (200 g) granulated sugar
grated zest of 1 orange

Combine the sugar and its flavoring in a small bowl. Reserve until needed.

Rose glaze

½ cup (200 g) glazing fondant
   (fondant icing)
2 tablespoons (30 g) rosewater

Lemon glaze

½ cup (200 g) glazing fondant
   (fondant icing)
grated zest of 1 lemon

Champagne-chocolate glaze

½ cup (200 g) glazing fondant
   (fondant icing)
¼ cup (50 g)
champagne-chocolate ganache

Warm the fondant in a small bowl in the microwave in 10-second intervals, stirring between intervals. When the fondant is slightly warm, about 20 seconds, add the corresponding flavor and stir until fully blended.

Ants and Pineapple

Alex Atala
D.O.M.
Brazil 2013

page 238

1 pineapple
4 saúva ants

Peel the pineapple and cut into four equal cubes.

Place a piece of pineapple on top of a serving dish and top with an ant. Serve immediately.

Crapaudine Beetroot Cooked Slowly in Beef Fat with Smoked Cod's Roe and Linseeds

Tommy Banks
The Black Swan
United Kingdom 2013

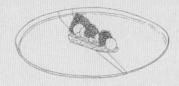

page 239

225 ml red beetroot (beet) juice
    (ideally from the peeled
    crapaudine trimmings/scraps)
Cabernet Sauvignon vinegar
2 large crapaudine beetroot
    (beets), peeled
100 g beef fat
20 g oak shavings for smoking
    (optional)
sea salt

For the horseradish goat's curd
100 ml whipping cream
15 g fresh horseradish, peeled and
    finely grated
75 g goat's curd
sea salt

For the smoked cod's roe emulsion
65 g smoked cod roe, skinned and
    deveined
30 ml water
15 ml lemon juice
1 teaspoon Dijon mustard
15 g egg yolk (about 1 yolk)
1 teaspoon sea salt
125 ml grapeseed oil

For the linseed crackers
60 g brown linseeds (flaxseed)
100 ml boiling water
pinch of sea salt
vegetable oil

For the pickled beetroot discs
1 golden beetroot (beet)
1 red beetroot (beet)
150 ml standard pickling liquor,
    cooled

First prepare the goat's curd. Bring the cream almost to the boil, stir in the horseradish, then remove from the heat. Cover the pan tightly with clingfilm (plastic wrap) and place in the fridge to infuse overnight. The next day, strain the cream through a fine sieve, squeezing it all out with the back of a ladle. Fold the strained cream into the goat's curd with a rubber spatula (do not beat) and season with salt to taste. Keep in the fridge in a piping (pastry) bag until needed.

To make the cod roe emulsion, combine all the ingredients except the oil in a small bowl and blend thoroughly with a hand-held blender so the mixture is smooth and completely homogenous. Begin gradually streaming in the grapeseed oil until it is all used up and you have a stiff and glossy emulsion. Transfer to a piping bag. Combine all the ingredients for the linseed crackers in a small container and leave to one side for 20 minutes. The linseeds (flaxseed) will absorb the water and form a caviar-like gel. Preheat the oven to 150°C/300°F/Gas mark 2. Spread the linseed mixture thinly on a silicone baking mat. Place on a baking tray and bake for about 30 minutes. The cracker will start to lift away from the mat when it is ready. Break it into pieces once cooled and store in an airtight container.

To make the pickled beetroot discs, peel the beetroot (beets) and slice about 2 mm thick on a mandolin (do the golden one first!). Using a 2-cm cutter, stamp out discs from both beetroot. Place the yellow discs in one vacuum-pack bag and the red discs in another. Divide the pickling liquor between the two bags and seal to full pressure. If you don't have a vacuum sealer, then you can heat the pickling liquor and pour it over the discs.

For the beetroot, bring the beetroot juice to the boil, reduce the heat, then simmer carefully, frequently skimming until you have a thick, syrupy glaze. Season to taste with salt and the vinegar. Cover and keep warm until ready to serve.

Top and tail (trim) the crapaudine beetroot (beets), and cut them into flat triangle shapes about 1.5 cm thick. Melt the beef fat in a large, heavy-based frying pan (skillet), add the beetroot portions and cook slowly over a very low heat for 4–5 hours, turning every 20 minutes or so and seasoning with salt as you go. When the beetroot portions are totally tender and shrunken and shrivelled almost like a steak, place them in a tray, bind tightly in clingfilm and leave to rest. If you are going to smoke the beetroot, then poke a hole in the clingfilm (plastic wrap) and smoke with the oak chips, using a smoking gun or similar cold smoker. Seal the hole and keep warm like this until ready to serve.

To serve, brush each warm, smoked beetroot portion thoroughly with the glaze and place in the centre of four plates. Pipe on alternate dots of the cod roe emulsion and the goat's curd to cover the whole surface of the beetroot. Finally, arrange small pieces of linseed cracker and well-drained beetroot discs on the top.

Mother Mole

Enrique Olvera
Pujol
Mexico 2013

page 240

For the mole negro – mole viejo

4 chiles chilhuacle rojo chiles
4 chiles chilhuacle negro
4 chiles chilhuacle amarillo
2 heirloom tomatoes
2 large garlic cloves
½ white onion
1 whole clove
1 allspice berry
1 sprig thyme
1 sprig marjoram
1 sprig oregano
1 small cinnamon stick
1 tablespoon powdered ginger
1 star anise
2 tablespoons white sesame seeds
2 prunes
¼ teaspoon nutmeg
¼ plantain, peeled
2 tablespoons roasted peanuts
1 tablespoon raisins
2 tablespoons whole almonds
3 tablespoons stone-ground
   chocolate
2 tablespoons pecans
3 tablespoons grapeseed oil
1 cup (240 ml) water
3 tablespoons kosher (coarse) salt

For the mole rojo – mole nuevo

15 chiles pasilla mixe
2 heirloom tomatoes
2 large garlic cloves
½ white onion

1 whole clove
1 allspice berry
1 sprig thyme
1 sprig marjoram
1 sprig oregano
1 small cinnamon stick
1 tablespoon powdered ginger
1 star anise
2 tablespoons white sesame seeds
2 prunes
¼ teaspoon ground nutmeg
¼ plantain, peeled
2 tablespoons roasted peanuts
   (groundnuts)
1 tablespoon raisins
2 tablespoons whole almonds
3 tablespoons stone-ground
   chocolate
2 tablespoons pecans
3 tablespoons grapeseed oil
1 cup (240 ml) water
3 tablespoons kosher (coarse) salt

For the corn dough

makes 2.2 pounds/1kg
1 tsp slaked lime (calcium
   hydroxide)
2 cups (510 g) dried corn

For the sesame seed tortillas

1 cup (280 g) corn dough
1 teaspoon kosher (coarse) salt
4 teaspoons water
3 tablespoons white sesame seeds,
   toasted

To make the mole negro – mole viejo

Place all the ingredients except the oil, water, and salt in a roasting pan and roast in a 450°F (230°C) oven for 8 minutes, checking to see that they do not burn. Remove from the oven and finely grind.

In a pan, sauté the ground ingredients in the oil over medium heat, stirring frequently, for 45–60 minutes.

Add the water and cook, stirring frequently, for 25 minutes. Strain and adjust the salt.

Reheat the mole every day, adding a new batch of black mole paste every 2 days.

To make the mole rojo – mole nuevo

Place all the ingredients except the oil, water, and salt in a roasting pan and roast in a 450°F (230°C/Gas Mark 8) for 4 minutes. Remove from the oven and finely grind.

In a pan, sauté the ground ingredients in the oil over medium heat, stirring frequently, for 45–60 minutes.

Add the water and cook, stirring frequently, for 25 minutes. Strain and adjust the salt.

Roast Suckling Pig

Chui Wai-Kwan
Seventh Son
China 2013

page 241

Mixed Rice with Vegetables and Korean Beef Tartare

Kim Sung-Il
La Yeon
South Korea 2014

page 242

To make the corn dough

Dissolve the slaked lime in 4 cups (about 1 liter) water in a pot and bring to a boil. Add the corn and cook for 45 minutes. Let stand for 12 hours. Drain the corn in a sieve and rinse until the water runs clear. Grind to a thin and compact dough.

To make the sesame seed tortilla

Knead all the ingredients in a bowl until combined and smooth.

Divide into 12 portions a little less than 1 ounce (25 g) each and roll each one into a ball. Using a tortilla press, form into tortillas.

Cook on a comal over medium heat, turning three times, for 45 seconds on each side for a total of 2 minutes and 15 seconds.

Plating
Reheat both moles. On each plate, spread ¼ cup (60 ml) of the mole viejo into a circle, using the back of a spoon. Place 1 tablespoon of the mole nuevo in the middle of each circle of the black mole. Serve with tortillas.

This recipe is not to be found. If you are inspired to make it at home, first find a young pig. Season it. Roast it on high heat in an oven with charcoal. To stay true to its origins, it should be served in two courses—first with the pig skin and steamed bread for a sandwich, then the meat with bones included.

Julienne vegetables such as bean sprouts, bellflower, shiitake, and aster (in-season ingredients), season and stir-fry.

Mix the seasoned herbs with Gimpo Gold Rice.

Spray soy sauce on julienned 1++ Korean beef chuck and serve it on top of cooked rice.

Serve soy sauce on the side.

Chicken Country Captain

Mashama Bailey
The Grey
United States 2014

page 243

2 whole fryer chickens, cut into
  8 pieces
2 quarts diced onions
2 quarts diced green peppers
4 serranno peppers (chillies) diced
  with seeds
2 cups chopped garlic
2 teaspoons curry powder
4 cups whole plum tomatoes
  without the liquid
1½ cups white wine
2 quarts rich double stock
1 cup currants/raisins
chopped parsley
butter
olive oil
salt and pepper

In a Rondue, add 2–3 tablespoons of butter and 2 tablespoons of olive oil.

On medium heat, brown off all of the chicken in batches without crowding the pan. Depending on the size of your pan, this may take 2–3 batches. Set the chicken aside to make the sauce.

Discard the fat, and in that same Rondue add 3 tablespoons of butter and 1 tablespoon of olive oil. Sweat the onions, peppers, and garlic on low heat until fragrant and translucent, Lightly season with salt and pepper. Add the curry powder. Stir together until the curry coats the vegetables.

Chop the tomatoes, add them, and continue to cook down slowly until the vegetables begin to caramelize and become really soft, with it's fond (caremelized bits) developing on the bottom of the pan. Once you have a good golden brown coloring and the vegetables no longer smell raw, deglaze with the wine and reduce. When the wine has cooked off, add the stock and another 3 tablespoons of olive oil. Add the chicken, bring to a boil, reduce to a simmer and cook on low heat until the chicken is tender. Check for salt and remove from the heat.

Before serving, add the currants or raisins and more chicken stock if needed. Finish with chopped parsley.

Cacio e Pepe in a Bladder

Riccardo Camanini
Lido 84
Italy 2014

page 244

1 dehydrated pig's bladder
300 g rigatoni pasta, such as
  Felicetti
135 g pecorino, aged black rind
  variety, grated
90 g extra virgin olive oil
3 g black pepper, freshly cracked
12 g salt, such as Guérande

Soak the dehydrated pig's bladder in cold water for about 10 days, changing the water daily.

When the bladder is adequately hydrated, insert the other ingredients into it using a funnel, then firmly secure the bladder opening with kitchen twine.

Cook the stuffed bladder in a large pan of boiling water, being sure to keep it submerged in the water and shaking it occasionally to mix the pasta inside. Cook for 30 minutes.

Serve in front of guests by cutting open the bladder with a sharp knife and spooning the rigatoni onto plates.

Superiority Burger

Brooks Headley
Superiority Burger
United States 2014

page 245

1 cup red quinoa
1 medium yellow onion, chopped
2 teaspoons ground toasted fennel
   seeds
1 teaspoon chili powder
1 cup cooked chickpeas, rinsed and
   drained
1 teaspoon white wine vinegar
1 cup small-diced carrots
½ cup coarse bread crumbs
¾ cup walnuts, toasted and
   crushed
juice of 1 lemon
1 tablespoon chopped fresh flat
   parsley
1 tablespoon hot chili sauce
2 tablespoons non-modified potato
   starch
grapeseed oil for searing the
   patties
salt and black pepper
Toasted buns, shredded lettuce,
   Roasted Red Tomatoes (see
   right), pickle slices, Muenster
   cheese (if you like), sauces
   (honey mustard, Special Sauce)
   of your choice, for serving.

Preheat the oven to 425°F.

Cook the quinoa in 1½ cups salted water until fluffy, about 45 minutes. Cool and reserve. In a separate pan, sauté the onion until translucent and browned, and season with salt, pepper, the fennel, and chili powder. Add the chickpeas and keep on the heat for 5–10 minutes, stirring constantly. Deglaze the hot pan with the white wine vinegar and scrape everything stuck to the bottom of the pan back onto the mix. Using a potato masher, roughly smash the onion-chickpea mixture. Mix the chickpea mash by hand with the cooled quinoa.

Roast the carrots in the oven until dark around the edges and soft, about 25 minutes. Add the chickpea-quinoa mixture. Add the breadcrumbs, walnuts, lemon, parsley, and chili sauce, and season again with salt and pepper, until it tastes sharp. Mix the potato starch with 1 tablespoon water to create a cloudy, thick slurry. Fold the slurry into the burger mix as the binding agent. Form the mixture into 8–10 patties and sear in grapeseed oil in a hot sauté pan or cast iron skillet (frying pan) until fully browned, about 3 minutes on each side. To serve, place each patty on a toasted bun with shredded iceberg lettuce, Roasted Red Tomatoes, 2 pickle slices, Muenster cheese (if you like), and sauces such as honey mustard or Special Sauce.

For the Roasted Red Tomatoes
makes enough for 4
any leftover tomatoes or not-so-
   great tomatoes, cut into large
   chunks
2 tablespoons extra virgin olive oil
1–2 tablespoons raw sugar
2 teaspoons crushed red pepper
   (dried chilli) flakes
2 teaspoons fennel seeds, toasted
   and crushed, plus more for
   garnish (optional)
2 garlic cloves, thinly sliced
salt and black pepper

Preheat the oven to 300°F.

Combine the tomatoes, olive oil, sugar, red pepper (dried chilli) flakes, fennel seeds and garlic in a shallow baking dish. Add some salt and be generous with black pepper. Stir to combine and put in the oven. Cook for as long as possible, 1–2 hours, until the tomatoes break down some and the tomato liquid concentrates and becomes thicker.

Spaghettoni in Butter and Fresh Yeast

Riccardo Camanini
Lido 84
Italy 2014

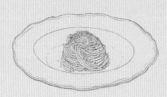

page 246

fresh brewer's yeast
320 g spaghettoni pasta,
    preferably artisinal
130 g butter (Riccardo uses
    Beppino Occelli)
salt
pepper

Crumble the yeast onto a baking tray and dry out in the oven or a dehydrator at 70°C for around 5 hours.

Cook the spaghettoni in salted boiling water for 8–12 minutes until al dente.

In a separate pan, soften the butter. Add the cooked spaghettoni and season with salt and pepper.

Neatly plate the pasta and sprinkle with the dried yeast to finish.

Curried Baby Goat with Sweet Potato Gnocchi

Nina Compton
Compère Lapin
United States 2015

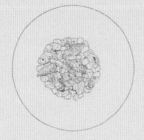

page 247

For the baby goat
4 onions, julienned
1 quart ginger, roughly chopped
1 quart turmeric, roughly chopped
1 head of garlic, halved
1 cup garam masala
1 spice sachet (5 cinnamon
    sticks, ¼ cup star anise, ¼ cup
    ground coriander, 1 tablespoon
    cloves, 2 cups ccurry leaves)
8 quarts. brown chicken stock
5 lb baby goat leg or shoulder
    (brined overnight)

In a large stockpot, sauté the onions, ginger, garlic and turmeric; add the garam masala and the sachet and sweat for 5 minutes on medium heat. Add the brown chicken stock and bring to a simmer. Pour the mix over the goat and roast at 300°F, basting the meat while cooking and turning it every 30 minutes, until tender. Take all the meat off the bone and reserve the stock.

For the finished ragù
4 onions, julienned
1 cup minced ginger
1 cup finely chopped tumeric
1 habanero pepper (chilli), minced
1 cup garam masala
8 cans (tins) coconut milk
roasted baby goat
reserved stock
1 spice sachet (5 cinnamon sticks,
    ¼ cup star anise, 1 tablespoon
    cloves, 2 cups curry leaves)

Sweat the onions, ginger, turmeric and habanero; add the garam marsala and cook for 5 minutes on low heat. Add the coconut milk, meat cut into 1 inch chunks and the reserved stock and simmer for 45 minutes.

For the sweet potato gnocchi
makes extra (enough for 10–15)
5 large egg yolks
2 lb sweet potato roasted at 350°F
    until tender and peeled
½ lb all-purpose (plain) flour
salt

Vegetable Pulp Burger

Dan Barber and Adam Kaye
Blue Hill
United States 2015

page 248

In a mixer, combine the sweet potato, egg yolks, and salt; then add the flour slowly. Pipe the mixture onto a cutting (chopping) board and then cut in to 1-inch logs, place on a floured sheet tray and freeze until ready to use.

To garnish

15 cherry tomatoes, halved and slightly dried in a 300°F oven for 30 minutes
3 oz arugula (rocket)
6 tablespoons toasted cashews
1 tablespoon pickled cilantro (coriander)

Cook the gnocchi in boiling salted water, and once floating add to the ragù and simmer for about 1 minute. Add the cherry tomatoes and arugula (rocket). Plate and garnish with chopped cashews and pickled cilantro (coriander).

For the burger

227 g raw button mushrooms, washed, dried and cut in half
114 g firm tofu, cut into 3 slices
400 g canned kidney beans
227 g roasted beet (beetroot) pulp
227 g roasted carrot pulp
58 g celery pulp
100 g toasted whole natural almonds, roughly chopped
30 g Panko breadcrumbs
58 g grated Parmesan cheese
3 eggs, beaten
86 g mayonnaise
30 g garlic confit
114 g tempeh, crumbled
90 g caramelized diced onions
85 g cooked barley
25 g harissa
25 g miso
15 g Worcestershire sauce
50 g butter, softened
15 g salt
oil for grilling
grated cheddar cheese for topping the burger
Grilled buns, beet (beetroot) ketchup (see below), pickles, lettuce, and honey mustard mayo (see below), to server

Preheat a convection oven to 375°F.

Place the mushrooms on a baking tray and drizzle with a little vegetable oil. Roast for 15 minutes until lightly browned. Remove and allow to cool completely.

Line a baking tray with parchment (baking) paper and arrange the slices of tofu on the tray. Bake for 15 minutes, until golden brown. Remove from the oven and allow to cool.

Spread the kidney beans on a parchment lined baking tray and bake for 10 minutes, until they begin to dry and crack open. Remove from the oven and allow to cool.

In a large bowl, combine all the ingredients and mix thoroughly by hand, breaking up the large pieces of roasted tofu.

Working in batches, transfer a third of the mixture to a food processor and chop to a medium-fine texture. Transfer the mix to a clean bowl and repeat with the remaining mixture. Mix well by hand to homogenize the mixture.

Heat a ridged, cast iron grill (griddle) over a medium-high flame. Preheat the broiler (grill). →

Vegetable Pulp Burger

Form the mixture into rounds approximately 90 g. Brush the burgers with a little vegetable oil and place on a well oiled cast iron grill. Grill the patties for 2 minutes per side and remove; place on a baking tray. Top with some grated cheddar cheese and place under a broiler (grill) for 1 minute, until the cheese has melted and begins to bubble.

Remove and serve on a grilled bun with beet (beetroot) ketchup, pickles, lettuce and honey mustard mayonnaise.

For the beet (beetroot) ketchup
2 tennis ball-sized red beets (beetroot), roasted until soft, peeled and diced
1 cup red wine, reduced to ¼ cup
1 cup port wine, reduced to ¼ cup
pinch of xanthan gum
salt
raspberry vinegar

Simmer the beets (beetroot) with the wines, stirring occasionally, until the liquid is reduced by half.

Add a pinch of xanthan, and blend until smooth.

Pass through a fine sieve, and season with salt and raspberry vinegar to taste.

For the honey mustard mayo
1 egg yolk
1 tablespoon Dijon mustard
2 tablespoons sherry vinegar
1½ cups grapeseed oil
½ cup mustard oil
½ cup honey
1 cup wholegrain mustard
2 tablespoons lemon juice
1 teaspoon salt

In a bowl, combine the egg yolk, Dijon mustard and sherry vinegar.

Starting drop by drop and progressing to a steady stream while whisking constantly as the mixture thickens, add grapeseed oil followed by the mustard oil to form a thick mayonnaise.

Whisk in the honey, wholegrain mustard, lemon juice and salt. Refrigerate, covered, for 1 hour to set for optimal texture.

For the buns
612 g whole-wheat (wholemeal) flour (freshly milled hard red spring wheat recommended)
500 g milk
12 g honey
7.5 g yeast
25 g sugar
116 g butter, chilled and cubed
20 g water
20 g breadcrumbs, darkly toasted and pulverized
5 g sesame seed oil
15 g salt

Combine the flour, milk, honey, yeast, salt and sugar in the bowl of stand mixer. Blend at a low speed (1) until the ingredients come together.

Incorporate the butter in two separate additions. Continue to mix until the dough pulls together from the side of the bowl and creates a window pane. Form the dough into a ball, wrap and place in the refrigerator overnight.

Combine the water, breadcrumbs and sesame oil (this will form the bun topping).

Divide the dough into 24 pieces and shape into rounds. Flatten each round, and pipe a small amount of the topping onto each roll. Set the rolls aside to proof at room temperature for 3 hours.

Bake in a 350°F convection oven for 12–15 minutes.

Wild Boar Cappelletti with Plum Broth

Antonia Klugmann
L'Argine a Vencò
Italy 2016

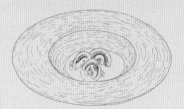

page 249

400 g boar meat
extra virgin olive oil, to taste
butter, to taste
1 onion
1 carrot
1 celery
1 clove of garlic
black pepper, to taste
rosemary, to taste
double (heavy) cream, to taste
500 g '00' flour
120 g eggs
200 g eggs yolks
2 kg plums
fleur de sel, to taste
black pepper

For the stuffing, roast the boar meat in an iron pan with a couple of tablespoons of extra virgin olive oil and some butter.

Chop the onion, carrot, celery and garlic. In a different pan, brown the vegetables with some extra virgin olive oil and water. When they are stewed, add the roasted boar meat and some boiling water; continue to cook for a couple of hours. Towards the end, add a couple of pinches of black pepper and rosemary to taste.

Reduce the mixture until it has thickened and got darker in colour.

Pour the mixture, still hot, into a food processor, add a couple of tablespoons of double (heavy) cream, and process until almost smooth.

To make the cappelletti, knead the flour with the eggs and yolks until a neat and uniform dough is obtained. Roll out the dough and cut it in squares. Put a spoonful of the stuffing onto each pasta square. Fold the squares into triangles. Close the triangles by the bottom ends to create the typical shape of the cappelletto.

Wash the plums and extract the juice. Add salt to taste. Cook the cappelletti in salty boiling water and serve them in the warm plum broth.

Kobe Beef
Cutlet Sandwich
Hisato Hamada
Wagyumafia
Japan 2016

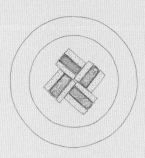

page 250

Whole Hog Barbecue
Rodney Scott
Rodney Scott's Whole Hog BBQ
United States 2016

page 251

1 piece Kobe beef Chateaubriand cut (center cut of tenderloin), trimmed of excess fat and sliced to 1.8 cm thickness, weighing approx. 100–150 g (dimension of the beef steak should be approximately the width of the toast), or prime grade, highly marbled beef if unable to source Kobe beef
2 slices Japanese milk bread, 1.5 cm thick, or pullman loaf or similar dense and fluffy white bread if unable to source Japanese bread
1 whole egg
all-purpose (plain) flour, enough for coating 1 piece of steak
Japanese panko breadcrumbs
Bulldog katsu sauce
about 1 litre vegetable oil, for frying

Fill a heavy pot or deep-fryer with vegetable oil and heat to 190°C (374°F).

Meanwhile toast the bread slices until a light-medium brown and set aside.

Prepare the beef for dredging. Arrange three individual shallow plates or bowls, one filled with a whole egg, whisked thoroughly, one for flour and one for breadcrumbs.

Ensure the beef isn't straight from the fridge to avoid a cold centre when fried. Coat the steak first in the flour, with an even and light coating, shaking off the excess flour. Dip the floured steak into the whisked egg and let the excess liquid drip off, followed by a generous coating of panko bread crumbs. Make sure to pat the steak with a gentle push into the crumbs to ensure they stick.

When the oil has reached temperature, drop the beef in gently and fry for 1 minute. Remove from the fryer after 1 minute and let rest for another minute.

While the beef katsu is resting, prepare the sandwich. Spread a thin and even layer of katsu sauce on one side of both slices of toast. Make sure the sauce covers the entire surface of the toast.

Place the beef katsu on the toast and layer the other slice, sauced side facing down. Trim off the crusts of all sides and slice the sandwich in half or quarters.

Best served immediately.

Rodney Scott has not divulged all the details about this barbecue. Though to make his whole hog, first build a hog pit in your backyard. Get some oak, hickory, and pecan hardwood, and smoke the hog with salt, black pepper, and Rodney's secret sauce (including vinegars, peppers, and citrus). Cook the hog for 12 hours on its belly, then flip and cook longer, seasoning again. Then chop the meat into rough pieces and serve (in a roll if you'd like) with sides, such as collards (spring greens). Then you too will know how to do this and can host a weekly feast like he does.

Meat Pie

Calum Franklin
Holborn Dining Room
United Kingdom 2016

page 252

Find some old tarnished British molds for savory pies. Decide on a pork or beef or vegetable filling, then and go to town making elaborately decorated pastry creations.

Duck Jelly

Claude Bosi
Claude Bosi at Bibendum
United Kingdom 2017

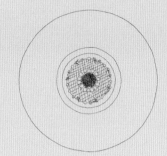

page 253

White chicken stock
20 kg chicken carcass
6 calves feet, split
45 litres water
mirepoix (6 onions, cut in half, then
    toasted on the stove, 8 carrots,
    1 whole celery, 1 sprig thyme)

Immerse the carcasses and calves feet in the water, bring to the boil, skim. Add the mirepoix and cook. It needs to be cooked longer than a normal chicken stock, as you want to optimize the amount of gelatin that comes from the ingredients (this varies with the produce). Pass through a fine chinois.

Brown chicken stock
20 kg chicken carcass
6 calves feet, split
35 litres water
mirepoix (6 onions, cut in half, then
    toasted on the stove, 8 carrots,
    1 whole celery, 1 sprig thyme)
125 g tomato paste (purée)

Roast the chicken bones. Immerse the carcasses and calves feet in the water, bring to the boil, skim. Add the mirepoix and and tomato paste, and cook. It needs to be cooked longer than a normal chicken stock, as you want to optimize the amount of gelatin that comes from the ingredients (this varies with the produce). Pass through a fine chinois.

Duck stock
40 kg duck bones
4 calves feet, split in half
red mirepoix (red onion, carrot)
celery
thyme
Madeira
white wine
coriander seeds
2 litres brown chicken stock (see
    above) 35 litres white chicken
    stock (see above)

Break the bones into smaller pieces. Roast the bones and feet in a pan or pot on the stove. Remove the bones. Drain the fat. Set the fat aside.

Sweat the mirepoix down with the duck fat. Add the thyme. Stir and roast until cooked.

Add one-third of the duck bones. Deglaze the pan with the white wine. Reduce by half. Deglaze with the Madeira. Reduce by half.

Add the crushed coriander seeds. Add the white and brown chicken stock. Cook for approximately 2½ hours. When cooked, strain in a colander, then chinois. Put in the blast chiller to ensure the fat rises to the surface. When the fat solidifies at the top, remove. Remove the fat and discard. →

Duck Jelly

Keep the stock in the refrigerator for at least 12 hours.

Clarification
1 bottle Madeira
diced celery
diced shallots
diced carrots
diced red beetroot (beet)
pasteurized egg whites
parsley stalks, finely diced
tarragon stalks, finely diced
ground pepper
toasted coriander, seeds ground
salt

Reduce 1 bottle of Madeira to one-third of its quantity.

Add your diced vegetables to a bowl and mix with the pasteurized egg whites, reduced duck jus and reduced Madeira. Add salt. Mix altogether.

Put the duck stock into one large casserole (the stock should be hard/set jelly consistency), melt it but do not heat. Add the mix, whisk, take to the heat, bring to the boil. Remove from the stove.

When the impurities rise to the top, make a peeping hole through the top to check if the liquid underneath is clear enough. It should reach boiling point – about 10 minutes maximum. Pass the stock through the chinois and muslin (cheesecloth) – through the hole – take only the liquid, not the vegetables. When all the stock has been passed, while it is still warm, infuse with tarragon stalks wrapped in muslin (cheesecloth). Infuse until it cools down completely. When it has cooled, take the muslin (cheesecloth) out. Put into the blast chiller. Remove the trace of fat from the top of the liquid by skimming with a cloth.

Onion bavarois
(white Cévenne onion purée)
Peel the onions. Slice very thinly on the slicer. Sweat in a pan with salted butter. Do not colour. Replace the lid. Let cook gently on side of stove until fully cooked. Blitz (process) to make a purée. Cool down.

Bavarois
6 gelatin leaves
100 g milk
800 g onion purée (see above)
400 g whipped cream
Soak the gelatin. Warm the milk. Dissolve the gelatin in the milk. Add the milk and gelatin to the onion purée. Mix together, then fold in the whipped cream.

Dill mayonnaise
Picked dill leaves (no stalks)
15 g Japanese mayonnaise

Blanch the leaves in boiling salted water; cool in ice water. Squeeze the leaves and place in boiling water. Cook. Return to iced water. Let cool down.

Squeeze the leaves. Put into a Vitamix. (Keep one part of the blanching liquid, because we need it to make the chlorophyll.) Blitz to make a liquid purée. Put in a wide casserole dish on the stove. Bring to the boil. As soon as the mix starts to split (water and chlorophyll separates), drain it into a Gastro tray (that has holes) with a muslin cloth (cheesecloth) on top. The idea is that the water drains away and the chlorophyll stays on the muslin cloth. Blast chill until cold.

Whole Turbot

Tomos Parry
Brat
United Kingdom 2018

page 254

Take 5 g dill chlorophyll and mix with the Japanese mayonnaise. Put into a piping (pastry) bag.

Sturgeon mousse

50 g smoked sturgeon
15 g dashi

Cut the sturgeon into small pieces, and blitz with the dashi until a smooth purée.

Feuilles de brick tube

clarified butter
feuilles de brick pastry

Take the feuilles de brick and cut into a circle. Dip in warm clarified butter to soak up the fat. Roll over a metal rod to make a narrow tube. Bake until golden. When warm, remove the rod and keep the tube.

Onion soubise

90 g egg yolk
110 g whipped cream
60 g milk

All goes into a bain marie on the stove – cook until it is scrambled dry. When dry, blitz with 60 g onion purée. Blitz until smooth.

To dress

Put the bavarois into a piping (pastry) bag with a small nozzle (tip). Pipe onto a tray horizontally. Blast freeze. When frozen, use a cutter to make a circle.

Take a round plate with a recessed centre (bowl-like). The centre needs to be a smaller circumference than the rest of the dish. Put into a blast chiller until the disc is frozen to the plate.

Warm the duck consommé. Remove the plate from the blast chiller. Pour gently until it covers the bavarois. Keep the plate still, otherwise it will set due to the coldness. Once it has set, place caviar on top.

Pipe dots of the onion soubise on the caviar, followed by dots of the dill mayo. On top of the onion soubise, put the tops of the dill leaves to garnish.

Fill the feuilles de brick tube with the sturgeon mousse and serve on the side.

1 whole wild turbot
a light vinaigrette (made from approximately 50% fish stock, 20% light wine vinegar, 10% lemon and 20% rapeseed/canola oil in a spray bottle – many of these elements are to taste)
fine salt

Burn down your charcoal to embers, making sure they are giving a gentle glowing and even heat.

Remove the gills from the turbot and season with salt, only inside the head. Place the turbot in a turbot cage designed to clamp a large fish, generously spritz with the vinaigrette, and place over the grill.

Keep turning every 8–10 minutes for 30–40 minutes, constantly basting with the spray. In order to develop the natural collagen in the fish into a delicious gelatinous sauce, the ideal temperature to maintain the fish at for the duration of cooking is 55°C.

Once the fish is cooked, cut out the spine of the fish, season with more salt, and place on a large white plate, adding more vinaigrette

Gently move the plate to release the gelatine from the fish – this will combine to make the "pil-pil" style sauce that you serve with the fish.

A

Acurio, Gastón, *500 Anos De Fusion* (El Comercio, 2008)

Adrià, Ferran, *elBulli 2005–2011* (Phaidon Press, 2014)

Adrià, Ferran, *A Day at elBulli* (Phaidon Press, 2012)

Aduriz, Andoni Luis, *Mugaritz* (Phaidon Press, 2012)

Ansel, Dominique, *Dominique Ansel: The Secret Recipes* (Simon & Schuster, 2014)

Alajmo, Massimiliano, *Ingredienti* (Turnaround, 2009)

Arregi, Aitor, and Cardenal, Juan Pablo, *Elkano: Paisaje culinario* (Planeta Gastro, 2016)

Arzark, Juan Mari, *Arzak: Recetas* (Bainet Editorial, 2012)

Atala, Alex, *Alex Atala: D.O.M* (Phaidon Press, 2013)

B

Bang, Esben Holmboe, *Maaemo* (Matthaes Verlag, 2018)

Banks, Tommy, *Roots: Recipes Celebrating Nature, Seasons and the Land* (Orion Publishing, 2018)

Barber, Daniel, *The Third Plate: Field Notes on the Future of Food* (Penguin, 2014)

Blanc, Raymond, *Le Manoir aux Quat'Saisons* (Bloomsbury, 2016)

Bloch, Barbara, *A Little New York Cookbook* (Appletree Press, 1993)

Bloomfield, April, *A Girl and Her Pig* (Ecco, 2012)

Blumenthal, Heston, *Historic Heston*, Bloomsbury (2013)

Blumenthal, Heston, *The Big Fat Duck Cookbook* (Bloomsbury, 2008)

Blumenthal, Heston, *The Fat Duck Cookbook* (Bloomsbury, 2009)

Bocuse, Paul, *The Complete Bocuse* (Flammarion, 2012)

Bocuse, Paul, *My Classic Cuisine* (Pyramid, 1989)

Bocuse, Paul, *Paul Bocuse's Regional French Cooking* (Flammarion, 1997)

Bocuse, Paul, *Cuisine de France* (Flammarion, 1990)

Bocuse, Paul, *Paul Bocuse: The Complete Recipes*, (Flammarion, 2012)

Bocuse, Paul, *Paul Bocuse's French Cooking* (Pantheon Books, 1977)

Bottura, Massimo, *Massimo Bottura: Never Trust a Skinny Italian Chef* (Phaidon Press, 2014)

Boulud, Daniel, *Daniel's Dish: Entertaining at Home With a Four-Star Chef* (Filipacchi, 2003)

Bras, Michel, *Essential cuisine Michel Bras: Laguiole, Aubrac, France* (Editions Rouergue, 2008)

Brazier, Eugénie, *La Mere Brazier: The Mother of Modern French Cooking* (Modern Books, 2015)

Brennan, Ella and Martin, Ti Adelaide, *Miss Ella of Commander's Palace* (Gibbs M. Smith, 2016)

C

Cámara, Gabriela and Watrous, Malena, *My Mexico City Kitchen: Recipes and Convictions* (Lorena Jones Books, 2019)

Cardenal, Juan Pablo, and Sarabia, Jon, *Etxebarri* (Grub Street, 2017)

Carême, Marie-Antoine, *Le Cuisinier Parisien* (Chapitre, 1828)

Carême, Marie-Antoine, *The Royal Parisian Pastrycook and Confectioner, From the Original of Carême*, edited by John Porter (F.J. Mason, 1834)

Carrier, Robert, *New Great Dishes of the World* (Boxtree, 1999)

Chang, David, *Momofuku* (Clarkson Potter, 2009)

Chapel, Alain, *La cuisine c'est beaucoup plus que des recettes* (Robert Laffont, 2009)

Charpentier, Henri, *Life à la Henri: Being the Memories of Henri Charpentier* (Simon and Schuster, 1934)

Chase, Leah, *The Dooky Chase Cookbook* (Pelican, 1990)

Chiang, Cecilia, *The Mandarin Way* (Little, Brown and Company, 1974)

Chiang, Cecilia, *The Seventh Daughter: My Culinary Journey from Beijing to San Francisco* (Ten Speed Press, 2007)

Choi, Roi, Nguyen, Tien and Phan, Natasha, *L.A. Son: My Life, My City, My Food* (Ecco, 2013)

Cipriani, Arrigo, *The Harry's Bar Cookbook* (Smith Gryphon, 1996)

Clifford, Michael, *Cooking with Clifford: New Irish Cooking* (Mercier Press, 1993)

Clifton, Denise E., *Tables from the Rubble: How the Restaurants That Arose After the Great Quake Still Feed San Francisco Today* (Tandemvines Publishing, 2017)

Coco: 10 World-Leading Masters Choose 100 Contemporary Chefs (Phaidon Press, 2010)

Cobb, Robert, *The Brown Derby Cookbook* (Original Hollywood Brown Derby, 2009)

Conran, Terrence, Harris, Matthew, and Hopkinson, Simon, *The Bibendum Cookbook* (Conran, 2008)

Corrigan, Richard, *The Clatter of Forks and Spoons: Honest, Happy Food* (Fourth Estate, 2008)

Crippa, Enrico, *Best of Enrico Crippa* (Giunti Editore, 2016)

D

David, Elizabeth, *French Provincial Cooking* (Penguin, 1960)

Diat, Louis, *Gourmet's Basic French Cookbook: Techniques of French Cuisine* (Gourmet/Hamish Hamilton, 1961)

Ducasse, Alain, *Grand Livre De Cuisine: Alain Ducasse's Desserts and Pastries* (Ducasse Books, 2006)

Dufresne, Wylie and Meehan, Peter, *wd~50: The Cookbook* (Anthony Bourdain/Ecco, 2017)

Dunlop, Fuchsia, *The Revolutionary Chinese Cookbook* (Ebury, 2006)

Dowding, Ian, *Secrets of the Hungry Monk* (Hungry Monk publications, 1971)

E

Escoffier, Auguste, *Ma Cuisine* (Paul Hamlyn, 1965)

Escoffier, Auguste, *The Escoffier Guide to Modern Cookery* (Heinemann, 1903)

F

Fidanza, Caroline, Dunn, Anna, Collerton, Rebecca, and Schula, Elizabeth, *Saltie: A Cookbook* (Chronicle Books, 2012)

Filippini, Alexander, *The Delmonico Cook Book* (Brentano's, 1893)

Fleming, Claudia, *The Last Course* (Random House, 2001)

Flores, Carlotta, *El Charro Cafe: The Tastes and Traditions of Tucson* (Fisher Books, 1998)

Fox, Jeremy, *On Vegetables: Modern Recipes for the Home Kitchen* (Phaidon Press, 2017)

G

Gagnaire, Pierre, *Pierre Gagnaire: Reinventing French Cuisine* (Stewart, Tabori & Chang, 2007)

Gagnaire, Pierre, *The Five Seasons Kitchen* (Grub Street, 2016)

Galvin, Gerry, *Drimcong Food Affair* (McDonald Publishing, 1992)

Gill, A. A., *The Ivy: The Restaurant and Its Recipes* (Hodder & Stoughton, 1997)

Gilmore, Peter, *Quay* (Murdoch Books, 2010)

Goodwin, Betty, *Hollywood du Jour: Lost Recipes of Legendary Hollywood Haunts* (Angel City Press, 1993)

Granger, Bill, *Bills Sydney Food* (Murdoch, 2011)

Gray, Rose and Rodgers, Ruth, *The River Cafe Cook Book* (Ebury Press, 1996)

Gutierrez, Sandra A., *Latin American Street Food: The Best Flavors of Markets, Beaches, and Roadside Stands from Mexico to Argentina* (The University of North Carolina Press, 2013)

H

Hamilton, Gabrielle, *Prune* (Random House, 2014)

Headley, Brooks, *Superiority Burger Cookbook: The Vegetarian Hamburger Is Now Delicious* (W. W. Norton & Company, 2018)

Hermé, Pierre, *Macarons: The Ultimate Recipes from the Master Pâtissier* (Stewart, Tabori & Chang, 2015)

Henderson, Fergus, *The Complete Nose to Tail* (Bloomsbury, 2012)

Hesser, Amanda, *The Essential New York Times Cookbook: Classic Recipes for a New Century* (W. W. Norton, 2010)

Hix, Mark, *Mark Hix: The Collection* (Quadrille, 2013)

Ho, Elizabeth, Liew, Cheong and John, Timothy, *My Food* (Allen & Unwin, 1996)

Howard, Philip, *The Square: Savoury: 1* (Absolute Press, 2012)

Humm, Daniel, *Nomad Cookbook* (Ten Speed Press, 2015)

I

i Fontané, Jordi Roca, *El Celler de Can Roca* (Grub Street, 2013)

K

Keller, Thomas, *The French Laundry Cookbook* (Workman Publishing, 1999)

Kennedy, Diana, *Cuisines of Mexico* (Harper & Row, 1973)

Khong, Rachel, *Lucky Peach: All About Eggs* (Clarkson Potter, 2017)

Kinch, David and Muhlke, Christine, *Manresa: An Edible Reflection* (Ten Speed Press, 2013)

Kitchin, Tom, *From Nature To Plate: Seasonal Recipes from The Kitchin* (W&N, 2009)

Klugmann, Antonia, *Di cuore e di coraggio* (Giunti Editore, 2018)

Koffmann, Pierre, *Classic Koffmann: 50 Years a Chef* (Jacqui Small, 2016)

Koslow, Jessica, *Everything I Want to Eat: Sqirl and the New California Cooking* (Abrams, 2016)

L

Ladner, Mark, *The Del Posto Cookbook* (Grand Central Life & Style, 2016)

Lee, Corey, *Benu* (Phaidon Press, 2015)

Lewis, Edna, Goodbody, Mary and Bailey, Mashama, *In Pursuit of Flavor* (University of Virginia Press, 2000)

Lutkins, Sheila and Rosso, Julee, *The New Basics Cookbook* (Workman, 1989)

M

Mackenzie, Nigel & Susan, *The Deeper Secrets of the Hungry Monk* (Hungry Monk Publications, 1988)

MacKenzie Hill, Janet, *Salads, Sandwiches and Chafing-Dish Dainties* (Little, Brown, 1899)

Marchesi, Gualtiero, *La cucina Italiana: Il grande ricettario* (De Agostini, 2017)

Masson, Charles, *Flowers of La Grenouille* (Crown, 1994)

Matsuhisa, Nobuyuki, *Nobu: the Cookbook* (Quadrille, 2001)

Maximin, Jacques, *The Cuisine of Jacques Maximin* (Severn House, 1986)

McDermott, Nancie, *Southern Soups & Stews: More Than 75 Recipes from Burgoo and Gumbo to Etouffée and Fricassee* (Chronicle Books, 2015)

McFadden, Joshua and Holmberg, Martha, *Six Seasons: A New Way with Vegetables* (Artisan, 2017)

N

Nilsson, Magnus, *Fäviken* (Phaidon Press, 2012)

O

Oliver, Raymond, *La Cuisine: Secrets of Modern French Cooking* (Tudor, 1969)

Olvera, Enrique, *Mexico from the Inside Out* (Phaidon Press, 2015)

Ono, Jiro, *Sushi: Jiro Gastronomy* (Viz LLC, 2016)

Ottolenghi, Yotam, *Plenty* (Ebury, 2010)

P

Passard, Alain, *The Art of Cooking with Vegetables* (Frances Lincoln, 2012)

Patterson, Daniel, *Coi: Stories and Recipes* (Phaidon Press, 2013)

Pic, Anne-Sophie, *Le livre blanc* (Jacqui Small, 2012)

Pic, Anne-Sophie, *Scook: The Complete Cookery Guide* (Jacqui Small, 2015)

Picard, Martin, *Au Pied de Cochon: The Album* (Douglas & McIntyre, 2008)

Pierangelini, Fulvio and Prandi, Raffaella, *Fulvio Pierangelini. Il grande solista della cucina italiana* (Gambero Rosso, 2005)

Point, Fernand, *Ma Gastronomie* (Overlook/Rookery, 2009)

Prudhomme, Paul, *Chef Paul Prudhomme's Louisiana Kitchen* (William Morrow, 1993)

Puck, Wolfgang, *The Wolfgang Puck Cookbook* (Random House, 1986)

Puglisi, Christian, *Relae: A Book of Ideas* (Ten Speed Press, 2014)

R

Ranhofer, Charles, *The Epicurean* (Charles Ranhofer, 1894)

Redzepi, René, *Noma: Time and Place in Nordic Cuisine* (Phaidon Press, 2010)

Ripert, Eric, *Avec Eric* (Houghton Mifflin Harcourt, 2010)

Robuchon Joël, *Tout Robuchon* (Perrin, 2010)

Robuchon, Joël, *The Complete Robuchon* (Grub Street, 2008)

Roca, Joan, *El Celler de Can Roca*, Grub Street (2016)

Rodgers, Judy, *The Zuni Cafe Cookbook* (W. W. Norton & Company, 2002)

Roellinger, Olivier, *Olivier Roellinger's Contemporary French Cuisine: 50 Recipes Inspired by the Sea* (Flammarion-Pere Castor, 2012)

Rogan, Simon, *Rogan* (Harper Collins, 2018)

Romito, Niko, *10 lezioni di cucina*, (Giunti, 2015)

Rosenzweig, Anne, *The Arcadia Seasonal Mural and Cookbook* (Harry N. Abrams, 1986)

S

Sailhac, Alain et al., *The French Culinary Institute's Salute to Healthy Cooking, From America's Foremost French Chefs* (Rodale, 1998)

Savoy, Guy, *Best of Guy Savoy* (Les Editions Culinaires, 2013)

Seal, Rebecca, *Cook: A Year in the Kitchen with Britain's Favourite Chefs* (Guardian Books, 2010)

Senderens, Alain, *The Cuisine of Alain Senderens* (Papermac, 1987)

Shewry, Ben, *Origin: The Food of Ben Shewry* (Murdoch Books, 2016)

The Silver Spoon (Phaidon Press, 2005)

Soyer, Alexis, *The Gastronomic Regenerator: A Simplified and Entirely New System of Cookery with Nearly Two Thousand Practical Receipts Suited to the Income of All Classes* (Simpkin, Marshall and Co., 1846)

Stein, Rick, *Rick Stein's Taste of the Sea: Over 160 Fabulous Fish Recipes* (BBC Books, 2002)

Stitt, Frank, *Frank Stitt's Bottega Favorita: A Southern Chef's Love Affair with Italian Food* (Artisan, 2008)

T

Tosi, Christina, *Momofuku Milk Bar* (Absolute Press, 2012)

Troisgros, Pierre, *Les petits plats des Troisgros* (Laffont, 1985)

Tschirky, Oscar, *The Cook Book by Oscar of the Waldorf* (Dover Publications, 1973)

V

Veyrat, Marc, *Fou de Saveurs* (Hachette, 1999)

W

Wakuda, Tetsuya, *Tetsuya* (HarperCollins, 2000)

Waters, Alice, *Chez Panisse Cafe Cookbook* (William Morrow, 1999)

Waters, Alice, *Chez Panisse Menu Cookbook* (Random House, 1982)

Y

Ying, Chris and Bowien, Danny, *The Mission Chinese Food Cookbook* (Ecco, 2015)

100-layer lasagne 218, 401

A
abalone: braised abalone 127, 317
  buddha jumps over the wall
    21, 261
Acurio, Gastón 80, 143, 189, 373
Andrés, José 199
Adrià, Albert 143, 185, 199, 385
Adrià, Ferran 38, 93, 99, 115, 143,
  150, 161, 173, 179, 185, 199, 200,
  201, 207, 249, 342, 361, 385
Aduriz, Andoni Luis 113, 179, 201,
  209, 217, 386, 393
Aizpitarte, Iñaki 93, 192, 224, 377
aka sea urchin in a lobster jelly with
  cauliflower, caviar, and crispy
  seaweed waffles 198, 383
Alajmo, Massimiliano 172, 249, 360
Alciatore, Jules 34, 267
almonds: Ispahan macaron 47,
  171, 359
  strawberry watermelon cake
    214, 397
  vegetable casserole in textures
    161, 168, 342
Amber 198, 383
Anaya, Ignacio 68, 280
anchoas a la brasa 179, 365
Anchor Bar 87, 235, 289
Andrés, José 99, 185
Anna potatoes 29, 265
Ansel, Dominique 237, 422
Antoine's 34, 267
ants: ants and pineapple 238, 426
apples: carrot tartare 234, 418
  confit tomato with twelve
    flavors 134, 322
  fried black pudding with oysters,
    apple, and onion in mustard
    sauce 148, 333
  tarte Tatin 44, 271
  Waldorf salad 39, 269
Arcadia 132, 321
Argentina 57, 276
Arguinzoniz, Victor 179, 365
Arregi, Pedro 89, 289
artichokes: artichoke soup with
  black truffle 114, 306
Arzak, Juan Mari 99, 150, 295
Aslam, Ali Ahmed 96, 294
*assoluto di cipolle, parmigiano e
  zafferano tostato* 220, 405

Astrid & Gastón 189, 373
Atala, Alex 238, 426
Attica 215, 398
Au Pied de Cochon 70, 186, 281, 371
Australia 145, 153, 155, 157, 158, 166,
  182, 214, 215, 227
avocados: avocado toast 158, 340
  California roll 79, 286
  chimichanga 73, 282

B
baba au rhum 137, 324
bacon: cassoulet 176, 363
  club sandwich 41, 270
  Cobb salad 65, 279
  devils on horseback 193, 378
  lobster club sandwich 132, 321
Bailey, Mashama 243, 430
baked Alaska 31, 266
Baker, Harry 58, 276
bamboo shoots: Buddha jumps
  over the wall 21, 261
  tsukemen 81, 286
bananas: bananas foster 77, 285
  banoffi pie 101
Bang, Esben Holmboe 230, 414
Bangkok 116
Banks, Tommy 239, 426
banoffi pie 97, 101
barbecue: whole hog barbecue
  251, 436
Bar Néstor 115, 307
Barber, Dan 54, 109, 202, 248, 433
Barcelona 125, 143, 199
Brazier, Eugénie 53, 274
basil: Caprese salad 55, 275
beans: cassoulet 176, 363
  vegetable pulp burger 248, 433
Beard, James 39, 82, 151
beef: beef carpaccio 133
  Big Mac 90, 290
  carpaccio 72, 282
  DB burger 184, 369
  French dip sandwich 51, 273
  green gumbo 75, 283
  husband and wife lung slices
    63, 278
  Kobe beef cutlet sandwich
    250, 436
  loco moco 71, 281
  pastrami sandwich 33, 267
  Philly cheesesteak 62, 278
  prime rib 66, 280
  shepherd's pie 152, 208, 336
  short rib taco 210, 394
  tartare of beef with watercress
    and rye bread 224, 407
  tournedos rossini 26, 264
beef heart 219, 404
beets (beetroot): beet rose, yogurt,
  and rose petal ice 228, 409
  crapaudine beetroot cooked
    slowly in beef fat with smoked
    cod's roe and linseeds 239, 426
  into the vegetable garden 212, 395
  beggar's purses 121, 311
Bellissimo, Teressa 87, 289
Bennett, Arnold 59
Bentley's 154, 337
Benu 222, 406
bergamot: Eternity by Calvin Klein
  188, 372
Bianyifang 23, 263
Bibendum 129, 253, 317
Big Mac 90, 290
Bills 158, 227, 340

biscuits: chocolate coulant 118, 309
Black Forest cake 49, 273
black pudding: fried black pudding
  with oysters, apple, and onion in
  mustard sauce 148, 333
  gâteau of Clonakilty black
    pudding 146, 329
Black Star Pastry 214, 397
The Black Swan 239
bladders: cacio e pepe in a
  bladder 244, 246, 430
  chicken in a bladder 61, 278
Blanc, Raymond 98, 130, 244, 318
le blanc du lait et le noir de la truffe
  181
Bloomfield, April 107, 142, 152, 193,
  378
Blue Hill 248, 433
Blumenthal, Heston 94, 185, 190,
  191, 208, 223, 229, 370, 375,
  412
Bocuse, Paul 29, 52, 53, 61, 76, 91, 93,
  94, 95, 99, 103, 120, 123, 125, 148,
  293, 297
bone marrow: bone marrow with
  parsley salad and toast 160
  roast bone marrow and parsley
    salad 163, 346
Bosi, Claude 253, 437
Bottura, Massimo 124, 165, 236,
  348, 421
bouchée à la reine 20
*bouillon de champignons comme
  un cappuccino* 93, 292
Boulud, Daniel 26, 29, 90, 95, 184,
  247, 369
Bourdain, Anthony 88, 186, 251
Bourdin, Michel 104, 297
Bourgeois, Marie 52, 274
Bowien, Danny 28, 193, 235, 420
Bras, Michel 113, 118, 131, 140, 146,
  161, 200, 207, 212, 217, 223, 232,
  303, 309
Brasserie Chaya 131, 133, 320
Brat 254, 439
Brazil 238, 426
bread: avocado toast 158, 340
  Caesar salad 56, 275
  club sandwich 41, 270
  French dip sandwich 51, 273
  French onion soup 70, 281
  Kobe beef cutlet sandwich 250,
    436
  lobster roll 60, 277
  pastrami sandwich 33, 267
  Philly cheesesteak 62, 278
  sea urchin toast 225, 408
  smoked eel sandwich 231, 415
  tuna tartare 131, 320
  Zuni roast chicken with bread
    salad 138, 324
Brennan, Ella 77, 110, 285
Brennan's 77, 285
broths: *tsukemen* 81, 286
  wild boar cappelletti with plum
    broth 249, 435
  see also consommés; soups
The Brown Derby 58, 65, 276, 279
buddha jumps over the wall 21, 261
Buffalo wings 87, 235, 289
buns, pork 136, 197, 211, 381
burgers: Big Mac 90, 290
  DB burger 26, 90, 184, 369
  loco moco 71, 281
  superiority burger 245, 431
  vegetable pulp burger 248, 433

C
cabbage: green gumbo 75, 283
  John Dory back from India 126,
    315
  Nagasaki champon 46, 272
cacio e pepe in a bladder 244,
  246, 430
cacio e pepe in vescica 244, 246,
  430
Caesar salad 56, 68, 275
Caesar's Place 56, 275
Café Ahrend 49, 273
Café Anglais 29, 265
Café de Paris 43, 83, 270
cakes: Black Forest cake 49, 273
  chiffon cake 58, 276
  chocolate coulant 118
  coconut pecan cake 147, 332
  strawberry watermelon cake
    214, 397
calamari ai ferri con peperoncini
  142, 328
California roll 79, 286
Camanini, Riccardo 244, 246, 430
Cámara, Gabriela 175, 362
Campeol, Alba 86, 288
Canada 84, 186, 288, 371
canard à la presse 38, 269
Caprese salad 55, 275
caramel: chocolate coulant 118, 309
Cardini, Caesar 56, 275
Carême, Marie-Antoine 20, 22, 26,
  29, 259–61, 262
carpaccio 72, 282
  beef carpaccio 133
  pig's trotter carpaccio 150, 334
carpaccio de manitas de cerdo
  150, 334
carrots: carrot and celery root
  ravioli 174, 361
  carrot tartare 234, 418
  Irish stew 154, 337
casseroles/cassoulets *see* stews &
  casseroles
cauliflower: aka sea urchin in a
  lobster jelly with cauliflower,
  caviar, and crispy seaweed
  waffles 198, 383
  cauliflower in a cast-iron pot
    205, 389
  caviar jelly with cauliflower cream
    117, 253, 307
  whole roasted cauliflower 202,
    239, 387
caviar: aka sea urchin in a lobster
  jelly with cauliflower, caviar, and
  crispy seaweed waffles 198, 383
  beggar's purses 121, 311
  caviar jelly with cauliflower cream
    117, 253, 307
  cyber egg 170, 358
  loup au caviar 98, 295
  pizza with smoked salmon and
    caviar 123, 313
celery root (celeriac): carrot and
  celery root ravioli 174, 361
Central 219, 404
cereal milk panna cotta with
  caramelized cornflakes 211, 394
ceviche 80, 286
Cevicheria Pedro Solari 80, 286
The Chairman 216, 399
Champagne: Cronut® 237, 422
  lasagne of crab with a cappuccino
    of shellfish and a champagne
    foam 167, 353

loup au caviar 98, 295
Chang, David 81, 112, 136, 153, 162, 169, 197, 211, 215, 381
Chantecler 109, 300
Chapel, Alain 61, 91, 93, 94, 149, 181, 292
Charpentier, Henri 43, 270
Chase, Leah 75, 283
chaud-froid d'oeuf avec sirop d'érable et vinaigre d'xérès 169
cheese: baked goat cheese with garden lettuces 111, 302
  Big Mac 90, 290
  cacio e pepe in a bladder 244, 246, 430
  Caesar salad 56, 275
  Caprese salad 55, 275
  chimichanga 73, 282
  Eccles cake and Lancashire cheese 34, 160, 342
  fettuccine Alfredo 48, 272
  French onion soup 70, 281
  grilled salad smoked over embers, Isle of Mull cheese, truffle custard, and cobnuts 232, 416
  Hawaiian pizza 84, 288
  nachos 68, 280
  onion reduction with Parmesan buttons and toasted saffron 220, 405
  Philly cheesesteak 62, 277
  pizza Margherita 35, 267
  veal Prince Orloff 104, 297
cheese curds: foie gras poutine 186, 193, 371
Chez Fonfon and Bottega Café 147, 332
Chen, Mrs. 28, 265
Chen Chunfu 28
Chen Xingsheng 28, 265
chequerboard of star anise ice cream, pineapple sorbet, and liquorice 145, 329
cherries: Black Forest cake 49, 273
Chez Panisse 111, 302
Chiang, Cecilia 82, 287
chicken: buddha jumps over the wall 21, 261
  Buffalo wings 87, 235
  chicken in a bladder 61, 278
  chicken country captain 243, 430
  chicken in half mourning 53, 274
  chicken Manchurian 105, 298
  chicken tikka masala 96, 294
  Chongqing chicken wings 235, 420
  club sandwich 41, 270
  Cobb salad 65, 279
  General Tso's chicken 78, 79, 96, 285
  Hainanese chicken and rice 139, 326
  hot chicken 64, 279
  large fried chicken 156, 338
  Nagasaki champon 46, 272
  piri-piri chicken 74, 283
  samgyetang 128, 317
  smoked chicken 194, 379
  snail porridge 191, 375
  stew of cockscombs and chicken kidneys 94, 292
  whole roast black leg chicken 203, 388
  yellow earth chicken 196, 380
  Zuni roast chicken with bread salad 138, 324

chickpeas: chickpea purée with red shrimp 112, 302
  Superiority burger 245, 431
chiffon cake 58, 276
chilies: General Tso's chicken 78, 285
  grilled squid with chile 142, 328
  mother mole 240, 428
  snapper a la Talla 175, 362
chimichanga 73, 282
chimichangas el charro 73, 282
China 21, 23, 28, 63, 261, 263, 265, 278
Chock, Helen 69, 281
chocolate: Black Forest cake 49, 273
  chocolate caramel tart 164, 347
  chocolate coulant 118, 309
  chocolate nemesis 146, 332
  chocolate truffles 195, 380
  Cronut® 237, 422
  Ispahan macaron 47, 171, 359
Choi, Roy 66, 210, 394
Chongqing chicken wings 235, 420
chrysanthemum tofu soup with fish balls and matsutake mushrooms 206, 390
Chui Fook Chuen 102, 297
Chui Wai-Kwan 241, 429
Cipriani, Giuseppe 72, 282
Claude Bosi at Bibendum 253, 437
Claude's 157, 339
Clifford, Michael 144, 329
Clifford's 144, 329
club sandwich 41, 270
  lobster club sandwich 132, 318
Cobb, Robert 65, 279
Cobb salad 58, 65, 279
coconut: coconut pecan cake 147, 332
cocotte de legumes des jardines le Provence mijotée à la truffe noire ecrasée 140, 327
coda alla vaccinara 37, 268
coffee: banoffi pie 101
  chocolate coulant 118, 309
  tiramisu 86, 288
Coi 228, 409
Collinet, Jean-Louis-François 25, 264
Combal 170, 358
Compère Lapin 247
Compton, Nina 247
The Connaught 104, 297
Connaughton, Kyle 113, 169, 212
consommés: shellfish rockpool 217, 400
  smoked salmon consommé 157, 339
Contramar 175, 362
Copenhagen 224, 235
cornets 159, 162, 340
Corrigan, Richard 154, 337
cotelettes de mouton à la Reform 24, 263
coulant au chocolat 118, 309
Coulson, Francis 97, 294
courgette à la fleur et aux truffles 109, 300
cream: Black Forest cake 49, 273
  cereal milk panna cotta with caramelized cornflakes 211, 394
  chocolate coulant 118, 309
  crème brûlée 125, 314
  Eternity by Calvin Klein 188, 372
  Key lime pie 92, 291
  rum baba 137, 324

crème brûlée 125, 314
crème Vichyssoise glacée 50, 273
crepes: beggar's purses 121, 311
  crepes Suzette 43, 270
The Cricket Club of India 105, 298
Crippa, Enrico 172, 200, 207, 386, 391, 432
Cronut® 237, 422
the crunchy part of the lasagne 165, 348
cucina povera 35
cucumbers: quick pickled 136, 197, 211, 381
currants: Eccles cake 34, 160, 342
  spotted dick 36, 268
curry: chicken country captain 243, 430
  chicken tikka masala 96, 294
  curried baby goat with sweet potato gnocchi 247
Cutò, Procopio 18, 258
cuy Pekinés 189, 373
cyber egg 170, 358

D
la dame et son chevalier 165, 348
David, Elizabeth 53, 266
DB Bistro Moderne 184, 369
DB burger 26, 90, 184, 369
Del Posto 218, 401
Delair, Frédéric 38, 269
Delligatti, Jim 90, 290
Delmonico's 31, 42, 266
Denmark 213, 223, 224, 407, 399
deviled eggs 178, 365
devils on horseback 193, 378
di Lelio, Alfredo 48, 272
Diat, Louis 50, 273
Din Tai Fung 100, 296
Diner 176, 363
Dinner by Heston Blumenthal 208, 229, 412
D.O.M. 238, 426
Dominique Ansel Bakery 237, 422
Dooky Chase's 75, 283
Dowding, Ian 101, 296
Drimcong House 148, 333
Dubai 195, 203
Dublin 148
Ducasse, Alain 44, 93, 94, 109, 118, 137, 140, 149, 192, 217, 246, 253, 324, 327
duck: buddha jumps over the wall 21, 261
  cassoulet 176, 363
  duck jelly 253, 437
  Peking duck 23, 263
  pressed duck 38, 269
  snail porridge 191, 375
  tea-smoked duck 82, 287
Dufresne, Wylie 113, 190, 211, 374
Dugléré, Adolphe 29, 265
dumplings, soup 100, 296
Duntoye, Raphael 203, 388
Durand, Louis 47, 272

E
Eccles cake and Lancashire cheese 34, 160, 342
edible stones 201, 386
eels: smoked eel sandwich 231, 415
Efendi, Iskender 30, 265
eggplant (aubergine): eggplant with buttermilk sauce 187, 239, 372
  four dances of the sea 166, 350

eggs: baked Alaska 31, 266
  chocolate nemesis 146, 332
  Cobb salad 65, 279
  crab omelet 116, 307
  crème brûlée 125, 314
  crêpes Suzette 43, 270
  cyber egg 170, 358
  deviled eggs 178, 365
  eggs Benedict 39, 42, 270
  Grand Marnier souffle 83, 287
  Ispahan macaron 47, 171, 359
  L'Arpège egg 169, 358
  omelet 32, 266
  omelet Arnold Bennett 59, 277
  oops! I dropped the lemon tart 236, 421
  oysters and pearls 162, 345
  pistachio ice cream 108, 298
  pistachio soufflé 108, 298
  rum baba 137, 324
  Russian salad 27, 264
  sorrel pesto rice bowl 227, 409
  Spanish omelet 115, 307
  spotted dick 36, 268
  strawberry watermelon cake 214, 397
  tartare of beef with watercress and rye bread 224, 407
  thousand-year-old quail egg, potage, ginger 222, 406
  tiramisu 86, 288
  tsukemen 81, 286
Ekkebus, Richard 198, 383
El Celler de Can Roca 150, 188, 334, 372
El Charro Café 73, 282
elBulli 38, 93, 115, 150, 161, 168, 173, 199, 200, 342, 361, 385
Eleven Madison Park 213, 229, 234, 418
Elkano 89, 179, 254, 289
escalope de saumon à l'oseille 85, 288
Escoffier, Auguste 8, 12, 20, 31, 39, 40, 43, 61, 85, 94, 104, 107, 119
Esposito, Raffaele 35, 267
espuma de humo 173, 361
Eternity by Calvin Klein 188, 372
Etxebarri 179, 365

F
Fairlie, Andrew 183, 368
Faroe Islands 213
The Fat Duck 185, 190, 191, 223, 370, 375
Fäviken Magasinet 213, 221, 226, 405, 409
fennel: confit of Petuna ocean trout with fennel salad 155, 337
Fidanza, Caroline 176, 363
fish: black cod with miso 136, 323
  blackened redfish 110, 301
  Caesar salad 56, 275
  canned sardines with Triscuits, Dijon mustard, and cornichons 177, 364
  ceviche 80, 286
  confit of Petuna ocean trout with fennel salad 155, 337
  cornets 159, 162, 340
  chrysanthemum tofu soup with fish balls and matsutake mushrooms 206, 390
  four dances of the sea 166, 350
  grilled anchovies 179, 365
  grilled turbot 89, 179, 254, 289

loup au caviar 98, 295
omelet Arnold Bennett 59, 277
pizza with smoked salmon and caviar 123, 313
red mullet with potato scales 95, 293
roast tronçon of turbot with hollandaise sauce 107, 299
salmon escalope with sorrel 85, 288
salmon rillettes 135, 323
smoked salmon consommé 157, 339
snapper a la Talla 175, 362
tuna nigiri and maccheroncini 200, 386
tuna tartare 131, 320
tuna, shaved chives, and extra-virgin olive oil 133, 322
whole turbot 254, 439
yellowtail sashimi with jalapeño 180, 366
Fleming, Claudia 164, 347
Flin, Monica 73, 282
foie gras: black truffle soup Elysée 103, 297
chicken in a bladder 61, 278
duck foie gras charcoal grilled with sea urchin caviar and a spicy touch 209, 393
foie gras and miso soup 192, 377
foie gras poutine 186, 193, 371
gourmet salad 91, 290
hot pâté 52, 274
meat fruit 208, 229, 412
salt-baked squab pigeons 130, 318
tournedos rossini 26, 264
whole roast black leg chicken 203, 388
Fook Lam Moon 102, 241, 297
The Forum 127, 317
four dances of the sea 157, 166, 350
Fox, Jeremy 205, 212, 223, 389
France 18, 20, 22, 25, 26, 29, 31, 32, 38, 44, 47, 52, 53, 61, 70, 76, 85, 91, 93, 94, 95, 98, 103, 109, 113, 113, 114, 117, 118, 119, 122, 126, 134, 134, 149, 168, 169, 171, 174, 186, 192, 195
Franklin, Calum 252, 437
Franny's 56, 204, 388
French dip sandwich 51, 273
The French Laundry 159, 162, 340, 345
French onion soup 70, 281
fuqi feipian 63, 278

G
Gage & Tollner 151, 335
Gagnaire, Pierre 94, 126, 168, 198, 356
Galvin, Gerry 144, 148, 333
Gambero Rosso 112, 302
gargouillou 113, 140, 161, 212, 217, 223, 303
gâteau de Clonakilty black pudding 146, 329
gateau de mille feuilles à la ancienne 22, 262
gelato 18, 258
gelée de caviar à la crème de chou-fleur 117, 253, 307–6
General Tso's Chicken 78, 79, 96, 285
Germany 30, 49, 273
Gilmore, Peter 145, 182, 366
Ginza Kyubey 67, 280

goat: curried baby goat with sweet potato gnocchi 247
goat's curd: crapaudine beetroot cooked slowly in beef fat with smoked cod's roe and linseeds 239, 426
a simple dish of potato cooked in the earth in which it was grown 215, 398
Gold, Jonathan 210
gold leaf: rice, gold, and saffron 120, 124, 172, 200, 312
Golden Century 153, 336
gourmet salad 91, 290
Gramercy Tavern 164, 347
Grand Hotel Quisisana 55, 275
Grand Marnier soufflé 83, 287
The Grange 166, 350
Granger, Bill 69, 158, 227, 340
grapes: panfried quail with country ham 151, 335
Gray, Rose 142, 146, 328, 332
green goddess dressing 54, 275
green gumbo 75, 282
greens: lobster club sandwich 132, 321
salad 21...31...41...51... 207, 391
The Grey 243, 430
grouse: red grouse 19, 258
Guérard, Michel 72, 91, 93, 94, 103, 122, 148, 174, 181, 183, 290
guinea pig: Peking guinea pig 189, 373
gumbo z'herbes 75, 282
gunkan sushi 67, 280
gunkanmaki 67, 280
Guo Zhaohua 63, 278
Guy Savoy 114, 217, 306
gyukatsu sando 250, 436

H
Hainanese chicken and rice 139, 326
ham: eggs Benedict 39, 42, 270
green gumbo 75, 282
Hawaiian pizza 84, 288
lamb cutlets Reform 24, 263
panfried quail with country ham 151, 335
Hamada, Hisato 250, 436
Hamilton, Gabrielle 177, 178, 364, 365
hare: royal hare 76, 284
Harry's Bar 72, 282
Hawaii 69, 71, 281
Hawaiian pizza 84, 288
Headley, Brooks 245, 431
heart: beef heart 219, 404
rømmegrøt with cured reindeer heart and plum vinegar 230, 414
Heijun, Chin 46, 272
Helena's Hawaiian Food 69, 281
Henderson, Fergus 34, 106, 107, 160, 163, 342, 346
Hermé, Pierre 47, 164, 171, 359
The Hermitage 27, 264
Hix, Mark 24, 152, 208, 336, 392
Holborn Dining Room 252, 437
hollandaise sauce: eggs Benedict 39, 42, 270
omelet Arnold Bennett 59, 277
roast tronçon of turbot with hollandaise sauce 107, 299
homard à la vanilla 122, 312
Hong Kong 102, 127, 153, 170, 194, 196, 198, 203, 216, 233, 241, 253
Hopkinson, Simon 97, 129, 167, 317
Hôtel Bourgeois 52, 274

Hôtel Tatin 44, 271
Howard, Phil 167, 353
Humm, Daniel 61, 103, 185, 213, 229, 234, 239, 248, 418
Hunan 78, 96
Hung, Uncle 153, 336
The Hungry Monk 101, 296
husband and wife lung slices 63, 278

I
ice cream: 18
baked Alaska 31, 266
chequerboard of star anise ice cream, pineapple sorbet, and liquorice 145, 329
pistachio ice cream 108, 298
Imada, Hisaji 67, 280
India 105, 298
Inouye, Richard and Nancy 71, 281
into the vegetable garden 212, 395
Ireland 144, 148, 329, 333
Irish stew 154, 337
Iskender kebab 30, 265
Ispahan macaron 47, 171, 359
Israel 202, 387
Italy 35, 37, 48, 55, 72, 86, 112, 120, 124, 165, 170, 172, 200, 207, 220, 236, 244, 246, 249
The Ivy 152, 208, 336

J
Jade Dragon 233, 417
jalapeño peppers: nachos 68, 280
sorrel pesto rice bowl 227, 409
Jamin 117, 119, 253, 307, 311
Japan 45, 46, 67, 81, 88, 250
Jean-Charles Rochoux 195, 380
jelly: aka sea urchin in a lobster jelly with cauliflower, caviar, and crispy seaweed waffles 198, 383
duck jelly 253, 437
Joe's Stone Crab 92, 291
John Dory back from India 126, 315
Ju Chun Yuan 21, 261
Jung, Susan 10, 12, 20, 21, 23, 32, 44, 45, 47, 60, 62, 66, 76, 77, 87, 88, 89, 98, 100, 113, 116, 119, 127, 128, 138, 141, 162, 163, 171, 186, 188, 191, 194, 195, 196, 198, 206, 216, 233, 237, 241, 242, 250, 252
Junsuta, Supinya 116

K
K-Paul's Louisiana Kitchen 110, 301
Kahn, Howie 10, 13, 43, 52, 53, 69, 75, 82, 83, 99, 100, 102, 113, 119, 123, 135, 138, 139, 140, 142, 147, 162, 163, 169, 171, 175, 176, 177, 179, 180, 185, 190, 192, 193, 197, 209, 210, 211, 219, 221, 222, 226, 227, 234, 238, 240, 243, 248, 251
kale: kale salad 204, 388
Katz's Delicatessen 33, 267
Kaye, Adam 248, 433
kebab, Iskender 30, 265
Keller, Josef 49, 273
Keller, Thomas 66, 93, 119, 159, 162, 198, 222, 340, 345
Key lime pie 92, 291
khai jeaw poo 116, 307
Kida, Motojiro 45, 271
Kim Sung-Il 242, 429
Kinch, David 94, 113, 121, 169, 212, 217, 223, 404
Kin's Kitchen 194, 379
The Kitchin 217, 400

Kitchin, Tom 217, 400
Klugmann, Antonia 172, 249, 435
kobe beef cutlet sandwich 250, 436
Koffmann, Pierre 106, 108, 152, 203, 217, 298, 299
Kogi BBQ 210, 394
Koslow, Jessica 227, 409
Kwok Keung Tung 216, 399
Kwong Bing-Kwan 194, 379

L
La Bastide des Gordes 149, 334
La Famille 192, 377
La Grenouille 83, 288
La Maison Troisgros 85, 181, 288, 366
La Mère Brazier 53, 98, 103, 274
La Mère Poulard 32, 266
La Petite Maison 203, 388
La Pyramide 61, 103, 278
La Tante Claire 106, 108, 203, 217, 298, 299
La Tour d'Argent 38, 269
La Yeon 242, 429
Ladner, Mark 218, 401
Ladurée 171, 359
lamb: Irish stew 154, 337
Iskender kebab 30, 265
lamb cutlets Reform 24, 263
shepherd's pie 152, 208, 336
L'Archestrate 122, 134, 312
L'Argine a Vencò 249, 435
L'Arpège 113, 134, 169, 253, 322–20, 358
L'Arpège egg 169, 358
lasagne: 100-layer lasagne 218, 401
lasagne of crab with a cappuccino of shellfish and a champagne foam 167, 353
Lau Kin-Wai 194, 379
L'Auberge de L'Éridan 174, 361
L'Auberge du Pont de Collonges 95, 103, 293, 297
Lawry's 66, 280
Le Beccherie 86, 288
Le Bernardin 133, 135, 322, 323
Le Calandre 172, 360
Le Cirque 125, 314
Le Coze, Gilbert 72, 133, 135, 322, 323
Le Grand Véfour 76, 284
Le Louis XV 137, 140, 149, 217, 324, 327
Le Manoir aux Quat'Saisons 130, 244, 318
Le Pavillon Henri IV 25, 264
Le Pot-au-Feu 91, 290
Le Procope 18, 258
Lee, Corey 82, 102, 198, 222, 406
Lee, Jeremy 231, 415
Leloir, Luis Federico 57, 276
lemons: Cronut® 237, 422
oops! I dropped the lemon tart 236, 421
L'Enclume 232, 416
Les Maisons de Bricourt 126, 315
lettuce: baked goat cheese with garden lettuces 111, 302
Caesar salad 56, 275
chimichanga 73, 282
club sandwich 41, 270
Cobb salad 65, 279
green gumbo 75, 283
Lewis, Edna 151, 335
Lian, Foo Kui 139, 326
Lido 84 244, 246, 430

Liew, Cheong 157, 166, 350
Lima 143, 189, 219
limes: Key lime pie 92, 291
  nitro-poached green tea and
  lime mousse 185, 370
Lincoln Grill 71, 281
Linguanotto, Roberto 86, 288
liquorice: chequerboard of star
  anise ice cream, pineapple
  sorbet, and liquorice 145, 329
loco moco 71, 281
London 19, 34, 37, 38, 42, 59, 104,
  106, 107, 108, 129, 140, 142, 146,
  152, 154, 158, 160, 163, 187, 203,
  208, 229, 231, 252, 253, 254
loup au caviar 98, 295
lychees: Ispahan macaron 47,
  171, 359

M
ma po dou fu 28, 265
Maaemo 230, 414
macarons, Ispahan 47, 171, 359
McDonald's 90, 105, 184, 290
McFadden, Joshua 56, 204, 388
Mackenzie, Nigel 101, 296
Maison Dorée 26, 264
Maison Pic 98, 295
The Mandarin 82, 287
mandarins: meat fruit 208, 229, 412
Manfreds 224, 407
Manresa 212, 223, 395
mapo tofu 28, 265
Mar del Plata Golf Club 57, 276
Marchesi, Gualtiero 120, 124, 172,
  200, 207, 244, 312, 314
Martínez, Virgilio 219, 404
Mashita, Ichiro 79, 286
Masson, Charles 83, 287
Mathieu, Philippe 51, 273
Matsuhisa, Nobu 79, 131, 136, 141,
  180, 328, 366
Maximin, Jacques 109, 149, 300
Maxim's 31
mayonnaise: green goddess
  dressing 54, 275
meat fruit 208, 229, 412
meat pie 252, 437
menestra de veduras en texturas
  161, 168, 342
meringues: baked Alaska 31, 266
Mexico 56, 68, 175, 240, 275, 280,
  355, 418
mignon de veau Prince Orloff 104,
  297
Milan 35, 120, 124
Miles, Dolester 147, 332
milk: white milk and black truffle
  181, 366
mille-feuille 22, 262
miso: foie gras and miso soup
  192, 377
Mission Chinese Food 28, 235, 420
Moisson, Casimir 26, 264
mole madre 240, 428
Momofuku Ko 211, 394
Momofuku Noodle Bar 197, 381
Monaco 43, 109, 137, 140, 149, 217,
  271, 324, 327
Monte Carlo 43, 140, 149
morels: stew of cockscombs and
  chicken kidneys 94, 292
  stuffed pig's trotters with morels
  106, 108, 298
mother mole 240, 428
mousse, nitro-poached green tea
  and lime 185, 370

Mugaritz 201, 209, 386, 393
Muhlke, Christine 10, 14, 18, 22, 25,
  26, 31, 33, 38, 42, 43, 48, 49, 55,
  61, 64, 66, 70, 76, 77, 78, 85, 91,
  93, 95, 97, 98, 103, 106, 111, 115,
  117, 118, 119, 120, 121, 122, 123,
  125, 132, 133, 136, 138, 140, 142,
  146, 151, 155, 158, 159, 163, 164,
  169, 171, 178, 184, 185, 186, 187,
  197, 204, 205, 211, 212, 223, 224,
  227, 234, 235, 236, 240, 245,
  247, 251
mushrooms: chrysanthemum
  tofu soup with fish balls and
  matsutake mushrooms 206,
  390
  gâteau of Clonakilty black
  pudding 146, 329
  loco moco 71, 281
  mushroom cappuccino 93, 292
  pig's trotter carpaccio 150, 334
  royal hare 76, 284
  veal Prince Orloff 104, 297
Myint, Anthony 28, 235

N
nachos 68, 280
Nagasaki champon 46, 272
Néstor 115, 307
New Basque Cuisine 99
New Nordic Cuisine 223, 230
new-style sashimi 79, 131, 141, 328
New York City 29, 31, 33, 35, 38, 39,
  41, 43, 47, 51, 60, 61, 64, 66, 72,
  78, 86, 95, 96, 117, 121, 122, 125,
  132, 133, 135, 146, 155, 158, 159,
  164, 177, 178, 180, 184, 190, 193,
  197, 202, 211, 213, 218, 224, 229,
  234, 237, 245, 247, 248
nigiri di tonno e maccheroncini
  200, 386
Nilsson, Magnus 169, 215, 221, 226,
  405, 409
nitro-poached green tea and lime
  mousse 185, 370
Noma 213, 215, 223, 228, 407, 399
noodles: four dances of the sea
  166, 350
  Nagasaki champon 46, 272
  shrimp noodles 190, 374
  steamed flowery crab with
  Shaoxing rice wine and chicken
  fat 216, 399
  tsukemen 81, 286
North Abraxas 202, 387
Norway 41, 230, 414
Nourse, Pat 12, 20, 21, 24, 27, 28, 29,
  30, 34, 35, 37, 38, 40, 44, 46, 47,
  49, 50, 51, 54, 56, 57, 58, 59, 63,
  64, 65, 67, 68, 71, 72, 74, 76, 81,
  84, 101, 103, 105, 106, 110, 113,
  118, 134, 138, 140, 141, 145, 153,
  155, 156, 157, 163, 166, 169, 177,
  178, 180, 182, 197, 213, 214, 215
nouvelle cuisine 85, 91, 94, 95

O
Oasis Seros 145, 329
oats: snail porridge 191, 375
octopus: four dances of the sea
  166, 350
  octopus in olive sauce 143, 329
  shellfish rockpool 217, 400
offal: buddha jumps over the wall
  21, 261
  husband and wife lung slices
  63, 278

Oliver, Raymond 76, 284
olives: octopus in olive sauce
  143, 329
  spherical-I green olives 199, 385
Olivier, Lucien 27, 264
Olivieri, Pat 62, 278
Olvera, Enrique 238, 240, 248, 428
omelets: 32, 266
  crab omelet 116, 307
  omelet Arnold Bennett 59, 277
  Spanish omelet 115, 307
onions: French onion soup 70, 281
  onion reduction with Parmesan
  buttons and toasted saffron
  220, 405
  smoked eel sandwich 231, 415
Ono, Jiro 88, 289
oops! I dropped the lemon tart
  236, 421
Oslo 230
Osteria Francescana 165, 236, 348,
  421
Ottolenghi, Yotam 187, 239, 372
oxtail: oxtail stew 37, 268

P
Pak Poy, Tim 157, 339
Palace Hotel 54, 275
panna cotta, cereal milk with
  caramelized cornflakes 211, 394
Panopoulos, Sam 84, 288
Paris 18, 25, 26, 29, 36, 37, 42, 44, 47,
  61, 70, 76, 91, 114, 117, 124, 134,
  140, 149, 164, 171, 183, 187, 192,
  195, 202, 203, 217, 224, 229, 235,
  250, 253
Paris-Brest 47, 272
Parry, Tomos 254, 439
Passard, Alain 109, 113, 122, 126, 134,
  169, 198, 202, 253, 322, 358
passatina di ceci e gamberi rossi
  112, 302
pasta: 100-layer lasagne 218, 401
  cacio e pepe in a bladder 244,
  246, 430
  the crunchy part of the lasagne
  165, 348
  fettuccine Alfredo 48, 272
  lasagne of crab with a cappuccino
  of shellfish and a champagne
  foam 167, 353
  onion reduction with Parmesan
  buttons and toasted saffron
  220, 396
  open raviolo 124, 200, 314
  spaghettoni with butter and dried
  yeast 432
  tuna nigiri and maccheroncini
  200, 386
  wild boar cappelletti with plum
  broth 249, 435
pastel de kabrarroka 99, 150, 295
pastrami sandwich 33, 267
pâté chaud de la Mère Bourgeois
  52, 274
Pâtisserie de la Rue de la Paix 20,
  22, 259–61, 262
Pâtisserie Durand 47, 272
Pat's King of Steaks 62, 278
Patterson, Daniel 228, 409
peaches: peach melba 40, 269
pears: confit tomato with twelve
  flavors 134, 322
  devils on horseback 193, 378
pecans: coconut pecan cake 147,
  332
la pêche Melba 40, 269

Peking duck 23, 263
Peking guinea pig 189, 373
Peng Chuang-kuei 78, 285
Peng's Garden Hunan Restaurant
  78, 285
Perry, Harry 60, 277
Perry's 60, 277
Peru 80, 143, 189, 219, 286, 329, 373,
  404
pescado a la talla 175, 362
Petrini, Andrea 11, 14, 20, 91, 93, 94,
  112, 117, 124, 134, 140, 144, 148,
  149, 162, 170, 172, 174, 181, 190,
  191, 192, 197, 200, 207, 209, 213,
  215, 220, 225, 228, 230, 238, 244,
  246, 249
Phillipe's 51, 273
Philly cheesesteak 62, 278
Piazza Duomo 200, 207, 386, 391
Pic, Jacques 98, 295
Picard, Martin 186, 193, 371
pieds de cochon aux morilles 106,
  108, 298
Pierangelini, Fulvio 112, 302
Pierre Gagnaire 168, 356
pies: banoffi pie 101
  Key lime pie 92, 291
  meat pie 252, 437
  rabbit and crayfish stargazy pie
  208, 392
  shepherd's pie 152, 336
*pigeonneau de bresse en croute
  de sel* 130
pigeons: salt-baked squab pigeons
  130, 318
pig's trotters: buddha jumps over
  the wall 21, 261
  pig's trotter carpaccio 150, 334
  stuffed pig's trotters with morels
  106, 108, 298
pineapple: ants and pineapple
  238, 426
  chequerboard of star anise ice
  cream, pineapple sorbet, and
  liquorice 145, 329
  Hawaiian pizza 84, 288
  piri-piri chicken 74, 283
pistachios: pistachio soufflé
  108, 298
pizzas: Hawaiian pizza 84, 288
  pizza Margherita 35, 267
  pizza with smoked salmon and
  caviar 123, 313
Pizzeria di Pietro e Basta Così
  35, 267
plums: wild boar cappelletti with
  plum broth 249, 435
Point, Fernand 53, 61, 93, 94, 103,
  278
poke 69, 281
pommes Anna 29, 265
pommes purée 119, 311
pommes soufflées 25, 264
pork: 100-layer lasagne 218, 401
  cassoulet 176, 363
  crisp confit of pork belly, seared
  sea scallops, shiitake, jellyfish,
  sesame 182, 366
  glutinous rice-stuffed suckling pig
  233, 417
  hot pâté 52, 274
  pork buns 136, 197, 211, 381
  roast suckling pig 241, 429
  royal hare 76, 284
  thousand-year-old quail egg,
  potage, ginger 222, 406
  tonkatsu 45, 271

tsukemen 81, 286
whole hog barbecue 251, 436
porridge, snail 191, 375
potatoes: Anna potatoes 29, 265
edible stones 201, 386
foie gras poutine 186, 193, 371
gâteau of Clonakilty black
pudding 146, 329
Irish stew 154, 337
potato purée 112, 119, 310
red mullet with potato scales
95, 293
Russian salad 27, 264
saffron mashed potatoes 129, 317
salt-baked squab pigeons 130, 318
shepherd's pie 152, 208, 336
a simple dish of potato cooked in
the earth in which it was grown
215, 398
soufflé potatoes 25, 264
Spanish omelet 115, 307
Vichyssoise 50, 273
Poulard, Annette 32, 266
poularde en vessie 61, 278
Poulet "La Petite Maison" 203, 388
poutine: foie gras poutine 186,
193, 371
pressed duck 38, 269
Prince, Thornton III 64, 279
Prince's Hot Chicken Shack 64, 279
Provençal garden vegetables
stewed in shaved black truffle
140, 327
Prudhomme, Paul 110, 301
Prune 177, 178, 364, 365
prunes: devils on horseback 193, 378
Puck, Wolfgang 122, 123, 313
Puglisi, Christina 224, 407
Pujol 240, 428
pulpo al olivo 143, 329

Q
quail: panfried quail with country
ham 151, 335
quail's eggs: thousand-year-old
quail egg, potage, ginger 222,
406
Quay 182, 366
Quilted Giraffe 121, 311
quinoa: Superiority burger 245, 431
Quo Vadis 231, 415

R
Raan Jay Fai 116, 307
rabbit: rabbit and crayfish stargazy
pie 208, 392
radishes: radishes in a pot 223, 399
Radium Beer Hall 74, 283
ragout de crêtes et rognons de coq
94, 149, 292
Ranhofer, Charles 31, 266
raspberries: Ispahan macaron 47,
171, 359
peach melba 40, 269
*ravioles de carotte et céleri-rave,
poudre de truffe* 174, 361
ravioli: carrot and celery root ravioli
174, 361
open raviolo 124, 200, 314
ravioli aperto 124, 200, 314
Reale 220, 405
Redzepi, René 112, 113, 116, 213, 215,
217, 223, 228, 238, 407, 399
Reform Club 24, 34, 263
Rengatei 45, 271
Restaurant Andrew Fairlie 183, 368
Restaurante Arzak 99, 295

rice: California roll 79, 286
four dances of the sea 166, 350
glutinous rice-stuffed suckling pig
233, 417
gunkan sushi 67, 280
Hainanese chicken and rice 139,
326
loco moco 71, 281
mixed rice with vegetables and
Korean beef tartare 242, 429
rice, gold, and saffron 120, 124,
172, 200, 312
sorrel pesto rice bowl 227, 409
sushi 88, 289
white risotto with coffee powder
and Pantelleria capers 172, 360
rillettes, salmon 135, 323
Ripert, Eric 93, 103, 119, 135
riso, oro e zafferano 120, 124, 172,
312
risotto: spelt risotto 149, 334
white risotto with coffee powder
and Pantelleria capers 172, 360
*risotto bianco con polvere di caffè e
capperi di Pantelleria* 172, 360
risotto d'épeautre 149, 334
Ristorante Gualtiero Marchesi 120,
124, 312, 314
Ritz, César 38, 104
Ritz-Carlton Hotel 38, 50, 273
The River Café 142, 146, 193, 328,
332
Robuchon, Joël 112, 117, 119, 174, 178,
198, 253, 307, 311
Roca, Joan 150, 334
Roca, Jordi 99, 188, 372
Rochoux, Jean-Charles 195, 380
Rodgers, Judy 138, 324
Rodney Scott's Whole Hog BBQ
251, 436
Roellinger, Olivier 126, 315
Roemer, Philip 54, 275
Rogers, Ruth 142, 146, 328, 332
Rogon, Simon 232, 416
Rome 35, 48
Romito, Niko 172, 220, 249, 405
rømmegrøt with cured reindeer
heart and plum vinegar 230,
414
Rose, Daniel 47
rose: beet rose, yogurt, and rose
petal ice 228, 409
Cronut® 237, 422
Ispahan macaron 47, 171, 359
strawberry and watermelon cake
214, 397
Rosenzweig, Anne 132, 321
*rouge en écailles de pomme de
terre* 95, 293
Roux brothers 104, 152, 167, 183
royal hare 76, 284
Rule, Thomas 19, 258
Rules 19, 258
rum: bananas foster 77, 285
rum baba 137, 324
Russia 27, 264
Russian Salad 27, 264
rye bread: pastrami sandwich 33,
267
tartare of beef with watercress
and rye bread 224, 407

S
saffron: onion reduction with
Parmesan buttons and toasted
saffron 220, 405

rice, gold, and saffron 120, 124,
172, 200, 312
saffron mashed potatoes 129, 317
Sailhac, Alain 125, 314
St. John 34, 107, 160, 163, 342, 346
Saint Pierre Retour des Indes 126,
315
Saison 225, 408
la salade gourmande 91, 290
salade Olivier 27, 264
salads: bone marrow with parsley
salad and toast 160
Caesar salad 56, 68
Caprese salad 55, 275
Cobb salad 58, 65
confit of Petuna ocean trout with
fennel salad 155, 337
gourmet salad 91, 290
grilled salad smoked over embers,
Isle of Mull cheese, truffle
custard, and cobnuts 232, 416
kale salad 204, 388
roast bone marrow and parsley
salad 163, 346
Russian salad 27, 264
salad 21…31…41…51…207, 391
Waldorf salad 39, 269
Zuni roast chicken with bread
salad 138, 324
Salazar, Diego 11, 14, 39, 41, 44, 56,
62, 72, 73, 79, 80, 86, 87, 90, 92,
99, 103, 111, 113, 118, 119, 123, 131,
136, 140, 143, 150, 159, 161, 162,
163, 168, 179, 180, 189, 197, 201,
218, 223, 229, 234, 236, 237
Salón Rosita 143, 329
salsa golf 57, 276
samgyetang 128, 317
San Francisco 54, 82, 101, 121, 138,
175, 198, 222, 225, 228, 235, 250
San Sebastián 99, 115, 209
sandwiches: club sandwich 41, 270
French dip sandwich 51, 273
Kobe beef cutlet sandwich 250,
436
lobster club sandwich 132, 321
lobster roll 60
pastrami sandwich 33, 267
Philly cheesesteak 62
smoked eel sandwich 231, 415
Saratoga Club House 41, 270
sashimi: new-style sashimi 79, 131,
141, 328
yellowtail sashimi with jalapeño
180, 366
Satellite Restaurant 84, 288
sausages: the crunchy part of the
lasagne 165, 348
green gumbo 75, 283
Savoy, Guy 39, 114, 195, 198, 217, 306
Savoy Hotel 40, 59, 104, 269, 277
Scabin, Davide 124, 170, 358
Schwarzwälder kirschtorte 49, 273
scorpion fish cake 99, 150, 295
Scotland 183, 217, 400
Scott, Rodney 251, 436
Scott's 208, 392
The Seafood Restaurant 107, 299
Searle, Phillip 145, 155, 157, 329
seaweed: aka sea urchin in a
lobster jelly with cauliflower,
caviar, and crispy seaweed
waffles 198, 383
Senderens, Alain 122, 126, 134, 149,
174, 312
Seoul 128, 158, 242
Seventh Son 102, 241, 429

Shani, Eyal 202, 239, 387
Sharrow Bay Country House Hotel
97, 294
shellfish: aka sea urchin in a lobster
jelly with cauliflower, caviar, and
crispy seaweed waffles 198, 383
California roll 79, 285
chickpea purée with red shrimp
112, 302
crab omelet 116, 307
crab steamed with egg white and
huadiao wine 102, 297
crisp confit of pork belly, seared
sea scallops, shiitake, jellyfish,
sesame 182, 366
duck foie gras charcoal grilled
with sea urchin caviar and a
spicy touch 209, 393
four dances of the sea 166, 350
fried black pudding with oysters,
apple, and onion in mustard
sauce 148, 333
home-smoked Scottish lobster
with lime and herb butter 183,
368
king crab and almost-burnt
cream 226, 409
langoustine five ways 168, 356
langoustine and sea flavors 213,
407
lasagne of crab with a cappuccino
of shellfish and a champagne
foam 167, 353
lobster club sandwich 132, 321
lobster roll 60, 277
mushroom cappuccino 93, 292
Nagasaki champon 46, 272
open raviolo 124, 200, 314
oysters and pearls 162, 345
oysters Rockefeller 34, 267
rabbit and crayfish stargazy pie
208, 392
roast lobster with vanilla butter
sauce 122, 312
scallop cooked over burning
juniper branches 221, 405
sea urchin toast 225, 408
shellfish rockpool 217, 400
shrimp noodles 190, 374
steamed flowery crab with
Shaoxing rice wine and chicken
fat 216, 399
stew of cockscombs and chicken
kidneys 94, 292
XO sauce live pippies 153, 336
shepherd's pie 152, 208, 336
Shewry, Ben 215, 238, 398
Shikairo 46, 272
Shish Mahal 96, 294
a simple dish of potato cooked in
the earth in which it was grown
215, 398
Singapore 139, 326
Skenes, Joshua 225, 408
smoke foam 173, 361
snails: snail porridge 191, 375
Solari, Pedro 80, 286
Solivérès, Alain 149, 334
sorbet: 18
almond sorbet 161, 168, 342
chequerboard of star anise ice
cream, pineapple sorbet, and
liquorice 145, 329
sorrel: sorrel pesto rice bowl 227,
409
soufflé aux pistaches 108, 298
soufflé potatoes 25, 264

446

soufflés: Grand Marnier soufflé 83, 287
  pistachio soufflé 108, 298
  soup dumplings 100, 296
  soupe à l'oignon 70, 281
  soupe aux truffles Elysée 103, 297
  soupe d'artichaut à la truffle noire 114, 306
soups: artichoke soup with black truffle 114, 306
  black truffle soup Elysée 103, 297
  buddha jumps over the wall 21, 261
  chrysanthemum tofu soup with fish balls and matsutake mushrooms 206, 390
  foie gras and miso soup 192, 377
  French onion soup 70, 281
  mushroom cappuccino 93, 292
  Nagasaki champon 46, 272
  samgyetang 128, 317
  vichyssoise 50, 273
  see also broths; consommés
South Africa 74, 283
South Korea 128, 242, 317, 429
Soyer, Alexis 24, 34, 263
Spago 123, 313
Spain 38, 89, 93, 99, 115, 115, 150, 161, 168, 173, 179, 188, 199, 200, 201, 209
Spanish omelet 115, 307
spelt: spelt risotto 149, 334
  spherical-I green olives 199, 385
spinach: the crunchy part of the lasagne 165, 348
  green gumbo 75, 283
  roast lobster with vanilla butter sauce 122, 312
spotted dick 36, 268
The Spotted Pig 152, 193, 378
spring greens: green gumbo 75, 283
  grilled salad smoked over embers, Isle of Mull cheese, truffle custard, and cobnuts 232, 416
Sqirl 227, 409
The Square 167, 353
squid: four dances of the sea 166, 350
  grilled squid with chile 142, 328
  Nagasaki champon 46, 272
  shellfish rockpool 217, 400
  stargazy pie, rabbit and crayfish 208, 392
Stein, Rick 107, 129, 299
stews & casseroles: cassoulet 176, 363
  green gumbo 75, 283
  Irish stew 154, 337
  oxtail stew 37, 268
  stew of cockscombs and chicken kidneys 94, 292
  vegetable casserole in textures 161, 168, 342
sticky toffee pudding 97, 294
strawberries: strawberry watermelon cake 214, 397
suckling pig: glutinous rice-stuffed suckling pig 233, 417
  roast suckling pig 241, 429
Sukiyabashi Jiro 88, 289
Superiority Burger 245, 431
sushi: 88, 141, 180, 289
  California roll 79, 286
  four dances of the sea 166, 350
  gunkan sushi 67, 280
Sweden 213, 221, 226, 405, 409

sweet potatoes: curried baby goat with sweet potato gnocchi 247
Sweetings 36, 268
Sydney 145, 153, 157, 158, 182, 214, 227, 250

T
Tachibe, Shigefumi 131, 320
taco, short rib 210, 394
Taipei 78, 100, 156
Taishoken 81, 286
Taiwan 78, 100, 156, 285, 296, 338
Tam Kwok Fung 233, 417
Tamimi, Sami 187, 372
tapioca: oysters and pearls 162, 345
Tarlow, Andrew 176
tartares: carrot tartare 234, 418
  tartare of beef with watercress and rye bread 224, 407
  tuna tartare 131, 320
tarts: chocolate caramel tart 164, 347
  oops! I dropped the lemon tart 236, 421
  tarte Tatin 44, 271
Tatin, Caroline and Stéphanie 44, 271
tea: tea-smoked duck 82, 287
  nitro-poached green tea and lime mousse 185, 370
Tetsuya's 155, 337
Thailand 116, 307
Thé, Christopher 214, 397
The 8 206, 390
thousand-year-old quail egg, potage, ginger 222, 397
Tian Tian Hainanese Kitchen 139, 326
tiramisu 86, 288
toffee: banoffi pie 101
  sticky toffee pudding 97, 294
tofu: chrysanthemum tofu soup with fish balls and matsutake mushrooms 206, 390
  mapo tofu 28, 265
  vegetable pulp burger 248, 433
Tokyo 45, 67, 81, 88, 158, 171, 180, 195, 197, 250
Tokyo Kaikan 79, 286
tomate confite aux douze saveurs 134, 322
tomatoes: 100-layer lasagne 218, 401
  Caprese salad 55, 275
  chicken tikka masala 96, 294
  Cobb salad 65, 279
  confit tomato with twelve flavors 134, 322
  the crunchy part of the lasagne 165, 348
  Hawaiian pizza 84, 288
  oxtail stew 37, 268
  Pierre Gagnaire 168, 356
  pig's trotter carpaccio 150, 334
  Pizza Margherita 35, 267
  shellfish rockpool 217, 400
  Superiority burger 245, 431
  vegetable casserole in textures 161, 168, 342
tonkatsu 45, 271
tortilla de patatas 115, 307
Tosi, Christina 211, 394
Tosokchon Samgyetang 128, 317
tournedos Rossini 26, 264
Troisgros, Jean and Pierre 61, 85, 91, 93, 94, 103, 104, 114, 288
Troisgros, Michel 94, 126, 181, 366

truffles: artichoke soup with black truffle 114, 306
  black truffle soup Elysée 103, 297
  chicken in a bladder 61, 279
  chicken in half mourning 53, 274
  chocolate truffles 195, 380
  gourmet salad 91, 290
  hot pâté 52, 274
  Provençal garden vegetables stewed in shaved black truffle 140, 327
  tournedos rossini 26, 264
  truffle custard 232, 416
  truffled zucchini 109, 300
  veal Prince Orloff 104, 297
  white milk and black truffle 181, 366
Tschirky, Oscar 37, 40, 43, 270, 269
Tse, Joseph 206, 390
tsukemen 81, 286
tunta 201
Turkey 30, 265

U
Ubuntu 205, 389
United Kingdom 19, 24, 36, 40, 59, 96, 97, 101, 104, 106, 107, 109, 129, 130, 142, 146, 152, 154, 160, 163, 167, 183, 185, 187, 190, 191, 193, 203, 208, 217, 223, 229, 231, 232, 244, 252, 253, 254
United States 21, 28, 31, 33, 34, 39, 41, 42, 46, 50, 51, 54, 56, 58, 60, 62, 64, 66, 73, 75, 77, 79, 82, 83, 87, 90, 92, 105, 110, 111, 121, 123, 125, 131, 132, 133, 135, 136, 138, 141, 147, 151, 152, 159, 162, 164, 176, 177, 178, 180, 184, 190, 193, 197, 204, 205, 210, 211, 212, 213, 218, 222, 223, 225, 227, 228, 229, 234, 235, 235, 237, 243, 245, 247, 248, 251

V
vanilla: Cronut® 237, 422
  Eternity by Calvin Klein 188, 372
  roast lobster with vanilla butter sauce 122, 312
veal: 100-layer lasagne 218, 401
  stuffed pig's trotters with morels 106, 108, 298
  veal Prince Orloff 104, 297
vegetables: gargouillou 113, 140, 303
  Provençal garden vegetables stewed in shaved black truffle 140, 327
  Russian salad 27, 264
  vegetable casserole in textures 161, 168, 342
  vegetable pulp burger 248, 433
  see also individual types of vegetable
Veyrat, Marc 174, 232, 361
Vichyssoise 50, 273
Victory Club 68, 280
Vienna 202
Vines, Richard 11, 15, 19, 36, 59, 96, 103, 104, 106, 107, 114, 119, 129, 130, 137, 140, 146, 152, 154, 160, 161, 163, 165, 167, 173, 183, 191, 201, 202, 203, 208, 217, 229, 231, 232, 236, 239, 253, 254
Virlogeux, Jean Baptiste 59, 277
vol-au-vent 20, 259
volaille demi-deuil 53, 274

W
Wagyumafia 250, 436
Wakuda, Tetsuya 153, 155, 337
Waldorf-Astoria 39, 43, 83
Waldorf Hotel 39, 42, 269, 270
Waldorf salad 39, 269
Wang, Nelson 105, 298
Wang's Large Fried Chicken 156, 338
wastEd 54, 248
watercress: green gumbo 75, 283
  tartare of beef with watercress and rye bread 224, 407
watermelon: strawberry watermelon cake 214, 397
Waters, Alice 82, 111, 138, 151, 181, 302
wd~50 190, 211, 374
wild boar: wild boar cappelletti with plum broth 249, 435
Wine, Barry 121, 311
Wong, Eric and Linda 153

X
xiao long bao 100, 296
XO sauce live pippies 153, 336
Xu Yuan, Margaret 196, 380

Y
Yang Bingyi 100
yellow earth chicken 196, 380
Yeung Koon Yat 127, 317
Yin Yang Kitchen 196, 380
Yip, Danny 216
yogurt: beet rose, yogurt, and rose petal ice 228, 409
Yiruma, Rosita 143, 329
yukhoe bibimbap 242, 429

Z
zabaglione 236, 421
Zhang Tianzheng 63, 278
Zheng Chunfa 21, 261
zucchini: truffled zucchini 109, 300
Zuni Café 138, 324
Zuni roast chicken with bread salad 138, 324
Zuo Zongtang 78

Acknowledgments

A project of this size requires the commitment and expertise of many people. The publisher would like to extend special thanks to the chefs and restaurateurs featured in the book, for their cooperation and great enthusiasm.

We would also like to acknowledge the crucial role of our curators, without whom the project would not have been possible. We are especially grateful to Christine Muhlke, for her excellent texts and continued support.

We are particularly indebted also to François Simon, for his vital contribution regarding the French dishes featured in the book.

Thanks also go to our illustrator, Adriano Rampazzo, who has been a joy to work with and whose talent and insight have allowed us to visualize these dishes as never before.

Special thanks are due to Caitlin Arnell Argles for her research and editorial input, and to all those who have helped us track down materials, information, and people: Pejman Ahmadi, Chihting Chao, Gif Jittiwutikarn, Hahyun Joo, Helen Hemblade, Mel Kara, Alfredo Romero, and Federica Sala.

Christine Muhlke would like to thank Chloé Charles, Julia Edelman, Jessica Merliss, Gila Schwarzschild, Kara Shure, Ali Slagle, and Charlotte Woodruff Goddu for their invaluable assistance.

Additional thanks are due to Theresa Bebbington, Vanessa Bird, Caroline Bourrus, Déborah Dupont-Daguet, Rebecca Federman, Julia Hasting, Cecilia Molinari, Hélène Gallois Montbrun, João Mota, Hans Stofregen, Ana Teodoro, Albino Tavares, Gisela Rosell, Matt Sartwell, and Kate Slate.

Phaidon Press Limited
Regent's Wharf
All Saints Street
London N1 9PA

Phaidon Press Inc.
65 Bleecker Street
New York, NY 10012

phaidon.com

First published 2019
© 2019 Phaidon Press Limited

ISBN 978 0 7148 7932 1

A CIP catalogue record for this book is available from the British Library and the Library of Congress.

Commissioning Editor: Emily Takoudes
Project Editor: Lucy Kingett
Production Controller: Sarah Kramer
Design: Lacasta Design
Artworker: Studio Chehade

Printed in China

448

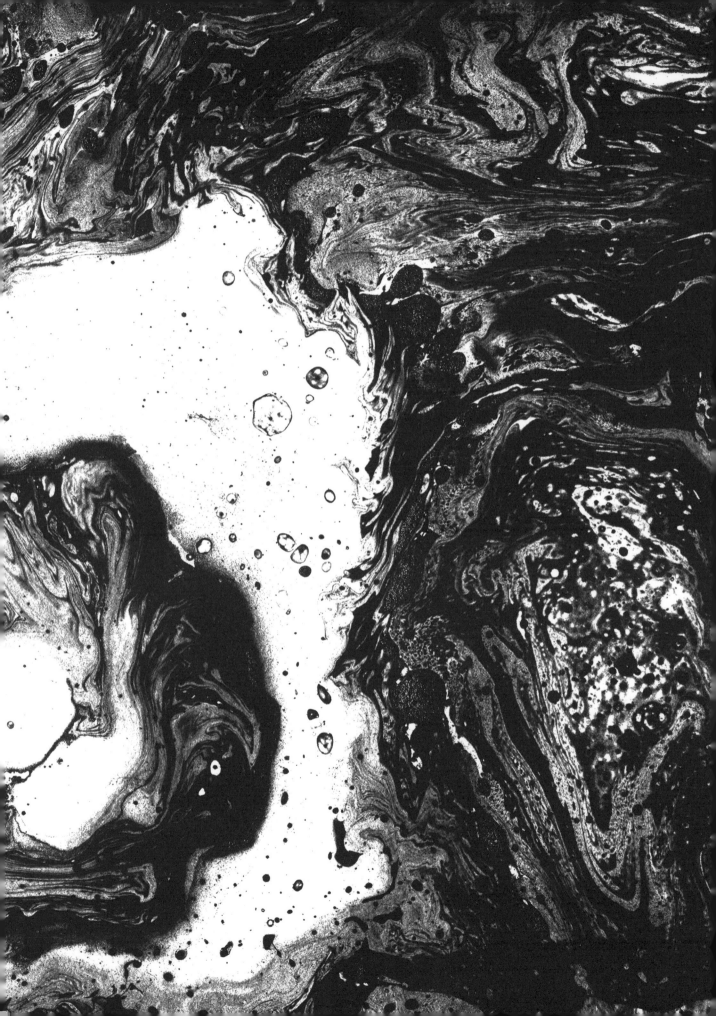

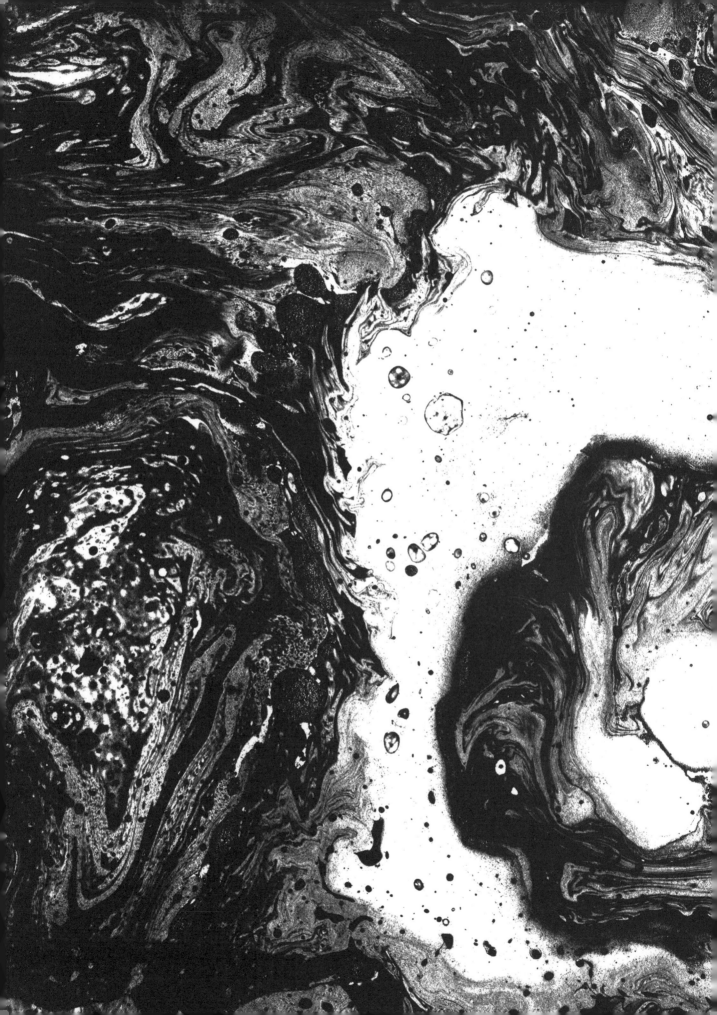